A BROWSER'S DICTIONARY

Among John Ciardi's other books

I Met a Man (Poems for children)

For Instance (Poems)

Dante's *Divine Comedy* (Translation)

How Does a Poem Mean? (An Introduction to Poetry)
Revised edition with Miller Williams

Too Gross (288 original limericks) With Isaac Asimov

A Browser's Dictionary AND

NATIVE'S GUIDE TO THE UNKNOWN

AMERICAN LANGUAGE

JOHN CIARDI

HARPER & ROW, PUBLISHERS, *New York*
Cambridge, Hagerstown, Philadelphia, San Francisco,
London, Mexico City, São Paulo, Sydney

Portions of this work originally appeared in the *Atlantic Monthly*.

A BROWSER'S DICTIONARY. Copyright © 1980 by John Ciardi. All rights reserved. Printed in the United States of America. No part of this book may be used or reproduced in any manner whatsoever without written permission except in the case of brief quotations embodied in critical articles and reviews. For information address Harper & Row, Publishers, Inc., 10 East 53rd Street, New York, N.Y. 10022. Published simultaneously in Canada by Fitzhenry & Whiteside Limited, Toronto.

FIRST EDITION

Designer: Sidney Feinberg

Library of Congress Cataloging in Publication Data

Ciardi, John, 1916–
  A browser's dictionary.
    1. English language—Etymology—Popular works.
2. English language—Terms and phrases. I. Title.
PE1574.C55   428'.2'03   79–1658
ISBN 0–06–010766–9

80 81 82 83 84 10 9 8 7 6 5 4 3 2 1

Signs used in this book

?   In doubt.

*   When placed before a root word, indicates that it cannot be traced beyond the form given.

=   Equals.

<   From.

→   To, yields, yield, leads to, lead to.

,   Indicates a vowel in an unattested form. Thus the stem *forfi-* may be more securely rendered as *f'rf'-* indicating "unspecified vowel."

/   Indicates a consonant shift, as g/h signifies "shift from *g* to *h*." Similarly, p/f, b/v, d/t, th/t, etc.

Roman numerals indicate centuries. "XVII" should be read "the seventeenth century." To avoid confusion, the first through the fifth centuries and the tenth are written out. All dates are A.D. unless otherwise noted.

General abbreviations

approx.	Approximately.
colloq.	Colloquially. Colloquialism.
dial.	Dialect.
dict.	Dictionary.
dim.	Diminutive.
esp.	Especially.
etymol.	Etymology. Etymological.
ext.	(Sense) extension (from one meaning of the word to another).
influ.	Influence. Influences. Influenced.
lit.	Literally.
obs.	Obsolete.
part.	Participle.
perh.	Perhaps.
p.p.	Past participle.
prob.	Probably.
pron.	Pronounced.
redupl.	Reduplicated form (as *heebie-jeebies*).
ref.	Reference. Refers to.

sthrn.	Southern American regional.
ult.	Ultimately. Ultimate.
usu.	Usually.
wstrn.	Western American regional.

Abbreviations of languages often cited

Am.	American English.
Brit.	British English.
Du.	Dutch.
Eng.	Modern English (since c. XVI).
Fr.	French.
Ger.	German.
Gk.	Greek.
Gmnc.	Common Germanic. Intermediate between Indo-European and the German, Scandinavian, and Dutch languages, as well as Scottish and English.
IE	Indo-European.
It.	Italian.
L.	Latin.
MD	Middle Dutch.
ME	Middle English.
MHG	Middle High German.
MLG	Middle Low German.
OD	Old Dutch.
OE	Old English.
OF	Old French.
OHG	Old High German.
OLG	Old Low German.
ON	Old Norse.
Port.	Portuguese.
Sc.	Scottish.
Sp.	Spanish.

Works frequently cited

AHD	*American Heritage Dictionary.*
Brewer	Cobham H. Brewer, *Dictionary of Phrase and Fable.*
EDD	*English Dialect Dictionary.*
Grose	Captain Francis Grose, *A Classical Dictionary of the Vulgar Tongue.*
Johnson	Samuel Johnson, *Dictionary of the English Language.*
MMM	Mitford M. Mathews, *A Dictionary of Americanisms on Historical Principles.*

NT	*New Testament.*
NWD	*New World Dictionary.*
ODEE	*Oxford Dictionary of English Etymology.* Edited by C. T. Onions (pronouced *On-ee-on*).
OED	*Oxford English Dictionary.*
OT	*Old Testament.*
P. *Origins*	Eric Partridge, *Origins, A Short Etymological Dictionary of Modern English.*
P. *Slang*	Eric Partridge, *A Dictionary of Slang and Unconventional English.*
Sc. Dict.	*Jamieson's Dictionary of the Scottish Language.*
Weekley	Ernest Weekley, *An Etymological Dictionary of Modern English.*

I owe a particular and grateful thanks to the AHD, whose appendix on Indo-European Roots has enormously simplified the hunt.

FOREWORD

It was Linnaeus, the great Swedish taxonomist, who risked his reputation by dubbing us *Homo sapiens,* literally, "sapient man," and in various common interpretations, "thinking man" or "rational man." *Homo,* at root akin to *humus,* is the biblical clay from which God allegedly kneaded Adam when allegedly giving him his "sapience."

And so much for in-group boasting. Certainly H. L. Mencken was not wildly astray when he reclassified us as *Homo boobiensis,* "boob man."

And yet there was Aristotle. Something like a rational civilization has sometimes been achieved by one man at a time. If *sapiens* won't stand the test, *boobiensis* slanders the best among us. Who are we? And what should we be called?

Linnaeus would have done better to call us *Homo loquens,* "speaking man," or "the clay that speaks." For though our racial sapience remains in doubt, our loquacity is beyond question, and sufficiently distinguishes us from the less savage brutes. Man is the animal that uses language.

Lewis Thomas in his *Lives of a Cell* describes the nonstop and precision labor of an anthill. Anthills have been known to endure for over fifty years, the daily labor within them continuing the same without interruption, though 3 to 5 percent of the workers die daily. By the first of August nothing is left, on racial average, of the population that was so busily little-footing it on the first of July. In fifty years the hill runs through over six hundred generations—enough to take man back to the forests and halfway up the tree. And in all that ant eon, the work goes on the same at the same tireless pace.

Thomas asks if there is any similar ceaseless activity of humankind, and he answers that of course there is, and that it is the endless making, multiplying, and changing of language.

No one knows when or how speech began. Science knows which area of the brain controls our speech mechanisms, and fossil evidence tells evolutionists that those centers were present about a million years ago. But to have the mechanism is not enough. The ancient Greeks could have gone hang gliding, but didn't. The human child needs the example of its parents before it can acquire even the notion of speech possibility.

Professor Julian Jaynes, the Princeton anthropologist, theorizes that human speech did not come into being until something like 40,000 years ago, when man became a pack hunter of large mammals. A man pack surrounding a mammoth or thinking to drive it over a cliff needed a hunt master who needed commands for "closer, back, toward the sun, give way on the left." In earlier times man was a stalker and trapper of small animals, and would have done better to stalk in silence. Only in pack pursuit would noise be survival-useful.

Others dispute Professor Jaynes's theory. Ashley Montagu, studying the intricately made stone tools found in the Olduvai Gorge, from a time millennia before mammoth-hunting European man, concludes that no stone-chipping father could have taught his son the precision of such work without names for the various parts. The fact is we don't know how language started, but such brilliant guesses may help us to understand not only how much we don't know, but in what great detail we don't know it.

Whatever the origin of language, it is certain that once started, it took off at an ever increasing rate. Once *Homo loquens* had two words, he had the possibility of combining the two into a third, then the three into more, then that more into ever more.

Our earliest known language ancestors were the Aryans. *Aryan,* if we can put aside Hitler's racist abuse of the term, means simply "a speaker of Proto-Indo-European," an adduced language spoken about 5,000 to 6,000 years B.C. The adduced Indo-European root *ni-* meant "down" (NETHER); the root *sed-* meant "to sit" (SEDENTARY). Early Aryans saw a way to put those two bits of language together to make a new and necessary label. They made *nizd'-,* bird's nest ("place where the bird sits"). Their Latin-speaking descendants took over the new word stem and made of it *nidus,* nest. The Teutons, however, took note of the fact that birds foul their nests and that the nests begin to stink in the heat of summer. At this end of the process we have the word *nasty* (at root "nesty"), "a foul and stinking thing."

The Indo-European root *pap-,* baby, was simply based on the sucking sound of a nursing infant. (*Infant* is from Latin *infans,* not able to speak, from *fari,* to speak.) The root *kak-,* probably either echoic or expressive of disgust, meant "dung," as in Latin *cacare,* to defecate. Combining them, with modifications in Dutch and English, we have *poppycock,* rubbish, nonsense, but at root, of course, "baby poop."

And by other combinations and adaptations *pap-* has given us English *pap, pabulum, poppet, pupa, puppet, puppy*—and more. Man is the language-making animal, and what he usually makes it of is other language. The more language he has, the faster he will make more.

Often the process is arrestingly poetic. English *liquid* is from Latin *liquere,* to be liquid, to liquefy, and that is in turn from Indo-European *leikwo-,* to leave, to depart. A liquid is that form of matter that "goes away." As in the nice ambiguities of poetry, a liquid may "go away" by flowing, by evaporation, by percolation, or it "may cause to go away" by dissolving things, or by wearing them away as rain wears mountains down. With all its consonant, and therefore welcome, ambiguities, the connection between the idea "to go away" and the substance "liquid" is a poetic figure. The word is a small fossil poem written by the race itself.

Having evolved English *liquid,* moreover, having the example of other suffixed words and variant forms, and needing other labels, it was easy to settle on *liquor* for strong spirits, and *liqueur,* simply the French form of the same word, for after-dinner cordials (*cordial* being compounded of the idea "taken to heart"). So we have not only words but labels and ideas we had no need to think out for ourselves because we inherited them from our language fathers. As we inherited the sweet "liquefaction" of Julia's clothes, a pleasure we had no need to contrive, and probably could not have contrived.

At root this process in its endless accumulation and variation is a language solution of the problem "What shall we call this to make it recognizable?" Our standard answers to this question are language conventions called *idioms.* Each language settles on its own idioms by voting to adopt them by common agreement. So we say *ball bearings* and Italians say *cuscini a sfera,* literally, "spherical cushions." But really, spherical cushions? What sort of sense does that make? But it does make sense. The fact is that just under the surface, we and the Italians have come up with an identical language solution. Among English-speaking mechanical engineers, a cushion is a weight-bearing, weight-distributing member. And isn't our ball, except on the gridiron, a sphere? I have known many tourists in Italy to be baffled by roadside advertisements for "spherical cushions." I also remember the delight of the few who made the connection after a while and not only saw what it meant, but how and why it meant it. Man is also the language-delighted animal.

Language conventions are what all or most of the speakers of a given language agree upon. There remains a fascinating book to be written (go ahead and write it—I won't find the time) on the language solutions of those who lack the conventions, as child babblers and speakers of broken English. "At last I grasp to see it!" a Frenchman once told me. Clearly he was not speaking native English, and yet he assembled what English he had into a form that made sense.

My daughter at age two discovered that the negative of *O.K.* was *no-K.* Father fondness aside, it was a fine language solution. The form is not common enough to be embraced by the language convention, but were it popularized, it could easily enough become standard idiom.

Lascar seamen who spoke only pidgin (a corruption of *business*) English often served as stokers on early tramp steamers. Inevitably they needed a label for ashes, for which there was no word in pidgin. The question "What are we to call these?" produced a language solution that may offend delicate ears but is directly to the point. Ashes became *shit belong-um fire.* And as a note on the likenesses of humankind, that solution is clearly akin to the solution made in Old English *scittan* (that's a *c*-kappa—the *c* is pronounced as *k*), to shit, the word having at root the same sense as *sect, bisect, sector,* the common root sense being "to divide, to take away from," that is, "to divide from the body," as, in pidgin English, ashes are divided from the fire or left over from it. The population changes; the process goes on forever in the psychic anthills of *Homo loquens.*

My uncle by marriage, Alessio DiSimone, migrated to America at age seventeen. He lived to be ninety-seven without acquiring a more than rudimentary broken English. Yet with it he invented the fascinating all-purpose tense *was-be.* "Gian," he would say to me, "you was-be good boy." Depending on the context—and in context it was always clear—that could mean "you are/you are being/you have been/you had damn well better be a good boy." There was even a conditional tense. If I looked up at the sky and said, "It looks like rain," he would squint at the sky and answer, "Could was-be." The language convention allows us to know who is native; any workable language solution, in or out of the convention, allows us to know there is a mind at work.

Such clear but unconventional language solutions come about in much the way I must suppose *Homo loquens* first learned how to combine his first few elements into more words, which made more, which made more. Today the momentum of language-making keeps accelerating as a consequence of its own acceleration. Somewhere I read someone's guess that an average working vocabulary consists of 15,000 words. I suppose such counting has its place within the anthill. I will accept the figure, if warily. If this statistical guess has any merit, it is at least an equal guess that we, in the twentieth century, generate that many new words in any ten-year period. If we include not only the lingo of science, technology, and semiprofessional blather, but also cant, catch phrases, and transient slang (as *twenty-three skidoo, it's the cat's pajamas, wafflebutt, hippie, cool cat*), I should be willing to take a chance on raising the neology count. *Homo loquens* is the language express, and forever highballing.

And in shaping language he is shaped by it. Our scornful word *barbarian* is based on Greek *barbaros,* itself scornfully based on *bar-bar-bar,* a mocking rendering of the way foreigners talk.

Spanish *gringo* (of seventeenth-century origin, not nineteenth) is based on *griego,* Greek. *Gringar* meant "to speak outlandishly," just as the Greeks' outlanders were given the scornful name of their own blather, *bar-bar-os,* one who baas like a sheep. We still say *it's Greek to me,* often by way of contemptuous dismissal. Dante, without scorn, came up with his own language solution: *non mi è latino,"* which may reasonably be rendered; "it is not Latin [native/understandable] to me."

So much for the root sense. Once established in Greek usage, *barbaros* came to mean both "stranger" and "enemy" (in both senses with that overtone of scorn). It had to follow that the Greek way of meeting a stranger was influenced by the fact that one label (and its implied scorn) did such double duty. Heroes have died of less.

Oedipus was born under a dark prophecy that he would live to kill his father and marry his mother. To spare the child and to avert doom, King Laius and Queen Jocasta sent their son out of the kingdom to be reared by a distant king. When Oedipus had grown to a man's strength, he set out on his manhood journey in the same tradition of manhood confirmation that sent Arthur's knights questing for the Grail. Oedipus hitched up his chariot and went faring.

Inevitably his journey led him toward Thebes, and as he neared it he met another charioteer, a contemptible stranger-enemy, a *barbaros.* The other met in Oedipus the same compound of senses. In basic Greek they disputed the right of way till words came to swords, and Oedipus killed the *barbaros,* who later, of course, turned out to have been his father.

But was it prophecy or language that made that corpse? I cannot speak for the gods, but suppose that by some anachronistic freak the story of the good Samaritan had reached into ancient Greece and that the Greek word for "stranger" had emerged as *Samaratinos.* The motivational doublet of the word for "stranger," with no scorn implied, would then have been not "enemy" but "kind and gentle person." The gods might still have insisted on that death, but certainly they would have had to work harder for it. With any luck, the gentler language might have spared Laius, Jocasta might have kept her husband and found no need to marry the young man, and a few dramatic revelations later, Oedipus might have been recognized and might in

time have succeeded peacefully to the throne of Thebes. Such a pleasant progression would have spoiled the looming darkness of great
drama, but let it be recognized that language not only describes our
actions but prompts us to them.

I am, of course, merely browsing in this respite from the gods.
But this book is for browsers, for those who will be pleased to ramble
beyond the standard dictionaries to a more intimate conversation with
words and phrases and their origins and shifting histories. It is not
possible—I will not live long enough—to treat all the words and idioms
in American-English use. By limiting the number of entries, I have
tried to discuss more fully those terms that are most interesting, and
I have been flatly subjective in my choices. A term is interesting if it
interests me, for only out of my own interest can I make these word
histories interesting to a reader—and informative, and *readable*. This
dictionary is meant for reading—not necessarily in sequence, and not
at a gulp, but browsingly, to pick up, to sample, to put down, and
then, I hope, to pick up again, and maybe even again.

My great original model, though I have introduced my own methods
and variations, has been Cobham H. Brewer's century-old *Dictionary
of Phrase and Fable,* my favorite bedside and coffee table book. I
cannot rival Brewer's learning but, exhilarated by it, and given the
additional tools made available by a century of etymological development, I can bring to the discussion a sort of detail unavailable to my
earlier betters, among whom I include in awe the moralistic but monumental Archbishop Trench, godfather of the *Oxford English Dictionary,* for it was from a suggestion made by Trench that the seventy-
year project of the OED took form.

I have tried at all points to be accurate in these histories, and I
think I have, in the main, succeeded. Yet having bored inch by inch
through many dictionaries, good, great, and not so great, I have found
none, whatever the resources of its editorial staff, that has not made
mistakes. It follows that, working alone, I must have made my own
mistakes. I shall welcome correction, and even admonition, from any
reader who catches me at it and will point the finger so that I may
correct my errors in future editions. My present plan is to bring out
at least several of these browser's dictionaries before collating the
whole into some future obsessive tome; for this word-tracking has become my happy obsession and I foresee that I shall be at it for the
rest of my life if—to run in an Irish bull—I live that long.

Now and then I have had to correct some of our standard dictionaries, but never in rancor, for I have depended on them gratefully, while
noting that no one of them tells me as much as I need to know about
the word, and that most have neglected the histories and origins of

even our choicest idiomatic phrases. The reader who cares to check
for himself the method of my disagreement with the master tomes
may browse such specimen entries (and disagreements) as *cheapskate,
galleywest, ghetto, honeymoon, kangaroo court, lead pipe cinch, nincompoop, posh, sycophant,* and *Yankee.* These, among many others,
are terms some or all of our best dictionaries have botched.

Even our best dictionaries, moreover, have insisted on being pointlessly safe at times, dropping the whole question of etymology with
an "origin unknown" when, in fact, a great deal is known about the
term, though not enough to permit an unqualified assertion. I cannot
argue against professional caution, but it would do well to avoid over-
caution. Where I have found substantial though not conclusively attested evidence for a derivation, I have stipulated what part of the
history is in doubt, and made a hypothetical offering of the rest.
Limehouse, for example (and its history is apart from that of *Limey*),
can be etymologized with a high degree of probability, and I have
thought that probability—clearly so labeled—more interesting and
more useful that an evasive "origin unknown." Some instances of my
more speculative etymologizing are the likely but not entirely conclu-
sive accounts of such terms as *Jolly Roger, Davy Jones, half seas over,
son of a seacook, cocksure,* and *hornswoggle. Homo loquens* has not
usually carved on a stone such messages as "Today I combined *horns*
and *waggle* into a new word for the sign of the cuckold, and I'll be
hornswoggled if it didn't catch on at once!" He must sometimes be
guessed out, and as long as the guess—clearly labeled as such—is based
on some evidence, I have preferred to guess rather than say nothing.

I have also found it interesting (to me—and, therefore, interesting)
to cite and to refute on evidence some of the most widespread wrong
etymologies, among them the derivation of *sincere* from Latin *sine
cera,* without wax; of *posh* from *port out starboard home;* of *love,* the
tennis score, from French *l'oeuf,* the egg, and of *cop* from *copper
buttons,* or variantly from *(c)onstable (o)n (p)atrol.* The fact is that
some among us have put almost as much ingenuity into misexplaining
the origins of words and phrases as the race has put into making language. I have welcomed these inventions as being interesting in themselves, and interesting again as a specimen behavior of *Homo loquens.*

Many terms, moreover, even when accurately etymologized, do
not make whole sense until they have been put into a historical context.
For that reason I have appended a historical note to many of the
terms here treated, and I confess to having found those histories not
only essential but a part of my obsession equal to my felonious footnotery of etymologies.

See *roué,* for example. The French word labeled a criminal so foul that he was executed by being broken on the wheel. English *roué* is not as dark as that. Nor can the difference be accounted for without a historical note on the *duc d'Orleans*, his regency, and the scapegrace court with which he surrounded himself, referring to his rakes and roisterers as his *roués* because every one of them fully deserved to be broken on the wheel. The duke, of course, was having his joke. And his followers welcomed the label, self-seekingly insisting that it referred to their valor and loyalty, because any one of them would endure the wheel sooner than be disloyal to the great patron.

The facts given, anyone is free to interpret them to his own pleasure, but without a knowledge of this court banter there is no way to understand how *roué*, so grim a word in its original sense, is used half humorously and usually indulgently in English.

That is how it is with *Homo loquens*. We have to look closely to see what he is really doing in his word hive, but he is always there, and forever doing it. He is also your ancestor and mine, as he is you and me. To browse his verbal relics is more than to learn his language: it is to catch part of his most basic nature in the most characteristic act of himself.

JOHN CIARDI

A BROWSER'S DICTIONARY

A

Aaron's rod   An epithet for any force that engulfs everything around it. [Exodus 7:9–12:

> When Pharaoh shall speak unto you, saying, Show a miracle . . .
> Take thy rod and cast it before Pharaoh, and it shall become a serpent.
>   . . . and Aaron cast down his rod before Pharaoh . . . and it became a serpent.
>   Then Pharaoh also called the wise men and the sorcerers: now the magicians of Egypt, they also did in like manner with their enchantments.
>   For they cast down every man his rod, and they became serpents: but Aaron's rod swallowed up their rods.]

aback   *Obs*. Once the standard form of *back*. Surviving only in **taken aback** Nonplused. Unexpectedly checked in one's course. [Originally nautical. Said of square sails blown back against the mast by a sudden wind shift, or by bringing the ship up into the wind as in *backing and filling*, which see.]

abecedarian   One who is still learning the alphabet; hence, a beginner. [So in XVI, based on earlier *abecedary* (XV), spelling book, and with precedent in Medieval L. *abecedarium*, based on a-b-c-d as first four letters of the alphabet, hence standing for all the alphabet, as in *to learn one's abc's*. (Such later senses as "teacher of the alphabet" and "grammarian" and even "scholar of the origins of the alphabet" are simple exts. of doubtful precedent.]

NOTE. *Solfeggio* and *gamut* are words formed on the sequence of musical notes. *Abc, alphabet*, and *abecedarian* are the only words in English based on the sequence of letters in the alphabet. See *kelemenopy*.

abracadabra   1. *Now*. A standard part of the gibberish of a performing magician-illusionist. 2. *Earlier*. A holy word charged with special powers to heal and to ward off evil. [In the arcana of magico-religion, first associated with the Gnostic cult of antiquity and the early Christian era. (Simon Magus, who is denounced in Acts 8 for attempting to buy for money the power of the sacraments—and from whom *simony* derives—was a late Gnostic leader.) Though the cult adopted bits and pieces of Christian ritual, it clung to the forms of early witchcraft. Its holiest conjure word was Gk. *abrasadabra;* perh. < the name of the god it worshipped, perh. from the name of an early high priest, and very likely both; for as with the pharaohs and with the later Roman emperors, it was a common practice to deify great leaders. Or perh. an altered acronym based on Hebrew *ab,* father; *ben,* son; and *ruach acadash,* holy spirit. Where there is no evidence, one guess does as well as another.

The word was commonly written over and over on parchment in various geometric crossword forms, and the parchment folded into a cross or a geometric figure. The talisman so formed was hung by a string around the neck of an afflicted person, who was instructed to wear it for a specified time while performing pre-scribed rites, and then to dispose of it as prescribed by the cult healer, almost certainly without opening the magic pack, and—presto!—the afflicted one was made whole.

What is more, it probably worked, just as faith healing still works for true believers in cases where the illness stems from a nervous disorder.]

accolade   1. An honor paid one, as by an especially ceremonious reception, or by a eulogy. 2. *Rites of chivalry.* The act of creating a knight by touching him on the shoulder with the flat of a sword while saying, "I dub thee Sir So-and-so." [L. *ad,* to; *colum,* collar. In Late L. prob. (unattested) *accolāre,* to embrace about the neck. OF *acolada.*]

Aceldama   (The *c* is pronounced as an *s.*) 1. Another name for the original potter's field outside Jerusalem. 2. Any scene of great car-nage. 3. Any place of death and horror. *the Aceldama of the Nazi concentration camps.* [Via Gk. *Akeldama* < Aramaic *haqel dama,* field of blood. Matthew 27:7–8: "And they took counsel, and bought with them (Judas's thirty pieces of silver) the potter's field, to bury strangers in. Wherefore the field was called, The field of blood . . ." The Aramaic original, here rephrased, probably referred to a field of bloody battle. There is no evidence that the potter's field had ever been such a battle site. The "blood" is prob. a double reference to Judas's blood money, and to the many obscure persons to be buried there.]

Adam As narrated in Genesis, the first man. [Hebrew *'adham,* man < *'adhamah,* earth, clay; hence, of mortal clay.] *Adamic* Ingenuous. One who behaves as if everything were happening for the first time. *Adamite* 1. A descendant of Adam; any human being. 2. A member of a sect that sought to live as Adam did. 3. *Now rare.* A nudist.

Adam's ale Water. [Whimsical. Because it was all Adam had to drink. Cf. *municipal beer,* tap water.] *the old Adam (in us)* The sinful trace inherent in our earthy natures. *Adam's apple* The bulge of laryngeal cartilage in front of the throat, commonly prominent in men, rarely so in women. [Said to be the sinful apple, which stuck in Adam's throat. Eve ate first, but in the legend as explained by a male-dominant society, deceitful woman swallowed her apple without a trace, whereas the misled but basically honest good old male was too open and honest to hide his guilt.] *not to know one from Adam* Not to know one at all. [The point is that Adam was the most recognizable of men. He lacked the rib taken from him for the creation of Eve. He had no belly button since he had not been born of woman and hence had not had an umbilical cord. And as a direct creation of God, only he among all men was perfect in beauty.] *not to know one from Adam's off ox* See *ox.*

admiral 1. *Now.* A naval flag officer. 2. *Earlier.* A sea lord. Columbus bore the title Admiral of the Ocean Seas. [Root sense: "sea lord" < Arabic *amir-al-mā,* emir (of) the sea. Shortened to Arabic *amir-al,* the emir, the lord; and so into XI It. *ammirale,* sea leader, but also with the senses "harbor master" and "port engineer" and so used by Dante in early XIV. In XVII Eng., Milton still used *ammiral,* but by XV *admiral* had become common, and was prob. construed as deriving from L. *ad-,* to; *mirare,* to look fixedly (ADMIRE). And this Latinate misreading may account for XVI–XVII *admiral galley,* the lead ship of a naval formation (not necessarily with an admiral aboard), to which other ships looked for sailing directions, directed by flags in daytime, stern lights at night.] *admiral of the head Naval slang.* The naval equivalent of an army latrine orderly.

affable Easily approachable. [Root sense: "easy to talk to." < L. *fari,* to talk; prefixed *a(d)-,* to talk to → *affābilis,* talkable-to. Akin to *fable* < L. *fabula,* a story (a spoken tale); and with side sense deriving from the wonders spoken in fables: *fabulous.*] *Most fables say that Fannie was fabulously affable.*

affidavit   *Law.* A written deposition sworn before a notary or officer of the court by a witness unable to appear in court. [The stem is *fid-,* faith, trust < L. *fidēs,* faith. Prefixed *ad-,* to, the assimilated form being *af-* → *affidare,* trust to, testify to → *affidavit,* he has testified (to).]

agnostic   One who does not know. [Based on Gk. *gnosis,* knowledge; with *a-,* negative prefix. Coined in 1869 by Thomas Henry Huxley, father of British novelist Aldous Huxley and of J. S. Huxley, Sir Julian, biologist and author. An early biologist and defender of Darwinian theory, and ardent in disputation with fundamentalists, Huxley tired of being labeled an *atheist,* one who denies the existence of God, and labeled himself an *agnostic* to indicate that he had no evidence on which to affirm or deny that existence.]

aisle   A passageway to one side of or through rows of seats or pews. [L. *ala,* wing. OF *aile,* wing of a building, ell (ELL). ME *eile* may have been influ. by *isle,* little island, and meant specifically "the side passages of a church between the outer wall and the first row of columns," that sense remaining primary in modern Brit.]
    two on the aisle *Theater.* The two adjoining seats nearest the aisle; regarded as choice seats because of easy access and departure. **lay them in the aisles** *Theater.* To score an enormous success. [Hyperbole. The basic idea is from comedy: to move the audience to such paroxysms of laughter that they roll uncontrollably in the aisles.] **go down the aisle** To get married. [Said of the bride only. The groom waits at the altar for the bride to come down the aisle. After the ceremony the two go up the aisle together.

There was a young man from Belle Isle
Who said to his girl, "If you'll, I'll."
    "I'm willing," said she,
    "But first I must see
How you look as I walk down the aisle."

a.k.a.   *Recent police jargon.* Also known *as.* [Replaces earlier *alias.*]

akimbo   Occurs only in *with arms akimbo* With hands on hips and elbows sharply bent outward, a body posture indicating impatience, hostility, or contempt. (But note that within the easily extended possibility of most idioms, one would be clearly understood in saying, "He has lived his whole life with his mind akimbo," or "Here comes Hot-pants Harrier with her legs akimbo.") [ON *kengboggin,* bent bows < *keng,* bent (KINK); *boggin,* bows. Akin to OE *bogan,* to bow (down to). (See *buxom.*) Into ME as *in kenebowe,* at root a rendering of the Old Norse but influ. in Eng. by association with *keen,* sharp, sharply.]

alcohol   In simplest form C_2H_5OH, the transcendental liquid classically produced by fermentation, and raised to the power of eternal life by distillation, and rarely, as in upper New England's field applejack, by freezing barrels of the ferment, causing the essence to draw to the center of the ice cake. [< Arabic *alkohl* < *al,* the; *kohl,* a cosmetic for darkening the eyelids. It is made from a powder of antimony. To achieve a fine even stain, this powder was vaporized and cooled. When, c. 1000 A.D., Arabian alchemists invented the distillation of alcohol by a similar process, they borrowed the name for their product from the cosmetic process, and alcohol has ever since been doing things to the eyes.]

alert   *adj.* Keenly watchful. Vigilant.—*n. Military and naval.* 1. An alarm signal. 2. The period during which such an alarm watch is in effect. *We had an all-night alert. red alert* The condition of maximum danger and the status of forces during such a period. [Root sense: "on the watchtower." It. *erta* < *torre erta,* watchtower; lit. "tower raised (erected) high < L. *erectus,* raised. With It. *alla,* to the, on the → *all' erta,* on the tower, on lookout. Eng. *erect* has primary sense "to construct" but is at root "straight, straight line"; here, such a line raised vertically. See IE stem *reg-* and its many derivatives.]

alibi   1. *In informal usage.* Any excuse. *Alibi Ike* Disdainful term for a person who never delivers on a promise but is always ready with an excuse. 2. *Legal.* In refuting a criminal charge, proof that one was somewhere else at the time the crime was committed. [< L. *alibi,* elsewhere < *alius,* other; *ubi,* where.]

alice blue   A pale blue. [So named during Theodore Roosevelt's presidency, 1901–1909, as a dress designer's homage to his daughter Alice, born 1884, later Mrs. Longworth. The still surviving popular song "In My Sweet Little Alice-Blue Gown" is of the same era and testifies to the popularity of the color. More remarkably, *alice* *blue* establishes the Roosevelts as a family that has given two eponymous words to the language, *teddy bear* (which see) having been named after T.R. I can find no other family that has produced two eponymous words. Samuel *Maverick* gave his name to the language, and his grandson Maury coined *gobbledygook,* but the latter is not eponymous.]

alkahest   *Alchemy.* The mythical universal solvent. (But if it dissolves everything it touches, what does one keep it in? and how does one keep it from dissolving the world?) [Pseudo-Arabic. Coined by *Paracelsus* (which see), XVI Swiss alchemist and self-vaunting mystifier.]

allemande right/allemande left   Square dance calls. And in corrupted forms *alleman, alley man, allez man* [The step called for, to the right or to the left, is from a popular late XVII French dance called *l'Allemande,* the German Woman. The corrupted forms have led to some curious etymologizing, but the origin is firmly traceable to that German woman.]

alligator   The amphibious New World lizard. Closely related to the African crocodile, but smaller on average, and having a shorter snout. [< Sp. *el lagarto,* the lizard; later modified to Sp. *alagarto.*]

allude   [Based on L. *ludere,* to play. Ult. < IE *leid-,* to play (LUDICROUS).] 1. *Properly, and with root sense functioning.* To hint. To suggest glancingly, as if posing a riddle. 2. *In common slovenly usage and by now prob. the primary Am. sense.* To refer.

amateur   1. An ardent nonprofessional, esp. in sports; but also *amateur artist,* one for whom art is a cultural passion but not a career. Whence, 2. An inferior performer; one who lacks professional qualification. So the fixed phrase *rank amateur* Clumsy beginner; one totally lacking in professional skill. [Loan word. Fr. *amateur,* lover, enthusiast of. See *love* as tennis term for zero. And cf. *for love* (without pay), and *not for love nor money* (not for any reason).]

amen corner/Amen Corner   1. A section of pews, usu. near the pulpit, reserved for church elders who lead the responses, esp. the amens. Variantly, such a section of pews regularly taken over by the vocally fervent. 2. *NYC machine politics.* In late XIX and early XX, a suite in a New York City hotel, permanently reserved as a meeting place for politicians. [For putting their heads together as if in prayer? For allowing the ward heelers to say "Amen" to whatever the bosses said?] 3. *Brit.* A former street intersection in London, destroyed in a WW II air raid. [On Corpus Christi Day, monks marched in procession over a fixed route to St. Paul's Cathedral, the streets they traveled acquiring the names of the prayers they chanted in regular order: *Paternoster Row, Amen Corner, Ave Maria Lane,* and *Creed Lane,* because on this last approach to the cathedral they chanted the Credo.}

amuck/amok   Frenzy. [Malay *amok,* bloody attack.] *run amuck/ amok* To be carried away by a murderous frenzy. [Especially associated with Maori males of New Zealand. Under circumstances not entirely understood by white men, Maori males went into ritual seclusion, from which they emerged, as if rabid, to race through the jungle and slaughter any living thing they encountered. Part of this trance was induced by hallucinogenic mushrooms (see *berserk*), but a more powerful agency was certainly a drug called "religious frenzy."]

Ancient of Days   God, conceived as the timeless dispenser of time. [Daniel 7:9: "I beheld till the thrones were cast down, and the Ancient of days did sit, whose garment was white as snow, and the hair of his head like the pure wool: his throne was like the fiery flame, and his wheels as burning fire." It is not easy to parse such effusion to logic, but the Hebrew word here rendered *Ancient* is *attiq,* removed; the prob. sense being "He who is removed from (apart from) time," i.e., "the Eternal One."]

anecdote   1. A brief narration of an incident as a way of making or of illustrating a point. 2. In history and biography, such an account of a previously undisclosed incident. (In this sense the plu. can be *anecdota.*) Also *anecdota* A collection of such previously unrevealed incidents. The adjectival forms are: *anecdotal, anecdotical, anecdotic.* [Root sense: "not previously made public." Based on Gk. *didonai,* to give; prefixed *ek-,* out → p.p. *ekdotos,* given out, made public; with negative prefix *an-* → *anekdotos,* not given out; not made public, (or as we might say today) not previously published.]

angel   [Gk. **aggelos,* messenger. (Gk. *gg* was pron. *ng.*) Akin to **aggaros,* mounted courier. Converted to present religious sense as a metaphor that became traditional among early Christian writers, the metaphor then passing into a new concept.] 1. A messenger from God. [Such messengers are common to many religions. Hermes, and Iris, the rainbow, were the commonest such messengers in Greek religion. Angels, though usu. anonymous in the OT, are more common than in the NT, much of their function as intermediaries between God and man having been taken over by Jesus while he was on earth, and continuing through his revelation and his vicar on earth. When, for example, the pope pronounces infallibly, he is performing the basic angelic function of announcing God's will to humankind.] 2. A heavenly creature. Hence, 3. A person so conceived as perfect and adorable. 4. A pet name for whatever one ends up with this side of adorable perfection. 5. A common given name, esp. in It. and Sp. *Angelo, Angelina, Angel.* 6. *Show biz.* A financial backer. ["Helper from on high." (And corresponding verb form, *to angel.*)] 7. *Aviation.* 1,000 feet of altitude. *at twelve angels* = at 12,000 feet.

Angelus, angelus 1. The R.C. prayer for heavenly protection beginning *Angelus domini nuntiavit Maria,* "Angel of God who announced to Mary," and followed by three Ave Marias with other versicles, and a collect in memory of the Incarnation. (In XIV it was recited only in the morning. In XV it was repeated at noon. In XVII an evening Angelus was added, this last known in Italy as the *Ave Maria.*) 2. The bell that sounds the call for these prayers, and that rings three times for each *Ave,* and nine times during the   collect.

angel food cake A light, fluffy cake, usu. with a hole through the center for better exposure to baking heat; made with egg whites only and no shortening. [Whimsical extravagance, perh. based on *panus angelicus,* bread of angels.]

guardian angel Nursery and pious legend. 1. A personal proprietary and protective heavenly spirit. 2. A person who undertakes such a protective role.

Hell's angels Fiends; messengers of Satan. *Hell's Angels* The most widely known of the reckless, antisocial, and often violent motorcycle gangs, this original group having formed in the San Francisco Bay area.

HISTORIC. Several studies have identified the original core of the gang as having been the sons of the Dust Bowl Okies of the 1930's. Migrants from childhood, accustomed to parental beatings and peer fistfights, and with no intellectual life, these young men formed a rebel society based on daredevil riding, personal filthiness, and contempt for the values of society. Bound by a rigid antisocial ethic, they valued risk and violence and even self-violence, their ethic prescribing massive violent retaliation for any real or imagined slight.

animus   A feeling of hostility. [A specimen evolution. Ult. < IE *ane-*, breath, to breathe, passage of air (ANEMOMETER). L. *anima* (fem.), the physical breath of life (ANIMAL); *animus* (masc.), the spiritual life essence (ANIMATION). L. *animus* does not in itself signify hostility, but implies it in the Roman assumption of the male as the aggressive, active principle; whence ANIMOSITY. Carl Jung, reviving this Latin implication, used *animus* to label a hazily described form of male aggression in the female personality (ANIMAL CRACKERS).]

anise and cumin   Superficial things, esp. when treated as more important than weightier matters. [Matthew 23:23: ". . . ye pay tithe of mint and anise and cummin, and have omitted . . . judgment, mercy, and faith . . ." *Cummin*, or *cumin*, is an Old World plant superficially rescmbling Queen Anne's lace. Its seeds, like those of anise, are used as a spice.]

anthology   A collection of literary pieces by many hands. [Root sense: "a bouquet." < Gk. *anthos*, flower; *logos*, word; in the generalized suffix *-ology*, study of ("that which puts words to").]

any more/anymore   1. No longer. (In negative constructions only. *We don't go there any more* = We no longer go there.) *But recently,* 2. Now. These days. *We do all our shopping at the A & P anymore* = Nowadays (of late) we do all our shopping at the A & P. (Which is not only a barbarism but defies all language sense, and yet is becoming increasingly common, even among those who might otherwise pass as literate.)

A-One/A-1/A number 1   Topnotch. The best. The finest. [In 1834 Lloyd's of London issued a classification of ships for insurance purposes, *A number 1* being the highest rating within the highest category; and so into general usage.]

aphrodisiac   *n.* Any substance or food said to increase sexual potency. —*adj.* Sexually stimulating. [< Gk. *aphrodisios*, of Aphrodite; *aphrodisia*, sexual pleasure.]

appaloosa   A boldly splotched, powerful, and spirited strain of range horse bred by the Nez Percé Indians of Idaho (and see *cayuse*).

[The Palouse River of Idaho and Washington is named after the Eng. distortion of the original Indian name. In the French of the voyageurs, *à la Palouse*, at the Palouse River (i.e., in the homelands of the Nez Percé).]

apple The fruit; the tree. [IE *abel-*, apple. With b/p in Gmnc. → OE *aeppel*, ME *appel*.]

   apple of discord *Greek myth.* Eris, goddess of discord, had a golden apple inscribed "For the fairest of all," and rolled it into a meeting of the gods, where Hera, Athena, and Aphrodite fell to squabbling over it, each claiming it had been inscribed for her.

   apple of one's eye 1. The pupil of the eye. [Conceived as a small apple (sphere).] 2. An especially cherished thing. *His daughter was the apple of his eye.* [In common use by IX. Prob. sense: "thing held in the center of one's eye" (attention). Perh. influ. by the apple of the Tree of Knowledge (which shone enticingly as it became the center of Adam's and Eve's attention).]

   apple knocker A yokel. ["One who takes a stick and knocks apples from a tree."]

   apple pie order Meticulous neatness. [*Pie* is known to derive from Fr. *plier*, to fold (PLY), as in *to pie a bed*, to short-sheet. Though unattested, the idiom probably derives from Norman-French *nape plié en ordre*, napery (household linens) folded (and put away) in order. French was the language of the manor house following the Norman Conquest, and menial work was done by the conquered Saxons. The steward of the manor instructed the Saxon laundry wench to wash, iron, fold, and store away the linens, using some such form as given above. She spoke no French and did not care to. *Nape plié en ordre* sounded to her like a garbled form of *apple pie order*, and that was good enough for her.]

   apple polisher One who seeks to curry favor. [As if by buffing an apple to a high shine, thereby making a common object seem to be an unusual thing. Am. Dating unknown.]

   apple sauce Bosh. Nonsense. [XVIII Am. *sass* for *sauce*. Prob. originally *don't give me any of your sass*, then *don't give me any of your apple sass*, then *apple sass, apple sauce*, as stuff not worth listening to.]

   The Big Apple The all-but-official nickname of New York City. [Charles Gillett, president of the New York Convention and Visitors Bureau, initiated (c. 1971–1972) the campaign to have the nickname officially adopted. Mr. Gillett calls the nickname a "positive upbeat symbol" and claims that it has become "the most successful city slogan in the history of tourism." So the robotics of enthusiasm.

The term originated among black jazz musicians of New Orleans c. 1910, as a translation of Sp. *manzana principal*. *Manzana* means "apple," but also "tract of land" (apple orchard), and in common usage "city block." *Manzana principal*, a main city block, downtown, the main stem, where the action is. The term later passed into show biz with the sense "the big time," and thence prob. to Mr. Gillett, but it has always remained a special term for jazz men. In his book *Hi De Ho* (1936) Cab Calloway defined the Big Apple as "the big town, the main stem, Harlem."]

apricot   The fruit, the tree, the color. [Ernest Weekley, *The Romance of Words*, London, 1912, traces the form through a circuit of the Mediterranean, starting with L. *praecox*, early ripe (PRECOCIOUS) → Vulgar L. *praecoquum* → Med. Gk. (exact form unknown) → Arabic *barquq*, apricot, *al barquq*, the apricot → Sp. *albaricoque*. The Shakespearean *apricock* reflects this clockwise excursion through Arabic. And even It. *albicocca* is based on the Arabic rather than the L. form.]

April Fool/April Fool's Day   *In Brit.* ***All Fools' Day.*** April 1 and a time for fools' errands, mock gifts, comic greetings, and practical jokes. In Scotland one is sent *to hunt the gowk* (the cuckoo). In France the person on whom a trick is played is called *le poisson d'Avril*, The April fish (fool). In Am. prison slang *fish* for gullible new prisoner has the same sense. [Variously attributed. Some refer it to the abduction of Proserpine in early spring, leaving her mother, Ceres, to walk the forests calling her name uselessly; others, to the Julian calendar, whose cumulative error over the centuries moved New Year's Day to almost the end of March (when Gregorian calendar reforms moved New Year's Day back to Jan. 1, a time for traditional gift giving, people continued to give mock presents on the false New Year, April 1). But all such efforts to fix a particular origin are wasted. As surely as man is sometimes prankish, festivals of mockery occur in many primitive societies, and their survival today in cultures scattered around the globe points to an origin lost in time. (Cf. *Halloween*, a survival of some lost early Teutonic festival, now Christianized as All Hallow's Eve.)]

apron   1. A protective garment worn over one's outer clothes, originally tied around the waist, later variants often with a haltered or sleeved bib. 2. *Ext.* a. *Theater.* The forward projection of a stage. b. *Aviation*. The hard top in front of a hangar or other service building. [< Fr. *napron,* a small tablecloth (NAPERY, NAPKIN). ME *napron* altered from *a napron* to *an apron*. (See *noncing.*)]

-ard A pervasive and generally pejorative suffix denoting "one characterized by." So *bastard, coward, dastard, dotard, drunkard, petard, shitard, stinkard.* But note also *wizard,* without the pejorative sense. [Prob. originally Frankish-to-French < Gmnc. *-ardt, -hardt,* able, able in. So the family name Hardy. So Ger. family name *Gerhardt,* able in war. And as so used in patronymics, without pejorative sense, and in fact affirming merit. The sense shift to a pejorative had already occurred in Norman French and must be assumed to have been a Frankish twist on the Gmnc. original.]

arena 1. Field of action in sports; by ext., in war. 2. *Primary sense in Am.* The building or stadium containing a playing field, boxing ring, or other sports area. *the municipal arena.* [But the *arena* is, specifically, the field, as distinct from the tiers around it. < L. *arena,* sand, sanded place < **harena, *arena* (perh. Etruscan). Because the floor of the arena was covered with sand, for footing, and in gladiatorial contests, to absorb blood.]
　enter the arena To compete. In politics, to campaign. **arena theater** Theater in the round. [The stage surrounded by the audience, as was the sanded central pit of Roman gladiatorial contests.]

assassin One who kills prominent political or religious persons for ideological reasons. Though a hired assassin may kill simply for gain, the ultimate reason for an assassination (and for hiring the paid assassin) is ideological. [Arabic *hashashin* (lit. "those who smoke hashish") was the name applied to zealots of an anarchistic sect founded in Cairo in XI by Hassan Sabbah, who planned to establish a single Mohammedan empire after killing off all Muslim rulers. In XII, under the leader called Jebel, or the Old Man of the Mountain, and until they were wiped out c. 1255 by Mongol invaders, they generally chose crusaders as their victims, hacking them savagely. Long a mystery drug to Europeans, hashish was customarily given as the cause for this blood lust. The use of hashish has since become more common and we now know that there is no such power of rabidity in the stuff, and that what was at work on the *hashashin* was a far more powerful hallucinogen called "religious fervor." (See *amuck, berserk.*)]

assbackwards   Messed up. Askew. Not in proper alignment. [Nor for that matter is the idiom, backwards being the only logical alignment for an ass. What would be really out of alignment is *assfrontwards*. But in vulgar exuberance, sweet style is always more than reason.]

authentic   Accurate. Based on truth. [Root sense: "authorial," asserted by a (reliable) author. Gk. *authentēs,* one who does, one who asserts. Late L. *authenticus,* verifiable, asserted by authority.]
    NOTE. *Genuine* (see *gen-, gene-*), with the Latin root sense "of an identified talent/genius," has an identical root sense; and *genuine* and *authentic* often function as synonyms, but Archbishop Trench, in a series of lectures published in 1882, points to an essential distinction: "Caesar's *The History of the Alexandrian War* is not genuine since Caesar did not write it; yet it is authentic in that its contents are accurate and verifiable. Thiers' *History of the French Empire* is genuinely his work but unauthentic in its content. And Thucydides' *History of the Peloponnesian War* is both genuine and authentic."

awkward   *adj.* 1. Clumsy. Graceless. 2. *Ext.* Uncomfortable. *an awkward situation.* [Root sense: "turned back upon itself." Second element is OE *weard,* in the direction of (TOWARD, FORWARD). First element akin to obs. Sc. *awk,* perverse; ON *afugr,* turned around. Ult. < IE *ap-,* off, away, turned from (APOGEE, ABDICATE).]
    awkward squad 1. *U.S. Army.* A group of recruits who are ungainly in close order drill and who are assigned to a single squad (drill unit) for remedial training. 2. *Army ext.* Any group of inept soldiers. 3. *General ext.* Any group of misfits.

B

backing and filling   Vacillation. Hemming and hawing. [Originally in nautical usage only: *backing*, in a square-rigged vessel, to have the wind blow the sails back against the mast; *filling*, to have the wind blow the sails toward the bow; *backing and filling*, to drift down a river while maneuvering broadside to the wind with partially set sails, alternately backing and filling to work the ship around obstacles and to keep it clear of the riverbanks; because on a set course in a narrow waterway the ship's momentum could leave it without room to maneuver.]

baggage   [OF **bague*, pack, bundle; with *-age*, collective suffix.] 1. Luggage. Aside from the clothes one wears and pocket items, the total of the possessions one takes on a trip. 2. *Since c. 1500.* Except for artillery and carried weapons, the total of supplies and equipment carried into the field by an army (which may move with, or apart from, its baggage train). 3. A woman camp follower. [OED cites, 1601: "Every common soldier carrying with him his she-baggage." In this sense certainly influ. by Fr. *bagasse*, slut. As late as XIX, Brit. regiments (and, for a time, ships: see *gun: son of a gun*) regularly took wives and camp followers into the field, esp. in empire outposts. When the regiment moved, the officers' ladies commonly traveled by private carriage; the women of enlisted men, with the baggage train. Hence, depending on one's sense of such wagonloads of gaggle, either of the two following senses:] 4. A woman of no redeeming social significance. 5. *With an indulgent connotation.* A saucy, pert, frolicsome girl.

   bag and baggage The total of one's transportable belongings. [*bag*, what one carries; *baggage*, what one ships.] ***clear out bag and baggage*** To leave with no intention to return. [Taking all that one can carry or ship.]

   NOTE. *Baggage*, once standard, has been replaced in Brit. by *luggage*. Both occur in Am. use, but *baggage* dominates the compound forms, as in: *baggage car, baggage check, baggage master, baggage room, baggage train.* Yet *luggage rack* is the fixed form for a baggage rack attached to an automobile, and shops sell no *baggage* but only *luggage.* If the salesperson in such a shop is saucy, one might refer to the *baggage who sells luggage,* but never to the *luggage who sells baggage.*

bail [L. **bajulus,* carrier. Root senses include: 1. A water carrier. 2. A woman bearing a child (and by ext. a nurse, i.e., one who takes charge of the child). 3. A person charged with the weight of any responsibility. Into Eng. via OF *baillier,* to carry, to handle, to take charge. ME *baile,* custody.] 1. To post a custodial bond for someone under arrest. 2. To remove buckets of water from a boat. [Rarely used *bail* with the sense "(rounded) handle of a pail" would appear to derive from L. *bajulus,* but is almost certainly from ON *beyla,* bulge, swelling, rounded thing.]

bailiff In Am. An officer of the court, or a sheriff's assistant, whose main duty is to serve and enforce writs and other court orders. *In Brit.* with the further sense: "steward of an estate." [Person charged with the responsibility for; suffixed *-iff,* ult. < Brit. *reeve,* an officer of a British shire (SHERIFF, shire reeve).]

bailiwick [Root sense: "specific area of authority." < ME *baile,* custody; OE *wic,* place of residence. Common in British place names, as *Chadwick, Fenwick, Warwick.*] One's native or chosen purlieus. (The sense corresponds closely to what juvenile street gangs call their "turf.")

baker's dozen Thirteen for the price of twelve. [Were bakers such notorious cheats that English law singled them out for heavy penalties for short weighting, thereby forcing them to throw in a thirteenth make-weight roll per dozen? Perhaps the bakers were worse scoundrels than butchers and other tradesmen, but though many sources refer to such a law, none identifies it. The OED does cite a related law in the *liber albus,* a codex dated 1859, but that law simply specified that hawkers who bought bread for resale be permitted a thirteenth loaf per dozen as their margin of profit. Legality aside, the practice of throwing in a "free" extra, for which the price has already been adjusted, is as old as mercantile man, and sufficiently explains the idiom.]

balance 1. A scale of the sort used as the zodiacal sign of Libra. 2. Equilibrium. 3. The remainder of an unpaid account; or the amount remaining on deposit in a bank account. [At root: "two large plates." < 1. *lanx,* a large plate; prefixed *bi-,* two. The form *bilanx* occurs in XVI as a holding from Latin, but the forms *ballance, ballaunce, balance* were established in OF and ME. It. retains the *bi- (bilancia).* The shift from *bi-* to *ba-* occurred in OF.]

ball [IE *bhel-,* swollen, bruised, rounded. And with early ref. to sexual swelling, whence BULL and BALLS (for testicles).] The most common idioms derive from games played with a ball. *be on the ball* To be alert and energetic. [As in soccer, to be at the center of play.] *carry the ball* To advance any given cause. To shoulder responsibility. [As in football, rugby.] *keep the ball rolling* To support any given activity vigorously. [To advance the play.] *have something on the ball* To be skilled, knowledgeable. [As a baseball pitcher who is able to control the spin and accuracy of his pitches.] *play ball* To go along with. To engage to participate and to follow the rules. [In baseball, the umpire's cry to begin play.]

(all) balled up Confused. Botched. Wrong. [Prob. a reference to a snarled ball of twine or yarn.]

ball of fire 1. A comet. 2. A dazzling person; a go-getter; one to set the world on fire. *balls of fire!* Exclam. of astonishment. [As if sighting many comets.]

balls and all Entirely. [Testicles and penis. The whole man.] *go for one's balls* To gamble everything. [Lose, and not much of the man is left.]

blackball Originally, to vote against. Later, to exclude, to ostracize. [In Greek election practice, voters placed clay balls in an urn, a ball of white clay to vote for, of black clay to vote against. The sense "to ostracize" is from the practice of British "gentlemen's clubs" in which a single vote against (a black ball) was enough to exclude.]

highball Now, primarily. A whiskey drink served with water or soda in a tall glass. *Earlier, Am. railroading.* A clear white signal at the top of the signal rack. Indicates clear track and full speed ahead. *balling the jack Am. railroading.* [*Jack* for throttle. To *(high)ball the throttle* was to run full speed ahead. So by extension:] To go sexually all out, and full animal-speed ahead. To engage in any activity to the energetic maximum.

[But *have a ball,* have an especially good time, is < Fr. *bal,* a dance < Gk. *ballizein,* to throw, to dance (to throw oneself and one's partner around).]

ballyhoo A noisy promotional campaign, as the preliminary hoopla of an advance agent who cares little for what he says so long as it is said loudly enough. The London *Times Literary Supplement*, July 19, 1934 (as quoted by Partridge, *Slang*), defined *ballyhoo* as "eloquence aimed at the pocket book." [Perhaps, as often asserted, from Ballyhooley, a village in County Cork, whose natives were said to be especially noisy-boisterous. But in that regard, how can any one Irish town be singled out from others? In the form *ballyhooly*, common in Brit. 1880's music halls, perhaps from Ballyhooley, but certainly influ. by *bally*, minced form of taboo *bloody*. So *ballyhooly truth*, the whole bloody (bloody-holy) truth, may well be entirely independent of Ballyhooley. Also, c. the same time and a bit earlier: *go to ballyhack, go to ballyhoo*, go to the dickens. Into Am. c. 1910.]

Ballyhoo A popular, mildly risqué, humor magazine of the Depression years of the 1930's. (See *zilch*.)

bamboozle To cheat. To swindle. To pull the wool over one's eyes. [Originally as noun and with the senses "a hoax, a swindle." Included by Jonathan Swift in a list of distasteful new slang words much in vogue in early XVIII. But in Am. as verb only, and commonly in the exclam. *well, I'll be bamboozled!*

Prob. a slang variant of Brit. *bombasine*, Am. *bombazine*, a fabric of silk and wool or silk and cotton which, dyed black, was traditional for a woman's mourning clothes. The sense "a hoax" may have developed because a cheat, dressed and veiled in such mourning clothes, would be effectively disguised to practice a confidence game as a bereft widow. < Fr. *bombasin*, which, via shifting L. and Late L. forms, is ult. < Gk. *bombux*, silkworm. And see *bombast*.]

bandbox 1. *Originally.* A small, circular, hard-leather box in which clergymen carried their bands, i.e., clerical collars, to keep them neat. 2. *Later.* A large, circular piece of luggage, esp. one for storing or carrying a ceremonial uniform. [Hence, the sense "immaculate, neat, immaculately dressed" in:] *neat as a bandbox,* and *he looks as if he had just stepped out of a bandbox.*

banjo A fretted, flat-surfaced string instrument. [Often asserted to be of African origin, our word based on untraced African roots of which Carib-Creole-pidgin *banjil, banjor* are intermediate forms. But the assertion of an African origin not traceable to a known African root is questionable etymology. Though attestation is partly lacking, the likely evolution is from Gk. *pandoura*, a guitar-like instrument → Portuguese *bandurra*, bandore. Prob. by Afropidgin (in which Portuguese was a strong element) → the Carib-Creole forms cited above, and then from *banjor* → *banjo*.] **banjo eyes** Large, round, wide open, protuberant eyes. Once a common nickname.

banquet   A more or less ceremonial feast, esp. one commemorating an occasion, an association, or a cause; or honoring a person. *fund-raising banquet* A "feast," usu. chicken and peas slop-served with cold coffee at $100 or more per plate, to raise money for a political or charitable cause. *banquet speaker* A speaker who attempts to be witty, persuasive, or both, after chicken and peas washed down with cold coffee. [A word that has risen and fallen in the scale of opulence. Originally It. *banchetto*, little bench, little table, signifying a snack taken at a small side table. In XVIII & XIX Brit., *banquet*, an elaborate ceremonial feast. In late XVI with ref. to dessert, which was customarily served at small tables—*banquettes*—set up in a room adjoining the dining room. And in early XVI with the original It. sense.]

barbarian   A word whose meaning depends on the speaker; at base a label applied to some other ethnic group and implying lack of culture and civilized graces. [Gk. *barbaros* is derisively echoic of how such people speak, their language consisting (to Greek ears) of *bar-bar-bar* (which was—or, in this case, wasn't—Greek to them).]

HISTORIC. Gk. *barbaros* meant both "stranger" and "enemy." To lock these two senses into one word is certainly to affect the way in which one meets a stranger. The young Oedipus, faring forth on his manhood journey, met a *barbaros* on the road, fought about the right of way, and killed the stranger-enemy, who turned out to be the unknown father Oedipus had been doomed to kill, according to the dark prophecy made at his birth. Is it too much to suggest that the language set of Greek predisposed Oedipus to that killing, which might perhaps have been avoided had the Greek word for stranger been conjoined with, let us say, *Samaritan* rather than *enemy*?

Barbary Coast   Roughly the African Mediterranean coast west of Egypt; the coast of the Berbers. [Both *Barbary* and *Berber* are based on L. *barberi*, Gk. *barbaros*, barbarian. But both forms have converged with It. *barba rossa*, red beard. *I barbarossi* (in extenso, "the red-bearded barbarians") was the Italian name for XVI Turkish pirates in the Mediterranean; and *Barbarossa* was the It. name of the Berber chief and dread pirate ruler Khair ud-Din, the Bey of Algiers. Algiers is on the Barbary Coast.]

Barmecide feast   Perhaps what the emperor eats while wearing his new clothes. The elaborate pretense of offering a luxurious abundance when there is in fact nothing. *adj. Barmecidal. American education set out to be a Barmecide feast.* [Barmecide was the name of the noble Persian family that, as recounted in *The Arabian Nights,* offered a beggar an elegantly served meal of platters heaped with imaginary food.]

barnstorm   1. *Mid XIX Am. theatrical.* The act of a theatrical troupe in playing a series of small towns. [The disastrous performance of the Royal Nonesuch in Twain's *Huckleberry Finn* was a barnstorming, and actually took place in a barn. It is unlikely, however, that American farmers would generally permit a theatrical troupe and an audience into their highly flammable barns, nor were working barns suitable places for a theatrical performance. Traveling shows were generally staged on wagons, under canvas, or in saloons. The idiom is best taken as a whimsical flourish for "out in the sticks," i.e., "taking the barns by storm."] 2. *Aviation.* To tour local fairs and small towns, landing in pastures and sleeping in barns. Barnstormers, with the consent of a farmer, staged an aerobatic show to attract a crowd and then sold aerial rides, in which they literally "stormed" ("made diving passes at") the barns. William Faulkner's *Pylon* is about barnstorming pilots. My father-in-law, the late Lyle J. Hostetter, barnstormed in a Mercedes-Benz biplane in the early 1920's.

baseball
    HISTORIC. Legend has it that Abner Doubleday, later a general, invented baseball in 1839. Whatever Doubleday's contribution, he did not develop the basic rules of the game as now played, nor did he invent the game. It was no man's invention, but an evolution from such colonial games of stickball as One Old Cat or One O' Cat, and Rounders, so called because players had to run around a prescribed course in order to score.

bash   To strike powerfully. Often with *in. bash his head in for him.* [Earlier *bask.* Of uncertain Gmnc. origin, prob. an expressive, the expulsive *b* and guttural *k* being forceful speech sounds.]—*n.* A riotous celebration, a wild party. [Cf. the equivalent metaphoric

force in *beer bust,* a guzzling carouse; and *fling,* a wild party.]
But *bashful* is < *abash,* at root: "to be taken by surprise."

bassackwards   All askew; not in right alignment, SNAFU. [Minced,
partially spoonerized form of *assbackwards.*]

bastard   1. An illegitimate child. Hence, 2. A nasty person. 3. An
unlucky because inferior person. *that poor bastard.* 4. *Printing.*
A type font combining elements of two others. (But in *a bastard
type* functions as an adjective.)—*adj.* In names of things, esp. of
plants, an inferior thing that resembles a better. **bastardize** To
corrupt by inferior admixture. [Ult. < Gk. **bastazein,* to carry;
which is stem of OF *bast,* pack saddle. *bast* with *-ard* → *bastard,*
corresponding to Fr. *fils de bast,* son of a pack saddle. Cf. Eng.
woodscolt for same sense and idiomatic flavor. (It. *basta,* enough,
is a side evolution from *bastazein,* with root sense: "all that I can
carry").]

bated breath   Held breath. *with bated breath* With tense and intense
eagerness, expectation. [The ref. is to the shallow breathing caused
by intense emotion. The form is the aphetic of *abated.*]

beam   1. A heavy structural supporting member, originally of wood.
2. *Ext.* A dense shaft, as of light. 3. *Ext. from preceding.* A directed
rather than diffused radio signal. [Ult. < IE *bheu-,* to exist (TO
BE]. Via Gmnc. evolution to Ger. *Baum,* tree ("thing that exists").
The early Teutons were tree worshippers, believing that trees
possessed souls that had to be propitiated. *Druid,* at root, means
"one who knows trees and how to propitiate their spirits." → OE
bēam, tree; and later, a wooden supporting member ("thing cut
from a tree").]
　　on the beam 1. *Aviation.* On course; within the path defined
by a radionavigation beam, as in sense 3, above. 2. *Ext.* Accurate.
Correct. Not off course.
　　broad in the beam 1. *Nautical.* Said of a vessel: wide in the
transverse beams. 2. *Ext.* Said of a woman: wide in the hips.
　　abeam Nautical. To one side of a vessel. (So placed as to be
within a sight line taken along a vessel's beams.) *on her beams
ends Nautical.* Said of a ship rolling so violently the plane of the
decks is vertical to the water. (A hyperbole. A vessel literally on
her beams' ends would almost certainly capsize or founder.)

beard   [The modern form is readily visible in IE *bharda,* beard, an
etymological point all the more interesting in that scholars have

been unable to adduce an IE root for *hair*. The old Aryans must have had hair, but their word for it has been lost.] A man's face hair, exclusive of his mustache. [As a distinguishing mark of manhood, the beard has been a male status symbol in many societies, and to pluck, tug, or even touch a man's beard has been a powerfully offensive gesture in several cultures. Among Orthodox Jews such an act comes close to violating a religious taboo. So *to beard*, to confront offensively, as in *Hamlet*, "Comes thou to beard me in Denmark?" This ancient point of honor underlies the first group of idioms below.]

beardless boy *Pejorative*. A stripling; less than a man. **beard the lion in his den** To confront with utter boldness. **twist one's beard** As above, to treat with ultimate discourtesy.

Bluebeard The title villain of a widespread folk tale. He married many women to rob and murder them, and under the foul compulsion to collect their severed heads. In what may be called the pure version, Bluebeard leaves on a journey, his wife discovers the grisly trophy room and is in turn discovered by Bluebeard, who is about to add her to his collection when her brothers rush in and kill the groom, she watching the proceedings calmly, or at least without losing her head.

beat generation The antiestablishment, under-thirty, mind-expansion-drug culture of the late 1950's and the 1960's. Disenchanted by middle-class values, by racism, and by the fear-conformity of McCarthyism and militarism, it "dropped out" (of the rat race), "turned on" (to drugs and hallucinogens), and "tuned in" (to a view of universal Allness as adapted from Zen and a mishmash of Oriental religion and philosophy). [Based on "I'm beat," meaning "I'm exhausted, I've had it." Jack Kerouac claimed to have invented the name. As reported by John Clellon Holmes, *Publisher's Weekly*, Oct. 5, 1959, Kerouac claims to have derived the named from "beatific"; but Kerouac's, in this case, is the sort of nonsense the establishment calls a PR gimmick.]

beaver 1. A full set of whiskers. 2. A cry in the group play of children, the first one to see a fully whiskered man crying "Beaver!" (A survival in child's play of an otherwise archaic form. For a similar survival, see *uncle: say/cry uncle.*) [Not a reference to the animal. Based on OF *biberon*, an infant's nursing bottle. (Akin to Eng. *bib, imbiber* and to Fr. *bavard*, a drooler.) The child's-game sense of whiskers is by association with chin and with earlier *beaver*, in one form of armor, the raisable lower part of a knight's face-

mask. Horatio tells Hamlet that the ghost "wore his beaver up"—
Hamlet, I.ii. *Beaver,* the animal, is a separate (Gmnc.) evolution
< IE *bher-,* brown, shining ("the glossy brown animal").]

bedlam   1. *Primary sense in Am.* Noisy disorder; the place of noisy
disorder. *The schoolroom was a bedlam.* 2. *Root sense.* Madhouse.
[Contraction of *Bethlehem.*] **Bedlamite, bedlamite** *Primarily Brit.*
1. An insane person. 2. Such a person who, being adjudged harmless, is released to wander the streets and beg for food. (Tom o'
Bedlam was such a one.)

HISTORIC. The Hospital (hospice) of St. Mary of Bethlehem
(in ME *Bethleëm*) was founded in London in 1247. In 1547, following the break with the papacy and the proscription of the monas-
teries, it became a lunatic asylum. Despite the many abuses practiced in Bedlam in various periods, it is notable as England's first
hospital for the insane, and the second in Europe, a similar institution having been established earlier in Granada, Spain.

Beecher's Bibles   Sharps rifles. [From the days of Bloody Kansas,
when proslavery and free-state forces were fighting for control
and both sides staged murderous raids. The antislavery Massachusetts Emigrant Aid Society raised money for arming the Kansan
Free-Soilers. According to Thomas A. Bailey, *Voices of America,*
the rifles were shipped in cases marked "Bibles," the shipment
arranged by Henry Ward Beecher (1813–1887), a prominent Unitarian clergyman of New England origin, and brother of Harriet
Beecher Stowe, who wrote *Uncle Tom's Cabin.*]

> An old Unitarian preacher
> Used to preach that the hen was God's creature.
>   The hen just for that
>   Laid an egg in his hat
> And thus did the Henry Ward Beecher.

belt   [L. **balteus,* prob. of Etruscan origin, prob. signifying "sword
belt."] 1. An encircling strip. 2. A geographical zone marked by
distinctive customs *(Bible belt)* or used for a distinctive purpose
(corn belt). 3. A continuous moving strip, as for transmitting power
or moving goods. *fan belt, conveyor belt.* 4. A powerful blow.
[As when Daddy removes his pants belt and starts swinging.] 5.
A drink of hard liquor, esp. one tossed back neat. **put it under
one's belt** To take a drink. **below the belt** Unethical. [In boxing,
a blow below the belt, esp. in the crotch, is a foul.] **loosen one's**

belt To prepare to eat heartily. [By allowing one's stomach to expand.] *tighten one's belt* To prepare for or to endure austerity. [As if squeezing one's stomach shut.]

berserk (May be pron. with stress on either syllable.) *adj.* 1. In a rage of blood lust. 2. *Loose ext.* In a rage. Irate. [ON *berserkr,* Norse warrior. *Serk* is cognate with Sc. *sark,* shirt (CUTTYSARK, short skirt). The first element may be from *bjorn,* bear, because Norse warriors sometimes wore a bearskin as an upper garment. But obs. Eng. *baresark,* without armor (i.e., "bare but for a shirt"), suggests an equally likely derivation from ON *berr,* bare. "I will go baresark (without armor) tomorrow to the war."—Kingsley, 1866.] *go berserk* To run amuck.

HISTORIC. Norse warriors inspired terror in the enemy by charging into battle in a bellowing frenzy and with no regard for their own safety. They attacked after prebattle rites akin to a war dance, and after eating a trance-inducing mushroom.

Drug-induced blood lust was common among early and primitive warriors. The Malays (see *amuck*) also performed prebattle rites and ate a hallucinogenic mushroom. The Mohammedan *hashishin* (see *assassin*) smoked hashish before killing. Recent knowledge of these hallucinogens suggests that they are not the powerful agents they were long believed to be, and that the principal spur to these acts of blood lust was the autointoxication of religious fervor.

Betsy/old Betsy The Am. frontiersman's invariable name for his long rifle. See *blunderbuss.*

HISTORIC. "Sweet Betsy from Pike," perhaps the best-known ballad of the post–Civil War western migration, is about the frontiersman's woman, but it is prob. equally about his long rifle. All versions recount that the plainsman walked hand in hand with Betsy, and that she had an explosive temper. It is a fair speculation that Old Betsy the rifle and Sweet Betsy the girl came together and that the girl dominated the merger, though the long rifle continues to ghost the narrative.

bhergh- There are two IE roots with this form; one meaning "high"; the other, "to defend." Yet "high ground" and later "high walls of a city" have to do with defense, and it is quite likely that the two roots are simply different sense extensions of the same root.
1. In the sense *high:* Ger. **Berg,** mountain; Eng. *iceberg*
2. Primarily, however, the root has developed the sense "pro-

tected place of common habitation" or "walled city." So in the parenthetical elements of *Pitts(burgh), Ham(burg), Canter(bury),* and in *borough,* a municipal unit.

Senses 1 and 2 prob. came together when humankind first began to settle into communities, choosing rocky *high* ground that was easy to *defend.* In time, however, cities naturally developed on low ground, at coastal points, or at the confluence of two rivers or trade routes. The cities still had to be *defended* and the defense was provided by *high* walls.

3. Aside from being a unit of defense, the walled city was also a cultural unit, whence such municipal identifications as *burgher;* Ger. *Burgomeister,* mayor; It. *burgo,* city, and *borghetto,* a quarter of a city (originally a small town outside the city walls, later swallowed by the expanding city); Fr. *bourgeois,* of the city (not peasant); and It. *in borghese,* in city (business) clothes.

4. (A speculation.) Grimm's Law has shown that the voiced stop *bh-* changes to *f* in Latin. Theoretically, then, *bhergh-* → f'rgh-; then, if suffixed *-t-* and perhaps with gh/k → f'rkt'- → *forti-* → *fortis,* strong, (strong place) (FORT, FORCE, FORTE, PIANOFORTE, EFFORT). And the same stem in Gmnc. underlies many words having to do with high fortified places. (It must be noted, however, that *fortis* might have evolved from other sources.)

5. *belfry* A mutant form. In the Middle Ages towers of German city walls were called *bergenfrei,* defenders of the freedom; → OF *berfrei.* Then by association with bells hung in such towers to sound alarms or to ring the hours, the form changed (certainly in ME and prob. earlier in OF) to *belfrei, belfri, belfry.*

bib and tucker   One's best clothes. Now usu. in the phrase *in one's best bib and tucker* Dressed in one's best. But originally of a "dolled up" couple, the form being *in their best bib and tucker* [From *bib,* a starched bib shirt worn by a man; *tucker,* a sort of feather boa tucked around the neck. There is no evidence that the phrase once implied tawdry finery, though I, for one, might think of a man wearing a boiled dickey and a woman flaunting a feather boa, as the cleaning lady and her garbage gentleman on a night out.]

biddy   A hen. *old biddy* 1. A brood hen. 2. *Ext.* An old woman, esp. a fussy and garrulous one ("forever clucking"). *here, biddy!* Traditional chicken call. [The commonly suggested derivation from *Bridget,* a generic name for the once generic Irish serving maid in England, is prob. apt to Brit. *biddy,* housemaid, which is prob. from baby-talk rendering of *Bidgie, Biddy.* But in the sense "hen," though unattested, almost certainly from *birdie, birdy.* Perh. influ. in Am. by *broody hen,* common sthrn. regionalism for brood hen. The metathesis of OE *brid* to Eng. *bird* is a relevant language process. And the omission and intrusion of *r* is common from Cockney to the Bostonese of JFK, who dealt with "Cuber" as a statesman, not as a "wadheelah."]

Big Bertha   One of the Kaiser's prized toys in WWI. An especially large long-range artillery piece mounted on a special flatcar. I believe (but have not been able to verify absolutely) that the Germans had only one of these showy monsters. In any case, Big Bertha was an experimental showpiece rather than standard artillery issue. [Named after Bertha Krupp, grande dame of the Krupp munitions cartel. Such comparison photographs as I have been able to find suggest a marked resemblance in the butt and mouth of the two pieces.]

bikini   The minimal two-string, three-cup (all demitasses) bathing suit. [After Bikini, the atoll in the Marshall Islands used as the site of the 1946 A-bomb tests.]
    HISTORIC. The next-to-nothing bathing suit was introduced in France at about the time of the tests and in the U.S. soon after them. The tale is told that in the slick chic of ad-agency jargon they were called bikinis, first, to suggest the state of nature, and second, because they would have the impact of an atomic bomb (bum?). The language, in its often easy tolerance of the absurd and even of the disastrous, accepted the term at once, and with no sense of indignation at this coupling of the poisoned islands and these little swishes of chic.

bimbo   A pejorative term for a hard-bitten girl. *That was some bimbo he was out with last night.* [Dating uncertain. < Sp. *bimbo,* infant, boy child. Prob. into SW Am. Perh. influ by *kid* for a gunfighter or boxer. Shift to "hard-bitten girl" unattested. Into Brit. c. 1940 with the sense "a guy."]

biscuit   1. A crisp unleavened wafer. [Medieval L. *bis cotum,* twice cooked. It. *biscotto.* OF *bescuit.* ME *bisquit.* Cf. *zwiebach,* lit. "twice baked."] 2. *Sthrn. regional.* Leavened quick bread, usu. baked in a size and shape resembling cupcakes. [This usage in no way corresponds to the etymology. Prob. connective sense is "quickness."]

bits   *Standard Am. colloq.* Units of money. *two bits,* 25¢. *four bits,* 50¢. *six bits,* 75¢. [Colonial America, lacking an official mint, suffered a constant shortage of small coins. Large transactions could be handled with letters of credit, but how did a traveler pay for a meal or for a drink? Coins of all nations were used in making change, the commonest being the Spanish silver piece of eight, very like the later U.S. silver dollar, and so called because it was stamped with a large Arabic 8 to signify a value of eight Spanish *reals,* a *real* having a value of about 12½¢. (There was a Mexican *real* of that value (later a peso), but there is no evidence that the coin had a general circulation in the early colonies.) A whole piece of eight, however, was a coin of substantial value. To provide small change, these coins were regularly cut into halves and quarters called "bits." I can find no evidence that they were cut into eighths, and they probably were not, for such a sliver would be uncomfortably sharp in the pocket. I had, in fact, believed that *one bit* had never come into use. Shelby Horton *(The Civil War),* however, cites a letter from a Union soldier to the effect that he would not pay "a bit an acre" for the land he had recently marched through.

When, circa 1798, the Philadelphia mint began to issue silver quarters and half dollars, the already established *two bits* and *four bits* were applied to those coins. There never was a six-bit coin, but any combination of coins adding to 75¢ was called six bits by analogy.] ***two-bit adj.*** Cheap. Especially in the fixed form ***two-bit whore*** The cheapest of sluts.

black and white (in European idiom)   Negro spokesmen are on record as objecting to such terms as *blackball, blackboard, blackmail, blackguard.* In a recent *N.Y. Times* interview, Mrs. Frank Hercules, a Negro and the principal of a NYC public school, referred to these and others as "racial digs."

There is no way not to mourn for the bitter history that has so sensitized the emergent and militant Negro to such idioms, but with the exception of *blackboard,* all these idioms evolved at a time when most Europeans were hardly aware of the existence of a black race. Beyond such idioms, early European religions developed an image structure based on night-day/devil-god/black-white/evil-good.

The IE root *dei-* had the senses "light, day, sky, brightness, deity." The opposite terms are "dark, night, the underworld (hell), darkness (blackness), devil." From that IE stem we derive such god names as Tiu (Tuesday), Zeus piter, Jupiter, the deity, and

L. *diem*, day *(per diem)*. This metaphoric assumption of European thinking is clear from even a short sampling of phrases, such as *black as sin, black as the pit, oh, my black soul* (the opposite being a white or immaculate one). Such language patterns are persistent. If not *black*, what shall the Bible-based preacher say to describe sin, hell, the devil, etc.?

No "racial digs" are implicit in such idioms; rather, the sense of implied prejudice arises from sensitivities exacerbated by a monstrous social injustice that took place long after these idioms had formed. That social distress will not be glossed away, but intellectuals of all races have some duty to recognize what forces are actually at work upon the language. There is enough intentionally offensive language to object to without finding evil where none is intended.

blackberry winter *Midwstrn. and Penna. regional.* A spell of relatively cool weather that occurs, or is alleged to occur, just as the blackberries blossom in May or, in the more southerly reaches, in late April. [A term akin to *Indian summer*, on which it may be based.]

blackmail Extortion under threat of exposing a dark secret. [But this sense is only since XIX. In IX–X northern and eastern England was occupied by the Danes and ruled by Dane Law, under which the conquerors exacted a tribute called *mal*, < ON *mal*, an oral agreement, a payment agreed upon. (But note OF *maille*, a coin; OHG *malaha, malha,* a coin purse; these forms indicating a generalized Gmnc. root brought into Fr. by the *Franks*, which see.) This tribute was collected not only from occupied territories, but from neighboring areas as the price of remaining unoccupied. These neighboring areas generally paid in silver, called *whitmal* (white mail). The occupied generally paid in labor, livestock, and wagonloads of produce, called *blackmal* (i.e., "not whitmal").

Later, and up to XVI, Scottish border chiefs exacted a tribute called blackmail, usu. paid in heads of cattle, as the price of leaving estates unmolested. They ran, in effect, what U.S. gangsters call a "protection racket" (pay up or get hurt). Then in XIX, as above.]

blivit *Whimsical vulgar exuberant.* A made-up word, which, when used, is supposed to lead to the question, "What's a blivit?" and the answer, assertedly a howler, is, "It's five pounds of shit in a three-pound bag." [I have never seen this form in print. It was common in street talk by 1932 (and how much earlier?). As a metaphoric element: *shit* for "trouble" (as in *up shit creek; that's*

when the shit hit the fan; well, I'll be dipped in shit!); the 5:3
ratio to express overabundance. *to get hit with a blivit* = to be
up shit creek and overboard.]

blockbuster   1. *WWII.* A large aerial bomb. [Conceived as large
enough to demolish a whole city block. No specified weight category, but in general understanding anything from a 500-pounder
to the ten-ton bombs sometimes dropped on Japan by B-29's. (Usu.
by planes on night weather reconnaissance. One ten-ton bomb
filled the bay and something in the boyishness of the bloody liked
the thought of dropping an egg big enough to fill the whole basket.)] 2. *Ext.* A startling announcement or disclosure. *The announcement of the oil embargo was a Wall Street blockbuster.*
3. *Show biz. Special adjectival or semiadjectival overstatement.*
Thing that has "impact" (stupid, overtheatrical word!). (The late
show on one of the TV networks was long listed as *The Blockbuster
Movie.*) 4. *Special extension.* An unscrupulous real estate agent
who seeks to spread panic and thereby to reduce real estate values
when a neighborhood undergoes a change, as when rezoned, or
when the first Negro moves into a previously all-white block. [He
seeks to "bust up the block," profiting from the panic. Now outdated by different patterns of social change. In effect, a latent
word in this sense, perh. destined to become obsolete; alternatively, to be revived if a new pattern of social change offers occasion
for the revival.]

bloody   Brit. taboo intensive; common in Am. only when one is affect-
ing an English air. [Said to be a contraction of *sblood,* His (Christ's)
blood; all bodily ref. to sacred personages having once functioned
as profanity. (See *Shock Language.*) Also said to be a contraction
of *by our lady, b'lady, bloody;* but both origins are in doubt, and
this second hardly qualifies as taboo.]

blue hen   A famous game hen of colonial Delaware. Long unofficially
(and since c. 1935, officially) the state bird of Delaware, which
has long been known as the *Blue Hen State.*
    HISTORIC. The Delaware regiment of the Continental Army
had a reputation for cockfighting, and all Crawthumpers (citizens
of Delaware) were said to be impassioned breeders of gamecocks.
In Delaware no gamecock was thought to be worth consideration
unless its pedigree could be traced to the blue hen.
    the blue hen's chick 1. A prized gamecock. 2. A special favorite.
One who can do no wrong. [A. B. Guthrie, Jr.'s book *The Blue*

Hen's Chick, an account of his days in Lexington, Kentucky, derives its title from the fact that his boardinghouse keeper signaled him out as her special pet and star boarder.]

blue moon   A proverbial never-never akin to the pot of gold at the end of the rainbow. [Despite various assertions to the contrary, there is no weather phenomenon that gives the moon a blue tint.] *once in a blue moon* Rarely. [But the earliest sense was, properly, "never." So the anon. early XVI rhymester who wrote "They say the moon is belewe," with the sense "the sort of nonsense fablers ask us to believe," in which the form is used as a long-familiar one, and clearly with the implication that the moon is never blue. By XIX the sense was firmly fixed as "rarely," but no one has been able to account for this sense shift.]

blunderbuss   The early, large-caliber, muzzle-loaded, scatter-shot, flared, short musket of the sort shown in illustrations of the Puritan settlers in Massachusetts. [Du. *dunder,* thunder; *bus,* box. The English modification from *dunder* to *blunder* certainly influ. by the awkwardness and unreliability of these early pieces. Later, improved muskets had stocks of glowingly polished brown hardwood, whence, with a slight modification of *buss* to Bess → *brown Bess,* an early standard rifleman's name for his piece. In crossing the Atlantic *brown Bess* seems to have been modified to *Betsy, old Betsy* (which see), the Am. frontiersman's standard name for his long rifle.

blurb   Any brief laudatory excerpt from a letter or review, especially when reprinted on the jacket of a book. [Coined in 1907 by Gelett Burgess (1866–1951), American humorist, illustrator of children's books, and author of the once pandemic poem "The Purple Cow." Perh. a portmanteau of *blurt* and *burble.* Burgess defined *to blurb* as "to make a noise like a publisher."]

blush: at first blush   At first appearance, at first consideration. The opposite of "after mature consideration." [*Blush,* here, a survival of OE *blyscan,* ME *blusshen,* to bloom, to redden, to show first color (and so, by analogy, to modern sense of *to blush*).]

board   Involves a whole family of English words and idioms and offers a specimen evolution based on IE *bherdh-,* to cut.
    By Grimm's Law, the voiced stops *bh-* and *dh-* change to *f* in Latin, whence *forf-i-,* the stem of L. *forfex,* scissors; the one

survival of this stem in English being the ornithologists' adjective *forficate*, describing the scissortails of certain birds. The sense progression over the centuries from *to cut → instrument for cutting → noncutting thing that resembles the instrument* is a fine illustration of the language process. See *carn-*, also at root "to cut" but which acquired the sense "cut of flesh" (CARNAGE) and then "flesh" (CARNAL, INCARNATE).

IE *bherdh-* was altered to *bord-* in Gmnc., acquiring the specific sense "cut piece of wood, plank, board"; a sense alteration probably traceable to the fact that the early Teutons were tree worshippers. Gmnc. *bord-* → English *board*, with many senses.

board, boardinghouse, boarder, room and board all derive from the associated sense "table." [Thing made of planks, i.e., cut wood.] So, too, **board of directors** [Those who sit around a table.] The related sense "flat surface" gives us **control board, chessboard.** And also **pasteboards,** playing cards. [Flat surfaces used in playing.] And the "flat surface" changed to a perpendicular gives us **bulletin board, blackboard, dartboard.** Also the horse racing idiom **across the board** A bet on a given horse to win, place, and show. [Because bets at English tracks were recorded on the bookmaker's blackboard.]

Early Teutonic ships making use of both oars and sails were essentially large open canoes, the most notable cut and shaped woodwork being in their sides, whence the sense "side of a ship," whence *larboard* and *starboard* (see below), and **overboard, on board, to board a ship** [All with the sense of coming or going over the side.]

And by a further extension to the sense "outer limit; boundary" → **Atlantic seaboard** and **border.** (In which last sense, English retained the Gmnc. *bord-*, earlier also *bourd-*, while most other derived terms changed to *board*.)

From the further sense "made of boards" we have **boardwalk** and the circular evolution through Italian of **bordello** from Old Flemish *bordel,* a hut made of planks (as distinct from stone or logs), and also with the sense "hut of the village prostitute." The prostitute in this case was nothing fancy; prob. an unwed mother (see *grass widow*), or a young widow who worked in the fields or as a laundress by day, and who eked out a poor existence by doing homework at night. The Italians borrowed and modified *bordel,* added chandeliers and drapes, and gave us the fancy whorehouse now implied by *bordello.*

starboard The right side of a ship when one is facing forward. [*Board* prefixed by OE *stēoran,* to steer; the ref. being to early vessels steered by a large sweep oar invariably extending over the right side.]

Since that side of the ship had to be kept clear for the movements of the steering oar, and since the ship could dock only on the side away from the oar, the left side was called the *hladanboard* < OE *hladan*, to load (LADE, BILL OF LADING), the side on which cargo was received. *Stēoranboard* was modified to *stēorboard* and finally to *starboard; hladanboard,* to *hladboard,* and then, under the influence of *starboard,* to *larboard.* So the old sea chanty:

> Tis larboard and starboard you jump to the call.
> *Yo-ho, blow the man down.*
> When Jumping Jack Williams commands the Black Ball.
> *Give us some time to blow the man down.*

But when Jumping Jack had to shout his commands in a high wind, *larboard* and *starboard* were easily confused and the men might too readily end up by jumping to the wrong side. In early XVII, therefore, probably on command of the admiralty, for the change was nearly instantaneous, *larboard* was changed to *port,* the new term being a logical successor to the old *hladanboard,* that being the side that was once put next to the dock (the side it came into port on), with the original sense further reinforced by L. *portare,* to carry, as cargo; and so, too, EXPORT, IMPORT.

bogus   False. Counterfeit. Spurious. [Am. 1827, a stamp or mill for coining counterfeit coins. Some say engraved plates for counterfeit paper money, but paper money was extremely scarce in 1827 and limited to (doubly suspect) large denominations. Americans, made wary by the failure of Continental currency, preferred hard coin in silver and gold. The first U.S. greenback paper dollars (redeemable for silver on demand) were not issued until 1862. The meaning established, the derivation remains in some doubt. Perhaps ult. < *bogie* < Welsh and Cornish *bug,* devil (BUGABOO, BUGBEAR), and with widely dispersed dial. variants *bogy, boogie, boogy.* In a letter to the editor of OED, Dr. S. Willard of Chicago noted that in common early Vermont, *tantrabogus* labeled any ugly object. *Tantra-* (in Devonshire dialect *tantarum*) may be a combining form of *tantrum,* foul-tempered. If so, *tantrabogus* may have had the root sense "ugly as a foul-tempered fiend," whence an easy sense extension to "false as a foul-tempered fiend." But whatever the ult. origin, the Am. evolution has been from substantive (in which sense now obsolete) to adjective. (Some refer the term to a XIX frontier con-man and counterfeiter named Borghese, but he has eluded my search.)]

bolt: shoot one's bolt   To use up one's resources (of energy, supplies, capital, talent) in a single effort. *John L. P. Ciardi, my son, shot his mental bolt just getting into college and has not been able to think since.* [Not to be confused with the bolt of *door bolt* or of *nuts and bolts.* The reference is to the bolt (short arrow, dart) of a crossbow, and not to using up one's total supply of bolts, but to a single shot. The crossbow was both powerful and accurate when handled by a good bowman, but it required slow and laborious recocking after each shot. For this reason, crossbows were generally used from parapets, behind which the bowman could withdraw to recock. In close combat on a field, the bowman would be defenseless between shots.]

NOTE. This bolt was always called a *quarrel,* a word I long thought to be resonantly martial, as in some such poetic line as *a flight of quarrels on the contested air.* I was disappointed at learning that this *quarrel* is < L. *quadrus,* square; and disappointed again at being unable to see how "squareness" is applicable. [Perh. a ref. to the grooves of the cocking mechanism. But ?]

bomb   [Gk. *bombos,* echoic of a rumbling sound, as of thunder. L. *bombus,* same sense. Late XV It. *bomba* is first to have the sense "an explosive device." Since XVI Eng. *bomb,* explosive, has taken over the entire function of the word, though it is common to refer to the rumble of distant bombardment.] *n.* 1. An explosive device, usu. one timed to detonate at a preset time. 2. An explosive device dropped from a plane. 3. *Earlier, now obs.* An antipersonnel artillery shell timed to detonate in the air. *the bombs bursting in air.* —*v.* 1. *Warfare.* To attack with aerial bombs. 2. To place and set a timed esplosive device. 3. *Theatrical.* To fail. *The show bombed in New Haven.* 4. To cancel or do away with.

the Bomb Atomic war power. *Today even India has the Bomb.*

bombshell 1. The casing of a bomb, esp. of an aerial bomb. 2. *In theatrical press agentry.* A performer, esp. a female, who gives the impression of explosive vitality. 3. A startling element suddenly injected into a situation. *His testimony dropped a bombshell into the trial.* [May seem to be a curious metaphor, there being no explosive power in a bombshell, but the presence of the shell is certainly enough to suggest a bomb within it and the likelihood that the bomb may go off.]

bombast Loud, pompously inflated language. [Root sense: "padding." < OF *bombace,* a sort of cotton batting used as padding for clothes. < L. *bombyx* (one of many variant forms) < Gk. *bombux,* silkworm. Perh. ult. from, or influ. by, Turkish *pambuk,* cotton.]

bonanza 1. *Mid XIX Am. mining.* A rich mining strike. 2. *Ext.* Any source of great wealth. *His discount store has turned out to be a bonanza.* [< Sp. *bonanza,* good weather; the sense shift being from fair weather to prosperity.]

bones: make no bones about it To have no scruples or reservations. [This sense first attested 1548 in Nicholas Udall's translation of Erasmus's *Paraphrase of Luke:* "He made no manier (manner of) bones . . . to offer up his only son Isaac." But earlier, most notably in John Skelton's *The Tunning of Eleanor Rumming* (1529): "she found therein no bones"; in which the sense is she met no difficulty. (Prob. a folk figure based on eating fish or soup or stew, the meal progressing best if the bones have been removed.) The sense "offered no difficulty" is confirmed by the 1459 OED citation: "And fo(u)nd that time no bonis in the matere." The sense evolution has been from "to encounter no difficulties" to "to be undeterred by, esp. by moral scruples or conscientious reservations."]

boob 1. A simpleton. [XIX Am. short form of *booby,* which has same sense in Brit. and Am.] 2. A woman's breast. And so vulgar: *what a pair of boobs on her!* She is notably large-breasted. [Prob. most immediately, via immigrant transmission, from Ger. dial. *bübbi,* woman's breast < IE *pap-,* baby (an echoic form based on the sound made by a suckling infant. So: PAP, PABULUM, POPPYCOCK). Perh., however, based on IE *bheu-,* to swell, a swelling (BUBO, BUBONIC PLAGUE). And very likely influ. by *booby,* the bird, because boobies swell out their breasts when preening and waddling. Quite likely all these sources conjoin.]
　　booboisie Lampoon name for the American middle class. [Portmanteau of *boob & bourgeoisie.* Coined by H. L. Mencken, c. 1925.] Similarly [also a Mencken coinage] *Homo boobiensis* The successor species (at least in small-town U.S.) to *Homo sapiens.*

booby 1. A simpleton. 2. A tropical sea bird akin to the gannet; especially graceful in flight, it is comically awkward on its feet. [XVII. < Sp. *bubo,* a simpleton; and early applied to the bird, with maritime transmission to Brit. and Am. Based on L. *balbus,* a stammerer, a stutterer. Ult. < IE *baba-,* echoic root expressing disdain for the way foreigners talk, their language being a stammered ba-ba-ba-ba. So Gk. *barbaros,* stranger, enemy (BARBARIAN).]

booby hatch 1. *XVII nautical.* A hatch with a raised cover forward of the foremast. [Because far-ranging boobies often lit on sailing vessels at sea and for some reason of bent instinct commonly gathered on this hatch cover.] 2. An insane asylum. [Originally a rough sailor's metaphor suggested by the cluster of boobies waddling, jerking their heads, and preening comically on the hatch cover. Eng. idiom has not been kind in its term for the afflicted. Some Am. terms for insane asylum are: *bat roost, bug house, cackle factory, cuckoo's nest, funny farm, loony bin, nut house.*

booby prize A mock "prize" given to the person who finishes last in a competition.

booby trap [Trap for fools. WWII.] 1. An explosive device concealed in a seemingly innocent or attractive setting, left by retreating troops to blow up the unwary among the advancing forces. 2. *Ext.* Any concealed danger made to appear inviting. *Dorothy Fredland should have known those wedding bells were booby trapped.*

boogie-woogie   *Jazz.* A piano style based on a heavy, insistent left-hand rhythm on which the right hand builds melodic variations and progressions. [C. 1920. Reduplication based on *bogie* or *bogy* for *bogie trunk,* a wheeled carriage attached to a train by a swivel pin which permits the train more easily to negotiate curves; hence, by association, the low rhythmic sound of train wheels.]

HISTORIC. The Am. Negro, bound to soil and toil for static centuries, felt a special affinity for the developing railroads of XIX U.S. The rush and whistle of the trains—powerful symbols of mobility and, hence, of freedom—passed almost instantly into Negro legend and balladry. The newly freed Negro was exploitable cheap labor in building the southern railroads, whence John Henry as folk hero. In 1867 George M. Pullman turned to the labor pool of newly freed slaves to be his obsequious and underpaid porters. (The once standard *George* for pullman porter was by association with Pullman's first name.) And terrible as were Pullman's exploitive working conditions, the railroad nevertheless offered the Negro an avenue of escape from the sun-up to sun-down fields. Everything to do with railroading became part of the idiom and feeling of the Negro, and especially of emerging jazz men.

boondocks   Always plu., always with *the.* Small-town America; out where the grass roots sprout in the shade of the sticks. *to stump the boondocks Political.* To campaign for the rural vote. [By U.S. armed forces transmission, c. 1910, from Tagalog *bundok,* mountain. The Philippines, volcanic in origin, rise jaggedly from the sea, the settled places being along the shore, the interior being often all but inaccessible. Dawn age tribes are still hidden away in those mountains. Tagalog *bundok,* therefore, meant "out back" in a special sense implying primitiveness, nearly impassable terrain, and even danger from headhunters.]

boondoggling   *n.* Puttery, pointless, fussy work. (And corresponding verb forms.) [Coined 1925 by scoutmaster R. H. Link to label such artsy-craftsy work as plaited leather neck cords and other (in his view) overemphasized make-work projects of the Boy Scout program.]

boot   [ME *bote* < OF **bote,* foot covering, shoe. So the second element of Fr. *sabot,* Fr. and Eng. *sabotage.*] 1. In Am. now signifies a shoe whose uppers extend above the ankles; in Brit. includes what Am. calls a shoe. So Brit. *bootery* for Am. *shoe store.* But up to c. 1920, except for dress pumps, men's shoes laced or buttoned above the ankle; and boots, still standard western footwear, were the common shoeing. 2. *Stagecoaching.* The rear compartment of a stagecoach, usu. covered with a tarpaulin and used for hauling freight or luggage. [In earlier Brit., a step at the back of a formal carriage on which the footmen (boots) stood when the carriage was underway. *Boot,* for footman, may derive from the fact that polishing boots was one fixed duty of such servants. In any case, Brit. still uses *boot* for what Am. calls a car *trunk.*]

    boot camp USN & USMC. Recruit training camp. [Reputedly, though without secure attestation, because the old iron men of wooden ships made it a point of pride to turn out for deck muster barefoot, even in the coldest weather. Uninured recruits turned out for muster shod and were scorned as *boots.*]

    Boot Hill A burial plot at the edge of a western frontier town, often on a rise, but not always. MMM cites an 1881 ref. to Dodge City's "Boot Grave-yard . . . called thus from the fact that 38 men had been buried there with their boots on." Natives of Tombstone, Arizona (or their resident PR men), claim that its cemetery was the first to be dubbed Boot Hill or Boothill. The fact is that any "Boot Grave-yard" situated on a rise is almost certain to be called Boot Hill. ***die with one's boots on*** An often expressed ideal of the western frontier. To die fighting or in the course of vigorous work rather than in enfeebled old age.

bootlegger A dealer in illegal liquor. [Fanciful; as if he carried pints and quarts in the legs of his (sea) boots. In this sense an Americanism. Standard in 1920's Prohibition era but first attested 1889 (at which time there were—in Iowa, for instance—regional dry laws.) The common assertion that *bootlegger* earlier meant *smuggler* is without support.] —*adj.* **bootleg** Illegal. By 1940 had been applied to things other than liquor, as *bootleg phonograph records,* records reproduced and sold in violation of copyright.

bet your boots Formula asserting certainty. [Equivalent to *bet your life, bet your ass*. To be left barefooted in unsettled country could easily be fatal. One would bet his boots, therefore, only when there was no fear of losing.]

pull oneself up by the bootstraps To succeed by one's own unassisted efforts. [Whimsical. Boots, esp. cavalry boots, are commonly equipped with straps as an aid in dressing. At times it must have seemed that one had, literally, to pull himself off the ground in order to get the things on.]

boot: to boot In addition to. [IE *bhad-*, good, a good thing. With d/t in Gmnc. → b't → BETTER. In Gmnc. form *bot-* → OE *bōt,* cure, assistance. ME *bote,* which in manorial England signified an additional right or usufruct of a tenant farmer, as *haybote,* hedge right (a tenant's right to cut branches for repairing his hedges and fences), *housebote,* house right (a tenant's right to cut wood needed for house repairs). And see *hook or crook*. Survives only in the form "and something to boot."] *what boots it?* What good does it do? [Long common in Brit., but except for dialect usage, had become a poeticism by 1900, and never really took root in Am.]

boots and saddles (The resemblance to preceding *boots* is accidental.) The once standard cavalry order to mount. [Based on Fr. *bout selle,* a cavalry saddle known in obs. Brit. as *butt saddle,* i.e., "flat saddle." See *butt*. The form of the Fr. command was either *boutesel* or *bout et sel,* meaning not "mount" but "saddle up."]

bored for the simples In the exclam. of surprise or vexation (rare but surviving; I last heard it in southern Ohio in 1970) *well, I'll be bored for the simples!* Well, I'll have my skull drilled to cure my lunacy! [*Bored,* trepanned; *simples,* mental simples, lunacy.

Prob. orig. Elizabethan; now obs. in Brit. but surviving in Am. rural dialect. Trepanning was a standard treatment for lunacy in *Bedlam* (which see), prob. based on some theory of drawing out the evil humors. See *humor.*]

HISTORICAL. Trepanning, for whatever reason, was practiced by Stone Age medicine men using stone or bone augurs. Such surgery, moreover, was not always fatal: skulls of that period have been found and show not only that the operation was performed but that the patient lived at least long enough for the skull to knit. The Stone Age medicine man, it is worth adding, almost certainly had opiates, hallucinogens, and herbal anesthetics unknown to the Elizabethans. But however grisly the image of a flint-boring session in a cave mouth, or its counterpart in a back room of Bedlam, such surgery is relatively painless, the skull having few nerves, and the brain proper, none.

Borgia   A generic name for infamy. [Rodrigo Borgia, father of Cesare and Lucrezia (known as his "nephew" and "niece"), became Pope Alexander VI (1492–1503). A libertine and a Machiavellian ruler, he was especially infamous as a poisoner of political opponents. Every crime, including incest, has been charged to him, most of the charges based on substantial evidence.] *you Borgia, you,* declares that the person so addressed is capable of and guilty of every   infamy.

HISTORIC. Returning from a hunt at the pope's country estate in 1503, Alexander and Cesare called for wine, and whether in error or as part of a counterplot, they were served a bottle of their own "social" wine. (In Italian, poisoning was called *una morte assistata,* not murder but "an assisted death.") Alexander died almost at once. Cesare, being young and powerful, and knowing special antidotes, recovered, but having lost the papal aegis with the death of his "uncle," went off to Spain as a free-lance knight and died in battle there. Lucrezia, herself a poisoner and debauchée in her youth, lived to old age and died a duchess much honored for her charities.

Cesare was the family's poison specialist. He had the stuff prepared by poisoning a hog, which was then hanged by its hind legs, the poisoned drool of its death agonies being caught in a basin and dried to a powder said to be both lethal and tasteless in wine.

Cesare's cure was based on various antidotes he knew and on an unusual heat therapy. Four stout posts were fixed into his chamber floor. Each morning during his cure, a bull or an ox was led in, thrown to the floor on its back, and lashed to the posts, one leg secured to each. The living animal was then gutted and Cesare was sewn into the abdominal cavity with only his head projecting, to sweat it out in the heat of the beast's dying fever. There are many arts to being a Borgia, most of which have been lost.

bosh Rot. Nonsense. [One of the few English words derived from Turkish, in which the word means "void, inane, stupid, useless." Into general Eng. acceptance c. 1824 following its frequent usage in James Morier's *Adventures of Hajji Baba of Ispahan*, subtitled "A Persian Romance."]

boss *n.* Person in charge. —*v.* 1. To give orders. 2. To be overbearing in issuing a constant flow of heckling orders. [Into early XVIII Am. < Du. *baas*, master; a borrowing from early Du. settlers of New Amsterdam (New York). Since late XIX in limited Brit. use.]

Boss/Bossie/boss/bossie The U.S. farmer's standard name for a dairy cow. [A mysterious form. The U.S. farmer's call *ho Boss* and *hey Boss* is almost pure classical Gk. for "the cow." Yet the form does not appear in general Brit. usage and the OED lists it only in its supplement as SW Brit. dial. for "a half-grown cow." Ult. < Gk. *bous*, L. *bos*, cow.

Perh. the Am. usage could have stemmed from that rare SW dial. Brit., but the use is so widespread and so firmly established as to invite further speculation.

In colonial times and into the early XX it was a professorial prerogative to graze a cow on campus. Through this same period, colleges were essentially theology schools, the curriculum based on Hebrew, Greek, and Latin. I have a curious vision of a professor emerging from his study before twilight and calling his cow whimsically in Gk. *hē bous*. Back on the farm at vacation time and for summer work, students imitated the professor's form, and were in turn imitated. There is not a shred of attestation for this speculation, and I would gladly hear another. But let the root question remain visible: How did the classical form get from Greece and Rome to New England and to general Am. usage, leaving no Brit. trace except for limited usage in SW Brit. dial.?]

Boston 1. A city in Lincolnshire, England. [The name contracted from *St. Botulf's stone*, so called because one pious legend had it that St. Botolph conducted his Christian mission near a large stone. More likely, however, *-ston* is at root Danish *steinn*, stone house, i.e., church; in which case the root sense is St. Botolph's church.] 2. The capital of Massachusetts, also known (to itself) as "The Hub (of the Universe)," though that designation was first applied not to the city but to the state house.

Boston bag A woman's handbag (and, rarely, a briefcase) with handles on either side of the opening. *Boston bull, Boston terrier* A standard breed of small, usu. black dog with white markings on snout, chest, and legs. Developed in New England by crossing the bulldog and bull terrier. *Boston cream pie* [So called everywhere but in Boston, where it is called George Washington pie.] A usu. two-layer sponge cake with a cream filling and light chocolate icing. *proper Bostonian* A descendant of one of the founding families, or of all of them, who has dedicated himself to the religion of being a self-committed provincial from the center of an expiring universe, the original existence of which is partly hypothetical.

boughten Obs. p.p. of *to buy;* now *bought.* [Once, and barely surviving, Am. ruralism, but still functioning commonly in the fixed phrase:] *store-boughten* Bought at a store for money; i.e., not made at home. (Note that it was once country pride to make do with what one could make or raise oneself, the pride largely dictated by a lack of cash. So *store-boughten bread,* bread not baked at home—and imagine throwing away good money on any such thing!)

bourbon Corn whiskey. [After Bourbon County, Kentucky.] *Bourbon* A line of French kings from XIV to XVI and again in XIX, with collateral branches in Spain and the Kingdom of Naples. [The naming of a county in Kentucky after a French royal line testifies to the strength of the French influence in the early Mississippi Valley. Bourbon whiskey, however, is a pure expression of native American genius.]

boy 1. A young male person. 2. An inferior. *bat boy.* 3. Lovable person. *Danny boy.* 4. Immature person. "All wars are boyish and are fought by boys."—Melville. 5. Used among adults as a term of affectionate intimacy. *a night out with the boys, just one of the boys, boyfriend.* 6. *Exclam.* Expresses surprise or enthusiasm shared with a friend. *boy oh boy! attaboy!* [< Gk. *boeiai dorai,* cowhide, oxhide. (Ult. < *bous,* cow, ox.) Because cowhide was used for the collars and fetters of slaves. Whence L. *imboiare,* to enslave → OF *embuier* → ME *boye, bye,* an inferior, a male youth.]

HISTORIC. Today in Am. a term in racial contention. Blacks,

long addressed as "boy" in the root sense "slave, inferior," and so called regardless of age, have a deeply felt reason for receiving the term as a racial slur. They insist on "man" after the habit long fixed in the English-speaking Caribbean. Whites, on the other hand, still have built into their natural vocabulary the fond male-intimate senses of *attaboy! boy oh boy!* and *one of the boys;* and this male-intimate affectionate sense has often given offense to blacks when none was intended. Perhaps, in time enough, if there is that much time, we may yet become one people and speak a single language.

Brand X/brand X   1. *Advertising jargon.* A brand other than the one being promoted. [In promotion-by-comparison, what the Rinso ad agency had to say about Duz in the days before advertisers could call names by name. (But now that new ground rules allow Rinso to say nasty things about Duz by name, Brand X has disappeared from advertising copy and may be on its way out of the language.)] 2. *Esp. when not capitalized.* An inferior product. 3. *Briefly, in the 1950's.* A brand name for a line of cigarettes advertised to be "for the man who always wanted to be vice president." [A spoof by two ad agency men who so packaged and promoted a good cigarette manufactured for them on contract. The project broke even nationally and actually made a profit in California, where anything is possible but the likely.]

brandy   A strong spirit distilled from wine; originally from grape wine, later from the wine of many fruits and berries, and still later directly from the fermented mash of such in the making of brandy liqueurs. [< Du. *brandewijn,* burnt wine, with ref. to the fact that the wine was "cooked" (distilled). *Brandewijn* seems to have appeared c. 1600, some say as a way of salvaging a bad year's wine, but there is more in doubt than in evidence. *Brandewijn* might also be rendered "wine that burns" (cf. Amerind "firewater"). Earlier Eng. forms: *brandewine, brandy wine.*]

brass hat   A high military or naval officer. *the brass hats* Command officers in general; those in charge of strategy. [Army and Marine officers in the rank of major or higher, and naval officers in the rank of lieutenant commander or higher, wear gold braid on the visors of their caps (called "scrambled eggs") and *brass hat* is commonly, but wrongly, referred to that braid. The ref. is to the cocked hats worn by Napoleon and his officers; worn fore-and-aft by the officers and athwart by Napoleon. These hats folded flat and were carried under the left arm when an officer went indoors. They were called, therefore, *chapeaux à bras*, (under the) arm hats; *bras* then Anglicized to *brass* in a partial translation.]

brass monkey: cold enough to freeze the balls off a brass monkey (A vulgar whimsical intensive for sweet style's sake.) Very cold. [One of the standard rhetorical intensives of self-elaborating slang, of a class with: *grinning like a jackass eating briars, slick as a button on a backhouse door, hot as a fresh fucked fox in a forest fire, running around like a lost dog in a meat market, crooked as a hound's hind leg, worthless as tits on a boar.*]

brass tacks: get down to brass tacks To get down to hard facts; to basic issues. [Though common, the idiom is unattested, and open to conjecture. Concealed brass tacks were used in upholstery because they did not rust and thereby stain the upholstery. They were also used (for the same reason) on the counters of old dry goods stores for measuring off exact yard lengths. A common way of measuring fabric from a bolt was to hold it to one's nose and spread it to the length of one's extended arm, that extension being taken to be a yard. If the buyer called the measurement into question, the fabric could be put down to the brass tacks for an exact measurement. Either reference seems to be adequate, but the second was once, and by much, the commoner experience of brass tacks, and prob. the more likely source of the idiom.]

brinkmanship *Diplomacy.* The questionable art of negotiating as if forever ready to drop atomic bombs sooner than grant any further concession. [< *(on the) brink* combined with *gamesmanship,* which see. Forever associated with the policy of John Foster Dulles, 1888–1959, Eisenhower's secretary of state, 1953–1959; but not invented by him. The first attested usage was by Adlai Stevenson in 1956 in a speech attacking Eisenhower-Dulles foreign policy. Stevenson remained uncertain about the term, telling reporters that he may have "dreamed it up," but also that he "might have read it or heard it somewhere." In any case, a word was born and now seems securely a part of the language.]

broadcast From the beginnings of English into the 1920's a broadcaster was a farm worker who sowed small seed, as barley, millet, rye, by dipping his hand into a cloth bag slung about his neck, and spreading the seed with a broad casting motion of his arm. The inevitable metaphoric ext. *don't broadcast it* meant "don't spread it about." And only these senses can be found in the 1925 *Webster's International Dictionary,* though Webster's was slow in recording the first radio use of this term, c. 1922–1923.

Picked up by radio as a metaphor, it became the firmly established term for a general radio diffusion as distinct from a specifically directed message from one radio operator to another. At the same time that radio was developing into a giant industry, mechanical drillers and seeders were replacing the old farmer broadcaster. Today the only broadcasting one is likely to see is a suburban man thickening his lawn by spreading new seed (and even he is likely to use a spreader rented from the hardware store).

So it is that the original sense is becoming obs. Certainly the radio sense is now primary, and has even given rise to a new generation of hybrid forms, as *telecast, simulcast, newscaster, sportscaster,* etc.

Brother Jonathan From the Am. Revolution to c. 1812, a variously depicted Yankee hayseed who personified the new U.S. as John Bull and later Colonel Blimp personify, or once personified, England. Brother Jonathan was replaced by *Uncle Sam* (which see). [Originally a ref. to Jonathan Trumbull, first governor of Connecticut, and one of the most reliable supporters of the Revolution. In serious need of supplies, and all other sources having failed him, Washington is said to have remarked, "We must consult Brother Jonathan." Trumbull did not fail him, and *to consult Brother Jonathan, to turn to Brother Jonathan* became, though briefly, a common phrase.]

brown study Deep and solemn contemplation. Often connotes gloom. In "Bells for John Whiteside's Daughter," an elegy for a little girl, John Crowe Ransom extends these senses to include, metaphorically, death:

> There was such speed in her little body,
> And such lightness in her footfall,
> It is no wonder that her brown study
> Astonishes us all.

[*Brown* for "somber, darkening" has a long history. Dante (early XIV) has *l'aer bruno,* lit. "the brown air" but signifying the coming on of night. Prob. into English via Fr. *reverie brun, reverie sombre,* which were interchangeable.]

bub *Am. only and only as a form of direct address.* 1. Fellow. Guy. *Hey, bub, got a light?* 2. An inferior person. *Say Mister when you speak to me, bub.* [XIX. Perh. based on baby-talk *Bubby, Bubba* for brother. But Ger. *Bube,* boy (itself derived from a similar or identical baby-talk form), is at least as likely. The resolution depends on the dating, which remains uncertain. If in use early in XIX prob. < *Bubby, Bubba.* If not in use till after mid XIX prob. based on Ger. *Bube* and a transmission from German immigrants.]

buckaroo 1. A cowboy. 2. *Ext.* One of the rough and ready guys. A guy. [Sp. *vaquero,* cowboy < *vaca,* cow; *-ero,* agential suffix. OED *Supplement* first attests in SW usage in a letter from Texas dated 1827: "peons and bukharos, or herdsmen," the clear implication being that peons walk and bukharos are mounted. And *bukharo* is the only form attested until *buckaroo* in 1889. Webster's NWD, 1974, is flatly wrong in glossing this word: "prob. < Gullah *buckra,* white man, boss, altered after Sp. *vaquero,* cowboy." The term is rather from *vaquero* and altered after the Civil War by *buckra* (which see).]

HISTORIC. Negroes, after first serving as troops in the Civil War, became western cavalry after it. Their enlistments served out, many became cowboys in the West and Southwest, and their considerable role in taming the West has been as much overlooked by white historians as it is now being overemphasized by blacks. *Buckra,* a SE regionalism, was unknown in the SW in 1827. It was after the war that Negro riders brought the term west to interact with *vaquero-bukharo.*

bucket [IE *beu-,* swollen rounded, lumpish, (and associated ideas, including) heavy. Suffixed -*k*- in Gmnc. → OE *būc,* rounded container, pitcher, belly, heavy thing. Suffixed -*et* < Fr. *ette,* dim. suffix → Eng. *bucket,* a little *būc.*] A pail or similar container of wood or metal.

bucket of bolts *Am. colloq. whimsy.* A car. A cheap car. [Because (1) it rattles when moved, (2) consists of nothing more.]

bucket seat [*Am. Dating?* Probably < early barrel chair, a rounded chair (as if cut out of an oak barrel). Hence a little barrel chair. ?] A seat tilted backward and rounded in the back. Popular in sports cars for the flamboyant young.

kick the bucket To die. [But not, as commonly supposed, by standing on a bucket to hang oneself, then kicking the bucket away. Into XVI *bucket* had the additional sense "beam, heavy structural supporting member," a survival of the root sense "heavy thing." Animals to be slaughtered had their hind legs roped, prob. separately, and the lines hauled over a heavy beam. When their throats were then cut, their feet *kicked the bucket* in their death throes.]

buckra   [< Efrik and Ibic (tribal languages of Nigeria) *mbakara,* master < *mba,* agential prefix, one who; *kara,* conquers, surrounds, governs. This form survived in Gullah, Negro dial. of the offshore Georgia and Carolina islands, with the sense transfer to "boss, white man, powerful person." Hence:] 1. Master. White man. [Attested 1737 as an endearing term for a white master.] 2. Both powerful and good. [So, 1775: "he owes his happiness to the good Buckara God"—MMM. And 1871: *buckra yam,* very good yam; good enough for a white man. (May also be a ref. to a white potato as distinct from sweet potato.)] 2. Oppressor. Bad person. 3. Boogieman. Powerful, punishing spirit. [And so used in a historical novel by Toni Morrison, *Song of Solomon,* 1977:

> O Solomon don't leave me here
> Cotton balls to choke me.
> O Solomon don't leave me here
> Buckra's arms to yoke me.

I must believe, if only on the evidence of the last line (the diction of which was never known to Negro dialect), that this ballad is literary and that it was invented by Miss Morrison for plot purposes. Obviously, however, *buckra,* of African origin, surfaced in Gullah. (The last imported slaves were sent to the offshore islands and most nearly kept their African speech and customs.) The term then escaped to the mainland and into general southeastern usage with various sense extensions based on the different possible views of "old master" and his power. It was finally taken west by black cavalrymen and cowboys after the Civil War and there blended with *bukharo* of Sp. origin to form Am. *buckaroo* (which see).]

buff[1]   [Gk. *boubalos* (prob. based on *bous,* cow, ox) referred to African animals such as antelope and buffalo, and especially to their treated hides, the hides rather than the animals having been items of commerce in ancient Greece. L. *būfalus* (with the regular b/f into Latin as noted by Grimm's Law) has often been taken to mean "buffalo," but its more likely sense was "scraped and tanned animal hide"; and that sense underlies all the widely varied senses of Am. *buff.*] 1. *Obs.* Buckskin leather. [Exactly the root sense.] 2. *Ext.* The color(s) of buckskin. 3. Devotee, aficionado, enthusiastic adherent. *Most women are marriage buffs. Civil War buff. Railroad buff.* [The original early XIX form was *fire buff,* applied to NYC volunteer firemen after the buff-color uniforms of professional firemen.] 4. *Rare.* A polishing cloth of chamois or other soft leather. Whence the common v. *to buff* To polish. [To rub with a buff.]

   in the buff Naked. [Dressed in one's own hide.] *Miranda's buff is the nicest thing to come out of the ancient Greek skin trade.*

buff²   To strike. [OF *buffe,* a blow. More commonly *buffet,* which, as the dim. form, should mean "a little blow," but has come to mean "a powerful blow." *the buffets of fate,* or more commonly, *the buffetings of fate.* Yet *buff* survives in variant form in such heady comic strip forms as *Zap! Pow! Boff!* And it is probably the base of show biz *boffola,* a joke or comic turn that elicits a striking (knock-'em-dead) response. And, in standard form, in:]

   buffer Anything that cushions a blow. [Sense shift from "blow" to "absorber of blows."] *buffer zone* A neutral zone between opposing forces. [And in chemistry a buffer is a substance that maintains the stability of certain compounds, as in *buffered aspirin.*]

   blindman's buff A child's game in which a blindfolded player attempts to tag (strike) one of the other players, who are not blindfolded and who seek to elude him or her. [ME *blindfellen,* struck blind. Modern *blindfold* is < the p.p. *blindfelled.* Root sense: "blindman's tag."]

buffalo   Originally the misnomer and now the standard form for the North American bison. [See *buff¹.* Vulgar L. *būfalus,* the buffalo of Africa and Asia (and once of Europe). *Bos bubalus.* In a 1544 report of his explorations, De Soto used the form *bufalo,* and thereafter *buffalo* is common in XVII and XVIII accounts for *Bison bison.* See *turkey* for a similar misnomer that has become standard Am.]

   to be buffaloed To be stopped/stumped. In such forms as *it had me buffaloed, don't let him buffalo you.* [Though unattested, the root image must be of having one's way blocked by a herd of buffalo, or most awesomely, by a buffalo stampede. A common explanation refers to an early wood-burning train having its way blocked by a buffalo herd. But by the time the first railroads had pushed any considerable distance into the western plains, the buffalo had been effectively wiped out and the ranges stocked with cattle. I suspect that the vanished buffalo herds had become quasi mythological in memory, and that the awe they had inspired had been transferred to cattle, esp. to trail herds. The dating, however, troubles all such conjecture, MMM's first citation being from 1948! The term was in use in this sense long before 1948, but how long? The dating is critical and information on it is missing.]

buffoon 1. A clown. 2. A stupid, clownish person. [< It. *buffare* (echoic), to puff out the cheeks and blubber out the air in an Italianate Bronx cheer. Agential form, *buffone, buffo*. And so *basso buffo*, in opera, a comic basso. Also *buffoonery*.]

bug [< Welsh *bwg* (*w* for *u*), a specter. Akin to the first element of Cornish *buccaboo*, devil, imp, goblin. And so: BUGABOO, BUG-BEAR, BOGIE, BOGEY, BOGEYMAN, BOOGIEMAN.] 1. An insect, esp. a beetle. [Attested XVI but prob. in use much earlier. Because many beetles are so grotesque in form as to suggest a fiend of hell.] 2. *Ext.* A microbe. [XIX. By analogy to insects. Again because of the extraordinary forms they take.] 3. *Ext. of 2 in Am. colloq.* An infection. *I think I've got a bug.* Or, during an epidemic, *Everyone seems to be down with the bug.* 4. *Plu. only.* A common imperfection in a mass-produced mechanical or electrical system. *It took over three years to fly the bugs out of the B-29* (to locate by trial and error in regular operation the causes of recurring systems failure). 4. A devotee. *Leonard Kasle is a golf bug; no one, in fact, has more bugs in his game.* 5. A concealed electronic eavesdropping device. (Also as v. *to bug*, to plant such a device.) [Because these devices are small, and because the wires attached to early unsophisticated models resembled the legs and antennae of insects.]

    bugs, buggy Am. slang. [Dating uncertain. Prob. late XIX.] Crazy. *He's bugs. He's buggy.* [Implies that queer things crawl around in his head. And because people suffering from *delirium tremens* commonly see enormous swarms of crawling insects. (Sometimes they carry away the pink elephants from the previous hallucination.) And so:] *bug house* Insane asylum. [Place of creepy-crawly visions.]

bugger Earlier also *booger.* 1. A catamite or a pederast. 2. A mean, low person. *dirty bugger.* 3. *Ext.* An ordinary guy as a sure loser. *the poor bugger.* (In these two senses almost synonymous with *bastard.*) —v. **bugger** To act as the pederast. *be buggered* To act as the catamite. *bugger up* To make a mess of. —exclam. *Well, I'll be buggered!* [Medieval L. *bulgaris*, Bulgarian, with ref. to members of the Eastern Orthodox Church in central Europe. They were held to be heretics. The Chartist movement of these ascetics became identified with the Albigensians (who were one part of the ancestry of the Amish and Mennonites). "Heretic" was the exclusive sense of the word in OF and ME. Later "pervert." Because, says Partridge, "the Albigensian heretics were often perverts." But the remark is random: they were more nearly ascetics who endured martyrdom rather than renounce their faith. Nor did the sense shift from *heretic* to *pervert* until mid XVI, the first OED citation to make this new sense clear (though a few ambiguous citations predate it) being dated 1652.

I suspect, though I cannot attest, that the sound values of ME *bougre* may have suggested the new sense. As I suspect that Am. child's usage *booger*, dirty thing, as snot, toe crud, is also from *bougre*.

bull¹   [Root sense: "animal with the swollen pizzle." And so: IE *bhel-*, to swell; with early ref. to the enlarged pizzle of an aroused bull. All senses follow by association.] 1. A mature bovine male. 2. A powerful man. 3. Also **harness bull**. A cop. [XIX and early XX crim. slang: "a large, menacing male."]

And in many compounds to express "large, powerful, aggressively masculine," as: *bull dyke* (a "male" lesbian), *bull fiddle, bullfrog, bullheaded, bull-necked.*

bull, bear On Wall St. a bull is one who buys in anticipation of a rise. [Prob. because bulls toss their horns upward.] A bear sells short, expecting to buy at a lower price the shares he will deliver to satisfy his obligation.] Also *bull market, bear market, bullish, bearish.* [*Bear* perh. by association with "to bear down." Or from once common saying *to sell the skin before you bag your bear.*]

bull pen 1. An enclosure for a bull. 2. *Baseball.* The ball park enclosure in which relief pitchers warm up, or wait to warm up, during a game.

bull's eye 1. The small central circuit of a target. 2. A shot that hits that circle. 3. *General ext.* Any skillful stroke. *As an exclam. of approval.* Well done! [Skulls fixed on posts or tied to a tree were once common targets for archers, and to put an arrow through an eye socket was the test of skill.]

bull²   An empty, exaggerated, lying, or misleading statement. [Though now associated with *bullshit* ("to shoot the bull"), the form is based on obscure OF **boule,* a fraud, a deceit (perh. an irreverent ref. to papal *bolla* or bulls, but the guess is unsupported).

ME *bull*, a false statement. And note modern Icelandic *bull*, nonsense.]

bull session A lengthy colloquium, as of idle college students, in which the arts of exaggeration and non sequitur are developed to the perfection of random.

Irish bull *Rhetoric.* A statement that seems to make surface sense but contains a ludicrous contradiction. *The weather of Dublin is so inclement that most of the inhabitants live elsewhere. This restaurant is so crowded it's small wonder no one ever comes here. Every time I order pancakes I remember why I never order them. He is so ugly he would look better if he were invisible.* [*Bull* was in use in this sense in XVIII. It was first called *Irish bull* by Maria and Richard L. Edgeworth in their *Essay on the Irish Bull*, 1802. The Edgeworths were probably moved by the general British tendency to attribute all absurdity, esp. rhetorical absurdity, to the Irish, who for their part have labored conscientiously in support of the British assumption.]

bulldog edition *Am. journalism of the 1890's.* The earliest edition of a morning newspaper. With metropolitan papers, as the *N.Y. Times*, the collector's-item edition rushed to the suburbs so that we in New Jersey may have all the typos intact. [*Encyclopedia of Advertising* (Fairchild Publications, 1952) suggests that the term evolved when New York City's *Herald, World,* and *Journal* introduced early editions and "fought like bulldogs for circulation." Perhaps. But this explanation has a taint of folk etymology about it. I mean to look further, and meanwhile welcome any comments from readers.]

bulldozer A heavy machine on tank treads and with a large adjustable steel blade for moving earth and for clearing scrub growth and debris. [Am. c. 1875, the first form being *bull dose,* with ref. to a flogging and with the root sense "a dose strong enough for a bull." Form changed to *bulldoze* by c. 1880, with a sense shift to "powerful political coercion," as in the related political idiom *to steamroller the convention.* Then, prob. c. 1890, as a name applied to the first steam-driven mechanical bulldozers.] *bulldoze* 1. To operate a bulldozer. 2. *Obvious ext.* To overwhelm. To come on strong.

bullet: bite the bullet 1. To stand firm under attack. Akin to *to stick to one's guns.* (See *gun.*) [The new Enfield rifle issued by the British in the 1850's took a cartridge with a paper tube. In loading his piece, the rifleman had to bite off the end of the tube to expose the powder charge to the spark. Thus the root sense: "to stand and reload calmly when under attack."] 2. To grit one's teeth and face adversity. [In performing surgery without anesthetics, or in probing to remove a slug from a wound, it was once common to have the patient bite hard on a wooden dowel or on a lead bullet, whereby the root image became "to set one's teeth hard." In both associations the root sense is "firmness in adversity," but to be given the choice of two root images is something of a language curiosity.]

HISTORIC. In 1857 Great Britain had taken over only part of India. Its best native regiment was made up of Sepoys, some of them Muslim (to whom pork was taboo), some Buddhists (to whom the flesh of the sacred cow was taboo). Whether as fact or rumor, word spread among the Sepoys that the protective grease coating on the new cartridges was a mixture of lard and beef tallow. The Sepoys, therefore, refused to bite their bullets. The refusal turned into a mutiny, and the mutiny into the Sepoy Rebellion, in which many Englishmen were killed throughout India. Eventually, ever secure in the knowledge that God was on their side, the British put down the Sepoys and their allies with great slaughter, and all India came under British rule.

bully　One who abuses the weak. [< Du. *boele* (pronounced as in the Yale cry *boolah-boolah*), sweetheart; and thereafter with long sense evolution in English XVI, *bully*, sweetheart, fine young man; XVII, fop, deceiver (shift from "well dressed" to "overdressed" to "impostor who seeks to deceive"); XVIII, swindler, pimp (note survival of XVI "sweetheart" with sense shift to pimp as "a criminal sweetheart"); XIX, a thug, a strong-arm man, a hoodlum. And so to present sense.]

HISTORIC. Theodore Roosevelt is forever associated with his favorite exclamation of approval, *bully!* So used, it is a XVI survival, probably traceable to the Dutch settlers in T.R.'s ancestry, and probably transmitted as a term in Roosevelt family talk, though this last point must be referred to Roosevelt biographers.

bum[1]　The buttocks. [ME **bom*.] ***bum's rush*** Forcible eviction of an undesirable person, as by a saloon's bouncer. [And, to be sure, responds directly to the cry "Throw the bum out!" But that *bum* is *bum*[2], an accident of convergence. The standard bum's rush consists of seizing the victim from behind by the collar and the seat of the pants and heaving him bodily into the gutter. Cf., therefore, Brit. *bum bailiff*, a court or sheriff's officer who seizes wanted persons (nabbing them from behind).]

bum² 1. A hobo. 2. A person who refuses to work for a living. Hence, 3. A worthless person. —*v.* 1. To loaf. 2. To beg. To mooch. Often with *around*, **bum around.** —*adj.* No good. Commonly, *it's a bummer* It's no good. It can't be made to work. And so: *bum rap Police & crim.* 1. An arrest on false charges or on insufficient or illegal evidence. 2. A sentence imposed on an innocent person. *bum steer* Bad advice. [Ger. *Bummler,* a loafer. Folk etymology persistently but wrongly attributes *it's a bummer!* to Johann Jakob Bommer, XVIII Swiss organ-maker, of whom *Musical Heritage* magazine (May 2, 1977) says, "his organs were so much admired they gave rise to the expression *it's a real Bommer!*" But both the dating and the sense refute this bit of enthusiasm.] **on the bum** 1. On the road as a hobo. 2. Mooching. Cf. *Hey, Mac, lemme bum a light.* 3. Not working. *This machine is on the bum.*

bumboat *Nautical.* A small, usu. bargelike and always stinking tub used by harbormen who traded with ships at anchor, esp. for refuse and greasy slops. [Du. **bom,* a small bargelike fishing boat with a blunt bow.]

bureau [< Fr. *bureau,* a government office. But originally a feltlike cloth covering a desk. < OF *buire,* dark brown (It. *buio,* dark, dark brown). < L. *burrus,* flame red. < Gk. *pyrrhos,* fire (PYRE, PYROMANIAC). The sense evolution has been < fire → color of fire → cloth of that color used to cover desks → the desk so covered → the place in which such desks are found. (See *carpet: to have on the carpet.*) The root sense "red" is curiously, but only coincidentally, akin to that of *red tape.*] 1. An office. (This sense is primarily European, but *travel bureau* is standard in Am. for a shop or office that arranges travel and sells tickets.) 2. A subdivision of government. *The Federal Bureau of Investigation of the Department of Justice.* Or of a large organization, as *the news bureau.* 3. Ext. (Based on likeness to a desk with drawers and cubbyholes.) A dresser for bedroom clothes storage.

bury the hatchet To make peace. [*Hatchet,* here, for "war ax, tomahawk." Amerind customs varied, but some Indian tribes kept a ceremonial tomahawk that was buried when peace was made and exhumed when war was declared.]

busman's holiday   A day off from work on which one does more or less what one would do on a working day. The mailman who goes for a walk is taking a busman's holiday. [XIX Brit. drivers of horse-drawn omnibuses, becoming attached to their teams, were uneasy about turning them over to relief drivers who might abuse them. On their days off, therefore, the drivers regularly went to the stables to see that the horses were properly harnessed, and returned at night to see that they had not been abused.]

bust   1. *Sculpture.* A portrait showing head, shoulders, and part of the upper chest. Hence, 2. A woman's bosom. Also *busty* Having a large bosom. [Originally a funerary memorial, but with the root sense "surrounded by fire." Based on IE *eus-*, to burn. L. *urere*, to burn. Prefixed *amb(o)-*, about, around → *amburere*, to cremate ("to surround with fire"). Via p.p. *(am)bustus*, cremated → *bustum*, place of cremation, of burial, of entombment. Because such sculptures, usu. atop a stone shaft that sometimes also showed male genitals at an appropriate point in the shaft, were common memorials in place of burial; and because they were surrounded by the funeral pyres in which the newly dead were being cremated.]

butler   The chief servant of a more or less opulent household. (The frequency with which Butler turns up as a surname testifies to the fact that butlers were once as common as they are now rare.) [At root, a variant of "bottler" < Fr. *bouteille*, bottle. Ult. < Gk. **buttinē*, cask. (Cf. earlier Eng. "butt of wine" for "small cask of wine.") Since the wine cellar was regarded as a precious storage, the person entrusted with the keys to it would be the most important member of the household staff, its chief steward.

Genesis 40:21: ". . . he restored the chief butler unto his butlership again: and he gave the cup into Pharaoh's hand." In some versions "butler" is rendered "cupbearer." Either rendering implies more than the modern reader is likely to understand. For the butler/cupbearer was also the wine taster. Because poisoning was an established political method in Oriental courts, the butler was a highly esteemed officer of the royal household and a member of what might be called the king's "cabinet." For a similar evolution from servant to high official, see *marshal* (which evolved to high status as *butler* did not).]

butt-   Widely dispersed Gmnc. root with the sense "heavy, lumpish, thick." Ult. < IE *bhau-*, to strike, to bruise. The connective sense is prob. "swollen like a bruise (result of a beating)."

butt 1. Thick end. *rifle butt.* 2. Buttocks. *a kick in the butt.* 3. A stub end. 4. *By association.* A cigarette. 5. Target. Esp. in archery. [Thing struck.] *butts,* a target range. 6. A steep earthen mound behind a target range (for stopping bullets). Hence, *Geology.* **butte** A natural feature resembling sense 6. *Butte, Montana.* **butt of the joke** The one on whom the joke is played. [Its target.] —*v.* **to butt** To strike with the head. (But *butt,* cask, is < Gk. **buttinē,* wine cask.)

butts and bounds *Obs. Brit.* Property lines and markers. [*Butts,* flat stones that mark corners; *bounds,* lines connecting the butts along the limits of the property.]

buttwife *Obs. Brit.* A fishwife who dealt only in flatfish. And so: **halibut** "holy flatfish." [ME *hali,* holy; with *-but(t);* because eaten on holy days. And so: *turbot* "spiny flatfish." [Scandinavian *steorobot* with same root sense; Old Swedish *tōrnbut,* spiny (thorn) butt; with ref. to its spiny fins.]

butter and egg money   Often simply *egg money* Money from the sale of eggs and home-churned butter. Hence, a small discretionary sum; a special allowance (akin to pin money except that it is earned and pin money simply given). [Because the henhouse and churn were the Am. farm wife's domain, the money so earned having been traditionally hers to spend as she pleased.] *butter and egg man, big butter and egg man* 1. A wealthy farmer. 2. *Roaring Twenties.* A rich yokel who has come to the big town to whoop it up and who has turned into a big spender on the nightclub scene. [And in this sense popularized by George S. Kaufman's play of that period, *The Butter and Egg Man.*]

butterscotch   Candy. [At root: "cut butter squares." Has nothing to do with Scotland. See *hopscotch.*]

buxom   *adj. Now applied only to women.* Robust in the bust. [But at root: "servile, obedient," and applied to both sexes. Based on OE *būgan,* to bow, bend, yield, obey. Ult. < IE *beug-,* to swell, to curve (BOUGH, BOW). ME forms, *buhsum, bowsom, buxum, ibucsum,* conveyed the cluster of senses "humble, obedient, cheerful, patient, submissive, hard-working, robust, comely," a syndrome, I submit, that expresses all the qualities an Old English lordling would most desire in his peasants: cheerful servility and bodily strength for drudgery. First became specific to women in XVI from the sense "powerfully built working wench." Among earlier usages note *Piers Plowman,* "and buxom to the law" (submissive to it); and Spenser, *The Faerie Queene,* who has Neptune (with ref. to young castaways) command "His mighty waters to them buxom be."] *Ah, when will Charlee Wilbur buxom to me be?*

B.V.D.'s   (If the singular form B.V.D. exists, I have never come upon it.) 1. *Originally.* A one-piece, short-sleeved, short-legged, button-front, slit-seat, light men's underwear. 2. *Ext.* Any underwear, even for women, but not including long johns. *I walked in and caught her in her B.V.D.'s.* (But usu. with ref. to men's underwear.) [Nothing seems to invite more random folk etymology than a possible acronym, and the ingenious have offered endless explanations of these three letters, from Back Vented Drawers through Body-Vest Doodads. But B.V.D. is, in fact, a trade name registered in 1876 by *B*radley, *V*oorhees, and *D*ay, the company that manufactured these *b*arely *v*isible *d*etails.]

by-law   [Not "an incidental law" (a "by-the-way" law), but a governing ordinance as a practical interpretation of the provisions of a charter.] 1. The procedural rules of an organization and its shalls and shall-nots. 2. *Obs.* Village ordinances. [< ON *bylog,* village law < ON *byr,* village. Second element < *log,* law. Ult. from IE *bheu-,* to exist, to be (BEING). With ext. sense "place of being, place where one exists," hence, "village."]

C

Caesar   (Anglicized pron. *sē′zar;* in L. *kī′sar.*) Gaius Julius Caesar,
signifying Gaius (given name) of the Julian clan (of Etruscan origin)
of the family Caesar. 100–44 B.C. Roman emperor 49–44 B.C. He
became the type of the emperor and no man's name has given
rise to more eponymous words in more languages.

   Caesarean section The delivery of a fetus by incision through
the abdominal wall and into the uterus. [Legend has it that Caesar
himself was so delivered. But the family name, signifying *caesus,*
the cut one, p.p. of *caedere,* to cut, was already long established
at his birth. The etymological evidence clearly points to some ancestor who had been delivered by cutting, that delivery serving
to name the family line.

   Caesar Emperor. ***the twelve Caesars*** Caesar and the eleven
emperors who followed in his line. ***kaiser*** Same word but with
Ger. spelling, and meaning emperor. Originally the title of the
German emperors of the Holy Roman Empire. ***Kaiser Bill***
Wilhelm, last of the Hohenzollern line, the pig-faced emperor of
Germany (and grandson of the Victorian sow), emperor of Germany in WWI, booted into exile in 1918. He was a favorite lampoon
target of WWI doughboys and popular songs. ***czar, tsar*** [Variant
of *Caesar* by way of *Cezar.*] The Russian emperor, the last of whom,
Czar Nicholas, with his family, was tumbled into an anonymous
ditch by the red revolutionists. And so in Am.: *czar* (never *tsar*),
one who has absolute rule over some specific sphere. *labor czar,
crime czar.*

   Jersey, Isle of Jersey As a conquering general, Caesar left his
name on various places in Asia Minor and Europe, among others,
on the English Channel island first named *Caesarea,* or Caesar,
and gradually modified by the natives to Jersey. Noted for its weaving, this island became known for its exportation of *jersey cloth,*
a warm, durable, slightly elastic fabric originally used by fishermen.
Whence, ***jersey*** the pullover part of various sports uniforms, in

Am. esp. *football jersey,* whence a sense shift, this shirt being called a *jersey* even when made of synthetic fibers, and the word connoting not the material but the various numerals, names, and insignia sewed to such shirts as blazonings of prestige; hence the honor of the regalia, as in *to turn in one's jersey* to give up the game; and *to retire one's number/jersey* a tribute paid to great performers: upon their retirement, their jersey number is never again issued to a player but remains specific to the man who gave it such glory.

The island also developed a valued strain of dairy cow noted for the high butterfat content of its milk, whence *jersey cow.*

New Jersey The state, said to consist largely of suburban New York City and suburban Philadelphia; in any case, the only state of the Union whose two principal cities lie outside its borders. [Sir George Carteret, 1610?–1680, was vice-governor of the Isle of Jersey during the English Civil War and held it for the Crown long after the rest of England had fallen to Cromwell. He was rewarded after the Restoration by a baronetcy and an equal share in an enormous grant of American land that was named in his honor *Nuova Caesarea,* New Jersey. The city of Carteret, N.J., is named for him.]

Additionally, *July* [< L. *Julius mensis,* the month of Julius. Seventh month of the Gregorian calendar.] The Gregorian calendar was a reform of the *Julian calendar* instituted in 46 B.C.

Among given names: *Julia, Juliana, Jules, Julian, Julius, Julio, Cezar, César, Cesare.*

And though *julienne* (*Cookery.* Cut into thin strips) is ult. < Julius, it is prob. so only by way of an unknown chef with one of the Julius names listed just above.

Caesar's wife should be above (even) suspicion   A semi-adage asserting that important persons must be not only above evil but above even the possibility of being suspected of evil.

HISTORIC. The ref. is to Pompeia, second of Caesar's three wives. In 62 B.C. she served as hostess of the festival of the *bona dea* patroness of women and of women's virtue. The festival was taboo to men, but Publius Claudius, a roué who was rumored to have had an affair with Pompeia, attended disguised as a woman. His disguise inadequate, he was identified and ejected by the women. Caesar, declaring that the scandal, though probably unfounded, was not to be ignored, divorced Pompeia, declaring that Caesar's wife should be above (even) suspicion. Caesar was not characteristically such a prim evader. He probably had other reasons for wanting to get rid of Pompeia and struck this pose of blemishless virtue because it was expedient.

Cajun   A general reference to the people, language, and customs of French settlers in the lower Mississippi bayou country. Corruption of *Acadia.* [Common dial. rendering of *-jun* for *-dian: Acadian* → *Cadian* → *Cajun. Indian* → *Injun.* And note the same shift in Brit. *India* → *Injah.*]

HISTORIC. By the treaty of Utrecht, 1713, France ceded to England that area of Nova Scotia and New Brunswick called Acadia, which the French had settled. When in 1755 a new war with France seemed imminent, the English forced the French Acadians to swear loyalty to England, those who refused being ordered to be transported and dispersed among the colonies to the south. Longfellow's "Evangeline" romanticizes the story. One group, which was landed at Bayou Teche, Louisiana, kept a basically French identity and became the Cajuns. Some of the original deportees returned to Acadia after the Treaty of Paris, 1763, and their descendants have retained an ethnic identity less altered than that of the Cajuns.

calculate   1. To express mathematically. 2. *Ext.* To appraise with cold logic. 3. *Upper New England colloq.* To reckon; to opine. *I calculate, I callate, I cally,* I reckon; in my opinion. —*adj. calculated* Adds the sense "premeditated" to those above. *a calculated insult.* [Root sense: "to add and subtract by using pebbles." < L. *calculi,* pebbles; with ref. to a crude form of abacus used by the Romans, with pebbles as counters (CALCULUS).]

HISTORIC. The Romans, hobbled by a clumsy numerical system, could calculate by thousands and tens of thousands, but seemed to lack even the concept of millions or of larger numbers except in such metaphors as "countless as the grains of sand/blades of grass/stars in the sky"—the last being even a poor poeticism since there are only about 3,000 stars visible to the naked eye and no man ever saw much more than half of those at one time. European mathematics remained crude until the adoption of the decimal-based Arabic numerals, and the enabling invention of zero, which is, of course, the opposite of mathematical infinity. As mathematicians, the Romans were almost literally pebble counters.

cameo/cameo bit/cameo role   *Theater.* A brief but featured part in a production. One of the classic cameos in English theater, though this name for it did not exist in Shakespeare's time, is the role of the gravedigger in *Hamlet*. [Based on the idea of a small (brief) but complete portrait; usu. a role involving a single appearance on stage, but one in which the cameo player dominates the scene and, ideally, projects a memorable character. (In that, distinct from a walk-on part.)

The term seems to have appeared in this sense just after World War II. On Broadway it survives in the sense given. In Foamrubbersville, Cal., it now generally refers to the appearance of a well-known star ("a known portrait") in an incidental appearance, in which case only the appearance is implied, and not a brief and memorable characterization. If Dean Martin orders a drink and the bartender, who does not again appear in the film, just happens to be Bob Hope, that, in Hollywood, passes as a cameo.]

Canary Islands A small group of islands of volcanic origin off the NW coast of Africa, now a Spanish possession. [Any association with canary, the bird, is an accident of English assimilation. Root sense: "dog islands." Sp. *Islas Canarias* < L. *insulae canariae,* Islands of the Dogs; so named by Pliny the Elder, A.D. 23–79, because these islands were said to be populated by many packs of large wild dogs.]

HISTORIC. One may only guess at the mystery of this name. Pliny followed an account of an expedition to these islands by Juba of Mauretania in 40 B.C. But the islands emerged from the sea in isolation from mainland evolution and no mammals are indigenous to them. Juba is the first known explorer of the islands, but the dogs he found on them must have been left by earlier unknowns—probably by Arab merchants who had been blown out to sea. The Arabs have never been known for large dogs. What Juba saw must have been inbred packs of small curs who lived on fish, sea birds, and eggs. Pliny's account was, of course, hearsay and a century after the fact. Hearsay dogs have been known to grow to enormous size in the course of a century.

candle A taper. [At root: "white-shining." < L. *candere,* to shine (INCANDESCENT) < *candidus,* white, shining white. (The same root yields CANDID, CANDIDATE, "one who wears a white toga.")]

burn one's candle at both ends To squander one's energy riotously. *the game is not worth the candle* The possible rewards are not worth what one must put into it. [Ref. to early card games at stakes so low the winner could not pay for the candles that lit the play.] *not (fit to) hold a candle to So-and-so.* Not fit to be his servant. [Servants customarily lit the way for their masters, by candlelight indoors or by lantern outdoors.]

canoe The light water craft, either with outriggers (and sometimes sails) and made of a hollowed log for sea use, or the lightweight fresh-water shell used by North American Indians, consisting of birch bark or hides stretched over a framework of boughs. [Worth noting as the first word from the languages of the Amerinds to pass into European usage. Columbus used Carib Indian *kanoa* in his report on his first voyage (written 1493). The ref. was to the seagoing outrigger *kanoas* of the West Indies, but by 1555 *canoa* was attested in English, the present form deriving from Fr. *canoë* and the specific reference being to the lake-and-river shells of the northern Indians and the early French voyageurs.]

cantankerous Quarrelsome. Testy. [< ME *contek*, *contack*, quarrel, dispute; *contekour*, brawler. Many guess derivations have been offered for these ME forms, but beyond them all is fog.]

capital: with a capital letter Formula indicating emphasis, intensity. "Making her first film in five years, Ali MacGraw feels Terror with a capital T, Fear with a capital F." *N.Y. Times*, Aug. 11, 1977. [Dating uncertain, but there are old precedents—at least since Middle Ages—for emphasis by upper-case first letter, as in God and pronouns referring to Him. I once received a "snappy" business letter that signed off with "Yours for everything that spells Service with a capital *S*," but not many things can do that.]

cargo [L. *carricare*, Sp. *cargar*, to load. Ult. < L. *carrus*, a wagon (CAR).] Goods in the process of transportation. (I have been unable to trace why, in English, a cargo goes by ship and a shipment goes by car.)

carn- (CARNAGE, CARNAL, CARNATION, INCARNADINE, INCARNATION, REINCARNATION, INCARNATE, CARNIVAL) An intermediate Italic stem functioning in English words of widely different meaning. Ult. < IE *(s)ker-*, to cut. With nasalized suffix in Ital. → *k'r-n'-* → L. *carō*, flesh (the stem visible in genitive *carni*). The sense evolution in Italic was from: cut, to cut → cut flesh → flesh.

The IE root *bherdh-* (see *board*) also meant "cut, to cut." In Gmnc. *bord-* it became specific to "cut piece of wood, plank, board." This Gmnc. association with trees may perhaps be explained by the fact that the early Teutons were tree worshippers.

As speculation only, what will explain the Italic specification from "cut" to "carnage"?

carnage A slaughter. (The sense is specific to a slaughter of human beings, as in war.) *carnal* Of the flesh; specifically of the desires of the flesh. *carnal knowledge* Sexual intercourse. [To "know" (Biblical sense) someone (or one another) "in the flesh."]

carnation The flower. [< the It. technical term in Renaissance painting *carnagione*, the treatment of flesh tones. Renaissance painters normally treated their acreages of lady flesh in glowing whites and pinks, readily associated with the basic (prehybridized) colors of the flower.]

incarnadine Of the color of blood. [A slant but firm association with cut flesh. Most if not all dictionaries give as one sense of *incarnadine* flesh-colored; but this is a persisting clerk's error, and to use the word in this way is to insist upon being misunderstood.]

incarnation 1. *Theologically*. The embodiment of Jesus Christ in human flesh. 2. *Ext*. Any related embodiment. *reincarnation* The belief that souls after death will be reborn in another body. *incarnate* Of an embodiment, personified. *the devil incarnate*, the devil in the flesh. And so the XVI It. lampoon of the English fop on the Grand Tour:

> *L'inglese italianato*
> *è diavolo incarnato.*

Which, with a small violence, may be rendered:

> *The Englishman Italianate*
> *Is the devil incarnate.*

carnival 1. The season just before Lent, a period of ten days to two weeks of riotous festival before the season of mourning. [Not, as commonly asserted, from L. *carne vale*, which would be poor grammar; but < It. *carne levare*, to put away the meat, the flesh. (It. *levare* has the root sense "to raise" but the effective sense "to put away," "to pick up in the act of removing.)] 2. A traveling street tent show with music, catchpenny booths, and "rides," traditionally a Ferris wheel and/or a merry-go-round. [Because such shows are supposed to produce the mad gaiety of the pre-Lenten carnival festivities.] *carny Am. slang*. One who works in a traveling street-show carnival.

carouse 1. *Originally*. A boisterous drinking festival in which toasts were given round and round till all hands were noisily drunk. 2. *In U.S.* Any boisterous drinking revel or chug-a-lug. —*v.* To engage in such a loud drinking party or pub crawl. [< Ger. salute *gar aus,* meaning lit. "quite (entirely) out," and with the effective sense "Bottoms up!" This was the cry of Germans at a sort of chug-a-lug contest to see which man could drain the largest stein of beer at a single draught.]

carpet   1. Woven floor covering. 2. *Ext.* Animal hides sewn together as a floor covering. *goatskin carpet.* (But note that when a single hide is so used, idiom calls for *rug;* so: *bearskin rug.*) 3. *Ext.* Any more or less extensive and even ground cover. *a carpet of pine needles/moss.* [IE *kerp-,* to pluck, to grasp. Here with ref. to the pulling and knotting of threads in weaving a carpet. And so: L. *carpere,* to pluck, to seize; whence, old It. *carpita,* carpet ("thing plucked and seized/knotted"). Same IE root with k/h and p/f in Gmnc. → OE *haerfast,* harvest (implying a different sense of "plucking and seizing"). Modern It., however, uses *tapeto* < Gk. *tapēs,* woolen carpet (TAPESTRY), which is based on IE *temp-,* to pull tight (TENSION), with ref. to stretching thread on loom. The Fr. form *tapis* can be translated "carpet" but has the primary sense "cloth covering of a desk; baize." In Europe, carpets were first used to cover beds and tables, the common floor covering of the manor house and palace being rushes, peasants making do with swept earth floors.]

   have on the carpet To interrogate and reprimand or punish. [Fr. *sur le tapis,* with ref. to papers placed on a desk for official review. The review could, of course, be favorable, but the natural tendency of this species is to associate "official consideration" with "in trouble." So with *omen,* divine sign (good or bad) and *ominous* (boding ill). We hope for the best from our ministers and gods, but we expect the worst. In Parliament, *to bring a question on the carpet* is to bring up an issue for official consideration and debate. But note also, following the mistranslation of *tapis,* the earlier, now obs. Brit. idiom *to carpet a servant,* to call a servant into the drawing room or parlor for a reprimand. (Those rooms were carpeted, as most other rooms, and the hallways, were not.)]

   sweep (slip) under the carpet This is the converse idiom, and though it now suggests a lazy housemaid hiding her sweepings under an edge of the carpet, it originally meant "to remove from official consideration" by slipping the papers under the cloth covering of the desk; in Fr. *mettre sous le tapis.*

   carpetbagger A northern opportunist, often a minor political appointee, who went South after the Civil War to exploit the poverty of the defeated southerners and the vote of the newly enfranchised Negro. [After the then popular traveling bag, a grip made of flowered carpeting, or of a tough material that resembled such carpeting.]

red carpet A symbol of ceremonious reception. Variously *red carpet treatment* and *roll out the red carpet* [From the fact that carpeting seems first to have been used under thrones and on approaches to them. Hence, "kingly treatment." And mixed, within the absurdities of majesty, with the idea that sacredly royal feet should not walk in the dust with the baseborn.] A related idiom is Brit. *carpet knight* (Usu. pejorative.) A courtier knighted at court (kneeling on the king's carpet) for services there, not on the field of battle, in recognition of valor.

magic carpet A carpet with a magic ability to transport through the air all that stand upon it. [Now associated with the tales of *The Arabian Nights,* but a motif widespread through all Middle Eastern folk tales. According to the Koran, the original was the green silk marvel of King Solomon, upon which his throne stood, and which could transport him anywhere on command, along with his armies, his court, and his attendant spirits. In flight a canopy of birds (with, one hopes, trained sphincters) shielded him from the sun.

The huckster being always with us, various airlines have taken over *red carpet* and *magic carpet* as labels for luxury flights.]

Casanova A ladies' man. The sort of fop known in Am. as a skirt-chaser. [After Giovanni Jacopo de Seingalt (1725–1798), in whose *Mémoires of Casanova* (*Casanova,* Newhouse) he describes his warm reception and amorous conquests in the capitals of Europe (though by reading between the lines of his bragging, one can see that once he had scored an elegant first impression, he soon managed to evoke a general dislike that rapidly had him packing for the next stop on the circuit).]

case *adj.* 1. The last card of a given value. *case ace.* [Mid XIX Am. cardplaying; esp. faro, in which the cards are dealt from a "shoe" or "case." When three aces have been dealt, the last one, still inside the case, is the *case ace.*] 2. *Ext.* The last one of anything. "If there was a case quarter in the house she'd have given it to him."—Toni Morrison, *Song of Solomon.*

case hardened 1. *Metallurgy.* A metal covered with a thin sheath of hard alloy. [*Case,* sheath; as in *case knife,* sheath knife.] 2. *Ext.* Same as *hard case:* one inured to evil by many instances, cases.]

case the joint   *Crim. Am. XIX.* To reconnoiter a place in close detail in preparation for a break-in or holdup. [Prob. < *to get down to cases.* But in faro the *case keeper* kept careful watch over the play and the scoring, using an abacus-like device that was also called a *case keeper.*] **hard case** A tough customer; a habitual criminal. [*Case,* instance, item, example; *hard,* tough.]

cash in one's chips   To die. [In poker, one turns in one's chips for cash when one leaves the game. By ext., to leave the game of life. The form is XIX Am. Brit. has adopted the phrase but in the form *to hand in one's checks.*]

cashier   To dismiss from the armed services or from a position of responsibility for cause, or at least under what the services would call "conditions other than honorable." [Into Eng. following the Netherlands campaign of 1585 < Du. *casseeren,* to break. Fr. *casser,* to break. It. *cassare,* to cancel ("to break off"). < L. *quassare,* to break, to invalidate (QUASH AN INDICTMENT).]

Cassandra   1. *Greek myth.* Princess and priestess of Troy, daughter of Priam and Hecuba, and half-sister of Aeneas. She made rather much of her virginity, rejecting even Apollo, who punished her with the gift of true prophecy, stipulating that she would never be believed. In effect, she was to live with the terrible knowledge of all the disasters to befall Troy and to be shut away as a lunatic for her dark prescience. (As a moral coda, she gave to Agamemnon what she had refused Apollo, and was axed by Agamemnon's wife, Clytemnestra, having had to live with the knowledge that the ax would fall.) 2. A prophetess of doom. One who always foresees the worst. *Don't be such a Cassandra:* Stop harping on the dark side of things. [Strictly speaking, a Cassandra should be right in her dark forebodings. In idiom she is dismissed as a compulsive alarmist, as was the original Cassandra.]

castles in Spain   Symbol of idle fantasies. [*Castles,* grandiose projects; *Spain,* romantic place, fabled home of El Cid.] **to build castles in Spain** To daydream. [Fr. uses *châteaux en Espagne* and *châteaux en Asie* interchangeably, and either Spain or Asia will do well enough for a faraway romantic place.]

catamite   A pederast's pink-cheeked boy. (See *gonzel kid.*) [In Greek myth *Ganymede,* said to be the most beautiful of boys, was translated to Olympus to serve as cupbearer and butt-barer for those goaty gods. In one version of the legend Zeus himself, in the form of an eagle, snatched up the boy and carried him to Greek heaven. Gk. *Ganymede* was altered to L. *Catamitus*, whence *catamite*.]

catawampus   Slaunchwise. Diagonally askew. *You've got it all cata-wampus.* [A coinage of early XIX exuberant rhetoric or "Davy Crockett" American. Origin unknown. As a guess only: *cata* < *cater, catty*, as in *catercorner; wampus* < *whomp* with *-wise*, ("all skitter-thump-wise"). But ??]

catbird   A usu. grayish southern songbird, *Dumetella carolinensis*, related to the mockingbird. [So called because one of its calls resembles the meow of a cat.]

> ***in the catbird seat*** Exultant. Sitting on top of the world. [Sthrn. regionalism popularized by sports announcer Red Barber, who called his autobiography *The Catbird Seat.* I am not familiar with the way of the catbird: I assume that the root image is of the bird perched high overhead and pouring out exultant song; in Red Barber's terms, a fair equivalent of the feeling a pitcher must have in his heart going into the ninth inning with a fifteen-run lead.]

caterpillar   1. The wormlike, hairy, many-footed larva of a butterfly or moth. 2. *Am. ext.* A tractor with tank treads. *Caterpillar* is a registered trade name, but *caterpillar* with a lower-case *c* is now a standard Am. word. Also *cat.* [Whimsical: "hairy cat." Based on L. *catta*, cat; *pilosa*, hairy (cf. the *pile* of carpets). But there is no evidence that this whimsicality was a Latin invention. *Catta pilosa* does not occur in Latin writings, the first form of this whimsicality occurring in OF *chatepelose*, hairy cat. The form *pillar*, as the ODEE suggests, was prob. by association in XVI with OF *piller*, to ravage, to plunder (with ref. to the damage done to foliage by such pests as the apple-tree tent caterpillar).]

Catherine wheel   *Fireworks.* A pinwheel. (Strictly speaking, a pinwheel is a small-scale adaptation for home use of the large Catherine wheels used by professional pyrotechnicians.) [After the wheel, instrument of torture and a fixed symbol of St. Catherine.]

> HISTORIC-MYTHOLOGICAL. Catherine of Alexandria, later St. Catherine, was ordered martyred by the emperor Maximinus in A.D. 309. She was to be lashed in place and torn to bits by a wheel that had hooks fixed in its rim. This much known, the rest is from pious legend.

Catherine was said to be of a patrician family. She converted to Christianity at a time when the emperor was determined to stamp it out. In deference to her family, the emperor is said to have sent a group of his most learned men to win her from her error, but she instead converted them. It was then Maximinus ordered her to be executed, along with his learned defectors.

The legend runs on miraculously that just as she was to be ripped by the wheel, it shattered in a blinding flash that left her free and unharmed. That one flash, however, seems to have used up her miraculous resources, and she was beheaded without further intervention *ex machina.* So the wheel became forever associated with her in church art; and so from martyrdom to the fireworks show.

cats and dogs   *Stock market.* Speculative, low-priced stocks, usually new issues; the opposite of established blue chips with a long record of dividend payments. [Dating ? *Cats and dogs* conceived as an animal rabble in comparison with, say, thoroughbred horses.]

cat's-paw   1. A dupe. [After the ancient folk tale in which a monkey used a cat's paw to pull his chestnuts from the fire, whereby the monkey got the nuts to eat, and the cat got a singed paw to lick.] 2. *Nautical.* A small isolated ripple on a glassy sea, the result of a single puff of wind during a calm. [Metaphor.]

cattycorner/catercorner   Diagonally across a square. (In Am. usu. with reference to street intersections, to indicate relative position diagonally across the intersection, as *The bar is cattycorner to/ from the bank.* Most dicts. list *catercorner* first, and I cannot object, but here enter my impression that I have heard *cattycorner* more often in Am.) [< *cater,* XVII Brit. slang for the throw of a four at dice, i.e., on a single die, the four dots forming a square. < Fr. *quatre,* L. *quattuor.* Ult. < IE *kwetwer-,* four.]

cayuse   1. Cayuse Indians. [After the English mangling of the Indian name of the tribe.] A tribe of what is now northeastern Oregon and parts of Washington. 2. An especially tough and unruly strain of range horse bred by the Cayuse Indians. 3. A mean and crusty person. Commonly *ornery cayuse* on western frontier, *ornery* being a corruption of *ordinary,* and perhaps a sufficient comment on the meanness of the ordinary on the frontier.

HISTORIC. The Cayuse and their neighbors, the Nez Percé, showed a natural aptitude for breeding range horses for strength, endurance, and wild spirit. See *appaloosa*. Being superb horsemen, they prided themselves on the wildness of their mounts. A. K. McClure wrote in *Three Thousand Miles Through the Rocky Mountains*, 1869 (cited by MMM), "The kiyuse is never perfectly trained."

cess: bad cess   Bad luck. *Bad cess to you.* [Erse and into Am. primarily through Irish immigrants. But *cess*, in earlier form *sess*, cognate with *assessment*, was originally a yearly tribute paid to a conqueror, and later a land tax. Hence, the root sense of *bad cess to you* is "may you be taxed out of existence," or at least "may your taxes be raised."]

champion   *n.* The preeminent person in a given field. Originally referred to combat; later, to sports; most recently, to other competitions, as in *championship bridge.* —*v.* To defend, support, uphold. *champion a cause.* [Root sense, first, "one who takes to the field to uphold a cause," then, by ext., "the winner," i.e., the one who has the field when the fighting is over. < L. *campus*, field, arena. Late L. *campion*, Fr. *champion*, the one of the field. (Into Ger. as *kämpfen*, to fight. Also the base of *Kemp*, common Eng.-Ger. surname.)]

HISTORIC. Medieval law permitted trial by combat on the assumption that God would give power to the litigant who was in the right. To assist God toward a more even-handed justice, the parties at issue could appoint *champions* (men who took the field) to do their sword-clanging for them as private defenders at law.

The common reference to "Charlemagne and his thousand champions (knights)" has a closely related sense, the knights being conceived as defenders on the field of battle of the Christian faith against Moors.

charisma   1. *Theology.* The God-given power to perform miracles. The empowering grace of God. That power symbolized in religious art by the halo. 2. *As a fad word of robotic illiteracy.* The ability to attract favorable notice. The same quality go-getter salesmen used to call "personal magnetism" or "animal magnetism." [Depraved sense 2 adapted from sense 1 in post-WWII sociopolitical jargon, prob. by Max Weber, German sociologist. Sense 1 is ult. < IE *gher-*, fervent desire. With g/k → Gk. *kharis*, God-given grace; *khairein*, to revel in.]

charity   The primary sense is now *almsgiving;* the secondary, *kindly forbearance*, as in "with malice toward none, with charity for all."

But neither of these senses is sufficient to explain the Christian graces of faith, hope, and charity, and why the greatest of these should be charity. The Christian root sense is "the active outgoing love of others; the condition of loving one's neighbor as oneself." [L. *caritas,* at root: "high cost of living"; by ext. in Ciceronian L.: "love, esteem (to set a great value upon)"; and then in early Christian preachment the gist of "Do unto others as you would have them do unto you." And note the modified survival of this sense in "to take a more charitable view."]

charlatan   A quack. An impostor. [Originally a traveling seller of cure-alls of the sort XIX Am. labeled "medicine man." [It. *ciarlatano,* a traveling self-styled doctor, dentist, and peddler of nostrums. Altered < *cerretano,* a citizen of Cerreto, an Umbrian village that traditionally sent many such traveling cheats throughout Italy and much of Europe.]

charley horse   A muscular cramp, esp. one in the legs. [Not used in Brit. In Am. via the internationalism of horse racing < early XIX Brit. *charley horse,* a horse that pulled up lame. In XVIII Brit. slang, a *charley* was a night watchman, especially a partially disabled veteran; so called after Charles II, in whose reign it became common to give such jobs to veterans. They stumped about their rounds partially lamed. A likely (but unattested) sequence would be: lame watchman → lame horse, and then, jumping the Atlantic, belaming muscle cramp.]

chauvinism   The insistence, often rhetorically loud and long, that all right and merit is on the side of one's country, party, or cause, and that the opposition has no claim to consideration. [After Nicholas Chauvin, much wounded in the service of Napoleon, who as an old veteran dedicated himself to the jingoistic adoration of the emperor, flourishing his rhetoric, his wounds, and his decorations in passionate affirmation of *la gloire.*]

cheap   [Prob. < L. **caupo,* peddler, trader, innkeeper. Prob. into Gmnc. with the stem **kaup-,* whence OE *cēapian,* to trade, to buy and sell. The OE *c,* originally a kappa, evolved before the soft vowel to *ch,* and so ME *chep,* a purchase made (TO SHOP, SHOPPING), a bargain (CHEAP), a market, esp. a street market (and so CHEAPSIDE in London); and so the common Brit. place name forms CHIP- (Chipstead, Kent), CHEP- (Chepstowe, Monmouthshire), CHIPPING (Chipping Norton, Oxfordshire), all of which identify market towns or market sites. From XIV to XVII the forms *good cheap, good cheaping,* and *to great cheap* were common, signifying good trading, good bargaining. In modern Eng., however, only as *adj.* 1. Inexpensive. (Worth more than the price.) 2. Trashy. (No bargain at any price.) 3. Vulgar. (Not up to the value you and I place on ourselves.) 4. Miserly. (Not willing to spend.)

    cheap shot 1. *In contact sports.* An unnecessarily rough check, tackle, or block, esp. one after the whistle has stopped play. 2. Any verbal "hitting below the belt," as a personal slur in debating an issue. [Sense 3.] *cheapskate* A mean, stingy person. [Root sense: "cheap shit." See *shit.*]

check [Now with a wide range of extended senses. Originally into MF. as the chess term indicating "your king is in danger." < OF *eschec,* check, chess. < Persian *shah,* king. Ult. < IE *ksei-,* king, to rule. → Old Persian *khshayathiya,* king; of which the modern Persian is a shortened form. With natural exts. in XIV to the senses: 1. Control. Arrest. Stop. 2. A pattern of cross lines (as on the chessboard). Whence, 3. A check mark. (Originally an *X,* later a *v* with an elongated right arm.) Whence in XVI, with ref. to check marks made beside the items on a list, 4. Identifying label, ticket, tab *(hat check, dinner check, certified check).* So the verb senses: 1. To stop *(check the German advance).* 2. Verify. Control *(check one's addition).* 3. Stanch *(check the flow of blood).* And these categories will explain the many common idioms based on *check in, check off, check out, check up, body check,* etc.]

    check Expresses agreement. *check?* Do you agree? *check and double check* Expresses emphatic agreement.

    checks and balances In the founding theory of the U.S. Republic, the investiture of restraining powers upon the executive, legislative, and judiciary branches.

    checkmate The final position in which the king, being subject to capture, is left no possible defensive move. [< Persian *shah mat,* the king is dead. Via OF *eschec mat(t)e.*]

checkpoint 1. *Military and police.* A control station through which all traffic along a given route must pass, usually being required to stop for inspection. 2. *Navigation.* A visual reference point. *Checkpoint Charley WWII.* An enemy unit, usu. a single airplane, that flies a reconnaissance on a more or less fixed schedule, usu. at night. (When such a plane came in to strafe and bomb more or less on fixed schedule, it was called *Pisscall Charley,* because it wakened everyone as if for latrine call.)

check rein 1. A special training harness, as a thong from bit to saddle to break a horse of the habit of lowering its head. 2. *Ext.* Any special form of restraint. *He keeps a tight check rein on his emotions.*

cheer 1. Mood, face, countenance. [L. *cara,* face < Gk. *karē,* head.] 2. A loud acclamation as by a large body saluting a leader. [Philip Howard, *Weasel Words,* Oxford, cites what may be a first Latin use in this sense in the obscure sixth-century African poet Corippus: *"Caesaris ante caram,"* before the face (presence) of Caesar: i.e., an acclamation sounded in his presence. And in 1720, Daniel Defoe, *Captain Singleton:* "We gave them a cheer as the seamen call it." "As the seamen call it," in seeking to explain what a cheer is, certainly indicates that the sense was then new in Eng.] **cheers** 1. Repeated acclamations. 2. Drinking toast. [As if: "May this put a good countenance on things."] 3. Also **cheerio** Goodbye. [Primarily Brit., but see Don Marquis's Mehitabel and her favorite refrain, "Cheerio my dearie-O." Also with the sense: "May the future greet you with a good countenance."]

cheese[1] [L. **caseus,* by transliteration → Gmnc. *kasjus* → OE *cēse,* the *c,* originally a kappa, changing before the soft vowel *e* to ME *chese,* cheese.] 1. Pressed curds variously treated and aged. 2. *Slang.* More or less moist body dirt that forms in creases.

cheesecake *Photography.* A photo of a pretty girl or girls with skirts hiked or windblown to provide a sampling of thigh or underwear or both. [Tame stuff in these X-rated days, but thought to be daring c. 1912, when the word was first coined, prob. by James Kane, a photographer for the *New York Journal,* prob. as an impromptu comment while watching a photo of peekaboo thighs firm up in the developing solution. Kane did not explain what he meant by the word. *Cupcake* is a standard endearment for a pretty girl; *cheese* is the standard word photographers ask their models to say. Alternatively, cheesecake is creamy white (like fluffy lingerie?). If some combination of these elements does not explain the term, it will have to remain unexplained.]

cheesecloth Coarse cotton gauze. [Originally (and still) used to wrap some cheeses for the aging process.] **cheesy** Cheap. Stingy. [Prob. < (now rare) *cheeseparing,* skinflinting.]

he thinks the moon is made of green cheese Commonly said of a credulous dolt. [*Green,* unaged, unripe. Hence, a natural metaphor based on seeing wheels of cheese wrapped in cheesecloth and palely aglow in the dark of the aging cellar, perhaps exuding a little moisture, the beading of which would suggest the markings on the moon.]

(cheese²) **the big cheese**   The important person. The top man. *He's the big cheese around here.* [Gift of the Brit. Empire < Hindi *chīz,* thing.]

(cheese³) **cheese it!**   *Warning cry.* Watch out! Stop it! *Cheese it, the cops!* Watch out, the police are coming. [Brit. early XIX. The following entry from the 1811 *Dictionary of the Vulgar Tongue* shows the term has not changed meaning:

> *Cheese it.* Be silent, be quiet, don't do it. *Cheese it, the coves are fly;* be silent, the people understand our discourse.

Though unattested, prob. < *cease it!*]

Cheshire cat   Not a specific breed of cat, but prob. a folk tale reference. *grin like a Cheshire cat* To grin so broadly as to show one's gums. [Since *Alice in Wonderland,* 1865, forever associated with Alice and Lewis Carroll, whose Cheshire cat could fade from view until only the grin remained. But Grose notes it in his *Classical Dictionary of the Vulgar Tongue,* 1785. The cat is prob. from a lost folk tale, the full form of the expression being *to grin like a Cheshire cat eating cheese/gravel.* Alternatively, the saying is a bit of self-consciously exuberant country rhetoric, a tradition still very much alive in Am. sthrn., as in *grinning like a jackass eating briers.* (I have found nothing to explain why cats of the nonexistent Cheshire breed should grin more broadly than cats of other nonexistent breeds, and so much more broadly than cats of existent breeds.)]

chess   The game. [Ult. < Persian *shāh,* shah, king, sheik. And see *check: checkmate,* the first element of which is another variant of the same stem. The intermediary form is OF *esches* (Fr. *échec*), plu. of *échec,* hence literally "king," the plu. form implying "game of the two kings."]

chess pie   A traditional colonial cream pie, the basic filling consisting of cream beaten together with eggs and butter, and commonly with a wide range of nut, fruit, and fruit juice additives. *Jefferson Davis pie,* a southern variant, adds flour and spices. [James A. Beard traces the earliest U.S. recipes to Virginia and Tennessee, and speculates that "chess" is a corruption of "cheese." There is, however, no cheese in a chess pie. One may argue that chess pie filling has approximately the same consistency as that of cream cheese pie. Though it smacks of folk etymology, "chess" is more likely a corruption of "jes' " for "just." "Jes' pie," as distinct from *apple pie, cherry pie, pumpkin pie,* etc.

Chichevache From medieval folk tales: a monster said to live only on the flesh of virtuous women and, therefore, to be forever hungry. (One of the hoariest of dull jokes: to this day every campus that sports a stone lion continues the so-called legend that it will roar whenever a virgin passes by.) [It seems to have been Chaucer who brought Chichevache to England from his prowling through European folk tales. In the *envoi* to his "Clerke's Tale" he warns women away from virtue "Lest Chichevache you swelwe (swallow) in hire (her) entraille (entrails)." < OF *Chichefache,* prob. "pinched face" or "ugly face." Chaucer rendered OF *fache* as *vache,* cow.]

chicken [The etymology offers two clear but different sources. Perh. < IE *ku-,* rounded, hollow (CUP. Ger. KOPF). This stem functions in Gmnc. in a wide range of words with the IE sense, and also to signify "lump, enclosure." (In the sense "rounded object," may be associated with egg.) Prob. suffixed *-k-* in Gmnc. → *kuk,* chicken, *kukin,* little chicken → OE *coccin, cīcen,* ME *chicken.* But Gmnc. *kuk* may as readily be echoic of the chicken's cry *kuk-kuk-kuk.* (Which came first, the *ku-* or the *kuk-kuk-kuk?*)] 1. The common domestic fowl bred for egg laying and meat. The group includes many hybrid strains as exotic as the parrots and the birds of paradise. The old hen may not look like much, but she has gaudily mutable genes. 2. Specifies a fryer (up to about 9 months) as distinct from an established egg-laying hen, and so a natural metaphor for young women as distinct from matrons. (See also *Cockney.*)

chick, chicken A young woman. Also *slick chick* In beat-generation slang, a specimen of lithe nubility. *chicken lobster* A young and tender lobster. (Must weigh at least one pound to be a legal catch.) *she's no chicken* She's not as young as she used to be. But *hen party* does for any social gaggle of females, young or old.

chicken feed An insignificant amount of money. [Disparagingly compared to the mash and swill commonly fed to chickens.]

chicken-hearted/chicken-livered Cowardly. [Because chickens are easily panicked.] *In current slang, simply chicken* Cowardly. *He chickened out on me.*

HISTORIC. In England the heart does as the seat and symbol of courage. *Richard the Lion-Hearted.* In the Romance languages the heart serves as the seat of love and compassion, the liver as the seat of courage. So: It. *uomo di fegato,* lit. "man of liver," a brave man.

chicken inspector A more or less standard party gag of the 1920's. [Joke stores commonly sold badges so stamped, and bumpkin gagsters made much of flashing these badges as their authority for a close inspection of all chicks at the party, including any— ha-ha—old hens.]

a chicken in every pot A Depression-era symbol of plenty. (See *fleshpots* in the Biblical sense.) **don't count your chickens before they're hatched** Proverbial. [There's many a pip twixt the *ku-* and *kuk-kuk-kuk.*]

chicken pox Medically, *varicella.* A highly contagious mild virus infection, usu. of children. [So called because said to be too mild to harm a chicken.]

chicken shit In WWII, the civilian soldier's name for service regulations and for the endless, pointless, make-work of service chores. [Because the one unending labor on any chicken farm used to be the shoveling up of droppings, which were forever immediately renewed in place.] *By association only, akin to* **chicken colonel** A full colonel. [Disparaging ref. to his insignia of rank, which is a spread-eagled eagle (or is it in fact a chicken?). The association because such chickens were commonly in charge of training-camp chicken shit. Also **light colonel** A lieutenant colonel. [*Light* as a mocking misreading of the form *lt. col.,* and because he/she/it is not "full."]

chickpea A round .45-caliber pea especially suitable for drying. Sp. *garbanzo.* In It. *cece,* It. dial. *cecere, ceccere.* [L. *cicer, pea.* Fr. *chiche.* ME *chiche.*]

HISTORIC. In the *Sicilian Vespers* (which see), dialect *cecere, ceceri,* or *cecceri* was used as a *shibboleth* (which see) to determine who might live and who must die.

Chick Sales An outhouse. [So named after Chick Sales, Am. comedian at the height of his popularity c. 1920. He had a particularly successful comic routine in which he explained how to build an outhouse.]

chiffonier A high, narrow chest of drawers, often with a mirror on top. [Root sense: "rag chest," or ult. "bin for wood chips." The *-ier* is a suffix of function. Fr. *chiffon,* a sheer rayon or silk fabric

< OF *chiffe*, old rag < OF *chipe*, which is ult. < OE **cipp*, chip: in the general Frenchification of early ME, an unusual instance of backflow from ME to OF.]

Chinaman's chance: not have a Chinaman's chance   To have no chance at all. [Because in the rawhide West, half-brutalized men who had learned to hate Injuns, breeds, and the Mex regarded Chinese immigrants as something less than human. Killing a Chinese was not, at one time, taken to be murder. A Chinese could not file a complaint at law. And in any legal dispute with a white man, the Chinese were sure to lose. This contempt was further fanned to hatred in the days when miners smuggled in coolies who would work for starvation wages to take over the jobs of white mine workers, who, already impoverished, often massacred parties of Chinese workers.]

NOTE. *Chinaman,* the standard Am. colloquial form, is generally regarded as offensive, the proper form assertedly being *Chinese.* I have been unable to locate the source of this nice distinction without a difference, it being rather overnice in view of the fact that *Frenchman, Irishman, Welshman, Cornishman,* etc., are standard and with no trace of a pejorative sense.

chippy/chippie   A prostitute. [Am. only. In Brit. slang, *chip, chippy* refers to a carpenter (< wood chips). *Am. Thesaurus of Slang* gives (undated) *chippy house,* brothel. MMM gives first known attested usage from a Colo. newspaper, 1890: "The leading dudes and chippies of Europe." Yet, despite these contexts, a chippy is specifically a streetwalker. Prob. < sparrow, chipping sparrow. Because lined along the street in a row? Because streetwalkers at times make chip-chip sounds? (I have heard them do so in London and I have supposed that were I a plainclothesman, they might then explain they were just chip-chipping innocently in the joy of heaven.) Perhaps into Am. via a chipped-at American abroad; though *chippy house* and the 1890 citation refer not to streetwalkers but to house whores or deluxe call girls. Whence ???]

chock-a-block   *Nautical.* Describes the situation of a two-block tackle when the two blocks have been drawn together, permitting no further purchase. [*Chock* may be argued to be the concave wheel through which the line passes inside the pulley; *block,* to be the whole pulley assembly; but in practice they are used as two different names for the same thing.] Hence, ***chock-a-block full*** Filled to the maximum. And so: ***chock-full*** Absolutely full. Full to the brim. [The etymology is uncertain. *Chokke-fulle* and *cheke-fulle* are XIV. Prob. from OE **cēoce*, cheek; whence the root sense of *cheke-fulle*, "filled to the cheeks." (Cf. "I'm stuffed to the eyebrows" for "I am absolutely full of food and can eat no more.") *Chock-a-block* is prob. later, and *chock* is likely a separate evolution from Norman French **choque, *chouque*, log, block of wood (especially one used as a wedge). In modern Fr. *souche*, the standing stump of a felled tree.]

chortle   To laugh. [A portmanteau word made by packing together *chuckle* and *snort*. Packed by Lewis Carroll (C. L. Dodgson) as part of the poem "Jabberwocky" in *Through the Looking-Glass*, 1871:

> "O frabjous day! Callooh! Callay!"
> He chortled in his joy.]

Christian   Of Christ. [< Gk. *Christianos*, originally a nickname (equivalent to modern slang *Christer*) applied by the people of Antioch (the capital of Syria in the first century, it is now in Turkey) and later proudly asserted by the followers of the new religion.] And see *cretin*.

HISTORIC. Richard Chenevix Trench, Anglican archbishop of Dublin, is, as he might have said of himself, "worthy to be heard" on this point (from a series of lectures published in 1882):

> . . . for imposed by adversaries it [the name "Christian"] certainly was, not devised by themselves, however afterwards they may have learned to glory in it as the name of highest dignity and honor. They did not call themselves, but, as is expressly recorded, they "were called," Christians first at Antioch; in agreement with which statement, the name occurs nowhere in Scripture, except on the lips of those alien from, or opposed to, the faith. [Acts 26:28; 1 Pet. 4:16] . . . it was plainly the heathen, and not the Jews, who were its authors; for Jews would never have called the followers of Jesus of Nazareth "Christians," or "those of Christ," the very point of their opposition to Him being, that He was *not* the Christ [the Messiah], but a false pretender to the name.

Christmas   [*Christ*; suffixed *mas(s)*, rite. (See *mass*.) Literally, "the mass of Christ," and understood to be specific to the celebration of the nativity. The twelve days of Christmas have both Judaic and Teutonic antecedents.]

HISTORIC. In Gmnc. **yul* or **jul* labeled the season just after the winter solstice, when the hours of daylight once more began to lengthen. The Teutons celebrated the return of the sun with an immemorial revel that, within traceable history, lasted twelve days or two weeks. The wild revelry of the ancient festival has disappeared from Christmas, but many of its features seem to have been transferred to the German pre-Lenten Fasching, still celebrated by many as a work holiday for all-night drinking and dancing. *Yul* is, of course, the base of English *Yuletide;* but also of *jolly,* as in Santa's ho-ho-ho, and the now fixed epithet *Jolly old St. Nick* (in which *jolly* is both *merry* and *Yuley*).

No one can trace how the Christmas tree and the special Yule log became central features of this ancient festival, but both are undoubtedly related to the fact that the ancient Teutons were forest dwellers and Druidical tree worshippers. [*Teuton* means at root: "the people who worship Tiu" (TUESDAY). *Druid* means at root: "one who has knowledge of trees (and of their tutelary spirits or daemons)."]

The tutelary spirit of the Teutonic festival was some sort of Old Man of the Woods, perhaps a pagan equivalent of Pan, and he was impersonated by some red-nosed, white-bearded jolly old guzzler who danced around the Yule fires and proposed toasts. He was probably attended by others, who impersonated forest hobgoblins, just as Santa Claus is today portrayed as being attended by dwarfs.

By the VI, Roman missionaries had begun to Christianize the northland, bringing Christmas to the Yuletide, and since the two festivals occurred at the same time, the resultant ritual became a curious hodgepodge. The old rites continued to be practiced by the heathens. [*Heathen* is, at root, "one who lives out in the heath" (the wild uncultivated back country away from the civilizing influence of settled places).] In this blending of the two festivals the Old Man of the Woods acquired a new name, which has survived. He became *Kriss Kringle,* the name deriving—unbelievable as it may seem—from Ger. *Christkindl,* the little Christ child. It is a bit like putting one of Santa's gnomes in a manger and calling that the Feast of the Nativity, but so goes the language, and so it is that this little Christ child has come down to us with a white beard, a boozer's red nose, and a gnomish twinkle.

Our Santa Claus is clearly related to Kriss Kringle and the Old Man of the Woods, but at a Christian remove. Dutch settlers brought him to New York as *Sinterclaas,* a dialect version of Du. *Sint (Ni)colaes,* Saint Nicholas.

Saint Nicholas was a fourth-century bishop of Myra, in Lydia,

Asia Minor. He hodges his way into this podge as the patron saint
of gift givers. Pious legend tells of an impoverished but good man
who could not provide dowries for his three daughters and who
was about to sell them into a life of sin. (Though impoverished,
they were probably too genteel to take in laundry, and one does
owe something to one's social position.) Saint Nicholas, hearing
of this lower-upper-class plight, threw a bag of gold through the
man's window on each of three successive nights, each bag providing a dowry for a marriage possibly made in heaven. . . . And a
Merry Xmas to all.

Many purists object to the form *Xmas*, yet it has ancient antecedents, X having long been a pious symbol of Christ and of the
cross (so much so that illiterate Jews at Ellis Island refused to
use *X* as a mark, signing instead with a small circle—in Yiddish,
a *kikl*). *Xmas* puts one not among the illiterate, but in the company
of early Greek and Roman saints. Our Christmas customs, having
absorbed so much else, can certainly stand a few of those, if only
to keep an eye on the hobgoblins.

chronic   [Gk. **chronos*, time. Also *Chronos*, the ancient supreme god
of the Greeks and father of Zeus (CHRONOMETER).] Continuing
over a long time, with ref. to a long-continuing disorder. So *chronic
federal deficits, chronic disease, Dinah Levy's chronic marriage
to Leonard.*

NOTE. *Temporal* [L. **tempus*, time] is etymologically distinct
from *chronic* only in that one derives from the Greek word for
time, and the other from the Latin. Yet *temporal* has no connotation of disorder but rather connotes transience and worldliness
as distinct from religious values said to be eternal. So two words
that might as readily have been identical have been assigned distinct senses by that self-sequential illogic called idiom, in answer
to the need to label distinct ideas.

Richard Chenevix Trench, Anglican archbishop of Dublin, in
a series of lectures published in 1882, offers a valuable list of such
paired words, here partially reproduced:

1. Paired words from Old English and Latin:
   shepherd—pastor
   feeling—sentiment
   handbook—manual
   anger—ire
   love—charity
   foresight—providence
   freedom—liberty

      to whiten—to blanch
      to soften—to mollify
      to unload—to exonerate
      unreadable—illegible
      unfriendly—inimical
      unchangeable—immutable
      boyish—puerile
  2. Paired words from Latin and Greek:
      revelation—apocalypse
      compassion—sympathy
      transparent—diaphanous
      digit—dactyl
      moons—lunes
      grief—dolor

Trench also cites the distinct meanings of *astronomy* and *astrology,* both from Greek and etymologically almost identical.

From Latin: *despair* (L. *spero,* I hope) and *diffidence* (L. *fide,* faith). Also: *interference* and *interposition; insolent, irregular, unaccustomed,* all with the Latin root sense "not according to commonly established rule"; and *invent, discover,* both at root "to come upon," yet so distinct as to make it ludicrous to say "Columbus invented America." (That invention was left to Henry Ford.)

chuck   [Prob. < OF **chuquer, *choquer,* to make a quick motion of the hand, as in throwing something away (which is prob. the origin of *shuck,* which see), but the sense included any quick hand motion, as in striking or tapping.] To throw.

    chuck it out Throw it away. ***chuck it, chuck that*** Am. *colloq.* Stop it. [Be done with that. And so also:] ***chuck the habit*** To break off an addiction or a habituated behavior. ***chuck under the chin*** To kitchy-coo by touching lightly under the chin, usu. with the knuckle of the bent index finger. [A gesture of endearment, as in playing with a baby.] ***dearest chuck*** Term of endearment. [For a person to be chucked fondly under the chin.] ***chuck hole*** A burrow or other hole in the ground. [Because it chucks a horse that steps into it. (The term is sometimes loosely used for breaks in a paved surface, but those are more commonly *potholes.*)]

chuckle   [Echoic of *chuck-chuck-chuck* as a rendering of a chicken's cry; with *-le,* substantive suffix. In XVI, to laugh uproariously. Present sense from XIX.] *n.* Subdued laughter. —*v.* To laugh so. *Civilization is the unachieved distance from the belly laugh at* *someone else's discomfort to the chuckle at one's own folly.*

chucklehead An oaf. [May be argued to signify "head capable of nothing but the chuck-chuck of a chicken," but more likely < Brit. dial. *chuck,* a lump (chunk).]

chum¹   Intimate companion. Pal. Crony. [XVII Brit. university slang, prob. based on *(cham)bermate,* roommate.]

chum²   *n.* 1. Chopped-up fish and fish guts, preferably ripe and redolent, spread around a fishing boat to attract school fish, as bluefish. 2. The area or track so spread on the surface. Also *chum slick.* —*v.* To fish by using chum. *We chummed for blues off Sandy Hook.* [Commonly glossed "origin unknown," but it must certainly be noted that Jamieson's *Dictionary of the Scottish Language* defines *chum* as "food, provision for the belly." I have been able to find no ref. to this Sc. chum in connection with fishing, but perhaps some reader familiar with Scottish can steer me to one (or show that the term is not so used).]

cigar   A roll of tobacco wrapped in a leaf. [Sp. *cigarro* < Mayan *sikar,* to smoke.] *close, but no cigar* 1. Almost, but not quite. 2. *In effect.* You lose. [A catch phrase of XIX Am. carny men who operated games (esp. the feat-of-strength game of driving a weight up a pole by a blow of a heavy mallet) in which cigars were given as prizes.]

cinch   A saddle strap. 2. A sure thing. 3. An easy thing. [Sp. *cincha,* belt. (< L. *cingere,* to gird; *cingula,* girdle, belt.) In Mex. Sp. *cincha* was specifically a saddle strap.] —*v. cinch (up)* To tighten a strap.
    lead pipe cinch A doubly sure or doubly easy thing. [Few idioms have so confused both folk etymologists and lexicographers. "Lead pipe," here functioning as an intensive, has nothing to do with plumbing, and is not a blackjack used by XIX Am. thugs. It is a much neglected midwestern and western form for galvanized iron pipe (which looks as if it were lead). People who say "red light" for "traffic light" are almost certain to say "lead pipe" for "galvanized pipe." So Willa Cather, *One of Ours* (1922): "He put his feet on the lead-pipe foot-rail and his elbows on the brown counter top." (In which "lead pipe" must mean "galvanized iron pipe," since lead pipe would buckle if used as a foot rail.)
    For saddling and cinching a blower (a horse that distends its belly), a short length of this so-called lead pipe was slipped under the saddle strap and turned like a tourniquet, the work assisted

by a few knee jabs in the belly. When the blower had been forced to deflate and the saddle was cinched tight, the length of pipe was tucked between the saddle strap and the horse's belly, that horse being cinched and double (lead pipe) cinched.]

cioppino An Italian version of bouillabaisse much featured in and around San Francisco, but increasingly common in eastern Italian restaurants, where it is often listed as *chop-in-o* or *chip-in-o*. [The word does not appear in Italian dictionaries, nor in menus in Italy, and all San Francisco restaurant owners seem eager to promote the story that the dish was invented by Italian immigrants on beach fishing parties. One of their number would fire up a communal pot and start a tomato sauce base. Then any fisher who *chipped in* or *chopped in* some of his catch could have some of the (a word is born) "cioppino."

A lovely tale, but it overlooks the fact that many of the Italo-Americans in San Francisco were from Genoa, and that in Genoese dialect *cioppin* or *ciuppin* labels the local fish soup.]

clabber The curds of sour milk that separate from the watery whey. (Little Miss Muffet was eating clabber and whey when the spider came along.) [< Irish *bonnyclabber*. First element from earlier Irish *bainne*, milk < Middle Irish *banne*, a drop of. Second element < Middle Irish *clabair*, curd.] *clobber* To beat (to a pulp), though unattested, is prob. from *clabber*.

clap Always with *the* Gonorrhea. *Dear Angela: It may come as a surprise to you, but I have good reason to know you have the clap. I am surprised.—Jerry.* As verb, takes *up: clap up* To infect with gonorrhea. *be clapped up* To have gonorrhea. [XIV. < OF *clapoire*, venereal sore < *clapier*, brothel. Which was an adaptation of Provençal dialect *clapier*, rabbit hutch < **clap*, a pile of stones, esp. stones of the sort turned up by the plow. Animal enclosures were commonly made by rough-mortaring these stones, for security, and because wood was scarce. (See *hook or crook* and *boot: to boot*.) The dating, however, indicates that the word entered Eng. well after OF, prob. via Du. *klapoore* (< *clapier*).]

claptrap Cheap, self-seeking blather. [Originally theatrical. Said of the antics of a performer who uses every sort of shoddy stage trick to wheedle (trap) applause (clapping).]

clergy The body of ordained ministers, originally of the Roman Catholic Church; later, the total of the ministers of all churches.

[But with the concurrent sense in early England "learned man," literacy and the knowledge of Latin being almost exclusively the possession of clerics. And this sense was already specific to L. *clericus* (the shift to *g* occurred in OF *clergie*), clerk, learned man, scholar. Ult. < the zero-grade (vowel omitted) form of IE *kel-*, to cut, to divide → Gk. *kleros,* mortal lot, inheritance; the word acquiring a religious connotation at the time of the Greek Testament with ref. to the sons of Levi, who were forbidden to inherit because God was their portion. Hence the extended root sense: "learned man of God."]

benefit of clergy In medieval legal L. *privilegium clericale,* the exemption of clergymen from civil trial, they being under the jurisdiction of church courts. By demonstrating an ability to read simple Latin, one could literally get away with murder.

Even if due to hang, a defendant could claim the benefit, whereupon the ordinary (chaplain) of the court presented a Latin Bible and pointed to a text. If satisfied with the reading, the ordinary announced, *"Legit ut clericus,"* He reads like a clergyman, and the man was released after being branded on one hand, probably as an information to his clerical superiors that he should be tried under church law.

The traditional text was, appropriately, the first verse of Psalm 51, beginning, "Have mercy upon me, O God." The verse was early known as *the neck verse:* read it and you save your neck.

The benefit was only slightly abused at first by rogues who, after some early training toward the priesthood, had returned to the world. And early church courts could yet punish as severely as the civil courts. With the gradual spread of learning and the decline of church courts, the benefit became available to any literate rogue, and even to a carefully coached illiterate one, the Latin of the neck verse presenting no great difficulties. In XVI the benefit was suspended in cases of high treason. In XVII it fell into general disuse but was not legally abrogated until late XVIII.

without benefit of clergy Now almost exclusively with reference to an unmarried couple who live as man and wife. Earlier with reference to the complex canons under which the church withheld the sacraments from the contumacious and the obviously damned, most notably from suicides, who by the act of self-destruction consigned themselves immediately to hell.

HISTORIC. Suicides were usually buried at crossroads (they and the contumacious being forbidden holy ground) and without priestly attendance. In ambiguous cases, the suspected suicide might be permitted burial in holy ground and with some priestly attendance but without full rites. In *Hamlet,* Ophelia's burial was with *maimèd rites* and with unlit tapers *(a lumi spenti).* Her madness partly exonerated her of guilt, and her social rank forced the church to make concessions it would not grant to a lowborn person.

clock A timepiece. [Root sense: "thing that rings bells." < OF *cloque, cloche,* bell. ME clok.]

   time clock A clock with a stamping mechanism by means of which employees punch their work cards with time in and time out. [Familiarity has blinded us to the curious redundancy of this form. (What is a clock for if not for time?) *Punch clock* would have been a more natural idiom (and note that *punch* takes over in related idioms, below), but *time* here is "time worked," as in the standard line from westerns in which the foreman says, "Draw your time and git."] *punch a clock* To do common work for hourly pay with the time worked determined by a time clock. *I'm not going to spend all my life punching a clock* = I mean to find better work to do. *clock puncher* Such a worker.

cloth 1. Woven or felted fabric. 2. *Maritime. Now rare.* A sail. Sails. [OE *clāthas,* ME *cloaths, close* are from a root scattered through the Gmnc. languages, prob. a late borrowing; a guess partly supported by the fact that early Teutons wore hides rather than fabric. The root is of unknown origin, perh. (?) akin to Gk. *klothein,* to spin, whence Clotho, the Fatal Sister who spins the thread of mortal life.]

   NOTE. Denham's praise of his fellow poet Waller (late XVIII) contains a choice example of the reawakening of the root sense of words:

> To him no author was unknown,
> Yet what he wrote was all his own.
> Horace's wit and Virgil's state
> He did not steal but emulate.
> And when he would like them appear
> Their garb but not their cloaths would wear.

Though *garb* and *clothes* are often used synonymously, note that *garb* (It. *garbo,* style) points to the cut; *clothes,* to the cloth so cut. The point is that Waller does not steal the rags of the classic masters but cuts his own cloth to their elevated style.

   the cloth The clerical vocation. *man of the cloth* A clergyman.

[Originally, any livery or traditional style of dress that indicated one's profession. Contraction of sense to specific clerical ref. in early XVII.]

cut one's coat according to one's (the) cloth To an extent hard to imagine today, clothing declared one's station in life and gentlemen of fashion made a display of the elegance and fullness of their costumes. Hence, this admonishment to the prudent to make do with what one has, and not seek a costume more elaborate than one has cloth for or can afford.

make up from whole cloth 1. *Earlier.* To stretch the truth. 2. *Then.* To make up out of thin air (based on no truth at all). [This common idiom has never been satisfactorily explained. In XV *brode cloth* indicated, not (as now) fineness of weave, but double width, it being woven 72 inches wide (sometimes 54 inches) and sold doubled over. Thus to make up (a costume) of broadcloth was to give oneself double latitude in the "cut" of one's story. (Which would be plausible, could *brode cloth* be firmly connected to *whole cloth.* I am unable so to connect the two, and must offer this much not as etymology but as a speculation toward a future demonstrable etymology. ???)]

cobweb   Spider web. [*Cob* for "spider" survives only in this compound form < OE *atorcoppe, attercoppe,* spider; lit. "poison head" or "poison cup." The form of the word reflects the old belief that all spiders were poisonous. The first element, *ator, atter,* is of unknown Gmnc. origin, prob. akin to *adder,* the poisonous snake. *Coppe* is ult. < IE *ku-,* hollow thing, rounded thing, the base of both Eng. CUP and Ger. KOPF, head. The ME form is *coppeweb.* (Some refer *copperhead,* the mildly poisonous snake of southeastern U.S., to this Gmnc. *coppe,* but the snake's coloration, I submit, is enough to explain its naming without arcane reference to word forms long obsolete before English-speaking people discovered the copperhead.]

cock¹   [IE *ku-,* hollow thing, rounded thing, is often cited as the source, and cannot be flatly denied, esp. with ref. to egg; but echoic *ku-ku-roo → kuk,* from the rooster's call, is more likely. (Which came first, the *ku-ku-roo* or the *kuk?*) In any case, Gmnc. **kuk-,* rooster, chicken → OE *ciccen,* chicken (the initial *c* originally a kappa, but softening to *ch* in evolving to ME.] 1. The mature male of most birds, and esp. of domestic fowl (though not of goose, swan, and duck, which are gander, cob, and drake). 2. *Ext.* An angle of tilt. *cocked at a sharp angle.* [< the jaunty strut of the rooster.] 3. Small protruding device, as the hammer of a gun, a faucet, the tap of a barrel.

cock and bull story A long, stupid, unbelievable yarn. An elaborate but transparent lie. [Refers to medieval folk tales in which animals regularly talked as if they were human beings, their rambling concluding in some intricate moral. One such yarn was about a cock that turned into a bull. In a French variant the cock was turned into a donkey and the equivalent Fr. phrase is *faire un coq à l'ane*, to make a cock into a donkey, the effective sense being: "believe that and I'll tell you another."]

cockhorse A hobbyhorse. [Lit. "a male-bird horse," a nursery whimsy, perh. influ. by cock robin and who shot him.]

cock² *Slang.* Penis. [Usu. explained as deriving from *cock¹*, rooster, but IE *kak-*, male genitalia, indicates that the slang term is a true ancient survival. See *hatch¹*.]

cockalorum 1. A strutting, crowing bantam rooster. 2. *Ext.* A boastful, self-important little man. 3. *Ext.* Self-vaunting talk. [Prob. < Du. *kokeloeren*, imitative of a cock's crow.]

cockamamie Cheap. Ridiculous. Unbelievable. *He gave me some cockamamie story.* [Late XIX Am. corruption of Fr. *de(calcomania)*, mid-XIX French fad (lit. "decal-mania") of ornamenting objects, and esp. one's skin, with transfer designs. The craze seems to have started when fashionable ladies began to apply more and more elaborate beauty spots to their upper cheeks. The Am. form may also have been influ. by *Cock-a-nee-nee*, the name of a cheap molasses candy popular in NYC in late XIX.]

cocked hat A triangular hat common in XVIII. [So called because brim was *cocked* up, and because often worn with a *cocktail* of feathers.] **be knocked into a cocked hat** To be left in a difficult situation. [The original ref. was to bowling, and to the situation when the first ball leaves the three point pins of the triangle standing, a split in the shape of the cocked (tricorn) hat. It is possible with luck and great skill to score a spare from such a split, but don't bet on it unless you are contemplating vows of poverty.]

cock of the walk A vain strutter. **cocky** Arrogant. **waathercock** Weather vane. **cold cock** To knock cold by hitting over the head with a blunt instrument. [*Cock* = barrel cock, barrel tap.]

cockle A small bivalve mollusk, either rounded or roughly heart-shaped, with slightly fluted ribs radiating from the hinge. [IE *konkho-*, shellfish (CONCH). Gk. *konkhē*, mussel; *konkhullion*, little mussel. OF **conquille, coquille*, shell, cockle. ME *cokille*, cockle.]

the cockles of one's heart *Lit.* The valves of the heart. *Effective sense:* One's innermost feelings. [*Cockles* for *valves* is based on the real or imagined likeness of the heart-shaped and ribbed shell to the shape and surface texture of the heart valves.] **warm the cockles of one's heart** To gratify one's deepest feelings. [*Warm,* to give pleasure; as in *warm feelings, to warm to a person.*]

Cockney A native of London's East End. To qualify as a Cockney one must have been born within sound of the Bow bells (the bells of St. Mary-le-Bow). The characteristic Cockney dialect is particularly marked by the omission of initial *h,* by the aspiration of initial vowel sounds, by the intrusive *r (I sawr it, I did),* and by the diphthongizing of many vowel sounds. [< ME *cockeney,* cock's egg, an exuberant formation with the senses: 1. Any unnatural thing (since cocks lay only square eggs). 2. A small or deformed egg such as young layers produce until they get the hang of it. 3. A contemptuous rural term for city dwellers so ignorant as not to know a cubical cock's egg from the real thing. Cobham Brewer, *Dictionary of Phrase and Fable,* says the sense was narrowed to Londoners only in XVII. As above, it has since been narrowed further.]

cocksure Cocky. As self-assured as a strutting rooster. (Some Madison Avenue pranksters once worked out an elaborate campaign to promote a new perfume to be called . . . Cocksure.) [But this sense is late XVIII and prob. by association with the strut and maleness of the rooster. The sense of the earliest (XVI) citations in OED is "absolutely sure," and the word was used in the most formal of contexts. OED, taking *cock* to the tap of a barrel, conjectures that its sense derives from the fact that the wine in the barrel is secure when the tap is firmly shut.

OED, however, curiously ignores Chaucer's use (*Manciple's Prologue,* line 9) of *cokkes bones* for "God's bones." Prof. F. Robinson, one of the great Chaucerian scholars, glosses ME *cok* as "corruption of God." John Fox (1516–1587), founder of the Society of Friends, wrote in his *Book of Martyrs:* "Whoso dwelleth under that secret thing and help of the Lord, shall be cocksure for evermore." Did Fox mean "God sure" or only "absolutely sure"? Was the Chaucerian usage based on some such epithet for Christ as "the cock that crew mankind's new day"? Scholarship must someday find an answer to this riddle of "cock/God."]

cocktail   An alcoholic mixed drink, often garnished with whole or sliced fruit and vegetable sprigs, these festive additives known as "garbage." [Origin unknown. The most substantial, though yet inconclusive, clue is in Washington Irving's: "those recondite beverages, cock-tail, stone-fence, and sherry cobbler" (1809). Irving's phrasing suggests that these terms are new ones, perhaps of last quarter of XVIII. Irving, moreover, seems to be listing specific mixtures. A stone fence is apple jack and cider mixed in about the proportions of Scotch and soda. A sherry cobbler is a few ounces of sweet sherry made even more disgusting by a spoonful of sugar mixed with fizz water, with which it is served over ice. But there is no known recipe for cocktail as such. There is the fact that *cocktail horse,* horse with a raised (cocked) bob tail, is also first attested 1809. Perhaps *cocktail* refers to a drink containing "garbage" which is taken to resemble the tail of a *cocktail horse.* (??)

The suggestion that such drinks are called *cocktails* because they inspire cockiness is hardly worth inscribing in granite. And the same may be said of J. B. Dillard's assertion *(Where Our Words Come From)* that it derives from West African *kaketal,* scorpion (because it has a sting in its tail). Surface resemblance is not enough to pass as etymology; the dating and line of transmission must be accounted for, and this scorpion fails both those tests.]

cocoa/coconut/cocoanut   These forms interplay through an accident of history and of language. *Cocoa* was first, and should properly have been *cacao,* the evergreen tree and its bean, which is the source of chocolate and of the drink cocoa; < Nahuatl *cacauatl,* in which *uatl* is tree. *Cacao* was altered to *cocoa* under the influ. of the accidentally similar but unrelated form *coconut,* whose variant *cocoanut,* shows that it was in turn influ. by *cocoa.* These new dietary products, moreover, were further linked in the minds of Europeans because they were introduced from the New World in quantity at about the same time in late XVII. *Coconut* is < Sp. baby-talk *coco,* ugly face; because at one end of the hairy nut the natural markings readily suggest a monkey face.]

codfish aristocracy   *Boston provincialism.* The *nouveaux riches.* [A term applied by the traditionally exclusive first families of Boston to families, not originally of Boston, that had grown wealthy in the fisheries and then bought or built mansions in the Back Bay area, once the exclusive preserve of old-line wealth. Ah, to be nouveau rich again!]

codpiece A pouch like the bag of a jockstrap fitted to the tights worn by men in XV and XVI and still used by Shakespearean actors. [Except for the fact that John Barrymore used to roll up a face towel and pad his codpiece for greater dramatic dimension, there is nothing fishy about a codpiece. The stem is OE *codd*, bag, pouch, scrotum; prob. ult. < IE *ku-*, hollow, rounded, suffixed *-d-* in Gmnc. CUTTLEFISH, COD(FISH), CUBBYHOLE.]

coffee-and Generic for a snack. *I'll just have coffee-and at my desk.* [Originally, from the jargon of short-order cooks, coffee-and-dough-nuts.]

cognomen Plu. *cognomens/cognomina.* 1. Family name. [Among Roman patricians, the third name, as Gaius (given name) Julius (of the Julian *gens*) Caesar (of the family Caesar).] 2. A nickname. (See *nickname.*) [< L. *gnoscere*, to know (learning being associated with knowing the names of things). Collaterally *nomen*, name, prefixed *co-*, with, name with (by) which one is known. Or perhaps, "a name one holds together with others (members of the family)."]

cold Lacking heat. [OE *ceald*, cold, is ult. < IE *gel-* via Gmnc. with g/k and suffixed *-dt-*. Of the many idioms based on the term, the most interesting are:]

cold-blooded *Zoology.* The classifying adjective for such life forms as invertebrates, fish, reptiles, and amphibians, whose blood temperature approximates the environmental temperature. *in cold blood* With reptilian indifference. Of a crime, esp. of murder, with premeditation and without mercy.

cold cock To knock unconscious with a blunt instrument. [*Cold*, to knock cold; *cock*, barrel tap, bung.]

cold deck *Am. gambling. Poker.* A stacked deck prepared before the game starts and switched into play at a critical point, usu. during a minor distraction by an accomplice. [*Cold* because it has been kept apart (unwarmed by human hands as in shuffling and dealing) until switched into the game.]

cold feet Symbol of cowardice. *get cold feet* To lose one's courage or resolution. [Though the dating and origin are uncertain, the idiom is based on the natural observation that anxiety and stress can impair circulation, causing the extremities to feel cold.]

cold turkey Out-and-out matter of fact. *I'll give it to you cold turkey* = I'll give you the blunt, dead-straight facts of the case. [*Cold turkey* for *dead turkey:* plain meat with no feelings left.] *quit cold turkey* To forswear a fixed habit with no preparation and with no tapering off. Esp. in narco slang, to kick the heroin habit, enduring the withdrawal symptoms without benefit of medication. [To quit the way a dead turkey quits.]

comet A heavenly body, prob. consisting of frozen gases, streamers of which trail behind it. Nonluminous, comets are visible to us only when they come close enough to reflect the light of the sun. [At root: "long-haired star," which is the sense of Gk. *aster kométes* < *aster*, star; **komē*, hair.]

NOTE. Our ancestors were not all bald, yet no scholar has adduced a secure IE root for *hair*. Eng. *hair* (which see) is based on Gmnc. *ker-*, which like Gk. *komē* is of unknown origin. L. *pilus*, hair, is another European stem and perhaps, but only doubtfully, traceable to IE *pil-o-*, *pil-so-*, hair (if there is such a stem). Russ. *vólasi* and Czech *vlas* are clearly cognate, the stem *v'l-* being within a standard v/p shift of L. *pil-*, or within a similarly standard v/f shift of L. *fil-*, *filus*, thread, which can be traced to IE *gwhi-*, thread, tendon. It. *capello* and Fr. *cheveux* are based on the stem *caput*. And to add to the confusion, modern Gk. has **mallia'*. I can find nothing to explain why the word for anything as common as hair should lead to so many etymological dead ends.

comrade [Root sense: "roommate." < L. *camera*, room; OF *camerades*, soldiers who sleep in the same barracks or who are billeted in the same quarters.] 1. XVI. A close and constant friend. 2. A companion in arms. [And so, too, in Am. till c. 1900, when the word became unpopular because of the associations of:] 3. A member of the Communist Party, but also a general term of address among Communists, the equivalent of "Mister" or of "Citizen" as used during the French Revolution.

kamerad The Ger. form with the same meanings as above but also as the cry that means in effect "I surrender," i.e., "Let's be friends," and ult., "I am ready to be your roommate"—the answer to which is usu. "No, thanks."

condom Brit. *cundum* The first to deal with this word was Capt. Francis Grose in his *A Classical Dictionary of the Vulgar Tongue*, London, 1785. More recent dictionaries have been at some variance. I take Grose to be definitive, and here quote him in full:

Cundum. The dried gut of a sheep, worn by men in the act of coition, to prevent venereal infection; said to have been invented by one Colonel Cundum. These machines were long prepared and sold by a matron of the name of Phillips at the Green Canister, in Half-moon St., in the Strand. That good lady having acquired a fortune, retired from business; but learning that the town was not well served by her successors, she, out of a patriotic zeal for the public welfare, returned to her occupation; of which she gave notice by divers hand-bills, in circulation in the year 1776. [*Ed. note.* What Grose is really saying is that the old hag sold her business and then set up competitive shop again, ruining the poor fool to whom she had sold out.]

Grose adds:

Also, a false scabbard over a sword, and the oil-skin case for holding the colors of a regiment.

HISTORIC. I do not know what Grose meant by his addendum; probably that *cundum* was extended as a name for these things. In WWII, bushel baskets full of these "machines" (but made of rubber) were kept in places frequented by soldiers, the combat infantry making standard (though not exclusive) use of them as covers for their rifle barrels, a use for which they were ideally suited, keeping dirt and water out of the barrel, yet leaving the rifle ready for instant use. Europe was largely liberated by the contraceptive rifle.

conniption/conniption fit A fit of violent emotion. [Origin much guessed at but unknown. The *English Dialect Dictionary Supplement* cites Cumberland dialect *canapshus*, ill-tempered, captious; seemingly a dial. corruption of *captious;* and *canapshus, coniptious, conniption* is a likely dialect sequence, but there is no evidence of such intermediate forms. Others have even guessed a derivation from *catnip*, but simply as a guess, without supporting evidence. *Da capo:* origin unknown.]

consider To evaluate, ponder, take under advisement. [But at root: "to cast a horoscope." < L. *sidera,* stars (SIDEREAL); prefixed *con-*, with; hence, "with the stars," i.e., studied with the influ. of the stars in mind, i.e., cast as a horoscope.]

constable 1. *Modern Am.* A minor police official, usu. serving writs for a sheriff. 2. *Earlier.* A municipal police officer. (And so the old vaudeville line, presumed to be very funny, in which the small-town cop is derided as "the constabula from Ashtabula.") Which is directly from: 3. *Brit.* A police officer. 4. *Earlier Brit.* A high officer of the realm commanding in the king's name. *constabulary* A police force. [Root sense: "count of the stable," i.e., chief groom.

< L. *comes stabuli,* count of the stable. The word has risen high in social status and then declined. Cf. *marshal, butler,* which have also undergone dramatic changes in social standing.]

contemplate   1. To be absorbed in observation, introspection, or foretelling the future. *to contemplate divorce* To consider the possibility of a divorce (action not yet decided upon). *the contemplative life* Religious reclusion devoted to visionary meditation. [Root sense: "to study the guts of ritually eviscerated animals." L. *contemplari,* to prophesy by studying plucked entrails. < *com-,* with (here used as an intensive); *templum,* a place marked off on the ground by a priest diviner (TEMPLE). Ult. < IE *tem-,* to cut, to score, to mark off on the ground as with a stick (TEMPLATE).]

HISTORIC. The term is ult. from primitive magic. In conjuring, it is common practice to mark off an area on the ground, often in some magical geometric shape. The *pentacle,* a five-sided figure, is much favored by Nordic witches and wizards. The conjuror stands inside the figure as a defense against the spirit he summons. Or he summons the spirit inside the figure, the magic power of its shape serving as a cage. Roman conjurors *(haruspices)* called such a figure a *templum.* The figure so marked and the area ritually purified, the haruspex entered, eviscerated the animal in a ritual way, and then "read" the entrails to forecast the future. When his auguries were especially accurate, the place of the templum came to be thought of as holy-magical. Bit by bit, such especially holy places were marked off by stones and later, roofed over, became *temples.*

coonskin   The hide of a raccoon. *nail the coonskin to the barn door* Get the job done. [After the preparations for the hunt and the hunt itself, the raccoon must be skinned and its hide stretched to be scraped and cured. A barn door offered a large, flat, easily available surface, and the skin so placed doubled as a sort of trophy. The phrase, rather jauntily country-bumptious, came into bad odor when President Johnson used it in the late 1960's to describe the desired end of the Vietnam horror.]

cop   A policeman. [A common folk etymology bases the term on *(cop)per* buttons, another on an acronym for *c(onstable) o(n) p(atrol);* both are fanciful. In generalized Brit. dial., *to cop* (of unknown origin), to seize, to snatch, to steal. So, still surviving: *I copped it in Macy's basement* = I stole it in Macy's basement. And common criminal slang: *cop a plea* To plead guilty to a lesser charge in order to escape prosecution on a more serious one, i.e., to snatch at the chance to accept the lesser charge.]

copper 1. The chemical element. [Named after best-known place of origin. < Gk. *Kuprios,* of Cyprus. L. *Cyprium aes,* copper of Cyprus. Late L. *cuprum.* Gmnc. *kupar,* OE *coper, copar* (and bear it in mind to distinguish the form from ME *coppe,* spider: see *cobweb*).] 2. A U.S. cent. [Because except in WWII, when steel was used for them, these coins were of copper alloy.] 3. Any small copper coin. *He threw the Egyptian street urchins a handful of coppers.*

copperhead The snake. One of four subspecies found as far north as Connecticut and as far west as Texas, but most common in southeastern states. It is viviparous, and though venomous, its bite is rarely fatal except to children and persons in poor health. [ME *coppe,* spider, has been suggested as a source of the name (see *cobweb*), but it is almost certainly sufficiently explained by this snake's coloration.]
   Copperhead 1. In common Civil War usage in the North, a Southern sympathizer or Confederate agent in the North. 2. *Ext.* Any treacherous person. [Because the copperhead snake, unlike the rattler, strikes without warning.]

coprolite *Geology.* XIX. A fossilized turd. [Gk. *kopros,* dung; with *-lite,* Eng. combining form of Gk. *lithos,* stone ("shit stone"). *Al Stein is a coprolite.* To date, the term has remained technical and specific to the study of fossils, but so long as there are so many Al Steins in this world, it is absolutely necessary to bring the term into general use.]

corndodger *Sthrn.* A lump of fried corn meal. [Root sense is prob. "clod of fried corn meal." < Brit. dial. *dodger,* a clod, a lump of food; *dodgel,* a large lump of food. See *dodge.*]

corny Rustic, lowbrow, trite. Schmaltzy. Kitschy. [C. 1890. Am. show biz. NYC-centered traveling actors, holding themselves to be slickly superior to the yokels for whom they performed—who did generally prefer their humor broad and low, or melodramatically sentimental—scorned their audiences as *corn-fed,* whence *corny.*]

coup de grace [Fr. *the mercy blow, the mercy stroke.*] The mercy consisted of putting a wretch out of his misery, and in the days when torture was a common form of legal execution, death could be mercy enough. There are cases on record in which family influence secured a victim's death before the prescribed torture was applied to his lifeless body. Until recent times, the officer in command of a firing squad customarily fired a pistol shot into the nape of the fallen victim's neck to make sure he was out of his misery.

NOTE. Not to be confused with the tradition that one man on every firing squad be given a rifle loaded with a blank, the mercy consisting of the fact that no man in the execution of a fellow soldier could be certain he was in fact his comrade's killer. The tradition is in any case pointless. The difference in recoil between the zing of a projectile and the pop of a blank is physical and would be immediately registered by any qualified rifleman: every man on the squad would know what he fired.

coward   A craven. What every intelligent person becomes in time enough. [Often mistakenly taken to derive from *cowherd,* a low bumpkin (lacking the valor the aristocracy claims as its trait). But properly < Fr. *coue,* tail; with the pejorative suffix *-ard* (as in *bastard, dastard, drunkard, stinkard*); lit. "a tail person," i.e., "one with his tail tucked between his legs."]

cowboy   1. A mounted cowhand of the American West. 2. A rough-and-ready young swaggerer. *drugstore cowboy.* Also **to cowboy around** To roughhouse. [An English rendering of Sp. *vaquero,* a mounted cowherd < *vaca,* cow, with agential suffix *-ero,* one who has to do with. The Spanish might have been rendered *cowman,* but *man* was inhibited by its use in *cattleman,* a rancher with many herds. Cowpunchers were, moreover, boys and young men in their vigorous prime, and with a high death rate from falls, gorings, gangrene resulting from frostbite, pneumonia, and the many other perils of open country, including "lead poisoning." *Cowboy* first came into general use about 1867 with reference to trail riders who drove Texas longhorns up the Chisholm Trail to Abilene, Kansas, for transshipment to eastern markets.]

NOTE. Tory guerrillas of the American Revolution used to lure into ambush Continental soldiers and farmers who sympathized with them. One of their bushwhacking tricks was to ring a cow bell from a thicket, summoning the farmer to strayed livestock or the hungry soldier to meat he might make his own. These Tories were accordingly, and contemptuously, called *cowboys.* In all likelihood, however, this sense of *cowboy* had become obsolete by the time the term developed again with its western reference.

cowslip   A fragrant yellow wild flower; in Europe, a variety of primrose, and in America, of marigold. [At root: "cow dung (flower)," because common in pastures. < OE *cūslyppe*, cow dung. The second element, *slyppe*, is ult. < IE *sleubh-*, slippery, slippery stuff (SLOP). *Where the cow slips there slip I.*]

Coxey's Army   Any bedraggled horde. Usu. half humorously. *The family got back from the rained-out picnic looking like Coxey's Army.* [Now rare. From 1894 to c. 1930, a specific reference to Coxey (see note) was generally understood; from then to WWII the idiom would have been understood by many who did not remember Coxey.]
   HISTORIC. On March 25, 1894, a time of economic bust, about a hundred unemployed Populists, moved by a religious fervor that led them to call themselves The Commonweal of Christ, left Massillon, Ohio, to walk to Washington, D.C., and to demonstrate for the passage of economic reform bills proposed by their leader and self-styled "general," Jacob S. Coxey. Picking up recruits along the way, the "army" arrived in Washington some 500 strong. Soon after their arrival and encampment, President Grover Cleveland showed his sympathy by arresting Coxey and his "staff" for trespass on public property, the movement broke up, and units of the "army" straggled home as best they could. It is this image of the retreat that underlies the idiom.]

crap¹   *n.* 1. Excrement. 2. Nonsense. —*v.* To defecate. Also *take a crap.* —*exclam.* Expresses disgust, revulsion, vexation. *crapper* A toilet seat. A toilet. [The story of Sir Thomas Crapper, who was knighted for inventing the flush toilet, is a hoax. < ME *crappe*, rubbish, stuff left over, stuff thrown out of. < MD **crappen*, to tear away from.]

crap²   *v.* To lose at dice by making an opening roll of two, three, or twelve. *craps* Such a roll. *crap out* To lose by making such a roll. [Brit. slang *crabs*, the roll of two (now called *snake eyes*) at hazard, an earlier form of dice or craps.] *crap shooter* 1. A dice player. 2. *Ext.* One who gambles recklessly. *This pension committee was appointed to invest the workers' money, not to shoot craps with it.*

crate   [Root sense (a small glimpse into the ways of man c. 6000 B.C.): "basket." < IE *kert-*, to bend, to intertwine, to weave. With k/h → Gmnc. h'rt-i → *hurdiz*, a movable section of woven brush fence (HURDLE). Brit. HOARDING, a fence. Variant IE *kr't-i-* → L. *cratis,* same sense as *hurdiz.*] 1. A large usu. wooden packing box. 2. *Aviation.* A jalopy airplane. —*v.* To pack for shipment.

crawthumper 1. A disparaging name for a Roman Catholic. [Because in prayers of contrition Catholics beat (thump) their breasts (craws).] 2. An early nickname for a Marylander. [Because Maryland was a Catholic colony.]

creek Though loosely used in Am. for watercourses that might elsewhere qualify as rivers, has the general sense: "small tributary, brook." [Root sense: "crooked (waterway)." ME *creke, crike,* prob. into English during the Danish conquest < ON *kriki,* a crook, a twist. Ult. < IE *ger-,* twisted, bent; the zero-grade form *gr-* evolving into Gmnc. with g/k → *kr-, kri-,* and suffixed *-k-* → *krik-.*] *up the creek* In a bad spot. *up shit creek without a paddle* In a worse spot. [Vulgar exuberant elaboration of *up the creek.* XVIII Am.]

HISTORIC. To an extent easily forgotten today, travel in the early colonies and the early United States was by river. In going up many American rivers it is easy for a voyager to mistake a tributary debouchment for the main channel. If he does not discover his error in time, he will eventually find himself lost in a maze of backwaters, or in a channel that has narrowed until there is no room for turning the boat around. Such a situation will lead to trouble generally, and the more so in the early American forest.

cretin An idiot, usu. one congenitally deformed by a thyroid deficiency. [< XVIII Swiss-Fr. *creitin, crestin;* Fr. *crétin,* Christian; but with no antireligious sense that Christian faith amounts to idiocy; rather to indicate compassionately a poor deformed creature possessed of a God-given soul and of the grace of baptism.]

HISTORIC. In most Romance countries, "Christian" has long been commonly used for "person." So in Italian, even today, *questi due poveri cristiani* means "these two poor souls (people)," the usage involving a semantic tug toward Christian charity, as if to remind the person addressed that all Christians are brothers and their brothers' keepers.

crocodile The large aquatic lizard most numerous in Africa. [< two Gk. words of untraced origin: *kroke,* gravel (with reference to the pebbly banks and bars on which these animals sun themselves); *drilos,* worm; lit. "the worm one sees on gravel banks."] *crocodile tears* Insincere sorrow. [Medieval bestiaries popularized the belief that crocodiles enticed their victims with moans and wept as they ate them.]

cropper: come a cropper   1. To suffer a serious setback. To be ruined. 2. *Originally.* To take a heavy fall from a horse, striking the ground with one's whole body length. [< Brit. horsy slang, c. 1800, *neck and crop,* said of a horse and meaning all of it; by ext., completely. *Crop,* here, for *cropped tail;* or as it might have been said in Am. (but wasn't), "neck and bangtail." In the oddly coherent illogic of idiom, the expression leaves the head of the horse out of the reckoning, but still means "the whole horse, all of it, entirely." And so: *to come a cropper* is "to fall entirely, to take a maximum fall."]

crosspatch   A more or less dear person who has fallen into a temporary ill humor. (Often defined as "ill-tempered person," and that definition can be supported, but Caligula was an ill-tempered person one would not think to call a crosspatch, whereas a small boy who is having the sulks is readily "mommy's little crosspatch." [*Cross,* not in a good humor; *patch* < It. *pazzo,* fool, zany; a common nickname in English for a court jester, who was often a dearly regarded intimate.]

crypt   [< Gk. *kryptos,* concealed; *kryptō,* I conceal.] 1. A burial vault under a church. [At root: "place for concealing a body" (as the pharaohs were hidden in death).] 2. A code; a cipher. [Short form of *cryptogram,* at root: "secret (hidden, concealed) writing."] *cryptic Of a remark or message.* Enigmatic. ["Concealed" in whole or part.]

crystal   [< L. *crystallum,* rock crystal < Gk. **krustallos,* ice (originally, but later) rock crystal. 1. *In the commonest form of a complex phenomenon.* A more or less transparent form of mineral fused into a series of identically shaped geometric units which may vary in size. 2. Such a unit. 3. *Ext.* A valuable kind of glass whose worked forms give off resonant tones when tapped. 4. *Ext.* A transparent cover for the face of a wrist watch or pocket watch. *crystal clear* Very clear.
    crystal ball A clear glass globe in which mumbo-jumbo diviners pretend to see the future. *crystal gazing* 1. The act of foretelling the future in this way. 2. *Derogatory.* Loose and unfounded planning for the future. *We need a detailed analysis, not this crystal gazing.*

crystal set An early simple form of radio in which a quartz crystal served to pick up the signal.

HISTORIC. Long outdated, the crystal set was part of the mythology of American boys c. 1925–1935, and a major adolescent project. It consisted of a large coil of copper wire (usu. meticulously coiled around a round Quaker Oats box and then shellacked), a slide bar with a contact to serve, with the coil, as a frequency selector, a crystal (always specified as "Brazilian"), a battery, earphones, and all the antenna one could string. The contraption was primitive, but the miracle of it fed at least a decade of Boy Scout projects.

I do not understand the signal-detecting characteristics of crystals, but in World War II the identification-friend-or-foe signal on airborne B-29's (called *bojangles*) was transmitted through a crystal and could only be properly received through a matching crystal in the base receiver, thus eliminating the possibility that an enemy plane might sneak in under cover of a forged identification signal.

cuckold   A man whose wife has committed adultery, an act in which she was said to "betray" him. (Adultery was a cause for damnation, duels, and murder before it changed into a subject for articles on modern living.) [Based on *cuckoo*. OF *cucualt*, cuckold ("one who has been cuckooed"); because the cuckoo, like the American cowbird, lays its eggs in the nests of other birds, the lusty fledglings ousting the natural heirs and taking over.]

cuckoo   1. An Old World bird brought to Am. awareness because of its use in once popular Swiss *cuckoo clocks* from which a mechanical cuckoo emerges to signal the time with an odd two-tone cry. [The name is echoic of the cry of this bird.] 2. A silly or demented person. *He's a cuckoo.* But also *he has gone cuckoo; you must be cuckoo.* [Because the cry and the jerkily mechanical movement of the clock cuckoo suggest zaniness.] *cuckoo's nest* An insane asylum. (And see *cuckold.*)

cue   1. *Theater.* The signal for a stage response. [Origin uncertain. Perh., as has been speculated, because actors marked their working scripts "q" (abbrev. for It. *quando*, when).] 2. *Ext.* Any signal for action by prearrangement.

come in on cue 1. *Theater.* To respond on time and as directed. 2. *Ext.* To respond to any situation smoothly, by prearranged signal, or as if by prearrangement. *as if on cue* As smoothly as if by prearrangement.

cue me in Explain the situation to me. [Explain the plot and the alignment of forces, and tell me how I should respond to what prearranged signals.]

culprit   *Now.* The guilty person. *Earlier, but ambiguously.* The person charged with an offense. (One may argue that to be charged is not proof of guilt, yet the word contains, at its roots, an assertion of guilt.) [L. *culpabile,* guilty; *praestus,* (we are) ready. The legal formula *culpabile, praestus* meant "He is guilty and we are prepared to prove it." The formula was spoken by the crown clerk (prosecutor) after the defendant had entered a plea of innocence. The formula in Norman French was *Culpable. Prit d'averrer,* and was entered on the outside of the indictment as *cul. prit.,* later *culprit,* to indicate the man had been charged in court.]

cunt   1. The female sex organ. 2. A woman conceived as nothing but a sex mechanism. [< IE *ku-,* hollow receptacle (CUP, Ger. KOPF, head). ME *cunte* is cognate with Ger. *kunte.* The form, however, does not occur in OE writing, its absence indicating an early language taboo, perhaps by association with the similarly taboo *fuck* (which see, and especially the note on its pre-Norman French taboo).]

curfew   1. In the Middle Ages, a common municipal edict setting a stated hour at which all household fires were to be put out for the night. [Because of the fear of conflagration. OF *cuevrefeu;* ME *couverfeu, curfeu,* cover (put out) the fire.] 2. *Later.* An ordinance requiring citizens, or certain classes of citizens, to be off the streets during stated night hours. 3. The period during which such a ban is in effect. 4. The signal, usu. a bell, signaling the beginning of the ban. *Curfew shall not ring tonight.* 5. *Today.* A police or military edict with the effect of 2, above.

curious   *adj.* 1. Disposed to learn, to be informed. 2. Inquisitive. 3. Unusual. [But James Fenimore Cooper, *The Pioneer:* "let him (Indian John) lend the doctor a hand, for old as he is, he is curious at cuts and bruises." Cooper means that Indian John has special knowledge of how to treat such wounds; and Cooper's is the root sense, now obs. but surviving from Latin through most of XIX (and would prob. be alive today were our graduates Latin-literate). < L. *cura,* care, management, supervision → *cūriōsus,* characterized by special care and ability. The connecting sense between *unusual* and *marked by special skills* (as in Cooper) is *ingenious.*]

curmudgeon 1. A mean, testy person. 2. *Of late.* A gruff, blunt, but honest fellow. [This sense shift, prob. only temporary, almost certainly dates from FDR's secretary of the interior, Harold L. Ickes, who billed himself as "an old curmudgeon," implying an encrusted heart of gold. Historically, however, a curmudgeon has been a mean one. Scrooge, before his reformation, was a curmudgeon, a grasping, cheese-paring skinflint. The suggestion that the form derives from Fr. *coeur méchant,* evil heart, may be an inspired guess, but it is an unsupported one. The earliest form cited by the OED (1626) is *curmegient.* The dialect of Fife has *curmudge,* a mean fellow. In obs. Hertfordshire dial. *mudgel-hole* was "dungill midden." *Cur-mudgel* might certainly be taken in this dial. for "dunghill dog." Except that it wasn't. And so the case rests on a secure foundation of unanswered question marks.]

curry favor To offer fawning service in the hope of ingratiating oneself. [A modified translation of OF *estriller Fauvel* or *torcher Fauvel,* to rub down the chestnut horse; a ref. to the curious allegorical *Roman de Fauvel,* 1310, in which Fauvel, a chestnut horse, symbolizes worldiness and duplicity.]

curtail To cut short. [< Fr. *court* < L. *curtus,* short; Fr. *tailler,* to cut, *tailleur,* one who cuts, tailor (TAYLOR). Though influ. by obs. Brit. *curtal,* which was specific to the trimmed bangtail (BANGS) of a show horse, *tail,* here, is an accidental resemblance to *tail,* animal caudal appendage.]

    curtail step Architectural. The widened, elongated, and often curved first step of an ornamental flight of stairs. [Brit. mid XVIII. So contrary a sense (increased rather than clipped) might well be enough to suggest a separate origin, and lexicographers have offered various more or less random speculation (e.g., *cur's tail* as a rounded and ornamentally furred thing). It is more likely, however, that the form is an ext. of *curtal,* the connecting sense being "done for ornamental effect" (in show horses by clipping, in stairway architecture by graceful, usu. curved, enlargement).]

cushy Soft, easy. Most commonly in the formula *cushy job* Sinecure. [Influ. by *cushion,* and there is nothing in the sense of the term to resist that influ. Etymologically, however, a gift of the British Empire < Persian *khush,* luxury, pleasure, opulence.]

cut and run   To leave at top speed. [*Nautical.* To cut the cable (wasting no time in raising the anchor) while making full sail for the speediest possible departure.]

cutlet   A thin, boneless rib cut, usu. of veal. [But not based on "to cut." Rather < L. *costa,* rib. Fr. *côte,* OF *cotel,* little rib. Modern Fr. *côtelette* is a double diminutive, "a little, little rib (piece)."]

cynosure   Thing, point, person looked to as a standard of comparison or as a ref. point for fixing one's location. (But this, the root sense, seems to be yielding to:) Center of attention. [Root sense: "dog's tail." Gk. *kynosoura* < *kynos,* of the dog (genitive sing. of *kyōn,* dog); *oura,* tail. *Kynosoura* was the Greek name for the handle of the Little Dipper. The last star in the handle is Polaris, the North Star, the altitude of which determines north latitude, hence the mariner's central reference point, hence a reference point.]

D

Dago   Pejorative name for an Italian. *dago red* Italian red wine. [But earlier with ref. to any dark-skinned person. MMM cites "ye negro Dago," Am. colonial, 1723; "Degos," 1832, as a ref. to natives of Minorca in the Balearic Islands; but by c. 1890 specific to Italian immigrants. < Sp. *Diego*, James, common given name.]

dainty   Delicate. Fastidious. Refined. (But as the pretty is to the beautiful, implying ornamental slightness rather than substantial worth.) [The evolved sense being a reversal of the original sense, ult. < L. *dignus*, worthy (DIGNIFIED, DEIGN, CONDIGN). And with the original sense in English "substantial and able," as in *a dainty steed*, a powerful and desirable (fit) war horse. XVI *a daintie capon*, a substantial roast bird (one fit for a trencherman's teeth). So when Prospero, in *The Tempest*, says, "that's my dainty Ariel," he means not "airy and delicate" (as students commonly understand) but "worthy, able, effective."] *dainties* A la-di-da term for cute little things, as tea cookies, and especially ladies' underwear. (These last perhaps designed to be able and effective in chosen context.)

daisy   The common wild flower. [OE *daegeseage*, day's eye; compounded of *daeges*, genitive form of *daeg*, of day; with *eage*, eye; and by later contraction *daisy*. This root image is a charmingly typical act of the English folk imagination and does not occur in any other language in the name of this flower. It. *maragarita*, daisy, has cognates in Sp., Fr., and Ger., and is ult. < Gk. *margaron*, pearl, also a charming root image but rather less poetic than the English root picture. The difference is worth noting, if only to demonstrate that many words are not translatable, not, that is, if one seeks to account for their root images.]

dally welter   Also *dally wstrn. v.* In roping, to coil the lariat around the pommel after an animal has been roped. —*n. Only in the first-given form.* One who ropes in this way. Among plains cowboys, a term of contempt for southwestern cowboys (also *Calipho-ney cowboys*) who worked in the Spanish tradition. [< Sp. *dar la vuelta*, give the turn to.]

HISTORIC. The plains cowboys (from eastern Texas to Oregon) were primarily the Pikes and the sons of the Pikes (the Anglo-Saxon reverted to barbarism) who went west from the various Pike counties of Missouri, Illinois, Kentucky, and Arkansas. A different breed from the Spanish and Spanish-influenced cowboys of the far Southwest, they took all difference as cause for contempt.

In roping, they tied onto the pommel before throwing a loop. When a *dally welter* explained the advantages of undallying in case of need, the plains cowboy would likely answer, "Why rope on to anything you don't mean to own?" In undallying, moreover, he would loose his rope and be disgraced as a tenderfoot.

The rhetoric of the plains cowboys favored a triple series of compound epithets. Caliphoney cowboys wore large rowels on long stems. They were therefore contemptuously dismissed as "spur draggers."

They ate bread or tortillas in the Spanish tradition, rather than sourdough biscuits. They were, therefore, "bread eaters."

The danger in dally weltering was that the rope might snap tight while one's fingers were between it and the pommel. Caliphoney cowboys tended, therefore, to be "short-handed," and even this mutilation was reason for rhetorical contempt. They were scoffed at as "two-finger" incompetents.

So in the full, round rhetoric of the plains, as set forth for me by William Decker, a cowboy would dismiss the whole "passel" of "them Caliphoney cowboys" as no more than "spur-dragging, bread-eating, two-finger dally welters."

Dan Cupid   Cupid. [*Dan*, here, as a variant of *Don*, in effect Sir Cupid. Cf. *Dan Chaucer* as a common epithet for Geoffrey Chaucer. < L. *Cupido* < *cupīdō*, eager desire; and with a sense shift to avarice, CUPIDITY. *Radix malorum cupiditas est:* Avarice is the root of all evil. L. *Cupido* labels this god's manifestation as the infant Eros, son of Aphrodite and Ares, usually portrayed as a beautiful babe with a bow and arrows. When struck by one of Cupid's shafts, men and even the gods conceive an overpowering passion for the first creature they see. (See *hermaphrodite* for Cupid's half-brother and more on this family's history.)]

dandelion   The weed (of which there are several variants), with yellow flower and jagged leaves. In all forms it is an excellent pot green if picked young and tender. [Anglicized from Fr. *dent-de-lion* (intermediately ME *dentdelyon*), lion's tooth (so named because of the jagged leaf edge).]

dander Temper. [Few simple words have so troubled etymologists. ODEE tentatively refers it to **dunder*, in West Indies usage, the working ferment of sugar cane being made into rum; and the sense and dating (early XIX) may be said to concur. But Sc. **dander*, an ember of a smith's fire, seems more likely, esp. in connection with:]

get one's dander up To become irate ("emotionally heated"). [In which case the root image would be from the act of blowing on coals to make the fire blaze. But ?]

dapple Esp. in ***dapple gray*** Originally specific to gray horses, whose mottled markings were taken to resemble those of many apples. [Earlier *apple gray*. The *d-* was prefixed in ME by the same language process that evolved *daffodil* from *aphodel*, prob. under the influ. of Du. *de affodil*, the aphodel. Chaucer, *Canterbury Tales, Prologue*, 616, has *pomely grey* < OF *gris pommelé*, apple(d) gray. And always with ref. to the markings of gray horses, It. has *grigio pommelato*; Ger. has *apfelgrau*; ON has *apalgrár*; and the same form can be attested in Russian *v yablokakh* (*yábloko* being "apple"). Though the origin of this "apple gray" metaphor cannot be traced, its spread through so many different language families is certainly evidence of its great antiquity.]

dark horse 1. *Politics*. An obscure candidate who comes, seemingly from nowhere, to win a nomination, usu. when the front runners are deadlocked. [In this sense the term is an Americanism dating from the Democratic convention of 1844. None of the leading candidates (Martin Van Buren, Lewis Cass, and James Buchanan) was able to win a majority on the first eight ballots. On the ninth, someone entered James K. Polk, who won the nomination, and later the election, running as the "dark horse candidate."] 2. *In the term's original reference to horse racing*. An obscure horse (not one with a "shining reputation") who comes from nowhere to win the race. [Coined by Benjamin Disraeli, British statesman and popular novelist. In *The Young Duke* (1831) he wrote: "A dark horse which had never been heard of (swept to triumph)." The term passed at once into Brit. race track idiom, was soon after adopted on Am. tracks, and then acquired its (now dominant in Am.) political sense.]

Davy Jones   The seaman's version of the devil as a snatcher of souls. *Davy Jones's locker* The bottom of the sea as the tomb of drowned men and sunken ships; hence, the seaman's equivalent of the land-lubber's hell. [With *(Jolly) Roger* and *Mother Carey's chickens* (see both), part of a seagoing trilogy long believed to be of untraceable origin. Yet a reasonable conjecture is possible.

Jones has long been known to be a corruption of *Jonah,* the bringer of bad luck to sailors. *Davy* (earlier also *Taffy*) has then been glossed (much too patly, I submit) as a simple seamen's impro-visation. In Afro-Carib-Creole, the pidgin of the slave trade, many roots of which still function in Caribbean dialects, *duffy* or *duppy* (*u* pronounced as $\overline{oo}$) is the name of a revenant voodoo spirit that seizes souls. A similar root (consisting of d/t-vowel-b/p/f/v-vowel) occurs in West African languages with the same sense.

Hebrew is an Afro-Asian rather than an Indo-European lan-guage. AA has not been studied as closely as IE, but if the roots of the two language families are distributed over similarly wide areas, Hebrew *dibok,* evil spirit < *dabhaq,* to seize, may be taken as attesting the West African root.

This reference to Hebrew is, in any case, a side speculation. With or without it, *Davy Jones* prob. means at root: "the devil as the revenant spirit of Jonah come to snatch the souls of men." Any final assertion, however, must await more research into AA and Afro-Carib-Creole pidgin.]

dead   [IE *deu-* with primary sense "to die," but also "to use up, to become exhausted." This secondary sense is prob. the base of XVII Brit. slang *to die,* to have an orgasm. The IE root, suffixed *-t-* or *-d-* in Gmnc. → OE *dēad,* ME *ded.*] *adj.* 1. *Primary sense.* No longer alive. But this sense readily extends to: 2. Inanimate. Unre-sponsive. *dead weight.* 3. Absolute (as death is). *dead center.* 4. As good as dead. *dead duck.* 5. Exhausted. *dead tired.* 6. Not func-tioning. *dead battery, dead in the water.* 7. At nadir. *dead of winter.* 8. Point beyond which all fails. *dead line.*

dead duck A goner. [Prob. suggested by its alliteration. Cf. the more recent *gone gosling,* with the same sense. But certainly influ. by common Am. XIX *dead as a duck drowned in a thunder-storm,* in which *duck* should be *duckling.* From the common obser-vation that ducklings were commonly found dead and half buried in mud after a very heavy rain, and looked as if they had drowned, though they had probably died of cold because they had not yet developed a full protective coating of body oils.]

dead eye 1. *Primary sense.* A crack shot. *Deadeye Dick.* [In

XV the form was *dead man's eye,* prob. with ref. to archery contests in which the eye sockets of skulls served as targets. In XIX Brit. slang, *dead hand* signified a person especially adept at a given task.] 2. *Maritime.* A wheelless hole in a block through which a lanyard is passed.

dead man's hand *Poker.* A holding of a pair of aces and a pair of eights. [And so generally understood, though various other holdings are argued by some. In any case, the ref. is to the hand held by Wild Bill Hickok (a murderer who hid behind a badge) when he was shot in the back while playing poker in Calamity Jane's saloon in Deadwood City, Dakota Territory, Aug. 2, 1876. His murderer, Jack McCall, was Calamity Jane's lover. He was hanged for interfering with a local poker game, and Calamity Jane (who never was much good at choosing her company) now lies beside him in the Deadwood cemetery.]

dead man's switch A fail-safe device that permits the operation of a machine or a mechanism only while a spring-loaded handgrip is depressed. [So called because if the operator dies or becomes unconscious, his hand falls from the switch, allowing the spring to open, thereby stopping the mechanism. The throttles of modern trains are so equipped to bring the train to a stop in case the engineer suffers a heart attack or a disabling injury.]

dead soldier An empty liquor bottle. [Whimsical. Because the "spirit" has gone out of it. In XIX Brit. slang, *dead marine.*]

dead: let the dead bury the dead   Let bygones be bygones. Leave the animosities and errors of the past out of present discussion. [Originally spoken by Jesus, as recorded in Matthew 8:21–22: "And another of his disciples said unto him, Lord, suffer me first to go and bury my father. But Jesus said unto him, Follow me; and let the dead bury their dead."

debate   Now signifies a formal presentation of arguments and counterarguments within parliamentary guidelines and time limits. As the formal rules of debate are lost, the discussion descends to wrangling. [Yet wrangling is the root sense. < L. *de-,* down (also functions as an intensive); *battere,* to beat (BATTERY, ABATE). This root sense is nicely expressed by the colorful It. word *battibecco,* hot argument; lit. "a beating of beaks" (as if two birds are fencing).]

declaim   1. To recite oratorically. 2. To speak forcefully, assertively, grandiosely. [L. *de-,* intensive prefix; *clamare,* to cry out.] *All the Kennedys have suffered from declamation of character.*

declare 1. To announce openly. 2. *Customs.* To state, usually in writing, all goods one is bringing into the country. [Root sense: "to make clear." < L. *de-*, intensive prefix; *clarare*, to make clear. Hence, "to make very clear."]

    I do declare! Rural colloq. Exclam. of surprise, vexation. Often as a form of greeting to a person unexpectedly encountered, in which context the extended sense is "I do openly assert (that it is a pure and pleasurable surprise to see you)!"

decoy 1. A lure, usu. a staked duck or a carved and painted imitation placed on a pond or lake to attract wild ducks. 2. *Ext.* Any lure to draw out a hidden enemy. In WWI, *decoy ships* that looked like defenseless merchantmen lured German U-boats and then fired at them with concealed guns. [Before modern shotguns, duck hunters caught ducks by spreading fowling nets from tree to tree across the natural flight approaches to a likely body of water. In this sense *decoy* can be explained as being from Du. *de kooi*, the cage; ult. < L. *cavea*, cage (CAVE). But such a "net cage" would also require a lure as in sense 1, above. *Duckcoy* and *duckoy* occur in XVII–XVIII, the form being close to that of the Dutch. But in XVI *to coy* was "to entice." OED cites the 1634 usuage: "the Art to coy the fonder sort into their nets." And I have in memory, though I cannot now locate the Shakespearean line, "I'll coy their hearts from them." All evidence points to a convergent evolution from these two sources, though all reference to a fowler's net has disappeared from modern usage.]

deep [OE *dēop*, of obscure Gmnc. origin. Akin to DIP.] *adj.* 1. Reaching far down. 2. *Ext.* Intellectually profound. *deep thinker.* —*n.* *Poetic.* Usu. with *the.* The sea.

    the deep six The bottom of the sea. [*Deep* for "deepest"; *six* for "fathom"; hence, the last fathom down. *give it the deep six* 1. Throw it overboard. 2. *If said of a ship.* Sink it. Also *deep six it.*

defense mechanism *Psychiatry.* A psychic compulsion to suppress or disguise a traumatic experience. [*Mechanism* is a robotically insensitive choice in the context of neurotic illusion, about equivalent to calling a poem a "word machine." I would much prefer *neurotic castling,* with its suggestion of building imaginary castles in which one may hide from the trauma, as do some neurotics, or sally forth to attack it in disguised form, as do others.]

delirious Describes a disordered and incoherent state of mental agitation. [The root image—a fossil poem—is "out of one's furrow" (not plowing a straight line but wandering all over the field). < L. *delirare*, to rant < *de-* out of, away from; *lira*, a furrow; ult. < IE *leis-*, course, track, trail.]

demijohn A large bottle covered with wickerwork and equipped with a wicker handle. There is no established size, but the fact that a gallon of water weights 8 pounds imposes a top limit of about 12 gallons as a manageable weight, with perhaps a lower limit of about 2 gallons if the thing is to qualify for the root sense: "an imposing personage of a bottle." [Not < Fr. *demi*, half. These bottles first appeared in XVI France and were given the whimsical name *Dame Jeanne*, Dame Jane, as if in tribute to some robustly slab-sided proprietress of a country inn. Into XVII Brit. as a mangled translation of the Fr. And note It. *damigiana*, Sp. *damajuana*, and Arabic *dāmājāna*. The old dame got around.]

derrick Though most dictionaries permit the term to include hoisting towers with movable booms, Am. usage labels such structures as *cranes* and reserves *derrick* as the name of the tall, tapering, latticed drill rig used in oil fields. [In early XVII Brit., a gallows; so called after Derrick (given name unknown), who from c. 1598 to 1610 was the public hangman of London, with offices on Tyburn Hill.]

derring-do Valor. [In literary convention the word is specific to tales of chivalry. Perhaps to prove that anything is a word once it becomes one. At root: "to do a daring deed," altered into a noun phrase. < OE *durran*, to dare; compounded with *don*, to do. The Chaucerian form is *durring-don*. *Derring-do* first occurs in Spenser, who may have taken his form from an error in transcription (or what is today called a typographical error). The form had just about expired, even in literary romances, when it was revived by Sir Walter Scott.]

deus ex machina Can mean: Any divine intervention into mortal affairs. But is used primarily as a literary term to signify: Any contrived injection into a plot of an outside element to extricate a character from an otherwise unsolvable situation. [L. translation of Gk. *theos ek mekhanes*, "god from a machine (mechanism)." The reference is to Greek drama, in which actors who portrayed gods were lowered to the stage by block and tackle (the "machine"). Usually, then, the gods proceeded to straighten out the mess of human affairs.]

devil [OE *dēoful*, devil; akin to Ger. *Teufel*, OHG *tiuful*. (Note resemblance of OE *dēo* to L. *deus;* of OHG *tiu-* to Tiu, god, as in Tuesday. But to render *-ful*, *-fel* as variants of *fall*, and to render the sense as "the God that fell," though tempting, is to guess beyond evidence.) These forms are ult. < Gk. *dia-*, across, away from; *bollein*, to throw → *diabolos*, devil ("he who throws across," what he throws being men's souls, the point to which he throws them varying with the state of the myth). *Diabolos* was used in first century to translate Hebrew *sātān*, Satan. The form of *diabolos* corresponds to that of *discobolos*, discus thrower.] 1. Satan or any of his attendant fiends. 2. Any supernatural evil spirit. 3. *Ext.* Any evil person. 4. *Ext.* An admirable person. *a devil of a fellow.* [Akin to *daredevil* in sense: "one who will take on any risk."]

devil's advocate One who argues the evil—i.e., the unpopular—side of an issue. *The devil's advocates who argue for every perversion in the name of individual freedom.* [From the R. C. Church ritual of canonization. As a precaution against the elevation of an unworthy person to sainthood, one cleric is appointed to search out any defects in the life of the proposed saint and to argue them against canonization. Officially titled Defender of the Faith *(promotor fidei)*, he is commonly referred to as the devil's advocate *(advocatus diaboli)*, the devil being reputed to be no friend of saints.] **there'll be the devil to pay** There will be a hard time coming. [But not, as often supposed, in the sense of standing before the devil's bar to atone for one's sins. The original expression was *the devil to pay and no pitch hot.*

Devil < OF maritime *diable* labeled a seam on old sailing ships; the reference being further confused because *devil-diable* was applied to different seams at different periods: in XVI to the keel seam; in XVII to the seam that joined the more or less vertical sides of the ship to the more or less flat bottom; in XVIII to the especially wide and overhanging seam that joined the main deck to the hull. *To pay* < OF *payer*, to apply pitch; ult. < L. *pix*, pitch.

In XVI, when it became necessary to "pay the devil" (as Captain Cook had to do in the Pacific), the ship was worked onto a suitable beach at high tide and careened. The pitch (preheated by a shore party assigned to the task) was then applied to the keel seam in frantic haste, for the work had to be finished before the tide returned and refloated the ship. And so the related expression *between the devil* (the seam to be pitched) *and the deep blue sea* (the returning tide). The expression further confused by the fact that in XVIII sailors who "payed the devil" would be suspended over the side in a boatswain's chair (also *between the devil and the deep blue sea*), their precarious position being made more nautical by the fact that they were working on a seam above their heads and receiving the full benefit of all hot pitch that dribbled down on them as hairdressing and facial cream.]

printer's devil A printer's apprentice. [Because he was given the dirty work of cleaning up and was forever black with ink.]

Tasmanian devil 1. An ugly, black-furred, rat-tailed burrowing marsupial of Tasmania. 2. A toy consisting of a rubber-capped tube of liquid in which a celluloid figure, usu. of Satan, was suspended. When the rubber was pressed, the increased pressure caused the devil to sink; when the pressure was released, it rose. (I have not seen one for fifty years. They may be beneath the interest of the electronic young, but they passed as a fair wonder in the child eyes of another era.)

diamond [Root sense: "adamant." < IE *deme-*, to dominate, to tame → Gk. *daman*, L. *domare*, to tame, to subdue, to break horses. And Gk. *adamas*, hard, unyielding (*a* as Gk. neg. prefix). Prob. Low L. form *adimas* by metathesis to Late L. *diamas*, OF *diamant*, ME *diamaunt*.] 1. The gemstone. 2. Its conceived shape as a rhomboid with acute angles at top and bottom (and so variously applied to anything so shaped, as various animals so marked: *diamondback rattlesnake, diamond terrapin;* in plu. a suit of cards, in sing. a card of that suit; in baseball originally the infield, then extended to signify the whole playing field).

diamond anniversary, diamond jubilee A 75th anniversary observance, but for marriages the 60th. [Because who lives to the 75th?]

diamond in the rough 1. An uncut, unpolished diamond. (It lacks luster in this state.) 2. *Ext.* A person of great but unrealized worth. [Implies that he/she will "shine" (be outstanding) when "polished" (trained and developed), but as often implies that he/she is a present nuisance and that someone ought to polish it off.]

dibs: go dibs (in) To share (in). *I went dibs in his canoe* (shared the use of it) *all summer.* (When I was a boy in Medford, Mass., the invariable formula for claiming a share of any goody, whether an apple core or the next use of a baseball bat, was *I howny dibs* or *I howny next dibs.* I have never seen *howny* in writing, and can only speculate that it is based on "I (claim to) own." Surely, however, others will remember this boy term. [In this sense *dibs* is prob. from *dibstones,* an old child's game involving the distribution and capture of small bones or stones used as counters. In capturing an opponent's counters one cried "Dibs!" with the sense "I claim." An ancient African version of this game is called *kabuki.*]

dickens/what the dickens   (Variant forms of mild exclam. or minced oath.) The devil! What the deuce! [Inevitably suggests Charles Dickens, but Shakespeare used the form 250 years before him, and in a way to suggest it was already well established. Of the many possible, and attestable, explanations, I prefer the derivation < Sc. *de'il,* devil; with dim. suffix *-kins* → *de'ilkins,* imps.]

dilapidated   To be partially but not totally in ruins. [At root, a precise metaphor: "to have stones missing from" (as in a neglected but not yet collapsed edifice). To say "the colosseum is dilapidated" permits the exact sense; to use the word in the generalized extension "shabby, decayed, worn," blurs it; to say "a dilapidated jalopy" slops it. < L. *dis-,* apart, away from; *lapis, stone.* (Stem, *lapid-.* LAPIDARIAN.) L. *dilapidare,* to throw away, is not so much a source as an intermediate evolution, and has the root sense "to throw (to shed) stones."]

diner   1. One who dines. [Agential of *to dine* < L. *dis-,* prefix indicating contrary action; *jejunus,* hungry, empty (JEJUNE). Fr. *déjeuner,* breakfast (the breaking of one's overnight fast) < OD *disner,* ME *dinen,* to dine.] 2. *U.S. Railroading.* A dining car. [Shift from "one who dines" to "place for dining."] Whence, 3. A short-order eatery traditionally built to resemble a dining car.
   HISTORIC. Diners as inexpensive short-order restaurants were first established near railroad stations and in railroad dining cars that had been condemned as rolling stock. Though today's diners have become elaborate affairs with attached dining rooms and with lengthy menus, their long counters still suggest those at which railroads fed their road crews, and many diners retain such architectural details as the bull-nosed doors reminiscent of doors into a rail car. Synonyms: *greasy spoon, sloppy Joe's, ptomaine palace, hash house, the Greek's, beanery.*

disaster   1. Widespread devastation or affliction. 2. (When applied to one person or a small group.) Utter ruin. 3. *Loose ext.* A fiasco. [Based on astrological belief, with root sense "ill starred." < L.

dis-, negative prefix; *astrum,* star. Cf. *consider,* similarly based on astrological belief, < L. *con-*, with; *sidera,* stars; root sense: "With the stars," i.e., "weighed according to one's horoscope."]

dismal   Dreary. Gloomy. Inauspicious. Whatever one does not like or want. [< L. *dies mali,* evil days. OF *dis mal.* (*Di* for *day* survives in operatic Italian—*un bel di*—and as the final element in Italian and French days of the week, as Fr. *lundi,* Monday—moon's day; It. *venerdi,* Friday—day of Venus.) It was common Roman superstition that two days of every month were unlucky ("Beware the Ides of March"), and these were the *dies mali.*]

ditto   The aforesaid again. In listing items, usu. indicated by the sign ". Sometimes by the abbreviation *do.,* a practice that has survived in Wall Street market listings. [It. *detto,* said (p.p. of *dire,* to say), the effective sense, in context, being "the aforesaid again."]

diva   (Anglicized plu. *divas.* It. plu. *dive.*) An operatic prima donna. [It. *diva,* goddess < fem. form of L. *divus, deus,* god. Ult. < IE *deiu-, dieu-*, to shine (as the heavens) and hence the root of both L. *die,* day, and *deus,* god (DEITY; also Fr. DIEU, God). A testimony to the regard in which Italians hold their first ladies of song: Italian opera-goers commonly cheer a fine performance with cries of *brava* but reserve the cry of *diva* for a supreme performance by a prima donna.]

Dixie/Land of Dixie   With the exception of Texas, which is its own mythology, those states that once formed the Confederacy. [From the title of a minstrel show song, "I Wish I Was in Dixie's Land" (later simply "Dixie"), composed in 1859 by Dan D. Emmett. The song became instantly and wildly popular North and South, but during the Civil War it became the all but official anthem of the Confederacy.

Despite various commonly asserted etymologies (see note), the one firm etymological fact is that the word does not appear in any written form before Emmett used it in the title of his song. Minstrel shows were performed by blackface non-Negro minstrels who loudly proclaimed their nostalgia for the South and their bondage. Emmett, an old showman, needed a place name that would identify his fake Negroes with the joys of slavery. All evidence is that he coined *Dixie,* perhaps after the Dixon of the Mason-Dixon line. That line, originally surveyed in 1763–1767 as the boundary between Md. and Pa., was established, together with the Ohio River, as the boundary between slave and free states.

Such a coinage, though unattested, is certainly not beyond the ingenuities of a showman. And the dating must suggest that if Emmett did not himself coin it, it fell from heaven in 1859, just in time to give him a title for his song.]

NOTE. One recurring but unattested etymology refers to a ten-dollar bill supposedly issued by a never identified New Orleans bank, and prominently marked with Fr. DIX, ten. These are said to have been nicknamed *Dixies,* whence New Orleans was the original *Land of Dixies,* the term later extended to include all of Louisiana, and later all of the South. Ingenious, but I find it impossible to believe that any early U.S. region could have been identified by the widespread use of ten-dollar bills, and bank notes at that, rather than federal currency.

Another refers to a never identified Johan Dixie, who is said to have worked Negro slaves on his farm on Manhattan Island, and to have treated them so kindly that when he sold them down the river to southern plantations (for kindly money?), they sang of their yearning to be back on Dixie's land. Perhaps, but Dixie's Negroes would probably have had to sing their nostalgia for at least a century before 1859, and to have done their singing unheard by anyone but Emmett.

you ain't just whistlin' Dixie You ain't just beatin' your gums. I.e., You said a mouthful. [Dating and origin unknown. As a reasonable speculation, "to whistle Dixie" would be to whistle the marching song of the South (without actually doing any fighting), i.e., to make empty sounds. Hence, the evolved sense: "You're not just mouthing sounds, but getting down to the real fighting gist of it." But ?]

dodge   *v.* 1. To evade by ducking out of the way. 2. To elude. *-n.* 1. An artful trick. *a tax dodge.* 2. *Crim. slang.* A racket. *What's your dodge?* [Though not into standard English until XVII, all that is known of this term is that it has had a long and complex history in various British dialects. Dialect *dodge, dodger,* a clod of earth, if thought of as something that can be thrown at a person, may, though only speculatively, be related to the primary verb sense as "the act of evading by ducking aside." *Dodge, dodger* has also functioned in dialect as "lump of food" (a clodlike chunk of food); and *dodgel* as an especially large chunk of food, whence Am. sthrn. *corndodger,* which see.]

Dodgers   The National League baseball team, once central to the mythology of Brooklyn and Miss Marianne Moore, which broke

Miss Moore's heart by moving to Los Angeles, where the earth-quake is already coiled to swallow the team into the pit for its perfidy. [In late XIX, when Brooklyn was still an independent municipality, Brooklynites were commonly called *Trolley Dodgers* because of the unusually large number of horse-drawn trolley cars that clanged through its crowded streets before the extension of the Brooklyn-Manhattan Transit subway. The baseball team was first known by the full municipal nickname, later shortened to *Dodgers.* Not—as fanciful persons have asserted—because a street-car line ran through the outfield of the team's first playing field, forcing outfielders to dodge a trolley when fielding a ball.]

dog days   The hottest days of summer. [< Late L. *dies canicularis,* days of the dog, applied to the period from mid July until the end of August, which is the time of highest heat and humidity in Rome. So called because the Dog Star (Sirius) rises with the sun during this time. Sirius is the brightest star observable from earth and was held to be an astrologically "hot" star. The Romans explained the heat and humidity of their unbearable midsummer as being due to the fact that during these days Sirius added its heat to that of the sun.]

doldrums   Always with *the.* (Various authorities assert this to be a plu. form taking a sing. verb, but can one say "the doldrums has me"?) The condition of being dull and listless. [The first element is < OE *dol,* ME *dold,* dull (DOLT). The second element has been conjectured to derive from the second element of *tantrum,* which is of XVIII origin. Such an influ., however, does not explain the fixed plu. form, which is of XIX origin. As speculation only, I suggest that the elements are not *dol-* and *-trum* but *dold* and *rum(s),* as in *rum go* (which see), with the root sense "the dull queers." But ???]

    in the doldrums 1. In a dull and listless state. 2. *Nautical.* (Dating uncertain.) Becalmed at sea. (See *horse latitudes.*)

dollar   [Based on Joachimsthal (Valley of St. Joseph) in Czechoslova-kia, site of a mint established in early XVI. The coins there minted were called *Joachimsthalern,* and in the sing. form *Joachimsthaler,* whence Ger. *taler* → Du. *daler.* When the U.S. declared its inde-pendence, it insisted on freeing itself from the British pound ster-ling and called its basic unit of currency the dollar.] The basic unit of U.S. currency as established by the Coinage Act of 1792; later adopted by Canada, Australia, New Zealand, and various smaller nations.

dollar-a-year Describes federal appointees who serve for patriotic reasons rather than for pay. [Popularized in WWI. *Dollar* for "token sum," but also as the standard "valuable consideration" without which a contract is not binding, as in the legal formula "for one dollar and other valuable considerations."]

dollar sign The symbol $, officially designated as having a single vertical, though often drawn with two. Prob. originally a *U* superimposed on an *S* for *U.S.*, the loop of the *U* being later eliminated.

the almighty dollar Money as the object of avaricious worship. [First used by Washington Irving, *Creole Village*, 1837, but c. 1600 Ben Jonson used "almighty gold" with the identical sense—and note how nearly *almighty gold* duplicates Almighty God.]

bottom dollar One's last dollar. [Poker. The chips being stacked, one takes chips from the top of the pile in betting. To bet one's bottom dollar is to bet the whole stack—all one has.]

to pay top dollar (for) To pay full value for, with possibly a premium for quality. To outbid. [The root image is, again, a stack of poker chips, the higher stack (the one whose top chip rises higher than others) representing the higher price (bet).]

doornail: dead as a doornail *Metaphoric intensive.* Very dead. [*Door* and *nail* are earlier; *doornail* is attested by mid XIV, and also *dum* (dumb) *as a doornail.* But this doornail is not a nail in the modern sense. It is, rather, a large-headed, malleable iron bolt longer than the width of the door and fitted into a prebored hole that extended through opposing iron plates that were either ornamental hinges or metal strips to strengthen and ornament the door. The protruding end was then hammered into another knob, forming, in effect, a large-headed rivet. *Dead,* because immovably in place.]

HISTORIC. Nails, as we know them, were rare in carpentry until almost 1800, as witness the wooden pegging of most Am. colonial carpentry and cabinetmaking. In building Monticello in late XVIII, Jefferson used some nails but had to establish his own forge, in which they were made by hand. Nor, in any case, can nails be driven through hard wood (as in oaken doors) without the strong likelihood of splitting it.

Modern carpentry, in rough construction with soft wood (as pine), drives nails longer than the door battens, then clinches them by hammering the protruding ends to one side; and this technique is called *dead-nailing,* but does not correspond to the old form of the doornail (door bolt, door rivet).

There is nothing to support the common assertion that *doornail* once meant the metal plate embedded in a door to be struck by a hinged door knocker (it being *dead* because the natural resonance of the metal was muffled by the wood in which it was embedded).

doozy   An outstanding thing. Usu. in the formula *it's a doozy* It's a oner. It's a humdinger. [Corruption < *duesie, Duesie,* short for *Duesenberg,* Am. auto produced 1921–1937 by Fred and Audie Duesenberg; the fastest, finest, most advanced, and most expensive U.S. production model of its time and now one of the great classics sought by antique-auto buffs. A well-kept Duesenberg in running order brought a touch over $200,000 in a late 1970's auction.]

dope   *Sthrn. colloq.* Coca-Cola. *gimme a dope Soda fountain order.* Gimme a glass of Coca-Cola. [The now world-famous drink was first marketed in 1865 by John S. Pemberton, a veteran of the Confederate Army and an Atlanta pharmacist, and was originally called "French Wine Coca—Ideal Nerve and Tonic Stimulant." The stimulant in the drink was a small amount of cocaine, which in those days before the Pure Food and Drug Act was a common additive to patent medicines. In 1886 the cocaine was replaced by caffeine, and the name changed to Coca-Cola. In 1888 the present company bought the product and tried to suppress the common nickname *Coke,* but failed, and eventually registered it as a trade name. Coca-Cola was named after the coca leaf and the cola nut, but prob. equally for cocaine and cola, cocaine being derived from the dried cola leaf. I doubt that southern teen-agers know why they order "dopes," but the name harks back to the brewing kettle in Pemberton's backyard, of which an assistant once remarked that you could guess when the mixture was right by smelling the fumes of the cooking cocaine.]

dosie-doe/dosie-dotes   Square dance call. The figure in which two dancers come together, circle one another back to back, and then dance backward to their original positions. [Sthrn. corruption of Fr. *dos à dos,* back to back. In XIV France also the name of a sofa and a carriage, in both of which the seats were arranged back to back.]

double in brass   To function in an additional skilled capacity. *Ernie Hansen, a master potato picker by trade, doubles in brass as president of the Perth Amboy Savings Institution.* [Early XIX Am. circus jargon, with ref. to the fact that every member of the troupe, whatever his or her performing specialty, was expected to pick up an instrument and play in the brass band when the circus paraded into town.]

double-talk 1. The act of saying one thing while meaning another. 2. Seemingly sincere but in fact evasive lingo. *All I got from him was a lot of double-talk.* 3. *Vaudeville.* A comic routine consisting of rapid well-modulated patter that uses normal syntax to connect meaningless words. [For which you will have to skim the amifactor before you can pertinate the synch that ventracizes the mean average stirpage.]

doughboy Now specific to the U.S. enlisted man of WWI, but in common use long before. [In late XVIII maritime, a lump of fried dough, a favorite food of sailors. Elizabeth Bacon Custer (Mrs. Col./Gen. George Armstrong Custer) in *Today in the Plains* (1867) asserted what must have been an accepted, though doubtful, army version of the term's origin: "A 'doughboy' is a small round dough-nut served to sailors on shipboard generally with hash. Early in the Civil War the term was applied to the large globular brass buttons on the infantry uniform, from which it passed by a natural transition to the infantrymen themselves."

If Mrs. Custer is right, there has been a convergent evolution, for M. M. Mathews, *A Dictionary of Americanisms,* points out that by 1850 *dobie-boy* (based on *adobe*) was "applied by Spaniards in the Southwest to army personnel" (prob. because their blue uniforms were forever dusty, as if covered with adobe).]

dragoon A name given to early blunderbusses. [Altered < *dragon* because they "breathed fire."] *dragoons* First applied in XVII to cavalry equipped with short heavy muskets in addition to the conventional cutlery, and then in place of it. Hence, *to dragoon* To coerce; to set upon with great force. [Because cavalry, always a powerful striking force, became doubly powerful when given fire power.]

NOTE. There is in the hamlet of Ripton, Vermont, a family surnamed Dragon that has continued there since white men first settled the land. Their original surname is lost. The present one derives from the fact that men of this line served as dragoons in the American Revolution, the evolution of their name exactly reversing that from *dragon* to *dragoon.*

dreary Dismal. Boring. Depressing. [But these senses are post-Elizabethan evolutions. Earlier with the sense "of mortal darkness."

Ult. < IE *dreu-*, to drip, a drop; via Gmnc. (in which the sense became "drop of blood, to bleed") → OE *dreōr*, gore (dripping blood). And prob. influ. by obs. *dree*, to suffer, to endure. So Scottish *to dree one's weird*, to endure one's fated lot. The sense "gory," implicit from OE to Spenser, no longer functions, and the word has lost its earlier fatal connotation. Cf. *shambles*, once specific to the gore of a butchershop but now, except among purists (who have lost their battle to keep the word specific), any scene of disorder, whether or not blood-spattered.]

drench [A changeling word. IE *dhrag-*, *dhreg-*, to pull along. And either in IE or in early Gmnc. acquired the sense now expressed by slang *to have a pull on the bottle*, i.e., to drink deep ("to draw liquid into oneself"). Via Gmnc. → OE *drincan*, to drink; and by association *drencan*, to make wet, to soak; whence ME *drenchen*, to drown. *Drench* and *drown* have since acquired distinct senses, but one coming in from a heavy rain will still say, if only as a hyperbole, "I'm drowned" for "I'm drenched."] *n.* (In Am. all but obsolete.) A dose of liquid medicine, especially for an animal (root sense: "to flood its insides"), but in New England, through XIX (and still rarely): *spring drench* The traditional bitter tonic, usu. sulfur and molasses, taken on putting away one's winter long johns. (See *moxie*.) —*v.* To soak, to wet through and through.

druthers *Colloq. Always plural.* Preference. *If I had my druthers* If I were totally free to choose. [Whimsical substantive formed by elision of dialect *I'(d ruther)* for *I'd rather*, the plural expressing not only choice but the sum of all one's choices.]

duck (idioms)
　　duck boards A boardwalk over a muddy place or over one likely to become muddy. *duck soup* Said of anything that presents no difficulties. Often *as easy as duck soup*. [Because ducks, being naturally fatty, easily make up into soup.] *dead duck* A goner. (See *dead*.)
　　lame duck A political officeholder who has not been reelected but who still has some time left in office. [And so in Am. since XIX, but in XVIII Brit. one who has defaulted on a debt; and in XIX with specific ref. to a trader who has walked off the floor of the exchange without settling his obligations for that day. In both senses of the British idiom the defaulter is thought of as having "waddled off limping."]
　　ruptured duck The lapel button issued to discharged veterans

of WWII. [It was intended to signify peace by showing an eagle on the ground in the act of folding its wings after its warlike flight. In the generalized oafishness of official art, what emerged looks at least as much like a duck as it does an eagle and the dangling wings still ajar suggest that it has a hernia. The naming was an immediate and inspired act of G.I. poetry.]

sitting duck An easy victim.

ugly duckling 1. A gawkish and ungainly child. 2. The least attractive child in a family. *It wasn't easy for Harry Crews to be the ugly duckling in this family, but he made it.* [After the Hans Christian Andersen story "The Ugly Duckling," in which a swan accidentally hatched by a duck, ridiculed by its accidental siblings as ungainly and ugly, achieves full growth and turns out to be an elegant swan. In general usage, however, this idiom refers almost exclusively to the early ungainliness, with no promise of a glorious transformation.]

ducks and drakes   The idle sport of skipping a stone across calm water. [The game must be immemorially old, but this name for it first attested XVI. The circular ripple made by the first skip was said to be a duck, the second a drake, the third another duck, and so forth. The object, of course, is to see how many ducks and drakes one can put on the pond.] *play ducks and drakes with one's money* To throw it away, as if skipping it across a pond. (Unlike bread cast on the waters, money so treated does not return a hundredfold.)

HISTORICAL. Legend has it that the young George Washington skipped a silver dollar across the Potomac. As a young surveyor he may have skimmed something clear across the narrow upper reaches of the Potomac, but not a silver dollar. Silver dollars were first minted in Philadelphia in 1794. The most likely coin for young George's squandering impulse would have been the Spanish piece of eight. (See *bits.*)

dudgeon   Survives only in the idiom *in high dudgeon* 1. Indignant. 2. In a rage. [An uncertain etymology. XIV Norman Fr. *digeon,* ME *dudgeon,* was a sort of wood favored for the handles of knives and daggers. "And on thy blade and dudgeon gouts of blood."— Lady Macbeth. It is tempting, therefore, to render *in high dudgeon* as "with dagger raised high," i.e., "in a murderous rage," with a later sense shift to "indignant." And perhaps so, but such a rendering cannot be supported by evidence, and nothing explains why the idiom reads "in" rather than "with" high dudgeon.]

dunce   A person stupid or ignorant, or both. [An etymological defamation of character. From the middle name of John Duns Scotus, c. 1265–1308, English priest, philosopher, and theologian, called "The Subtle Doctor." A master of logical analysis, he acquired a following of scholars called *Dunsmen* or *dunsmen*. After the master's early death, however, his disciples became so absurdly snarled in the subtleties they admired but could not manage that they came to be mocked as Duns's, whence *dunces.*]

dust: bite the dust   To die. [Am. XIX. Popularized as a standard phrase in Westerns. *and another Indian bit the dust* (was shot off his horse and landed on his face as if biting the dust). Borrowed by RAF in WWI, it became Brit. service slang for "to be shot down" or "to die in a crash landing."]

Dutch   [MD *dutsch,* Dutch. Akin to Ger. *Deutsch,* German.] 1. Of the Netherlands. 2. *Archaic in Brit. but surviving in Am. slang,* German. So *Dutch Schultz,* Prohibition era NYC gangster of German immigrant parents, born, as I recall, Arthur Fliegelheimer.
    HISTORIC. The Dutch and the English, near neighbors, once dealt with mutual respect, many words of Dutch origin passing into English. Bear in mind that bad weather could easily drive Dutch fishermen into British channel ports and British fishermen into Dutch ports. Then, in what seems to have been the early XVII, the adjective *Dutch* began to acquire loutish connotations in English, and these have persisted except in such straightforwardly identifying forms as *Dutch doors, Dutch oven,* etc. Some typical uses, among many others:
    Dutch courage False courage brought on by drunkenness. *Dutch treat* An invitation to a meal, drink, the theater, with the guest expected to pay his share. But *let's Dutch it* = let's each pay his share. *Dutch uncle* A well-intentioned but boorishly blunt adviser. *in Dutch* In trouble. [Perh. associated with the sort of dressing down one gets from a Dutch uncle.]
    Pennsylvania Dutch (*Dutch* for *German.*) XVII & XVIII German and Swiss-German settlers in Pennsylvania, primarily the plain folk of the Mennonite and Amish religions, at root, forms of family monasticism.

d.v.   God willing. [Abbreviated form of L. *deo volente,* God willing.] *D.v. it won't be v.d.*

ε

eagle   [L. *aquila,* OF *aigle.*] Long the most symbolic of hawks, *eagle* does standard metaphoric service for: 1. An aviator. 2. A rank in Boy Scouting, 3. A hole in golf played at two strokes under par. 4. A former gold piece stamped with the image of an eagle. Also: *double eagle.*

   eagle eyed Having sharp vision. *eagle eye* One who is sharp of eye. In ext. connotes marksmanship. Also the quality of an overseer who misses nothing. *Don't try to get anything funny past old eagle eye.* [The eagle was once believed to be able to stare directly into the sun without blinding itself.]

   It took the G.I., beginning with the eagle as the national bird and as a symbol on money, to find the characteristically coarse but metaphorically vivid possibilities of *eagle shit* G.I. pay. [Squeezed out of the national bird the hard way.] *The eagle shits today* It's payday. *squeeze a dollar till the eagle shits* To be miserly. (In these two usages *shits* is sometimes minced as *screams.*) And the variant: *squeeze a nickel till the buffalo shits/roars.*

easel   A frame for holding a canvas on which a painter works. [XVII. One of several painterly terms from Du. to Eng. following the XVI flowering of Dutch art. (Cf. *landscape.*) < Du. *ezel,* ass ("beast of burden"). Essentially the same metaphor works in the Fr. word for easel, *chevalet,* which is "little horse." And cf. Eng. *clothes horse* for clothes rack. Variantly a fop.]

ecdysiast   A stripteaser. [A whimsical coinage by H. L. Mencken, c. 1920. Adapted from Gk. *ecdysis,* the process of shedding an outer layer, as a snakeskin or a carapace. Based on **duein,* to put on; prefixed *ek-,* of, from (here indicating "the opposite of").]

Echoes   A common nickname in the ethnic slums of early XX, usu. in combination with a first name, as in *Joe Echoes, Sam Echoes,*

Eddie the Echo. [Because in the patois mixture of ancestral tongue and Am. that was spoken by many ethnic groups, there was a marked tendency to repeat opening constructions at the end of a sentence. *I told him it was no good, I told him. Ya gotta remember who ya dealing with, ya gotta. He gives me a bad time, he gives me.* The tendency was common to many, but with some it was a fixed speech trait, and it was these obsessive repeaters who were nicknamed *Echoes* or *the Echo.*]

economy   The basic sense, now with many extensions and variations, is "the prudent management of one's resources." [Ult. < Gk. *oikos,* house; *nemein,* to manage → *oikonomia,* management of a house, of an estate. L. *oeconomia.* OF *economie.*]

ecstasy   Rapturous delight. [But root sense is "madness." < Gk. *ekstasis* (STASIS, STATUS), out of one's place/condition, i.e., "out of one's senses." Ult. < IE *sta-,* stand, standing, to exist in place.]

egg money   Money from the sale of eggs. By Am. farm tradition, the farm wife's prerogative for small expenditures because she traditionally tends the hens. Hence, pin money. [In full, *butter and egg money* (which see), because she churned too, the money from the sale of butter also being, traditionally, hers to keep.]

eh?   Ques. How does one say in Yiddish: "I did not understand what you just said; would you repeat it, please, more slowly?" Ans. "Eh?"

eight   [IE *okto,* eight (OCTAGON). With k/h in Gmnc. OE *eahta,* ME *eighte,* eight.] The cardinal number between 7 and 9. Arabic 8. Roman VIII.
    behind the eight ball In a bad situation. Snookered. Stymied. [In many games of pocket pool the eight ball is the final object and one loses if one sinks it out of turn. Usually in such games, the balls must be sunk in numerical order, or one must first strike the ball next in order or lose his turn. If one is behind the eight ball he has no clear shot at his object ball, and may be in danger of sinking the eight ball out of order, thereby losing the game.]
    piece of eight A Spanish silver coin, closely corresponding to the later U.S. silver dollar. It was so called because it was stamped with a large Arabic 8 to signify a value of eight Spanish *reals.* Pieces of eight became legendary in stories of pirate treasure. They were in common use in the American colonies, and were often cut into quarters and halves for small change. See *bits.*

straight eight 1. An automobile engine with eight cylinders in line. 2. An automobile with such an engine. **V-eight** The same with the cylinders arranged in two rows of four at an equal inclination to a central shaft.

elbow [IE *el-*, forearm, elbow; *bheug-* to bend, to bow, to curve. Via Gmnc. → OE *elnboga*, forearm bending point. ME *elbowe*.] 1. The central joint of the arm. 2. *Ext.* Any device with a right-angle bend, as a road curve, a pipe fitting, a variety of pasta. —*v.* To jostle, thrusting with one's elbow.

elbow grease Hard work, esp. in rubbing and scrubbing. [Folk fanciful: nothing polishes better than this grease. In use by at least late XVII with a precedent in Fr. *huile de bras,* arm oil.] *elbow room* Uncrowded space. Room enough to bend an elbow without being crowded. [In use by mid XVI.] *bend an elbow* To drink alcoholic beverages. [From the act of bending the elbow in raising a glass to one's lips. As an inspired word play based on this idiom and the preceding, a chain of midwestern cocktail lounges calls each of its branches The Elbow Room.] *rub elbows with* To hob-nob. [As at stand-up-and-shout cocktail parties in which the human sardines are arranged elbow to elbow. Hence, "on intimate terms."]

electric 1. Pertaining to any of the forms of electricity. 2. *Metaphoric ext.* Emotionally charged. *an air electric with excitement.* [It seems a long way from *electron* to *amber,* yet it is the concept that has changed rather than the form of the word. < Gk. *elektron,* amber. Because the first man-made form of (static) electricity was produced by rubbing amber, esp. with wool.]

eleven Arabic 11, Roman XI. [Root sense: "one left over after ten." IE *oino-*, one → Gmnc. *ain-* → OE *end-*, which suffixed *-leofan*, left over → *endleofan*, (ten and) one left over. ME *enlevene, elle-vene*. And so, too, OE *twelf*, twelve, which is Gmnc. *twa*, two, suffixed *-lf*, an extremely contracted form of *leofan*.]

eleventh hour The last moment. [Based on the idea "last hour of the day," *twelfth hour* would seem more accurate, but *eleventh* was Biblically set in the parable of the workers in the vineyard (Matthew 20), in which the owner of the vineyard hires workers at the beginning of the twelve-hour day, promising each a penny. Returning at the third, sixth, and ninth hours, he hires more workers, promising to pay "whatsoever is right"; and still others at

the eleventh hour, with the same promise. At the end of the day
he pays each man a penny (parable of Christ's gift of grace), and
when the first-hired complain, the owner defends his action, saying: "So the last shall be first, and the first last: for many be called,
but few chosen." Eleventh, therefore, is the last hour at which
the generous owner could hire men for any semblance of a day's
work. (And yet, in terms of the parable of grace, there is still
the twelfth hour, and even the last minute of the twelfth hour,
in which to plead for Christ's grace and, in pleading, to receive
it: "ask and it shall be granted unto you." In any case, the sermon
has more or less faded from the idiom, the one sense functioning
as given.]

eliminate   1. To remove, do away with, get rid of. *The pocket computer has all but eliminated simple training in math.* 2. To knock
out of a competition. *eliminated in the quarter finals.* 3. To excrete.
to eliminate from one's system. [Root sense: "to put outside the
threshold." < L. *e(x)-*, out of; *limen,* threshold. "Please eliminate
the cat" is hardly standard English, yet it means, at root: "Please
put the cat out," i.e., across the threshold.]

emeritus   Plu. *emeriti* An adj. but often used as a noun. (See *paregoric,*
originally *paregoric elixir* but now a noun as *paregoric.*) *So professor emeritus* → *an emeritus.* Specific to academics, a professor (dean,
president) who upon retirement retains the title of his tenure by
formal order of his college and under the same authority by which
it confers degrees. [L. *ex-*, of, out of, from; *merēre, merēri,* to merit
→ *ēmerēri,* to merit by right of service; p.p. *ēmerītus.*]

end: bitter end   The last extremity of hostility or affliction. *to the
bitter end* Unyieldingly. To the last limit of endurance. [Proverbs
5:4: "But her end is bitter as wormwood." But in a specimen example of two distinct but converging sources, equally from nautical
English *bitt, bitts,* (a) stout inboard post(s) to which a ship's cable
was attached, the last inboard length of the cable being called
the bitter end. A ship riding out a storm with all her cable payed
out had no more room for maneuver and was said to be at her
bitter end.
   Since this last length remained inboard, it was not submerged
in salt water, and was even partly protected from the weather.
It remained, therefore, in better condition than the rest of the
cable, whence the common variant (and so Defoe) *better end.*
Obviously, however, the sense "last extremity" is not well ex-

pressed by "better end," and perh. with the reinforcement of the Biblical usage, *bitter* has become the fixed idiom.]

endorse/indorse   1. To validate a check by putting one's signature on the back (thereby pledging personal assets for the amount of the check). 2. To cosign a monetary note, not necessarily on the back. 3. To vouch for: to lend the support of one's name and reputation in pledge for a cause or candidate. *I endorse Edward Kennedy as the oblivion candidate.* [The sense shift can, perhaps, best be measured by citing Milton's Latinate reference to howdahs in an Oriental procession: "elephants endorsed with towers." < L. *dorsum*, back; *en-*, on. To endorse a check is to sign *on the back*, though the endorsement is generally understood to be the *signature itself* rather than its placement. This sense shift occurred in XVI Eng.]

enthusiasm   Intense interest and eagerness for. Zeal. [Root sense: "God seizure," i.e., the condition of being possessed by a god. < Gk. *enthousiasmos*, inspiration < *en-*, in; *theos*, god; the effective sense being "god-possessed." The idea of having one's identity (one's body and personality) taken over by another being is now a science fiction theme. Among earlier men, however, spirit seizure involved all sorts of magical protective practices.]

-eroo   Am. slang suffix as an intensive *(he's a real stinkeroo)* or intimate knowledge *(watch it: here comes the old switcheroo* = watch it, here comes the critical trick (that I know all about). [Based on the Sp. agential suffix *-ero*, as in *vaquero*, cowboy < *vaca*, cow; *-ero*, one who has to do with.]

erotica   Any collection of sexually stimulating writings or objects, esp. the word booksellers use to classify what my neighbor calls "dirty books." *In my sectarianism, Oscar, women are the only true erotica.* [< Eros, the Greek god of love, said to be the most beautiful of the gods. He was the son of Aphrodite and Hermes (or, variantly, of Ares). In his manifestation as the precocious infant who shot arrows of love into the hearts of humankind (and even of the gods) he was known to the Romans as *Cupido* (< *cupīdō*, desire. CUPIDITY), whence Cupid.]

escape   *v.* 1. To break loose, as from confinement, peril, danger of capture. [The root image is of running right out of one's clothes after they have been seized by a pursuer. < L. *ex-*, out of; *cappa*, cape, cloak.] But, 2. To elude. *to escape notice.* [And this sense, far from the root image, should be rendered *to elude*, though this reduced sense of *escape* is now about standard.] —*n.* The act of breaking loose or of eluding. —*adj.* Providing freedom from. *escape hatch, escape literature.*

esoteric Unusual. *Raffiné.* For those of special tastes only. [Root sense: "for the initiates of a religious mystery." < Gk. *hesōteros,* within; *hesō* (comparative), more deeply within. In the Greek Testament 1 Corinthians 5:12, *hoi hesō* was used for "those within the received faith," i.e., Christians. The antonym (2 Corinthians 4:16) is *ho hexō anthrōpos,* the exoteric man ("man outside the faith"), i.e., pagan. (See *pagan, heathen.*) Nothing in current Am. usage approximates the root sense; and the word is often confused with *exotic,* which is "foreign" (also from *hexō,* but with the sense "not of our sort, an outside thing.")]

essay The more or less academic name for a short prose exposition of the sort known to publishers as an article or a piece. [But earlier, with root sense *to essay,* to attempt, an attempt. As the name of a sort of writing it originally implied a modest disclaimer that the work was rather less than a full treatise. Francis Bacon was the first to call a collection of writings *Essays,* 1597. Of his pieces he wrote: "certain brief notes . . . I have called *Essays."* The word is late, but the thing is ancient.]

ethnic Of a tribe or nation related by language, customs, religion, and, given many variations, a more or less common genetic pool. But a Janus word that can mean either "of our kind" or "of their (other) kind." **ethnics** In sociological jargon, members of a minority ethnic group. [IE *seu-, se-,* his, their, is the base of all such third-person reflexive pronouns as L. *sui,* It. *suo,* Fr. *se,* etc. Variant IE root *su-,* suffixed *-edh-no-* → Gk. *ethnos,* like one another, of a kind, hence "of a related group," but connoting "of that other kind (not ours)"; and so Gk. *ethnikos,* of a (foreign) people. Hebrew *goyim,* the gentiles, is rendered in the Greek Testament *ta ethnē,* lit. "the ethnic," in effect, "of that other kind." And so Udall, 1545: "An athnike and a pagane king."]

excelsior Shredded wood, originally used as mattress stuffing; later, commonly as padding in packing crates, and now variously (see letter below). [L. *excelsior,* higher, comparative of *excelsus,* high. In the Great Seal of the State of New York, *Excelsior* functions

as an imperative: "Yet higher, ever higher." The motto was borrowed into the name of the Excelsior Mattress Co., then became
the name of the stuffing used by the company. OED cites U.S.
Patent No. 75728 (1868): "A machine for manufacturing that article of commerce called 'excelsior' for filling mattresses." Since
the "article" existed before the machine so patented, the earlier
stuffing probably consisted of wood shavings from lumber mills.
I do not know when excelsior passed out of use as mattress stuffing,
but up to c. 1935 and the proliferation of synthetic packing materials, excelsior was the commonest packing material for shipping
crates.

HISTORIC. I have not seen excelsior for many years, and had
assumed it was no longer being manufactured. Recently, however,
I learned that there is an American Excelsior Co. in Arlington,
Texas, and its vice-president, W. E. Johnson, writes me:

> American Excelsior Company was founded in 1888 to manufacture
> curled shavings for packing material or mattress stuffing, perhaps for
> the Excelsior Mattress Company. Our sales and company continue to
> grow each year, and the primary uses of excelsior have gone far beyond
> mattress stuffing. The greatest use today is as a fiber that is mixed with
> a binding agent to produce structural board . . . [for] ceilings. Excelsior
> is used extensively as an erosion control material, by Highway Depart-
> ments to stabilize banks along cut and fill roads . . . as the cooling
> medium (when air is drawn through a wet excelsior pad) in evaporative
> coolers . . . also as filler in caskets, in poultry nests, and is probably
> the best material that can be used in archery targets.

exception proves the rule   See *proves.*

excruciating   Intense. Originally with ref. to agony, as *this excruciating headache;* but extended to any sort of intensity, as *the show
was excruciatingly funny;* or in simple reply to the question "How
were the comedians?" one may simply say, "Excruciating!" [But
the root sense, all pain, is: "to crucify." < L. *ex-*, functions as an
intensive; *cruciare,* to crucify, (but with generalized sense) to torture. Ult. < *crux,* cross.]

expend   To spend; originally, money; by ext. anything, as effort, time,
emotion. "An expense of spirit and a waste of shame."—Shakespeare. [Root sense: "to weigh out (money)." And payment by
weight, revived in XIX Am. mining camps, was once common
in the early days of imprecise (and later of clipped) coinage. <

L. *ex-*, out, out of; *pendere,* to weigh (PENDULUM, PONDEROUS, POUND).]

exquisite   *adj.* 1. Of rare esthetic perfection. *an exquisite cadenza/ vista/sense of design.* 2. *Loose ext.* Intense. *an exquisite pain.* —*n. Obsolete.* A fop. (English foppery was largely based on an imitation of Italian manners, dress, and affectation. By XVI it had become established tradition for young British gentlemen to go on the grand tour of the Continent, with a protracted stay in Italy. Returning with an Italian wardrobe and a full range of Italian-ate affectations, the young fops were successively called: macaronis (XVI); fantastics (XVII); enthusiasts, exquisites (XVIII). [< L. *exquisitus,* choice, chosen; p.p. of *exquirere,* to search out. Fr. *recherché* is an exact synonym of the root sense.]

fancy   [Ult. < *fantasy* by way of ME *fantsy*, at root "the ability to project mental images" < Gk. *phanein*, to show, and intermediately *phantazein*, to make appear. In Milton it is the highest quality after reason itself. So *Par. Lost*, V, 100–106:

> . . . But know that in the soul
> Are many lesser faculties that serve
> Reason as chief; among these Fancy next
> Her office holds; of all external things,
> Which the five watchful senses represent,
> She forms imaginations, airy shapes,
> Which Reason joining or disjoining, frames . . .

Dickens, esp. in *Hard Times*, intends by it all the good and graceful impulses of warm human sensibility, as opposed to the sterility of Mr. Gradgrind and his School of Hard Facts. Yet in the interim since Dickens, the word has lost its equivalence to "imagination" and has acquired a lesser, and even pejorative, meaning. That decline prob. began with such Brit. colloq. expressions as: *I fancy it is,* I imagine (but do not know for certain) that it is; *fancy that,* imagine (let your imagination play on) that; *take a fancy to,* to be more or less whimsically attracted to.] *In Am.* 1. Ornate. *fancy scrollwork.* 2. Overly ornate. *city slickers and their fancy clothes.* 3. Flashy but unreliable. *Judith Ciardi and that ex-fancy man she married.* 4. *In merchandising and slang only.* Choice. *fancy fruit and produce; that's some fancy car.*

    fancy Dan 1. A flashy dude. 2. A boxer who is all ballet dancer and no punch. [*Dan* is a generic, prob. based on earlier *fancy man,* a dude, and prob. influ. by *Dan Cupid* (which see), the fanciest boy.]

    fancy-schmancy/fantzy-schmantzy [Yiddish-Am. patois. In Yiddish, reduplication tends to express scorn. Perh. no expression serves better to show how low the word has fallen since its exaltation by Milton and Dickens.] A generalized pejorative. Hoity-toity.

faro The most popular XIX Am. casino game. In it, the players bet against the dealer on the cards that will be turned up from the shoe or "tiger" (and many of the Am. idioms based on *tiger* are based on faro). [A simplified spelling of *pharaoh,* so called because in a faro deck, kings are represented by pharaohs.]

farrago A hodgepodge of inferior stuff. [IE *bhares-,* grain (BARLEY). With bh/f in Latin by Grimm's Law → *farr-* → *farrago,* mixed grain, cattle mash (FARINA).]

fast and loose Irresponsible, esp. with money, esp. with someone else's. *He has been playing fast and loose with company funds.* He has been running through company money. [The ref. is to a medieval street fair swindle; the root sense not, as commonly assumed, "rapid and easy," but "bound and unbound." The swindler doubled a leather thong and made a circle of it on a table in which holes were drilled. The sucker, placing pegs in holes, bet that the pegs would be *fast* (encircled by the thong) or *loose* (not inside the loop) when the thong was drawn tight. Since the showman could manipulate the doubled thong at his pleasure, to play the game with him meant to lose one's money. The game has long since disappeared (it was called *prick the garter* in XVI), but the sense "to make money disappear/to run through money" has remained.]

fastidious Meticulous. Demanding. Overcritical. Difficult to please. [But at root: "squeamish, easily moved to disgust." < L. *fastus,* disdain; *fastīdiōsus,* a sense of loathing. The root sense is expressed exactly in It. *non darmi fastidio,* do not make trouble for me (lit. "do not move me to revulsion").]

feather [IE *pet-,* flying, to fly. (In zero-grade form *pt-* and suffixed *-r-* → Gk. *pterodactyl,* lit., flying finger; though the word is English but compounded of Gk. roots.) With p/f, t/th, and suffixed *-r-* in Gmnc. → OE *fether,* feather.] *n.* 1. The outer covering of birds. Plumage. 2. Ornate human dress. *in fine feather,* gaily clad. 3. An inconsequential thing. 4. A least clue. *a feather in the wind.* —*v.* 1. *Rowing.* To turn the blade parallel to the water on the backstroke. 2. *Multiengine aviation.* When shutting off an engine in flight, to turn the edges of the props till they are vertical to the air flow. [The props, ungoverned by the engine, would otherwise windmill, spinning faster and faster, often to such a velocity that the heat of friction melts the propeller shaft, the windmilling prop pulling it forward like taffy, and often breaking off unpredictably, sometimes scything into the body of the plane.]

featherbed n. A bed made of a tick stuffed with goose down. ["Feather" is a misnomer since the quills of feathers would stick through the cloth of the tick. Good featherbeds were made exclusively of down. A farm wife might spend many years collecting enough down for a good bed, and such beds became both symbols of luxury and family heirlooms frequently mentioned in wills. Shakespeare's bequest of his "second-best bed" was almost certainly a reference to a featherbed. It was "second-best" probably because some feathers were mixed in with the down.] —*v. Union-industry relations.* To overstaff a work assignment by contractual agreement in order to provide more jobs, though some of the workers are simply in attendance, with little or nothing to do. [As if lying about on a featherbed.]

a feather in one's cap A mark of distinction. An honor won. [The idiom entered English in XVI when a traveler in Hungary wrote: "It hath been an ancient custom among them that none should wear a feather but he who had killed a Turk." But the warrior custom of wearing feathers to indicate an enemy killed or a battle fought is immemorial and worldwide, though perhaps best known to us in the use of feathers by Amerind braves.]

feather one's nest Make comfortable provision for oneself.

featherweight 1. A boxer (now also wrestler) in the 118–127 pound class. 2. An insignificant person.

show the white feather Show cowardice. Turn and run. [Cockfighters believe that any gamecock with so much as a single white feather is no fighter. Trainers have been known to clip stray white feathers from a bird or to dye them. But the cowardice, real or alleged, remains. The white feather is not, therefore, a visible thing, but a character trait, a flaw of breeding. In cock or man it becomes visible in the act of turning and running.]

fee 1. Payment for discrete services, as distinct from salary or wages for continuous employment. 2. Payment for the exercise of a right. *license fee.* 3. *Legal.* The legal right to property. *fee simple* Unrestricted title to a property. [Like *pecuniary* < IE *peku-*, wealth expressed in herds, esp. in heads of cattle. (This form of wealth is still the standard in parts of Africa. When metal first became established as a medium of exchange, bars of silver or gold were commonly stamped with a cattle head, and the same symbol was common on early coins.) *Peku-* with p/f in Grmnc. → *fe(ku)-* → Frankish and OF *fe, fief,* hereditary landholding. And note ME *fee house,* which meant both "treasury" and "cattle shed."]

fee splitting In referring a case to a professional colleague, the practice of taking a percentage of the fee he charges. In law and medicine the practice is commonly held to be unethical. **retaining fee** (So in Brit.) In Am. **retainer** A fee paid on engaging a professional, esp. a lawyer, and legally establishing one's right to demand his services. (A lawyer who has accepted a retainer must generally secure his client's permission to return it or to transfer it to another lawyer, who agrees to represent the client. If the client will not release the lawyer, the lawyer remains bound to serve the client.)

feisty [Root sense: "farty," but see below. Born in New England, I first heard this word when my Missouri-born wife described someone as "fat and feisty." I have since heard it in Oregon, Colorado, Michigan, Pennsylvania, and the South. AHD classifies it as *regional,* but what region is that? (Prob. the Accelerated Mobility Belt.) NWD is wrong in marking it as an Americanism. OED lists it only in the *Supplement* and then as a variant of *fist,* to fart; which is IE *peiz-,* to blow, to pass wind. Suffixed *-d-* → L. *pedere,* to fart (PETARD). IE *peiz-* with p/f in Gmnc. → *fis-* → OE *fistan,* ME *fisten,* to fart, which became obs. in standard Brit. c. 1650.

But in some variant Gmnc. form cognate with Du. *vijst* → Sc. *feist,* curiously defined by Jamieson, *Dictionary of the Scottish Language,* as, "The act of breaking wind in a suppressed manner from behind." And so in Lancashire dial., but in East Anglia with the sense: "a closed in smell, fustiness, mildew." Also akin to Sc. *fissle* (FIZZLE), a sustained low sound.

I cannot find the dial. source of *feist* in the sense "small mongrel dog," but if the low sound is taken to be its growl, the two senses current in Am. use follow, both implying brisk bubbling energy, but in two different modes:] 1. Lively. Frisky. Raring to go. Full of beans (and sputtering some of them). 2. Irascible. Crotchety. Spoiling for a fight.

fellow [Root sense: "one who puts down money (as in paying for drink or food); one who stands treat." OE *fēolaga,* companion < *fē,* fee (money); *lag,* to lay down, a laying down. ME *felawa.*] 1. *Now, in common colloq.* A male companion. A chum. A guy. *one of the fellows (fellers).* 2. *But earlier.* A companion of similar caste, inclination, commitment (of either sex). "The virgins that be her fellows shall bear her company." —Psalms 45:14. 3. A member of a learned society, or a recipient of a grant for study ("one on a fellowship"). 4. One of a pair. *the fellow to this glove.* (This usage primarily Brit.; Am. tends to use "mate.") 5. *Colloq.* A boyfriend. *Mazie is out with her fellow.* 6. (Brit. only and more or less obs.) A low person. —*adj.* Sharing in common. *fellow man, fellow feeling, fellow worker.*

fellow in Christ A Christian cobeliever. *fellow traveler* 1. A traveling companion. *But primarily,* 2. A crypto-Communist. One who does not openly declare himself to be a member of the Communist Party, but who shares its beliefs and aids its work. *regular fellow/reglar feller* An average nondescript joe. One of the boys. *fellowship* 1. Convivial company. 2. The congregation of a particular faith. 3. A group organized for a particular purpose. 4. An appointment to a learned society. 5. A grant-in-aid for scholarship, travel, work in the arts, research.

felt   A heavy fabric compacted from wool, fur, hair, and other fibers by soaking, filling, heating, kneading, and beating. (The heavier and stiffer felts used in hats were similarly worked on a base of animal hides, usu. rabbit or beaver, treated with mercury.) [IE *pel-, peldo-,* pelt. With p/f in Gmnc. → OE *felt,* a pelt.]

HISTORIC. According to pious legend, felt was invented by St. Clement. Forced to flee Rome in the first century A.D., he suffered blistered feet, and to ease them he padded his sandals with balls of wool, noticing later that the sweating and kneading of his feet, along with road dust as filler, had worked the wool into a heavy but still pliable fabric. [Felt in Latin is *coactum* < *coactare,* to compel, hence, "substance forced (by being worked on)."]

Clement is said to have introduced felting as an early Christian cottage industry. He later became Clement I, the fourth pope (A.D. 92–101), though probably for other reasons, but he is still the patron saint of hatters.

fend/fender   [ME *defenden,* to defend, also occurs in the contracted form *fenden.*] Root sense: "Defender. To defend." *fend off* To defend by thrusting away some threatening thing. *fend for oneself* To protect oneself from want without assistance.

fender 1. *Can mean.* One who fends. 2. *But primary Am. sense.* The curved metal shield over the upper part of an automobile wheel. ["Defends" against water and mud thrown by the wheel.] 3. *And also.* A metal fireplace strip. ["Defends" against the spilling of hot coals on the floor.]

fender bender 1. A minor automobile accident. 2. *Agential.* A poor driver. [One who regularly bends his fenders.] *play wrin-*

kle-fender To weave aggressively through traffic, cutting so close to other cars that wrinkled (bent) fenders seem inevitable.

fetish [Root sense, with ref. to the arts of primitive magic: "made thing." < L. *facere,* to make (FACTITIOUS); artfully made (with "art" here implying "sorcery.")] 1. *In primitive magic.* Any object believed to have magical powers, esp. in warding off or summoning evil spirits. 2. *As a metaphor borrowed by psychologists.* Any object that attracts compulsive and excessive attention from a person or a cult. *fetishism* An emotional fixation, esp. an erotic obsession with some object not in itself markedly sexual. So *foot fetishism* (Also, by transfer) *shoe fetishism* An obsessive attraction to feet (shoes) as sexual stimuli. *make a fetish of* To be obsessively attracted to; to be compelled by.

fey *adj.* Seemingly under a spell of doom. [Sc. *fey,* doomed, touched by impending death. Often but wrongly confused with *fay,* which as a noun means "elf" and as an adjective "elfin, sprightly, charmed." Old superstition believed that as death drew near, otherworldly forces began to possess human beings, giving them clairvoyant powers. It was in this doomed sense that the *fey* person became enchanted, as distinct from the elfin powers of the *fay* person. This dark sense is a survival of the ult. IE root *peig-,* inimical, of malicious (black magic) intent. With p/f in Gmnc. → OE *faege,* fated to die; and then the common g/y shift from OE to Eng.]

fiasco An absurd failure. [< It. *far fiasco,* to make a flask, but in effect, to fail absurdly and utterly. The origin of the Italian idiom has been much guessed at but never resolved. The one certainty is that It. *fiasco* is not simply any bottle, but specifically a long-necked bottle with a rounded base (such as is commonly used for imported Chianti). Such *fiaschi* cannot stand upright until they are plaited with reeds that provide them with a flat base. Hence, the progression from "thing that cannot stand" → "thing that will surely fall over" → "project that will surely fail." Some annotators attribute the idiomatic sense to the fact that only an expert can blow such a bottle and that any nonexpert who attempts to will fail ridiculously (but as much could be said of any bottle or any glass-blowing project). Another attributes the idiomatic sense to the fact that a *fiasco* is nothing but a bubble of air. Others become more fanciful. On the assumption that when all is conjecture the simplest adequate explanation is the most likely, I lean to the round-bottomedness of the *fiasco* as the source of the idiomatic sense.]

fickle Flightily unreliable, of shifting affections. [The sense has softened considerably since IE *peik-*, evil, inimical. With p/f in Gmnc. → OE *ficol*, ME *fikel*, false, treacherous, inconstant. In feudal England the term tended to refer to betrayal of a liege lord by a sworn underling, a sin approaching sacrilege in the breaking of a solemnly sworn vow. By XIV the sense had become "inconstant," prob. still implying treacherous default, but since then the sense has moved away from "evil treachery" and toward "flighty inconstancy."] *fickle finger of fate* (See *finger.*)]

fiddle 1. What the violin becomes when it goes to Nashville. 2. More or less ornate nonsense. "things . . . more important than all this fiddle." —Marianne Moore. —*v.* 1. To play a violin country style. 2. To fidget and putter. *fiddle about* To putter at. *fiddle away (one's money/time)* To squander. [A word that has fiddled away its inheritance, a ref. to the obscure Italic goddess of victory and of rejoicing, Vitula; whence L. *vītulāri*, to celebrate a victory. Prob. into Gmnc. with v/f and t/th → OE *fithele*, ME *fidle*, fiddle (as the name of some primitive stringed instrument played with a bow, but nothing we would today call a violin). It must have been a crude and squeaky instrument that played the sense of the word from the arms of the triumphant goddess to mere fiddling about.] *fit as a fiddle* Vibrantly well. *play second fiddle* To be subservient to. *fiddlesticks Exclam.* Bosh. [Note that *violin bows* does not convey this sense. It is the phrasing of the title in the least dignified semantic terms that conveys the idea of nonsense.] *fiddle-faddle* The same pejorative sense. [Redupl. is a standard form of ridicule.]

   fiddle while Rome burns To be blithely frivolous in the face of an emergency. [Nero is supposed to have done so, but whatever his instrument, there were no violins in his day.]

fig [Gk. **sukon*, of untraced Mediterranean origin. (See *sycophant.*) The Gk. stem *suk-*, *syk-* with s/f → L. *ficus*.] 1. The tree and its fruit. 2. *By ancient association in Mediterranean usage.* The vulva.
   fig leaf A stylized carving of a fig leaf in lieu of (usu.) male genitalia on statuary; or sometimes a later appliqué on what was originally carved from nature. Also in paintings, but there usu. replaced by a stray fold of drapery. (In various periods of resurgent modesty, whole generations of stonecutters were kept busy carving

fig leaf addenda to the Greek and Roman genitals in the Vatican's enormous collection.) [The fig leaf, being common in Mediterranean countries, and of an appropriate size, was said to have been used by Adam and Eve to cover their suddenly shameful genitals after the fall from innocence. This legendary precedent, together with the resemblance of a split fig leaf to the labia, must be taken to explain the generalized Mediterranean usage of the fig (It. *fica*, vulva; *fico*, fig) as a female sex symbol.]

not worth a fig Worthless. [Once inevitably accompanied by, or at least implying, a snap of the fingers. So XVI *figge of Spaine*, a finger snap. So Fr. *faire la figue*, to snap one's fingers. So Elizabethan *a fig for, a figo for* (accompanied with a snap of the fingers), a formula of contemptuous dismissal. But though the finger snap is central, the sexual connotation of *fig/fica* cannot be ignored as a formula expressing contempt in a male-dominant society. (Cf. Brit. and Am. street slang, *not worth a cunt*, worthless.)

sign of the fig An ancient obscene gesture. (See *sycophant*.)

And as a converging evolution (rare in Am. but common in Brit.) *in full fig* All dressed up. [And so in XIX Brit. for human "glad rags," but in XVII with particular ref. to ornate panoply for horses. The form then, *feague*, is prob. akin to Du. *vegen*, Ger. *fegen*, to spruce up, to clean and polish. Whence ME *fager*, fair, of which the (hypothetical) verb form would be *fagen*, to make fair, to adorn, to embellish.

finagle To manage by trickery, sharp practice. *Judith Hostetter finagled me into (wholely) matrimony.* [Prob. altered < *fainague*, which the *English Dialect Dictionary* cites as being widespread by c. 1850 with the senses: 1. To cheat at cards. To renege. 2. To court and then abandon a woman without explanation and with no apparent reason. And though I know of no lexicographer who has cited the roots, the second element, *ague*, cannot fail to suggest Fr. *aigu, aigue*, sharp; and the first element, *fain*, Fr. *fine*, fine; suggesting a root sense "fine-sharp practice." (But ???)

Not listed in OED, prob. because considered to be colloq. Not listed in the various editions of Webster's till the 1930's and then glossed as "prob. respelling of Feinagel, Ger. mesmerist and whist expert of the Regency" (1812–1820). And the later form *finagle* and the sense "cardsharp" support this derivation. On the other hand, later editions of Webster's variously gloss the term as "origin unknown" or, again, with ref. to the elusive Feinagel. As the best available guess: based on dial. *fainague* but altered by association with *Feinagel*.]

fine Italian hand A form of elegantly precise and flowing penmanship developed by papal scribes druing the Renaissance. [Called in It. *cancelleresca,* of the (papal) chancellery < Late L. *cancellarus,* scribe, secretary < L. *cancella,* the latticed screen behind which secretaries worked. Some of the choicest type faces of XVI were developed in Italy and modeled on *cancelleresca.*

Not to be confused with *hand of steel in a velvet glove,* with ref. to subtle political intrigue, which was also an Italian Renaissance specialty.]

finger [IE *penkwe,* five. (With associated sense: "what a hand has five of.") With p/f and k/g in Gmnc. **fingraz* → OE *finger,* finger.] 1. A digit of the hand, usu. excluding the thumb. 2. Anything resembling a finger in being long and thin. *Finger Lakes, lady finger, fingerling.* 3. The width of the finger as a measure. *Give me three fingers of rye* = Pour rye into the glass to the width of three fingers.

finger food Snacks (as hot dogs, hamburgers, tacos, etc.) to be eaten out of hand.

the fickle finger of fate The vagaries of fortune conceived as bad. [Exuberant vulgar alliteration based on the idea of "up yours" for being "done in." And so:] **fucked by the fickle finger of fate** Done in by bad luck. Akin to **give one the finger** To dismiss with a gesture of contempt consisting of a clenched fist with one finger extended, signifying "up yours," or "fuck you—rudely." (See note on "sign of the fig" under *sycophant.*) **finger fuck** To use a finger as if it were a penis. And so: **social finger** *Arch vulgar.* The finger with which one "socializes" sexually. *Leggo! You're hurting my social finger and my girl won't like me.* **stink finger** A contemptuous epithet for a person. [Implies that he stands around with his finger up his ass.]

finger-lickin' good *Sthrn.* Said of food eaten out of hand (barbecued ribs, fried chicken, etc.) and so tasty that one licks every last bit from one's fingers. (Now more or less preempted as an advertising catch phrase by the Kentucky Colonel fried chicken franchise chain.)

burn one's fingers/get one's finger's burned To suffer for one's greed. [As if in snatching food from the fire and finding it too hot to handle.]

have a finger in the pie To have a share in a venture. [As if thereby entitled to stick in one's finger and lick the sweet filling that sticks. (Or to stick in your thumb, and pull out a plum, and say what you have to to IRS.)

point the finger at Accuse. *point the finger of suspicion* Calumniate. *put one's finger on* Locate. Identify. *put the finger on* Identify and accuse. Single out as the guilty one. So *finger man Criminal.* One who identifies the victim for robbery, murder, etc.

jump at the crook of one's finger To attend in servile response to one's least gesture. *wind around one's little finger* To bring to complete and abject subservience. *sticky fingers.* Descriptive of a thief. *at one's fingertips* Ready to hand.

to finger 1. To feel a fabric between thumb and fingers. 2. What a finger man (above) does. *finger through* To leaf through a book, as in skim reading.

finicky   Also *finnicky* And, primarily in Brit. *finnicking* Overly fastidious. Fussy. Hard to please. Hence, quick to find fault. [< XVI *finical,* tending to be overly fine. In XVII Brit. university slang, *finicking.* In XIX *finicky.* Prob. akin to MD *fijnkens,* neatly, precisely. *Jim Dickey woke the next morning feeling very Mickey Finnicky.*]

finnan haddie   Rarely *finnan haddock* Smoked haddock. [Earlier *findhorn haddock* < Findhorn, Scotland, a fishing port.]

five-and-ten   Variantly *five-and-dime* Before inflation, a department store in which all the merchandise was priced at either five or ten cents. Woolworth's was once, and strictly speaking, a five-and-ten, but such stores were once a national institution, there being many independent stores of this sort, and many chains other than Woolworth's.

flabbergast   To astonish; to render speechless with amazement. [*Flabbergasted* is listed in the *Annual Register,* London, 1772, as a newly fashionable bit of slang. (*Bored,* to suffer from ennui, was similarly listed.) A fanciful coinage and above all a fine expressive formation. Additionally, *flabber* is prob. < *flap,* and second element < *aghast.* Note that *flap* suvives as current slang for a quarrel, a to-do, a commotion.]

fleshpot   A pot for cooking meat. *the fleshpots* 1. Feasting. 2. Brothels. [Sense 2 is a late and untraced evolution, prob. by association with *pot,* belly, and *sins of the flesh.* The original sense is as in Exodus 16:3: "Would to God we had died . . . in . . . Egypt, when we sat by the flesh pots, and when we did eat bread to the full."]

fleshpot school (of painters) 1930's. Those who painted heavy, sensual nudes more or less in the manner of Picasso's period of monumental nudes.

Florida   Became the 27th state in 1845. Though it is the southeastern-most state, its northern panhandle strip extends westward into the Central Time Zone. [Not, as often asserted, < Sp. *tierra florida,* flowered/flowering land; but Sp. *pascua florida,* the flowering season (Easter), during which Spanish churches were decorated with enormous masses of flowers; because it was during the *pascua florida* that Ponce de León discovered the peninsula in 1513. (Exactly as Easter Island was named after the day of its discovery.)]

flummox   To bewilder, disconcert. *He has me flummoxed.* [Charles Dickens was prob. the first to use this form in English literature. Prob. < dial. of East Anglia **flummocks* to embarrass. But in related dials., to mangle. And as an adj. *flummocky,* slovenly.]

fly in the ointment   A small flaw that destroys a much larger good. (But increasingly with the extended sense:) Minor imperfection. *There is one fly in the ointment* = There is one problem we must resolve, one thing we must take care of. (As if the fly could be picked out and the ointment restored; whereas the force of the original is that one such blemish destroys the total good.) [And so Ecclesiastes 10:1: "Dead flies cause the ointment of the apothecary to send forth a stinking savour, so doth a little folly him that is in reputation for wisdom and honour."]

fly: Spanish fly   1. *Entomology.* The beetle cantharides, called blister beetle because its body fluid is a skin irritant. 2. *Slang.* An aphrodisiac powder made of the dried bodies of these beetles. [Origin and dating of the term are unknown, but it is a fixed language custom to name sexual practices and devices after a neighboring nation (cf. *French disease* for venereal disease). *Fly* was prob. influ. by Brit. slang *to be fly,* to be aware, to know what's what, to be in on the secret. Hence, with the likely root sense: "(the) Spanish secret (of how to win lady friends and influence pupils)." Cantharides, however, is not specific to Spain, but may be found through all Europe.]

focus   *n.* Point of convergence, as of rays, attention. —*v.* To converge; to cause to converge. ***bring into focus*** To make clear. [A logical but radical sense shift < L. **focus,* hearth ("point at which the

Roman family converged"). In It. the same root evolved to *fuoco*, fire, whence Fr. *feu.*]

foghorn Originally an animal horn blown with a low penetrating sound in fog to alert other vessels of the presence of one's ship; now a mechanical device for the same purpose. *Senator Foghorn* The type of the legislative windbag, his drone penetrating and repetitive, he himself in a mental fog with nothing to assert but his presence there. [A fanciful invention of Al Capp in his once popular comic strip *Li'l Abner,* which appeared from c. 1935 to c. 1975.]

folderol Nonsense. *Why publish such folderol?* [After the common, meaningless syllables sung in the refrains of many English folk songs, as *Fol-de-rol de-ray; fol-de-rol de-rah.*]

fool [Bag of wind. So L. *follis,* bellows. Ult. < IE *bhel-,* to blow. With standard shift of the voiced stop *bh-* to *f* in L. → stem *f'l-, follis* → OF *fol* (modern Fr. *fou*). But Sc. *fou,* drunk ("out of one's wits"). "We are na fou" (we are not drunk). —Burns.] *n.* 1. A court jester. 2. A witless person. 3. An obsessively silly person. *a fool for love.* 4. An outstandingly skillful person. *a flying fool.* [One willing and able to take on the impossible (which is foolish) and to carry it off skillfully (to the awe of observers).] And corresponding verb forms for sense 2.

    fool around To act aimlessly. *fool away (one's time/money)* To waste aimlessly. *fool with* To putter at. *refuse to fool with* Have nothing to do with. *foolhardy* Brash. Mindlessly daring. *foolproof* Secure against all hazards. *a fool and his money are soon parted* Old adage. (Variantly *are soon partied.*)

    foolscap A sheet of paper 13 × 16 inches, folding to 8 × 13, now called *legal size,* to distinguish it from *letter size* or common typewriter paper, which is 8½ × 11 inches. [Surviving documents on such paper show that it was watermarked with the belled cap of a court jester, a "fool's cap," and that watermark (still in use as part of the tradition of papermaking) is an evident source of the term. But this paper was originally imported from Italy, and is attested in early XVIII as *Genoa foolscap.* In It. such a sheet was called *un foglio capo,* a chief (large) sheet. If *foglio* is given an English plural as *foglios capo,* the resultant form is very close to *foolscap,* whereby one must conclude that the term derives from both the watermark and the It. name.]

    fool's errand A foregone labor. *fool's gold* 1. Iron pyrites. [Because it gleams like gold but is worthless.] 2. Any false lure. *fool's paradise* Any seemingly ideal condition that is certain to lead to unhappiness.

And see *April Fool.*

fornicate/fornicated *Architecture.* Arched. Vaulted. [Root sense: "built like an arched brick oven." And so: It. *forno,* oven. Based on IE *gwh'r-,* heat, hot. Via *(g)w'r,* with w/v/f, and suffixed *-n-* → L. *fornŭs, fornax, oven* (FURNACE). Then with sense shift to "arched construction of a brick oven." Then, because the Romans used the same sort of arched brickwork in the underground parts of great buildings, and because the poor and the prostitutes of Rome lived in such undergrounds c. the time of Christ, early Christian writers evolved the verb *fornicārī,* to frequent brothels. The whores of Pompeii worked in similar stone cribs.] *n.* **fornication.** —*v.* **to fornicate** To have sexual intercourse, esp. adulterously. What the upper classes do while the rabble is fucking.

forty acres and a mule Up to mid XIX, the basic farm unit. Thought to be as much land as a vigorous man and a good animal could work; and if the land needed clearing, as much as he could make fruitful in four or five years of the sweat of his prime time. As such, a motto from the American dream of a free man on his own land. Indentured servants were common in the colonies, men and women who had sold themselves to a term of virtual slavery as payment for their transatlantic crossing. For them, forty acres and a mule was a definition of the freedom they were working toward.

On Jan. 1, 1863, the same day on which Lincoln issued the Emancipation Proclamation, the Homestead Act went into effect. Its purpose was to encourage the settlement of western lands, which, being generally less fertile than those east of the Mississippi, were made available in quarter sections, thus raising the norm of the farm unit to 140 acres.

found Room and board. [Common until early XX, now rare. Usu. in the wage formula "*X* dollars a month and found" for farm hands, lumberjacks, and others who lived on the job. But also *how's the found?* = how are the (on the job) living accommodations? < Fr. *tout trouvé, et tout trouvé,* and all (the necessities of life to be) found (on the job).]

four corners of the earth The remotest points on earth. [In some sense related to the four cardinal points of the compass, but essentially based on the ancient belief that the world was flat, a belief that persisted until XVI sailors had circumnavigated it; and still sufficiently alive in early XVII to permit John Donne a point in the lines, "From the round earth's imagined corners, blow/ Your trumpets angels."]

fourflusher A poseur who makes large claims with nothing to support them. [Poker. *Flush,* a rather powerful hand consisting of five cards of the same suit. *Four-flush,* a hand containing four cards of the same suit. In draw poker a player holding a four-flush is generally well advised to draw to it in the hope of making a flush. If a player so draws, and failing to make the flush, bets his hand as if he had made it, he is bluffing. If the bluff works, he may think of himself as an excellent player. If, despite his bluff, he is called, he has nothing to show, and must think of himself as a bum caught with his hand in the cookie jar; and hence the pejorative sense of fourflusher in general usage: a person caught trying to work a stupid trick.]

four hundred Always with *the.* High society. [Coined in 1889 by society reporter Ward McAllister, who remarked that only 400 people qualified as New York society. Perhaps related to the fact that Mrs. Astor's NYC town house was built with a ballroom designed to accommodate 400, there being only that number worthy of an invitation. But if so, Mrs. A. raised her estimate in 1905 when she invited 800 (without expanding her ballroom).]

four-letter word An obscenity. [Because most of the Gmnc.-OE words for digestive and reproductive parts and processes are four letters long; and because the Norman Conquest established the view that such words are offensive whereas their Fr.-L. equivalents are acceptable. See *Shock Language.*]

fourth estate The press conceived as a social power in its ability to influence national opinion. [The three traditional estates of the realm were: the lords spiritual, the lords temporal, and commons. In an essay published in 1840, Carlyle declared that Edmund Burke, speaking in Parliament, had referred to the three estates and had then added: "but in the reporters' gallery yonder there sits a fourth estate more important far than all." And most have followed Carlyle in attributing the phrase to Burke; but he had spoken c. 1790 and Carlyle, writing fifty years later, may have misremembered, for no such phrase occurs in Burke's collected speeches. Whatever the fact of Carlyle's memory, the phrase first occurs in a piece published in 1828 by Thomas Babington Macaulay (1800–1859) with no attribution to Burke, who died in 1797.]

fracas   (In Am. the first *a* is pronounced as in *hay*.) A noisy confrontation. A set-to. A brawl. [< It. *fracasso*, which has the same meanings, but is of uncertain origin. Perh. < L. *frangere*, to break, perh. an unattested Medieval L. past participle. *American Heritage Dictionary* suggests that it may be a telescoped form of *frangere* and L. *quassare*, to smash to pieces. Maybe.]

framis   Double-talk. *All I got from him was a lot of framis.* [Double-talk, a form of rapid, smoothly articulated, and well-modulated bafflegab with a normal syntax but with meaningless key words, has long been a popular specialty of comedians, and widely popularized in comic movies of the 1930's. The word (or rather the nonword) *framis* surfaced frequently in these comic routines; then, as Pinocchio turned into a real boy, *framis* turned into a real word by biting off its own comic nose and becoming a label for what it once was. "The endomylogical concurrence of framis-analysis integration is parietal to the *sui generis* transcendence of the implicit." —Fabrique du Jour, *Tergiversations*, trans. by John F. Nims.

frank   A many-tiered word, deriving in all its senses from the Franks, a Germanic tribe that conquered Gaul circa A.D. 500, establishing an empire from which France (named after them) evolved. [Ult. < Gmnc. *frank-*, javelin.] A proud and conquering people, the Franks practiced, or at least attributed to themselves, those traits of openness, honesty, and straightforwardness expressed by the adjective *frank*.

Under Frankish law, full freedom was only for the Franks themselves, but people who accepted them as their protectors could be **enfranchised** as free men.

In OF *franc* also meant "strong, free," and is so used in **frankincense**. [Because the stuff is volatile and the odor strong.]

The conquest of the Franks is obviously at the root of the place name **Frankfurt** [The ford of the Franks, place where the Franks crossed the river.] And so **frankfurter** Frankfurt sausage; now the American hot dog. So, too, in the given names **Frank, Francis, Frances,** and their many variants; in the **franc,** French coin and unit of currency. And in **franking privilege** [< *frank*, free.] The right to send a letter through the mail on one's signature, without paying postage. (It. *francobollo*, postage stamp, is a curiosity. <

Earlier *bola,* a seal in wax, franking a letter for delivery. Hence the root anomaly: "a free seal one pays for.")

Less obvious is the name *Franklin,* freeholder [< earlier *frankelien,* one who holds an estate in fee simple (free of liens)] and *lingua franca,* an international language ("language of free passage"). An evolution from the time when all cultivated Europeans had French as a common language.

free lance   A free agent, esp. a nonstaff writer who accepts commissions for special assignments. *to free-lance* To work in this way. (*Free* in the sense "not regularly attached." The point of free-lancing is, generally, to charge all that the traffic will bear.) [Originally, esp. after the Crusades (XI through XIII), a knight not in service to a feudal lord who offered his lance as a mercenary. In Italy from XIV to XVI war lords called *condottieri* organized bands of such knights sworn to them in at least temporary fealty, and, along with other troops, gathered mercenary armies for sale to the highest bidder. Cesare Borgia (see *Borgia*) died in Spain in early XVI, fighting as a free lance.]

French   The people and the language of France. [Gmnc. *frank-, frankon-,* javelin, spear, became the name of the tribe called the Franks, conquerors of Gaul circa A.D. 500. (See *frank.*) OE *frencise,* in which the *c* was originally a kappa but softened to *ch* before the soft vowel *i;* and so → ME *French.*]

In Eng. usage *French* is neutral with ref. to cookery *(French dressing, French fries)* and to arts and crafts *(French cuffs, French doors).* But in the common language pattern of assigning one's own worse traits to one's neighbor, *French* is commonly pejorative in Eng. and especially so in matters of sex, great licentiousness being associated with the French. So:

to French it, to engage in oral sex. *French disease* Venereal disease. *French kiss* A mouth-open, tongue-mingling kiss. *French safe* A condom. Despite the fact that the condom was invented in the XVIII by a British army officer (see *condom*). Similarly, *Frenchified Always used pejoratively.* In the French manner, i.e., mincingly, foppishly, overly sophisticated, lecherously, deceitfully, etc.

French leave Unannounced departure. [Because it was customary in XVIII French society to leave a party without saying goodbye to the host or hostess (who might already have left for the next party, at which one might meet them as guests). *take French leave* 1. To leave unannounced, especially without paying one's bill. 2. *Armed services.* To go over the hill. To decamp. To desert. To go AWOL. [The Eng. term is always pejorative, but as two can play the same game, the Fr. equivalent is *s'en filer à l'Anglaise,* to take English leave, i.e., to run up a bill for board and lodging and skip out without paying. In XVI Fr. *un Anglais,* an Englishman, had the effective sense: "one who skips out without paying his bill."]

frog   Derisive epithet for a Frenchman. [Commonly, but erroneously, said to derive from the fact that the French esteem frogs' legs (and properly so) as a choice food. The epithet, however, is based on the coat of arms of the French kings, the so-called lilies of France. The fleur-de-lis is, actually, a stylized iris. And in the Middle Ages, the forerunner of the royal shield was emblazoned not with "lilies" but with frogs rampant, prob. the heraldic bearing of some feudal lord of a marshy region. See diagram below. Cobham Brewer, *Dictionary of Phrase and Fable,* from whom the diagram is adapted, describes the device as "three toads erect saltant," and cites the fact that Nostradamus (XVI) called Frenchmen *crapauds,* toads, frogs, with reference to this heraldic device.]

fleur-de-lis   crapaud saltant

fuck   *v.* To copulate. —*n.* 1. A copulation. 2. A woman or a man conceived as a sex mechanism. *She/he is a good fuck.* **fucking** 1. *Adjectival or adverbial intensive. You're fucking well told:* You're damned well told. 2. *n.* Any act of being abused, cheated, shabbily treated. *The trouble with fucking is the fucking one gets.* [It is commonly argued that the Norman Conquest made this native Eng. form a taboo word. Thus one may say *fornicator* in a court of law or in a sermon, but not *fucker.* Yet though ME *fucken* is attested, which must certainly indicate a corresponding OE form, perhaps *fukkan, fokkan,* the word is not attested in OE, a lack that would indicate a reluctance to use the word in writing, which would in turn indicate that the word was taboo before the imposition upon the language of French attitudes.

That taboo may perhaps (?) reflect the surviving root senses of IE *peik-*, enmity, evil, malicious. With p/f in Gmnc. → unattested OE verb cognate with MD *fokken,* to beat against, penetrate, copulate. *Fickle* (which see) is from same IE base. Also *fey,* which is OE *faege,* fated to die (which may be the base of XVI slang *to die,* to have an orgasm).

Word magic was still a powerful survival among the Anglo-Saxons, and these dark root associations may have made the early British peoples uneasy about the word for reasons that had nothing to do with propriety.]

fun [ME *fon, fonne,* fool, clown; *funnen,* to poke fun at. Of uncertain dial. origin. (And so surviving Am. sthrn. regional, *we was just funnin'.*) Johnson (1755) dismisses *fun* as "a low cant term," but he never had much.] 1. Amusement. Merrymaking. 2. Noisy children's play. —*adj.* Amusing. *We had a fun party. It's a fun thing.* [A recent excrescence. The language process here is natural and even perhaps inevitable. But why does it grate on my ear? Maybe because I've never had any fun with people who talk this way.]

funky *In Creole Negro.* Smelly, mildewed, smoky (as a smoked ham). [Prob. < Creole *funkier,* to smoke (as a ham). Perh. < Fr. *fumer,* to smoke; but poss. from a yet untraced West African root via Afro-Carib-Creole pidgin.] Sidney Bechet once explained to me that c. 1900 *funky* had the sense "back on the plantation," and *funky jazz* now labels primitive (back on the plantation) pre-Dixieland jazz. *In art criticism (already obsolete or obsolescent).* The work of more or less trained artists who pretend to be primitives. *In mod slang.* Term of general approval. *We had a real funky time* = the current equivalent of 1920's "It was swell-elegant peacherino."

funny (See *fun.*) *adj.* 1. Amusing. 2. Queer. Odd. Peculiar. (And so the common Am. phrasing: *Do you mean funny-peculiar or funny-haha?*) The sense "peculiar" functions in *There's something funny going on* (and I don't like it). *There's something funny about him* (that I distrust).

funny bone 1. A point near the elbow at which pressure or a blow can force a nerve against bone, causing a numb tingling. 2. *Ext.* A sense of humor. *tickle one's funny bone* To make one laugh. (I have never found an explanation for this idiom. What's funny about the so-called funny bone?)

funny business Something suspect. *funny money Crim.* Counterfeit. *funny papers/funnies* Comic strips. *fun's fun but* I can take a joke as well as the next man, but it's time to be serious.

G

galaxy *Astronomy.* 1. A more or less discrete cluster of stars and luminous dust and gases. 2. With *the.* The cluster containing our sun; i.e., the Milky Way. *Metaphoric ext.* 3. Any large gathering of social luminaries. [The root ref. is to the Milky Way. < Gk. *galaxia kuklos,* milky circle (Gk. name of the Milky Way) < *gala,* milk; *kuklos,* circle. *Kuklos* is akin to Yiddish *kikl,* little circle. See *kike.*]

galleywest: to knock galleywest With ref. to a person, to deliver a stunning blow; with ref. to a thing, to smash to smithereens. [It is a fixed habit of lexicographers to refer this idiom to Brit. dialect *Colley West, Colley Weston, colleywest,* meaning "awry, bungled, all in a mess," explaining it as an eponymous tribute to some unidentified bumpkin who left a reputation as a bungler.

Galleywest, however, is an Americanism first attested in Mark Twain's *Life on the Mississippi,* and with so marked a difference in meaning as to suggest some other source. At the gratefully acknowledged suggestion of E. K. Liberatore of Ridgewood, N.J., I offer the following complicated and not fully attested, yet persuasive etymology based on maritime usage and the old sailors' game called "building the galleass."

< OF *galleass* < Old It. *galeaza,* a war galley with oars, two or three lateen-rigged sails, and a high sheer that allowed gunners to fire down (and to pour boiling pitch) upon the enemy's decks when at close quarters. In XVI and XVII the *galleass* dominated the Mediterranean. In 1571 at the battle of Lepanto, galleasses destroyed the Ottoman fleet, turning back a Turkish bid for the conquest of Europe.

In the sailors' game of "building the galleass," an off-duty watch chose a "builder," who had men stretch out on the deck, head to heel, to form a "keel." At right angles to them and in a sitting position on either side, he placed other men to serve as "ribs."

He then singled out one of the new hands, told him he looked like a lion of a fellow, and that no other would do as his figurehead. The victim was placed in the "prow" and made to lean forward, chin out, while the forward keel man held his ankles and the two forward ribs held his wrists behind him. The "buyer" then came forward to inspect the work and decided that the figurehead, though handsome, needed gilding, whereupon a confederate standing by with a mop dipped in a slop bucket smacked the victim in the face with the "gilding brush," knocking him galleass. The form *galleywest* may have been influenced by *colleywest*, though neither is attested before XIX. Or *galleywest* may have come about as a natural English modification of *galleass*.]

gallivant   Also *galivant/galavant.* To gad about in search of pleasure, esp. among the ladies. [Often referred to Fr. *gallant,* ladies' man; with *avant,* forward. Hence, "to go forth playing the gallant." But behind *gallant* is OF *galer,* to revel, to live festively (the sense not restricted to being a ladies' man). (GALA, REGALE.)

galluses   Suspenders for trousers. (Though the term is standard, it passes for dialect in modern Am., *suspenders* being the common term.) [The plu. form of *gallus,* earlier variant form of *gallows* ("what it all hangs from").]

galoot   Also, but rare in Am. *galloot.* And earlier *geloot.* A guy. A working stiff. An able-bodied lout. [Am. 1866, and into Brit. soon after. Partridge, *Slang,* refers the form *geloot* to Du. *gelubt,* eunuch. If it comes to simple cognate-snapping, I suggest that Du. *galoop,* the act of running about at random, might be more to the point. But neither is persuasive, especially since Dutch was not a natural influence upon mid XIX Am. Origin unknown.]

galore   In abundance; in profusion. [< Gaelic *go,* to; *leór,* utmost. This adjective always follows the noun it modifies. *girls galore, fun galore.* Common in the language of advertising and press agentry, but not to be found in the language of, say, Supreme Court decisions. Words of Irish-Gaelic origin are few in Eng. and are often glossed as substandard English (so *kibosh, shebang, blarney, shenanigans*). Can this reduced status be attributed to the long-established Brit. tendency to look down on things Irish?]

galoshes   (The sing. *galosh* is rare.) Waterproof overshoes. New light-weight overshoes are now often called rain boots. Galoshes are heavier than these. Before zippers, they latched well above the ankle with a row of metal clamps. In the 1930's it was a collegiate fad to wear them unbuckled and aflap. [Earlier, heavy work shoes that laced above the ankles. At origin the heavy thonged sandals of the Gauls, their thongs crisscrossed over wrappings that reached to midcalf, and called by the Romans *gallica solea,* Gaulish shoes. Late L. *gallicula* → OF and ME *galoches.*]

gamesmanship   The art of remaining one up on those one deals with without actually cheating. [Coined by Stephen Potter in his book *The Theory and Practice of Gamesmanship, or The Art of Winning Games Without Actually Cheating,* 1947. Obviously based on *sportsmanship,* the term has yet been influential in its own right (see *brinkmanship* as one derivative). And how can several of our leading dictionaries list the word without reference to Potter?]

gamin   A waif of the streets. [Fr. has *gamin* for a boy of the streets, *gamine* for a girl. Of unknown origin. Efforts to relate it to Gmnc. roots remain inconclusive. Brought into English by Thackeray, *Paris Sketch Book,* in 1840.]

gamut   The total range of experience or possibility. **run the gamut** To go through the whole range. *Calvin Coolidge ran the whole gamut of emotion from ho to hum.* [The early six-tone musical scale consisted of *ut, re, mi, fa, sol, la.* In XI Guido d'Arezzo extended it by adding a low G he called *gamma* after the Greek letter. This seven-tone scale (Guido's scale) became known as the *gamma-ut* and later *gamut* in much the same way that ABC stands for "alphabet." (Guido later added a tone he called *ela* at the top of the scale, thereby establishing the eight-tone scale.) The term fell out of musical usage and acquired its present sense in XVII.]

gandy dancer   A worker on the eastern stretch of the transcontinental railroad. (The western stretch was built by coolie labor; the eastern, primarily by Irish immigrants.) [*Gandy* after the track-laying tools which were manufactured by the now defunct Gandy Mfg. Co. of Chicago, and prominently marked with the company name; *dancer* after the rhythmic motions of long lines of laborers swinging their tools as if performing a tribal dance. A fossil poem.]

NOTE. The gandy dancers are memorialized in American folk music by a jig called "The Gandy Dancers' Ball," the chorus of which runs:

We danced on the ceiling
And we danced on the wall
At the gandy dancers' ball.

garbage   1. Refuse, esp. the discarded remnants of food. 2. *Ext.* Any
worthless and messy hodgepodge. *His arguments are sentimental
garbage.* 3. *Improper ext. but increasingly common in Am.* Any
trash, whether or not it contains discarded food. 4. *Whimsical.*
The fruit and vegetable garnishes of a cocktail. [ME *garbage,*
animal dung. Prob. via Norman Fr. < It. **garbuglio,* a mess.]

garden   Unless qualified by an adjective (as *vegetable garden*), a more
or less formally arranged plot of ornamental plants. [L. *hortus,*
cultivated land (HORTICULTURE). In Vulgar L. *hortus gardinus,*
cultivated plot inclosed (guarded) by a wall. (See *paradise,* at root
a *hortus gardinus*). The English word takes the name of the inclosure as the name of the thing inclosed.]
       garden spot   A loosely used term for any place located in
an attractive landscape. New Jersey officially designates itself the
Garden State with a double reference to itself as a garden spot
and to the fact that it was once a leader in truck gardening. *truck
gardening* The overlapping cultivation of seasonal vegetables to
be trucked to more or less local markets.
       lead one up the garden path   To deceive. To lead astray
by sweet enticements. [Perhaps influ. by *primrose path* (which
see), but the dating is surprisingly recent, the OED *Supplement's*
first attestation being dated 1926.] *Yes, I led Ruth up the garden
path, but she never let me pick any flowers.*

Garrison finish   *Am. sporting slang.* A victory won in a last-minute
surge. [Because Snapper Garrison, popular XIX jockey, was famous
for winning races by coming from behind in the stretch.] *Marriage,
my son, is the opposite of a Garrison finish.*

gas   [Coined by Dutch alchemist J. B. van Helmont (1577–1644) as
a metaphysical name for "the essence of a thing," i.e., its indwelling
spirit. *"Halitum ilum* Gas *vocavi, non longe a Chao veterum secre-
tum":* "I have called that spirit *gas,* as being not far removed
from the Chaos of the ancients." Gk. *chaos* was the unformed
(vaporous, gaseous) state of matter before the Creation gave solid
form to some of it, the rest remaining unformed but potential
matter, its metaphysical essence being in its potential for formal
existence.]

1. *Science*. Matter in a vaporous state. 2. *Common colloq. since the introduction of illuminating gas in early XIX*. Illuminating gas. *gaslight era* The period in XIX and into XX in which city streets were lighted by gas, lamplighters making the rounds at twilight to light the lamps, and again at dawn to turn them off. *take the gas pipe* To commit suicide by inhaling this asphyxiating gas. 3. Cooking gas. First introduced before WWI, the gas range all but eliminated the old wood and coal burning cook stove. Whence, to express powerfully effective action: *now you're cooking with gas*. And variant: *that's really putting it on the front burner*. 4. *From c. 1900*. Gasoline. [*Gas* with *-oline* < L. *oleum*, oil. And so the Am. form, but note Brit. *petrol* (< *petroleum*, rock oil), Fr. *essence*, and It. *benzina*, as each language reached for its own term for this new product.] *step on the gas* Hurry up. [Step on the accelerator, increasing the flow of gas to the engine.] 5. Lethal gas used for executions as in California. *get the gas chamber* To be sentenced to death.

And general forms: *just gassing* Just talking along in no particular order of discussion. [Exhaling hot air.] *gas bag* A pompous, long-winded person. In mod slang: *it's a gas* It is highly pleasurable. [From the habit of the sub-drug culture of inhaling various hallucinogenic vapors to achieve a euphoric mood. And so full circle from physical to mental chaos.]

gates of mercy: close the gates of mercy, shoot the wounded, and sink the lifeboats A standard phrase of rhetorical exuberance often heard in a friendly (i.e., nonprofessional) poker game when one of the players raises the permissable limit in order to drive the weak out of the pot and make the strong pay mercilessly for staying in the play. [*Gates of mercy* has a Biblical ring but does not occur in the Bible. (Psalms 118:19 has "gates of righteousness.") *Shoot the wounded:* once a common practice of partisans, especially among the Moors and Gypsies, who shot their own wounded to spare them torture if taken by the enemy, and to keep them from revealing secrets under torture. (In Hemingway's *For Whom the Bell Tolls*, one of the Gypsy leaders so shoots a wounded comrade.) *Sink the lifeboats:* in sea warfare, an unforgivable act. The appearance of this term in the rhetorical flourish may derive from Hun-atrocity stories of WWI.]

gazabo *Slang, originally sthwstrn.* A wise guy. A smart aleck. Also *a wise gazabo.* [Not to be confused with *gazebo*. *Gazabo* is < Mex. Sp. *gazapo*, a wise guy.]

gazebo   In Brit. a pavilion with a pleasant view. In Am. a screened-in outdoor sitting place, often with a view, but primarily for enjoying a summer breeze, or the hope of one. [An arch formation in which English *gaze* is joined to -*ebo,* a L. first-person-future suffix as in *videbo,* I shall see. I can find nothing to support the assertion in various editions of Webster's that the term may be "< an Oriental word." What word, gentlemen, in which language?]

geek   A side-show freak who caters to the boob taste for revulsion by biting off and eating the heads of live chickens and rats. [A piece of human refuse, usu. an alcoholic in the terminal stages of syphilis. His pay consists of cheap alcohol. Unable to speak coherently, and his coordination destroyed by drunkenness and disease, he twitches about making animal sounds, *geek* being not only an expressive involving speech muscles associated with the vomiting reflex, but a fair approximation of his dialogue. A geek is not an actor but a demented person exploited by another, who must necessarily be more demented, and a spectacle for yokels who must be more demented than both.]

geezer   Commonly *old geezer.* (Generally glossed as slang, and generally not in the pope's English vocabulary, but certainly a standard colloquialism by now.) A queer old gaffer, especially one with eccentrically antiquated views and manners. [Root sense: "a mummer." ME *giser,* a masquerader; *gisen,* to masquerade < OF *guise,* disguise, mask. All with ref. to the antics of people dressed for a masquerade or for carnival time. Hence, antic, eccentric, zany.]

gen-, gene-   This IE stem with the sense "to bear, to give birth to" underlies many seemingly unrelated English words.

    1. From the root via Graeco-Latin, words having to do with sexuality and procreation. *generation, gender, congenital, (pro)genitor, progeny.* As a special extension, (electrical) *generator,* but note also *to generate interest.*

    2. Via L. *gens,* clan, in the sense: "kinship unit." *gene, genus* (biological kinship unit), *general* (< L. *genera,* plu. of *genus*), *genetic, genealogy, congenial* and *genial* (being, at root, "of one's clan," hence, "approved of, of like views and manners, likable"), and *indigenous* ("of the clan," hence, "native").

    3. Via L. *gens* in the sense: "unit of social caste and political power." *gentry* ("members of the dominant caste"), *gentleman* and *gentlewoman* ("of the gentry"), *gentle* ("having the traits of the gentry"), *genteel* (once synonymous with *gentle* but now pejorative and applied to members of the aspirant middle classes who,

in attempting to ape gentle manners, overdo the imitation), **degeneracy** (the condition of having fallen from the standards of the *gens*). And as a special case, **gentile** ("member of one of those other clans"—see *ethnic*. Usually a non-Jew, but among Mormons a non-Mormon: Utah may be the only place in the world that instantly converts a Jew into a gentile).

4. Based on extended L. form *genius* with the senses *(a)* tutelary spirit of childbirth, **genie**, tutelary spirit (the form also influ. by Arabic *djinni*, with same sense, whence **djinn, djinni**); and *(b)* innate ability, whence, **genius, ingenuity, ingenuous, ingénue, engineer, engine.** (*Engine*, though now specific to mechanics, once meant simply "an ingenious contrivance." Othello refers to his cannons as "engines." John Webster in *The Dutchesse of Malfy*, c. 1612, has "Raised by that curious engine your right hand.")

5. Via the IE zero-grade form *gn-* and variously prefixed and suffixed. **benign** ("of good birth"), **malign** ("of bad birth"), **pregnant** ("before birth; before giving birth"), **cognate** ("of like birth").

6. Via the same stem altered *(g)na-a-* and suffixed *-t- →* L. *nascire*, to be born (the stem visible in the past participle *natus*, born). **connate** ("born with/together/at the same time"—and note that in an age dominated by astrology, to be born at the same time was to share the same zodiacal influences), **enate** ("born out of," hence, "related on the mother's side") **innate** ("in, i.c., from, birth"), **nativity, native, nature, naturalize** ("make native to").

7. IE *gen-, gene-* with g/k in Gmnc. **k'n- →* OE *kin*, kin; Ger. *Kind*, child. **kin, kind, kindly** (like *gentle*, has the root sense "having the manners of our kind"), **wunderkind.**

George   1. Masculine given name. [Ult. < Gk. *gēorgos*, tiller of the earth, farmer. < *gēos*, earth (GEOGRAPHY).] 2. As a once standard name for a Negro pullman porter and extended as a generic for any Negro serving man, is by association with George M. Pullman. (See historic note to *boogie-woogie*.)

let George do it Leave it to someone else. [Originally a common saying of Louis XII of France (misruled 1498–1515), who, incompetent in affairs of state, referred them to his prime minister, George Cardinal d'Amboise, a tireless and devious schemer who conspired to become pope and who snarled all state policy toward that ambition.]

Georgia cracker   Any native of Georgia conceived as a yokel with a high opinion of his own wit and merit. [From *wisecracker* <

wiseacre, which see. Localized to Georgia in late XVIII, but *cracker* had Brit. dial. precedent for "yokel," and reinforced in Am. by *cracker barrel,* an invariable feature of general stores, around which country locals commonly gathered to exchange verbal shots. The reasons for the localization to Georgia are not specifically traceable, but are of a piece with the general regional low opinion of people in the next region, as in the common sthrn. labeling of North Carolina as "a valley of ignorance between two mountains of conceit"—which manages to undercut three regions with one snip.]

gerrymander   (Pronounced *jerrymander.*) n. and *v.* In political trickery, to reshape electoral districts, esp. congressional districts, in a way to minimize the vote of the opposition party. [In perpetual tribute to Elbridge Gerry, 1744–1814, Madison's vice-president 1812–1814. In 1812, as the governor of Massachusetts, he redefined the state's voting districts to his own advantage. So intricate was his manipulation that the redrawn lines of Essex County moved one politician who studied the map to say it looked like a salamander rampant, whereupon another admirer of governmental artwork replied that it looked rather more like a *Gerrymander* or *Gerrymaunder.*]

gestalt   [Ger. *Gestalt,* shape, form < *gestalt,* p.p. of *stellen* (akin to STALL), to set in place.] *In psychology.* Configuration. The perception of a form as somewhat independent of its parts, or as more definite than its parts. (If one clearly prints *physcology* on a card, flashes it to a test group for an instant, and asks the group to write down the word, most will write *psychology* or *physiology,* registering not the word written but the familiar word pattern nearest to it.) **gestalt modification** As used in the etymological notes of this book, the alteration of an unusual word form into one more or less approximating it but more familiar. See *galleywest, hangnail, sea cook.*

gestation   1. The period between conception and delivery of an offspring. 2. *Ext.* The period between an original idea and the carrying out of a plan, scheme, project. [Root sense: "act of carrying on, waging, conducting." < L. **gerere,* to wage, to carry on; most commonly in the L. form *bellum gerere,* to wage war. And from p.p. *gestus* → GESTURE ("an action performed"), JEST (the obs. sense was "deed, exploit": BEAU GESTE), BELLIGERENT, INGEST.

ghetto   Now, esp. in Black English, a Negro or Hispanic inner-city slum. (Never, for example, Chinatown, and rarely Little Italy.) But originally a crowded section of a European city in which Jews were forced to live. (See historic note.) In questioning New Yorkers, especially those born since WWII, I was surprised to learn how few knew that the ghetto was once specific to Jews. In any case, both the now current and the original sense connote "ethnic slum" and "place in which one is forced to live against one's will." *golden ghetto* A city or suburban area of more or less imposing houses set aside for prosperous Jews. Under restrictive real estate covenants in force as late as the 1960's, real estate agents would not sell to Jews except in such areas. Some property conveyances, moreover, specified that the property could not be resold except to non-Jews.

[Though I can find no English dictionary that has not confused the case, the etymology of *ghetto* can be positively asserted: < L. *jactare,* to throw, to cast (as metal in a foundry) → Venetian dial. *geto,* foundry. The curious XVI church Latin form *ghectum* is intermediate to *geto* and L. *jactum,* thing cast. It was on the island that contained *il geto,* the Venetian foundry, that the first ghetto was established. (See historic note.)

Our lexicographers have been confused by the fact that the *g* in It. *geto* would normally be pronounced *dj,* and they have properly noted that *dj* does not evolve to a hard *g* in It., but they have failed to note that in Venetian dial. *geto* was, to begin with, pronounced with a hard *g.* Venetian *geto* was altered in XVI to It. *gheto* to bring the spelling into conformity with Italian practice; and altered again, almost at once, to *ghetto* under the influ. of *-etto,* the common dim. suffix.

Jewish scholars have further confused the etymology by referring *ghetto* to Hebrew *get,* divorce, explaining the root sense as "place of our divorcement." I have no doubt the ghetto Jews so rendered it in their Hebrew-Yiddish-Italian patois, but after the fact, the evolution having been firmly Italian. (Italian-American patois once rendered *'Mericano*—American—as *merda (di) cane,* dog shit, but without altering the etymological trace of Amerigo Vespucci.)]

HISTORIC. The Third Lateran Council (1179) forbade the faithful to lodge among the "infidel" but without declaring specific restrictions. The first formally decreed ghetto (and that only for certain classes of Jews) was established in Venice c. 1500 in the area around *il geto.* In 1555, Pope Paul IV, taking example from Venice, decreed (in the bull *Cum Nimis Absurdum,* amid very great discord) the first Roman ghetto, and the first by papal edict. In 1556 that ghetto was established in a few swampy blocks of what is now Trastevere ("trans-Tiber").

Most European ghettoes were walled in, the cost of the walls being assessed upon the Jews. Confined by the walls as the population grew, ghetto tenements were raised higher and higher as their area became more and more crowded. Jews were subject to strict curfews and often remained sealed within ghetto walls on holy days. In a custom revived by the Nazis, who required Jews to wear a prominent yellow star of David, ghetto dwellers were often required to wear distinctive dress, probably to help identify violators of the curfew. In most of southern Europe, however, the ghettoes were allowed substantial self-government within their walls—so long, of course, as the special taxes levied upon them were promptly paid.

G.I. 1. Government issue. *G.I. can* A standard-issue garbage can. 2. An enlisted man, esp. in the army. [The term in sense 2 evolved sometime after WWI, becoming standard in WWII to express the civilian-soldier's new sense of himself as a piece of disposable government property. Of regular army noncoms, the ex-civilian was fond of saying, "He wasn't born; he was issued."]

 gyrene [< *G.I. (ma)rine.*] 1. An enlisted man in the USMC. 2. *Ext.* Any marine.

gink A man of no consequence. A stiff. A guy. [Origin unknown. Am. first attested 1910. Introduced into Brit. by P. G. Wodehouse in 1920, but the form never came into general Brit. use; which should refute the assertion that the term is Brit. dial. < *ginkie, a slatternly woman.] *Hotel de Gink* A generic name for a flophouse. (In the name of an unsystematic curiosity, I have checked telephone directories in many cities, looking for a *Hotel de Gink.* So far I have not found one, but still half expect to, in California if nowhere else.)

HISTORIC. In WWII, when Marines and G.I.s had more or less secured an island area and had time to improvise shelters a bit more substantial than pup tents, they often hung hand-lettered signs on these quarters. One of the commonest of such signs, as photo coverage of the Pacific island war shows, was *Hotel de Gink.*

gird (up) one's loins To prepare physically and spiritually for a hard task. [From the time when men wore skirts. Root image of pulling up one's skirts and tucking them into one's belt (girth), leaving the legs unencumbered. A pervasive image in both OT and NT, as, among many other instances: Exodus 12:11: "your loins girded, your shoes on your feet"; 2 Kings 4:29: "Gird up thy loins, and take my staff"; 1 Peter 1:13: "Wherefore gird up the loins of your mind."]

girl [Gmnc. **gur,* child (of either sex); with dim. suffix *-wil → gurwil,* an infant → OE *gyrele;* ME *girle, gurle.* In ME *knave gerlys* was used for "small boys," but by c. 1530 *gurle* had become specific to female children.] 1. Female child. 2. A maiden. 3. A hired female menial. 4. A sweetheart. 5. A woman of a "certain" age with a surviving interest, gossipy or physical, in the social competition for male attention.

    girl crazy Also *girl chaser* Labels a boy or man obsessively interested in every girl in sight. *girl Friday* A faithful female secretary or assistant. [After *my man Friday* of Defoe's *Robinson Crusoe,* 1719.] *girl friend* 1. A sweetheart. 2. A boy's or man's date. (If a man, usu. "lady friend.") *girlie* Low-status form of address to a female. [Cf. *dearie.*] *girlie show* A theatrical or cabaret performance that presents groups of girls in scanty costumes. *les girls* [An arch combining of the Fr. plu. article with English *girls.*] Generally with ref. to women in sense 5, and implies the cattiness of socially and sexually competitive women. *a-girling and a-boying* Doing what comes naturally.

given name Specifically one's first name; can include one's middle name(s). [Because unlike the family name, which is inherited, it is given by the parents. See *surname, nickname, cognomen.*]

    HISTORIC. The common form was long *Christian name,* because it was officialized at baptism, but the term gives reasonable cause for offense to non-Christians, esp. to Jews—and what, for that matter, is the "Christian" name of Li Po? In colonial America, the punctilious Puritan forefathers also objected to "Christian" on the grounds that this (these) name(s) was given at birth, before the infant had been made a Christian by baptism.

glamor/glamour Romantic allurement, esp. by contrived means, as press agentry. *the glamor of Hollywood,* the (advertised) enticements of Foamrubbersville. [Root sense: "the art of contriving magic spells." A complex evolution slightly obscured by ambiguous dating. Norman Fr. *glomerie* for *gramarie,* grammar, is an unexplained shift but has precedent in Medieval L. ODEE cites *magister glomerie,* master of grammar (of learning), the title of a medieval master of Cambridge University. The sense connection with *grammar* is from the fact that a *grammarian* was a man of learning in a much larger sense than is now implied in parsing sentences, and that magic was a learned art (cf. *Faustus*). *Glamour* functioned primarily in Scottish from XI. It is attested in XVIII with the sense "magic spell." Then popularized in early XIX in the novels of Sir Walter Scott with the sense "the magic of romantic beauty," which sense is perturbed in modern Am. by the press agentry that has labored to "cast a magic spell" (of ballyhoo) over selected publicity dolls, male and female; the press agentry asserting the quality to be inherent, but many understanding it to exist only in the aura of contrived publicity.] Also *glamorous, glamor puss, the glamor game, to glamorize.*

goat: get one's goat   To rile. [Because herd animals tend to become uneasy when they are alone, it was long a custom in England, and later in America, to provide a stall companion for a high-strung race horse, and especially for a stallion. Since another stallion would be a challenge, and since a mare might "tease," a customary companion was a goat. Once the two animals became accustomed to one another they tended to become restive when parted. *To get the goat* was to steal into a rival's barn the night before a race and lead the goat away, a common dirty trick. No one much cared how the goat felt about it, but the horse tended to become restless, which left it in poor shape for the race.]

gobbledygook   Linguistic utilizations intermediate to finalized specification and rhetorically structured to maximalize optionalization of alternatives while preserving deniability interim-wise. [Coined sometime during World War II by Congressman Maury Maverick of Texas. Improvised on the spur of the moment, the term passed immediately into general usage. Maverick, as reported in the *N. Y. Times Magazine*, May 21, 1944, explained: "Perhaps I was thinking of the old bearded turkey gobbler back in Texas who was always gobbledygobbling and strutting with ludicrous pomposity. At the end of this gobble there was a sort of gook."]

NOTE. Am. is indebted to the Mavericks for two now standard words, Maury's grandfather having been the eponym of *maverick* (which see). The Theodore Roosevelts are the only other family I know that has given us two words. The *teddy bear* (which see) was named after T.R. and *alice blue* (which see) after his daughter.

God's little acre   *Sthrn.* An acre of farmland whose yield was designated for the church in lieu of tithing. [Popularized as the title of Erskine Caldwell's enormously successful novel published in 1933. Prob. < Brit. *God's acre,* a rural cemetery outside the churchyard. (Originally the churchyard itself, but churchyards fill up in time and death spills over.)]

Goldberg, Rube   From 1904 to c. WWII a popular comic strip cartoonist. Later a political cartoonist. *a Rube Goldberg (contraption)* An absurdly elaborate mechanism for accomplishing an absurdly simple task. Hence, any unusually complicated mechanism. [Because Goldberg's most popular comic strips were based on mock mechanical drawings of such devices. In Goldberg fashion, for instance, the design for an alarm clock might show:

> Shot put in cup *(a)* is counterbalanced by water in cup *(b).* Water evaporates, tipping shot into ice-covered pail *(c)* containing piranhas *(d).* When ice *(e)* is smashed, piranhas seize bait *(f)* attached to string *(g)* which pulls pin *(h),* releasing 500 lbs. of ball bearings *(i),* which roll down chute *(j)* striking bass drum *(k)* next to the head of sleeper (1).

A common expression c. 1920–1940, but now used only by gaffers who came of age in the time of Goldberg's popularity, and likely to pass out of use as the gaffers die out.]

golgotha   [Root sense: "the place of skulls," hence, "burial place." < Aramaic *gulgutha,* skull.] 1. A burial place. 2. A place of lamentation. *Golgotha* Calvary, the hill on which Jesus and the robbers were crucified. [Because it was said to be domed like a skull.]

gonzel kid/ganzel kid   1. A young punk. [William Decker, an editor of Viking Press, reports its use in this sense by an old Oregon cowhand in 1930.] 2. A catamite boy who is the traveling companion of a homosexual hobo. [Dating unattested, but its association with hoboes on the transcontinental railroads makes 1880 a likely date. Now rare, but listed by Bruce Rodgers in his *The Queens' Vernacular: A Gay Lexicon,* 1972, and noted as "known in 1930's & '40's." < Yiddish *ganzl,* duckling (dim. form of *ganz,* duck. Cf. English "duckie" as a term of endearment.) Whatever the original dating, its use by hoboes would have spread it rapidly across the country.]

   HISTORIC. There were many reasons for taking to the road as a railroad hobo in late XIX America. One among them was certainly the difficulty—the near impossibility—of surviving as a homosexual in the goldfish bowl of the American small town. For various other reasons, many runaway boys also took to the hobo trail, and these were regularly picked up as companions by homosexual tramps.

goober Also *goober pea.* A peanut. [< Angolese *nguba,* peanut. One of the few accurately traceable Africanisms in southern regional Am. There must be many more, but the traces have been obscured by time. And even in this case there is a mystery, for the peanut was not native to Africa, but rather was imported from South America. It would be useful to know more about Angolese *nguba.* Was it an earlier Angolese word adapted to this new plant? Or did it come into Angolese as an effort to approximate the (now lost) South American name?]

good old boy *Sthrn.* The rough and ready white supremacist who can be counted on for any social activity from barroom brawling, to a shivaree, to coon hunting, to a lynching, all being about equal sports to him. He made a helluva fighting man in the Civil War and, except for moonshine, has not made anything since. *Peter Taylor was born to be a good old boy but incurred civilization.*

good scout An obliging fellow. [Origin in doubt. Am. only. First attested by MMM, 1912, which dating precludes a reference to the Boy Scouts, a movement not founded until 1908 (in England) and not widespread in U.S. until after WWI. Nor does the implied genial permissiveness of the idiom conform to the idealism of honor-bright youth, a true good scout being as genially obliging in hell-raising as in moral improvement. Similarly there is no evidence of a reference to military scouts, and no visible sense conformity.

Mary Helen Dohan, *Our Own Words,* suggests a derivation from Du. *schout* (pron. *skaut*), a bailiff of the early Dutch settlements in N.Y. "who combined the powers of mayor, sheriff, and district attorney, and whose title may have given us the phrase *a good scout* for one not unduly harsh," but this guess, though modestly tentative, ignores the dating.

Scout, a university servant (one who scouts about to provide the needs of young gentlemen scholars), was in use at Oxford by 1798, and at Harvard and Yale in early XIX. Assuming that it survived to 1860 and the Civil War, and that its compounding into *a good scout* was in verbal use twenty or thirty years before its attestation in 1912, the dating and the sense conform well, and this university usage emerges as the likeliest source. But ?]

gook   *WWII. Pacific Theater.* The standard derisive G.I. name for a native of the Pacific islands or for a Southeast Asian. [The sometimes suggested derivation from Scottish *gowk,* cuckoo, April fool, is based only on surface similarity, without allowing for the dating and means of transmission. The term is better glossed as an expressive of disdain based on its sound values, which, like those of *yuk* and *gunk,* involve speech muscles associated with the vomiting reflex.]

goose   [Cited by ODEE as "one of the few bird-names of IE age; prob. ult. of imitative origin." The probable IE form was *ghans.* (Ger. *Gans,* goose.)] 1. The bird. 2. *Ext.* A stupid person.

   to goose To jab in the anus, usu. with a stiffly extended thumb. [The thumb so extended may be said, at least roughly, to resemble a goose's bill, but many a farm worker bent over some task has been goosed by the bird itself.]

   goosey, goosy [The earlier, and Brit., senses "like a goose" (silly) and "causing goose flesh" are not common in Am.] 1. Nervous. Tense. [As if expecting to be goosed.] 2. Sexually aroused.

   As direct metaphors: *goose flesh* A temporary roughening of the skin caused by erection of the papillae in reaction to cold or to emotional stress. Emily Dickinson: "That desirable goose flesh which is poetry." [Like the bumpy skin of a plucked goose.] *gooseneck* A flexible shaft, as on a desk lamp. *goose step* A march step in which the legs are swung parallel to the ground with the knees locked. *goose egg* Zero.

   cook one's goose To do one in. *his goose is cooked* It's all up with him. [Origin unknown. A persistent folk etymology tells how a besieged town, to show how plentifully it was victualed, hung a fat goose from the flagpole, then mockingly sent to ask the besieging captain why he had come; to which he answered, "I have come to cook your goose." Another refers the idiom to the goose that laid the golden eggs (once it was killed and cooked, no more was to be had of it).

   These ingenuities aside, a likelier source is in the English custom of the Christmas goose, and in the rogues' countercustom of stealing poultry. A small tenant farmer might go to year-long pains to raise a fat goose for Christmas (and for its down). To have it stolen (and cooked by someone else) was a calamity that could mar not only Christmas but the whole year.]

   gone gosling A person who is beyond hope. [Dating unknown, but prob. a recent slang elaboration of the (alliteratively selected) *dead duck,* with the same sense. In XIX rural Am. *dead as a duck drowned in a thunderstorm* had some currency. It referred to the fact that ducklings (not ducks) were often found dead after a real gully washer. They were found half embedded in mud, as if they had drowned, but the ducklings probably died of cold because they had not yet developed as adequate covering of protective body oils.]

what's sauce for the goose is sauce for the gander A proverbial assertion that what is good enough for one is good enough for another of the same kind. (Yet note the curious inversion of the form. Though an idiom from a society in which women were held to be inferiors, it asserts that what is good enough for the wife is good enough for the husband, whereas every assumption of a male-dominant society would require the case to be put the other way round. Perhaps an early subconscious victory for Women's Lib.) [There are two possible explanations. *Sauce* may be an alteration of *souse* for "mash," in which case the root sense is "what is good enough for the wife to eat is good enough for the husband." Or *sauce* may be < Fr. *sauce*, the common Am. equivalent being "gravy," in which case the root sense is "what does as gravy for the wife does as gravy for the husband."]

sound on the goose In favor of slavery. [A mysterious idiom of Bloody Kansas when the issue of incorporating the territory as a slave or free state was to be settled by a vote. A commonly put question was: "How do you stand on the goose?" The answer "I am sound (all sound/all right) on the goose," indicated that one was a Southern sympathizer and would vote for slavery. The idiom passed into Brit. in late XIX with the sense "politically orthodox." I have found no historian who has been able to explain the term. Could *goose* be a corruption of *as it goes? As it goes* might explain the Brit. sense, but the question is no more than conjecture. Origin unknown.]

gospel 1. The teachings of Christ as set forth by Matthew, Mark, Luke, and John, in the first four books of the NT. 2. *Ext.* Any system of beliefs said to resemble these in one way or another. *the odious gospel of* Mein Kampf. 3. *Ext.* Anything accepted as unquestionably true. *If you say so, that's gospel as far as I'm concerned.* [OE *godspell*, good news; can also be rendered "news of God," *God* and *good* being cognate. The second element ult. < IE *spel-*, to say, to recite (as an incantation). In OE *spell*, news, story, account, fable, recitation, magic incantation. With changed senses, the form survives in *spell:* 1. To recite the letters of a word in order. 2. A magic trance. (Thing brought on by an incantation.) 3. A period of time. (Duration of a trance.) SPELLBINDER, SPIEL.]

gossip   *n.* 1. A rumormonger. 2. The tittle-tattle spoken by rumormongers. —*adj. gossipy.* (And all corresponding v. forms.) [Originally either of the two godparents who served as baptismal sponsors. In late OE *godsibb, godsibbe* (SIBLING). ME *godsip, gossyp.* The sense shift from *godparent* to *tittle-tattler* took place in late XVI.]

    HISTORIC. A man and a woman sponsored an infant at its baptism, taking a vow to oversee its religious development. So sacred was this vow that *godsibbes* were forbidden to marry, they being already joined in a sacramental obligation. That vow, when conscientiously fulfilled, would require regular intimate discussions between the godparents, whence the sense shift to "people often seen with their heads together in intimate conversation about someone else." The dating of the sense shift suggests that with Henry VIII's break with Roman Catholicism, the role of godparents in the Church of England lost the intensity of its earlier religious imperative.

Gotham   Once a common nickname for New York City. [Given it by Washington Irving in *Salmagundi* (written c. 1807). The original Gotham is in Nottinghamshire, England. Whether legend or fact, the story is told that in XIII King John visited Gotham, thinking to build a castle there. The townspeople, afraid that a royal presence would impose restrictions and higher taxes, conspired to act like lunatics during his visit, so persuading him that the town was an open insane asylum and unfit for his royal seat. Gothamites were thereafter known as "the wise fools." But Irving's sense of the term was more nearly "city of self-important but ignorant slickers." New Yorkers, in accepting Irving's label as a fond nickname, may be said to have proved its accuracy.]

go that   To accept. To agree with a proposal. [Prob. < *to go along with.*] *N. Y. Times,* Aug. 13, 1976, p. 11: " 'I could go that,' Mr. Holmes said."

grain: against the grain   Against one's nature. [A common error takes "grain" to be the organic set of wood texture. The base, however, is Fr. *gré,* natural capacity for pleasure (AGREEABLE) < L. *gratus,* gratifying, welcome. Fr. *contre le gré,* disagreeable (Lit. "not to one's natural inclination.") See also *ingrained.* In French "against the grain (of the wood)" is *à rebours* or *au rebours.*]

grass widow *In XX Am.* A divorced woman. [And so firmly has this sense become entrenched that it has brought about *sod widow* for a widow whose husband has died (and is under the sod rather than on the grass.) But in earlier English, an unwed mother. (This sense is attested in XVI but its much greater antiquity is indicated by related forms in Germanic usage, as MLG *grasswedewe* and Ger. *Strohwitwe*, straw widow.) The reference is obviously to country maids who so-to-speak married on the grass (in the hay) and who became so-to-speak widowed when their so-to-speak husbands so-to-speak withdrew.]

greaser (*s* pronounced as a *z*) Early sthwstrn. derisive term for a Mexican; later extended to any swarthy person. [Also *greaseball* (in which *s* often does not take the *z* sound). Because their sweat is asserted to be oily!]

great Scott! Exclam. of surprise, astonishment. [< Ger. *grüss' Gott*, hello < *Gott grüsse dich*, may God greet (receive) you; the idiomatic form being closely akin to that of Eng. *goodbye* < *God be wi' ye*. Am. only, mid XIX, which suggests a borrowing from the loud greetings exchanged by German immigrants, their boisterous cordiality contributing to the exclamatory sense of the Am. adaptation. The insistent survival of the capitalized *Scott* may have been side-influenced by Gen. Winfield Scott, who as hero of the Mexican War (1846–1848) was at the height of his popularity just as the idiom was coming into general use. There is, however, English precedent in the use of *hello* as an exclam. of surprise, as in *hello! what's this?*]

Greek The people and the language of Greece. [In Gk. the country is *Hellas*. *Graikos* was the Gk. name of a single, probably Illyrian, tribe that lived near Epirus. By some historic accident the Romans rendered *Graikos* as *Graecus* and made that name do for all Hellenes.]
    it's Greek to me I don't understand it. [Because not only the language but the alphabet are unknown to most non-Greeks. In XIV Dante expressed the same idea in the reverse idiom *"non mi è latino"*: "it is not Latin to me."]
    the Greek's Common Am. way of referring to a diner. [Because the first Greek immigrants in U.S. often opened small restaurants. In a common immigrant pattern, then, they sent for relatives, who normally joined in their work, and sent for others. At this

end of that progression, it is common for diners to be owned and operated by Greeks and their descendants.]

Greek god An especially handsome and muscular man. [As the gods were portrayed in ancient Greek statuary.]

Greek it To practice anal sex. [Because homosexuality was not only common in Greece but encouraged in the army on the theory that soldier lovers would fight the more fiercely to defend one another.]

HISTORIC. The Greek has acquired a general reputation as a foreigner given to sharp practices. In XVII Brit. *to greek* meant "to cheat at cards." The pejorative Sp. *gringo* (which see) is ultimately from *griego*, Greek. *Nick the Greek* is a standard name for a professional gambler, and the all-but-official title of the chief odds-maker of Las Vegas, whatever his ethnic origin. That the Greek ethic has prized shrewdness is attested at least as far back as the Trojan Horse.

green cheese Unaged cheese. *think the moon is made of green cheese* To be a dolt. [First attested in the writings of Sir Thomas More (early XVI) but probably already long established as a folk metaphor, the naturalness of which becomes evident if one thinks of large wheels of cheese set to ripen in a dim, cool place. In addition to their roundness, green cheeses tend to "weep," i.e., to exude small amounts of moisture, and these on a pale round surface in a dim place might readily suggest the markings of the moon.]

greenhorn 1. An inexperienced person. Implies gullibility. A once standard term for a newly arrived immigrant who lacked knowledge of native ways and had to accept instruction on trust. [*Green* is, of course, a general term for "immature, inexperienced, gullible." But *green horn* is more specific. The newly formed horns of deer are covered with a skin that later splits and peels. While it still clings to the horns, fungus spores often develop on the tatters, giving the horns a greenish cast. Thus *green* both as a metaphor and as an accurate observation from nature. (On the western frontier *greenhorn* was scoffingly synonymous with *tenderfoot* and *pilgrim*.)]

gringo *S.W. regional since c. 1850, then generally diffused.* The standard Mexican pejorative term for a *Yanqui* or *Norte Americano*. But earlier, any foreigner, the term becoming more or less specific to *Yanquis* because they were the most prominent (and usually the most offensive) foreigners in Mexico. [No end of non-sense has been invented in explanation of the term, most of it having to do with XIX and XX interventions by U.S. forces in Mexico. The fact is that the form was already established in early XVII Sp. with the sense "the gibberish spoken by foreigners," whence the ext. to "foreigner." Altered from Sp. *griego*, Greek, perh. with some such intermediate form as *griengar,* to speak like a Greek (which was Greek to the Spaniards).]

NOTE. *Gringo* in the sense "that barbarous language spoken by foreigners" can be said to close a language circle begun by the Greeks themselves. Greek *barbaros,* foreigner (hence, "stranger, enemy"), was based on *bar-bar-bar,* the Greek version of the gibberish spoken by non-Greeks.

growler *Am. slang.* 1. A keg of beer equal to about one-eighth of a barrel. 2. A usu. tin receptacle, usu. with a lid, usu. of about two quarts, for carrying draft beer away from a saloon. [Sense 2 attested 1888. Sense 1 prob. somewhat earlier.]

rush the growler To run to the saloon for a growler of beer and to hurry it back to workingmen, or to good old Dad once he got home from work, an errand usu. assigned to children. [The saloon keeper commonly tried to fill the growler as much as possible with suds. It was common, therefore, to grease the growler in the belief that it kept a large head of suds from forming; and perhaps a film of oil did cause some of the suds to slide back into the liquid, but aside from oiling the beer, the practice could not have made much difference. *Growler rushing* also connoted in late XIX "a drinking spree," i.e., growler after growler as in modern chug-a-lug. *Growler* also labels a relatively small iceberg, usu. encountered as one of a group broken from a larger one, and prob. called *growlers* because they tend to rub against one another with a sound akin to growling. One of the functions of the iceberg patrol is to break large bergs into relatively harmless growlers.]

Grundy, Mrs. A personification of the narrowest orthodoxy of public opinion. *Grundyism, grundyism* Moral pecksniffery. [Mrs. Grundy is a constant presence, though never an onstage character, in Thomas Marston's play *Speed the Plough* (1798), in which Dame Ashfield repeatedly asks, as if in terror of social disapproval, "What will Mrs. Grundy think?" The name may have been suggested to Marston by the nursery rhyme beginning "Solomon Grundy/ Born on Monday."]

guerrilla warfare   [< Sp. *guerra*, war; with dim. suffix *-illa:* little war.] The more or less hit-and-run resistance of partisans to the occupation of their country by formally organized military forces with superior equipment. *guerrilla* A native partisan fighter.

Guinea   Pejorative name for an Italian. [In this sense from c. 1900, the earliest form, *Guinea-Wop*, having the sense "nigger-wop," Guinea having been first used in Am. c. 1800 for a Negro slave from the Guinea coast of Africa.]

gumbo   [Many sthrn. regionalisms are based more or less uncertainly on slave-imported words of African origin. This is one of the few that can be traced positively. < Bantu *gumbo*, okra.] 1. Okra. 2. A soup or stew thickened with okra. 3. *Ext.* A clay soil that becomes especially sticky when wet. [Thick as gumbo soup.] 4. *By association with the original region of gumbo cookery. Gumbo* The patois of French and Carib Creole pidgin with smatterings of Am. spoken in southernmost Louisiana. Some remnants of a cognate patois can be traced in Haiti, though minus the few touches of Am.

gun   [ME *gunne, gonne.* Prob. < Gmnc. *Gunhild, Gunhilde.* So ON Gounghildr (*gunnr* and *hildr* both mean "war"), a fond girl's name for a piece of siege machinery, esp. for a catapult. (So, in WWI, *Big Bertha* (which see) for a particularly long-range German artillery piece.] 1. A firearm or artillery piece. 2. *Ext.* Any tubular device for propelling a projectile. *blow gun.* 3. *Ext.* A trigger-operated tool. *air gun, ray gun, caulking gun.* 4. *Ext. Aviation.* A throttle. *give 'er the gun, gun it.*
    big gun 1. An artillery piece. 2. *Ext.* An important person.
    great guns British coastal artillery. (See Hardy's poem "Channel Firing.") *going great guns* Proceeding vigorously, powerfully, unstoppably. [With the power of a coastal artillery barrage.] *great guns!* Exclam. of surprise. [As if jolted by the opening salvo of coastal artillery.]
    son of a gun A variable phrase: 1. Mild exclam. of surprise. 2. An epithet for a mean, low person. 3. An epithet or form of greeting for a good old guy. (Always in this sense when used with "old.") [In the early days of British sea power, women commonly sailed with men, esp. on long voyages. When, therefore, a birth occurred aboard ship, the ship's surgeon commonly delivered the child in a screened-off section of the covered gun deck. The birth took place "under the gun," and the infant commonly slept in a small hammock slung from the gun barrel. The log entry "son

of a gun" is on record in cases of unknown paternity. No one
has reported finding "daughter of a gun"—the admiralty had probably directed that only strong sons be born on British vessels. Senses 2 and 3 are implicit in the origin: for those who thought of
sailors as riffraff, sense 2; for those who thought of them as fine
stout fellows, sense 3.]

spike one's guns To frustrate an opponent by blocking his intended plan of action. [But at root, a sort of scorched earth policy
in which one spikes his own guns to deny the enemy the use of
them. Early cannon were muzzle-loaded and were fired by lighting
a fuse inserted in a small hole on one side of what would now
be the breech. In falling back and abandoning close-support field
artillery, the simplest way to jam the guns was to jam a spike
into this fuse hole. In time the enemy gunners could clear this
fuse hole, but not in time to turn the guns on those who had
abandoned them. It was, therefore, one's own guns one spiked,
the original frustration of the enemy consisting of denying him
use of them.]

stick to one's guns Stand firm to a position taken. [Field artillery
in close support often came under attack, esp. by cavalry. To stand
and continue firing when so attacked took courage, esp. since artillerymen usu. lacked infantry weapons. When artillerymen broke
and ran under attack, the enemy could turn the guns to his own
use. There have been many instances of artillerymen chained to
their guns as a material aid to bravery.]

Gunpowder Plot Guy Fawkes (1570–1606), incensed because
the king and Parliament had permitted an increased representa-
tion of Roman Catholics, smuggled a cache of powder kegs into
the cellar of the House of Parliament and planned to set it off
on Nov. 5, 1605, when Henry VII was due to attend the sitting
of Parliament. The plot was discovered and Fawkes was executed.
Guy Fawkes Day is still observed as a holiday in England, especially
by children, who roam the streets begging "a penny for the old
Guy," much as children in the U.S. go "trick-or-treating" on Halloween.

gunwale/gunnel The projecting edge at which the main deck
of a sailing ship joins the hull. [Because it was once used to help
secure naval cannons. ME *gunnewalle*. *Walle* is akin to *welt*
(ridge).]

gunk Any repulsive, more or less viscous stuff. [XX Americanism.
Expressive of revulsion. Akin to *yuk*, a revulsive expression that
employs speech muscles associated with vomiting.]

gun moll   The woman companion of a criminal. [Originally his confederate in crime. < Yiddish-American *gonif's Molly* < *gonif,* thief; *Molly,* generic term for a woman (MOLLYCODDLE). Not, as often asserted, because Prohibition era gangsters had their guns carried by their women to avoid arrest on the charge of carrying a concealed weapon. Such gun toting was generally left to bodyguards, and the women generally chosen by gangsters were very much not dressed to conceal anything.]

gunzel/gunzl   Contemptuous name for a gangster. [Yiddish-American: English *gun, guns,* with Ger. dim. suffix -*l,* "a little gun." Originally with ref. to a Jewish gangster, then generalized.]

gussied up/all gussied up   Dressed in one's best (go-to-the-city) clothes. [Originally a Georgia regionalism, now widely diffused. < *Gussie, Gussy,* fond local nickname for Augusta, Ga.]

gyrene   A U.S. Marine enlisted man. [Altered and combined form of *G.I.* and *(ma)rine.*]

H

haberdasher   A dealer in all items of men's wear. (So in Am. In Brit. a dealer in hats, shoes, socks, shirts, and other accessories, but not suits, coats, etc. [Like *isinglass* and *mushroom* (which see), the word is made up of elements without English analogues and with no certain and translatable foreign base. Ult. < OF *hapertas,* of unknown origin, and perhaps (but uncertainly) meaning "cloth, fabric, stuff." XV Anglo-Norman *haberdasshrie.* Eng. XV–XVII *haberdash,* incidental small wares (clothing accessories?). Obviously a label was needed for a recognized sort of tradesman, and the idiom settled upon this form, rather than on (the equally likely) *haptasser, happyteaser, haptassler,* etc.]

hair   [An etymological mystery. As surely as our ancestors were not bald, there must have been an IE word for hair, but scholarship has not found it. OE *hāer,* hair, is from hypothetical Gmnc. **khāer-, xāer-, hēr-.* ME *haire, hare.*] 1. The threadlike growth on the skin of terrestrial mammals. 2. *Ext.* A generalized measure of narrowness. ***by a hair*** Just barely. Also *hairbreadth, hair's breadth.* And see *r.c.h.,* below.

   hair of the dog (that bit one) Now, a morning-after drink as a cure for a hangover. [But earlier based on a received medical principle that like cures like; in Latin, *similia similibus curantur;* and traceable to the earliest practice of witch doctors. So in the Middle Ages a common cure for dogbite was to place a hair of the dog in the wound (which would then infallibly heal), or to burn the hair of the dog, put the ash in water, and drink it. (Even today nothing is more effective than a witch doctor or two in treating a hangover.)]

   hair-raiser A terrifying experience. ***hair-raising*** Terrifying. [Intense emotion, esp. fear, causes hair to stand erect. Various commentators have noted that the hair of a man about to be hanged sometimes stands straight up briefly. So ***make one's hair***

stand on end To fill with terror. And so *hairy* A terrifying or emotionally trying experience.

hair shirt Among the sublimities of penitential religion, an undershirt woven of coarse hair, or a stubbly goatskin worn with the fur side against the body, usu. permanently. (The odor of sanctity may be said to have begun in the unwashed and unaired biostratum between the hair shirt and the suppurations of chafed and poisoned flesh.)

hair trigger A gun trigger adjusted to fire at the slightest pressure. [As the weight of a hair.] *hair-trigger adj.* Explosively irritable.

get in one's hair Annoy. [All sorts of things can catch in the hair annoyingly, but in the days when almost every house had a barn or a stable, crab lice spawned in hay and stable heaps were most common, the standard treatment being a coal oil (kerosene) shampoo.]

short hair/short hairs Pubic hair. And in the variant forms *get one by the short hairs/get one where the hair is short* To have one securely in a difficult and painful situation. Equivalent to *have one by the balls* (which no one wants to be had by).

split hairs To insist on overly fine distinctions.

take hair/lift hair To scalp.

not turn a hair Remain cool and unruffled [Brit. horsy-set jargon, c. 1800. A hard-ridden horse becomes lathered and loses its grooming; i.e., its once curried hair "turns."]

r.c.h. (A common exuberant vulgarity of U.S. mechanics.) The finest possible measure of mechanical adjustment. *Give it two r.c.h.'s to the left and you'll have it right on the tit* = give it two least turns to the left and you will have it in perfect alignment. [Based on such forms as m.p.h. and r.p.m. Here, *r.c.h.* for "red cunt hair." Which also functions as rhetorical bait. Ask any mechanic why he assumes red pubic hair to be finer than any other, and every man in the shop joins in pointing out your ignorance while expounding on his intimate researches into such matters.]

halcyon days   1. A period of serene weather. 2. *Ext.* A time of prosperity. [After the halcyon, ME *alceon* < Gk. **halkuōn,* a mythical bird uncertainly identified with the kingfisher. A sea bird, it was reputed to build floating nests, hatching its young in the fourteen days that center on Dec. 22, the winter solstice. Through the magic powers of the halcyon, the sea remained calm and the weather bright and fair through these days, a sort of Aegean Indian Summer. Like *bonanza,* in Sp. "fair weather," and in Am. mining strike, "great good fortune," *halcyon* has gone from the sense "good weather" to the sense "good fortune."]

half seas over   1. *Maritime.* Halfway across the sea. [*Seas* is a frozen genitive form; as if from "half the sea's width over." In this sense first attested by OED 1551. Shortly before his death in 1700, John Dryden wrote in a letter, "I am half seas over to death," his usage being a metaphoric extension of the literal maritime "halfway to the other side." 2. *In common usage.* Drunk. Half drunk. Halfway to passing out of the picture. [In this sense first attested 1700.]

NOTE. A number of authorities have asserted the derivation from Du. *op zee zober,* export beer (lit. "beer to be sent upon the seas"). And if so, the connection with drunkenness together with the similarity to the Eng. form *half seas over* would readily give rise to the sense "drunken." But the Du. form is not attested, there simply is no evidence to support this Du. origin, and there is fair reason to dismiss it as folk etymology.

halibut   A flatfish. [Root sense: "holy flatfish," i.e., "flatfish eaten on Fridays and R.C. holy days of obligation." *hali* < OE *haelig,* holy. *butt,* lumpish, bruised, swollen (and so IE *butt-*). In earlier English *buttwife,* fishwife who sold flatfish; *butts and bounds,* property lines (being flat stones that marked corners—*butts*—and the lines between them—*bounds.*) *Turbot* is, similarly, "spiny flatfish" (BUTT); and ON *steorn,* thorn, spine.]

Halifax: go to Halifax   *Minced curse.* Go to hell. [Now rare, but once common in U.S. and prob. understood to be with ref. to Halifax, capital of Nova Scotia, to which many Tories moved during the Revolutionary War. So *Hal* for *Hell* with added connotation of contempt by association with Tories.

But also has Brit. antecedents. Cobham Brewer, *Dictionary of Phrase and Fable,* cites an old beggars' prayer quoted by John Taylor (1580–1653), known as the "water poet":

> From Hull, Hell, and Halifax
> Good Lord deliver us.

Because it was known that beggars could get nothing in Hull without laboring for it, and that Halifax summarily beheaded anyone caught stealing kerchiefs (a once common form of street theft). *Go to Hull* might have done as well, but is too close for a true minced form; and Halifax was clearly the worse place, for if a person could get nothing to eat in Hull, he might end up in Halifax with no way to eat what he might get.]

halo   1. *Physics.* An aura that seems to surround a light source when its rays reach an observer across a misty, dusty, or smoky atmosphere. 2. *Religious art.* An aura or nimbus around the head of a saint, a symbol of God's enabling power within. See *charisma.* [Based on Gk. **halos*, threshing floor, because the dust of the threshing diffused the sun's rays. Sense 2, based on L. *halō*, elevated, the original metaphor for religious purposes; but note that Gk. *halos* also acquired the meaning "nimbus around the sun," the sun being a fixed ancient symbol of God, hence of godliness.]

ham/ham actor   A strutting, bellowing emoter. [Heavily blackfaced clowns of the minstrel show (see *minstrel*) are said to have removed their make-up with lard, which they slanged as *hamfat.* Or *hamfat* may have been their slang for the face cream they used. In any case, the term emerged c. 1900 in a popular minstrel show song, "The Hamfat Man." On the reasonable assumption that the term was in actors' use for twenty years before appearing in print, the term may be dated 1880. Minstrels were, of course, clowns, and the shift to *ham, ham actor* in XX is an easy adaptation.]

NOTE. Partridge, *Slang*, notes that the term entered Brit. usage from Am. c. 1939 and speculates that it derives from *hambone*, a bumbling amateur musician among professionals, a Brit. slang term c. 1880. Perhaps, but unlikely, and wholly unattested. MMM cites *ham*, an inferior boxer, in Am. use in 1888; and if the sense is taken to be "one who clowns about instead of fighting," the sense and dating conform persuasively with *hamfat.*

The sometimes suggested derivation from Cockney *hamateur* is obvious folk etymology. The derivation from *(Ham)let* because of his speech to the players leaves one to ask why the term waited in the wings for 400 years before emerging in the U.S. There remains to be noted that Hamish McCullough, 1835–1885, toured the Middle West after the Civil War. And that fact has led some to claim that the troupe was called *Ham's actors;* but that label is almost certainly a willful invention and there is no evidence that it was ever applied to McCullough's troupe until well after *ham actor* had become a fixed term in Am.

Haman: hanged high as Haman   To be destroyed by one's own plotting. Hoist on one's own petard. (See *petard.*) [Esther 3–7, tells how Haman, counselor to King Ahasuerus, plotted the extermination of the Jews, and especially of Mordecai, for whom Haman ordered a gallows "of fifty cubits high" (5:14). Esther, however, changed the king's mind for him, and the story ends (7:10): "So they hanged Haman on the gallows that he had prepared for Mordecai. Then was the king's wrath pacified."]

HISTORIC. For persons of aristocratic pretension, to live and die by steel was warrior-honorable. To be hanged, aside from being fatal, dishonored one's name and lineage. The hanging of highly placed persons was basically an act of mockery and the general rule ran: The higher the crime (or the king's wrath), the higher the gallows. On such specially high gallows, corpses were often left dangling on dishonorable display, as, in a common variant, the heads of especially notable criminals were impaled on high spikes to serve as crow-pickings.

ham-and-egger   1. *Boxing.* A fighter who has never advanced beyond preliminary bouts, or a has-been who contines to fight for "eating money." 2. *Show biz.* A plod-along performer who has never risen to prominent billing. 3. *Ext.* Any plod-along person.

handicap   1. An advantage. 2. A disadvantage. *handicapped person* One who suffers from a physical or mental disadvantage. *handicapper* 1. The track official who assigns the different weights carried by race horses (assigning relative advantages and disadvantages) 2. One who studies the racing forms and selects horses, ideally winners. [Based on the old game called *hand in the cap, hand i' the cap, hand i' cap,* a form of which is mentioned in *Piers Plowman.* The game seems to have involved the drawing of money or of forfeit or betting slips from a hat. Earliest OED form (1653) is *Handy-Capps. Handicap* became a horse racing term in XVIII.]

handwriting on the wall   Dire forewarning. *see the handwriting on the wall* To know things have come to a disastrous end. [Does not function as a warning. By the time the handwriting becomes visible all is lost. Daniel, 5, tells of the feast of Belshazzar, king of Babylon, at which the gold and silver vessels taken from the temple at Jerusalem were brought out and (5:4) "the king and his lords, his wives and his concubines drank from them." At the instant of this sacrilege a disembodied hand appeared and wrote (5:24) MENE MENE TEKEL and PARSIN, which none could decipher until Daniel was summoned, and interpreted (5:26–27): "MENE, God has numbered the days of your kingdom and brought it to an end; TEKEL, you have been weighed in the balances and found wanting; PERES, your kingdom is divided and given to the Medes and Persians." The account concludes (5:31): "That very night Bel-shazzar . . . was slain. And Darius, the Mede, received the king-dom." (So the Westminster Study Bible. The message as rendered in the more familiar King James Bible was MENE, MENE, TEKEL, UPHARSIN.)]

hangnail A flap of dead skin at the base of a toenail or fingernail. [Earlier *agnail.* Ult. < IE *angh-*, pain, constriction. (Ger. ANGST, anguish, anxiety.) OE *angnaegl*, lit. "angst-nail," thorn in the flesh. As the *ang-, agn-* became less and less recognized in common usage, it was gestalt-modified (see *gestalt*) to the nearest familiar pattern, in this case *hang.*]

harass (Commonly pronounced with accent on the second syllable, and that pronunciation seems to have become American standard, but properly with the accent on the first syllable.) To attack or annoy repeatedly. To persecute. [Root sense: "to set the dogs on." < OF. *harasser* < *harer* < *hare*, sic 'im, sic 'em (command to a dog).]

harbinger (Pronounced with the accent on the first syllable; the sound of the *g* is soft.) A forerunner. A presage. [When great per-sons traveled, a servant called a *harbinger* (Fr. *vauntcourier*, one who runs ahead) preceded the retinue to arrange for food and for lodging for the night. There are numerous tales of harbingers leaving signs and chalk marks on inn doors to rate the quality of their wine, food, and lodging. *Harbinger* is a complex form akin to OE *here*, Ger. *Heer*, army, attacking force. Akin also to *harbor* < OE *herebeorg*, lodging, but lit. "army encampment" < *here*, as above; *beorg*, root sense: "hill"; effective sense: "defended camp." (See *bhergh-*.)]

harbor A sheltered body of water for the mooring of ships. 2. *Earlier.* Any refuge or lodging, this sense now surviving primarily in *harbor a criminal.* (*Note.* There is no etymological reason for not harboring a friend, but the idiom has become associated with the legal prohi-bition on giving refuge to a fugitive felon. There is in New York State a retirement home for seamen, *Sailor's Snug Harbor,* but the sense here is prob. "last port of call" rather than from the root "lodging.") [< OE *herebeorg*, lit. "army hill" < OE *here*, army; *beorg*, defended encampment ("high place"). (See *harbinger* and also *bhergh-*.)]

harlot   A whore. [But the sense was not specifically female until XV. Earlier: vagabond, rogue (XIII); wandering clown, manservant (XIV). ME *herlot, harlot,* OF *herlot, arlot,* vagabond, young fellow, low fellow < Medieval L. *erlotus,* glutton ("vagabond begging food which he consumes greedily." In Am. slang, "a hobo chow-hound.")]

hat   A covering for the head, usu. consisting of a crown and a brim. [IE *kad-,* shelter, protection, cover. With k/h and d/t in Gmnc. → OE *haett,* hat.]

hat trick In Am. with ref. to hockey only. The star feat of a single player who scores three goals in one game. [In Brit. with ref. to any triple star feat, but originally specific to cricket: the feat of knocking over three wickets in three successive bowls. So called because such a feat was once signalized by passing the hat among the spectators for the benefit of the star athlete. The Am. usage of this idiom only with ref. to hockey is due to the fact that the game (prob. originally Irish) was introduced into Canada from England and into U.S. from Canada. (Canadian ice hockey was an adaptation of Irish-English field hockey. The English winter does not normally produce enough ice to make the ice game likely.)]

hard hat   1. A protective metal or plastic helmet worn by workers in mines, on construction sites, and in many factories. Hence, 2. The blue-collar worker who wears it. Hence, 3. A truculent political reactionary.

high hat 1. *Now rare.* In various forms, a stovepipe hat with a stiff brim. 2. A gentleman of fashion. [One who wears such a hat.] Hence, 3. A snob. —*adj.* Snobbish. —*v.* To snub.

mad as a hatter Quite mad. [Earlier, felt hats were made by treating furs, usu. rabbit or beaver, with mercury. Prolonged exposure to the fumes of mercury damages the nervous system. Old hatters, therefore, developed a twitch, they tended to become incoherent, and they suffered a loss of coordination that made them appear to be zany, a condition once known as *the hatter's shakes.*]

throw one's hat in the ring To accept a challenge. Now, usu. in the political sense, to announce one's candidacy for office. [Am. XIX, during which the traveling "strong man show" was common. John L. Sullivan, once world heavyweight champion, was billed as "the strong man of Boston." The strong man, sometimes after an exhibition with sparring partners, challenged all comers, offering a prize to any man who could stay in the ring with him for a specified time without being knocked down or knocked out.

To throw one's hat into the ring was the standard signal that the challenge had been accepted. ***Hat in the Ring Squadron*** A famous U.S. aerial group of WWI [Its planes were marked with an Uncle Sam hat inside a ring, signifying "We came to fight."]

   cocked hat/be knocked into a cocked hat See *cock*.

hatband: tight as (queer as) Dick's hatband   Very tight. Very queer. In fact, ludicrously so. [A catch phrase intensive. Still in Brit. use. Once common in Am. but becoming rare, prob. because of the slow but steady de-Anglicization of the U.S.

    An idiom in dispute. If meaning is what one thinks one means when using a given form, then most people mean by *hatband* the crown of England and by *Dick,* Richard Cromwell, son of Oliver Cromwell, Lord High Protector of England. Oliver died Sept. 3, 1658, and Richard was proclaimed his successor Jan. 27, 1659. Oliver had planned to have Richard crowned king, with the protectorate as an intermediate step, but Richard fumbled and was forced to resign May 25, 1659, passing instantly into obscurity. Most who have used this phrase have meant it in contempt of the absurd notion that so high a "hatband" could be made to fit so gross a Roundhead.

    The OED, however, questions this rendering, giving *Nick* in place of *Dick,* and (non)explaining: "Dick or Nick was prob. some local character whose droll sayings were repeated." It offers nothing, however, to support this nonassertion. There is, though, the fact that the phrase is not attested until 1785, when Grose lists it in his *Classical Dictionary of the Vulgar Tongue,* giving *queer* as the only form, and defining it as "Out of order, without knowing one's disease."

    And there the trail is lost. If Richard Cromwell occasioned the idiom, the lag of more than a century before attestation seems long; but even longer if, as the OED suggests, the expression is grafted on some earlier, lost form. The Cromwellian reference has certainly been intended by English-speaking people since the eighteenth century, and the OED demurrer is certainly insubstantial. In the end a person is left to mean by a phrase whatever he thinks he means when he uses it, and even more so when he isn't sure.]

hatch[1]   [< IE *kak-*, male genitalia (in which slang COCK, penis, is readily visible, substantially rebutting the derivation from COCK, rooster, though the latter prob. influ. the former). Via Gmnc. with k/h and k/g → OE *hagen,* male genitals; ME *hacchen* with sense shift to "to produce life"; and at some point I have been unable to determine, specific to "producing life from an egg."] *v.* 1. To bring forth fledglings from eggs. 2. *Ext.* To bring a plan to action. *hatch a plot.* —*n.* 1. The act of hatching. 2. The brood brought forth by a given hatch. 3. The total of chicks hatched. *The spring hatch in the Carolinas has been 11 percent above last year's.*

hatch²/hatchway   Opening in a deck. The cover of such an opening. [Of obscure Gmnc. origin → OE *haeccan, hecc,* deck covering, hole in a deck, cover of such a hole. ME *hacche, hecche.*

down the hatch A drinking toast. Signifies: "Stow it away." *booby hatch* See *booby.*

haversack   A canvas bag carried by a single strap over the shoulder. [Lit. "oat sack." < Ger. *Habersack* < *Haber,* oats. Because first used by field workers in broadcasting (see *broadcast*) small seed such as oats. Millet's once much-reproduced painting *The Sowers* shows field workers broadcasting from a haversack.]

hay   [IE *kau-,* to fell (a tree), to cut. With k/h and suffixed -*g*- in Gmnc. → OE *heig,* hay; and with regular shift of terminal OE *g* to *y* in later English → ME *hei,* hay.] *n.* 1. Grass cut and dried for fodder —*v.* 1. To make hay. 2. To feed animals with hay.

haymaker 1. One who makes hay. 2. A powerful roundhouse blow. [After the motion of swinging a scythe.] *hayseed* 1. A barbed seed of any of the various grasses used for hay. 2. A yokel. [Because the barbed hayseeds are forever stuck to his clothes.] *hit the hay* To go to bed. [Originally on a tick stuffed with hay.] *roll in the hay* To have a lusty, bucolic sexual go. [In a haystack or haymow.] *that ain't hay* (Usually said of money.) That's something of value. [Not as worthless as hay underfoot.]

make hay (while the sun shines) Seize the opportunity while you can. 1. On a literal level, because hay, once cut, can only cure in dry hot weather. 2. In the extended sense, get what you can while you can. *Carpe diem.* Gather ye rosebuds while ye may. [But note that "gather ye rosebuds" is delicate, and "make hay," lusty. Many a father of a teen-age daughter has wondered, when a young man came to call, whether the boy was gathering rosebuds or making hay, the difference being of some parental concern.]

hayburner   A horse. [A variable term, sometimes disparaging (creature good for nothing but to "fuel up" on hay); sometimes merely whimsical (creature that uses hay for fuel). Mid XIX Am. Note that the term could not come into being until *wood-burner* had been established for the "iron horse" locomotive.]

haywire   1. Stiff wire used for baling hay. Also called baling wire. [Beginning circa WWI, hay balers began to be common in the U.S. and haywire and baling wire began to be perhaps the most common farm article next to cow dung.] 2. Wrong. Crazily unpredictable. All snarled up. [Because this wire was twisted tight around the bales and popped up at unpredictable sharp angles when cut; and because any accumulation of the stuff became a hopeless snarl.]
     NOTE. Though identical in literal meaning, *haywire* and *baling wire* have firmly different idiomatic senses. By language convention *haywire* is the symbol of something gone wrong, whereas *baling wire* is the stuff used in making emergency repairs to machinery and farm tools. It is out of idiom to use *baling wire* in such a construction as *it's all haywire* (all wrong). When the old Model T Ford went *haywire,* the ingenious farmer put it back in order with *spit and baling wire.*

head[1]   *Nautical.* (In common use by 1875, but prob. with long antecedents.) Shipboard equivalent of a latrine. [The *head* of the ship was in the bows and in early ships it was there sailors relieved themselves, prob. at first simply by holding on to ropes, and later from a small platform in the head (bow) with a hole through it. In a sailing ship underway, a man in the bow would be eliminating downwind. In the stern he would be discharging into the wind and likely fouling the stern sheer (of the captain's cabin).] *admiral of the head* Sea lord (see *admiral*) of what a landlubber would call a latrine. A mock title for a seagoing latrine orderly.

head[2]   *Slang. Post WWII.* Oral sex by a woman. (The ext. to "oral sex by a man" would be obvious, but I have not come upon it.) *Do you give head?* Do you take the penis into your mouth? [*Head* for *mouth,* the third orifice.]

heathen   1. *At root.* One who lives in the wilderness, on the heath, on the moors (in wild, untilled land). 2. Among Christians, one who lacks the "true" (their own) religion. (See *pagan* for an identical development based on other roots.) Because those who lived out in the wilds were the last to be reached by Christian missionaries and clung to ancient religious rituals long after the cities had become Christianized. [IE *kaito-,* wilderness, untilled land. With k/h and t/th in Gmnc. → OE *haeth,* heath; *haethan,* heath dweller, savage. *Piers Plowman* provides an unusually early etymology (xv. 451): "*Hethene* is to mene (mean) after *heth* (heath),/ And untiled (untilled) erthe."]

heel [IE *kenk-*, heel. Via obscure evolution in Gmnc. prob. involving a double k/h and dropping the nasal → OE *hēla*, heel.] *n.* 1. The back of the foot. 2. *Ext.* The end of a bluntly rounded thing, as some loaves of bread. 3. *By a similar ext.* The end of a golf club nearest the shaft. 4. A mean, worthless person. [The lowest part of a man.] —*v.* To follow closely, as in command to a dog.

at heel/close on the heels of Close behind. *dog one's heels* To follow closely and persistently. *down at the heels* Needy. Shabby. In financial straits. [Down to worn-out shoes.] *ward heeler* A minor politico; the local runner for the political boss. [As if he followed at the big man's heels on local visits, waiting to run errands.] *under the heel of* Oppressed by. *take to one's heels/show a clean pair of heels* To run away from a fight.

lay by the heels To bring low. *leave one to cool his heels* To keep one waiting [Both derive from the once legal practice of placing people in the stocks for minor offenses.]

head over heels Utterly and uncontrollably. (The root idea is of falling: *He lost his footing and went down the slope head over heels.* And so, by metaphoric extension: *He is head over heels in love.*) [But the idiom is curiously perverse in implying that head over heels is an abnormal situation. One would expect the abnormal situation to be expressed *heels over head.* Idiom, however, is its own patterned illogic. Cf. *time clock* (what else is a clock for?). *Punch clock* would certainly have been a more logical name. But idiom, remarkably sensitive in some ways, is just as remarkably tolerant in others, the evident absurdity of some details being subsumed into the understood gestalt configuration. See *gestalt.*]

heeled Armed, esp. by a concealed handgun. [From cockfighting, in which razor-sharp spurs (called heels) were strapped to the legs of fighting cocks, turning the normal cock tussle into a mortal engagement.] *well-heeled* Affluent. [An ext. of *heeled.* Originally said of someone carrying a fat wad of bills, a roll that would make his pocket bulge as if he had a pistol in it.]

hell: come hell or high water In the face of whatever difficulties. No matter what. [Partridge, *Slang*, gives the Brit. form as *hell and high water.* Both at once would obviously be intended as an intensive, but do not those Britishers realize that high water would put out the hellfires and the fires turn the water to steam, turning all muddle into a massive sauna? Origin unknown. P. finds no attestation before 1935!]

hell-bent for/hell-bent on   All out. Do or die. [Perh. akin to upper New England regionalisms, *in spite of Hell, in spite of Christ,* common intensives. *bent,* bound to, determined; *hell,* ultimate penalty; hence, determined at all costs. First attested in Maine, the election of 1840 (the same election that popularized O.K., which see), in which Edward Kent ran for governor; whence the rhyming slogan long common in U.S. electioneering: "Hell-bent for Edward Kent." Charles Earle Funk, *A Hog on Ice,* quotes a post-campaign song:

> Oh, have you heard how old Maine went?
> She went hell-bent for Governor Kent,
> And Tippecanoe and Tyler, too!]

   hell-bent for election As above. But early extended as a generalized intensive. *He lit out of here hell-bent for election.* He left in a hurry.
   hell-bent for leather [*Leather* for "saddle."] Galloping at top speed and in total disregard of danger. ***hell for leather*** Later variant of preceding.

hell-on-wheels   1. Originally (c. 1870) a railhead encampment depot in the building of the transcontinental railroad. 2. A catchall expression of violence, either in revelry or assault. *We had a hell-on-wheels party* (riotous revelry). *John L. Sullivan was hell-on-wheels in the ring* (violent physical action). *Joe's wife is hell-on-wheels when he comes in drunk* (violent temperament). *Reggie Jackson was hell-on-wheels in the last game of the 1977 World Series* (expresses admiration of one who performed powerfully).
   HISTORIC. At regular intervals of the railroad's transcontinental extension, railhead depots were established as bases for the next extension of the right of way, sometimes at an established town, sometimes at a geographically convenient unsettled point. There the railroad set up supply cars, sleeping cars, cook wagons, rolling offices, service wagons, and a supply dump. This rolling community was followed by horse-drawn wagons that offered whiskey, prostitutes, gambling, and whatever else could lure the pay from a *gandy dancer's* (which see) pocket, including a chance to get mugged. When the line had been extended a suitable distance, the whole anthill moved down the line to the next railhead, the horse-drawn

wagons followed on their own, and the entire transportable hell-hole was reestablished at the new end-of-track.

helter-skelter   Every which way; in more or less total disorder; at random. [The redupl. is based on *skelter*, which is ambiguously < ME *skelte*, haste, in disorderly haste; and/or dial. *kelter*, working order (see *kilter*). Hence, "in disorderly haste," or simply "in disorder."]

hermaphrodite   1. *Biology.* A creature, as the earthworm, with both male and female sex organs. 2. A person having secondary characteristics of the opposite sex; a man-woman, a woman-man. 3. Anything marked by contradictory elements or sets of elements. So *hermaphrodite brig* A two-masted sailing vessel with square-rigged sails forward and schooner-rigged (triangular) sails aft. [In Greek mythology Hermaphrodite was the son of Hermes (Mercury) and Aphrodite (Venus), whose two names he combined. Note that he is therefore a brother of Eros-Cupid, or since Ares is variantly given as the father of Eros, his half-brother. One day Hermaphrodite went swimming in a pool whose tutelary spirit was the nymph Salmacis, who for love of Hermaphrodite prayed that they might be indissolubly united, whereupon their two bodies, with some shouted protest by Hermaphrodite, merged into one. Note, moreover, that love had to be inspired by brother Eros-Cupid. There are some family relationships here that are certainly worth looking into.] *adj.* **hermaphroditic**

heyday   In Brit. also *heighday.* 1. The prime of one's life and vigor. *Tom Swales was a powerful man in his heyday.* 2. The peak of popularity, as of a fashion or a fad. *in the heyday of the Flapper.* [In early XVI the exclam. *heyda!* expressed wonder, vigorous gaiety, enthusiasm. Akin to LG *heidi, heida,* hoorah. In late XVI *hey-day, heyday,* a time of notable excitement (lit. "hurrah day"). And by XVIII, the shift to the present sense.]

hey-derry-down   Traditional Brit. song refrain. [Eliezer Edwards, *Dictionary of Words, Facts, and Phrases,* London, 1901, notes: "Blackwood's Magazine (July 1878) says this has been traced to a Druidical chant *Hai down, ir, deri danno,* 'Come, let us hasten to the oaken grove.'"

I have not yet located a copy of the cited issue, but the note will certainly do as a high-water mark of inventiveness, even for folk etymology, which here ventures into a detailed derivation from an unknown language.

Intuitively, of course, I agree with *Blackwood's* writer. My own intuition has long since demonstrated to me that the popular song refrain "Yessir, that's my baby" derives from the Proto-Cursive Pre-Hieroglyphic Egyptian prayer *Ia shah Thot smeib abi,* meaning "The great God Thoth has been gracious to me (in granting me this child)." *Abi* (dative of *o-boi,* the pronoun *I*) is akin to *ibis,* the bird sacred to Thoth; and has the additional sense "person," ie., "one of God's ibises." Cf. the related Am. Negro form "all God's chillun (ibises) got wings." And with them a license to practice folk etymology.]

high-falutin(g)/hifalutin   High-flown. Affected. Hoity-toity. (Said of language or manners.) *Miller Williams, he come back to Arkansas all nosed up with them high-falutin big-city ways he took in Joplin.* [Am. latter XIX. Prob. (?) a la-di-da variant of "fluting" ("toodlin' high"). Am. dial. readily inserts a schwa, as in *slippery el'm.* And singers commonly do the same in an exaggerated way, as in *you're da-riving me ca-razy.* Into Brit. usage c. 1900. Eliezer Edwards, writing c. 1901, noted, "The word is becoming domesticated in England," adding, as the ultimate attestation, "and has even crept into a *Times* leader."]

high horse   A great horse. [Knights wanted powerful chargers to carry the weight of armor, and the taller the charger, the greater the knight's advantage in a tilt. Persons of rank sought out long legged impressive Arabians. The higher one's rank, the higher the horse.] *on one's high horse* Aloof. Snobbish. [In the full dignity of one's rank, real or assumed.]

hind leg   Either of an animal's back legs. [< earlier *hinder,* rear, surviving into XIX Brit. *hindermost,* farthest back, but now *hindmost* in Am., with *hindermost* obsolescent if not obs.]

stand up on your hind legs Stand up and face adversity resolutely. [Said to persons, but the image is of an animal, as a bear, rearing to fight. Or is this an avatal image of an ape changing into a man by learning to walk erect?] *crooked as a dog's hind leg Rural intensive flourish.* Very crooked. *by the left hind leg of the lamb of God* Today an arch minced oath with a rural rhetorical flourish; in the context of an earlier, more fundamentalist society, the form must have been offensive, blasphemy consisting of associating the holy with the profane.

hinterland   1. Back country. *In the hinterlands of Cambridge there is a region called Harvard College.* [In XIX German colonization, Ger. *Hinterland* labeled any region lying behind a coastal or river-bank strip. < *hinter,* behind; with LAND. The Eng. equivalent, used only in bodily reference, is *hinderparts,* one's backside. So Herrick's dedication to his book:

> Who with these leaves should wipe at need
> The place where swelling piles do breed,
> May every ill that bites and smarts
> Perplex him in the hinderparts.]

hip   *Mod. slang (and prob. becoming passé).* Aware, knowing, up on, in the know. [Earlier *hep* with the same senses, perh. modified from the military usage for counting cadence, itself a modification of "left" as in *hep-ri'-hep* (because "hep" is easier to say with great expulsive force). MMM attests *hep* in this military usage by 1862; with the sense "aware, knowing," as of 1903; the sense shift being from military alertness to alertness in any sense.

J. L. Dillard, *Where Our Words Come From,* asserts a straight-line connection between West African *hipi* and mod. slang *hippie;* but this assertion addresses only the present form *hip* without considering earlier *hep,* it suggests no conceivable line of transmission, and must be dismissed as a fetch based on surface resemblance only by a Negro scholar who is a bit overzealous in his otherwise admirable desire to show how much African culture has contributed to American life—as it has done richly, though that contribution is not assisted by willful etymology.]

hippopotamus   The semiaquatic African pachyderm. [Root sense: "river horse." Gk. *hippopotamos* < *hippo,* horse (PHILLIP, HIPPODROME); *potamos,* river: MESOPOTAMIA, lit. "between (two) rivers."]

hitch   [ME **hytchen,* to raise by block and tackle (in a series of separate tugs). The form has precedents in East Anglian dialect.] *n.* 1. *By association with block and tackle.* A more or less temporary knot consisting basically of a loop-and-turn around a post. 2. *By association with the separate tugs needed to work a block and tackle.* A jerky motion. *He gave his pants a hitch. He hitched up his pants.* A snag (as when a rope catches in block). *Ext.* A limp, a stumble. 3. A military or naval enlistment. [One segment of a career.] —*v.* To fasten temporarily. To tie. *hitching post, hitch* *(up) a horse to a wagon.* (Note that both fastenings are temporary and easily undone.)

go without a hitch   To go smoothly. [In maritime usage, *to go with a run.* (With ref. to a line through a groove or pulley. If a coil snags, the line *catches a hitch.)*] **get hitched** Get married. [Team up in harness. (The connotation "temporary fastening" is muted here.)] **hitch up with** 1. Same as preceding. 2. To team (temporarily, as a rule) with someone as a traveling companion, partner, or buddy. **hitchhike** To travel by "thumbing" rides. [Go one's journey in a series of separate units.]

Hob   A familiar dialect nickname for Robin Goodfellow, also called Puck, a sprite more mischievous than evil. [XV < *(hob)goblin.* But *Hob* was also a standard nickname for the once common given name Robin.] **raise Hob** 1. *Lit.* To summon Robin Goodfellow (to his mischief). 2. *Effective sense.* To act up. To play pranks. **play Hob with** To spoil; to destroy. *Jean Borup keeps saying no, which raises Hob with my fantasy life.*

NOTE. In *A Midsummer Night's Dream*, II. i. 32–41, the Fairy, addressing Robin Goodfellow, sums him up:

> Either I mistake your shape and seeming quite,
> Or else you are that shrewd and knavish sprite
> Called Robin Goodfellow: are you not he
> That frights the maidens of the villagery;
> Skim milk, and sometimes labour in the quern,
> And bootless make the breathless housewife churn;
> And sometimes make the drink to bear no barm;
> Mislead night wanderers, laughing at their harm?
> Those that Hobgoblin call you and sweet Puck,
> You do their work, and they shall have good luck:
> Are you not he?

(*Quern,* a hand mill for grinding grain; *barm,* froth.)

hobbledehoy   Rarely, and only in Brit. **hobbadehoy.** A teen-age boy in his awkward stage. [An etymological *kelemenopy* (which see), the origin confused by a surplus of clues, one following from another, the total leading nowhere. A XVI verse describing man's life as divided into seven-year periods reads in part:

> The first seven years bring up as a child.
> The next to learning, for waxing too wild.
> The next keep under Sir Hobbard de Hoy.
> The next a man, no longer a boy.

Sir Hobbard de Hoy, a fanciful name of unknown origin, must be either the master to whom a boy is apprenticed from 14 to 21, or a composite don at public school and the university.

Hoy may be akin to *hoyden* (now an impudent girl, but earlier a trickster, blusterer) < Ger. *Heiden*, Gypsy, wandering rogue (but at root: "heathen"). And earlier *hoy* was also a loud noise (cf. nautical *ahoy*). *Hob*, a common nickname for Robin, Robert, is also associated with imp, hobgoblin. Whence *hob o' the hoy* has various permutations of meanings, with "roguish noisy imp" central to them.

Shakespeare has *Hoberdidance* and *Hobbididance* as names of fiends or goblins. (Cf. *Flibbertigibbet*.)

But in the nature of kelemenopy, once these many and seemingly sequential clues are assembled, we find they lead nowhere.]

hobnob with   To be on intimate terms with. To be palsy-walsy with. [ME *hab-nab* < *habben*, to have; *ne habben, n' habben, nabben*, to have not. In Shakespeare with the sense "give or take" (we would say "give and take"). So *Twelfth Night*, III. iv: "hob, nob is his word, give't or take't." In XVIII with ref. to two men buying drinks for one another in turn and exchanging toasts; hence being cronies. Thence in XIX to present sense.]

hobo   A knight of the road. From time to time one comes on a newspaper interview with some eccentric who bills himself as King of the Hobos, and who has prepared a public relations philosophy for himself as one who has chosen a particular way of life which includes a minimum of work when absolutely necessary, but which is primarily a quest for freedom. These hobo image-makers insist that they are not tramps (tramps will not work, and will steal when they can), and not bums (bums are alcoholic). These distinctions, though much cherished for publicity purposes by the various "kings of the hobos," disappear in common usage, and the three terms become interchangeable. [The most common gloss, "origin unknown," is an evasion. Though not securely attested, the term can reasonably be parsed from *ho*, variant of *hi*, *hello*, a common greeting; with *bo*, guy (Got a match, bo?) *Bo* may be ult. from baby-talk version of *brother*. But it is also a common Sthrn. nickname < *Beau* < once common plantation South given name *Beauregard*. Whence, *ho, Bo* or *ho, bo*, hi, guy → *hobo*.]

Hobson's choice   The choice of the one thing that is offered or nothing at all. [After Thomas Hobson, early XVII innkeeper and liveryman known to generations of Cambridge students. The university bloods were passionate horsemen. Allowed a choice, they would have ridden Hobson's best horses to exhaustion. He therefore let out his horses in strict order of rotation, the most rested horse nearest the stable door, and one might have his choice of that horse or no horse. Addison memorialized Hobson in a *Spectator* essay, and Milton wrote two epitaphs for him.]

hock *v.* To pawn. [OED *Supplement* glosses the term as an Americanism, first attested 1859. Prob. < Du. *hok,* hovel, prison, and with the slang sense (by association with debtors' prison) debt. Perh. so, but I do not understand how OED can overlook: *Hocktide* The second Monday and Tuesday after Easter, which up to XVI were days of a folk revel surviving from lost heathen sources. On *Hock Monday* the country women ganged up on the men, hog-tied them, and held them until a ransom was paid for getting them out of hock. On *Hock Tuesday* the men did as much for the women. All proceeds were then turned over to parish charities.]

in hock In debt. *go into hock* To go into debt. (And conversely *out of hock/get out of hock.*)

hock one's soul for To go to any lengths for. [As if, in the common medieval folk tale motif, one pledged his soul to the devil in return for the thing desired. (My personal devil has turned down all my best pledges, alas.)]

hocus-pocus 1. An old jiggery formula used by conjurors, medicine men, and other performing street cheats. (Earlier forms: *hocas pocas,* 1624; *hokos pokos,* 1625.) 2. *Ext.* Any deceit. *the hocus-pocus of politics.* 3. *Ext.* Nonsense. Double-talk. *You'll get nothing but a lot of hocus-pocus from him.* [Redupl. based on *hoc est* from liturgical Latin *hoc est corpus meum,* this is my body, from the communion service. The ODEE offers a derivation from XVI pseudo-Latin gibberish formula used by XVI wandering student beggars and street performers, *hax pax max Deus adimax,* and certainly all such frummery is relevant, but all Catholics, which is to say everyone in early Europe, were familiar with the service of the mass, and certainly the liturgical Latin must be taken as the obvious source.]

Hogan A generic Irishman, the archetype of the shabbiest XIX Am. shanty Irish. *Hogan's goat* 1. A goat that stinks unbearably. 2. Anything that stinks unbearably. [This idiom had about expired when it was partially revived c. 1965 as the title of a play by William Alfred.] *Hogan's brickyard Am. XIX. Prob. obs.* A baseball diamond. [Anything associated with Hogan was run down and cluttered. Perh. originally a dumping ground used as a baseball diamond. Or perh. (??) so called because of the bricks hurled by irate fans.]

hog on ice In full form *independent/stubborn/stand-offish as a hog on ice Metaphoric intensive.* Very independent/stubborn/stand-offish. [Of a class with such country rhetorical flourishes as *slick as a button on a backhouse door.* Origin uncertain, but less than mysterious. Prob. a ref. to a hog that has been slaughtered but left whole to be spitted for a barbecue. A whole scalded and scraped porker bedded down on ice to await the spit will do as a fair country metaphor for indifference. The round stone-cum-handle used in the Scottish ice game called curling is known as a hog, and various renderings of the obscure rules of the game can argue contexts in which such a "hog" may be called "independent," but though such a gloss can seem ingenious, it falters on the fact that the idiom is unknown in Scottish.]

hoi polloi The ragtag and bobble-tail rabble. A snob name for the common people, i.e., you and I; unless I am doing the talking, in which case, just you. [A transcription of Gk. for "the many," nominative plu. form. In classical times the ever shifting populace (*mobile vulgus;* see *mob*); the lowest classes of free citizens, for whom the Roman state provided "bread and circuses."]

hoity-toity *adj.* Fussily affected. Snobbish. High-falutin. La-di-da. [And so in Am., but in Brit. with the primary sense "frolicsome"; and, as a noun, "a riotous fling." C. 1600. Redupl. based on dialect *hoit, to romp riotously, as at a country festival. Selden's *Table Talk* contains a curious variant in a contemporary account of the court of Charles I (crowned 1625, beheaded by Cromwell 1649). After mentioning the "gravity and state" of the preceding courts of James and Elizabeth, he writes: ". . . but in King Charles's time there has been nothing but Frenchmore and the cushion dance, omnium gatherum, tolly-polly, and *hoite-come-toite."* A puzzling usage: if Selden had in mind Fr. *haut comme le toit,* high as the roof, he was certainly associating good English idiom with bad French. In any case, everyone seemed to be having a good time at Charles's court—while it lasted.]

hollow [Akin to *hole.* OE *hol,* hole; *holh,* hollow. Ult. < IE *kel-,* to hide away. With k/h in Gmnc. HOLE, HOLD (of a ship), HELL.] *n.* A hole or depression. —*adj.* 1. Empty. 2. Without substance. *hollow words and empty threats.* —*v.* 1. To make a hole or depression. Usu. with *out.* 2. To preserve the outer covering while removing the internal substance.

 hollow leg Symbolizes the ability to drink much without becoming tipsy. [Fanciful metaphor: as if the booze by-passed one's stomach and went into a special storage hollowed out of one's leg. Dating uncertain.]

 beat all hollow 1. To beat overwhelmingly. 2. To be better than in every way. *Drinking beats working all hollow.* [*Beat hollow* is attested in Brit. 1759. *All hollow,* which is Am. only, attested 1762. *Hollow* is prob. a corruption of *wholely.* If so, the original Brit. form may have been *to beat wholely;* and the Am. *all* may be a root echo of the lost *wholely.*]

holy 1. Sacred. *Holy Church, the Holy Land.* 2. Devout. *holy man.* [IE *kail-,* of good omen, hale, intact. With k/h in Gmnc. to OE *haelig,* blessed; Ger. *Heilige,* saint. The terminal *-ig* of OE regularly changes to *-y* in Eng.]

 Holy of Holies The innermost room of a Jewish temple. The Ark of the Covenant is stored there. Only the high priest is permitted to enter, and he only once a year on the Day of Atonement. The Latin form is *sanctum sanctorum,* holy place of all holy places.

 holy mackerel Common Am. exclam. of surprise, awe, vexation. Or used as one of the mildest of minced oaths. [Though a simple form, a complex evolution. Invokes contemptuous ref. to Roman Catholics as mackerel snatchers (because they ate fish on Friday). Also the second century A.D. acronym *ichthus,* the Greek word for fish, but also *I(esous) CH(ristos) TH(eou) U(ios), S(oter):* Jesus Christ, Son of God, Savior. And also the profane reference to the Holy Ghost in the common exclam. *holy smoke!* or in full mock form *holy smoke, the church is on fire!*

 holystone Nautical. A piece of coarse pumice or sandstone once used to scour wooden decks. *v.* To scour decks with such a stone. [Both so called, whimsically, because to do the work sailors had to kneel (as if in prayer).]

holy Toledo! Once common exclam. of surprise, awe, mild vexation. [Now rare, but still understood. Medieval Toledo, noted for both its cathedrals and its mosques, was an important religious center for Moors as well as Spaniards, a city holy to both. It was also the scene of solemn coronation pomps. In *Don Quixote* Cervantes apostrophizes it as "O holy city!" El Greco painted it as a place of great architectural and scenic splendor.]

Homo sapiens   In taxonomy, the label for mankind as now constituted, the genus consisting of a single species. [< L. *homo*, man; *sapiens*, sapient. The term was first applied by Linnaeus, Swedish taxonomer, 1707–1778, born Carl von Linné. Linnaeus meant to indicate that man was distinct from all other creatures in being rational. On the other hand, no one has undertaken to prove the rationality of aggregate man. Linnaeus might more rationally have labeled his creature *Homo loquens*, talking man, for whether or not he has learned to think, he has certainly learned to talk faster than anything can think, and is clearly distinct from all other creatures in his loquacity.]

honeymoon   *n.* 1. The first (blissful) month of marriage. [*Moon*, month; *honey*, sweetness. And see note below.] 2. A blissful time. *Their marriage was a lifelong honeymoon.* —*v.* To spend the honeymoon. *They honeymooned at the corner cafeteria.*

HISTORIC. *Honeymoon* is generally associated in Am. with the tender love time, but was the root sense "month of sweet joy" or "month of the waning of joy"? On that point the Nordic and the Mediterranean traditions seem to be at odds.

L. *mel*, honey, was an established term of endearment. It. *luna di miele* is simply "month of sweetness." And so for Fr. *lune de miel* and Sp. *luna de miel*. All rings of nothing but joy.

Among the Nordics, moreover, and in early England, it was long a fixed custom (as it still is in Wales) to drink mead (honey wine) at the marriage feast. (The custom began because the stuff was supposed to be an aphrodisiac, but the later association was with sweetness.) Attila the Hun died in 453 of guzzling too much of the stuff at his wedding feast. It was long custom, too, for newlyweds to share a glass of mead each night of the first month, prob. for its legendary powers as an aphrodisiac. Once again, all is sweetness, or at least hoped-for sweetness. And so it was long understood, at least in the south.

Then the OED (citing Dr. Samuel Johnson as its authority on love and marriage) glossed *moon* as: "originally having no ref. to the period of a month, but comparing [italics mine] *the mutual affections of newly married persons to the changing moon which is no sooner full than it begins to wane.*"

Successive Webster's dictionaries, after more than a century of bracketing *honeymoon* and *honeymonth* as "the first month after marriage," picked up from the OED and Johnson, and fumbled at a change of mind. The 1925 *New International Dict.* adds a close paraphrase of the italicized portion of the OED gloss. The 1953 *New World Dict.* adds, "cf. Flitterwochen, lit., tinsel weeks," implying falseness and waning of love. By 1970 the note, bristling with question marks, has become:

> (? in ref. to the waning of affections of newlyweds) but ? folk-etymol. for ON *hjūnōttsmānathr*, lit., wedding night month.

The OED further cites several English authors from 1552 to 1656 who used "honeymoon" with this Nordic connotation of "waning affections." Its later citations, however, though some are ambiguous, tend to imply "time of sweetness."

The doctors being in disagreement, I can only suggest that the liberated reader go look at his/her wife/husband and lean to the northern or the southern tradition according to the weight of the evidence.

honky/honkie   *Am. Negro.* A derisive term for a white person. [Though now firmly established in the vocabulary, and of recent origin, the origin is in dispute, the dating being all-important.

The term first came to the awareness of whites during and just after WWII. At that time many southern blacks moved to Chicago and Gary to work in factories, and found themselves for the first time working side by side with white workers. Because the labor force in and around Chicago contains a large percentage of people of Middle European descent, the newly arrived blacks may have altered *honky* from *hunky*, a derisive term for Hungarian, perhaps taking the strange term to mean any white worker, hence any white man. And if the term cannot be attested before c. 1941, the dating would favor this derivation.

Alternatively, it may derive from *honky-tonk*, a southern Negro barrelhouse in which early jazz musicians played. At one time, white jazz buffs made a big thing of visiting *honky-tonks*, where they would be naturally resented by the Negroes whose privacy they invaded, but welcomed by the proprietor for their cash. If they were slurringly called *honky-tonkers* and that term then shortened to *honkies*, the progression would be natural and from native sources, and therefore to be preferred. I cannot, however, find its use attested before WWII, though it may have been in use without having found its way into print. I warmly welcome from any reader firm evidence of the term's earliest use.

Among other implausible suggested origins is *honker* for "goose," with the evolved sense "white (stupid, noisy) goose."]

hooch 1. Rotgut. 2. Any hard liquor. [< *Hoochino*, the Am. rendering of the name of a Tlingit tribe of Eskimos of southern Alaska, the name in its unpronounceable original meaning "the people of the strait of the grizzly bear."]

HISTORIC. No Amerinds had developed fermented or distilled drinks before the coming of the white man, though many then developed a disastrous taste for firewater. Under the Russian occupation, the Alaskan Indians seem to have acquired no knowledge of alcohol. With the arrival of the Americans in mid XIX, however, the Alaskan Indians became riotous drunkards.

The Americans ate sourdough bread. A bucket of sourdough starter, if left for a few days, exudes a slightly fermented liquid, a sort of noxious flat beer for which the Tlingits developed a taste; but "hooch" was yet to come.

Regulations forbade hard liquor on the military post, and a still would be too fragrant to conceal. An American army sergeant, therefore, scrounged the parts for a still, rigged up a cooker and coils in the Hoochino village, and showed the natives how to distill.

With access to sugar and molasses from the American trading post, and with a natural talent for throwing into the mash anything else they could find, the Hoochinos soon became manufacturers of a perilous rotgut which they not only drank in binges that involved the whole village and all nearby white men, but took to distributing through most of southern Alaska. In a memoir of Alaskan travels in 1880, John Muir tells of meeting a party of Chilcat Indians on a 200-mile trek to a Hoochino village to demand blood money for a Chilcat woman who had died of drinking their rotgut.

hoodwink To dupe. To pull the wool over one's eyes. [*Hood*, the head piece of a cape as worn by friars, shepherds, and many others; *wink*, that which covers the eyes.]

hook or crook By one means or another. By fair means or foul. [But fair-or-foul is a late evolution by association with slang *hook*, to steal; *crook*, a thief. The original reference was to the feudal *bote* (see *boot: to boot*) that gave peasants the right to gather as firewood any fallen branches together with any that could be broken off by a shepherd's *crook*, or by a *hook*, a curved knife fastened to a pole. Felling of trees, except by special permission or under specified circumstances, was strictly forbidden. The original sense "by limited means only" has changed to "by whatever means one can devise."]

hooligan   A street tough. A brawler. A minor thug. [Said to derive from *Hooligan,* surname of an Irish family that lived in Southwark, London, c. 1900, and that seems rather notably to have enlivened the neighborhood, but never trust an Englishman to be accurate in ridiculing the Irish; with the English the ridicule comes first and the details may be freely invented along the way.]

Hooverville   A bitter eponym for the shack towns made of crates, and lacking plumbing and electricity, that sprang up in city dumps and open land during the 1930's. They were the only shelters the dispossessed could find during the years of the Great Depression. [Named after Herbert Hoover, U.S. President 1928–1932. Hoover took the blame for the nation's financial collapse, and the fact is that despite his great personal integrity, Hoover was economically an illiterate.]

HISTORIC. During Hoover's administration a famous Hooverville sprang up on vacant land in Washington, D.C., when jobless veterans of WWI gathered there from all over the nation on what was called a "bonus march," a demand by impoverished veterans that they be given their service bonuses. The veterans remained until Hoover, in a display of statesmanship, ordered the army to evict them. As a footnote on the intricacies of history, the eviction proceedings were handled by Gen. Douglas MacArthur, whose aide was Maj. Dwight D. Eisenhower.

hopscotch   The child's game played on a court marked on the ground, now by chalking a pavement, earlier by scratching bare ground with a stick. [Earlier *scotch-hoppers* (XVII), *hop-scot* (XVIII); but with no reference to Scotland. *Scotch* < OF *escocher,* to cut, with ref. to marking (cutting) the playing court on the ground with a stick. *Escocher* was originally with specific ref. to cutting a *notch* (which see) in a counting stick. Hence, to cut. Hence, to destroy (cut out), as in *scotch a rumor.*

And so, too, **butterscotch,** a yellow (butter-colored) candy which is cut (scotched) into squares. [There is no evidence that this candy was first made in Scotland. The Japanese ape-alls have entered the market with their own brands of Scotch whiskey, a practice the Scots are eager to scotch.]

horn spoon   *Am. prospecting, mid XIX.* A cow horn used by quartz prospectors as placer miners used a pan to shake out the dross and isolate the ore, the quartz miners' process commonly called horning. [First attested by MMM 1855.] **by the great horn spoon** Variantly **by the sacred horn spoon** A mild minced oath. [But what is it a minced form of—the trump of doom? The minced oath, first attested in a ballad dated 1842, probably preceded the mining term, and prob. explains why a whole cow horn was called a spoon.]

hornswoggle To be deceived, cheated, outdone, made a fool of. As an exclam. *Well, I'll be hornswoggled!* [One of the most colorful of Am. exuberant formations. MMM first attests it in 1829, and again in 1866 with the form *hornswaggled.*

In one of the most curiously persistent errors of our etymology, our dictionaries have universally (or so to the best of my knowledge) glossed it "origin unknown." Their bafflement, I submit, could only follow from a misdivision of the elements into *horn* and *swaggle.* It should be divided into *horns* (symbol of cuckoldry) and *waggle.* To place the hands on either side of one's head, knuckles to the temples, and index fingers extended, and then to wave the head from side to side, is an ancient gesture of mocking a man as a cuckold. The exclam. *Well, I'll be hornswoggled!* can only mean at root: "Well, I'll be cuckolded!"]

horrid *At root:* Inspiring horror, mortal terror. *But through long, more or less petulant use as a hyperbole:* Unpleasant. *a horrid child.* [< L. *hōrrere,* to cause to tremble, to inspire fear, to bristle (as hairs on the neck or an army with spears), to be rough and shaggy. Winston Churchill had the classical sense in mind when he said, "War is above all words horrible." He was, in fact, all but translating Virgil's *"Bella, horrida bella"*: "War, horrid war." And so Milton, *Comus:*

> . . . where every desolation dwells
> By grots and caverns shagged with horrid shades

in which *horrid* and *shagged* reinforce one another's root sense of bristly, rough, emotionally upsetting.]

horse latitudes Either of the two belts of the Atlantic between 30 and 35 degrees of north and south latitude. In these latitudes (see note) Spanish transports to the New World commonly found themselves becalmed for long periods. [The term first appeared in Eng. in 1777 as an approximate rendering of Sp. *el golfo de las yegnas,* the gulf (sea) of the mares. Spanish transport regularly carried cavalry to the New World. When ships were long becalmed, water and provisions ran low, and it became necessary to dispose of the horses. Some dictionaries have been so far from a sense of the real world as to suggest the Spaniards threw the horses overboard. Out of respect for the Spanish fighting man's instinct for survival, I will insist that he did not throw good meat to the sharks; he ate the horses, after first drinking their blood to supplement his water ration.]

NOTE. Long held to be a mystery of the sea, the windlessness of the horse latitudes is a phenomenon of the planet's primary atmospheric circulation. Warm air rises at the equator, cooling as it rises, but thrust onward by the impulse of the air rising behind it. At the top of the upward flow, the air divides more or less equally and flows to the poles. Cold and heavy then, it tends to settle into the rarer air below. A first major zone of settlement occurs in the horse latitudes. Warming as it descends, the air from above mingles with the surface air with relatively little lateral motion (wind) until the normally high barometric pressure of these latitudes forces a lateral breakout; the long-becalmed ships being finally released by a storm.

horseshoe   Symbol of good luck.

HISTORIC. As superstitions go, this one developed late, for horses were not generally shod, at least in Europe, until about IX, at which time the inventions of the horseshoe, stirrups, and the horse collar combined in a technological revolution that one may say changed the very nature of the horse. It may be the extraordinary transformation brought about by these inventions that invested the horseshoe with its sense as a potent symbol.

Shoeing made possible a sort of hard riding previously unknown. The introduction of stirrups revolutionized cavalry by permitting a spearsman to brace himself as part of his thrust, and a swordsman or lancer to lean far to the right or left. The horse collar, by putting the strain on the neck and shoulder muscles instead of across the chest, which constricted the heart and the flow of blood to it, made it possible for a horse to plow all day long instead of for a few hours at a time.

hot pillow joint   A No-Tell Motel or Hotel which rents rooms by the hour for sexual assignations, often by prearrangement with streetwalkers and cruising prostitutes from its own bar. [Whimsical exuberant, the pillows conceived as being still warm from contact with the heads of the previous occupants. *Joint,* common slang for a public establishment ("place where things meet").]

howdy [Contracted form of "how do you do" via regional "howdy-do."] 1. An informal back country greeting. 2. *Ext. by association.* A yokel. 3. *Whimsical.* A more or less sharp dip in a roadbed. [Because it causes passengers riding in an automobile to dip their heads as if saying "howdy" or "howdy-do."]

we've howdy'd but we ain't shook Self-relishing sthrn. idiom with ref. to a nodding acquaintance. We've nodded in passing but we have never shaken hands (as in acknowledgment of a formal introduction).

Hoyle Edmund Hoyle, Sir Edmund. Died 1769. Author of the definitive book on the rules of games, esp. of card games. *according to Hoyle* According to the rules. *Hence.* Fair. Aboveboard. Sportsmanlike.

hubba-hubba WWII. A variable expressive. When shouted by troops, a cry of enthusiasm. When shouted by an officer or a noncom, a command to react enthusiastically and on the double. [Based on *hubbub??* It is the fixed dementia of the military mind that troops can be made enthusiastic by being ordered to shout.]

huckster 1. One who hawks his wares. *If there is a heaven, poor Oscar Williams is huckstering through it, bent under a back pack of definitively immortal poems.* 2. A fast-talking, hard-sell salesman who deals not with customers but with suckers. 3. In an uncharacteristic honesty, a name applied to themselves by executives and salesmen of ad agencies. (*Hawk, hawker,* are prob. cognates.) [ME *huccstere,* itinerant peddler, was borrowed without change from MD. Based on Low German root *hok-,* prob. ult. < IE *keu-,* to curve, to bend (which evolved in Gmnc. with k/h and suffixed *-k-*). The double root sense is prob. 1. Container (peddler's basket made by bending reeds). 2. Man bent under the weight of basket (back pack). On both counts, a ref. to a wandering peddler.]

hue and cry 1. A repeated cry of alarm. 2. An uproar of shouted demands by a street crowd, as of demonstrators or protesters. 3. Any sustained public utterance of opinion, whether aloud or in print. *All our newspapers have joined in the hue and cry against permissive education.* [But in British law, a duty required of all citizens from the time of the Norman occupation to the repeal of the last "hue and cry" statutes in 1827. Mary Helen Dohan, *Our Own Words,* specifies it further:

> *murdrum* was a heavy fine imposed upon the whole community for the death of a Norman, any murdered man being presumed Norman unless four freemen of the community could give "proof of Englishry." (Then, obviously, the murder did not matter.) The legal phrase *hu-e-cri* (both words meaning in French "to cry out against") . . . compelled all men by law to join with "horn and voice" in the hunt for the murderer, whose guilt was considered theirs as well.

By XIV special reprisals for the death of Normans and legal indifference to the murder of Englishmen had largely passed, but the duty of citizens to join in the pursuit of criminals with a hue and cry (as in "Stop, thief!") remained legally stipulated until early XIX.]

hugger-mugger   Disorder. Confusion. [And so in *Hamlet,* though the form appears earlier with many variants, among them XV *hoder moder,* which is traceable to a dead end (prob. < old dialect) in ME **hoder,* huddle heap; **mokere,* a store of goods ("makings"? "made things"?), hence, "disorderly heap of stuff," and when applied to a person, "clumsy, disorderly lout."]

humble pie   The dish of humility. *eat humble pie* To abase oneself. To eat crow. [A nonced word. In ME *numble(s) pie,* a meat pie made from the lesser organs of an animal. After a hunt, the lord of the manor and his guests ate roast venison and the hunt attendants ate the chopped organs, intestines, and tripe baked in a pastry shell. Later, the cheapest of meat pies were made of the chopped intestines and least desirable organs of domestic animals. Ult. < L. *lumbus,* loin; *lumbulus* (dim. form), a little loin cut. Modified in OF to *noumbles* with sense shift from "loin" to "those organs nearest the loin" (intestines, tripe, testicles, etc.). Nonced (see *noncing*) in late ME from *a numble pie* to *an umble pie.* Then, prob. because *umble* sounded like a Cockney mispronunciation of *humble,* the *h* was tacked on by those who thought they were speaking "correct" English.]

humbug   1. Nonsense. Bosh. 2. A deception. A hoax. 3. An impostor. A fraud. One who offers a persuasive sort of nonsense as reason. (Common in Brit., this agential form is rare in Am.) [Appeared in mid XVIII Brit. with senses 2 and 3 above, became immediately popular, and was firmly fixed in English by Scrooge's repeated use of "Bah, humbug!" in Dickens's *Christmas Carol.* Despite many fanciful folk etymologies, nothing is known of its origin. A whimsical invention.]

humor   *n.* 1. *Now.* That which moves to laughter. 2. A mood. —*v.* To cajole. To play up to and allay someone's bad mood. *humoresque* A whimsical musical composition. *humorist* One who evokes laughter. *out of humor* Grumpy. Not amenable to pleasantries. [But a much altered word. Ult. < IE *uegu-, ugu-*, wet. With g/h and suffixed *-m-* → hypothetical intermediate form *(u)hu-m-* → L. *umere, humere*, to make wet, to be wet (HUMID); and also *ūmor*, bodily fluid.]

HISTORIC. Early medical theory, persisting into XVIII, was based on four humors, or bodily fluids: blood, phlegm, yellow bile, black bile. A healthy person was said to have all four humors in "balance." When there was an excess of blood, one tended to be physically apoplectic and emotionally irate; when of phlegm, to be physically sluggish and emotionally torpid; when of yellow bile, to be physically jaundiced and emotionally choleric; when of black bile, to be physically listless and emotionally melancholy.

From XVI to early XVIII English playwrights produced a great body of comedy based on these theories of the humors. The more a character was dominated by a single humor, the more eccentric his manner, and the more risible the stage effect. It was so that *humor* (in Brit. *humour*), once specific to a medical condition, came to mean "that which calls forth laughter."

hussy   (The *ss* may be pronounced as a pure sibilant or as a *z*.) 1. An impertinent girl. 2. A shameless wench. 3. A prostitute. [Up to XVI merely a contraction of *housewife* (of which earlier forms were: *hussif, huswif, huswife.* < Scandinavian *hus*, house (see *hustings*); *wif*, woman, wife. For alteration of terminal *-if* to *-y*, cf. *goody* < *goodif, goodwife.* (*Goody* for *Mrs.* remained in use in Am. until early XIX.) For the male chauvinist slander whereby the good English housewife evolved into a hussy, see Women's Lib.]

hustings   (Only with *the* and in the plu. form. Some authorities insist that the form be treated as a singular, but I refuse to say "the hustings rings with acclaim.") The field of political campaigning. "[Dole's] demeanor on the hustings turned some voters from the Ford-Dole ticket." —N. Y. *Times,* Nov. 5, 1976. [< ON *husting*, legislative assembly. < *hus*, house; *thing, ding*, legislative assembly.

In Scandinavia *thing, ding* was roughly equivalent to "parliament," i.e., a general legislative assembly. The "house thing" was a meeting of high councillors called by the king at his castle *(hus);* hence, more nearly, a cabinet meeting.

Husting(s) has had the following meanings in Britain, the Am. sense deriving from the last, and all, of course, deriving from the Danish occupation of England: XI, an assembly of peers; XII, a court that sat in Guildhall, London; XVII, a platform on which members of this court sat; XVIII, a platform from which parliamentary candidates were nominated.] *stump the hustings* To campaign for political office. (see *stump:* to campaign.)

hybrid   [L. **hibrida,* mongrel.] Crossbred. Now, as in *hybrid corn,* labels the product of a scientific crossing of genetically different strains in order to achieve especially desirable characteristics (which breed out after two or three generations). The sense "specially chosen strain," along with the chance resemblance of the forms, probably underlies the common folk etymology < "high bred," as if "thoroughbred," but the earlier sense was "mongrel" ("that which does not breed true").

hysteria   The more or less total loss of emotional control. [The term is from the smug sequences of male-dominant thinking. Greek males, priding themselves on their emotional steadiness, ascribed loss of emotional control to the behavior of women. Concluding that it stemmed from the malfunctioning of some organ specific to women, they imagined they had located the source in *hustera,* the womb, whence *husterikos,* of the (malfunctioning) womb. And so, too:] *hysterectomy Surgery.* The partial or total removal of the uterus.

I

ice [OE *īs*, ice. < a similar Gmnc. form of untraced origin, perh. (??) echoic *(hiss)* of the sound of sliding on ice.] 1. Water frozen into a solid. 2. A dessert based on crushed ice. *icing* Frosting on a cake. [Perh., by ext., an added sweet.] *put the icing on it In ext. sense.* To put the last touches to any project. 3. *Crim. slang.* Diamonds. Jewelry in general. [See *crystal* and note that root word, Gk. *krustallos, first meant "ice" and only later "rock crystal." Here the reversal of the same association.] *iceman* 1. A mythological deliveryman of prerefrigerator U.S. 2. *Crim.* A thief or fence who specializes in jewelry. 3. *More recent crim. adds the sense:* Killer. One who ices people. *to ice* To kill. [To make cold in death; together with, to put on (morgue) ice.] *on ice* 1. To put away to chill. 2. Dead. [Corpses were once literally packed in ice during the wake.] 3. A sure thing. *it's on ice* It's dead sure.

icebox An insulated food chest with a usu. zinc-lined compartment for a block of ice and an outlet for melt water. [Once a standard Am. kitchen device, now replaced by the refrigerator. Old gaffers still tend to refer to the refrigerator as the icebox, but come one or two more rounds of mortality and the idiom will pass to the exclusive use of antiquarians.]

break the ice To dispose of the formalities and establish a more intimate level of discussion. *cut no ice* To make no difference; to have no effect upon. *that cuts no ice with me,* that makes no difference to me. [From the time, up to the 1920's, when blocks of ice were literally cut (with specially made ice saws) from ponds, and stored in cold cellars and sawdust packing. And see *ice trade,* below.] *on thin ice* In danger.

ice trade In late XIX fast New England packets found a profitable trade in taking pond ice to India, where it fetched a good price as a delicacy. Seeking passengers and cargoes of chance, these packets usu. first crossed to England, then sailed around the Cape of Good Hope, then to the Indian Ocean. Despite two equatorial crossings on the long passage, the ice, once massed and properly packed in sawdust, survived the passage. In Central City, Colorado, once a mining boom town of the 1870's, ice so packed in a cave for sale to the miners is still preserved, and the present owner of the icehouse assures me he is still selling it to tourists a century later.

ice cream suit   A light-colored lightweight summer suit for men. [< earlier (c. 1900) *ice cream pants,* white pants said to be the color of vanilla ice cream; these with a dark blue blazer made up the standard near-formal men's dress for outings, teas, and Sunday go to meeting. For young men they were the near-official uniform for "heavy" dates, school graduations, confirmations, etc. (See grandfather's high school graduation picture.)]

ichthus   The Greek word for fish, wherefrom the fish became a symbol of Christ (see *holy: holy mackerel*) because of the pious acronymic: *I(esous) CH(ristos) TH(eou) U(ios), S(oter):* Jesus Christ, Son of God, Savior. (And note that *CH* and *TH* are single letters in Greek.)

idiot   A person of the lowest measurable intelligence. [But earlier, a person of no social rank. So in XVII, Jeremy Taylor, ". . . great ones (in social position) as well as idiots." And Taylor's is one sense of Gk. **idiōtēs.* 1. A private person (one not in public office). 2. An ignorant member of the hoi polloi (one not fit to be in office). The first sense survives in ID, IDIOSYNCRASY; the second in modern *idiot.*] **idiot card** *Movies and TV.* A placard on which an actor's lines are printed in bold letters. [And held up to one side of, or above, the camera so that the "idiot" need not memorize. This work is now done by a printer attached to the camera, the lines put in view by remote control.]

ignoramus   An ignorant person. Readily implies "stupid" as well as ignorant. [L. *ignoramus,* we take no notice of, we ignore. Formerly in legal Latin the notation entered upon a bill of indictment by a grand jury that has decided to take no action. The sense in common usage is not that of the legal language but developed from *Ignoramus,* 1615, a play by George Ruggles, the title being from the name of an assertive but incompetent lawyer who was a leading character of the play. It is unlikely, however, that the term could have survived in common usage without its sound values and without the common confusion with *ignorant* conjoined to the last two syllables of *hippopotamus* to suggest clumsiness.]

immolate   To sacrifice. *Darling, I have gone to immolate myself for the rent.* [And implies a burnt offering, but only by association, the root sense being "to sprinkle with fine-ground meal in preparation for burning as a sacrifice." Based on L. *mola,* a fine-ground meal; this *mola* was specially blessed by the temple priest somewhat in the same way in which the R.C. Church blesses holy water.]

imp   1. A small fiend. 2. A mischievous child. [A much changed form. Root sense: "plant shoot, plant graft (implanted shoot)." < Gk. *emphuein,* to graft, to implant a shoot. Via Late L. → OE *impa,* plant shoot, sapling. (*To imp* survives in falconry, meaning "to graft new feathers to a hawk's wing to repair damage or to improve flight characteristics.") The basic sense shift was from "plant scion" to "scion of a family." Up to XIV "our gracious king and his royal imp" would serve as formal usage. Then, c. early XVI, by association with such formulas as "imp of hell," the word came to mean "a fiend." And in XVII the root sense, "scion," and the XVI evolved sense, "fiend," met in the new sense, "mischievous child."]

impasse   A roadway that leads to a dead end. [Fr. *passer,* to pass, to proceed; with neg. prefix *in-,* the form syncopated to *im-* before *p.* On Fr. street signs commonly used as if *Lane, Place, Alley.* A Parisian street sign reads *Impasse des Deux Anges,* for which Am. would have to use some such form as *Two Angels Place* and then add *Dead End* or *No Thoroughfare* or *No Thorofare.*

As a cliché of Am. journalism, labor negotiations are commonly said to be *at an impasse,* which is later said to have been resolved, a slovenly usage: the way out of an impasse is not by resolution but by backtracking; and the form might more sensitively be *in an impasse* or *at a dead end,* the dead end being to the impasse as the landing is to the fall, the one implicit in the other, and yet distinct.]

impediment   A burden. [Often, but wrongly, used in the sense "obstruction." Based on the stem *ped-,* foot (L. *pēs,* foot) → L. *impedimenta,* baggage, burden ("the sum of things carried on a march or journey").]

impetuous   Brash. [< L. *petere,* to assault; prefixed *in-,* in (the syncopated form *im-* before *p*), lit. "to rush in upon" (IMPETUS).]

imply   To suggest indirectly, by a logical extension of what one says rather than by overt statement. [Root sense: "to fold into (one's

remarks)." < L. *implicare,* to involve. < *im-,* in; *plicare,* to fold
(IMPLICIT, IMPLICATE).]

NOTE. If literacy is in some part defined by the accuracy with
which one uses words, the common confusion of *imply* and *infer*
is a mark of illiteracy. *To imply* is an action by the speaker or
writer (who "folds into" his remarks an unasserted intent); *to infer*
is an action by the listener or reader, who "carries into" (L. *in-,*
into; *ferre,* to carry) what is said or written his own intent.

indenture   [The root sense at law is "document with serrated edges."
< L. *dens,* tooth. It. *indentare,* to make a serration, to indent.
The ref. is to the once common practice of cutting a document
in two with serrated edges, one half to either party of the agreement, to permit authentication of the document by fitting the
two jagged edges together. In Medieval L. *carta indentata,*
indentured paper, indenture; which is also the sense of (rare in
Am.) *charter party,* legal term with exclusive ref. to ships and
signifying a paper so divided with jagged edges. < Fr. *carte parti,*
divided paper.] *Law.* 1. A document with indented edges. 2. A
contract in which two parties bind themselves to an exchange
of services and observances. 3. *Earlier, and esp. common in Am.
colonies.* A contract binding party A to a specified term of service
to party B, often with a specified payment at the termination of
the service. As practiced in the Am. colonies, a period of virtual
enslavement in return for the expenses of the voyage to the New
World. *indentured servant* A person so bound to service for a
period of years. (Shipmasters sailing to America once regularly
carried indentured passengers, whose indentures were sold at auc-
tion on arrival. The terms of indenture, therefore, often depended
on the captain and might be fair or might amount to practical
slavery. The Colonial Court of Massachusetts once sentenced two
incorrigible offenders to indentured slavery for life.)

index   A system of references or correlations. (Plu. *indices.*) [Root
sense: "that which points to." Root image: index finger. Ult. IE
deik-, deig-, to point to, to show → L. *digitus,* finger. Also *indicare,*
to indicate, point to (INDICATE).] *index finger* The first finger.
[Root sense: "pointer, finger used in pointing"; an agential form
of *indicare,* thing that indicates. (The heart-stimulant drug *digitalis*
is cognate at one metaphoric remove, because derived from fox-
glove, genus *Digitalis,* which is L. "fingerlike" because the corollas
of these flowers occur in finger-shaped clusters, as if a small
hand.]

Indian Strictly speaking, a native of India, but in consequence of Columbus's epic navigational error, an American aborigine, and so the primary sense in all Am. idioms. Sometimes, for clarity, *American Indian* or *Amerind* [Formed by telescoping *Amer(ican)* and Ind(ian).] Similarly *India* and *West Indies*. And see *Injun*.

Indian file In single file. [After the manner in which Indians commonly traveled narrow forest trails.]

Indian giver One who makes a gift and then demands its return. [Culminating in the potlatch ceremonies of the Kwakiutl Indians, gift-giving had elaborate ceremonial implications among the Amerinds. In their custom, the gift-giver often expected a more valuable gift in return for what he had given. If dissatisfied with the exchange, he was within his right-by-custom to reject the countergift and to demand the return of what he had given.]

Indian sign An intimidation. A hex. *Who put the Indian sign on you?* [In various senses. Indians marked their territories and sacred places with symbols indicating death to trespassers. Signs (tracks) of prowling Indians once meant a war party and danger. A lance driven into the ground was a declaration of war. And perh. with ref. to charms used by Indian medicine men. All could be cause for fright.]

Indian Summer 1. In North America, a period of warm bright days after the first frost, usu. c. Nov. 1 in northerly states, but sometimes in early winter. 2. *Ext.* A happy and prosperous time in late middle age. [A common weather phenomenon of North America when dry southerly air interrupts the normal west-to-east flow of the weather. *Indian,* here, for indigenous.]

infant A baby. [Root sense: "not yet able to speak." IE *ba-, bha-,* to speak. Prob. echoic. *ba-ba* in several IE languages is the root of the word for "foreigner" ("one whose speech sounds like ba-ba-ba"); so Gk. *barbaros,* stranger, enemy (BARBARIAN).

By Grimm's Law the voiced stop *bh-* changes to *f* in Latin. So stem *fa-* → L. *fari,* to speak. With neg. prefix *in-* → L. *infans,* baby ("nonspeaker").

The modern sense is once again the root sense, but intermediately: a child (XIV); a legal minor (XVI) ("person without a legal voice"). In Spain and Portugal XVI, XVII, *infante, infanta,* prince, princess ("child of the king"). At same time It. *infante,* young man, (and also) foot soldier, whence *infanteria,* infantry. The sometimes asserted derivation of *infantry* < Sp. *infante* ("soldiers of the *infante*") is refuted by the dating. (But I will accept *adult* < *adultery,* should anyone insist.)]

infer   See *imply.*

influence   *n.* An affective power. —*v.* To affect. [Root sense: "a flowing in, to flow in upon." < L. *in-*, in; *fluere*, to flow. Whenever
this word is encountered in writing prior to c. 1800, it is reasonable
to assume an astrological ref. to the influence of the stars.]

   NOTE. One of the most graceful effects of poetry (or of any
precise writing) occurs when the author sets a word in a context
that allows a counterpoint of the root sense and the extended
sense. Assume the poet to be standing on an eastward-facing beach
just at dawn with the surf running high. Then assume him to
have written, "And dawn is all one rosy influence." The surf, tinged
red by the level rays of the new sun, flows in (root sense) rosily;
and it has (extended sense) an affective power upon the beholder.
Language is rarely used at this depth, but the rareness of excellence
should not be made into an excuse for the failure to recognize
it. In the days when the school system still taught languages (and
sometimes even English), the recognition of root senses was as
common as it is now rare. This book is in part an effort to reawaken
an awareness of the root depths of words.

ingrained   *adj.* So deep-seated as to be ineradicable and unchangea-
ble. [Commonly, but wrongly, taken to be a ref. to the grain of
wood as an essence of the material. Root sense: "indelibly dyed."
Ult. < L. *granum*, a seed, a grain of wheat; with an ext. to "thing
the size of a small seed"; and further ext. used as the name of
the small insect from which the Romans extracted a fine and very
fast red dye (the cochineal insect). So *granum*, this insect → OF
graine, the dye → ME *in graine*, unfadably dyed; with metaphoric
ext. to "unalterably set (as in one's ways)." So Shakespeare, *Twelfth
Night*, I.v: " 'Tis in graine, sir; 'twill endure wind and weather."]

Injun   Indian. [The corruption of *di* to a soft *g* sound before *a* is
common in Am. but not specific to it. Cf. Brit. *Inja* for *India*. In
Am. *Cajun* for *Acadian.*] **honest Injun** Now a boy's formula for
asserting the truth of a statement; about equivalent to "Scout's
honor" or "cross my heart and hope to die." In XIX western frontier: 1. An intensive. *Honest Injun, there was forty of them!* 2.
For asking if one is speaking the truth. *Forty? Honest Injun?* 3.
Adverbially. *I tell you honest Injun, I seen it with me own eyes.*
= I tell you truthfully. [In all senses based on the palaver-pidgin
worked out with Amerinds, and with the ritual assertions of sincer-
ity and truthfulness expected during such palavers, as: "Me honest
Injun. Speak with straight tongue."]

ink Writing and marking fluid. [An intricate evolution beginning with IE *keu-, kau-,* to burn → Gk. *kaiein,* to burn; whence *enkaustikos,* encaustic (root sense: "heat-sealed"), with ref. to Gk. encaustic painting in which colors were mixed with beeswax and heat-sealed after being applied to a surface. By association with the heated wax into which a seal was pressed, L. *encaustum* came to mean first "signature" (see *endorse* for a similar sense shift) and then "the ink used in signing"; whence OF *enke, enque* (mod. Fr. *encre*); and so ME *enke,* ink.]

  ink in To insert a handwritten change into a typed or printed text. **ink out** To delete a word, phrase, or passage by superimposing an inked line. **ink slinger** [Am. XIX. Rare since the typewriter's total overthrow of penmanship.] A newspaper reporter. **inky** Dark. **clear as ink** Not clear at all. **red ink** *Bookkeeping.* Indicates a loss. So **in the red** [*Ink* understood but never said.] Showing a debit balance. Hence, in debt. **to ink** *Sportswriter's slang.* To sign a contract.

inkling An intimation. A slight clue. *I made it my pleasure to leave the revised but unimproved* Saturday Review *and have only a red inkling of where Carll Tucker is going with it.* [ME **inkel, *inkle,* to mutter. (Cf. "he hasn't a whisper" for "he hasn't the ghost of a chance.")]

innuendo 1. An oblique hint or implication, usu. derogatory. 2. *Law.* *a.* A specification. *b.* In a libel or slander action, the plaintiff's interpretation of the allegedly libelous or slanderous statements at issue. [But earlier, and through XVI, used in British law with the senses: "viz., to wit, namely," in serving to specify what had earlier been in doubt. So "that a person unknown (*innuendo,* the defendant) did break and enter . . ." < L. *innuare,* to nod; *innuendo,* by nodding to. This earliest legal usage of *innuendo* is now often expressed by "let the record show that the witness pointed to the accused." Thus, though the root sense is "tacit," i.e., by sign and without speaking, the effective legal sense evolved to "specified by word."]

INRI These letters are commonly found on a scroll fixed to a crucifix above the head of Jesus. They are an acrostic of the L. *I(esus) N(azarenus) R(ex) I(udaeorum),* Jesus of Nazareth King of the Jews. There is no evidence that the Roman executioners scrawled or carved these letters into the cross. Early Christians were much drawn to pious rubrics. This one prob. evolved from the "crown of thorns" offered to Jesus by his executioners to mock his assertion of spiritual kingship. By preserving the rubric, the faithful convert the original mockery to a renewed piety.

intoxicate   1. To inebriate. 2. *Ext.* To stimulate powerfully. *Pussy Galore was intoxicated by the beauty of Conrad's money.* 3. *Medical (and the root sense).* To poison (TOXIN, ANTITOXIN). [And at ultimate root, as the various temperance unions will be delighted to note, the sense is: "shot full of arrows." < Gk. *toxon,* bow; the plu. form *toxa* having the curious accumulated sense "bow and arrows." The sense "poison" is from the ancient practice of dipping arrowheads in poison in order to make even a scratch potentially fatal.]

irony   1. The act of meaning the opposite of what one says, in speech or writing. Jonathan Swift's *A Modest Proposal* purports to improve the condition of the poor by legalizing the sale of infants as a table delicacy for the rich; it is in fact a bitter attack on the oppression of the poor. 2. *Ext.* An incongruity in manners or in the arrangement of events. *the irony of having to pay interest on the money one does not have for paying his taxes.* (*Irony* is specific to saying the opposite of what one means. *Sarcasm* is any cutting remark.) [Root sense: "to speak (but not say what one means)." < Gk. *eirein,* to speak; *eirōn,* a person who says something but means the opposite; *eirōneia,* the act of speaking in this way.]

irregardless   *adv.* Without regard. Regardless. [A double negative and substandard form; but irregardless to the contrary notwithstanding, a double negative does not disqualify a word from standard usage. *Irregardless* has been adjudged illiterate by idiomatic convention. It has, therefore, come into standard use for joshing effect. "Irregardless of that, Mrs. Lincoln, how did you like the play?"]

isinglass   A form of mica, usually in thin laminated sheets, once commonly used for windows in the snap-on side panels of touring cars, and as the rear windows of what were first called roadsters and later called convertibles. [But earlier a more or less transparent gelatin or fish glue made from the air bladder of the sturgeon and sometimes of other fish. MD *huusblase* < *huus,* sturgeon; *blase,* bladder. In XVI Eng. *blase* was modified to *glass* by association with transparency; *isin,* earlier *isom, ison,* is simply an attempt to fit strange syllables into the Eng. voice box. The transfer of the name to mica "window glass" was, again, based on the partial transparency of the stuff. ". . . seen through lenses/of old scratched isinglass." —Elizabeth Bishop.]

ish kabibble   1. Meaningless nonsense spoken by immigrant Jews. 2. *Ext.* Any stupid chatter. *Ish Kabibble* A grotesque name for a Jew. *Calm down, you sound like Ish Kabibble.* [Not enough is known about this (prob. disappearing) idiom. It first came into Am. use in mid XIX, and it has been glossed (overcraftily, I believe) as deriving from Ger. *ich,* I; *ka-* for *ge-,* Ger. collective prefix; Ger. *Bibel,* Bible; hence, "I from all over the Bible." Perhaps. But the term seems better explained as a bigot's effort to reproduce Yiddish speech as an example of ridiculous human utterance, the sound values striking the Am. ear as ludicrous. Cf., for the same reason, the comic use of the standard It. surname *Bacciagaluppi.*]

ivory tower   The now standard symbol for the artificial world of ideas into which esthetic dreamers and impractical intellectuals are supposed to escape from the "reality" of stockbrokers at a four-martini lunch. [< Fr. *tour d'ivoire,* tower (made) of ivory, a striking image of the poet's imaginary residence. By Charles-Augustin Sainte-Beuve in the poem *"Pensées d'Août"* ("August Thoughts"), 1837.]

Ivy League   *n.* A term for the first-founded U.S. colleges, specifically: Brown, Columbia, Cornell, Dartmouth, Harvard, Univ. of Pennsylvania, Princeton, and Yale. Rutgers, though founded in 1766, suffered a long eclipse and is not included in this more prosperous association. —*adj.* Labels the shifting fashions, manners, and attitudes affected by students of these colleges. [A mid 1930's coinage. The generally reliable AHD attributes the coinage to Stanley Woodward, then sports editor of the *N.Y. Herald Tribune.* Woodward was the first to use it in print but acknowledged in his column that the term had been coined the day before by Caswell Adams of the *N.Y. Journal American.* The term was based, of course, on the ivy-covered walls of these schools, but originally expressed Adams's disparagement of them as inferior football powers: "that's just Ivy League," meaning, "that's of no real interest to football fans."]

𝒥

jackanapes 1. *Earlier.* A scoundrel. An impertinent rogue. 2. *Now.* A saucy and worthless but not necessarily evil fellow; and when applied to a small boy can even be a term of endearment. 3. *In XVI.* A common name for a tame monkey. [Etymology confused by too many clues. *Napes* may be a nonced form of apes (see *noncing*); or from OE *cnapa,* rogue; which with *c*-kappa and p/ v is recognizably later *knave* (which may explain why *Jack of Hearts* and *Knave of Hearts* are used interchangeably). In any case, first attested as a derisive nickname for William de la Pole, duke of Suffolk, a swaggering adventurer who was beheaded (murdered, not executed) at sea in 1450. His heraldic badge sported a clog and chain of the sort used to fetter tame apes. Prob. root sense: "the Jack (knave) of apes." Some have sought to derive *napes* from *Naples,* but that error is explainable as a misassociation with XV *fustian-anapes* for *fustian of Naples,* a sort of coarse cotton or linen cloth then imported from Naples. Samuel Johnson, prob. holding the term to be a vulgarism, excluded it from his dictionary.]

Jack and Jill The boy and the girl of the nursery rhyme. [But what were they before they evolved into a boy and a girl? Note that they went *up* a hill to fetch a pail of water, a hilltop being the least likely place for finding a spring, pond, or brook. As with much else in Mother Goose, the rhyme is probably based on some now lost reference. In early Eng. and still in dial., there is *jack,* a waxed leather pitcher with a spout; *gill,* a liquid measure (now ¼ pint, earlier ?). There is small point in speculating on the possible allegorical, political, or historical significance of the tumbling *jack* and the following *gill,* but the boy and girl may (??) have evolved from them.]

Jack Ketch Generic for a hangman. [From c. 1663 to his death in 1686, the hangman of London was called Jack Ketch, but prob.

in lieu of his legal name. The London gallows was on Tyburn Hill on ground that once belonged to the manor of Tyburn, whose squire was formerly Richard Jaquett; *Jack Ketch* being in all likelihood an alteration of his surname, with the added word play that "once Jack Ketches you, you stay caught."]

Jack Robinson   A semiproverbial but unidentified figure dating from XVIII. He is firmly fixed in idiom in *quick as one can say Jack Robinson* In no time at all. [Grose, *Classical Dict.*, 1875, attempts to make him a specific person: "A very volatile gentleman of that appellation, who would call on his neighbors and be gone before his name could be announced." But no notable "gentleman of that appellation" has been located in XVIII. And a ballad of that time refers to a sailor so named who, returning after many years' absence to find his wife remarried, disappeared "fast as you can say Jack Robinson."]

jade¹   A variously colored stone, most commonly green or white, long prized by the Chinese as a gemstone and for delicate carving. Forms of jade can be found in many places, but high-quality jade is becoming rare due to the depletion of known deposits, and some, as the dark green variety known as spinach jade, has eluded seekers for more than a century. [The English name derives from ancient medical superstitions as to the efficacy of certain stones, as amethyst was believed to avert or cure drunkenness, and the stone called heliotrope was purported to make the bearer invisible. So *jade* < Sp. *piedra de ijada,* stone of the side (iliac), because it was believed to be effective in treating disorders of the kidneys.]

jade²   1. *XIV.* A no longer workable horse. A crowbait. [Of unknown ME origin.] 2. *XVI ext.* A worthless woman. One who has no good qualities. (See *termagant* as an example of how invidious terms were regularly applied to women by writers of a male-dominant society.) *jaded adj.* 1. Worn out. Hence, 2. Surfeited. Cloyed. Bored. [No longer capable of a lively response.]

jargon   [Root sense: "bird twitter." < OF & ME *jargoun,* gibberish; but echoic of the sound made by flocks of birds, as by rooks, rendered *jargoun-jargoun.*] Specialized in-group or shop talk that is more or less unintelligible to the merely literate. As in the root sense, the term remains pejorative, often implying pretentious elaboration of nothing to say. So: *All I got from my broker was a lot of jargon.* So, too: *computer jargon* for *the specialized termi-*

nology necessary in programming computers, the first being pejorative; the second, neutral.

jay   1. A bird. Most commonly in Am., the blue jay. [L. *gaius,* jay, is ult. echoic, based on *gai! gai!* the squawk of this bird.] 2. *Ext.* A yokel. A bumpkin. [One who lives back there among the jays.] 3. *Ext. from 2.* A loud, stupid person. 4. A contemptible and despicable person. [This sense in Am. certainly stems from John Jay, Washington's envoy to the Court of St. James's to negotiate peace terms; later first U.S. Chief Justice. At the Court of St. James's he worked to reconcile the differences that eventually led to the War of 1812, but made so many concessions that he was much detested in the U.S. as a traitorous Anglophile. The strongly pejorative sense of *jay* in many Am. idioms is certainly a survival of this early hatred of John Jay.]

   jay birds. 1. *Colloq.* Blue jays. 2. Followers of John Jay. *it's a scandal to the jay birds! An intensive form.* It is indeed a scandal. [A possible joint evolution. Jays scream and squawk; and the idiom may, accordingly, mean: "It's enough to scandalize even these scandalmongering birds." But as likely a ref. to John Jay: it is scandalous enough to scandalize even one of those traitorous jays that support John Jay.]

   jayhawker A guerrilla in the days of Bloody Kansas. Now (so language goes from bloodshed to folksiness) a more or less self-chosen nickname for a Kansan. *jayhawk* There is no hawk specific to the blue jay. A nonexistent bird, the idea of which derives from *jayhawker,* a ferocious raptor. Now, as a logo for the University of Kansas, a grotesque cartoon of a bird resembling a dwarf pterodactyl with a thyroid deficiency.

   jaywalk To walk more or less heedlessly through city traffic. [< sense 2. Does not suggest opprobrium, but simply the folly of a yokel gawking his way through the big city.]

jazz   The only truly original American art form, the music of the Negro, ultimately based on a mixture of spirituals, blues, and African rhythms. [Ult. based on **jass,* Afro-Carib pidgin root with general reference to the sex act. According to Sidney Bechet, *Treat It Gentle,* the name *jazz* became attached to the music because c. 1900 the first paid work Negro musicians could find was in New Orleans *jass houses,* houses of prostitution, and it was there that *Dixieland* developed from earlier *primitive* or *funky* jazz. The original sexual sense of *jass* survives in such expressions as *don't jazz me, man; don't give me none of your jazz.*]

jeans/blue jeans Pants of heavy twilled cotton, traditionally dyed blue. Once worn by laborers. Now a unisex uniform of the young and in a wide range of colors. [Earlier *jean*, the fabric. < *geane fustian*, coarse cloth of Gene, Jene, ME names of Genoa. So at root: "cloth of Genoa, pants made of cloth of Genoa," because it was first imported from there. See *levis*.] **get into one's jeans** Usu. in some such form as *I'd sure like to get into her jeans* Enter sexually.

jeep The basic military car of the U.S. and allies in WWII. [Military slang from *G.P.* for General Purpose (vehicle); the form perhaps influ. by the comic strip *Eugene the Jeep* by E. C. Segar, 1894–1938. Eugene, a comical animal, regularly made a sound ballooned as "Jeep!"]

jeopardy At risk. In danger. [Anglicized < Fr. *jeu parti*, divided play. The ref. is to gambling; and the root sense: "with the odds still about evenly divided," i.e., that either side has an equal chance to win or lose. But *jeopardy* tends to imply the danger of losing rather ¹.an the equal likelihood of winning. The common *in great jeopardy* violates the evenly balanced sense of *jeu parti*, and is, in fact, a simply substitution of *jeopardy* for *peril* or *danger*.] **double jeopardy** In law, to be tried twice on the same charges. (A defendant found to be either guilty or innocent cannot be charged again. It is for this reason that felons found guilty on one charge confess to past crimes for which they have not been tried, lumping these offenses into the one guilty verdict so that they may not later be charged with them.

jerkwater town The most primitive of small towns. [Originally a town on the railroad line, but too backward to have even a water tower. Early steam engines had an insatiable appetite for water. When they ran out at a town without a water tower, the train crew had to "jerk" water in buckets from the local wells and haul it laboriously to the locomotive. Needless to say, jerking water was not their most popular sport, whence the contempt with which they labeled the place a jerkwater town.]

Jersey cow, jersey cloth, football jersey, Isle of Jersey, New Jersey are all ult. < *Caesar*, which see.

jest A quip. [Root sense: "action intended to amuse." Obs. *jest(e)*, deed, exploit, was a simple variant of Fr. *geste*, deed, exploit; *beau* *geste*, a chivalric deed. Then later, a tale about such exploits. (The connecting sense is "tale told to amuse.") Ult. < L. **gerere*, to wage, conduct (so in *bellum gerere*, to wage war); p.p. *gestus*, done; OF *geste*, deed done (JESTER, GESTURE, GESTATION).]

Jew's harp   A subspecies of musical instrument: a small lyre-shaped metal device with a single protruding metal tongue which is strummed when the "instrument" is held between the lips, the mouth cavity serving as a sort of sounding box, the lips as modulating devices. [There is no known association of this device with Jewish history. *Jew's* is almost certainly a corruption of something else. *Jaw's harp* has been suggested, and also Fr. *harpe de jeu*, play(thing) harp; but neither suggested form has been attested. The XVI form was *Jew's trump*.]

jib   *Nautical.* A triangular sail stretched from the foremast to the bowsprit. [Origin in doubt. Perh. < Danish *gibbe*, to sway from side to side. But ??]
   the cut of one's jib 1. *Nautical.* The style of a ship's rigging. 2. *Ext.* One's style. *not like the cut of one's jib* To dislike a person at first glance. *like the cut of one's jib* To take to at first glance; to be easy with. [Originally nautical only. Other senses are metaphoric extensions.]
   HISTORIC. Sailing ships of different nations tend to cut and rig their jibs distinctively. In the days of privateers and in sea war between sailing vessels, it was an urgent matter to know the nationality of a vessel as soon as it hove into view, and the cut of the jib most readily served to identify the stranger as friendly or hostile.

jig: the jig is up   The plot has been discovered. The cat is out of the bag. The trick has failed (and we have been caught). [< Brit. slang *jig*, trick, fraud < *jiggery-pokery*, fraud, deceit < XVII Sc. *juwkry-pawkey*, later *jookery-pawkey*, redupl. based on Sc. and dial. *jouk*, to duck, dance, dodge about.]

Jim Crow   Anti-Negro bigotry with all its implications from segregation to lynching. [Ult. < an anonymous XIX Am. song so titled. Then popularized by acclaimed vaudevillian Thomas D. Rice (first half XIX), one of whose skits presented a Negro character so named. Obviously based on *Jim*, common name; and *Crow*, black(bird).]

jim-dandy   All fine and dandy. Swell-elegant. Labels anything to be vastly approved. *We had a jim-dandy time at the party.* [Am. colloq. c. 1875. Prob. compounded of earlier *fine and dandy*, with *jim* as a common male-name intensive as in *tomcat*, but prob., too, by association with *jimminy* (which see), from exclam. of enthusiasm *by jimminy!*]

jimminy/Jimminy/jiminy/Jiminy   Mild exclam. *by Jimminy/by Jiminy* (rarely, with lower-case *j*) One of the mildest of minced oaths. [XVII. Corruption of *Gemini.* The sometimes offered suggestion that the term arises from *Je(su) (Do)mine,* has in its support the fact that most minced oaths are a form of *Jesus Christ* (and *geez,* they really are); but this is an ingenuity after the fact.] *Jimminy Christmas/Jimminy Crickets* Also minced oaths. The first is obviously based on *Jesus Christ.* The second is a twice-minced form. [So very mild have these mincings become that even the saintly bland of Walt Disney Productions features an animated cartoon character called Jimminy Cricket. (But Jesus Christ, don't tell them what they are doing!)]

Jingo: by Jingo!   *Mild expletive.* By God! [Prob. the only English term derived from the Basque tongue, perh. transmitted by Basque sailors, perhaps by Basque mercenaries used by Edward I (reigned 1272–1307) in his wars against the Welsh, but the first OED attestation is not till 1694, when Motteux used it to translate Fr. *par Dieu* in Rabelais. Common in XVII as a conjurer's formula, *hey jingo!* or *hi jingo!* or *high jingo!*] *jingoism* Also *jingo* (As in: *another of his jingo pronouncements.*) Chauvinism. Redder-whiter-and-bluer-than-thou patriotism. [An unusual second evolution < 1878 music hall ditty by G. W. Hunt, addressing the threat of war with Russia. "We don't want to fight, yet, by Jingo! if we do/We've got the ships, we've got the men, and got the money, too!"]

jinks: high jinks   1. *Originally.* Festivity. Fun and frolic. [Sir Walter Scott, *Guy Mannering,* describes *high jinks* as a Scottish party game of forfeits, but this sense is almost certainly a localism, prob. based on the idea that claiming a shy kiss as a forfeit amounts to high fun and frolic. < Sc. *jink* (akin to *jig, jouk*), to elude, to play a trick, but with the root sense "to skip about rapidly." And almost certainly influ. by the once popular Highland jig tune "Hey, Jenks!"] 2. *Ext. Am. late XIX.* Shenanigans. (Already implicit in the sense of the Sc. stem, but now made explicit.) *The city council has been up to some high jinks with the taxpayers' money.*

jinx   1. One who brings bad luck. A Jonah. 2. An evil spell. *to put a jinx on one. I've been jinxed.* [One is tempted to look to *jinx* (< L. *iunx*), the wryneck, a squawking European bird that can twist its neck in an extraordinary way. The wryneck was long associated with witches and witchcraft. But though the form and this association fit neatly, *jinx* does not appear in Brit. dialect dictionaries, and the OED, noting it only in its *Supplement,* glosses it as an Americanism not attested before 1912. (MMM notes it as of 1911.) It is this surprising dating that has moved etymologists to be wary of L. *iunx* as the source, and to gloss the term as "origin unknown," and so be it.]

jitney   1. A nickel. 5¢. Also commonly *jit.* 2. A horse-drawn streetcar. [Both senses seem to have developed simultaneously in Am. c. 1915, and there is no way of saying which came first. A nickel was the standard fare on the horse-drawn streetcar and on the electric trolleys that replaced them. These streetcars had a glass-sided box into which one placed a coin. Perhaps < Fr. *jeton,* now primarily a metal token for a pay telephone. (Also means "chip used by a gambler," but has the root sense "thing thrown (into a slot)," ult. < L. *jactare,* to throw, to cast. Cf. *ghetto.*) I have seen the suggestion that it derives via Yiddish from the name of a small coin in circulation in late XIX Russia, but I cannot locate the name of that coin.
    jeepney Philippines. An eight-seat bus built on a Jeep body and run by independent operators between downtown Manila and outlying points. [Not an Americanism but a curious American export. In Manila after WWII, surplus jeeps were fitted out with benches and a canopy and put into service as one-man bus lines, their name arising from the blend of *jeep* and *jitney.*]

Jno.   Also *Jnº.* Common written forms of John, Jonathan. [Like *ye* for *the* by a misreading of OE alphabet character *thorn* (which looks like a *y* but represents *th*), the form is a now established typographical error. The name John was earlier *Johan* (L. *Johannes, Iohonnes;* Hebrew *Yohanon,* meaning "God is gracious (in giving us this son)." The name was earlier commonly written *Jho* or *Jhº.* But the early cursive *h* was easily confused with cursive *n,* whence h/n. *Sneeze,* earlier *fneosan,* came about by a similar confusion of early cursive long *s* and long *f.*]

jock   [< Scottish *Jock* for *Jack.*] In the lower-case form *jock:* 1. Penis. 2. Jockey. 3. Athlete. [This last prob. from *jockstrap,* a strapped-on protective shield for the penis. Sense 3 = "a prick in a jock-strap."] *jockey* 1. The rider in a horse race. 2. *Ext.* One who rides and guides any apparatus. ***airplane jockey*** A pilot. ***barstool jockey*** A barfly. ***plow jockey*** A yokel. ***truck jockey*** A truckdriver. —*v.* ***to jockey*** 1. to maneuver for position, advantage. [As race jockeys do in trying to get a position on the rail.] 2. *Ext.* To outsmart. *I jockeyed Gil Gallagher out of five bucks at gin rummy, but he made it easy for me.*

Joe Miller   The name is received in Am. as that of the master "joke-smith," Joe Miller being to joke telling what Hoyle is to card games. [Joe Miller of London was a comic actor and much sought after raconteur. His tombstone at St. Clement Danes, on the Strand, bears the dates 1684–1738.]

HISTORIC. Joe Miller never compiled or published a jokebook. It was John Motley, a failed playwright, who produced *Joe Miller's Jest Book,* shortly after Miller's death, so titling it in order to capital-ize on the popularity of Miller's name. The various Am. editions titled *Joe Miller's Joke Book* were not reprints of the original but variant collections modeled on the *Jest Book.* Motley died in 1750.

johnnycake   A corn meal cake, originally baked on a hot stone. Now also oven baked or fried. It is thinner and crisper than corn pone. [Variously explained as deriving < *journey cake,* because easy to prepare when traveling, or < *Shawnee cake,* because white settlers learned to prepare it in the manner of the Shawnee Indians. Nei-ther derivation is entirely satisfactory, and both are perturbed by the New England form *jonakin, jonikin* (often with a capital *J*). The similarities of *journey, Shawnee, jonikin* suggest that all three are corruptions of some lost Indian word.]

HISTORIC. Though *johnnycake* is now firmly associated with the South, James Russell Lowell wrote of New England (1840) as "the land of johnnycake." The earlier form was *jonakin* or *jonikin.* James Fenimore Cooper, *Rural Hours* (1850) wrote: "We have . . . Jonikin, thin, wafer-like sheets, toasted on a [greased] board; these are all eaten at breakfast with butter." Note that Cooper's description would do rather well for a thin tamale-like corn cake baked by an Indian over a hot stone. (Though *jonakin, jonikin* recurs in colonial Am. and early U.S., I have not found the word in any Webster's dictionary, nor the recipe in any early Am. Cook-book.)

Johnny-come-lately   A parvenu. An upstart. [Originally, as *Johnny Newcome, Johnny Newcombe,* a derisive name for a green recruit in the British Navy, c. 1825. Into Am. use in this changed form very soon after.]

Joneses: keeping up with the Joneses   Overspending in order to keep up a life-style competitive with that of one's neighbors. [Invented by Arthur R. ("Pop") Momand as the title of his popular comic strip, which ran from 1913 to his retirement in 1941.]

joss   God; esp. a Chinese idol. [Now standard in special context; earlier Chinese pidgin < Port. *Deos,* God, by *d/dj* and monophthongizing.] *joss house* A Chinese pagoda. [Lit. "God house."] *joss stick* A scented prayer stick burned before an idol.

journal   [< L. *diurnalis,* daily, of the day, diurnal → OF *journee,* of the day, *jurnal, journal,* of the day.] 1. A daily record; a diary. 2. Common name for a daily newspaper. [Record of the day's events.] 3. *Ext.* A summary of daily records published at weekly, monthly, quarterly, or irregular intervals. *The New England Medical Journal.* Whence *journalism* The total effort involved in producing newspapers and magazines.
　　journey [From same source via OF *journee.*] An extended land trip as distinct from a sea voyage. [Because broken into daily units of travel interrupted by overnight periods of rest.]
　　journeyman [At root: "one who works for a day's wages" (as distinct from an apprentice, who worked originally on a years-long service contract, and a master craftsman, who originally operated his own shop).] 1. In craft unions, one who has served out his apprenticeship and is qualified to work for a master craftsman for day wages. 2. *Ext.* A competent craftsman.
　　adjourn To close an officially stated meeting; an action decided by a chairman after a motion, a second, and a vote. [But the root sense is not "to end deliberations for the day." Rather, "to suspend discussion until a stated day and hour." A bastardized form compounded of L. *ad-,* to; with Fr. *jour,* day. Hence, "to (until) the day (stated)." If no day is stated, the meeting is said to have *adjourned sine die* < L. *sine die,* without a day (having been set); in which case the next meeting takes place at the call of the chairman.]

jovial   In a happy mood. Mirthful. [Originally based on astrology: "born under the sign of Jupiter" (the influence of which so disposes the soul). Similarly, *martial* is, at root, "born under Mars";

mercurial, "born under Mercury;" *lunatic,* "born under the moon (Luna)"; *saturnine,* "born under Saturn"; and *venereal* (earlier sense), "born under Venus."]

joy [L. *gaudere,* to rejoice in; ult. < IE *gau-,* pleasure-giving. It. *gioia;* OF *joye, joie;* ME *joye, joy.*] 1. delight. 2. The source of one's delight. *Even J. Edgar Hoover was once his Daddy's joy— or is that possible?*

joy-juice 1. Hard liquor. 2. A sexual emission. *joy popper* 1. A not (yet) addicted user of heroin who takes a pop now and then at a party. [And so in Nelson Algren's *The Man with the Golden Arm,* 1949. But addicts' jargon changes rapidly, the current sense being:] 2. One who takes (pops) mood- and mind-altering pills (which are called *joy-pops*). *joy ride* 1. A fast auto (or plane, or speedboat, etc.) ride nowhere, for the thrill of going. 2. *Ext.* Any reckless venture. *He went on a Wall Street joy ride and cracked up. joy stick* 1. The control stick of an early airplane. [Perh. because it was the means to the exhilaration of flight.] 2. *Inevitable ext.* Penis erectus.

jubilation *n.* Exultation. Loud rejoicing. —*v.* *jubilate.* —*adj. jubilant.* [Root sense: "exultant hunting call (as *view halloo*)." So the root sense of L. *jubilare* with the extended sense "to rejoice." Ult. < IE *yu-,* an exultant cry. An early metaphoric borrowing by writers of the Christian era with the sense: "to rejoice in the Lord as the hunter in his quarry." So the It. musical direction *immenso giubilio,* to be played or sung exultantly.]

jubilee [Not etymologically akin to *jubilation,* though the similarity of the two forms has caused an interaction.] 1. A fiftieth anniversary. [In Jewish religion (Leviticus 25) a jubilee year occurs at fifty-year intervals. So called after *yobel,* the ram's horn that announces such a year. The *yobel* is sounded on the Day of Atonement, the tenth day of the seventh month, but the jubilee year does not start till the 49th year is over. (The *yo-* of *yobel* resembles IE *yu-,* but no conclusions are to be drawn from this similarity because, first, Hebrew is not an Indo-European but an Afro-Asian language; and second, the first element of the word is probably *yob-,* not *yo-.*)] 2. *Loose ext.* [And influ. by *jubilation.*] A festive celebration.

diamond jubilee A 75th anniversary. [The fiftieth being designated the *golden anniversary,* the 75th is designated *diamond,* it being rarer and more precious than gold. (Here, too, the sense *jubilee* seems to have merged with *anniversary jubilation.*)]

jumble   *n.* A disorderly piling together (of things, words, ideas). — *v.* To heap together in a confused way. To strew at random [Usu. glossed "origin unknown," but *The Lady's Cabinet,* 1666, by Lord Ruthven, gives a recipe for *jumbles,* which were cakes (cookies) made of an unusual number of ingredients; in which the root sense, "everything mixed up together," agrees with the XVI verb *jumble,* to mingle in confusion. These clues may be pointing, in some jumbled way, to a source in Brit. dial. that may have functioned in altering ME **jumpere, *jombre,* to mix confusedly, < which alteration, *jumble.* (But ??)]

jury-rigged   Adjective describing temporary repairs, esp. to a ship at sea. [And accordingly, some have rendered *jury* as a corruption of *journey,* explaining the sense as "repairs made in the course of a journey." There can be no objection to that sense, but *jury* ult. < L. *adjutare,* to help (ADJUTANT), It. *aiuto,* help, OF *ajurie,* aid. Into English XVI with sense "temporary remedy; field expedient." Commonly but not exclusively nautical.]

Kaiser   The German emperor. [Originally with reference to the German line of emperors of the Holy Roman Empire (962–1806); to the emperor of Germany from 1871 to 1918, when, at the close of WWI, Wilhelm, the last of the line, had his overpadded royal butt kicked into exile. < *Caesar,* of which Ger. *Kaiser* is a near phonetic rendering. See *Caesar.*]

kaleidoscope   1. A tubular toy sealed at one end by usu. frosted glass, and at the other by a clear glass sight. The tube contains bits of colored material (originally bits of colored glass) which shift about when the tube is turned. An arrangement of angled mirrors reflects these shifting colors as complex symmetrical patterns, the degree of complexity determined by the number and arrangement of mirrors. 2. *Ext.* Any subtly shifting display of colors. 3. *Ext.* Any fast-moving series of events that flow one from the other in intricate confusion. —*adj.* **kaleidoscopic.** [Root sense: "instrument for viewing beautiful forms." Compounded as a descriptive name by Dr. David Brewster, inventor of this toy. Based on Gk. *kalos,* beautiful; *eidon,* form; and *scope,* instrument for viewing, based on Gk. *scopein,* to view, to examine.]

HISTORIC. Eliezer Edwards, *Dictionary of Words, Facts, and Phrases,* London, 1901, writes of Brewster and his toy: "He intended to patent it, but having inadvertently shown it to a London optician, he was forestalled, and missed the opportunity of acquiring a large fortune. It was computed that in three months a quarter of a million were sold."

I do not know how one demonstrates an optical device to an optician "inadvertently." Brewster was later knighted by Queen Victoria, though probably for other reasons: it is impossible to imagine her seated on the throne with a kaleidoscope to her eye.

kangaroo court   1. *Now.* A mock court in which dominant prisoners tyrannize the defenseless, trying them on trivial or merely fanciful

216

charges, as loitering with intent to breathe someone else's air, and sentencing them to beatings, extortion, servitude, rape, and even death. 2. *In first Am. use among the miners of the 1849 gold rush.* A vigilante committee for hanging claim jumpers after a speedy "fair" trial. (Since claim jumping was the act of killing a man in order to take over and work his claim, any man who was found working a murdered man's claim, and who could not produce witnessed documents of a transfer of ownership, was held to be self-evidently guilty and to be hanged, his trial being a mere formality.) [The practice of prisoners' mock courts is immemorial and they would certainly have been held in the Australian penal colonies. Kangaroos have little fear of man and commonly stand (squat? sit?) staring at groups of people. A band of them might fancifully be taken to be a watchful jury. By that or by some other association, *kangaroo court* emerged as a new name for an old thing. The term was then transferred to the gold fields with the special association with vigilantes that it has since lost. There were many Australians in the '49 gold rush: the sea voyage from Australia to California was much easier than the voyage from the east coast of the U.S. and around the Horn.]

keester   Also *kiester/keister/keyster/kister.* [Into Am. prob. via Yiddish < Ger. *Kiste,* box, chest, basket < L. *cista,* chest, box (in which the *c* is a kappa) < Gk. **kistē,* basket. Old Irish *cess,* basket, is prob. cognate.] 1. The buttocks. [Prob. because rounded like a basket. But later senses function in the now rare forms:] 2. *In the thieves' cant of pickpockets c. 1900.* A back pocket on men's pants. [This sense by propinquity.] 3. A salesman's sample case, or the suitcase in which a street pitchman carries his wares. [A sort of chest or box. The same sense functioning in:] 4. *Obs. crim. slang.* A strongbox, a safe.

kelemenopy   (Accent on penultimate.) The one essential trope neglected by classical rhetoricians: a sequential straight line through the middle of everything, leading nowhere. "Teddy Kennedy's career has been the classical kelemenopy of the American twentieth century." —Angelo Registratore. [Based on k-l-m-n-o-p, the central sequence of the alphabet, having ten letters before and ten after it. Hence, a strictly sequential irrelevance.]

NOTE. Drudges lost in felonious footnotery regularly become kinkospectic if not tergivercentric. *Kelemenopy* is from my own psychic warp, to see if anyone would notice, and because I have always dreamed of fathering a word. End message. Xyzed—and out.

Kelsey   In the formula, now with many variants: **dead (cold) as Kelsey's nuts,** an exuberant intensive meaning "very dead (cold) indeed." [The ref. is to Kelsey Allen, who as a very old man in the 1920's was the drama critic for *Women's Wear Daily*, a newspaper published in NYC. Old Kelsey praised everything lavishly and his colleagues seemed to have concluded that he was as dead in the head as he was in the scrotum. Whether fact or mere rumor, he was said to work for a percentage of the theatrical advertising he generated, and he therefore praised everything in the hope of encouraging more advertising.]

ker-   Intensive prefix, usu. with words for a dull blow, as in *kerbang, kerflop, kerthump, kerwallop, kerwham;* but also *kerzap,* and in a common variant pronunciation *ca-rash* for *crash* (functioning here as in *caboodle:* see *kit and caboodle*). [Early XIX Am. Onions, ODEE, glosses it: "U.S. vulgar echoic . . . perhaps representing German or Dutch (collective) prefix *ge-.*" I do not see how it can be both. If echoic, echoic of what? But it is almost certainly altered from that Gmnc. *ge-,* prob. transmitted by Dutch settlers, and into Am. with a standard g/k and the common intrusive *r.* Hence, not an echoic but an expressive intensive.]

ketchup   A thick, spiced tomato sauce used originally as a condiment, but now, by the young, as the main course of all meals, the ultimate aim of American junk cookery being to subsume all savor into a universal red smear. [Originally a Chinese "rotten fish sauce." < Chinese *koë,* finely minced fish; *tsiap,* brine → *koëtsiap,* brined (pungent, rotten) minced fish sauce. Into Eng. prob. via Malay pidgin *kech'p.* Eng. variant forms are *catchup* and *catsup,* the latter suggesting, I will hope, "the cat's up (chuck)" or perhaps "the cat's sup(per)"—and if she will eat it, let her have my share.]

kettle   1. A more or less capacious vessel for boiling water. "Polly put the kettle on./ We'll all have tea." —Folk rhyme. 2. *Earlier.* A pot. [At root: 'little pot." Strictly speaking, a large kettle is a cauldron. < L. *catillus,* dim. form of *catinus,* cooking pot.]
    pretty kettle of fish A mess. ["Pretty" is always ironic in this idiom. First attested mid XVIII in Fielding's *Joseph Andrews* and Richardson's *Pamela,* both authors using it as a familiar established phrase, hence of at least XVII origin, if not earlier. Prob. sufficiently

explained as a folk tale ref. to some charred or spilled kettle of fish soup. But in XI *kiddle, kidillus* was a fishing weir; whence XVI *kettle net*, a fishing net. It is at least possible, therefore, that the original sense may have been "a good haul; a good netful"; or, if the ironic "pretty" already functioned, then the opposite, an empty or snarled net, a fiasco. This is conjecture only; but there is good reason to suppose that *kiddle* and *kettle* may have converged in forming this idiom.]

kibosh: put the kibosh on   To put an end to. To squelch. To put a stop to. [1836. Dickens, *Seven Dials*, has *kye-bosk:* "put the kye-bosk on her" = finish her off, knock her out (with reference to a fistfight between two slatterns). The origin has long been in doubt, but is now fixed by a letter from Padraic Colum to Charles Earle Funk (*Hog on Ice*, p. 22):

> "Kibosh," I believe means "the cap of death" and it is always used in that sense—"He put the kibosh on it." In Irish it could be written "cie bais"—the last word pronounced "bosh," the genitive of "bas," death.

Colum does not explain the nature of the cap. Is it the one put on by the judge about to pronounce a death sentence, or the hood sometimes slipped over the head of a person about to be hanged? In any case, though not otherwise attested, Colum's explanation seems authorative and is partially corroborated by the earlier form used by Dickens.]

Kickapoo joy-juice   *WWII slang, Pacific Theater.* Sub-hooch. Any improvised form of alcoholic drink, as fermented fruit juice drunk green and raw, with whatever additives of paregoric, lemon extract, or worse could be stolen from supply. Also mashed and crudely distilled garbage. Nothing alcoholic was too loathsome and all had to be rushed through the process and gulped raw. (See *hooch.*) [*Juice* has a wide currency in slang for "alcohol." So *juicehead, juicer,* an alcoholic. *Torpedo juice,* alcohol intended as a propellant for torpedoes but stolen for drinking purposes. *Kickapoo joy-juice* was coined by Al Capp, whose popular comic strip *Li'l Abner* regularly featured a besotted Kickapoo Indian and a demented hulk who was a throwback to man's animal past. These monomaniacal and inseparable buddies spent all their time cooking and drinking a foul brew that could dissolve anvils.]

kickshaws   Bric-a-brac. Trinkets, usually on display as items of interest and some worth. As food, little festive delicacy. [In XVI

quelkchose, kickchose, kikeshawes; corruption of Fr. *quelque chose,*
something, (but also, with the idiomatic force in context) something
special.]

kike   Perhaps the most derisive and offensive word for a Jew. [Am.
c. 1900. Its emergence in Am. coincides with the great wave of
migration from Eastern Europe. Leo Rosten, *The Joys of Yiddish,*
derives it from Yiddish *kikel, kikl* (pronounced as if *keekle*), little
circle. Illiterate Jews at Ellis Island refused to sign with an *X* (symbol of Christ and of the cross—see *signature*). They drew a *kikel,
kikl* as their mark. Rosten then credits immigration officials with
having derived *kike* from *keekle,* a phonetic alteration of which
I cannot believe their appointed stupidities to be capable. Rosten
is trying to explain an Americanism after the fact, as if it were a
Yiddish evolution. (Jewish scholars have similarly tried to derive
ghetto (which see) as if it were from Hebrew *get,* divorce, when
it is a purely Italian evolution from L. *jactare,* to cast, to throw.

A far more natural source is in the taunting cries of children
who followed bearded Jewish peddlers (to the children, grotesque
sights), singsonging *Ikey-Ikey-Ikey,* which naturally transposes to
Kikey-Kikey-Kikey. When I was a boy in Boston in the early 1920's
Ikey (from Isaac) and Jew were synonyms, and *Ike-the-Kike* was
a natural rhyming taunt.]

kilter   *In Brit.* Good operating condition. In good order. *But in Am.,
only in (all) out of kilter* Not in good working order. Askew.
Messed up. [< generalized Brit. dial. **kelter,* condition, which,
unless qualified, means "in good working condition." In c. 1800
Brit. thieves' cant, *kelter* was "money" (that which puts things
in good order). Akin to *helter-(s)kelter,* all messed up, not in order.]

king   1. A male monarch. 2. By association, a label for any preeminent
form. *king pin, king crab. The King* Jesus Christ. [Variant of *kin,
kind* (see 7 under *gen-, gene-*). Specifically < Gmnc. *kuningaz*
("of the royal kindred"). Cf. Ger. *Koenig,* king. OE *cyning,* king
(in which the initial *c* is a kappa).]

kinnikinnik   A non-tobacco smoking mixture of ground bark, leaves,
and plant tassles used by the Indians and the early white settlers
of the Ohio Valley. [The form is the white man's version of the
Algonquinian word for "mixture."]

NOTE TO PLAYERS OF WORD GAMES. In this spelling, one of
several given by *Webster's, kinnikinnik* is notable as the longest

palindromic word in the language, having eleven letters. The slightly strained forms *releveler* and *redivider* are probably in second place with nine letters, followed by *deified* with seven.

The Bible according to *St. Palindromos* begins: Verse One. *Madam I'm Adam.* Verse Two. *Eve.* Verse Three. *Sex at noon taxes.*

kissing cousin   *Sthrn.* Not a cousin by blood, but so close a friend as to be treated as one of the family ("cousin by affection") and normally addressed by the children as Cousin Tom or Cousin Jane. (In northern usage, such close friends are called Uncle and Aunt by the children.) [I venture this definition cautiously, basing it on an informal poll of hundreds of Southerners questioned over the years. Though every Southerner claims sure knowledge of this idiom, many disagree on its meaning, or understand it in more than one sense. Southern manners do not permit noisy argument, but to ask a group of Southerners to define it can lead to what I must call "heated politeness." The definition as given satisfies a bit more than half of those questioned. Others define it as: 1. A cousin too close to permit marriage—which makes it all right to kiss. 2. A cousin far enough removed to permit marriage—which makes it all right to kiss. 3. A cousin one sees all the time and has an especial fondness for—which makes it all right to kiss. 4. A cousin one sees only rarely and, therefore, greets with particular pleasure—which makes it necessary to kiss. 5. A cousin who takes part in all family counsels and who is always ready to assist—and whom one kisses out of gratitude. 6. An acknowledged cousin as distinct from some redneck to whom one is distantly related but with whom one "does not claim kin."

In connection with this last definition, it is necessary to remember that region by region the South developed a high degree of cousinage, the most successful of the original stock often taking over the rich bottom lands on which alone cotton and tobacco could be king, while the less competitive took to the hard scrabble hills and "bred down" to become rednecks. So Faulkner notes the redneck Workitts, even their name corrupted from that of their plantation-owning cousins the Uhrquarts. And as never to be acknowledged though always known cousins, there were the Negro issue of Daddy's tomcatting nights.

In some southern usage *cousin* functions as a common form of greeting—as a Quaker might say *friend.* Chill Wills, the late actor who played the wily but genial East Texas oaf, saluted everyone as "cousin." Had he remained in his home town, it would have been likely that anyone he so addressed was in some degree a cousin.]

kit and caboodle   All of it. The whole shebang. [In the double form, *kit and caboodle*, attested 1848. *Boodle* (in a later form, *kerboodle*) is attested in a N.Y. State legal document of 1699 with the sense: "estate, goods and chattels." *Ca-* is an Am. variant of the Germanic collective prefix *ge-*, which is also the base of Am. prefix *ker-*. *Kit* is the disputed element. Perhaps "gear" with root sense: "the estate and all equipment for working it." Perhaps a corruption of *kith*, people, with the sense: "the estate and all who live on and work it." In either sense, "all of it and all appertaining."]

kite   A flying toy of paper or cloth attached to a variable framework of light wooden strips. [In earlier Eng., and still in some Brit. use, a hawk. And so ME *kyte*, OE *cȳta*, ult. < an obscure Gmnc. root, prob. echoic of the hawk's shrill cry *ki-ki-ki*.] *go fly a kite* A formula of contemptuous dismissal. [Implies the person addressed is fit for nothing but foolish child's play.]

 kite a check Not, as often implied by lexicographers, fraudulent. The key is *money in transit*. It often takes three or more days for a check to clear. A businessman with two checking accounts, preferably in two different cities, if hard pressed for immediate cash, can issue a check from account A which he covers with a check from account B, leaving himself the clearance time of the check in which to cover the check from B out of accounts receivable or other anticipated cash flow. A bad check is drawn against no funds and with no intention of paying; a kited one, against anticipated funds, and made out in the blood of perforated ulcers.

kitsch   1. Glossy insipidity in art, usually marked by surface technical skill. *Norman Rockwell's painting is the mother of kitsch.* 2. The equivalent quality in intellect, writing, style in general. [Prob. a passing cant term of popular critics. *Am.* I first heard the term in the Village in 1965; first saw it in print in *Harper's*, Sept. 1969. Prob. via Yiddish transmission from Ger. *Kitsch*, trash, gewgaw finery; when said of a painting, a daub.] *Adj.* **kitschy.**

K ration   A WWII army field ration. It contained a small can of high-protein, high-fat processed meat (or sometimes a form of cheese probably fortified by cow dung); hard tack; stone-hard, unmeltable chocolate (for quick energy, all of which was used up in consuming the stuff); sometimes an actually appetizing dried fruit bar; a packet

of dehydrated sugared whale drool for making lemonade; sometimes an insect repellent tastier than the menu; and always a few
cigarettes. Packed in a wax-coated cardboard box, it passed as a
meal, its double function being to sustain the G.I. while making
him angry enough to kill. [*K* is an army supply code. Perhaps
indicating an alphabet sequence of menus. Though note that C
ration, introduced (at least to me) only in 1945, was so tastefully
edible as to be uncharacteristic of the army. If C was in fact developed before K, it must have been withheld as a bonus for those
who had survived or almost survived the war.]

Kriss Kringle   See *Christmas,* historic note.

L

lady [At root: "the one who kneads the dough," hence, "the bread-maker," hence, "mistress of the house" (she who has the key to the larder). OE *hlaef,* bread (LOAF); *digan,* to knead (ult. < IE *dheigh-,* to knead) → *hlaefdige* → ME *lafdi, laudi, ladi, lady.* (For common *-ig* to *-y* shift, cf. OE *hunig* → Eng. *honey.*)] 1. Mistress of the house. *lady of the house.* Hence, 2. Woman of property and social rank. *milady.* 3. Common colloq. for "madam." *You wanna cab, lady?* 4. Any woman for whom no other label is readily available. *lady bowlers, saleslady, cleaning lady.* (Cleaning ladies, one gathers, used to go out with garbage gentlemen before they became sanitary engineers.) 5. A woman of propriety and social graces. *ladylike.*

> I met a lady cold as ice.
> I would not care to meet her twice.
> She was a model of decorum.
> I ain't no lady, but I'm worum.
> —Frances Hansen

lady fair 1. One's betrothed. 2. One's female companion for the night. (An arch survival from the diction of chivalric romances.) *ladyfinger* A small sponge cake more or less in the shape of a (mashed) finger. [*Lady* to suggest delicacy.] *lady's man/ladies' man* 1. A gallant. 2. A skirt chaser. *lady of the night* A high-class hooker.

lalapalooza/lallapalooza/lolapalooza/lollapalooza An outstanding person, thing, creature. A oner. [XIX Am. slang. Because attestation is lacking, most dicts. gloss as "origin unknown," and perhaps properly so. Yet the appaloosa horse (which see), a dramatically outstanding animal, is a likely sense paradigm; and how can so distinctive a word form be withheld from its only Am. analogue? Fr. *à la Palouse,* at the Palouse River, meant "in the country of the Nez Percé." Fr. *l'appaloosa*, the horse, might readily have altered in usage to *lappaloosa*, which might in turn have been given a Sp. fem. article *la lappaloosa*. These intermediate forms cannot be attested, but certainly it is a language impossibility for two forms as distinctive and yet as similar as *l'appaloosa* and *lalapalooza* to evolve at the same time without an interrelationship.]

lambaste   To beat severely. [Root sense: "to beat lame." *Baste*, to hit, to strike; *lam-*, a form surviving only in this compound, is < OE *lemian*, to thrash, to cudgel, which is akin to OE *lama*, lame.]

lampoon   A bit of usually light-hearted personal satire. (As a verb, has the sense: "to ridicule." Originally a satiric drinking song.) [OF *lampons*, let us drink, first person plural imperative of *lamper*, to guzzle. Of obscure Gmnc. origin. The *m* is prob. a nasal infix, the root being *lap-*; and if only as a curious coincidence, the sense of *lamper* can be exactly expressed by Am. slang *to lap it up*, to guzzle. Into XVII Eng. with the sense "a scurrilous personal vilification." In satiric Fr. songs of the XVII, and in England in XVIII, the refrain was sometimes called a *lampon*.]

land office   Under federal provision, a local agency for filing land and mining claims on public lands. Now under the Department of the Interior, created by Act of Congress Mar. 3, 1849; but land offices were first authorized directly by Congress in 1800, four of them being then established in Ohio to handle claims on public lands by migrants from the east coast. ***doing a land office business*** Very busy. Going like hot acres.

Land of Goshen   An exclam. of surprise or dismay. [In Exodus, the name given to Egypt as the place of Jewish captivity, hence, a place of lamentation, and prob. originally used to express regret, though now it conveys primarily surprise, being used expressively rather than with a particular reference. So far as I can determine, the usage is restricted to the American Bible belt.]

landscape   1. A painter's depiction of inland scenery. 2. A view of inland scenery. (And by analogy, *seascape*, a marine view.) [The normal Eng. form would be *landship* < OE *landscipe*, in which the suffix *-scipe*, *-ship* denotes "a holding, the condition of owning (land)." But the term does not occur in ME. Following the great flowering of Dutch art, the term came into England in late XVI

< Du. *lantscap.* The XVI Eng. form was *landskip.* In XVII Milton had *lantskip.*

The British have characteristically adjudicated the interplay of native *-ship* and Du. *-scap,* by spelling the suffix *-scape* and pronouncing it *-skip.* If that adjudication seems even slightly illogical to you, you have no ear for English speech and English idiom will never flow natively from you.]

Laodicean   A reputedly religious but actually worldly person indifferent to the things of the spirit. [Strictly speaking, the Laodicean sin is sloth, the condition of knowing the good but of being lax in its pursuit. St. John the Divine excoriates the Laodiceans in Revelation 3:15–18: "I know thy works, that thou art neither cold nor hot. . . . I will spue thee out of my mouth. . . . Because thou sayest, I am rich . . . and have need of nothing. . . . I counsel thee to . . . anoint thine eyes with eyesalve (i.e., the true and ardent faith), that thou mayest see."]

larboard/starboard   See *board.*

larrup   To thrash. To beat severely. [Widespread in Brit. dial., sometimes in variant *lerrup.* Prob. either from or akin to Du. *larpen,* to lambaste.]

larva   (plu. *larvae*) The newly hatched stage of various creatures that undergo a radical transformation into their adult form; primarily of insects, and among them a usually wormlike form, as the caterpillar is the larva of the butterfly. [The name, based on demonology, is < L. *larva,* a daemon, a revenant spirit of the dead. Since such spooks were conceived as being faceless and shrouded, the word acquired the second sense "faceless, disguised." And both senses function in the application of the term to this stage in the life cycle of the insect as "the thing that creeps about disguised as something else." Nor is anything more natural than that superstitious early man should have been moved to awe by these creatures that vanished into a tomblike cocoon, to emerge as radically transformed adults usually capable of the mystery of flight. (If a worm can be so transformed, the thought would run, what can man not become in his glorious rebirth? And so one more stone of the temple of faith.)]

lavaliere   A usu. large pendant or jeweled medallion worn on a chain around the neck. [Fr. *lavallière.* After *Louise de La Vallière,* mistress of Louis XIV, who liked large medallions so worn (their size gave Louis a chance to fit in more diamonds).]

lavish   *adj.* In free-flowing abundance. —*v.* To offer in free-flowing abundance. Often *to lavish upon.* [Up to XVI a noun signifying "profusion." So Caxton, early XVI: "Ther was no laves in their speche" = their speech was terse (contained no profusion of words). < L. *lavare*, to wash (LAVE). The essential image is of overflowing waters, as at a Roman bath. OF *lavasse*, deluge of rain; *lavis*, outpouring of words.

From the same root: *lavatory* Place for washing oneself. *lava* Molten rock as volcanic overflow. *lavender* The aromatic plant; the scent of the plant. Because used as perfume in the tub, and as a scenting agent scattered among washed and stored linens.]

lead pipe cinch   An absolutely sure, safe, or easy thing. (See *cinch.*)

lease-breaker   A riotous marathon party in someone's apartment. [In an earlier day in NYC, tenants usu. signed yearly leases and landlords actually held them to their leases. If one wanted to move but could not afford to pay off the remainder of the lease, one invited friends to a prolonged disturbance of the peace, hoping to force the landlord to evict.]

leatherneck   A U.S. Marine. [Because for about 12 years circa 1880, a gift of the idiot there always is, the marine uniform had a leather lining in the collar of the dress uniform tunic. An instrument of torture, this lining became gritty with summer sweat and cracked and chafed in winter cold. In time even the marines gave it up.]

leer   A lascivious or cunningly avaricious look. [Root sense: "sidewise look." A specimen slant evolution based on IE *kleu-*, to hear. With k/h in Gmnc. → OE *hlēor*, cheek; the sense evolution being < ear (organ of hearing) → next to the ear → side of the face → cheek → cheeky look → sidewise look.] *v.* To look in this way. *leery adj.* Apprehensive. Wary. [The adjectival form first recorded in Francis Grose, *A Classical Dictionary of the Vulgar Tongue,* 1785. Defined as "on one's guard," with cross ref. to *peery,* inquisitive, suspicious. (Prob., though Grose does not say so, based on *to peer.* So *the cull's peery* = the fellow suspects something. But note that even without the influ. of *peery,* now long obs., the root sense "sidewise look" would readily suggest "warily alert look."]

leg [ON **leggr,* limb, leg.] 1. A limb on which a creature walks. 2. A supporting member, as of furniture. 3. One section of a more extensive course, as the first leg of a three-day race, or the distance a sailing vessel covers in a single tack. 4. The part of a garment that covers all or part of a lower limb.

make a leg In courtly tradition, a deep bow with one leg thrust forward. [In body language, to make a leg is an act of submission: by placing oneself so off balance one symbolically puts oneself at the mercy of the person bowed to, who could send one sprawling with a slightest touch. Since the act of making a leg is innately awkward, it became one of the courtier's graces to make it gracefully.]

break a leg Traditional salute to an actor about to go on stage. [This formula has been influenced in English by "to make a leg," and has been interpreted to mean: "May you receive so many curtain calls that you break a leg in making legs to acknowledge the applause." As such, then, a supreme wish for good luck—for what, to an actor, is a broken leg if it wins applause?

It is, however, ancient theatrical superstition that it is bad luck to wish one good luck. The German formula was and is *Hals- und Bein bruch,* Break your neck and leg bone. And in this form, the idiom rests entirely on the old theatrical superstition.]

get up (rear up) on one's hind legs To react aggressively. [As a horse rears when aroused.]

give a leg up To assist. [Specifically by joining two hands, fingers intermeshed, to form a stirrup in helping one to mount a horse or get over a wall.] *not have a leg to stand on* To lack all basis for an assertion or a claim. *on one's last legs* Approaching one's end. [Perhaps with the sense of "the weak legs of age" as opposed to the sturdy legs of youth. Perhaps from sense 3, on the last laps of one's course. Or the two senses may function to reinforce one another.] *have good legs* 1. *Of a girl.* Have shapely legs. 2. *Of a boy or man.* Be powerful or speedy in striding or running. Be a good walker. *pull one's leg* To josh. To tease. [As if to make one leg longer than the other. Prob. akin to "stretching the truth."] *shake a leg* Hurry. [*Shake* for "rapid motion." Singular *leg* in the pattern of "lend *a hand,*" which in no way excludes two-handed help.] *stretch one's legs* To go for a walk. *leg it* To walk. *legman Business and crim.* An agent who makes calls, delivers messages, works in the field.

legend 1. A more or less mythic story from the dim past. 2. *Ext.* One who achieves mythlike fame. *Babe Ruth became a legend* *in his own time.* 3. A motto, as on a coat of arms; an inscription, as on a monument or as part of a painting. 4. *Ext.* A subscribed explanation, as of map symbols. [Root sense: "thing(s) read about (but not experienced). < L. *legenda,* thing(s) to be read < *legere,* to read (but also "to select and assemble, to anthologize").]

leghorn 1. A type of straw hat. 2. A breed of chicken. [Both *leg* and *horn* are accidents. *Leghorn* is the English rendering of the Italian city of *Livorno* and the English rendering will seem arbitrary unless one notes that the earlier Italian name was *Ligorno,* of which *Leghorn* is a slovenly but reasonably close English approximation.]

lemon A flatfish. [F. *limande,* flatfish < OF *limande,* barrel stave. A curiously redundant survival, seen in Am. only in *lemon sole,* flatfish flatfish. Brit. has the same and also *lemon dab,* with the same redundancy. The word has survived on menus prob. only because *lemon,* a common accompaniment of fish, suggests an esp. flavorful specimen. Empty promise.]

levis (Pronounced *lē' -vīs.*) Heavy work jeans with copper rivets to reinforce the pockets and seams. The pants that finished winning the West. [After Levi Strauss, who began to manufacture them in San Francisco soon after the '49 gold strike. *Levi's* is a registered trade name, but *levis* is now a standard term in Am.]
   HISTORIC. Levi Strauss's rivets, design, and long dominance of the western market have set his product apart from others, but it is of a class with *jeans* (which see; at root: "cloth of Genoa"); *denims* < XVII *serge de Nîmes,* cloth of Nîmes, France; and *dungarees* < XVII *dungaree* < Hindi *dungrī,* a coarse calico woven in India.

lewd Licentious. Lascivious. [Root sense: "not of the clergy." Hence, XIII, illiterate (since literacy was almost exclusively a clerical accomplishment). Hence, as used by the upper classes by XIV, "ignorant, vulgar" (and that despite the fact that few of the upper classes were literate), and so, in self-lauding condemnation of others for one's own faults, "marked by the coarseness and lasciviousness of the ignorant lower classes." OE *laewede,* laic.]

libido *Post-Freudian psychology.* The erotic component of one's personality. The total of one's procreative drive. [*Libidinous,* given to/ characterized by lust, was in use from XV but *libido* is a XX psychiatrist's coinage. < L. *libet, lubet,* it is pleasing; *libido, lubido,* lust. Ult. < IE *leub-,* to desire, to love (Ger. LIEBCHEN, loved one; Eng. LIEF).]

lief   In Am., most common in New England regionalism *I'd as lief/ I'd liefer* I'd as soon, I'd sooner; which are XII forms with the sense "I'd as dearly, I had more dearly." Also as a flourish in pseudo-vacuo-ecstatico poesy: "Lief would I vouchsafe all but that I know . . ." [Ult. < IE *leub-,* to desire, to love. With b/f in Gmnc. → OE *lēof,* beloved, dear.]

lieutenant   A subordinate officer. *a. Military & Naval.* A junior officer. One who exercises authority in the name of a commander under whom he serves. *b.* An assistant. One who serves next in line. *lieutenant governor, lieutenant general.* Also *the gang chief and two of his lieutenants.* (L. *locum tenens,* one who holds a place (in lieu of another). OF *lieu,* (in) place of (a captain); *tenant,* holder. The Brit. pronunciation *leftenant* (not reflected in the spelling) is a survival of XIV *levetenant, lievtenant, leeftenant.*]

lights   *Plu. only. Primarily Brit.* Animal lungs as a cheap food. [Lungs being spongy, *lights* represents "the lightest part of the pluck." ME *lihte,* akin to Ger. *licht,* light (not dark), but here with the sense "not heavy." Survives in Am. primarily in the exclam. or oath:] *by my liver and lights!* By my liver and lungs! [Hence, *Upon my life!*]

like sixty   At utmost speed. [Root sense: "at sixty miles an hour." Cf. *going a mile a minute.* C. 1900 and early automotive age.]
   HISTORIC. In an age when thirty miles was a long day's pull for a wagon and a bone-wearying journey for a walking man, the idea of going a mile a minute was an eral dream, about akin to the idea of walking on the moon. One of the dreams of early automobilists was to find a car and a road that would make possible this magical speed. Just as we have grown half indifferent to space exploits (once you've seen one moon-walk, you've seen them all), so the thought of a mile a minute seems paltry to the supersonic age, and the idiom is already much fallen from use, but it did once ride the tail of a dream.

Limehouse   A section of London along the Thames and within sound of the bells of Bow, the home of the Cockney, and the oldest and most widely known slum of England. [< *Lime oast* → *lime*

oas' → lime 'ouse → Limehouse. Because in the earliest days of
the city, lime kilns (oasts) for making cement were located there.]

NOTE. A persistent folk etymology attributes the name to the
late XVIII, when the British Navy is alleged to have established
in this section of London a warehouse for storing limes and lime
juice to be used as an antiscorbutic (see *Limey*). But, 1. *Limehouse*
was in use for centuries before the XVIII. 2. No such warehouse
is recorded. 3. All the limes the British Navy could use at any
one time could easily have been stored in an odd corner of any
existing naval warehouse.

limerick   A popular five-line form of light verse rhymed AABBA,
the A lines trimeters, the B lines dimeters. Edward Lear, XIX
popularizer of the form, repeated the first rhyme word in the
last line, but since his time a new third rhyme has generally been
found to be more satisfactory and is now standard. I have been
a passionate limericker in my time and there is no way to stop
me from quoting myself by way of example, if only to prove that
the limerick can *(a)* be innocent:

> Said a salty old skipper from Wales,
> "Number One, it's all right to chew nails.
> > It impresses the crew.
> > It impresses me, too.
> But stop spitting holes in the sails!"

but *(b)* likes to be suggestive:

> There once was a lady named Wright
> Who simply could not sleep at night
> > Because of the ping-
> > Ping-ping of her spring,
> And the glare of her little red light.

or *(c)* more explicit:

> There once was a girl from New Haven
> Whose pubic hair was not shaven
> > But missing because
> > She slept without drawers
> Within range of a nest-building raven.

Examples *d, e, f,* and so forth are best referred to Victorian
England, in which donnish gentlemen found in the limerick an
excuse for letting out all the four-letter words they had stored

up from an obscenely repressed boyhood; and some of their output remains obscenely admirable, but the Am. limerick (whose shrine is the Saturday night faculty booze-up) tends to the subtleties of *single entendre,* to the *roman à cleft,* to the leer rather than to the full-fisted goose-direct.

HISTORIC. Though the limerick is a recent form, its name and origin remain a bit obscure. The first known examples of the form are from early XVIII and are in French, yet the name is from Limerick, Ireland. The Irish Brigade served in France for most of XVIII. It was probably the officers of the brigade who first popularized the form in English, their central base being in Limerick. Carousing drunkards of the time (see *carouse*) commonly sang solo ballad verses in turn, all joining in the traditional chorus "Will you come up, come up, come up? Will you come up to Limerick?" The chorus predates the limerick but was easily adapted to it, the form being easy to sing to various simple airs. Whether from the home base of the brigade, or from the traditional refrain, *limerick* became the name of the new form, and *limerick* it remains. But note that Edward Lear never wrote a limerick, for the word is not attested (OED) before the 1890's.

Limey 1. *Original sense, late XVIII.* A British sailor. 2. *Ext.* Any Englishman. [In late XVIII, the British Navy, having found that citrus juices could prevent the scourge of scurvy, instituted a daily ration of lime juice for all men on sea duty, whereupon Australian and then American sailors dubbed the British "limejuicers," whence *Limey, Limeys* for British sailor(s) and the early ext. to Englishmen in general. Limey is undoubtedly influ. by *Limehouse* (which see), but the two terms are etymologically distinct.]

linen [Gk. *linon,* flax < IE *lino-,* flax. L. *linum* → OE *linnen, linen,* (cloth) of flax.] 1. Thread, cloth, or garments made of flax. 2. Light clothing resembling linen, with esp. ref. to shirts, shirtwaists, and underwear (those articles of clothing one changes most often). *linens* Sheets (bed linens), tablecloths, and other common household cloths.

not wash one's dirty linen in public To avoid exposing one's most intimate affairs to general view. [A modified rendering of the French phrase attributed by Honoré de Balzac (in *Eugénie Grandet*) to Napoleon, but in fact proverbial and of unknown very early date: "'Il faut laver son linge sale en famille,' disait Napoléon." —"'One should wash one's dirty linen in private (within the family),' Napoleon used to say."]

loaded for bear Equipped and prepared for serious business. [In the days of muzzle-loading flintlocks, the powder charge and shot were variable. One loaded the gun according to what one expected to shoot. A man out for bear would load and charge up to the maximum capacity of his gun.]

loan/lend A *loan* (noun) is properly that which one *lends* (verb), the verb forms being *lend, lending, lent.* And so, except in semi-literate dial., from the beginning. Then c. 1800, esp. in the usage of the semieducated new business class, *loan* began to function as a verb. Today *to loan* has become standard in government and business, and is prob. on its way to becoming standard usage. In the late 1930's President Roosevelt still remembered enough basic English to call his prewar aid to Britain *lend-lease.* Under the verbally insensitive Eisenhower, such a program would likely have been *loan-lease.* It is possible to foresee that even *lend a hand* may become *loan a hand.*

Nor will language be admonished from a course it has set. C. 1710, for instance, Jonathan Swift held *mob,* now standard English, to be an ignorant cant form. If you have forgotten the verb *to lend* and have *loaned* your tin ear to this usage *anymore* (which see), you are probably speaking the language of the future; and may your ghost and Eisenhower's join in happy heavenly jargon, but stay away from my future ghost at the risk of its inconsequential wrath. [Both forms via a complex hypothetical Gmnc. evolution < IE *leiku-,* to leave → OE *laenan,* to give, to lend ("to leave in the possession of another").]

loan car Now rare. From c. 1920's, a car, usu. an old wreck, that garage owners lent to customers while their cars were in the shop for repairs. Purportedly because of insurance problems, but actually to spare an expense and to squeeze an extra dollar, the loan car has been superseded by a contractual rental car at a daily fee for use and insurance.

loan shark Usury, classified by Dante as a sin against God, nature, and art, must be nearly as old as money itself. And loan sharking has been practiced in various forms since. Only recently, however, as organized crime has acquired legitimate fronts, has the loan shark sought out hard-pressed businessmen, lent them money with compound interest at 20 percent a week, with fanciful additional penalties for tardiness or failure to pay, and so bank-rupted them and taken over the business under threat of violence. (I cannot date the origins of the practice, but in the 1930's I worked in a factory, and it was then common practice for a worker who ran short to borrow from a fellow worker against his next week's pay, the fixed scale being to borrow $4.00 and to repay $5.00—the same 20 percent weekly interest rate called *vigorish*, which see, by racketeers.)

loan word A word borrowed from another language and naturalized, though retaining its original form.

NOTE. *Brass hat* (which see) is a partially modified, partly translated Fr. term, now a purely Eng. form. *Seraph, cherub* are Hebrew loan words, now standard English, but retaining the Hebrew plural form *-im* in *seraphim, cherubim. Goy, goyim* is prob. in process of becoming a loan word, but is still generally treated as an unnaturalized Yiddish-Hebrew form, as witnessed by the fact that most writers still italicize it to indicate that it is a foreign term. When writers are no longer moved to italicize, it will have become a loan word.

lend an ear Listen to. [Long-established fanciful construction; as if lending the ear for someone else's use. (Will you bang it here, or take it out?)]

lobster shift *Journalism. NYC c. 1900.* The newspaper work shift (also *tombstone shift*) beginning at 4:00 A.M. [Because the newspaper people coming to work mingled with the lobstermen who were about to put out. (So at least the one reference I have been able to run down, but do not fishermen put out with the tide rather than by time of day? I am further told by an old newspaper hand that the term prob. originated with the *Journal-American*, whose plant c. 1900 was near the East Side fishing docks. Why are newspaper people, otherwise so garrulous, so short in explaining their own jargon?)]

locofoco The name given to the first friction matches c. 1810, in both Brit. and Am. [Some have suggested that the element *loco* is taken from the, then, newly developed *loco(motive)*, the first element being mistakenly taken to mean "self-(moving)," i.e., automatic. But *locofoco* can also be construed as "crazy fire" < Sp. *loco,* crazy; It. *fuoco,* fire; and these matches did tend to shoot smoking sparks when struck, making for a while a favorite new plaything for boys. For *fuoco,* see *focus,* which in L. is "hearth" ("place where the family comes together").

HISTORIC. In 1834, a John Marck of NYC opened a new shop on Park Row, contributing to American know-how and promotional come-on two brilliant new gimmicks: a soda fountain with champagne on tap; and *Locofoco Cigars,* one end of which had been dipped in match-head paste, allowing them to be lit like a friction match (and certainly contributing a choice flavor of sulfur and phosphorus to those first fine puffs).

Locofoco *U.S. politics. 1835–c. 1900.* A member of the Democratic Party. **Locofocos** The Democrats. (Originally the N.Y. Democrats, who called themselves the Equal Rights Party. Later, and for most of the rest of the century, any Democrat.

HISTORIC. In 1835 the Equal Rights Party called an important meeting at Tammany Hall. Their opponents, to disrupt the meeting, planned to shut off the main that supplied the gaslights. The Democrats, having been forewarned of the plot, quietly supplied themselves with candles and locofoco matches. When the lights were shut off, they took candles from their pockets, lit them with locofocos, and went calmly on with their business, their ingenuity providing them with a new political label.

locomotive Railroad engine. [Compounded of L. *locus,* place, the ablative *loco* implying "from, away from"; with *motio,* motion < *movere,* to move. In Thomistic terminology *in loco moveri,* to change one's position in space. The immediate Eng. source was *locomotion,* the ability or the act of self-movement, which was first used in XVII.]

HISTORIC. The first locomotive operated on a short railroad at Merthyr Tydvial in South Wales in 1804, having been built by the partners Trevithick and Vivian under a patent issued in 1802. Their first engine embodied all the essential principles found in later steam engines.

logger 1. *In Brit. dial. of unknown origin.* A wooden block. A chopping block. A knob. [Perh. ult. < *log,* but ??] 2. *Am. whaling.* A snubbing post built into the bow of a whaleboat. The line attached to a harpooned whale was coiled around the logger. [This usage also suggesting a poss. derivation from *log.*] **loggerhead** A knob head. A blockhead. [The root ref. is to a knob on the end of a stick. And so in the names of various animals with unusually large heads, as the *loggerhead turtle.*]

at loggerheads In hot dispute at close quarters, as if bumping heads. *By ext.* In hot argument, giving it to one another head to head and verbal scald for verbal scald. [A long-handled large iron ladle used for pouring melted tar and molten metal was earlier called a *loggerhead.* In naval engagements up to early XVII, ships often grappled while sailors used such loggerheads for scalding the enemy with tar, oil, or water that had been brought to a boil in cauldrons set up on deck in brick-and-sand pits. The *galleass* of the XV and XVI in the Mediterranean, with its very high sheer, was esp. well designed for such warm outpourings upon lower-lying vessels. See *galleywest.*]

long green Money. A lot of money. [Exuberant, as if counting out greenbacks in a long line laid end to end. Prob. c. 1870, since the first greenback U.S. dollars were not printed until 1863 and won acceptance only slowly. Up to that time U.S. dollars were always silver dollars, Americans having acquired a deep distrust of paper money after the failure of the Continental paper currency issued during the Revolution.]

long in the tooth Getting on in years. *Roger Fredland used to be a bit of a heller, but he's getting to be short of breath and long in the tooth.* [There being no truth in horse traders, the potential buyer checks the horse's age by examining its teeth. Constant grinding of fodder causes the horse's gums to recede, whereby the teeth of old horses seem to grow long. *Tooth* for *teeth* is an idiomatic fix. Dating unknown. Prob. of remote folk origin.]

longshoreman [Earlier Brit. *along-shore man.*] One who works on ships, primarily to load and unload, only when they are tied up along the shore, usu. at a pier.

long shot *Gambling and esp. horse racing.* A bet given small chance of winning and therefore paying long odds if it does win. *not by a long shot* Highly unlikely. Not nearly. [It is easy to explain this idiom as based on the distance of a bow shot: the longer the shot, the less likely the hit. And I see no way to deny this source as a possibility. But it is more likely a disguised evolution with "shot" substituted for "chalk," the earlier form being "not by a long chalk"; and so such surviving idioms as *chalk it up to experience,* to write off a loss by what one has learned from it; *chalk it up,* to put it on credit, to enter a bet; *chalk one up,* to score a point. In the days before modern writing implements and ubiquitous paper, records were commonly kept by chalk marks, as odds are still posted at British tracks. A long chalk would be one capable of marking many bets and charges, up to a high total, hence the extended sense, "not by a great deal."]

loop [ME *loupe,* a small hole or slit in a castle wall for firing weapons (originally bow and crossbow) from a protected position. Though generally glossed "origin unknown," it is certainly cognate with Du. *loopgat*, escape way, escape opening < *loopen*, to run, leap (LOPE); *gat*, gate.] *n.* 1. A roughly circular or oval coil of wire, string, ribbon, or rope, as the snaring end of a cowboy's lariat. *throw a loop over* To lasso. 2. To form such a coil. 3. *Aviation.* An aerobatic maneuver in a vertical circle.

loop the loop 1. *Aviation.* To perform a loop. 2. *Amusement park.* A roller coaster. *inside loop* A loop performed with the pilot's head inside the circle. *outside loop* The rarer maneuver, possible only in certain planes, in which the pilot's head is outside the circle of the maneuver. *As a naval ensign, Smith Kirkpatrick performed an outside loop and the evidence is that he hasn't landed yet.*

loophole 1. *As in ME* loupe, *above.* A protected firing post. 2. *Same sense as Du.* loopgat, *above.* A sly way out of a difficulty. 3. *Legal.* A way of evading the law's intent by a crafty interpretation of its letter. *loophole specialist* A tricky lawyer.

The Loop The center of downtown Chicago. [Because the El runs in a loop around the district.]

knock for a loop Exuberant hyperbole. To astonish. [As if to hit so hard as to cause a person to perform a back somersault.] *If you knew the whole truth about Bud Orenstein it would knock you for a loop—well, at least for a limp.* [I am unable to date this common idiom but am strongly tempted to associate it with the convention of late XIX (and surviving) comic strips in which astonishment is indicated by having the, so to speak, astonee perform a backward flip.]

loot 1. The booty of pillage or theft. (With corresponding verb forms.) 2. *Am. slang.* Money. Wages. Profit. [A gift of the British Empire, brought from India c. 1850. < Hindi *lūt*, booty, plunder.]

love *In tennis scoring.* Zero. [< *for love*, for nothing. Common in XVII Brit., the essential idiom survives in such combined forms as *labor of love* and *not for love or money.*]

NOTE. Not, as commonly asserted, from Fr. *l'oeuf*, the egg (as in current sports talk *goose egg*, zero). French idiom has never used egg in this way. Had it done so, moreover, the likely form would have been not *l'oeuf* but *oeuf*, *un oeuf*, or *'n oeuf*; in which case the common British slurring of borrowed terms might likely have led to *off*, *noff*, or (by mistranslation) *nine*, yielding such tennis scores as *fifteen-off*, *fifteen-noff*, or *fifteen-nine.*

lowbrow A person with a low forehead, and therefore believed to have small mental capacity. **middlebrow** Average forehead, average intellect. **highbrow** An intellectual, an egghead, an esthete.

HISTORIC. In the 1960's, NYC in-group jargonauts retooled from the New Criticism to kitsch-kultur by way of Kierkegaard, the analyst's couch, and blintz seminars at the local cafeteria, substituted *mass-cult, mid-cult,* and *high-cult* (*cult* for *culture*) for these terms, asserting a distinction without a difference, but their occult has passed into the quaint and the three brows remain firmly in idiom.

lower the boom 1. *Nautical.* To lower and secure the freight-loading booms once cargo is stored. Hence, 2. To finish off. *lower the boom on* To conk. To knock out. [To put away an opponent in a fight.] 3. To trap or corner, as stowed cargo. *He lowered the boom on me for a double sawbuck:* He cornered me and borrowed (put the arm on me for) twenty dollars.

luck [ME *luckel,* luck, is based on hypothetical Gmnc. **luc* as deduced from MHG *gelucke, ge-* serving as the collective prefix and surviving in elided form in mod. Ger. *Gluck,* lit. all sorts of good luck. Also a common Ger. surname.] Fortune. When unqualified, usu. implies good fortune, but *just my luck!* is a common lament of one who has been unfortunate. And so, too: *I wish Robert Bly lots of luck—all of it bad.*

luck of the Irish Commonly a blarney self-assertion that the Irish must triumph. (As witness the history of Ireland?) But equally to express a bad turn of fortune. *Dead in a fall off the ladder, say you? Now ain't that just the luck of the Irish?*

luck out To win by pure chance. **down on one's luck** Having suffered reverses. **in luck** Having good luck. **out of luck** Having bad luck. **lucky strike** *Mid XIX mining.* A rich discovery. [The Brit. form is *to strike lucky,* which Am. renders as *to strike it rich.*] **have the devil's own luck** *Primarily Brit.* Extraordinary fortune, either good or bad, depending on the context. (And on whether the devil is taken as a sure loser or as a wizard at manipulating the odds.)

Lady Luck The obsessive gambler's tutelary spirit. [A semi-mythological figure traceable to Fortuna or the Lady of Permutations as conceived by the Middle Ages to account for the shifting tides of fortune that alter the affairs of mankind. Dante, *Inferno,* VII, 70–96, treats her as an angelic agent of Divine Justice who distributes the good of the world evenly as one empire falls and another rises.] ***whore luck*** What the lady (now uncapitalized) turns out to be when the gambler loses.

    good luck piece Surviving primitive magic: anything conceived to have the protective power of an amulet, fetish, scapular, talisman.

lucre Money. Financial profit. (Has a pejorative overtone, which emerges explicitly in the fixed form ***filthy lucre*** Ill-gotten gain. Money as a morally corruptive power. [< L. *lucrum,* money, profit. Prob. ult. < IE *lau-, leu-,* gain. But ?]

    HISTORIC. There is no clear evidence that L. *lucrum* had a pejorative overtone, yet from the first introduction of money as a means of exchange, there is evidence of a feeling that true value consisted of land, crops, and livestock, and that minted money upset a natural balance. Money was proverbially said to be the root of all evil *(radix malorum pecunia est).* Dante (XIII–XIV) took the medieval view that God had meant man to earn his bread in the sweat of his brow, hence, that to lend money at interest was usury per se and a mortal sin against God's clear intent. And Christ drove the moneychangers from the temple. Humankind has always been ambivalent about money, eager for it because it became a means of life; afraid of it because it forced life into unnatural patterns. All of these racial attitudes are implicit in *lucre* and explicit in *filthy lucre* (but, Lord, let my hands be dirty with the stuff).

lulu¹ A oner. ***ain't he/she/it a lulu!*** Ain't that something. [Am. mid XIX. M. M. Mathews, *Dictionary of Americanisms,* offers a first attestation from Parker's *Spirit of the Times* (1857): "Well, he had a daughter; and she, O Bob! she was then, in my eyes, the looliest looly of the loolies, she was!" Mathews, along with all dictionaries I have consulted, glosses the term "origin unknown"; yet it is obviously < Fr. *loulou,* term of endearment; *mon gros loulou* (for feminine, *ma louloute),* my ducky-wucky. Ult. based on Fr. *loup-loup,* which may be rendered either as wolf-wolf or lupin-lupin (the flower).]

lulu² *N.Y. State Legislature.* A nonaccountable allowance for expenses N.Y. State legislators have voted to themselves on charitable impulse. [A reduplication of "lieu" from the phrasing of the legislation that authorizes this form of graft *in lieu of* this and *in lieu of* that. As *lulus²* go, the legislation is a bit of a *lulu¹.*]

lurch In some card games, to defeat by a penalizing margin (to skunk in cribbage, to schneider in gin rummy—which in either case doubles the loser's penalty). Otherwise only in *leave (one) in the lurch* To abandon in bad straits. [Prob. based on MHG *lurz,* clumsy, incorrect, defeated. OF *l'ourche, lourche,* with the root sense "defeat," was the name of a game resembling backgammon; *demeurer lourche,* to be left badly defeated (the equivalent of a skunk or a schneid, as above).]

lust 1. Intense (implies unrestrained) sexual craving. (But the root sense is better preserved in:) 2. Any intense craving. (Usu. with *for,* or in Brit. *after.* The British lust after lewd women; the Americans weep after them for having lusted for them.) So *lust for life, lust for power, to lust after riches.* [Root sense: "compulsive inner force." < IE *las-,* signifying "an inner force so strong as to lead to the breaking of all bounds" (WANDERLUST). Suffixed *-dt-* and later *-t-* in Gmnc. → OE *lystan,* to take pleasure in ("to satisfy one's inner drive"). So obs. *if ye so list,* if it please you, if you please (to) (LISTLESS). OE *lustig,* joyous, pleasing ("accordant with one's strongest feelings") (LUSTY). XIV. Powerful. *A lusty ale.* And see *luxury,* which through XVI expressed the now primary sense.]

luxury Rich and sumptuous living. [And this is now the only functioning sense. But Dante, *Inferno,* has *"Cleopatra lussuriosa,"* lustful Cleopatra ("abandoned to the gratification of her eroticism"). And Shakespeare, *Hamlet:* "To make the royal bed of Denmark/ A couch for cursed luxury," i.e. "lust." And note that through XVI the Gmnc. root *lust* (see above) signified "joyous, powerful, according to one's deepest desires."

Ult. < IE *leug-, leuk-,* to turn and twist, with special ref. to rank plant growth. → L. *luxus,* unrestrained plant growth → *luxuria,* unrestrained self-indulgence, uninhibited gratification.

Luxuria was adopted metaphorically by early Christian writers to express the opposite of the Four Natural Virtues (justice, prudence, temperance, fortitude). It may have been early associated with the Roman orgy, which began with abandoned gluttony and proceeded to abandoned sexuality; hence, the opposite of Christian restraint, whence easily narrowed to "carnal abandon, lust." The sin, be it noted, does not lie in sexual desire, which is a God-given appetite, but in the unrestrained abandonment to lust. Dante defines the sin as beginning at the point at which one thinks of lust to the exclusion of God.]

mad   [IE *mei-* expresses "motion, change." Suffixed *-d-* or *-dt-* in Gmnc. → OE *gemād,* changed (out of oneself). The prefix *ge-* functions as an intensive here.] 1. Insane. [Changed out of oneself, not in possession of oneself.] 2. *But more commonly in Am.* Angry. [Raving insanely.] 3. Infatuated. [Changed out of oneself by.] *I'm mad about her.* (Is also rendered in Am. *I'm wild about her.*)

   like mad Without restraint. *have a mad on* To be surly, angry. *madcap n.* A waggishly impulsive person. *—adj.* Whimsically impulsive. *His merry madcap ways. mad dog* A rabid person. *madhouse* 1. Insane asylum. 2. *Loose ext.* A place of noisy (but not evil) disorder. *mad money* 1. Money a girl takes on a date in case she becomes angry and decides to cab home on her own. 2. Money set aside for indulging some (mad) impulsive whim.

   mad as a hatter See *hat. mad as a March hare* Hopping and posturing erratically. In effect, "very mad." [Because March is the mating season for the English hare and its courtship ritual impels it to behave erratically. Erratically, that is, from the point of view of an Englishman. From the point of view of another hare, and especially from that of a doe, such behavior is not only socially acceptable but is probably regarded as romantic.]

magazine   [It. *magazzino,* storehouse for various commodities (as on a pier) < Arabic **makhazin,* storehouses (plu. of *makhzin,* storehouse). And this root sense has led to Fr. *magasin,* department store ("place for selling a variety of commodities") but this sense ext. has not come about in Am., in which the working senses are:] 1. A periodic publication, usu. weekly, monthly, or quarterly, containing work by many hands. ["A variety storehouse."] 2. *Military & naval.* A storage place for ammunition and explosives. 3. In a repeater rifle or machine pistol, the place in which rounds are carried. (Now more commonly called the "clip.") 4. *Ext.* In various machines and tools, the chamber containing materials for use.

magnet   1. *Now.* Variously charged and formed metallic devices that attract iron. 2. *Earlier.* An iron oxide stone with the property of attracting iron. [< Gk. *ho Maganēs lithos,* the stone of Magnesia, earlier name for Thessaly, the district of Greece in which such stones were found. *Magnesium* is a co-derivation from this place name, for it was in the mining of magnesium ore there that magnetic stones turned up.] **magnetic** 1. Having the power to attract iron. 2. *Metaphoric ext.* Having the power to attract. *a magnetic personality.* **magnetic field** The pattern of lines of force between the two poles of a magnet.

mahatma   [Sanskrit *mahatma,* great soul.] In India and parts of Tibet, a spiritual leader and teacher, and a master of the theosophical disciplines of body control whereby the soul is released for "pure" contemplation. **Mahatma** A Hindu title of honor.
　　HISTORIC. Mohandas Karamchand Gandhi (1869–1948), renowned as Mahatma Gandhi, is certainly the mahatma best known in the western world, and perhaps the one most revered in India. He led the nonviolent civil disobedience movement of 1914–1947 which was so important in bringing about India's independence from the British Empire. Freedom was plagued by a bloody internal conflict between Hindus and Moslems, and on Jan. 30, 1948, Gandhi was shot and killed by a fanatical Hindu who believed Gandhi had betrayed India to the Moslems. Shantih.

mainbrace   *Nautical.* On square-rigged sailing ships, either of two lines from the ends of the lower mainspar to cleats fixed far astern and usu. secured to the hull.
　　splice the mainbrace To have a drink. [Because the mainbraces were so awkwardly placed, it was necessary to call out the entire crew for an especially difficult labor when the braces had to be repaired or replaced. It was customary for the extra work to be repaid by an extra ration of rum for all hands; whence the present sense: "to have a round of drinks, to have a drink."]

malaprop   The incommodious subsidization of one word in lute of another, as in making a parsing reverence to allegories sunning themselves on the banks of the Nile. [After Sheridan's play *The Rivals,* 1775, in which the character Mrs. Malaprop uxuriated her vocalizations in this way. The name *Malaprop* is based on Fr. *mal apropos,* inappropriate.]

manor   The more or less impressive house of a landed estate. *to the manor born* Born to rank and wealth. Born with a silver spoon in one's mouth. [Cf. *born to the purple,* of royal birth. ME *manor, maner* make *manor* and *manner* almost the same word, whereby some have interpreted the original to be "to the manner born," but it is a distinction without a difference, the *manner* (the bearing of the landed gentry) being available only in the manor house.]

mantelpiece   A shelf or ledge, often ornamental, on the front of a fireplace. [< mantle, cape; because wet capes were once commonly hung to dry on such a ledge or shelf equipped with pegs.]
HISTORIC. This mantle/mantel association will be difficult to envisage unless one thinks not of the small modern fireplace, but of the old-style cooking and warming pit, often as large as a small room, with a fire at its center, and ample space to either side for hanging things to dry, and even for people to sit on ledges or benches to warm themselves.

Mardi Gras   1. *Primary Am. sense.* The pre-Lenten Carnival season whose festive observation has become traditional in New Orleans. 2. Any revel, festival, or promotional event in imitation of the New Orleans festival. [Note that in Am. people commonly say they are going to New Orleans for Mardi Gras when they mean they are going for the Carnival. *Carnival* is properly the entire pre-Lenten festival, lasting from ten days to two weeks. *Mardi Gras* is Fr. for "Fat Tuesday," the last day before Lent; so called from the custom of using all the lard in the house for festive baking before the meatless Lenten fast. In Brit. called *Shrove Tuesday.*]

mare's nest   1. A hoax. 2. A hopelessly snarled situation. [Attested 1619 < earlier but obs. *horse nest.* Sense 1 because mares do not build nests. Sense 2, I must suppose, because if they did they would make a mess of it.]

marine   A soldier who serves aboard ship as well as upon the land. [Contracted from earlier *marine soldier.*]
HISTORIC. The Earl of Torrington and the Earl of Pembroke were commissioned in 1690 to form the first British marine regiments. Marine detachments soon became common on British ships. Seamen scorned the marines for their ignorance of the workings of the ship, and hated them because they served as a shipboard police force.
tell it to the marines (the sailors are too smart to believe you) Formula of contemptuous rejection or dismissal. [Is based on the sailors' scorn of the marines for their ignorance of seaman-

ship. Prob. in XVII British maritime use in the full form (only the unparenthesized portion now surviving). The first attested usage was by Byron, "The Island," 1823.]

horse marines A nonexistent branch of the service, hence used in joshing the foolish, as, when asked what one did in the war, to answer "I was in the horse marines," the effective sense of which is "Mind your own business." [Partridge, *Slang*, notes that in 1796 the 17th Lancers, en route to the West Indies, served aboard ship as marines.]

maronna/maronn'/maronna mia   Exclam. of surprise, dismay, vexation. Equivalent to "My God!" [Common in street talk and among blue-collar workers. Borrowed from southern It. dialect rendering of It. *Madonna*, the Virgin Mary. In illiterate Italian usage, in various forms of New World Spanish, and in the patois of It.-Am. and Span.-Am, *d* between two vowels commonly becomes a trilled *r*. So the commonly heard "I ron' o" for "I don' o" (I don't know). And as a master stroke of its own sort, "stupor iriot" for "stupid idiot."]

maroon   To abandon in a wild and unpopulated place. *marooned on a desert island.* [Not akin to the color, which is from Fr. *marron*, chestnut. This form is from Sp. *cimarron*, wild, describing an undomesticated animal or an uncultivated region. Intermediately, in XVII–XVIII West Indies French, *cimarron* and *marron* labeled a runaway slave hiding out in the jungle far from settled places. I have not been able to track the shift from Fr. *marron*, in this sense, to Eng. *maroon*, but suspect it was a maritime and pidgin transmission.]

marshal   1. In most European armies, the highest military grade, the equivalent of a U.S. five-star general. (Pershing, commander of the American Expeditionary Force in World War I, was the first five-star general since Washington with the title General of the Army. He was raised to that rank to make him the military equal of the French and British marshals. After the war, he was promoted to General of the Armies, the pluralization implying a sixth star, but to the best of my knowledge, no one has ever seen that insignia.) 2. *In Brit.* An officer in charge of royal ceremonies and protocol. *In Am.* The official in charge of a ceremony, as a commencement exercise. Also called *marshal at arms* because he carries a mace. 3. *Obsolete. Preliminary to sense 1.* The officer in command of a substantial body of cavalry. [A word that has risen high from low origins. OE *maracalc,* groom, stable boy (at root: "horse servant"). < Gmnc. *mara,* horse (MARE); *calc* (of unknown origin; perh. a borrowing), slave, servant. But since horses were a prized possession, the officer in charge of the king's horses would have to be a trusted lord of the realm and a high officer of the court. Cf. *butler* for a similar up-and-down history.]

mask   1. A covering fastened over the face to conceal one's identity. If a full mask, usu. with holes for the eyes and mouth. Partial masks cover either the upper or the lower part of the face. Theatrical and ceremonial masks can be elaborate affairs into which one slips one's whole head. 2. *In various exts.* Anything that conceals. *a mask of friendliness over his deceit, a mask of trees hid the entrance.* (And corresponding verb forms.) [Via It. *máschera,* mask < Arabic *maskhara,* clown. I have not been able to run down accurate information on the style of Arabian clowns, but *mascara,* cosmetic for darkening the eyebrows and eyelashes, is from the same root, and clearly suggests that Arabian clowns did not slip a mask over the face, but painted themselves in some form of the practice yet followed by modern circus clowns.]
    death mask A mold of the face of a corpse made by greasing the features and covering the face with plaster of Paris. When the plaster of the mold has dried, castings of half the face can be made from it. Once a common memorial practice. Death masks of Beethoven were especially common in the studios of XIX musicians and artists, and many survive. *life mask* A cast made in much the same way from the face of a living person, but with straws and protective padding placed in the nose to permit breathing and to keep the plaster from going into the nose. Using various materials, the Am. sculptor George Segal has developed piece-mold body castings into an impressive art form.

mass   In R.C. (and in some High Anglican) churches, the solemn celebration of the Eucharist with its attendant ritual. [< L. *missa,* p.p. of *mittare,* to dismiss (MANUMIT); because the priest's last words are *"Ite, missa est,"* "Go, you are dismissed." Altered to *messa* in Late L. and Old It., to *maessa* in OE, to *masse* in ME.]

mate   [Root sense: "person with whom one shares food." < IE *mad-,* wet (in words having to do with the preparation of food). With d/t in Gmnc. → OE *mete,* food (MEAT). But note that OE *mete* was not "flesh as food" but "any food." Into XVI *meat for horses* meant "fodder." Sense ext. from "person with whom one eats" to "constant and intimate companion."] 1. Either of a married pair. A sexual partner. *mating season, mating game*. 2. *Nautical. a*. A fellow seaman. [A messmate.] *b*. By XIV. A ship's officer. [The captain's messmate and companion.] 2. *Ext*. [Based on the sense "two that go together."] Either of a like pair, as a sock, a shoe. (For *mate* in chess, a Persian evolution, see *check: checkmate*.)

    helpmate/helpmeet A wife. [The first form is a corruption of the second, which is based on *meet*, in old style, "suitable, fitting." Genesis 2:18: "I will make him an help meet for him."]

    inmate Now implies more or less enforced confinement as of a hospital patient or a prisoner. [But earlier, a fellow lodger; an inn-mate.]

Maui wowie *Pothead jargon*. A species of Hawaiian marijuana, esp. the pod and its tassels, prized because it has a much higher than usual amount of the hallucinogenic agent. In 1977, when the best Colombian marijuana was fetching up to $40 an ounce on the street, Maui wowie was going for $150. [*Maui*, place of origin; with rhyming redupl. *wowie*, variant of *wow*, exclam. of enthusiasm, a tribute to the strength of the stuff.]

maverick 1. *Mid XIX, Texas*. An unbranded range animal. Except for unweaned calves (which were supposed to take their mother's brand), unbranded animals on open range belonged to the first man to brand and claim them as his own. 2. *Ext*. An unorthodox person. One who leaves any metaphoric herd to go his own way. [Eponym. After Samuel E. Maverick, 1803–1870, Texas rancher who refused to brand his stock and who claimed all unbranded range stock as his.]

    HISTORIC. Am. owes two standard words to the Mavericks, Samuel's grandson, Congressman Maury Maverick having coined *gobbledygook*, which see. (The only other American family to put two new words into the language was the Theodore Roosevelts. *Teddy bear* (which see) is named after T.R.; *alice blue* (which see) after his daughter, later Mrs. Longworth.

May Day May 1. Now an international socialist workers' holiday. Originally a time for primitive rites of spring. And intermediately the date of the great annual witches' sabbath. *mayday Radio voice code*. The equivalent of S.O.S. [< Fr. *m'aidez*, help me.]

mazuma Money. [Am. < mid XIX wave of immigration. < Yiddish *mezuma*, lit. "ready" but effectively "ready cash." Based on Hebrew *m'zumān,* of Chaldean origin, with the sense "the ready necessary" with a ref. to money.]

McCoy: the real McCoy   The genuine article. The real thing. [Commonly attributed to Norman Selby, 1873–1940, popular boxer who, as Kid McCoy, was welterweight champion from 1896 until he outgrew the class in 1898. Said to have arisen from a barroom brawl over his identity, the Kid settling matters by slugging a doubter, who came to fingering his jaw and saying, "That's the real McCoy, all right." But it is of just such stuff that folk etymologies are made. The original was prob. from early XIX Sc., with ref. to a prized brand of Scotch whisky, "the real Mackay." MMM cites a 1908 usage of *the clear McCoy,* an interesting conformation of Mackay, for though it occurred after the modification to McCoy, it retains the earlier ref. to whisky. Another common folk etymology attributes the idiom to New Orleans crim. slang, c. 1900, with ref. to pure heroin arriving at that point as *the real Macuo*—which may in fact have been in use, but as a variant of Mackay-McCoy, not as its (after-the-fact) source.]

mealy-mouthed   *adj.* Describes, pejoratively, one who speaks little and evasively; one who is not straightforward; a hypocrite. [XVI *mealmouthed, mealmouth.* Some seek to derive the form from L. *mel,* OE *mell,* honey; hence, with the sense "honey (but lying) mouth." But the form is obviously based on the Ger. saying *Mehl im Maule behalten,* lit. to have (hold) meal in one's mouth (and to be afraid to speak for fear of losing some of the meal); with the effective sense of Eng. *mealy-mouthed.*]

meander   To proceed by slow windings. To wander aimlessly, not in a straight line. [< *Maiandros,* Gk. name of a slow, winding river in Asia Minor → L. *maeander,* winding, winding course.]

megillah   [Hebrew *magillah,* scroll.] 1. The scroll containing the Book of Esther, traditionally read in the synagogue on the festival of Purim. It is an especially lengthy scroll, and thus: 2. *Ext.* Any endlessly detailed and tedious account. **the whole megillah** Any endlessly spun story, account, preachment. *Do I have to listen to the whole megillah?* Do I have to listen to every overembroidered detail? Effective sense: "Get to the point!"

melon: cut the melon/slice up the melon   To divide the profits or some special bonus. [Wall St. c. 1900. Country metaphor. *Melon,* metaphorically = 1. a good thing. 2. Too much for any one person. Cf. the same metaphoric function of *pie* in *to slice the pie*, to divide the profits. So basic is the image of a pie that it has even become one of the standard forms for economic graphs showing the breakdown of expenditures.]

menial   Now implies baseness. *menial labor.* Intermediately, a servant. [But root sense: "member of the household." Vulgar L. *mansionatus*, one of the household < *mansio*, house (MANSION, MANSE). OF *mesne*, servant. ME *meynial*, servant. The sense shift in OF to "servant, inferior" was already implicit in *mansionatus*, the exact sense of which would be rendered "lesser member of the household and family," in a context in which the chief lord of the manor would be the *dominus*.]

meticulous   Exactingly careful in the handling of details. (Most dictionaries give as a second sense "excessively precise, overcareful," but though this derogatory sense is justified by the root, I must report that I have never felt it to function in modern Am., *meticulousness* labeling an honored quality of accountants, lawyers, surgeons, etc., the pejorative occurring only when qualified, as in "overmeticulous, excessively meticulous.") [Root sense: "in dread; as if one's life depended on it." < L. *metis*, fear; *(per)iculōsus*, fearful, perilous → *meticulōsus*, fearful, in dread.]

Mick   Pejorative name for an Irishman. (Paddy was also so used.) [< *Mick*, nickname for *Michael*, a common Irish name. And see *Mickey Finn*.]

Mickey/Mickey Finn   Also *Irish cocktail/slip one a Mickey* All forms refer to an incapacitating substance put into an alcoholic drink. [Efforts to identify a particular Mickey Finn are pointless. The name is generic for an Irishman. The reference is to the tough Irish bars of the XIX in the NYC *Tenderloin* (which see), though the expression did not become general until the practice of slipping someone a Mickey was revived in sleazy speakeasies of the 1920's.]

HISTORIC. The usual Mickey consists of a drop or two of chloral hydrate (knockout drops). It may have been used originally for quieting an obstreperous customer. It could certainly be used for robbing an unconscious drunkard before dumping him in the alley.

A variant Mickey consisted of a powerful laxative that would send the person so treated running for the toilet, which in XIX NYC was often a backhouse behind the saloon. This treatment, too, could function to get rid of an ugly customer; or for having any selected victim robbed by a confederate who waited by the backhouse.

mickey-mouse/Mickey-Mouse *Slang.* Gibberish. Double-talk. *All I got from him was a lot of mickey-mouse.* [After Mickey Mouse, a wildly popular animated cartoon figure introduced by Walt Disney in 1928 (originally as Mortimer Mouse), because he was given a fast-paced squeaky voice that sounds rather like the gibberish of a voice tape played backward at high speed.]

midwife A woman who attends another at childbirth. (Because hospital birth has become standard in the U.S., it may be well to say that until very recently almost all births occurred at home with only a midwife in attendance. Midwife delivery is still standard in most of the world.) [Root sense: "with-wife: a woman who is *with* another (at childbirth)." OE *mid,* with, *wif,* woman. Cf. *obstetrics* < L. *obstetrix,* midwife; < *stare,* to stand, prefixed *ob-,* before, and with agential suffix *-ix:* lit. "she who stands before (another woman at childbirth)."]

mile a minute: going a mile a minute And variantly *going sixty/ going like sixty* 1. Moving at incredible speed. 2. Doing anything at an incredible speed. *When she gets started gabbing, her tongue goes a mile a minute.* [Lit., of course, "at 60 mph." Such a pace will hardly seem impressive to one sitting in a jet plane, but in late XIX when railroads began to go at 60 mph and in early XX when automobiles began to race, the equation of one mile with one minute seemed an awesome change in humankind's ways, previously limited to the speed and endurance of horses. A people that had so recently trekked across the Great Plains must certainly have been awed by the prospect of crossing 3,000 miles of the American continent in fifty hours. Like the first moon-walk, it suggested a miracle to which everyone became inured almost at once, the sense of wonder surviving in this idiom, which is now probably obsolescent.]

miniature *n.* 1. *Originally.* A small painting illuminating a parchment or vellum manuscript. 2. *Ext.* Anything small; though in the most precise sense, a small-scale reproduction of a painting, a sculpture, or an object. —*adj.* Small. On a small scale. [But the idea "small" is an accident. Root sense: "painted in red." < L. *minium,* red lead, the pigment most used in early monkish illuminations. *Rubric* (the ornate initials worked in red, the red titles, subheadings, and marginalia of such manuscripts) is a sibling word < *rubrica terra,* red lead, the pigment of the ink used for these purposes.]

minister One who serves. To serve. [IE *mei-,* small, less; suffixed *-n-* → L. *minimus,* least; but L. *minister,* a servant (an inferior, a lesser one), took its form in response to *magister,* master (the great one), which is ult. based on IE *meg-,* great. *Minister* (clergyman) follows as "one who serves God *and* his congregation." (Cf. the official papal title, among others, *servo servorum,* servant of servants—"of the Lord" being understood.) So *to administrate, administrator,* for though the root is obscured in these words connoting an important office, it remains "to serve (the particular purpose)." The sense "small" survives in MINUTE, DIMINISH, MINOR, MINI-. And see *minstrel,* a special evolution.]

minstrel A wandering singer who accompanies himself on a stringed instrument. [Based on L. *minister,* servant (see *minister*); Late L. variant *ministeriālus* → OF *menestrel,* one who serves to entertain (earlier, one who chanted poetry to musical accompaniment, a rhapsode; later a ballad singer). ME *ministral.*]

minstrel show From mid XIX until well into XX, a form of blackface musical revue. In its time it was the most popular theatrical entertainment in the U.S.

HISTORIC. The first minstrel show, a four-man group called The Virginia Minstrels, was organized in 1843 by Dan D. Emmett, who later wrote "Dixie" (which see); but the final form of such shows was established by The Christy Minstrels, who opened a highly successful New York City run in 1846, after which many companies of at least twelve minstrels began to tour all of the United States.

The central figure, a combination M.C. and straight man called Mr. Interlocutor, was not in blackface make-up (the "Massuh" figure); all others (his "slaves") were. There is no record of a Negro playing in a minstrel show.

The troupe entered with a big musical number and with singing, dancing, and strutting, until Mr. Interlocutor said, "Gentlemen, be seated," at which all sat in a shallow arc facing the audience. There were two end men, always called Mr. Tambo (tambourine) and Mr. Bones (the tuned wooden bones). Mr. Interlocutor then began a fast comedy routine, primarily with his end men (they would today be called second bananas), with side remarks, antics, and musical flourishes from the rest of the line. This banter continued throughout, but the second half of the show presented a series of solo and small-group specialty numbers by members of the line, the whole buffoonery concluding with an ensemble number in the manner of the opening.

All such productions were a sentimentalized travesty of the Negro as a shiftless, fun-loving, ignorant-shrewd, shuffling, subhuman organism forever nostalgic for the joys of slavery. After World War I, vaudeville replaced the minstrel show except in local amateur productions, but the same blatant assumptions continued to mark the work of blackface performers, the once great stars of this form being "Mammy" singer Al Jolson and singer-dancer-comedian Eddie Cantor.

mister   1. Formal title of address to an adult male. 2. The title of a midshipman or cadet. [Two clear evolutions converge here. 1. < L. *magister*, master (MAGISTRATE); *master* altered to *mister* under the influ. of mistress. 2. < L. *ministerium*, trade, art, craft (and what would now be called a profession). So OF *mestier*, Fr. *métier* (cf. MYSTERY, with ref. to the secrets of a craft; the arcana of such arts as astrology and alchemy). Whence *mister* in use by XIII as a title for artisans and craftsmen, to distinguish them from simple laborers and farm workers.]

HISTORIC. In XIII surnames were still rare except among Norman artistocrats. See *nickname, surname*. The knights of Arthur's court, for example, were Sir Lancelot, Sir Bors, Sir Gawain, Sir Galahad. Beginning about the XIII, *mister* functioned in this way: Mister Richard, Mister William: then later Mr. William the carpenter; then Mr. William Carpenter; then Mr. Carpenter.

Something like the same practice persists in the U.S. South with various degrees of formality: Mister Jim; Mister Jim Tom; Mister Jim Tom Shotwell; Mr. Shotwell. Women are similarly: Miz Glessie; Miz Glessie Jane; Miz Glessie Jane Shotwell; Miz Shotwell.

mistletoe   A tree parasite, a bushy evergreen with white berries. The Eurasian species is *Viscum album,* the name signifying both "white mistletoe" and "sticky (viscous) white stuff," because the birdlime used for snaring small birds, like flies in flypaper, was made of the mistletoe berries. A traditional Christmas decoration, a sprig of mistletoe licenses a man to kiss any woman caught under it, and it is accordingly hung over doorways through which women must pass. [The root sense, a combination of etymology, legend, and natural observation: "bird-squirt plant," because it was believed to grow only from bird droppings. The bird specific to the mistletoe is the missel thrush, which feeds on the white berries. The English form is < OE *mistel*, misteltoe; *tān*, twig. But *mistel* is ult. < IE *meigh-*, to piss (MICTURATE). So "the plant propagated by bird-squirt."]

mitten   A sort of half glove consisting of one pocket for the thumb and one for the other four fingers together. [Etymology uncertain. Prob. < L. *medietās*, half → OF *mitaine* → ME *mytayne*.] *give a man the mitten* To reject his proposal. Hence, to jilt. [In XIX Am. and Canadian courtship. A whimsy based on asking for the lady's hand. If turned down, one gets not the hand but the mitten, probably understood to be a politely distant handshake, now called "the brush-off."]

mob   1. A crowd. 2. An unruly rabble. *lynch mob.* 3. *Crim.* An organized criminal gang. *mobster* A member of such a gang. *mobocracy* [Coined in 1920's by H. L. Mencken.] 1. Rule by the rabble. 2. Rule by criminal gangs. *Under Capone, Chicago was a mobocracy.* (And in late XIX, Baltimore was so notorious for its roving gangs that it was known as Mob Town.) [By back formation from L. *mobile vulgus*, the fickle (mobile, ever-changing) hoi polloi. Cicero: *"Non est consilio in vulgo, non ratio"*: "There is neither (wise) counsel nor reason among the rabble."

The L. was often written *mob. vulg.;* whence in late XVII *mob* emerged as Brit. slang. In 1710 Jonathan Swift inveighed against it as an offensive neologism. To him it must have sounded much as "rep" for "reputation" sounds today to a fastidious ear. Yet by 1755 the newly published *Dictionary* of the fastidious Dr. Johnson listed *mob* as standard English and cited its use as such by Dryden and Addison.]

moll   1. Earlier generic for a woman (as "Tom, Dick, and Harry" is generic for "any old guy." 2. Now specific to the woman companion of a gangster. [< *Molly.* Cf. *to be mollycoddled,* to be oversolicitously tended by a motherly woman.]

gun moll The woman companion of a gangster. [Often but wrongly explained as deriving from the fact that the moll carried her gangster's gun for him to prevent his arrest on a charge of carrying a concealed weapon. But important gangsters had bodyguards for this purpose, and molls did not dress in a way that could conceal anything. The term, identical with 2 above, is < Yiddish-American patois *gonif's molly*, the female companion and accomplice of a thief. The same patois gives us *gunzl, gunsel* (English *gun* with Yiddish diminutive suffix -*l*), an armed gangster, a hood.]

mollycoddle   *v.* To overindulge a person dotingly. To spoil by such overindulgence. Said usu. of a child or husband, but also a favorite rhetorical cliché of those who dismiss all prison reform as "a molly-coddling of prisoners." —*n. Rare.* A person spoiled by doting women. [*Moll, Molly,* a widespread dial. term for milkmaid. Here as a generic for woman. With *coddle.* i.e., "woman-coddled."]

Monday-morning quarterback   An expert after the fact; one who calls the plays after the game, and who is, therefore, as infallibly right as hindsight makes any fool. [Because, until recently, football games were played on Saturdays, allowing the Monday-morning quarterback most of the weekend for sharpening his hindsights. Originally specific to second-guessers of football, but extended to include anyone who "ifs" infallibly once a thing is over and done.] *All wives become Monday-morning quarterbacks by the tenth anniversary; mine made that varsity in six months.*

money   If you don't know what it is, I suspect you did not buy this book, but stole it, and are not entitled to a definition. [The Roman mint was in the temple of *Juno Monēta,* the epithet commonly, but carelessly, glossed as Juno the Admonisher (MONITOR). That epithet, however, was an Etruscan survival, its original form and meaning unknown. In any case, L. *monēta* came to mean, first, mint, and then, money ("thing minted"); whence It. *moneta,* OF *moneie,* ME *moneye,* money. (And see *fee.*)]

    blood money Money gained by betrayal or murder. **easy money** Money easily come by. But note the extension in *She looks like easy money to me:* She looks like one easily to be had.

    egg money Also **butter and egg money** See *butter and egg money.*

    found money A windfall. Any stroke of good fortune. [Even easier than easy money.]

    pin money A woman's allowance for small personal expenses. [Now, about synonymous with butter and egg money, implying a trivial amount. But in the days when pins were made by hand, and when the term encompassed ornate hat pins, pin money could be a substantial sum; and bequests of up to 200 British pounds for "pin money" can be found in British wills of XIV–XVI (at a time when many a tenant farmer did not see a pound a year in cash.)]

ready money Cash on hand or in easily converted securities.

moneybags A rich man. *money in the bank* A sure thing. A cinch. *money changer* 1. An agent who deals in international currency, converting from one to another for a small fee or agio. 2. *By Biblical association with the money changers Christ drove from the temple.* A usurer. *money man* A financier. The backer of a project. *money player* An athlete who performs best when under pressure. [When the chips are down.]

go for the money To strive to win. To bet daringly. *put money on* To bet on. *put your money where your mouth is* Standard argumentative formula by B when A has asserted a contrary opinion; in effect, "Back up what you are saying by betting on it, or shut up." *run out of the money* In any competition for (usu. cash) prizes, to be an also-ran. *take the money and run* Forgetting moral scruples, to grab what cash one can and clear out of a situation. (Cf. Omar Khayyám, "Ah, take the cash and let the credit go.") *your money or your life* Holdup man's command to stand and deliver or be killed.

moniker/monicker 1. *Among hobos.* One's "road" name. (Not a legal name, but a label one makes up for oneself and chooses to be known by. CB radio has revived the term in exactly this sense.) 2. *Crim.* An alias or nickname. *What's your monicker?* What are you known as? What do you call yourself? [Origin unattested. *Moniker* was prob. the original form, the *c* added later as a guide to pronunciation. Perhaps a corruption of *monogram* with ref. to the Gypsy sign language scratched on gates, walls, and the entrances to towns, and with especial ref. to the identifying mark of the person who scratched the signs.]

monkey shines Foolish antics. [Prob. < Gaelic *sindeag*, to leap, skip about, gambol; which is also the root of *shindig, shindy.*]

monster *n.* An odiously deformed, "inhuman" creature. 2. *Ext.* One who is cruel, savage, inhuman. 3. *XVI ext.* (By association with huge legendary monsters such as ogres, titans, and dragons.) A huge person or thing. *I have a monster of a headache* (can mean "a cruel one" but also "an enormous one." And cf.:) *monster rally,* in which the noun serves as an adjective meaning "enormous," where *monstrous rally* would have an entirely different meaning. Also **monstrosity** A monstrous person or thing. [The root sense is from divination, "portent of the gods." Based on IE *men-*, a

stem functioning in words pertaining to the mind (MENTAL). →
L. *monstrum,* an omen, a prodigious thing (MONSTRANCE), akin
to *munire,* to warn. The sense evolution from "sign from heaven"
to "dire warning" parallels that from *omen* (which see) to *ominous,*
threatening.]

HISTORIC. Deformed births or any other occurrences held to
be "unnatural" were taken by early man to be warnings of divine
anger and were referred to priest-magician-prophets for interpretation. In theory, such reading of signs allowed for good omens,
but within the experience of the race on this planet, notable signs
from on high seem to have foretold notably bad luck ahead (or
the bad luck was there for everything to point to).

month of Sundays   A long time. Almost exclusively in the greeting
form *I haven't seen you in a month of Sundays* It seems an eternity since I saw you last. [Am. but dating uncertain. In use by
early XIX but prob. older. To compile a month of Sundays would
be to cull one from each week, whence a month of them would
be from 28 to 31 weeks long, and some so render the idiom, though
seven or eight months is too short a time for the feeling of the
term. It is better referred to the interminable Sunday services
of some denominations. The Puritan congregationalists, for example, followed a four-hour morning service with an hour or two
for Sunday dinner, resumed for a three- or four-hour afternoon
service, and after a second rest period, met again for an evening
prayer service. The members of the congregation, mostly vigorous
farm folk, had to sit still and at rapt attention in their confining
Sunday best. At the back of the church stood beadles with long
poles tipped with a feather and a knob: one nod and you were
tickled, a second nod and you were knocked on the head. Any
day of such pious restraint while fighting off sleep must have
seemed in itself an eternity. A month spent in such a way would
outrun any sense of bearable time. It is this weary length the
idiom implies.]

mooch   *v.* 1. To wheedle, to get without pay. 2. Root sense. To skulk
about. (In *Hamlet, miching:* "Marry, this is miching mallecho, it
means mischief." *moocher* One who hangs about, getting whatever
he can get for nothing. [Though insistently rated as slang, the
term has a pedigree back to IE *meug-,* to skulk about. Prob. with
g/k into Gmnc. and k/ch in Frankish-Gothic → OF *muchier,* to
skulk, to hide → ME *mouche* (the exact sense in ME being in
doubt, but certainly implying some sort of surreptitious action).]

moot   Arguable. Subject to discussion and debate. Rare in Am. usage except in the fixed phrase *moot question;* but common in law school, where students argue hypothetical cases in *moot court.* There, such a case is a *moot,* and to argue such a case is *to moot.* [Often but wrongly confused with "mute," but based on IE *mōd-,* a meeting. Via Gmnc. → OE *mētan,* to meet (as in a representative gathering of freemen). With OE variants *mōt, gemōt;* ME *mot, moot.*]

morganatic marriage   Marriage below one's social station. [< Medieval L. *matrimonium ad morganaticam,* lit "morning gift marriage." < OHG *morgangabe,* a gift traditionally made by the bridegroom to his bride on the morning after the wedding night (a sort of token return for the dowry she had brought him). Because of the laws of primogeniture governing entailed estates, the lesser partner in such a marriage (usually the woman) signed away all claim to titles and inheritance, the children of the marriage also being excluded. The Duke of Windsor's marriage to an American widow, Prince Rainier's to an American actress, and Princess Margaret's to a British commoner were all morganatic. John Ciardi is known to have contracted a morganatic marriage to a Missouri farm girl, the children of the union being not only self-disinheriting but self-destructing.]

Morpheus   In Ovid's *Metamorphoses,* the god of dreams, son of the god of sleep. [< Gk. *morphē,* shape, form (because of the images called up in dreams) (MORPHOLOGY, MORPHINE).] **in the arms of Morpheus**   Asleep. [Strictly speaking, should mean "having a dream," but the root sense has been obscured by illiterate usage, and Morpheus is now commonly taken to be the god of sleep. (Of 300 college students recently asked to identify Morpheus, 121 could not identify him at all, 23 made merely random guesses, and the remaining 156 said he was the god of sleep.)]

mosey   To amble. **mosey along**   Amble off. **mosey around**   Amble about. *I'll just mosey around for a look-see.* [The earliest citations, c. 1836, imply rapid motion in the senses now associated with *vamoose* (which see), and those earlier senses, together with the dating, confirm the derivation of both *mosey* and *vamoose* from Sp. *vamos,* we go, let us go. The later sense evolution into slow moseying and fast vamoosing is unexplained unless one is willing to attribute it to the sound values of the two words (as I incline to, but inconclusively).

There are the British XVIII (and prob. earlier) dialect forms *to mouse, to mousey,* to skitter about like a mouse; and to *mose,* to smolder, *to mose about,* to bumble about; but these are prob. best dismissed as accidental resemblances, or at most as reinforcing the word's evolution from the Spanish.]

mother [< Baby-talk syllable *ma-* with suffix denoting relationship *-ter,* as in *(sis)ter* and *(bro)ther.* L. *mater;* Gmnc. *mothar;* Ger. *Mutter;* OE *modor; ME moder.*] 1. A female parent. 2. A woman who has borne children. 3. A creature that has "borne" young. *mother hen.* 4. Any conceived figure of loving attention. So *Mother Goose, Mother Nature,* and even, from the lyrics of a maudlin popular song of c. 1900, "Daddy, you've been a mother to me." 5. *In compounds.* A quality or thing acquired by birth. *mother wit, motherland, mother tongue.* 6. A generative principle. *Necessity is the mother of invention.*

The idea "generative principle" also functions in **mother-of-pearl** Nacre, once wrongly thought to be that which causes pearls to form. **mother of vinegar** The yeastlike bacterial slime that often forms on ferments, causing wines to sour to vinegar. [Certainly influ. by its likeness to the afterbirth, but in essence, "the begetter of," since this slime added to wine begets vinegar.]

And the special case from Black English **mother** [< motherfucker, prob. the ultimate term in *shock language* (which see). From Black English and now widely dispersed. Also *muffa.*] 1. A hard, mean, dangerous man who will stop at nothing—*and therefore* to be admired. (Sometimes intensified as a *mean mother.*) A *mother,* in being totally unfettered, is totally free, and admired for his freedom, as one who "takes no shit from nobody" (as the Negro was historically forced to bow to all abuse). Related idioms expressing this admirable-though-evil desire for total freedom are *outrageous* for "admirable," and *righteous* for "powerful" (including what is powerfully evil). 2. *Ext.* A person contemptibly cited. [As one so low as to commit incest with his mother.]

Mother's Day 1. The second Sunday in May, an unofficial holiday conceived in sentiment and dedicated to promoting the sales of flowers and greeting cards. 2. *In NYC's inner cities.* The day on which the mailman delivers the welfare checks. [So called because most welfare payments are for aid to dependent children.]

NOTE. Easily negotiable, and usually arriving in a single mail delivery that floods the inner city with money, such checks are regularly stolen from the mailboxes, the flow of cash causing a festive surge in spending, gambling, drinking, drug use, street crime, and crimes of passion.

Mother Carey's chickens Stormy petrels. (See *petrel*.) [It is said to be a sailor's superstition (I believe it to be a bit of lore based on close observation) that these small sea birds fly especially low when a storm is approaching. With their legs dangling, they seem to be walking on the water. Hence their name from L. *mater cara*, dear mother, an epithet for the Virgin Mary, here conceived as the patroness of seafarers. She, of her love, was believed to send her birds (chickens) to warn sailors of the approaching storm.]

mountebank A charlatan. A quack who travels about selling cure-alls. [It. *montimbanco* < *montare*, to mount; *in banco* (*in* syncopated to *im* before *b*), on a bench; hence, "one who climbs up on a bench (counter, table, etc.) to deliver a spiel."]

NOTE. The eminent New England family name *Saltonstall* is a related evolution: < Fr. *saulter*, to jump; *en*, upon; *stalle*, bench, counter; hence, with same root sense as *mountebank*.

mouthpiece *Music.* The part of an instrument that goes into or against the player's mouth. 2. The part of a telephone into which one speaks. 3. *Crim.* A lawyer. [The one through whom the client speaks.] 4. *Boxing.* A rubber guard piece into which a boxer sets his teeth at the start of each round. [The current cast-rubber mouthpiece could not have been in use much before 1900, but the use of cloth mouth padding by brawlers who see a fight coming is a trick that long predates the development of rubber, and was likely used by pugs all the way back to the gladiators.]

moxie *Slang.* Pluck (includes the whole range from raw courage to brazen effrontery). *The Kid took a beating but fought back on pure moxie; You have a lot of moxie to tell me I don't know my own business.* **Moxie** *Registered trade name.* A bitter herbal carbonated soft drink popular in New England. [Origin unknown. Some refer lower-case *moxie* to Yiddish, but none, to the best of my knowledge, suggests a Yiddish word that could be the base. Capitalized trade name *Moxie* also of unknown origin. Could it be from the herb mugwort, *Artemisia moxa?* This suggestion is a pure speculation: I do not know that mugwort is used in the soft drink. Yet whatever its origins, Moxie has had a language effect.

It was once standard New England custom to come out of winter long johns in early April and to take a "spring drench" of sulfur and molasses at the time of the change. That drench was a tonic, a body toner. New Englanders seem to have developed a taste for their dreadful dosage and that depraved taste is perpetuated not only in *Moxie*, but in the fact that in New England all carbonated soft drinks are called *tonics*, as *lemon tonic, orange tonic, cherry tonic*.

As a further speculation: to take one's spring tonic was believed to make one fit for the labors of plowing and planting, hence, ready to face anything. It is so, I conjecture, that *to have one's moxie*, originally "to be toned and fit," came to mean "ready for anything." But this is conjecture only and, therefore, ???]

muck-a-muck/high muck-a-muck/muckety-muck/high muckety-muck Mock title of dignity for a pompous person. [Chinook Indian *hiu*, plenty; *macamuc*, to eat. Into Am. sense by 1856, but the question remains: How did *plenty to eat* come to mean *(mock) important person?* The mockery, I speculate, arose from the sound values, vaguely ridiculous to the Am. ear. The idea of importance goes deeper.]

HISTORIC. In many cultures, the possession of ample food stores and supplies has been and is the mark of an important person. Kwakiutl chiefs made an elaborate ritual of giving away and destroying great stores of goods in potlatch ceremonies designed to show their personal importance. In herding cultures, wealth was measured in heads of cattle (see *fee*), for only a man of consequence could amass and protect a herd that would keep him ever abundantly supplied with food. And as a note on the survival of attitudes, let me add, from Lincoln Barnett's *The Treasure of Our Tongue:*

> In Nigeria . . . a boy who finishes grade school is known as a *megotbuk* [me-got-book], a boy who graduates from college is a *bigbigbuk*, and the exceptional young man who has studied at Oxford and returns home . . . is a *bintojaguarfridgful*—a contraction for "He has been to England and come home with a Jaguar and enough money to keep a refrigerator full of frozen foods."

mud [ME *mode, mudde* is akin to various untraced Gmnc. roots *mud-, mod-, mot-* with the senses: "mud, bog, earth, mire,"] 1. Soft, wet earth. Mire. 2. *Ext.* Baseness. "Born of the mud of the people."—Sidney, *Arcadia*, 1486. 3. Defamation. *to throw mud at.* [First so used in XVIII.]

muddy the waters To obfuscate. **Here's mud in your eye** A common toast. [Unexplained, but in no sense a bad wish. Can

the root sense be "May this (drink) confuse things (for the better)"?]
as clear as mud Ironic. Not at all clear. *wallow in the mud* Sink
oneself in degradation. [Make a pig of oneself.]

　　stick in the mud A person who does not participate in a good
time. [*Stick,* here, not as a piece of wood, but as one who sticks,
as in "he's a sit-on-his-tail."]

　　your name is mud You are in trouble. [The Maryland papers
continue to assert at intervals that this idiom derives from Dr.
Samuel Mudd, Maryland physician who in 1865 set a broken leg
for a traveler who turned out to be John Wilkes Booth, assassin
of Abraham Lincoln. In the post-assassination hysteria, Mudd was
tried as an accomplice and sentenced for life to Fort Jefferson in
the Dry Tortugas. He was later pardoned for heroic service during
an epidemic of yellow fever, but though his innocence of complic-
ity in the assassination has been established, his conviction was
reversed only recently by President Carter. His name, one may
say, remained Mud(d) in the root sense of the idiom, but Maryland's
claim is whimsical. Partridge, *Slang,* cites this idiom in use in 1820
with the senses "defeated, in disgrace," which were already implicit in XVIII *to throw mud.*]

muff　[L. **muffula,* mitten. OF *moufle,* overgarment, glove.] 1.
Women's wear. A small, usu. fur roll in which to insert one
or both hands against the cold. 2. *Slang.* Female pubic hair.
[Metaphor based on "furry" and on the fact that the muff,
with both hands inserted, is often carried at or just above the
crotch.]

　　muff diver One who performs cunnilingus. [Goes "headfirst"
into muff, sense 2.]

　　muffler 1. A shawl. [Overgarment.] 2. *Mechanics.* A device
for suppressing engine noise. [The XV sense of *to muffle,* to wrap
in cloth, developed the further sense "to stifle," and in XVII, "to
deaden the sound of" *(with muffled drums).*]

　　to muff Slang. To bungle. To botch. *You had your chance and
you muffed it.* [The form and origin are unattested. Is this a root
image of acting ineptly because one's hands are snagged in a muff?
Cf. *tanglefoot,* clumsy, inept person. But ??]

mug　1. A face. An ugly puss. *Bill Crane has a mug. I, sir, have a
visage.* [Brit. XVIII. After ceramic drinking mugs made in the
form of a grotesque face.] 2. A ruffian, a plug-ugly. [Brutish person.]
3. A dupe, a patsy, a victim. [Early XIX Brit. Because the faces
on drinking mugs were often distorted as if the "mug" were being

assaulted.] ***don't be a mug*** Don't be a patsy, a simpleton.

mug shot A police identification photo.

mugger 1. One who grimaces. So ***to mug*** To grimace. ***mug at the camera*** To make faces while being photographed. 2. One who assaults and robs, originally by coming up from behind and strangling or garroting. [Causing the mug (sense 1) to grimace.] So ***to mug*** To socialize in the manner of a mugger.

mugger   One who assaults, usu. violently, with intent to rob. Mugging, long associated with racial warfare on city streets, has come to imply as much the bodily violence as the robbery. [Origin uncertain. Prob. by association with *mug* for "face," because mugging once implied the act of seizing from behind and across the face or around the neck, to stifle any outcry. Philip Howard, *Weasel Words* (Oxford Press), quotes from *The Swell's Night Guide,* 1846: "and then we should have a mugging match." But the context, if I understand it, does not imply an act of mugging in the modern sense, but a stand-up-and-knock-down set-to; a face-to-face bareknuckles confrontation.]

mugwump   1. *Early Massachusetts powwow pidgin.* Chief. Big man. [Algonquinian *mugguomp, mukuamp,* chief.] 2. In the presidential campaign of 1884, an opprobrious epithet for Republicans who found the party nominee, James G. Blaine, so distasteful that they bolted to vote for Grover Cleveland. Hence, 3. *a. When spoken reproachfully by loyal party members.* A political turncoat. *b. As a proudly asserted maverick label.* An independent. A rugged individualist. 4. *Dating uncertain. Prob. early XX.* A crude graffiti cartoon figure of a face staring from behind a fence with an exaggerated nose projecting over the fence. [Whimsical. By association with the campaign of 1884, a fence-strider, one who works both sides of the fence; and as a word play, one who has his "mug" on one side of the fence and his "wump" on the other.]

mum¹ [Traceable to OE *mumme,* echoic of the sound made when the lips are closed. There is no basis for the often suggested derivation from *mummy,* a notably silent figure.] Silent.
mum's the word Say nothing.

mum² Chrysanthemum. [At root: "gold flower." < Gk. *chrysos,* gold; *anthemon,* flower.]

Murphy bed A folding bed attached to a closet door which, when shut, attempts to conceal the fact that the room is used as a bedroom. [After William Lawrence Murphy (1876–1959), who in 1898 founded a firm for the manufacture of such beds. The Murphy In-A-Dor Bed Company is still listed in the Manhattan *Yellow Pages* as doing business at 40 E. 34th St. From the beginning, however, it has called its product the *In-A-Door* or *In-A-Dor* bed. Several firms co-listed under "Beds-Concealed" offer "convertibles." The Lockwood Cabinet Co. of 163 E. 61st St. calls its product "The Murphy Bed." and Lew Raynes, Inc., of 40 E. 34th St. offers "The Original Disappearing Murphy Beds in Cabinets and Wall Components." W. L. Murphy, having established the name in Am. usage, has left it to competitors of the company he founded.]

muse [Gk. *mousa,* spiritual patroness, inspirator. Perh. < *maō,* I create, I invent, I seek out. But this verb, prob. of Illyrian origin, was obsolete in the Greek of the Golden Age.] *v.* To ponder. To meditate. To be absorbed in. —*n. Usu. capitalized.* A goddess of the arts. One who inspires.
The Nine Muses The daughters of Zeus and of Mnemosyne, goddess of memory; hence, "heavenly memory," the godlike reverie of the arts.
In the evolution of Greek myth, their names, number, and functions vary. In a more or less settled final form of the legend, in which they dwell on one peak of Parnassus under the protection of Apollo (who is presented as their father), they are nine and their often overlapping functions are: Calliope, epic poetry; Clio, history, Erato, lyric poetry, amatory poetry; Euterpe, music, lyric poetry; Melpomene, tragedy, music; Polyhymnia, sacred music; Terpsichore, dance, drama; Thalia, comedy, pastoral poetry; Urania, mathematics, astrology, music.
Mnemosyne, in a separate manifestation as *Mnesme,* memory, was sometimes numbered among the muses; as were Aoide, song; Melete, contemplation; and Thespia, drama. The Muses (also the Sacred Sisters, the Virgin Daughters) inspired artists by nursing

their infant souls at their breasts, filling them with divine milk (and substance). No one has explained how these virgin daughters came by their milk, but mythology is self-inseminating and autolactative.

In any case, once *muse* is recognized as the root, the following Eng. words are in clear sequence: *to muse* To be absorbed in, to be enraptured. *museum* Place of the Muses. *music* Muse-inspired sound. *amuse Earlier.* To enrapture. To bewilder, as if by a spell. *Now.* To entertain, to divert, to put in a good humor. *bemuse* Had the same earlier senses as amuse. *Now.* To confuse, bewilder.

amusement park [Root sense: "place that offers diversions."] A place much like a carnival (traveling street show) except that it is fixed in one place and offers, in addition to a Ferris wheel, merry-go-round, etc., such large, not movable diversions as roller coasters, tunnels of love, fun houses. [The form is an extended extension of an extension. There are no Muses to be found in amusement parks.]

mushroom   *n.* A usually umbrella-shaped fungus, variously a delicacy or poisonous. —*v.* To grow rapidly. [As these fungi sprout overnight.] *the mushroom-shaped cloud* Symbol of the A-bomb. [Earlier *mushrump,* and some have sought to relate *mush* to *moss,* but the root is of late, irregular Latin and of unknown origin, the second element being some sort of noun suffix. First attested as OF *mousseron* → ME *musseroun, muscheron.* The OED lists some twenty variant forms from XV to XVI, all being efforts of the language to establish an acceptable form to label a common object when both elements of the available word are without an English analogue or a translatable foreign base. *Isinglass* and *haberdasher* (which see) are similar evolutions of a word made up of seemingly nonsense elements.]

mustard: **cut the mustard**   To be able to perform a task. But I have never heard this idiom except in some negative form, as *he just can't cut the mustard* He doesn't measure up to the job. [An idiom from the self-elaborating tendency of much slang. *Cut,* to act, to perform; as in *cut a caper, cut a pretty figure. Mustard,* a synonym, c. 1900, for "hot stuff," as in *he thinks he's hot stuff,* he thinks he's admirable. Hence, before being cast in the negative: to act/perform admirably.]

mutton   The flesh of an adult sheep. (Implies a yearling or older. If the animal was younger, the flesh is lamb or kid.) [Earliest origin uncertain. L. *multo,* sheep → OF *moton,* but with the altered sense "castrated ram." (Such a ram was called in OE a *wether,* ult. based, via Gmnc., on IE *wet-,* year; hence, with root sense "yearling" because castrated when one year old. Survives in Am. as *bell wether,* earlier *bellèd wether,* because it carried a bell around its neck and served as leader of the flock.]

HISTORIC. *Mutton* is no longer used for the living animal, but it continued in use for several centuries after the Norman Conquest as a term distinct from *sheep.* In XII the Earl of Salisbury, bastard son of Henry II, bequeathed toward the construction of a monastery 1,000 *sheep* and 300 *muttons.* And an inventory dated 1337 lists 140 muttons (worth 10d. each) and 100 sheep (worth 8d. each).

mutual admiration society   A company of friends in which every member praises every other. [Now a fixed phrase in Am. Altered from *Society of Mutual Admiration,* coined by Oliver Wendell Holmes in *Autocrat of the Breakfast Table,* two chapters of which were written for the *New England Magazine* in 1831–1832; the rest for *The Atlantic Monthly* starting in 1857. After the 25-year interim, Holmes began again with the calmly underplayed, "I was just going to say when I was interrupted . . ."]

nabob   A wealthy and powerful personage. [Gift of the Brit. Empire Hindi *nawab, nawwab,* governor, viceroy. First used in Brit. as specific to one who had grown rich in the India trade. (With the form modified, but with same sense → Nob Hill (San Francisco), on which those who had "struck it rich" built their mansions.)]

namby-pamby   Sentimental, insipid, puny. [Based on baby-talk *Amby* for *Ambrose,* Amby nonced (see noncing) as *Namby,* as in baby-talk *some nother time;* the rhyme redupl. for derogation. All these modifying patterns are standard in English but seldom are so many instanced in a single idiom, and that a literary coinage rather than a folk evolution. The original Amby was Ambrose Phillips, 1671–1749, a poet whose limping assertions of the high inane moved Harry Carey, an almost equally obscure contemporaneous playwright, to satirize the poems as *namby-pamby.* Today no more than three condemned Ph.D.'s (two of them dead already) can quote a line of either Phillips or Carey, but this fragment they have shored against their ruin.]

name   [IE *nomen-* → L. *nomen,* name (NOMENCLATURE, COGNOMEN). But the Eng. form is prob. < Gmnc., prob. via the hypothetical form *namon-* → OE *nama,* name.] 1. A verbal identification or label. 2. An epithet, esp. a pejorative. So **call names** To apply judiciously invidious epithets to the dirty rats. 3. Reputation. [Perh. based ult. on aristocratic notions of the honor of the family name.] 4. Essential being. *the Holy name, the ineffable name of Jahveh.*
    HISTORIC. In many earlier societies, a child, esp. a man child, was given two names. One, known only to the parents (or only to the father) and to the priest and medicine man, would be revealed to him during the rites of his initiation into manhood. That was his true name, the name of his essential spirit identity or daemon, and anyone who knew it had power to summon and

control that spirit. The surviving folk tale of Rumpelstiltskin is based on this ancient belief: R. could work his power upon others but came under their power once he was identified by his true name.

Not even God was exempt. Tibetan monks have labored for centuries to compile the billion names of God, believing that once the true name in all its forms has been decoded and spoken, God will have been identified, the Creation will come to an end, and the next phase of being will begin. Among many others, the Jewish religion has a number of sacred and mysterious tenets about the true name of God.

And though these notions may seem remote from us, an awareness of them can provide an insight into a number of the idioms listed below.

name brand An established (well-recognized) trademark. (For antonym, see *brand X*.) [*Name* for *famous name* implies "the honor of the house" as in sense 3, above. Almost inevitably, *Famous Name* is now itself a brand name.]

a name to conjure with The name of a powerful person, hence, likely to make a powerful impression when a proposal is made in his name, or as if approved by him. [But earlier, the name of a spirit whose patronage is sought in summoning another spirit, or in casting a spell. Lit. "a name with which to work black magic."]

name the day To set the wedding date, traditionally the prerogative of the bride-to-be. (For other events one generally "picks" or "sets" the day.) *name day* In R.C. and other religions, a feast day of a saint for whom one is named, as June 24 is St. John's Day.

namedropper A person who strives bumptiously to impress others by sprinkling his conversation with the names of famous persons with whom he is, purportedly, on intimate terms.

name of the game 1. The object of the game. [Many games are named after the call that announces a win, as "gin" in *gin rummy*.] 2. An essential principle. *After a con man has taken the mark's bundle, the name of the game is "get out of town."*

name names In bringing charges of wrongdoing, to get down to cases, identifying the persons charged by name (rather than by reference to "certain parties").

namesake A person named after another as a tribute or title of honor. [Strictly speaking, the namesake is the original after whom another is named, but in usage the term includes both "the person named for" and "the person named."] *for His name's sake* Prayer formula beseeching in the name of God.

in name only In the form and title of a thing but without its essence. *Joseph was married in name only.*

in the name of 1. By authority of. *I arrest you in the name of the law.* 2. For the sake of. *in the name of the poor.* 3. Out of regard for. *in the name of mercy.*

good name Reputation for honor. *lend one's name to* To announce oneself as a sponsor. *make a name for oneself* To establish one's reputation, status. *know by name only/know only by name* To know one by reputation without deep knowledge of. *Even Richard M. Nixon knows himself by name only.*

nickname Separately listed. [ME *eke name,* an also (another) name.]

no-name A name for something (usu. a geographic feature) that has no name. *No-Name Creek.* (And see *Nome.*)

take His name in vain To blaspheme. [To juxtapose a sacred name with low or ordinary things is the essence of blasphemy. (See *Shock Language.*) *His name* should be uttered only in prayerful, devout, and ritual context. Even then, the true name of God can be too sacred to be pronounced by mortal man. Jewish religion, for example, uses *Adonai,* the Lord, instead of God's true but hidden name.]

to one's name Formula for labeling personal assets. In the affirmative, usu. *to his credit. He has several successful scripts to his credit.* But in the negative: *He hasn't got a nickel to his name.*

namely As hereinafter to be listed by name. To wit. (See *viz.*)

nary (Also sometimes *ary,* in which case usu. pronounced as if *airy.*) Not any. Not a one. [More or less generalized ruralism. Corruption of *ne'er a,* never a one, as in archaic "Ne'er a soul did I see."]

nasturtium The common garden flower, the leaves of which are a seasoning, esp. in vinegar. [Root sense: "nose twister," but not, as sometimes supposed, because of the odor, which is only mildly pungent; rather, because of its pungency when eaten, the "nose twist" being like that caused by Chinese mustard. (And the nasturtium is related to the mustard family.) < L. *nasus,* nose; with *tort-,* p.p. base of *torquere,* to twist. (And see *queer.*)]

naught Nothing. [IE *wekti-,* thing, living thing. With k/h in Gmnc. → OE *wiht,* thing, person (WIGHT); with neg. prefix *na-* → OE *nawiht,* ME *nau(g)ht.*]

naughty 1. Mischievous. 2. *Ext.* Risqué. (Sexually suggestive but not overtly immoral.) [But in XIV, having naught, needy. And so *Piers*

Plowman, "needy men and naughty." Whence in XVI, "lacking in goodness, having no moral merit"—which is the sense of Shakespeare's "so shines a good deed in this naughty world."]

Nazi [< Ger. *Na(tional) (So)zi(alist).*] 1. The National Socialist party of Adolf Hitler. 2. A member of this party. 3. *WWII.* Any German. 4. Any harshly dictatorial person.

need [The sense is much altered from the base, which is IE *nau-,* dead ("having used up one's life"), exhausted ("having used up one's energies"). Suffixed *-dt* in Gmnc. → OE *nēod, nēd,* distress, deprivation; ME *nede.* The evolution has been from "mortal privation" to "requisite but lacking."] 1. The lack of what is necessary for a specific purpose. *He needs a sharper saw to get that tree down.* 2. What is lacking for one's happiness. *All I need is you, baby.* 3. General necessity. *He needs some way of earning a living.*

needs/one's needs One's normal requirement for living. **needful** Necessary. **needy** Impoverished, destitute. Also **in dire need** [These last two forms being closest to the OE sense.] And now obs. *needs must I go,* it is necessary that I go.

New Jersey *Nuova Caesarea.* See *Caesar.*

nibs: his nibs/his Nibs Mock title of respect modeled on *his honor.* [Altered from XVII Brit. slang *nob,* head, head man. In XIX Brit. university slang, fellow of a college (a head man). The earlier sense survives in Am. *that's using your nob,* that's using your head. There was prob., though unattested, an intermediate form, *his nobship, his nibs(hip).*]

nickel Popular name of the U.S. five-cent piece of nickel and copper, first minted mid XIX. *No matter how high the tax rate, the U.S. Treasury never has a nickel to its name.* (Because no coin has ever been officially designated a "nickel.")

not worth a plugged nickel Worthless. [As a nickel with a bullet hole through it (or, more accurately, as one knocked out of shape by a bullet). A nickel was a popular challenge target in marksmanship.]

don't take any wooden nickels Whimsical formula of friendly leave-taking: a piece of worthless but kindly advice. (Except in California, no one is known to have accepted counterfeit wooden nickels. I once saw a lead nickel, but with the rising cost of lead, that game is hardly worth the candle.)

nickel-and-dime one to death (Originally in poker.) *He has been nickel-and-diming me to death.* He hasn't won any big bets, but he has been bleeding me dry with a long series of small wins. Also applied to a moocher who is forever wheedling small sums. Whence, *a nickel and dimer* A petty gambler or petty moocher.

nickelodeon An early movie house. [The standard admission fee was a nickel. *Nickel;* with *odeon,* a music hall < Gk. *ōideion,* place of musical performances < *ōidē,* song (ODE).]

nickel bag *Narc. slang.* A glassine envelope containing one dosage of heroin.]*Nickel,* five dollars; *bag,* the envelope. (*Nickel* is standard street-criminal slang for "five." Here, "five dollars." But also *a nickel-dime* is a five-to-ten-year sentence. So, too: *get a nickel,* draw a five-year sentence; *do a nickel,* serve a five-year sentence.)]

squeeze a nickel till the buffalo shits (In minced form *roars*) To be miserly.

nickname An additional name, familiar, descriptive, or simply identifying. [Based on obs. *eke,* and, also, in addition to. ME *eke name.* Then nonced (see *noncing*) from *an eke name* to *a neke name,* whence *nickname.* What the name was in addition to was one's given name, patronymics having been a late development in England.]

HISTORIC. What we call patronymics or cognomens were standard among the Romans. *Gaius Julius Caesar* signified "Gaius of the Julian clan of the family Caesar." Such "family names" did not, however, come into use in France until IX, nor in England until after the Norman Conquest, and then only slowly, the first such being generally estate identifications of landed gentry. The knights of King Arthur, for example, had no surnames (see *surname*), but were Sir Bors, Sir Giles, Sir Galahad, etc. Nor, at first, were such names inherited. John Peterson, for instance, could be the son of Peter Wilson, who could be the son of Will Johnson. Or two brothers might adopt different "second names" (also called "twa-names").

The *eke name* functioned well enough into the XVI (and in some areas, as in Wales, until later) as a necessary identification in any situation in which several persons bore the same first name (later often called the "Christian name," but see *given name*). Most such names, as nicknames still are, were based on place of origin (John Whitehill), physical characteristics (Fat John), trade (John the Barber), or personal history (Fortunate John, John Fortune). It was primarily these *eke names* that developed into family names, often with such evolutionary changes that the original form is hard to see. So: Bicknell (beacon hill), Pardow (par dieu), Quaynt, Queynte (known person, acquaintance).

Camden, *Remaines Concerning Britaine,* points out that even among the aristocracy, *sir-names* or *twa-names* were rarely given to illegitimate children. When Henry I (reigned 1100–1135) proposed the marriage of his bastard son, Robert, to a great lady, the coy minx is said to have replied in limping rhyme:

> It were to me a great shame
> To have a lord withouten his twa name.

Whereupon Henry named him Fitz Roy, son of the king. [*Fitz,* son of < OF *filz, fiz* < L. *filius,* son. *Roy* < Fr. *roi,* king. (Robert Fitz Roy, later Earl of Gloucester, left a reputation as a great war lord.)]

nigger   Contemptuous term for a black person. [Altered from *Negro* by way of sthrn. *nigra.* For the alteration of the first vowel to short *i,* cf. such sthrnisms as *since* for *sense, sinator* for *senator, pin* for *pen, cynic highway* for *scenic highway.*]

nightmare   A deeply disquieting dream. [This *mare* is no horse but akin to the *mar* of Fr. *cauchemar* < *caucher,* to trample, *mar,* evil spirit. Hence, with the root sense: "demon—trampled," Gmnc. folklore attributing these unquiet dreams to a goblin or an evil spirit that sat or danced on the sleeper's chest. *Mare, mar,* via Gmnc., ult. < IE *mer-,* to harm, with an early extension to the sense "harmful spirit."]

nincompoop   Dolt. Blockhead. Simpleton. [Few words have given our dictionary-makers so much needless trouble. Johnson, wrongly, sought to derive it from L. *non compos (mentis),* not (mentally) competent. The OED rejects Johnson's suggestion, only to dismiss the form as "prob. only a fanciful formation," and that clerk's guess has been aped by all subsequent dictionaries, which dismiss the form as "origin unknown." Yet the OED provides all the necessary clues in its own citations of the earlier form: 1676, *nicompoop,* and 1694, *nickumpoop;* which, if taken to be of Du. origin, as the sound suggests, present no difficulty. Du. *nicht,* niece, female cousin; *om* (prep.), for, of, about; *poep* (pron. as if Eng. *poop*), fool, clown.

And if that does not work out to be at root "(female) relative of a fool," I will be a monkey's uncle.]

nine The number of fingers one has left on both hands after stopping a hole in the dike. [OE *nigon*, nine. There is a standard tendency for OE *ig* to become a vowel in modern Eng. Telephone operators who pronounce the word in the exaggerated form *nigh-en* are sounding the probable intermediate form. Ult. < IE *neun-, newn-,* nine.]

The Nine (Sisters) The Muses. *the local nine Sports.* The home-town baseball team.

a nine days' wonder Any matter of intense but brief interest. [*Nine* cannot be dismissed as a generic number, the idiom being firmly based on the proverb "A wonder lasts nine days, and then the puppy's eyes are open." Puppies do take nine days to open their eyes, and even the foolish can make out a false "wonder" in nine days.] *ninety day wonder* In WWII, a 2nd lieut. or an ensign who has not won his commission at a service academy but by attending a three-month officer candidate school; and a fair wonder it is to create an officer and a gentleman in ninety days when God had proved unable to do so in the more or less twenty years before OCS.

cloud nine/Cloud Nine Bliss. The highest heaven. [It would be neat to assert this idiom as deriving from the Ptolemaic concep-tion of the universe as nine concentric spheres, the highest of which is Heaven (the circumference of everything, or as Ptolemy called it, the *Empyrean* < Gk. *empuros,* fire). So rendered, moreo-ver, it would correspond to the common *in seventh heaven,* identi-cal in meaning, but based on the Islamic conception of a seven-tiered heaven.

And perhaps the term is ultimately a Ptolemaic reference, but the fact is that it was first used in the Johnny Dollar radio show of the 1950's. As a standard formula of the show, Johnny managed to get knocked on the head in one way or another and to lie in a daze until he came to babbling of the bliss he had just experi-enced on *Cloud Nine.* Perhaps Johnny had read a book at some time and from it adapted Ptolemaic mysticism to radio patter.

Others have tried to explain the idiom as a reference to the International Classification of Clouds. In that system, which is basi-cally in descending order of mean altitude, cloud nine is cumulo-nimbus, the anvil-headed black thundercloud. But the sense of the idiom is clearly "topmost place of bliss," and though cumulo-nimbi can tower to about 25,000 feet, they are not the highest known clouds. Nor can those ominous black anviltops, shot through by lightning and churned by extraordinary turbulences, readily suggest a seat of bliss.]

nines: dressed to the nines   Dressed to perfection. [Probably not, as often suggested, from ME *to then eynes*, to the eyes (in which *then* is the dative of *the*), later nonced (see *noncing*) to *to the neynes;* the form is unattested. It is not possible to be certain, but the form is likely based on numerology, once a "science" as seriously regarded as alchemy and astrology. Numerologically, 9 (a trinity of trinities) stood for perfection. The use of plural *nines* would imply "the sum of all perfections."]

ninny   A fool. [Root sense: "an innocent." < the dial. variant of *innocent→ inny-cent→ an inny-cent (person)*, and then by *noncing* (which see) from *an inny* to *a ninny*.]

HISTORIC. Folk sensibility, as befits a man who gets up to shovel out the cowshed before breakfast, is hard-nosed. To be innocent in the contest for survival is naturally to be foolish. So *silly* < OE *saelig*, blessed, pure in heart, of heaven's elect (which may be well enough for sermons but puts nothing in the cook pot).

And so, conversely, *shrewd*, clever, calculating, ingenious, from a stem meaning "mean," as if only those who are sufficiently mean-minded may be clever enough to survive. (There is some uncertainty about the origin of *shrewd*. Perhaps from *shrew*, the small but vicious rodent, whence *shrew*, mean, vicious-tempered person. Perhaps from obs. *beshrew thee*, curse thee. But whether based on viciousness or damnation or equal parts of both, *shrewdness*, an admired folk quality, does not arise from sweetness and innocence. Your countryman expects the worst but fights on against it. See *omen*.)

nix   *A generalized negative. n.* Nothing. —*v.* 1. Stop it. *Hey, nix! Someone is coming!* 2. Turn thumbs down on. (And so the famous headline in *Variety*'s most exuberant style:) "STIX NIX HICK PIX": "Small-town audiences turn thumbs down on (recent rash of) movies about small-town life." *put the nix on it* To forbid it. To turn thumbs down on it. [Attested in early XIX Brit. < Ger. *Nichts*, nothing (which is ult. neg. prefix *ni-* with Gmnc. *wiht*, thing, person (obs. Eng. WIGHT).]

Nome   Originally a cape in northern Alaska. Later the city that developed there. [According to a variously told tale of the first mapping of Alaska, an early cartographer, working in pencil, is said to have written beside this cape the notation "Name?" The next cartographer in line, inking in the details, is said to have read "Nome" for "Name" and to have inked it so, ignoring the question mark. The story smacks of folk etymology, but sometimes the fantastics win. One may note, among others, the *Encyclopaedia Britannica:* "It (the city) was first called Anvil City; the name 'Nome' is derived from Cape Nome, first so called on a chart dated 1849, and said to have been a draughtsman's mistake for the query '? Name' on the original chart."]

nonce: for the nonce   For this one time. For the time being. [< ME *for then anes,* for that one time; the form then *nonced* (see below), the *n* shifting from *then* to *anes* → *for the nanes,* which was modified to *for the nonce.*]

noncing/to nonce   More commonly labeled *nunnation/nunation* after Arabic *nun,* the letter *n.* But Arabic nunnation is the addition of a declensional *n* at the end of certain words, whereas Eng. (and Fr.) *noncing* occurs at the beginnings of nouns, the *n* shifting on or off by some undefinable force in the sequential illogic called idiom. In these notes, therefore, I have taken *for the nonce* to be the eponym of the process and have used the forms *nonce word, nonced, noncing* as preferable to *nunnation, nunnated.*

In Eng. the process usually involves an *n* shift from the article *an* to the beginning of a word with an initial vowel; or conversely in words beginning with an *n,* a shift of the *n* to the article *a.*

So *an ewt* → *a newt; a nuncle* → *an uncle* (but also in XVI the almost interchangeable forms *my nuncle/mine uncle*). Some variously nonced Eng. words are: *apron, nickname, to the nines* (perhaps), *notch, ninny, humble pie,* their evolution explained under each entry and further referred to "see *noncing.*"

Noncing seems to have been most common in English up to early XVII, though generally earlier. So natural is this tendency, however, that infant prattlers still do natively what the language itself did some centuries back. So modern baby-talk *some nother time, neither* for *either, Nauntie* for *Auntie, Ana* for *Nana, my ame is* (or often *my yame is*) for *my name is.*

NOTE. Most dictionaries give *nonce word* with the sense: "a word coined for a single occasion (for the nonce), presumably not to be used again." I have found none, however, that has supplied an example answering to the definition given. I cannot, in fact, believe there is any such thing as a one-time-only-and-never-again word (unless I have just coined a hyphenated example—in which case I hereby uncoin it). I have not here entered "nonce word," on the grounds that there is no such thing, and I mention it here only to avoid confusion. In these notes *nonce, nonced, noncing* refer only to the *n* shift phenomenon of English and French.

nook Small recess. [Ult. < a widely dispersed but hypothetical Gmnc. root, prob. *hnekk-, narrow part or place (NECK), or Variant *hnokk-, prob. base of MD *nocke,* notched tip of a bow (NOCK). In ON dial. *nok,* hook, tip. All have the root sense: "narrow, recessed place or part." So ME *noke, nok,* a recessed place. So *inglenook,* a small recess where one may sit by the fire. (But note that *ingle* is not altered from "angle," but derives < Gaelic *aingeal,* fire, the root sense being: "recess by the fire.")

    nook and cranny In the formula *search every nook and cranny* To search every smallest recess and crack.

    nooky A sex act. [Brit. c. 1900 and immediately into Am. Perh. exuberant vulgar in which the vagina is conceived as the penis's chosen nook. But as likely a separate evolution from an alteration of earlier Brit. slang *to nug* To penetrate the vagina. (From *nudge* ???)]

    lackanooky [Exuberant vulgar whimsical, as if the medical name of a disease. (Cf. medical school slang *fecalemia* for "shit in the blood.") Am. only. Dating uncertain but the form is recent, prob. c. 1920.] Sexual deprivation. *On discharge, he claimed a 100 percent disability for an advanced state of Pacific rock-lackanooky, the one possible treatment for which would make him incapable of gainful employment for the rest of his life.*

noon Midday. [The sense has shifted from L. *nona hora,* ninth hour (after sunrise), originally 3:00 P.M., and in the first century associated with the crucifixion, earlier with the heat of the day. Our dictionaries too commonly assert the absurdity that the Romans calculated sunrise at 3:00 A.M. The Romans calculated it, as a norm, as 6:00 A.M., and so, too, Dante, who was a careful astrologer/ astronomer. The sense "12:00 o'clock midday" does not occur in English until XIV.] *high noon* 1. The moment when the sun is at zenith. 2. *Sense altered by our differing time zones.* The stroke of noon. *nooning Upper New Eng.* The midday work pause. *Roger Fredland took his nooning early today. nooner* Labels any midday habit, as a drink or a sex act. *He went to the bar for his nooner. On-duty firemen sleep in the firehouse but run home for lunch and a nooner.*

Norman French vs. Old English As many have noted, the English names for cuts of meat—beef, poultry, pork, mutton—are commonly of French origin, whereas the names of the corresponding animals—cow, bull, steer, chicken, hen, pig, shoat, sow, sheep, ewe—are of OE origin; and this language trait is easily explained by the fact that the conquered Saxons worked in the fields and sheds with the living animals, whereas the meat was served in the Norman manor house to French-speaking masters.

A related distinction can be noted in the names of the parts of the urogenital and digestive systems, the OE names passing from vulgarity to obscenity (asshole, prick), whereas the Latinate-French names (rectum, penis) acquired a sort of clinical propriety.

A third, and less noted, such distinction separates the military and naval vocabularies of English. Military ranks are almost exclusively of french naming—general, colonel, major, captain, lieutenant; naval ranks, of OE naming—mate, midshipman, boatswain, coxswain, skipper. A manual of military tactics is an exercise in French roots—army, battalion, column, defile, enfilade, fort, grenade, regiment, tactics. A naval manual is as typically an exercise in OE roots—abaft, boat, deck, gunwale, hawser, luff, tack, yard.

The explanation is not far to seek. Norman lords developed military power early and drilled it to their language. The English, on the other hand, did not formally organize a navy until the early XVI under Henry VIII. In the time from the Norman Conquest to XVI, English seafaring was left to fishermen and coastal traders too humble to attract the ambitions of Norman lords. Seamen, therefore, were left to speak to one another in their own terms, and by the time England developed a navy the seagoing vocabulary was too firmly set to be Frenchified, the conquerors themselves having become Britons.

notch 1. The root sense, from the days before clipboards and easily available writing implements, is the V-shaped cut a farmer made in a counting stick to tally sheep through a gate, shocks of grain placed on a threshing floor, etc. 2. *Geology.* Such a cut as an earth feature, as Crawford Notch, N.H. 3. A degree. *He moved up a notch in my estimation.* **notch (put a notch on) one's gun** To kill a man. [After the gunslinger's custom of notching the butt of his six-shooter to tally the number of men he had killed.] **notch one up** To score in any sense. [A more than usually complicated evolution from IE sek-, to cut (which is the stem of L. *sēcare,* to cut, It. *sega,* saw). So L. *absecare,* to cut off → OF *o(b)schier, schier.* (Akin to OF *escocher,* to cut, to score. See *scotch a rumor, butterscotch, hopscotch.*) And so to OF *oche,* a notch, ME *otch,* thing cut (HASH, HATCHET). Then by *noncing* (which see) from ME *an otch* → *a notch.*]

nut   An ambiguous slang term. 1. Head. [Attested in mid XIX Brit., but prob. in use from at least 1800. Prob. based on the fact that most nuts are round, and that many, such as the walnut, have a meat roughly resembling the shape of a human brain.] 2. An eccentric person, or a lunatic. [Prob. because nuts must be cracked; *cracked, crazed* having had long colloq. usage for "not mentally sound."] So in Am. *nut house/nut farm* An insane asylum. *be nuts/be off one's nut* To be eccentric or lunatic. *be nuts about Mazie* To love her with a mad passion. 3. An investment; expenses incurred in setting up a project, as a carnival game. *get off the nut* To recover expenses (ideally before beginning to take in a profit). [Originally U.S. carnival, but now general business slang. Perh. based on the image of a nut and bolt, the bolt being what one puts into a venture; so, when it is recovered, one has broken even. But ???] 4. A testicle. [Obvious metaphor.] *nuts* 1. Testicles. 2. Exclam. of derision. [A slightly minced form of *Balls! My balls to you;* which is in turn a minced form of *Fuck you!* But commonly also influ. by *nuts* in the sense "you're crazy!"]

HISTORIC. Toward the end of WWII in Europe the Germans mounted a fierce counterattack at Bastogne. Believing he had won, the German general asked the American general to surrender in order to spare the lives of his men. The one-word reply from what was artfully elaborated as The Battered Bastards of the Bastion of Bastogne was "Nuts!"—in which both "Balls!" and "You're off your nut!" clearly function in an expression of total contempt.

oaf A large, clumsy, dim-witted person. [Earlier a deformed child, a changeling left by elves (i.e., a rejected child-goblin exchanged for an infant human being—there's one in every family). Intermediate sense: "elf," the earlier forms being *ough, aufe* < OE *aelf,* elf. But ult. < IE *albho-,* white, with the associated sense *albino,* i.e., deformed person, unnatural person.]

Oakley, Annie Phoebe Ann Oakley Mozie, 1860–1926, famous sharpshooter and star of Buffalo Bill Cody's Wild West Show. *Annie Oakley* (C. 1900.) A complimentary ticket to a performance. [Whimsical. Advance agents regularly gave away complimentary tickets which they validated with a distinctive punch, as railroad conductors still punch tickets. One of Annie's stunts was to shoot the pips out of playing cards. Hence her name given to the "comps" as if she had shot the punch marks into them.]

objcct *n.* (Accent on first syllable.) 1. Any physical thing. 2. Thing or goal sought. —*v.* (Accent on second syllable.) To oppose. To protest. To place one's disagreement on record. [Though the n. and v. senses are discrete, both meet in the root form of L. *ob-,* toward; *jactare,* to throw. An object is something encountered ("thrown in our way"); to object is "to throw something against, in the way of." Cf. *abject,* at root: "thrown (cast) down," hence, downcast.]

obligation A binding commitment. [< L. *ob-,* to, toward (here functioning as an intensive); *legare,* to bind. The colloq. *it's my bounden duty* renders the root sense.] *obligatory adj.* Required under special bond. *holy days of obligation R.C. Church.* Days on which the faithful are specifically bound to perform certain acts and to practice certain abstinences. *I'm obliged to you* I am indebted to you. [A polite form functioning as "thank you" but meaning literally "your kindness binds me to offer you a future kindness in return." Cf. *religion,* the root sense of which is not "faith, body of belief" but "but the condition of being especially bound by the rule of a monastic order."]

obvious   Self-evidently clear. [Root sense: "like a thing met on one's way (in broad daylight)." < L. *ob-,* to, toward, against; *viam,* accusative of *via,* way.] *obviate* To prevent. [By intercepting and disposing of a thing on its way to happening.] *Richard Nixon seems to be the last to understand how obviously he has been obviated.*

odious   Hateful. *odium* 1. Hatred. 2. The stigma resulting from having acted in a hateful way. *hold one in odium* To detest. [The stem is unchanged since IE *od-,* hatred, to hate. L. *odio, I hate.* It. *odio,* hatred, revulsion. (*Odor* is based on IE *od-,* to smell, to stink, and the two stems may be simple homonyms, but they are more likely sense extensions of a single stem with the root sense "stinking, hateful, causing revulsion"; this conjunction of senses still functioning when we call a hateful person a "stinker."]

odor of sanctity   1. The state of grace. *He died in the odor of sanctity.* 2. *Originally.* A heavenly fragrance said to emerge from the tombs of the blessed.
    HISTORIC. Many pious legends have asserted that when the tombs of the blessed have been opened, usually for reinterment elsewhere, such a fragrance emerged from them as if the mortal remains partook of the sweetness of Heaven, to which the souls had mounted. Pious exaggeration aside, it is known that some corpses mummify rather than rot: on Saipan in WWII, I myself saw Japanese corpses, unburied for over a year, that had leathered without rotting. It was common medieval custom, moreover, to wash the dead with aromatic oils and to perfume their cerements. It is readily possible, therefore, that the first waft from an opened tomb would be scented with the trapped aromatics of the burial rite, which if not precisely heavenly, would at least be not notably tainted by putrefaction.

Oedipus   Son of Laius and Jocasta, king and queen of Thebes. To circumvent the natal prophecy that he would kill his father and marry his mother, the infant was sent out of the kingdom. When it came time for the young man to make his manhood journey (cf. the grail quest and tribal manhood-faring), Oedipus set off in his chariot. Wandering toward Thebes, he quarreled with a stranger (his unknown father) and killed him in a duel. He then went on to Thebes and married the widowed queen (his unknown mother). So the legend was fulfilled in darkness. Oedipus, having sworn to remove the guilt from Thebes, stabbed his own eyes out when he was revealed as the felon. The legend was dramatized by Sophocles in *Oedipus Rex* and *Oedipus at Colonus*. **Oedipus complex** Psychiatry. In the normal development of the male child between three and five, a libidinal attraction to the body of the mother accompanied by hostility toward the father because he has access to her body. In abnormal development, a more or less strongly incestuous attraction to the mother by an older child or by a man. The converse condition, in which a daughter is attracted to the father and hostile to the mother, is the *Electra complex*.

oeuvre   A work of art. ***oeuvre/oeuvres*** The body of an artist's or writer's output. [Fr. *oeuvre*, work. < L. *opus*, work (which is now reserved for a musical composition). *Opus* is standard in music; *oeuvre* is an affected arty-chic for Eng. *works*. But the same Fr. stem in *maneuver*, lit. "a work of hand," has become naturalized and unpretentious.]

ofay   *Black Am*. A white person. A honkie. [Pig Latin for "foe."]

offal   1. The "waste" parts of a slaughtered animal, primarily the pluck (stomach, intestines, lungs, etc.). "Or ere this/ I should have fatted all the region kites/ With this slave's offal": Hamlet on his uncle-stepfather. (And note that Hamlet did not propose simply to kill King Claudius, but to hack him open and throw his guts to the hawks and carrion crows.) 2. *Ext.* Any foul refuse. [Root sense: "what falls off/out." Ger. *aus-*, out; *fallen*, to fall. ME *offal, ofall* is prob. < MD *afval*, lit. "the outfall."]

ogle   1. *Earlier.* To look amorously. To make cow eyes. 2. *But now.* To leer. *Jay Rubero boggled his ogle and ended up married.* [IE *okw-*, to see. With k/g → Gmnc. *og-*, → Ger. *Augen*, eyes; *liebaugeln*, to make love-eyes. Same IE stem suffixed *-l-* in Italic → L. *oculus*, eye. It. *occhio*, eye, has dropped the suffix and returned very nearly to the IE root. Fr. *oeil* has retained the suffix but dropped the kappa of the IE root.]

oil on the waters   To pour oil on troubled waters is to bring calm from tumult, an ancient metaphor for the work of the peacemaker. [The Venerable Bede, 673–735, recounted how St. Aidan gave a flask of holy oil to a missionary about to set sail, and that when a great storm arose the young priest calmed the waters with the oil and was spared to reach his destination and to preach God's word to the heathen. And the metaphor still implies the act of calming raging seas. Yet no ancient ship could have carried oil enough to produce a significant oil slick, what it did carry being, in any case, in amphorae. The idiom must have originated with ref. to sacramental anointment calming the troubled waters of the soul.]

O.K.   Also *OK/Oke/Okay/okay* and as a reduplicated form *okey-dokie.* Verb forms *okays/okaying/okayed* or *O.K.'s/O.K.'ing/ O.K.'d.* A generalized expression of affirmation, approval, consent. [After Martin Van Buren (1782–1862, U.S. President 1837–1841). A native of Kinderhook, N.Y., he was popularly known as Old Kinderhook, or O.K.]

HISTORIC. In support of Van Buren's 1840 campaign for reelection, the New York Equal Rights Democrats, also known as the *Locofocos* (which see), formed the O.K. Democratic Club. The cry "O.K.," indicating enthusiastic approval of Old Kinderhook, soon began to resound at rallies, and the letters *O.K.* became common on placards and in political cartoons.

Foreign coverage of the campaign, which included reproductions of the cartoons, soon spread *OK* or *O.K.* through Europe and Latin America as a formula of approval. From that start, for reasons anyone is free to theorize, *O.K.* spread to become naturalized into practically every language on earth. *O.K.* is the most widely diffused word form in history, rivaled only by *Coca-Cola.*

But though the 1840 campaign popularized the form, it had a prehistory. About fifteen years earlier, Boston wits took to playing a waggish game of "murdering the King's English," and in that game *O.K.* became fixed as the abbreviation for *Orl Korreck.* The game had about played itself out by 1840, but the Locofocos remembered it. When Van Buren was crushingly defeated by William Henry Harrison, the Locofocos let it be known that *O.K.* stood for *Orful Kalamity* and *Orrible Katastrophe.*

Okie   1. A former Oklahoman become a migrant field worker in California. 2. An Oklahoman.

HISTORIC. In the 1930's many Oklahomans were forced off their land by the combined forces of the Depression and the natural disaster known as the Dust Bowl, which impoverished their land. Lured to California by false promises of good jobs, they trekked west in jalopy-truck caravans to become stoop labor. *Okie,* first developed as a term of contempt for these bedraggled and homeless drifters, was later accepted as a proud label by those who stayed in Oklahoma. See *jay: jayhawk, jayhawker* for a similar acceptance by Kansans of a once odious label.

old fogey/old fogy   A person, usu. a man, hard set in outmoded views and manners. *My adolescent children were unbearable young fogies about my behavior.* [< Sc. *old fogey,* an old, retired, usually invalided soldier. In common U.S. Army usage through WWII (but now rare), a *fogey* or *fogy* was a small increment in pay for each enlistment served, and for specified decorations won; and such increments were called *fogey/fogy pay.*]

olive branch   An ancient symbol of peace. In medieval Italy, mounted messengers arriving with good news carried an olive branch. [First recorded in the story of Noah's dove, which returned to the ark with an olive branch as proof that the waters were receding and that the deluge was over. But how does a dove break off even a twig from an olive tree, or scoop one up from the surface of the water? The olive branch as a symbol of peace probably goes back to primitive magic. The dove, too, must have had some special significance in totemistic belief. The two probably came together without regard for literal accuracy.]

olla podrida   (Pronounced *oy'-a/o'-lya.*) [Sp. "rotten pot."] A highly seasoned thick stew made of whatever fish, flesh, fowl, and vegetables come to hand, and usu. simmered in a covered pot. [The Fr. version is *pot pourri,* a literal translation of the Spanish, and later blended into one word as *potpourri.* Sc. *hotch pot, hotch potch* ("pot of hashed-up stuff") is akin (and so HODGEPODGE). All these terms function in Eng. for any random or messy collection, anthology, or rambling discourse. Also *omnium gatherum.*

omelet   Beaten eggs cooked in a thin layer. [Though now specifically an egg dish, the root sense is simply "thin layer" or "crêpe"; and omelets are often folded over a filling as crêpes are. Ult. < L. *lāmina,* layer, dim. form *lāmella* → OF *lamelle, la lamelle,* altered to *alemelle,* and then by metathesis to *amelelle,* and then with dim. suffix to Fr. *omelette. Amelette* still functions in south of France dialect.]

omen   A sign from Heaven. [And so L. *ōmen,* ult. < IE *o,* a mystical syllable of prayerful address and affirmation. Cf. *om,* the mystic

syllable of Oriental meditation.] *ominous* Darkly threatening. Foreboding ill.

HISTORIC. Strictly speaking, an *omen,* a sign of divine intention,
can presage good or ill; yet *ominous* is always "of ill omen." As
a view into one of the commonest of racial assumptions, "sign of
God" has always tended to mean "sign of wrath."

On the carpet (see *carpet*) makes the same point. The root
sense is "under official review"; the effective sense is "in trouble."
The official review might be favorable, but humankind is not inclined to think so. We may hope for the best from higher authority,
but racial experience moves us to expect the worst.

omnibus [Dative plu. ("for all") of L. *omnis,* all.] *n.* 1. *In earlier
English.* A horse-drawn large coach available to the public for
service along a more or less fixed route ("a for-all"). [*Bus* by back
formation from *(omni)bus.*] 2. An omnium gatherum, as an anthology of widely diverse works. —*adj.* Containing all sorts of things.
As, *a.* A roundup review of many different books. *b.* A sweeping
law or judicial decision. *Despite laborious pretenses to definition,
all laws and court rulings on censorship are an omnibus jumble.
The censor may know what he dislikes, but no censor pronouncing
in legalese has been able to describe what he seeks to ban.*

omnium gatherum A hodgepodge. An everything-in all-together. [L.
omnium, of all, everything (gen. plu. of *omnis,* all; with Eng. *gather*
given a mock L. declensional ending.]

one [The modern form of the word is recognizable in IE *oino-,* one.
Prob. via Gmnc. **ain-* → OE *ān* → ME *an, on,* one.] The first
whole number, a surd, with extended senses: individual,
unique, and, pronomially, a certain person. Generically, any individual; hence, all. *One doesn't do that sort of thing:* No one, or
at least no one of our sort, does such a thing. Also as an intensive
form of the indefinite article. *That's one great horse*—which does
not mean "that is one among other great horses," but rather "that
is a uniquely great horse."

All other idioms based on *one* may be taken to be self-evident,
but as language is to relish, I will certainly note the natural metaphor *one jump ahead of the sheriff* On the verge of bankruptcy
and foreclosure. (And was ever an idiom more precisely made
to order for the cartoonist?)

onion The sweetly pungent, aromatic, bulbous vegetable. [Root
sense: "thing joined into one," with ref. to the many layers that

conjoin into a single onion. Ult. < IE *oino-*, one. L. *unus*, one; *unio*, onion. OF *oignion*. ME *unyon*.]

oodles Many. A great amount. [Alteration of earlier *huddles*, as in *huddles of mice in a nest*.]

oomph An all-purpose term of approval of the qualities of strength, vigor, sexual attraction. [Am. Dating uncertain; prob. early XX. Perhaps, as some assert, simply an expressive; but if not based on, then almost certainly influenced by, *oompah-oompah*, common echoic for the stirring and positive sound of a brass band in the XIX, when every American town of any consequence had at least one bandstand in a park, and band concerts were a standard and regular public entertainment.]

oop/oops *Exclam.* An involuntary language reflex expressing recoil from an inadvertent minor mischance, as in dropping a glass or bumping into someone. Hence, used for comic effect in reaction to a major mischief, as when the mad scientist, inadvertently touching off the Omega bomb, says, "Oops!" [Though as native as any language form in English, *oop/oops* does not appear in most Am.-Eng. dictionaries. As conjecture only, since no evidence is available, I take the *oop* to be a reflex inhalation, the *s* to be the beginning of a bitten-off "sorry," for one often hears "Oop—sorry" and even "Oop—so'."]

ooze *v.* To emit liquid slowly. 2. To exude. To overflow. To leak. *Liberace just oozes charm—or shall we say he just oozes?* —*n.* Any seepage. [OE *wōs*, ME *wose*, juice. Ult. < IE *wes-*, wet.]

open sesame The verbal alkahest that dissolves all difficulties and opens all doors. [From the *Arabian Nights* tale of "Ali Baba and the Forty Thieves." The thieves stored their treasure in a cave with a magic stone door that would open only at this command. Ali Baba, in hiding, heard the magic password and was able to enter the cave and loot the treasure. His brother Casim extorted the password from him and also entered the cave, but forgot it and was unable to reopen the door to get away. He was trapped inside and killed when the robbers returned. Sesame (seed) is a small grain used for food, as a seasoning, and squeezed for oil. Casim tried *open barley* (and various other grains, but only *sesame* (three syllables) would move the stone.]

oracle 1. A divinely inspired prophetic utterance. 2. The speaker of such prophecies. 3. The place at which such prophecies are uttered. 4. *Loose ext.* A seer. A pundit. One believed to be wise enough to foresee the future. **oracular** 1. Foreseeing the future. 2. Enigmatically wise. Pompously obscure in utterance. [IE *or-* in various senses having to do with ritual and the incantation of spells. → L. *orāre*, to speak (ORATE), but with the root sense: "to incant, to pray." The root sense is accurately rendered by common Am. revivalist *to speak in tongues,* to fall into a trance and to utter gibberish believed to be divinely inspired. Greek oracles were priest-attended psychics and mediums who "got through" to "the other world" while in a trance which was autoinduced, assisted by herbal drugs, or both. Suppliants asked the oracle to foretell their future and were answered in a gibberish that the attendant priests "interpreted" for a fee.] **oratory** (Now most commonly from the evolved sense of L. *orāre.*) Speechmaking. (But originally, from the root sense of *orāre.*) Place for prayer, esp. a private chapel. **oratorio** A musical composition for orchestra with a more or less extensive chorus that chants a sacred story.

orange 1. The fruit. 2. The color. [The name of the fruit came first, the color following by association. Ult. < Sanskrit *nāranja* → Arabic *nārandj, nāranj* → Sp. *naranja.* And Portuguese variant *laranja.* And cf. *Naranja,* a citrus-processing and -shipping town south of Miami. In all these cases, the fruit kept its original name as a loan word. In XIII–XIV, however, other European languages began to develop their own terms, basically metaphors to label this new thing. (There is no classical word for the orange, and the first appearance of names for it in XIII–XIV Italian and French are evidence of its importation shortly before that time. See historic note.)]

HISTORIC. XIV Italian used *melarancia,* orange apple (now *arancia*). The same pattern occurs in OF *pomme d'orange,* orange apple, orange fruit (Fr. *orange*). German also has *die Orange,* but earlier, and surviving, North German used *Apfelsine,* lit. Chinese apple, but in effect, apple of the east. (Du., Russ., and all the Scandinavian languages, even including Finnish, use native variants of the same form.) And earlier, and still surviving, So. Ger. used *Pomerantze,* orange apple, orange fruit, which is the form borrowed by all the Slavic languages except Russian. See *potato* for a closely similar example of how European languages evolve terms for a new common object.

oreo   *Black English.* A Black who tries to talk, think, and act like a White. [After *Oreo,* registered trade name of a chocolate wafer sandwich with a white creamed-sugar filling; because it is black on the outside and white inside.]

Orestes   *Greek myth.* The archetypal matricide. [Son of Agamemnon and Clytemnestra. Clytemnestra killed Agamemnon for, among other things, messing around with Cassandra, and Orestes slew Clytemnestra because he was really Daddy's boy.]

orgy   Plu. *orgies* [Ult. < IE *werg-*, to do (WORK). Gk. *ergon,* work (ENERGY). The basic sense is "intense activity." So Gk. *orgia,* a secret rite involving intense worship (and so sense 3, below). In fertility rituals as in the cult of Dionysus, the *orgia* involved feasting, drinking, dancing, and open copulation, whence sense 1, below.] 1. A revel in which many sex partners are available for, usu., witnessed copulation. 2. *Ext.* Any rendezvous involving plural sex partners. 3. A period of intense activity. *Van Gogh's final years were an orgy of bursting colors.*

orient   The east. *Orient* The East. [L. *oriri,* to rise; *oriens,* a rising (esp. with ref. to the sun). Hence, "point at which the sun rises."] *orient oneself* To get one's bearings. [By ref. to the sun.] *orientation* 1. The act of orienting oneself. 2. *Ext.* The process of becoming familiar with a new environment. *During orientation week at Yale the boys find out where the girls live and vice versa. origin* Source. Point of beginning. [Also from *oriri,* via *origo,* I arise. (As the sun does, from nothingness.)]

original sin   The inherent sinfulness of mortal clay that led Adam and Eve to their disobedience, and which, in Judeo-Christian tradition, makes us sinful by birth. As the Puritan adage had it, "In Adam's fall/We sinnèd all." *After ninety years of tireless research, George Blair died bewailing the fact that he had not found a truly original sin.*

ostracism   [Ult. < IE *ost-*, bone. Gk. *osteon,* bone. And related forms *ostreon,* oyster, shellfish; *ostrakon,* sea shell, with exts. potsherd, tile ("bonelike things").] 1. Any general act of social exclusion. 2. *In ancient Greece.* A formal act of banishment from the state. [Because banishment was by a vote, the traditional ballot being an *ostrakon.*] —*v. To ostracize.*
    HISTORIC. In ancient Athens a person could be accused of being

a danger to the state and a vote taken to banish him for a period of ten years. Socrates, on being so banished, chose rather to drink poison.

The votes were marked on a ballot called an *ostrakon,* but though the word has the three meanings given above, it is obvious that the citizens did not collect sea shells or smash vases for voting materials, but used terra-cotta tiles easily marked with chalk.

In Syracuse, the period of banishment was five years and the ballot used was a large leaf (Gk. *petalon*), whence the rare but standard English term *petalism.* But though *to ostracize* is common, *to petalize* does not occur.

Today *to ostracize* does not mean to banish, but to exclude from all dealings. The Amish formally ostracize members who have seriously offended, even to the point of requiring parents to shun a sinful son or daughter. Excommunication from the R.C. Church is a form of ostracism.

Less formally, ostracism is a general social shunning as in the British idiom **send to Coventry,** to ignore an offending member of a group, refusing even to speak to him. [Because in the XVII English Civil War, Oliver Cromwell established at Coventry a prison in which his opponents were held incommunicado.]

outlandish   Queer. Barbarous. Ludicrously not of "our" custom. Unheard of (by "us"). At root: *congenial* (see *gen-, gene-*) is the antonym. [OE *utland,* foreign parts, *utlendisc,* foreign. Akin to Du. *uitlander,* Ger. *Auslander.* OED cites Aelfric's rendering of Leviticus 24:22, "as well for the stranger as for the native born," as *si he landesman, si utlendisc,* "be he native, be he foreigner." And John Donne, early XVII, uses the form neutrally in *outlandish ground* for "foreign soil." But in current usage, always connotes the barbarian's "we-they" sense of the ludicrousness of all difference from "our ways."]

ox   With the Gmnc. plu. form *oxen.* 1. A born-to-be-but-castrated bovine bull. 2. *Ext.* A hulking, powerful, stupid, clumsy fellow. [Origin in some doubt. Prob. < IE *uegu-,* wet; the prob. (and ironic) sense being "to make wet (the female)," i.e., "to inseminate." But if this is the case, the earliest sense must have been not "ox" but "bull." It is likely, therefore, that some untraced sense shift occurred; and the OE forms *oxa, oxan* suggest that there was some intermediate Gmnc. form, prob. *uks'-, uksen.*]

not to know one from Adam's off ox Not to know one at all. [Certainly a whimsical elaboration on "not to know one from

Adam." To understand the force of the idiom, one must envisage the ox driver as walking, not riding. Afoot, he directs his yoked oxen by prodding the near ox with a stick in his right hand. Therefore he must walk to the left of the lead (left) ox, which must be the better trained (hence, better known) one. The off ox is yoked to the right of the lead ox, i.e., away from the handler. The off ox is newer, less well trained, hence, less known. That much understood, the rest is exuberant flourish for sweet style's sake.]

oyer and terminer   *U.S. law.* A sometime designation for a high court trying a felony. *Brit. law.* An order to a judge to hear a case and arrive at a verdict. [Anglicized form and pronunciation of OF *oyer et terminer,* legal phrasing, "to hear and determine." *Terminer* not to be confused with *terminate.*]

oyez/oyes   (Any pronunciation conceivable by a court bailiff is acceptable.) Hear ye! [Fr. *oyez,* 2nd person plu. imperative of *oyer,* to hear. Repeated, this was the cry with which the bailiff opened crown courts in French, the form persisting in English; and once also employed by town criers.]

ozone   1. Chemically O_3, an allotrope of oxygen most commonly produced in the atmosphere by lightning, and having a distinctive odor. Ozone in an unaired enclosure is poisonous. [Root sense: "stinking (air)." < Gk. *ozein,* to stink.] 2. Fresh air, esp. "pure" country air. [This common colloq. sense despite the etymology and toxicity of ozone. So Ozone Park, N.Y., may be rendered colloquially as Fresh Air Park or etymologically as Stinking Air Park.]

P

pachyderm   Labels the largest of terrestrial mammals, as the elephant, the hippopotamus, and the rhinoceros. [Root sense: "thick-skinned." < Gk. *pachus*, thick; *dermos*, skin, hide.]

pagan   1. Esp. in Europe, a non-Christian believer in the ancient idol-worshipping and magic rituals. A heathen. 2. *Loose ext.* An unreligious person, or one not of the "true faith." (Jews and Moslems, though superstitiously feared, were not regarded as pagans; except that the variant form *paynim* was applied to the Moors against whom Charlemagne and his paladins fought.) [IE *pak-*, *pag-*, to bind. With the sense: "a binding agreement" → L. *pax*, peace. Also L. *pagus*, a bounded area within a country but away from the cities; hence, a village or district (at root: "a land area with agreed-upon bounds" ("land no longer subject to dispute") and with the effective sense: "far from the city." Whence *paganus*, a peasant who works outlying land; and in military usage, "a civilian." Metaphorically then, in this military sense, "one not of Christ's militia"; but also "one not yet reached by the missionaries." See *heathen* for a parallel evolution.]
   HISTORIC. Christianity had its first growth in the cities. Travel was rare and dangerous, and peasants, bound to the land, had small reason for traveling. In remote districts of Italy the worship of pre-Christian gods continued well into the Middle Ages. It was not till the fifth century that St. Benedict established a monastery at Monte Cassino, after converting the worshippers of a still surviving temple to Apollo in that place.

palace   1. A royal or viceregal residence. 2. *Ext.* An imposing and more or less ornate house. 3. *Ext.* A common name for a theater; and in Vegas for a casino-hotel. *Caesar's Palace.* [Via Fr. *palais* < L. *Palātium*, the Palatine Hill (on which stood the residences of the Roman emperors).] **palatial** Palace-like.

palaver   1. Prating or self-seeking talk. 2. A powwow. (Corresponding verb forms.) [< Portuguese *palavra,* talk. In XVI applied to more or less formal powwows between African natives and Portuguese explorer-traders, the natives intent on the formalities (and all they could get), the Portuguese putting up with the formalities (for the sake of all they could get for as little as possible).]

   NOTE. This sense shift from "talk" to "self-seeking talk" is paralelled in French *hableur,* a braggart < Sp. *hablador,* one who speaks; and conversely in Sp. *parlador,* braggart < Fr. *parleur,* one who speaks.

Pall Mall   (Pronounced *pell mell.*) An avenue in London's fashionable West End. [Named after the croquet court Charles II ordered built there. *Pall* < It. *palla,* ball; *Mall* < It. *maglio,* wicket.]

palooka   1. Any inept athlete, especially but not exclusively a prize fighter who seldom, if ever, wins. 2. *Ext.* A born loser. [Coined in *Variety* by sportswriter Jack Conway (1886–1928).]

pamphlet   A booklet. Earlier a short, unbound, usu. polemic, printed essay. [Root sense: "collection of love poems." Ult. eponymous < *Pamphilus,* XII Latin writer of popular love songs. *Pamphilet* had the sense: "collection of Pamphilus," *-et* serving as OF collective suffix. So the translation of Aesop's *Fables* by Marie de France was called *Ysopet,* Aesop-ery (Ernest Weekley). So *Pamphilet* → OF *Pamphlet* → ME *pamphlet.* (Then, the word having passed to English, it disappeared from Fr. and was borrowed back to label a short polemic.)]

pandemonium   Uproarious confusion. [Root sense: "(place of) all (howling) demons." < Gk. *pan,* all; *daimon,* devil. In the form *Pandemonium,* coined by John Milton, *Paradise Lost,* as his name for the capital city of Hell.]

Pandora's box   1. A present that turns out to be a curse. 2. An act or situation that spawns a tangle of interrelated troubles. [Pandora (the name means "all-gifted") was the Greek mythological equivalent of Eve as the first woman, though Pandora came into being only long after the Creation. Before her the earth was populated only by Titans, brutish male creatures not born of woman but sprung from the bowels of the earth. When the Titan Prometheus offended the gods by stealing fire from heaven and bringing it to earth, Zeus (so runs one version of the myth) revenged himself by ordering Vulcan (the magician-mechanic of the gods) to create

the first woman as a plague upon the earth creatures. Each of
the gods gave her as a gift a special talent for bringing men to
grief. These gifts Zeus sealed in a chest (symbolically, within her)
as the dowry she would take to Prometheus. (In another version,
Prometheus is punished by being chained to a rock to which an
eagle descended each day to eat out his liver. The Greeks, it seems,
could not decide whether a woman or a surgical eagle was the
greater plague.)

Prometheus, however, knowing the treachery of the gods,
would have nothing to do with her and her box. It was his younger
"brother" (so the legend runs, though creatures without mothers
or fathers are hard put to it to have brothers), Epimetheus, who
married her and opened the box, out of which flew all the afflictions
of mankind. In some versions of the myth, hope was the last snare
out of the box; in others, it alone stayed inside, there being no
hope of escaping the griefs born of woman.]

panhandler   A beggar. [*Pan* for begging bowl, tin cup, or other receptacle for coins.] *to panhandle* To beg.

HISTORIC. Begging by holding out some receptacle is of great
antiquity, perhaps from a time before there were coins and beggars
held out their bowls for bits of food. The purpose of the receptacle
is, at gist, to avoid bodily contact. Beggars have historically made
themselves as hideous as possible in order to awaken sympathy,
and a natural revulsion can partly explain the fixed habit of avoid-
ing contact. But a deeper explanation lies in the taboos of the
"untouchables," and in the fact that many beggars were once lep-
ers and forbidden by law to touch nonlepers.

panic   [< Gk. *Panikos,* of Pan. For though we tend to associate goat-
footed, pipe-playing Pan with frolicsomeness, he was at root a
prankish forest goblin, given to terrifying travelers, especially those
benighted in the forest.] 1. Uncontrolled terror, either in one person or in a group. 2. Commonly applied to times when stocks
drop ruinously in value. *the panic of 1929.* **hit the panic button**
Can mean, loosely. 1. To be filled with terror. *But better.* 2. To
sound an alarm, especially when a cooler response would have
been better. [Dating uncertain. Prob. from WWII in connection
with air raids.]

pants   [Earlier *pant(aloon)s.* < It. *pantalone,* flirtatious old miser,
an epithet applied to Tarriano, a traditional figure in Italian comedy. He wore pants after the fashion imported to Venice from

Byzantium. The epithet derived ult. from *San Pantaleone* ("the all-merciful"), patron saint of Venice. The uncertain sense connection between the comic epithet and the saint may be based on the fact that San Pantaleone was martyred in the East, perh. by Turks who wore pants, but ??] 1. Trousers. 2. *Loosely.* A woman's step-ins. [< *Panties.*]

anything in pants Any male.

fly by the seat of one's pants To pilot a light aircraft by feel rather than by reliance on instruments. [As if sensing the plane's attitude by the feel of one's buttocks against the seat.]

get into her pants Have intercourse with. [*Pants* in sense 2.]

gets into his pants one leg at a time (just like anyone else) Egalitarian catch phrase applied to any emminent person, to assert that he is, in the last analysis, only one more human being.

have hot pants To be sexually eager. *have ants in one's pants* To be restless. *hot pants Adj.* Labels a sexually eager person. —*n.* A recently contrived name for a girl's shorts cut off about $\frac{1}{16}$ inch below the crotch.

still in short pants Still a boy. [Because boys once commonly wore short pants and men, long ones.]

he/she wears the pants in the family He/she is the dominant figure of the household. [*Pants* for "male"; hence, in male-dominant society, "master."]

panty raid A once (c. 1950) collegiate foolishness in which male students raided women's dormitories, taking panties as their triumphant loot. (Prob. forever passé since the establishment of coed dormitories.)

Paracelsus   Aureolus Philippus Paracelsus, nom de plume of a Swiss alchemist and charlatan much given to metaphysical treatises and self-vaunting claims of mysterious powers. The surname signifies that he was (above and) beyond A. Cornelius Celsus, first century physician and writer, esteemed for *Artes* and *De Medicina.* [Gk. *para-,* beyond; with Celsus. And see *alkahest.*] Paracelsus may perhaps be forgiven his adopted name in light of the fact that his real name was Theophrastus Bombastus von Hohenheim (1490–1541).

parachute   A cloth canopy with a rigging to be strapped to a person or to an object for retarding the rate of fall through the atmosphere. [Gk. *para-,* against; Fr. *chuter,* to fall; hence, at root: "anti-fall (device)." This sense of *para-* is also visible in Eng. *parasol,* device against the sun; Fr. *parapluie,* umbrella (device against the rain);

and It. *paravento,* (automobile) windshield (device against the wind).

The first OED citation is dated 1785: "Mr. Blanchard (a balloonist) brought his parachute to England." M. Blanchard (as the name should have been rendered) did not, however, use it. The first recorded parachute jump was made October 22, 1797, from 2,000 feet, by the French balloonist André Jacques Garnerin.

In *The Laodiceans,* published 1871, Thomas Hardy uses *parachute* to label a flat stone shield raised, by metal or stone supports, above a chimneytop to prevent rain, birds, or thrown objects from falling into the flue. This sense of the word is now obsolete, but did respond exactly to the root words, though with a radically different effective sense.]

paradise The place of bliss; usu. with ref. to Heaven, but also to the Garden of Eden (the Earthly Paradise). [The root sense: "walled-in pleasure park," refers to the formal gardens so much prized in the Middle East, of which the Hanging Gardens of Babylon are the most famous example. < Old Persian *païridaēza,* walled-in place; the Persian form borrowed into Gk. as *paradeisos.* The word does not occur in the Hebrew of the Old Testament but is used three times in the Greek New Testament, once with reference to the place in which the souls of the dead await the Resurrection, and twice with reference to Heaven.] *a fool's paradise* The condition of blissful ignorance.

paramour *A slightly archaic word in Am.* A lover not sanctioned by whatever legal or moral rules may be said to remain in effect. [< Fr. *par amour,* by means of/for the sake of love. Hence, a lover (of either sex). In XIII meant simply "a sweetheart," but in Chaucerian use in XIV the sense changed to "illicit lover." Yet in devotional language the sense "loved one" continued for nearly two more centuries. The Virgin Mary was called by the devout "God's paramour." And in a carol of c. 1500, Christ addresses Mary as "my swete moder, myn paramour." The shift from "loved one" to "illicit lover" prob. stemmed from a confusion of Fr. *par,* for, by, with Gk. *para-,* to one side of (PARALLEL), whereby the word was understood to mean something like "side lover" or "lover one keeps on the side" (not within the bounds of matrimony).]

paraphernalia 1. Personal articles. *the paraphernalia of a woman's handbag.* 2. The tools and equipment of scientist, artisan, sportsman. *a roomful of chemical paraphernalia.* (Often with plu. verb.) [But these senses have evolved only since XVII. Earlier, in Brit. law, personal articles a wife can claim as exclusively her own, apart from her dowry. Based on the Gk. legal term *parapherna* (nom. plu.), articles and property not forming part of the marriage contract and belonging exclusively to the wife. < Gk. *para,* alongside, beyond, away from; *phernē,* dowry.]

pardon   1. Remission of a punishment or legal sentence. [Through Medieval L., *perdun,* Sp. *perdonar,* OF *pardoner,* was specific to papal indulgences; and so *pardoner,* in the Chaucerian sense, a priest, monk, or brother licensed to sell indulgences.] 2. *Since XVI.* Forgiveness of a fault, offense, injury. [< L. *per,* through (here functions as an intensive); *donare,* to give; hence, with the effective sense: "thing freely given."]

paregoric   A tincture of camphor and opium taken internally for relief of stomach distress, but perhaps best known to U.S. parents in the mild form rubbed on the gums of babies to relieve the pain of teething. [Root sense: "not engaged in politics." (It would follow that the Kennedys never used the stuff on their children.) < Gk. *parēgorikos,* soothing, inducing peace. The Greek association of the ideas "serene" and "not in politics" is a recognizable human response. The form of the word < *para-,* to one side of, outside; with *ēgora,* variant of *agora,* place of legislative assembly; and cf. the adj. *agoros,* engaged in making a speech. In XVII Eng. originally as an adjective in the label *paregoric elixir,* soothing elixir. Now as noun only, meaning "a substance that soothes."]

patsy   *Slang.* A dupe. The butt of a joke. *In crim. usage.* A fall guy. [Am. only. Late XIX, early XX. Origin uncertain. It may be that XIX and XX *patsy* are discrete evolutions.]
     NOTE. Perhaps < It. *pazzo,* crazy; *uno dei pazzi,* one of the crazies. Some refer the term to the XV Pazzi family of Florence, which had the arrogance to attack the Medici. The Pazzi were summarily wiped out, the hacked bodies of many of their leaders being dragged through the streets and dumped in the Arno while crowds mocked them. The family name and foolishness left it a place of ridicule in Italian history. It is too much, however, to assert that Am. slang waited five centuries to pick up this Florentine reference. And though one may argue that It. *uno dei pazzi* was something like It. idiom, the derivation then runs into the fact that in late XIX *patsy* meant "fine, wonderful, admirable."

I am inclined to think (?) that *patsy* in this obsolete sense evolved from Irish-immigrant *Patsy*, a fond nickname for *Patrick*, with the side sense "one of our boys," hence, "a helluva fellow," hence, "fine and dandy."

But soon thereafter, and, in fact, overlapping, *Patsy* was the standard Italo-American patois for the common man's name *Pasquale* ("of Easter"). Briefly, too, Patsy was a generic for the Italian immigrant greenhorn, a "patsy" for the foreman who clipped his wages and added abuse for good measure. This derivation is speculative but conforms, as the others do not, to the sense and the dating.

patter[1]   A glib line of fast talk. A spiel. (Clearly implies insincerity.) [XIV. Based on *paternoster*, with ref. to rapidly garbled recitation of Latin prayers by a priest saying mass but in a hurry to get to lunch.]

patter[2]   *n.* 1. A series of light pats. 2. The sound of such. *the pitter-patter of little feet.* —*v.* To walk with rapid light steps. [Echoic. Frequentive of *pat*, the sound of a light stroke.]

peach   [L. *persicum malum*, Persian apple. The name indicates that the peach tree, botanically *Prunus persicum*, of Chinese origin, reached Europe via its cultivation in ancient Persia. The naming of fruits as *malum* (which is "apple" but also a generic for "fruit"), together with the name of the place from which it was first imported, is common. In Late L. shortened to *persica* → It. *pesca*, peach (not to be confused with It. *pesce*, fish, *pesca*, the act of fishing) → OF & ME *peche*.] 1. The fruit and the tree. 2. *Am. slang from late XIX through the 1920's and then less and less common.* Epithet of general enthusiastic approval. *It/he/she is a peach:* It/he/she is swell. —*adj. peachy/just peachy.*

peaches and cream Symbolizes high living. [*Cream* perhaps as "fat of the land"; *peaches*, delicious fruit. Militant labor leaders of late XIX–early XX were much given to "we'll all eat peaches and cream" as a way of describing the abundant life when the workers came into their own. And c. 1875 Atlanta natives referred to Peachtree St., a main thoroughfare lined along one stretch with great houses, as *Peaches-and-Cream St.* with ref. to its elegance. Lacking firm attestation, I can only speculate that these usages stem not from "fat-of-the-land delicious fruit" but from the ideal of beauty expressed by "peaches and cream complexion," below.]

peaches and cream complexion Labels rosy blond beauty. [But the dating is uncertain. Clearly, however, all the foregoing senses function in:]

Peaches Common girl's nickname of the 1920's. [Almost certainly after the much publicized "flapper" who married an elderly "sugar daddy" named Browning and who, as Peaches Browning, flashed through NYC night life and gossip columns in full fluffery.]

gee, baby, we'd make a peach of a pair A common fad phase of the 1920's. [In the days when pomaded gents practiced "a smooth line" (of patter), such stuff passed as a dazzling pun among those whose lives were firmly based on the classicism of Tin Pan Alley.]

peccable   Given to sinfulness. At fault. *impeccable* Faultless. Free of error. [In which the root sense "sin" has been replaced by the sense "flawless taste." (*Peccable* is rare in Am.; *impeccable*, common.)] *peccant* Sinful. At fault. *peccadillo* [Sp. *pecado*, sin; with dim. suffix *-illo*, a little sin.] A quirk. Implies an endearing flaw not so much charged against one as noted to be forgiven. *Nancy's marriage to John Williams is best dismissed as one of her peccadilloes.* [Common in all Romance languages, the root *pecc-* is largely replaced in English by Gmnc. *sin. Pecc-* is ult. < IE *ped-*, foot; suffixed *ped-ko-* (assimilated form, *pekk-*) → early L. *peccare*, to stumble ("not walk right"), and so borrowed by early Christian writers as a metaphor for "not walking right in the ways of the Lord," whence the Christianized meaning "to sin."]

pecker   *In Am. slang (from earlier Brit., in which this sense is now obsolete).* The penis. [The root ref. seems to be to the woodpecker ("repeated thrusts of the projecting member"). In Brit., on the other hand, *pecker* has become associated with the "upper lip (of the woodpecker)," and so, across the barriers of a common language, the two senses bump heads in:]

keep one's pecker up To keep up one's courage. [But in Brit. firmly with the sense of "to keep a stiff upper lip," whereas in Am., though with the same extended sense, as firmly associated with the root image of "maintaining one's erection," i.e., not wilting in adversity.]

pedant   One, esp. a teacher, who makes a display of learning while missing the spirit of intellectual inquiry in a fussy devotion to minor rules. [But earlier, simply "teacher of boys," which is the exact sense of Gk. *paidagōgos.* The sense shift from the neutral "teacher" to the pejorative "dogmatic old nit-picker" is prob.

a judgment delivered by generations of bored schoolboys. But though this pejorative sense has attached to *pedagogue, pedant, pedantic,* and *pedantry,* it has not touched the adjectival *pedagogic,* "of the art of teaching."]

penthouse 1. An apartment, usu. with a terrace or terraces, on the roof of a high-rise building. 2. *Loose ext.* The top floor of a high-rise apartment house, sometimes slightly recessed for terraces, but a floor as distinct from a rooftop. 3. *Still looser ext.* The top floor of a tall building. [In XX Am. *penthouse* has acquired a connotation of highly sophisticated urban chic. Even a popular cleft-and-cleavage girlie magazine has been named *Penthouse* to suggest the goings-on in the quarters of a rich, fashionable big-city bachelor. Yet the root sense of this changeling word is "lean-to" or "attached shed." < Medieval L. *appenticium,* appendage < *appendere,* to attach < *pendere,* to hang (from), prefixed *a(d)-,* to. ME *pendis, pentis,* attached shed with a sloping roof. Late XIV *pentis* altered to *penthouse,* shed. The sense "rooftop apartment" is late XIX, and almost certainly by association with the rooftop sheds that covered the stairway to the roof and the elevator control machinery.]

person 1. A human being as distinct from other creatures. 2. A distinct individual. *He may be only a child, but he is also a person.* 3. One's body. *to seize the person and possessions of.* 4. *Trinitarianism.* The Father, the Son, and the Holy Ghost as three aspects of one godhead. [A surprisingly late evolution for so necessary a word. Sense 4 is closest to the root. Originally L. *persona,* a mask worn by an actor to signify a usually symbolic identity. Such masks had large mouth openings through which to speak, as in the commonly portrayed masks of tragedy and comedy. Hence, the word is prob. < L. *per,* by way of; *sonare,* to sound, to utter.]

    persona non grata [L. unwelcome person.] An undesirable person, esp. a diplomat who is no longer welcome in the country to which he has been assigned. (When a government declares a diplomat to be *persona non grata,* it is demanding that he be recalled.)

    Related words: *personable, personality, personalize, personification, personal, personnel, impersonate, dramatis personae.*

petard *Obs.* An early (c. 1500) explosive charge of black powder fired by a lighted fuse and used in siege warfare for breaching walls and blowing up gates. [L. *pet, peditum,* a fart < *pēdere,* to fart; with *-ard.* Hence, the root sense: "a noxious fart"; because early black powder was not only noisy but stank when exploded.]

hoist on one's own petard 1. To be blown up by one's own explosive charge. 2. *Ext.* To be done in by one's own trickery. [A Shakespearean coinage, *Hamlet,* III. iv: "For 'tis the sport to have the engineer/Hoist with his own petard."]

peter [Gk. **petros,* L. *petra,* rock, stone. So in Petra, a city in what is now Jordan, celebrated by John William Burgon, XIX Brit. poet (with ref. to the red sandstone of which it is built): "A rose-red city half as old as time." So in the given name *Peter,* rock.] 1. *Common slang since mid XIX. Am. only.* The penis. [Prob. on the principle of a male name for a male member, as in Am. *dick,* Brit. *John Thomas.* (*Peter* has also been a jack-of-all-trades term in Australian slang.] 2. *Crim. slang.* A safe. So since early XIX. But in XVII–XVIII (prob. from resemblance to a slab of rock) a piece of luggage (which, strapped to coaches and carriages, was a common plunder for thieves called "peter claimers"). Now rare, but *peterman, peteman* for "safecracker" was in Am. crim. use till c. WWII, with specific ref. to one who blows up a safe with nitroglycerine. *Lingo* distinguishes between *peteman* and *ripper,* one who cuts open a safe with drills and/or acetylene.

sneaky Pete *Skid Row slang.* 1. *Now.* Any of the cheap alcoholic liquors put down by derelict alcoholics. 2. *Earlier.* Any liquid containing alcohol in whiskey-like amounts, including the juice squeezed from Sterno, denatured alcohol, lemon extract, bar slops, or any mixture of such with which a dedicated alcoholic derelict can hasten his suicide. [Prob. < *peterman, peteman,* with ref. to the nitroglycerine soup with which he blows safes.]

peter out 1. To diminish gradually to nothing. 2. *Ext.* To run out of energy. *He started strong but petered out in the sixth inning.* [Originated in mid XIX Am. mining, passing immediately into Brit. use. First, with ref. to mineral veins, esp. of gold or silver, in hard rock, the vein said to *peter out,* the sense of which might well have been "to go back to rock." But it can with equal force be argued to derive from Fr. *péter,* to fizzle out, to fart < L. *pēdere,* to fart. (See *petard.*) *Isaac Asimov did well enough in his first 200 books but began to peter out by the 500th.*

Peter's pence An annual collection taken up around the world by Roman Catholics toward defraying the expenses of Vatican administration. [In England until Henry VIII broke with Rome, every household was taxed one penny for this purpose. *Peter*, the first pope, was a symbol of the Holy See.]

Peter Principle The principle of corporate organization whereby every man who does well in one capacity is promoted to another until he is frozen into the structure at his highest level of incompetence. [From the book *The Peter Principle*, 1969, by Dr. Lawrence C. Peter and Raymond Hull.]

rob Peter to pay Paul To take from one's right pocket to put into one's left; as in borrowing from rent money to pay the grocer, or in juggling funds from one department to another within the same firm. [Sts. Peter and Paul being equal symbols of the R.C. Church.]

blue peter Maritime. A signal flag, a white square on a blue ground, advising that the ship is about to leave port. A call to all passengers and crew still ashore, and a notice to all who have business with the ship to present their claims, speed deliveries, etc. [A separate evolution. *Blue* for the color of the flag's ground. Peter < Fr. *partir*, to depart, to leave.] So **time to hoist the blue peter** Time to leave.

petrel *Procellaria pelagica.* A small deep-sea bird usu. observed in flocks, the flight of which resembles that of swallows. **stormy petrel** A petrel, esp. one of a dense flock that flies so close to the surface of the sea that it seems (with its legs dangling) to be walking on it. [At such times called *stormy* because it was sailors' superstition (or close observation) that this behavior of petrels was a warning of an approaching storm. The present word form is attested 1703; earlier *pittrel*, which is prob. < It. *Petrello*, Little Peter, a name given to the bird after St. Peter, who, in imitation of Christ, is said to have walked on the water of Lake Gennesareth, also known as the Sea of Galilee. Also called *Mother Carey's chickens* (which see) because this warning flight of the petrel was said to be sent to sailors by the Virgin Mary, as Our Lady of the Seas (in L. *mater cara*, dear mother; and corrupted to Mother Carey).]

Philadelphia lawyer A legal trickster specializing in loopholes and fat fees.

HISTORIC. The original Philadelphia lawyer, a man maligned by the language, was Andrew Hamilton (born Scotland, date of birth unknown, brought to America at an early age, died 1751 in his seventies).

In 1743 John Peter Zenger (1697–1746), a printer of the NYC *Weekly Journal*, was charged with libel not for writing but for printing articles that exposed the corruption of the colonial governor. The charge was probably brought against Zenger instead of against the writer because Zenger's print shop could be attached for damages, whereas the writer probably owned no more than his quill and inkwell.

British law did not recognize truth as a defense in an action for libel. "The greater the truth," one jurist had declared, "the greater the libel." It seemed certain that Zenger would be found guilty and assessed a fine that would ruin him.

Then Andrew Hamilton of Philadelphia came out of retirement to defend Zenger, and argued so eloquently for freedom of the press that Zenger was acquitted, that finding establishing a precedent in American law, and causing a sensation in the colonies, in which it was commonly said, "If you are innocent, trust in God; if you are guilty, get a Philadelphia lawyer."

In repetitions of the story, Hamilton's coup turned out to be a triumph of legal trickery, whence the present sense of the idiom, which certainly libels a distinguished American, for Hamilton not only defended Zenger on principle and without fee, but even paid his own expenses for travel and for housing himself in NYC.

Phoebe Snow   *Railroading*. A girl dressed in white (Snow) as an advertising symbol of the Lackawanna Railroad, whose freight trains still bear the legend "Lackawanna—The Route of Phoebe Snow," leading many to suppose she was a historic personage. [She was, in fact, invented c. 1920 by the road's advertising department, her white dress and her name symbolizing cleanliness. The Lackawanna also called itself "The Road of Anthracite," because until WWI, when U.S. railroads were federalized for the duration, the Lackawanna burned only anthracite, thus eliminating the gritty soot of soft coal smoke which not only rained upon the cars but soon permeated all the upholstery. The Lackawanna's original conception of the spotless white Miss Snow was based on the nursery rhyme: "Here is the maiden all forlorn/Who milked the cow with the crumpled horn"; whence a series of such advertising jingles as.

> Says Phoebe Snow
> About to go
> Upon a trip
> To Buffalo,
> "My gown stays white
> From morn till night
> Upon the Road of Anthracite.

(These data from *Railroad* by James A McPherson and Miller Williams.)]

phony   *adj.* Fraudulent. Counterfeit. Sham. —*n.* A fake (thing or person). [The many ingenious folk etymologies based on *telephone* must yield to the dating, the root form *fawney* being attested 1781 (Partridge, *Slang*) with ref. to an Irish bunco scheme involving a purportedly gold ring. < Irish *fá inne*, finger ring. The swindle, called *fawney dropping* or *fawney bouncing*, prob. resembled the dropped-wallet or found-wallet pitch still worked by Am. flimflam men, and probably consisted of selling a gold ring which was switched for a brass one in the course of the swindle.]

   phonus balonus Am. *slang.* 1. A false and fraudulent person. A big-talking four-flusher. 2. His line of talk. *Here he comes now, still spouting a lot of phonus balonus.* [Arch reduplication. A mock-Latin modification of *phony* and *baloney.*]

pickle   [An eponymous word. After Wilhelm Beukelz, XIV Dutchman. *Buekel(z)*, with b/p and vowel modification → MD *pekel*, ME *pekille*, pickle. But pickled what? Though the derivation is firm, Beukelz is known only to have been a fisherman, perhaps one who pickled fish, possibly extending his pickling methods to other foods. Though his name now labels the process in Eng. and Du., pickling in vinegar, oil, brine, and various combinations of these mixtures is known to have been practiced by first-century Romans, and was probably an ancient method by then.] *n.* 1. A cucumber preserved in a variable but basically briny solution. (When other vegetables are so treated they are specified as *tomato pickles, pickled peppers, pickled corn,* etc.) 2. The preservative solution. (But more usually *pickling* or *pickling solution.*) —*v.* 1. To preserve food in this way. 2. *Ext.* To treat various metals in an acid solution. 3. To make drunk. *to pickle oneself, to pickle one's liver.* **pickled** *adj.* 1. Labels food (or metal) preserved or treated as above. 2. *Slang.* Three sheets to the wind and half seas over.

   pickle puss A sourpuss.

   pickle patch A vegetable garden. [Am. XVIII. In part a synecdoche, as if the cucumber vines were the whole garden (or allow them time, and they will be). But prob. equally because anything in the vegetable garden, excepting lettuce, was commonly pickled.]

   the pickle Baseball. The outfield. Commonly *left pickle,* left field; *right pickle,* right field; but though *center pickle,* center field, would follow logically, the form simply does not occur. [< *pickle patch.* Whimsical. A ref. to improvised playing fields, as if outfielders had to chase fly balls through a neighboring pickle patch (as must have happened often enough, the gardener berating the players as vandals). Cf. *bush league,* a playing association out in the bushes of the backwoods, and with bushes growing on the playing surface.]

you're way out in left pickle You're all wrong. You don't know what you're talking about. You're way off base. [Variant of *way out in left field,* i.e., far from home plate and the center of the action. *Right field* is as far removed but does not occur in the idiom. And certainly this fact points to a subtle survival of the ancient sense of *right* as honorable, superior, and of *left* as dishonorable, inferior.]

in a (pretty) pickle In a bad way. In a terrible mess. [Literally soaking in brine or some other pickling solution.]

HISTORIC. The ultimate sense, which the idiom softens, may be not just *in a mess* but *done in, dead.* When war leaders fell on foreign fields, it was long the custom to bury their hearts where they fell and to ship the bodies home for interment in the family plot or in some public monument. The usual way of getting the bodies home was in a barrel of pickling solution. Nelson, dying aboard his ship, was in effect in England, and his heart was not removed, but his body came home in a barrel of rum—a pretty enough pickle; nor can one suppose that the rum was improved by the association.

pidgin/Pidgin/pidgin English [*Pidgin* is a corruption of "business" as pronounced by a Chinese or other Oriental. Effective sense: "trade English."] A trader's language with multilingual roots and a standardized minimal syntax. It was developed beginning in XVI as a means of communication between European sailing men and the natives they met and dealt with.

HISTORIC. Pidgin commonly, but wrongly, is received to mean the pidgin evolved in the Far East. There are, however, many pidgins, among them the Afric pidgin of the West Africa slave trade, and its descendant, Afric-Carib-Creole pidgin. These pidgins are compounds of Portuguese, Spanish, English, and native roots. In North America the various expedients developed for powwowing and trading with various groups of Indians also qualify as pidgins. A close study of Afric-Carib-Creole is lacking and would probably shed light on many southern regionalisms.

pie (One of the highly complicated little words characteristic of English.) 1. Magpie. [In this sense already established in ME. < L. *pica.* Ult. < IE *(s)peik-,* a bird name. Magpies are two-colored, and they characteristically steal small objects which they store in a clutter. Most senses of *pie* are extensions of one or another of these characteristics.] 2. A more or less chopped mixture of fruits, meats, cheese, and vegetables baked in a shell (and usu. cover) of pastry. [Origin obscure. Perhaps because the filling is thought to resemble that clutter of small things the magpie stores. (??)] 3. *Printing.* Jumbled type. [Same as preceding.]

    piebald With ref. to a horse. Two-colored, esp. streaked or blotched or black and white or brown and white. [Norman Fr. *Pie,* two-colored; **bald,* dial. for "white face of a horse." *pieface* 1. Large, round, and flat of face. 2. A pejorative term for a person with such a face. *pie in the sky* Rewards in Heaven promised as false hopes and to turn one's attention from bad working and living conditions here on earth. [A standard term in the rhetoric of militant labor leaders since c. 1880. Prob. based on Karl Marx's "religion is the opium of the people," *opium* given an exaggerated pronunciation as *o-pie-um.*]

    pied bed A short-sheeted bed, the lower sheet folded back. The bed looks neatly made, but the pieing leaves no room for one's feet. (A dormitory joke. One must remake the bed while all fools guffaw.) [< Fr. *plier,* to fold.]

    apple pie order See *apple.*

pig *Slang. c. 1960.* A policeman. [The *1811 Dictionary of the Vulgar Tongue* defined *pig* as *a police officer.* There is nothing to connect the later term with the earlier. What we seem to have is a rare example of a bit of slang that was coined, lost, and recoined independently.]

pig Latin [Date and source unknown.] A cant form supposed, like Cockney rhyming slang, to be unintelligible to outsiders, yet practiced by children for at least 100 years, and prob. earlier. Pig Latin [mock Latin; Latin as pigs might speak it] transposes the initial consonant to the end of the word and suffixes the altered form *-ay.* "*Ixnay! opscay! is igpay atinlay for "Nix! (the) cops!*"

piker A cheapskate. [The standard sense, "one who fishes for pike," is not relevant here. Nor is the passing mid XIX form, "a westward migrant on the Great Plains," i.e., one from Pike County. (See *Betsy*—she was from Pike.) In the sense here given, MMM cites an 1898 passage: "A 'piker' is a tolerated collapse who makes a stray bet when he can borrow a 'check.'" So the first reference with the sense "cheapskate, floater," the origin uncertain. Perhaps (??) < tramp ("one who wanders down the pike").]

pilgrim [< L. *per*, through, by way of; with *agere*, to act, to go. But also influ. by *ager*, field, countryside (AGRICULTURE). Hence, "one who passes through the country(side)." It is well to remember that in Europe, and especially in Italy, well into the Renaissance, journeys through open country were journeys through robber baronies, and dangerous. Some dictionaries (e.g., NWD) give the primary meaning as "wanderer, sojourner," but if that was once the root sense, it has yielded in Am. to:] One who travels to a holy place for religious reasons, commonly in fulfillment of a vow, or in search of a faith cure. *Pilgrim* One of the religious band that settled the Massachusetts Bay Colony. *a pilgrim in this life* A pious person who moves through this life as if on a journey to a holy shrine (Heaven). And on the western frontier, *pilgrim*, originally with ref. to Texas cattle driven north to stock the ranges of the northern prairies, then applied to people newly arrived on the frontier as *greenhorns* or *tenderfeet*.

pillar to post Occurs in two distinct idioms.
   from pillar to post Here and there at random. [In this sense prob. a ref. to an old form of handball played against one wall of a courtyard. After a missed shot, the loose ball bounced about in the architecture from pillar to post.]
   be driven from pillar to post To be driven from one bad situation to another. Roughly equivalent to modern *between a rock and a hard place*. [*Pillar*, a modified form of pillory (stocks in which one stood upright with head and hands clamped in place). *Post*, whipping post. These were legal punishments for such minor offenses as swearing, brawling, drunkenness, and being adjudged a common scold (at a time when even minor theft was commonly a hanging offense). It was common for such minor offenders to be sentenced to a stated time in the pillory, followed by a turn at the whipping post to receive a stated number of lashes. Thus, his standing time served, the offender would be driven from the pillory to the post.]

pip 1. A disease of birds that causes a usually fatal crust of mucus in the mouth and throat. 2. *Loose ext.* A minor ailment. [ME pippe < Du. *pippa;* prob. < L. *pituita*, phlegm (PITUITARY), which in

Vulgar L. was prob. rendered *piptuita, pipuita, pipita.*]

   she gives me the pip She upsets me. (I can't stand her.)

   But *ain't he a pip?* (Usu. said in mockery.) Ain't he a great big something? [From *pippin,* an apple. The root sense, therefore, is: "Ain't he some special apple?"]

pipsqueak   An insignificant runt. [Echoic. In WWI, a name given to a small German shell, because it exploded with a *pip* after giving off a *squeak* in flight—or so rendered by British and American troops by comparison with the shrill whistle and boom of heavy artillery. Then, by extension, any insignificant thing; and then the original reference fading from memory. (Later in the war the name was applied to a British rifle grenade for the same echoic reasons. Early in WWII the name was revived and used to label an airborne radio transmitter whose *pip* and *squeak* signal identified an aircraft as friendly—called Identification Friend or Foe, or IFF. A later, more sophisticated IFF used in the USAAF was called bojangles.)]

piss   *n.* Urine. —*v.* To urinate. [Origin obscure but ult. echoic.]

   piss call 1. In boarding schools and camps for young boys, a common middle-of-the-night call to go to the urinals; a measure against bed-wetters. 2. In armed services, such a call jokingly made, or any middle-of-the-night summons. *Piss-Call Charley WWII.* An enemy reconnaissance plane that made night passes, usu. dropping a bomb or two; not quite a raid but enough to waken everyone.

   piss cutter Vulgar exuberant. A remarkable thing, either good or bad. [Based on an elaborate conception of a strand of female pubic hair dividing the flow of urine into two streams.]

   piss and moan To grumble and complain. To complain and do nothing about it. *All you guys do is piss and moan.* [Unattested, hence undated. Common in G.I. talk of WWII but prob. of earlier origin. A ref. to gonorrhea, which at some stages causes swelling and hypersensitivity of the penis and intense pain when urinating. So, from the bald intimacy of barracks-and-latrine life, the image of a man clutching a urinal and moaning with pain, a sufficiently apt metaphor for the G.I. condition.

   it's a pisser It is a remarkable thing. (Can imply remarkably good or remarkably bad.) [Unattested because until recently said to be "unprintable." Prob. from rough paternal pride when an infant boy, lying on his back, squirts a stream clear across the room. "Ain't he a real pisser!" says the proud father. And so *little pisser* as a term of endearment, with related forms in many languages; as in modern Gk. *skataki* (*skata,* shit; *-aki,* fond dim. suffix), little shitard, a fond term for a small child.]

pismire [ME *pissemire* < ME *pisse,* urine; *mire,* ant; prob. < Scandinavian, ult. < IE *morwi-,* ant. Because formic acid, secreted by ants, esp. in the concentrations found in an anthill, has a urinous odor.]

full of piss and vinegar *Vulgar exuberant.* Cockily peppy. [Bursting with vital juices. (*Vinegar* prob. for meanness.)]

And more or less obviously: **not worth piss** Worthless. **beat the piss out of** An intensive form of "to beat." **piss pot** 1. A chamber pot. 2. A low person conceived as being a chamber pot. **piss it away** (Said of money or opportunity.) Waste it. Squander it. **panther piss** Moonshine whiskey. **go piss in your hat** Formula of contemptuous dismissal. Also **go piss up a rope.**

plant 1. Categorically, any flora; but in common usage refers to small vegetation lacking woody stems, the loose distinctions being expressed in *plants, shrubs,* and *trees.* [The root ref. is in L. *planta,* bottom of the foot, but with an early sense ext. to "plant, vegetable growth, small flora." The associated sense implies "thing set in a hole stamped in the ground with the bottom of one's foot," but even if one takes that to mean "stamped with the heel (rather than with the whole foot)," there is neither evidence nor any likelihood that man ever farmed in this way; whereby this curious sense evolution must be taken to be a quirk of language. If the generalized root sense is taken to be "thing set in place," all senses follow.] 2. A factory. [Brit. uses *works* < Ger. *Werke. Mill* is both Am. and Brit.] 3. A confederate secretly set in place among an audience or group to encourage it to the response one wishes. 4. *Ext.* A ruse. A trap. [So a criminal suspecting treachery in the course of a robbery: *Get out—it's a plant (to trap us).*] And so all the verbal senses: **plant one's feet** To take a firm stance ("set one's feet firmly in place"). **plant an idea** ("Set the seed in place.") So **plant a (misleading) clue.** And **they planted him on Boot Hill** They buried him ("set him *very* firmly in place").

plaudits Applause. Enthusiastic approval. Praise. [Roman actors concluded their performances by asking the audience to applaud, saying *plaudite,* 2nd person plu. imperative: "(You) applaud"; much as a modern master of ceremonies says, "Let's have a big hand for the little lady." So Ben Jonson, *Every Man out of His Humour* (1599): "Beg a plaudite for God's sake." Most dictionaries assert the sing. *plaudit,* but does it occur? Oh, very well: *American history will certainly give Bob Dole a plaudit; well, half a plaudit—a one-handed clap; well, the clap.*]

Plimsoll line   One of a series of lines marked on the hull of a steam vessel to indicate the legal limits of cargo displacement under given conditions. A safety measure to prevent foundering due to overloading. [After Samuel Plimsoll, 1824–1898, British M.P. who introduced the legislation requiring such lines on the hulls of merchant vessels. As a language curiosity, *plim* in Brit. dial. means "heavy, full" (akin to *plump*) and OE *sol* means "muddy place, animal wallow," the form surviving in such Brit. place names as Solway Moss, Bradsole, and—modified to *zel*—in Grazely. The name *Plimsoll,* like an overloaded ship, has the root sense: "wallowing heavily."]

point-blank   Directly. Straight from the shoulder and without qualification. [Many sources refer this idiom to Fr. *point blanc,* the (white) bull's eye of a French target; and to *de point en blanc,* from (aiming) point to bull's-eye (without any elevation allowance for distance). This explanation would be flawless except for the fact that nothing resembling *point blanc* in this sense occurs in Fr. idiom. The sense is exactly as given—in a straight line from aiming point to target without allowances for distance, hence the extended sense: "straight from the shoulder." It is the origin that is in doubt. The ref. may be to archery (but did archery targets have a white bull's-eye? and if so, why is the idiom not recorded back to the days of Robin Hood?). It was the custom for archers to fire at animal skulls mounted on posts, and the star feat was to put the arrow through one of the eye sockets. Was that the "blank" here referred to? If so, why has no trace of it turned up in early commentary?]

poker   The card game, with its many variants, as stud, draw, seven-card stud, and many, many more. [The origin is not firmly attested, but Ger. has *pochen,* to brag; *Pochspiel,* bragging game. And Du. *pokken,* to brag, is clearly cognate; whence *pokker,* a braggart. If one may speculate an easy sense ext. from *brag* to *bluff,* one has the essence of the game; and that will have to do for placing an etymological bet, noting that it is a bet, and not a sure thing.]

    poker face Am. XIX. An expressionless face as required in playing poker. [Poker-related idioms are: *tip one's hand,* to betray one's holding and intentions by not playing the cards "close to the vest"; and *a tell,* a small habitual motion, facial twitch, or expression. Shrewd players study such *tells* (indications), which may be read to indicate a strong hand or a weak one.]

pokey/poky *Slang.* Jail. [Prob. ult. < Fr. *poche,* pocket ("small inclosure"). Cf. Brit. slang, *a pokey furnished room,* a small, drab one. And certainly influ. by *to poke along* (where is there to go?) and by *to poke* (because in the role-playing of cops and guards nothing is more common than to grasp a prisoner by the arm, or to direct him by nudging or poking with the hand or with a night stick, as part of the body language of dominant possession. So one who puts the wrong pig in his poke may be poked into the pokey by another pig and left there to poke about.]

polecat 1. A skunk. 2. A person conceived as a stinker. ["Pole" is not a slant ref. to the white stripe on a skunk's back; nor is the creature a cat, though it has been associated with the feline by superficial resemblance (as Am. *woods kitty, woods pussy);* nor is the form of Am. origin, as witness ME *polcat,* which is of uncertain origin, though the first element, *pole,* derives from OF *pole, poule,* poultry—skunks (and esp. the European polecat) being at times chicken-coop raiders. Perh. originally OF *poulchat, poule chat,* chicken cat (but no such form is attested).]

polliwog/pollywog The gilled, underwater form of an immature frog or toad. [Root sense: "head that wiggles." Earlier Eng. *Poll,* head (as in *poll tax*). The sense of *wog* is indicated by the Brit. dial. variant *pollywiggle.* Also *tadpole,* which see.]

pontifex A high priest of ancient Rome. *pontifex maximus* 1. The chief high priest of ancient Rome. 2. One of the official titles of the pope. [L. *pontus,* bridge; with bastard agential form *fex,* having the sense "bridge builder"; with *maximus,* greatest, foremost; hence, "master bridge-builder," the bridge being understood to be from this world to the next.] *pontifical* Of the priestly function. *pontificate n.* The term one serves as a priest, and especially as a bishop. —*v.* To speak with sententious self-assurance. [Like a priest.]

pooh-bah 1. A pretentiously ridiculous person. 2. A pompous but ineffective figure of public authority. *Pooh-Bah* The Lord-High-Everything-Else of W. S. Gilbert's libretto of *The Mikado,* 1885. [The name based on the two common expressives of contempt

pooh and *bah,* Gilbert being perhaps, but not certainly, the first
to combine them into a single term.]

poontang   [Sthrn < Fr. *poutaine,* whore, via Louisiana Fr. and its
corruption.] Variously, a woman as a sexual object, her cunt, the
sexual act. Spoken with a leering drawl by southerners in the army,
Ahm goin' inta town and ahm gonna git me some poooooon-tang,
it was probably the most lascivious sound I have ever heard out
of the mouth of man.]

pope's nose   In a chicken or other fowl about to be carved, the fatty
rectal bump. [Whimsical. This bump does, roughly, resemble a
flattened nose; hence, the irreverent metaphor. Variantly *parson's
nose.* This whimsicality provides the occasion for the family argument in the opening scene of James Joyce's *Portrait of the Artist
as a Young Man.*]

poppycock   Stuff and nonsense. [Root sense: "baby shit." A specimen
case of root survival in only slightly altered form. IE *pap,* baby,
is echoic of the sucking sound made by a nursing infant ("little
thing that sucks and sputters"); IE *caca-,* shit, still in Am. nursery
use < L. *cacare,* to defecate (and the same stem functions in all
Romance languages). This second element slightly modified to
cock. Aunt Jane may not realize what she is saying when she dismisses a statement as *poppycock,* but the roots would have been
clear to an Aryan of 8,000 years ago.]

posh   Swanky. Deluxe. [A direct borrowing of the form but not the
sense of Romany *posh,* half. Brit. Gypsies commonly, if warily,
worked with Brit. rogues. *Shiv,* Romany for "knife," came into
Eng. through this association. Similarly *rum go* is at root *Rom
go,* "a Gypsy thing," hence, a queer thing. Brit. rogues came to
know *posh* in such compounds as *posh-houri,* half pence, and *posh-
kooroona,* half crown, so associating it with money, and from XVII
to mid XIX *posh* meant "money" in thieves' cant, the sense then
shifting to "swank, fashionable, expensive" ("the good things
money can buy").]
    NOTE. A pervasive folk etymology renders the term as an acro-
nym of *p(ort) o(ut), s(tarboard) h(ome),* with ref. to the ideal accommodations on the passage to India by way of the Suez Canal, a
packet service provided by the Peninsula and Eastern steamship
line. The acronym is said to explain the right placement of one's
stateroom for being on the shady or the lee side of the ship. On

the east-west passage it is true, the ship being north of the sun, that the acronym will locate the shady side (though time of year will make a substantial difference). The lee side, however, is determined by the monsoon winds, and since they blow into the Asian heartland all summer and out of it all winter, only the season can determine which side will be sheltered. The earlier dating of *posh* as glossed above sufficiently refutes the ingenious (but too late) acronymic invention. And as a clincher, veterans of the Peninsula and Eastern, questioned about the term, replied that they had never heard it in the acronymic sense.

pot [At root: "what a potter makes." < Vulgar L. *pottus,* potter; of uncertain origin, perh. < a Celtic word brought home by legionnaires who had served in Britain.] 1. A large, usu. rounded container for cooking or storing food, originally made of fired clay. 2. Its contents. 3. A lot. *It will take a pot (pots) of money.* 4. *Poker.* The total amount bet on a single hand. 4. A protuberant belly. Also *potbelly.* **potbelly stove** A once common round, bulging iron stove that burned wood or coal. **go to pot** 1. In any activity, to be finished as a participant or competitor; to lose one's former ability and drive. [By analogy to an animal shot and tossed into the cooking pot.] 2. To develop a potbelly.

potash A compound of potassium. [Earlier *pot ashes,* because derived from the wood ash of cooking fires. In early Du. *potaschen,* pot ashes.]

potboiler A piece of writing, esp. a book, scribbled hastily for money on which to live. [To keep the cooking pot boiling with (understood) something in it.] *pot of gold* A folk symbol of riches, and esp. of illusory great fortune. [Said to be found at the foot of the rainbow. (Which is, of course, unreachable, its refraction moving ever farther away from an observer who approaches with the sun at his back.)] *take pot luck* In accepting an invitation to a meal, to eat whatever happens to be prepared or in preparation [i.e., in the pot.] *pot shot* 1. A hunter's shot aimed simply at providing meat (for the pot), with no thought of sportsmanship. 2. An unsporting easy chance; a cheap gesture. *take pot shots at (a person)* [From preceding.] To snipe verbally, bluntly, crudely

Brit. only. *pot* A large drinking mug. "Look into the pewter pot/ To see the world as the world's not." —A. E. Housman. *pot house* A pub. *pot valiant* Full of drunken courage that will evaporate as one sobers up. *pot* for marijuana is prob. from this sense, at root: "that which intoxicates."

put the big pot in the little pot *Mississippi Valley regional.*

To prepare food in festive overabundance. To make festive preparations for welcoming arrivals. [Root sense: "to overflow," which is what would happen if the contents of the big pot were poured into the little pot.]

potato   [< Taino (an all-but lost language of the Carib Indians) *batata,* sweet potato, yam. → Sp. *patata.*] A starchy edible tuber of the New World. (Its introduction into Europe in XVI and the rapid expansion of its cultivation in XVII provided Europe with a major new source not only of food but of alcohol. Distillation had been known since IX but was not common because small grains were needed for bread. The starchy abundance of the potato made alcohol cheap and hard liquor common for the first time. England's heavy XVIII switch to gin drinking was a gift of the potato—and concurrently rum became plentiful from West Indies sugar cane. The original *batata, patata* (yam) was believed to be an aphrodisiac.)

HISTORIC. The sudden introduction of a new common object demands a new name from our languages. One typical process is to keep the native name of the new thing, either intact or with a modification natural to each language. Portuguese kept the Taino form *batata.* Spanish modified it to *patata,* English to *potato.* Fr. evolved (and has kept) the metaphoric name *pomme de terre,* ground apple, ground fruit. In XVI, Italian evolved *tartúfollo,* which is really the name for truffle, but since truffles grow underground, the metaphoric impulse is clearly akin to that of the French form. Italian has since switched to *patata,* but German picked up the abandoned Italian form, varying it to *Kartoffel,* which is now standard. Earlier German, however, evolved *Erdapfel,* earth apple, now obs., but clearly a version of Fr. *pomme de terre.* As an example of how terms spread, note: Danish *kartoffel,* Rumanian *cartof,* Russian *kartofel,* Dutch *aardappel,* Yiddish *erdepel,* Swedish *potatis,* Norwegian *potet,* Greek *pata'ta,* and outside the Indo-European language family, Turkish *patates,* Arabic *batatis.* One may explain each term as it develops, but why it developed in that particular way in that particular language, and why a term is tried and dropped in one language only to be picked up in another, are matters for the elves of idiom.

So, for further example, the late forms: Am. *gas(oline),* Brit. *petrol,* Fr. *essence,* It. *benzina.* One of these forms or another labels the new product in most world languages. And see *orange* and its various European names, for another example of this language process.

hot potato Anything too hot to handle. *small potatoes* Labels anything as insignificant. *sweet potato* 1. An ocarina. [Physical resemblance.] 2. Term of endearment. One's honey bun. [Influ. by "sweet," one hopes, and not by direct physical resemblance. Not related to *sweet patootie*.]

potato Slang. 1. The head. [1930's.] 2. A girl. [Sweet potato.] 3. A dollar. [?] *potato trap* The mouth. [Rural dialect *tater trap*, same sense. Common in upper New England. Prob. XIX.]

potter's field A burial ground, in U.S. usu. municipally owned, for unidentified or unclaimed dead. [After Matthew 27:7, which recounts that Judas, in remorse, flung down the thirty pieces of silver; and these, gathered from the dust, were used to buy, as a burial place for the poor, a field that belonged to the potter. See also *Aceldama*.]

pound A weight of 16 ounces. Abbrev. *lb.* [The word and the distinct abbrev. derive alike from L. *libra pondo*, a scale weight. < *libra*, scale (the two-pan scale as in the zodiacal sign of Libra); *pondo*, a premeasured weight to be placed in one of the two pans (PONDEROUS, TO PONDER).]

pound sterling expressed by the sign £ The sign is an abbrev. for L. *libra*, pound. [Earlier written l̄ib̄. and overlined, as shown, in the traditional way of indicating an abbreviation. In dotting the i, hasty writers took to using a second dash rather than a dot, as if the form were written with a double overline. Later the *i* was dropped as superfluous. Then as *lb.* became the established abbrev. for pound weight, the *b* was dropped from pound sterling, the basic symbol becoming a capital *L* in cursive form, with the curiously surviving parallel line through the stem.]

powder Any dry mixture of fine solid particles. [OF & ME *poudre* < L. *pulvis*, ult. < IE *pel-*, dust.]

powder and paint Cosmetics. *keep one's powder dry* Be prepared to fight. [With ref. to muzzle-loading guns into which loose gunpowder was poured from a powder horn and tamped in. If the powder was allowed to become wet, it would not be fired by the spark of the flint.]

take a powder 1. To clear out fast. 2. *As a command.* Get out of here! Scram! [In the days before modern methods of pill-making and encapsulation, *powder* was a standard usage for "medical dosage," and medical powders were commonly folded into small paper packets to be dissolved in water or mixed with it. So *a headache powder.* The powder at the root of this idiom is a laxative, and by intention, a strong one, the root sense being a crude joke: "Take a (laxative) powder and clear (yourself) out."]

powder keg Symbol of a potentially explosive situation. *sitting on a powder keg* In a potentially explosive situation.

And as a Brit. idiom never in Am. use but notable: *pie powder court* A court formerly authorized at country fairs with authority to deal summarily with wandering vendors who attempted to cheat. [Earlier *pie poudre* < Fr. *pieds poudreux,* dusty feet (the Fr. term also means "vagabond"), hence, "dusty-foot court."]

prairie   In Am. the term is specific to the open grazing lands of the middle continent, over which the bison once grazed. [Ult. < L. **pratum,* grazing land, but into Am. via early French explorers < Fr. *prairie,* meadow land, *pré,* meadow, open field.]

prairie chicken Either of two wild birds resembling both a grouse and a pheasant. *prairie dog* A rodent that tends to form a prairie community of burrows. *prairie oyster Whimsical.* Testicle of a yearling calf gelded to make it a steer. (At the time of the gelding, westerners commonly feasted on these "oysters," which, if one puts aside the squeamishness associated with sex organs, rank just behind sweetbreads as a delicacy.) *prairie schooner* [Whimsical association of its canvas cover with the canvas sails of a schooner.] One of the heavy horse-drawn, usu. Conestoga wagons that crossed the prairie in the great post–Civil War westward migration. *Prairie State* The officially adopted nickname of Illinois.

precocious   Premature, prematurely developed. "precocious Figgs" (early-ripening figs). —Sir Thomas Browne, *Religio Medici* (XVII). [Root sense: "cooked (to cook) before ripening." < L. *praecos,* with effective sense: "premature," lit. "cooked before its time"; < *prae,* before; *coquere,* to cook. (Note that such a compound could readily have the supermarket sense "precooked." As one of the mercies of the classical ages, however, that concept of "just heat and serve" had not yet sullied the human gullet.)]

prehistoric   Before recorded history. [The word offers no etymological problems, but must be noted for the astonishing fact (and yet not so astonishing on reflection) that the OED's first attestation is from the title of Sir Daniel Wilson's *The Archaeology and Prehistoric Annals of Scotland,* published 1851!]

HISTORIC. Though the idea this word labels is now taken for granted, it is well to remember that many of today's commonplace assumptions were yesterday's intellectual battlefields. The Scopes trial, for instance, whose central issue was the legal right to teach evolution in the schools of Tennessee, was a passionate issue within living memory, the trial having taken place in 1925. Similar passions were aroused in England in mid XIX by the idea "prehistoric." England was still a nation of Biblical fundamentalists. The Creation (which scholars had even dated as having occurred circa 6000 B.C.) was Biblically recorded, and how could anything have happened before there was a world for it to happen in? The idea, had it occurred at all, would have been dismissed as absurd. When, therefore, early studies of geology, archaeology, and evolution (such as Wilson's) offered this new concept seriously, it was passionately denounced, not only as an absurdity, but as a dangerous assault upon established religion.

preposterous Ridiculous. Absurd. [Root sense: "back frontward; cart before the horse." < L. *praeposterus,* lit. "before-behind"; < *prae,* before; *posterus,* coming after (POSTERITY). (Every parent understands the etymological connection between posterity and the preposterous.)]

pretty [OE *praettig,* cunning, crafty, wily, ingeniously contrived. With regular shift of OE terminal *-ig* to *-y* → modern *pretty.* Ult. from obscure Gmnc. root, perh. (?) akin to L. *praetus,* ready; with sense shift to "enticingly prepared for use." Since which the sense has developed in many different directions:] 1. Attractive to the eye (but always superficially: by definition, the pretty is never the beautiful). 2. *Ironic.* Messy. *a pretty kettle of fish, a pretty pickle.* 3. Very much. *a pretty penny* A substantial sum. [Root image: attractive sight of mounds of coins (pennies).] —*adv.* Moderately well. Satisfactory if not ultimately good. *We had a pretty good time. pretty up* To make superficially attractive. Also *prettify* But in this form always connotes disparagement. *sitting pretty* Well situated and provided.

pretzel A glazed biscuit in the form of a stick or twist and with coarse salt embedded in the glaze; a standard bar item for beer drinkers. [Ult. < L. *bracchium,* arm. Prob. via Medieval L. dim. form *bracchiatelle,* little arms, because the shape of the love-knot twist roughly suggests little folded arms. Borrowed into Old Ger. as *bretzitella,* whence Ger. *Brezel, Pretzel.* An etymological legend, common but unattested, has it that monk bakers first rolled leftover dough in this way and salted and baked it as little prizes for boys who had done well in their day's lessons. The legend is almost certainly a folk etymology designed to support a mistaken derivation from L. *pretium,* prize.] *beer and pretzels* A combination (with the same force as Brit. *beer and skittles, cakes and ale*) taken to symbolize the good life among those who do not know how to order from a menu.

prevaricate   To lie. [But the root sense is: "to wander around; to evade the truth." Owen Barfield, *History in English Words,* renders the root sense as "to plough in crooked lines," and a lovely root image that would be if true, but this rendering must be noted as one of Barfield's very rare errors, probably by confusion with *delirious,* which see. The IE root is *wa-,* bent apart, which with simple w/v → L. *varus,* bent (VARIATION, VARICOSE) → *varicari,* to walk crookedly ("in a bent way"); *varicare,* to straddle, prefixed *prae-,* beyond. The root sense, therefore, though it can be associated with plowing, is "to walk in a crooked, knock-kneed, straddling way."]

primrose   In Am. primarily *Primula vera,* a spring-blooming garden plant, usu. yellow, though there are many hybrid varieties. In Britain, a common early wild flower.

> A primrose by a river's brim
> A yellow primrose was to him,
> And it was nothing more.
> —William Wordsworth

[The resemblance to the adj. *prim* is a language accident; and *rose,* here, is a generic term for "flower." The primrose is not a rose. < L. *prima rosa,* first flower (of spring). But though it is an early bloomer, many bulbous plants and also many violets bloom before it. Everything about this simple flower name is etymologically confused, and the term and its variants have labeled different flowers at different times: in OF the name of the hollyhock; in Old It. *primerverola* < *flor di prima vera,* flower of spring, but it is not known what flower was so labeled; in XI Eng. *pryme rolles.* And though ME had *primerose,* Chaucer used *primerole.*]
    primrose path Lit., a winding flower-bordered path through the wildwood. Symbolically, the life of easy self-indulgence; hence, to the puritanical mind, the sinful life. *take the primrose path* To lead a lazy, self-indulgent life. [As opposed to the sermonized

straight and narrow. And certainly there is a root suggestion of a country lad and a country lass wandering off into the greensward for purposes both premeditated and *ad libitum.*]

private [< L. *privatus*, of an individual; i.e., apart from the state; not a public holding. As *private property*, property not belonging to the state.] 1. The lowest rank in the army. [Which is, of course, very much "of the state," but in this sense based on a secondary connotation of *privatus*, not in (deprived of) public office (PRIVATION, DEPRIVE). All other senses in Eng. are based on the sense "personal; not public."] 2. Reserved to an individual. *private room, private parts, privy. private investigator, P.I., private eye* A detective not on a public police force. 3. Intimate; secret, not for public announcement. In old form *privy to* In on secret information. *privy counsellor* An official close to the British king. [In on state secrets.] *Privy Council* Through XVI, a British deliberative and legislative body roughly corresponding to what Am. calls the President's cabinet.

prodigy [L. *prodigium*, omen, with the root sense: "a foretelling." < *pro-*, before; *dicere*, to say.] 1. *Old sense.* An omen; an awe-inspiring occurrence. 2. Anything seemingly beyond nature, or at least beyond the norm. Most commonly in *child prodigy* A child especially gifted in certain ways (often, but not necessarily, implies an insufferable brat whose talent inhibits emotional balance).

HISTORIC. *Omen,* a sign from the gods, good or bad, evolves to *ominous,* of dark foreboding. In the same way neutral *portent* goes to darkly looming *portentous; awesome* to colloquial *awful;* and *prodigy,* a foretelling, to *prodigious,* looming darkly. So, too, *on the carpet,* under official consideration, converts to: in trouble. Language tends to convert all heavenly or official utterance into a sense unfavorable to man. Is pessimism an evolutionary adaptation? The language evidence is that man has sensed the supernatural and the official to be inimical. Perhaps because utterance from on high forebodes changes. Man, the master adapter, has always been scared silly by change. Can it be that fear is his true adaptive gift?

prodspondor An intricate but nonexistent machine or machine system. [Variant of *transpondor,* a device (the telephone, for instance) that receives energy in one form and transmits it in another. A WWII double-talk coinage by military men instructing greenhorns in more or less complicated machine systems. To relieve the boredom, some instructors prepared elaborate spoof-manuals for strange devices and systems. For reasons unknown, *prodspondor,* one fantasized name among many, took hold, and prodspondor framis-analysis became the *sine qua doodledum* of gizmotic heuristics.]

proletariat   1. *Since XIX communism.* The once oppressed working classes; by releasing their strength, energy, and native genius, communism will forge the glorious future—or break the proletariat's back trying. 2. *At origin.* A free Roman citizen of the lowest class; he was all but worthless to the state, and even a liability upon it, since work was reserved for slaves and the proletariat had to be fed and amused, but he was needed to beget children, and especially sons for the Roman legions. [Root sense: "good only at stud." < *proles,* offspring; *proletarius,* begetter of children (PROLIFIC).]

protocol   1. *The now primary meaning.* The etiquette and ceremonial order of precedence of diplomacy. 2. *The surviving but obscured root sense.* A preliminary draft, as of an international agreement, before ratification. [< Gk. *prōtokollon,* a sheet of papyrus glued to the beginning of a scroll and listing its contents. < *kollan,* to glue < *kolla,* glue (COLLAGE); prefixed *proto-,* first; the effective sense being "outline (description of contents) attached to the beginning."]

proves: the exception proves the rule   In common usage, a formula asserting the ridiculous proposition that no rule, generalization, or formulation of a scientific principle is valid until an exception to it can be found. [By mistranslation of Latin *exceptio probat regum,* which properly rendered is "the exception probes the rule," in which "probes" should be understood as "disproves"; for if the probe reveals an exception, the rule is shown to be invalid, at least until it is restated to encompass the exceptional case. This rendering of *probat* as "proves" has a fair claim to first dishonors as the most mind-fuddling mistranslation in history.]

prude   An overly proper person; implies righteousness rather than right, the assertion rather than the possession of high moral qualities. [The evolution has been from an honorable to a pejorative sense. Archbishop Trench, the distinguished churchman and etymologist of the latter XIX, inveighed against this sense shift as an act of cynicism. The form is based on L. *prodesse,* to be good;

which is L. *esse,* to be, with the stem *prod-, prud-,* of high merit
(PROUD, PRUDENT). Into XVIII Eng. < Fr. *prudefemme,* fine, honorable, virtuous woman (as if **pru de femme,* fine thing of a woman,
fine specimen of a woman). By association with *prudhomme,* good
man and true. And *Prudhomme* is a common French surname.
So the sense shift has been from "high moral quality" to "the
sham of moral pretension," whence the archbishop's clerical indig-
nation.]

psyche   Non-somatic being. What "soul" was before Tillich checked
the census and found that God had died. [In Greek myth *Psyche*
was the nymph who represented the soul, i.e., an immortal essence
of each person's identity.] *psychology* 1. The science that studies
the emotional, motivational, and cognitive elements of one's existence. 2. *In loose but persistent usage.* The ability to sense a person's
inclinations and to direct them. *A good salesman has to use a
lot of psychology. psycho Slang.* 1. A psychotic personality (one
who cannot distinguish between fantasy and "reality"). 2. *Loosely.*
A neurotic or eccentric person (one who can distinguish but who
is uneasy about the difference). *psych out* To use ploys that put
an opponent at a psychological disadvantage. *psych oneself up*
To work oneself up to a confident enthusiasm in expectation of
victory. *psychological hazard* An obstacle of no real consequence
that nevertheless causes emotional tension and consequently impaired performance, as, in golf, a small pond just in front of the
tee. *Marriage, as I explained to the former Miss Hostetter, does
not preclude love, but imposes a psychological hazard upon it.*

Pudding and Tame   From the common mocking child's rhyme:

> What's my name?
> Pudding and Tame.
> Ask me again and I'll tell you the same.

[The XVI work called *Popish Impostures* lists the names of various
fiends, among them Pudding of Tame. Both *Pudding* and *Tame*
remain unexplained, but the total follows the common formula
(cf. *Flibbertigibbet*) of giving a grotesque name to a grotesque
creature. The rhyme, however, is Am. and prob. originated in
early Maryland (in which R.C. colony *Popish Impostures,* an attack
on Roman Catholicism, may have been given particular scrutiny).]

pumpernickel   German dark, sour rye bread. [Ger. *pumpern,* to fart;
Nickel, devil (OLD NICK). Because this bread is coarse (sometimes

wonderfully so) but was said to be so hard to digest that it would make the devil fart. (The story that Napoleon, retreating from Moscow on his horse Nichol, fed it this bread, calling it *pommes pour Nichol,* apples for Nicholas, is not an etymology but a strained joke.)]

pumpkin   1. The vine. 2. The fruit. 3. The color, various shades of bright orange. [The word is not, as often supposed, of Amerind origin, though some species of pumpkin are indigenous to the New World. < IE *pekw-, peku-,* to cook, and so Gk. *peptein,* to cook, but also *pepon,* melon. L. *pepo,* a sort of squash (thing to be cooked). OF *popon,* nasalized pompon. In XVII *pumpion.* Then terminal *-ion* altered to *kin,* dim. suffix, for no apparent reason, the pumpkin being generally the largest vegetable in any garden.] *pumpkin head* A dolt. [Originally a taunting early colonial reference to the Massachusetts Bay Puritans, of whom it was said that they had their hair cut as if half a pumpkin had been jammed onto their heads, the hair being cut along the bottom edge. They probably did, in fact, use a bowl in this way.]

   some pumpkins Something special. *She thinks she's some pumpkins:* She has a high opinion of herself. [Always in plu. form. Prob. because farmers on harvesting their pumpkins proudly displayed the largest on their porch or at fairs, and those with especially large ones were said to "have some pumpkins."]

punch-drunk   Dazed, incoherent, clumsy. [Commonly said of prize fighters who have lost too many fights, the condition being usually attributed to repeated heavy blows to the head with resultant damage to small blood vessels and causing small cerebral clots and impaired flow of oxygen to the brain. Hemingway, however, in *Death in the Afternoon,* insists that the condition is due to advanced syphilis: "Boxers, bull fighters, and soldiers contract syphilis for the same reasons that make them choose their professions. In boxing most sudden reversals of form, the majority of cases of 'walking on the heels,' are products of syphilis. You cannot name the individuals in a book because it is libelous, but anyone of the profession will tell you of a dozen recent cases."]

pupa   Plu. *pupae/pupas* In the life cycle of most insects, the intermediate stage between larva and adult. [Commonly spent in a cocoon, in which it is conceived as being swathed like a baby, and it was this imagined resemblance to a swathed baby that moved the naturalist Linnaeus, in 1758, so to name this stage of insect development < L. *pupus,* boy, *pupa,* girl, baby, doll. So It. *pupa,* doll; OF *poupee,* doll (PUPPY). Ult. < IE *pap-,* baby (an echoic stem based on the sound made by a suckling infant (PAP, PABULUM, PUPIL, PUPPET). And see *poppycock.*]

pusillanimous   Meager. Puny. Cowardly. *Isaac Asimov is a pusillanimous figment of his former imagination of the man he never was.* [Root sense: "having the soul of a mere boy (not that of a man)." A Latin portmanteau word < *pusillus,* weak, meager < *pusus,* boy conceived as an unformed being (in army parlance, "here's where we separate the men from the boys"); with *animus,* virile impulse (masc. of fem. *anima,* soul).]

python   A large nonvenomous snake that crushes its prey to kill it, and for easier engorgement. [< Gk. *Pythō,* an early name for Delphi in Greece. There Apollo was said to have killed an enormous snake or dragon named the *Python.* Hence, *Pythiad,* the four-year period between the Delphic or Pythian games. Cf. *Olympiad.*]

Q

quack   An untrained person who claims special abilities as a healer. [Earlier a European medicine man, a wandering seller of cure-alls. Shortened from *quacksalver* < Du. *kwaksalver,* one who quacks like a duck in delivering the spiel for his "miracle" salves and ointments.]

quail¹   The small chicken-like wild bird. (The one form does for sing. and plu. Most dictionaries offer *quails* as an alternate plu., but use it in Am. and you will be taken for a foreigner.) [Ult. echoic of this bird's cry rendered as a clucky *co-a cu-la;* and so Vulgar L. *coacula,* modified to *quaille* in OF & ME.]
   ***San Quentin quail** Whimsical slang alliterative.* A girl or group of girls who are sexually available and eager but below the legal age of consent. [Because an adult male who tumbles one, though with her consent, can be charged with statutory rape and serve time in the penitentiary (San Quentin) for felonious entry. Leave them to the boys at school, gentlemen, bopping between minors being no more than an extracurricular activity.]

quail²   To cower. [L. *coagulare,* to curdle. (COAGULATE). Etymologically distinct from *quail¹,* but note the surprising accidental resemblance of *coacula* for the bird's cry, and *coagulare.*]

quaint   Engagingly unusual. [And so since XVIII. But the root sense is: "artful, skillful, clever"; the connecting sense being: "ingeniously wrought work of a knowing master hand." Ult. < L. *cognitus,* knowledgeable, p.p. of *cognōscere,* to know, to understand (the craft of). Cf. *cognoscenti,* those who know (they are becoming a quaint minority).]

Quaker   A member of *The Society of Friends,* the official name of the denomination founded in England by George Fox (1624–1691).

[Not an official designation but an accepted nickname. In mid XVII George Fox attributed the nickname to Justice Bennet, who so dubbed the Friends, he wrote, "Because I bid them Tremble at the Word of the Lord."]

Because the Friends are conscientious objectors to war, there was some minor and mildly mocking use of *Quaker* in WWI, as *Quaker bullet* A blessing. *Quaker rifle* A dummy wooden gun used in drilling recruits.

quantify   1. *Logic.* To specify a proposition as absolute or partial by prefixing or infixing it "no, all, some." The false syllogism: (1) Some dogs have spots; (2) My dog has spots; (3) Therefore my dog is some dog, is a quibbled quantification. 2. *In robotic corporatese and federalese.* To define the parameters of an operation quantity-wise to access them for the qualification prerequisite to finalization. [And what is the point of writing one's own subdictionary, if not to assert that any dean or corporate or federal cookie-pusher who lets the word *quantify* cross his lips is a personagerial humanoid who should be given social last rites with crank-case oil before he manages to have an ongoing, in-depth impact on the language ripple-effectwise.]

quarantine   A period of isolation in which a country holds arriving strangers and returning nationals when there is reason to believe they may be carrying a contagious disease. [Now a period of various length; originally forty days. < It. *quarantina,* a forty < *una quarantina di giorni.* Because forty days was held to be the incubation period for the black plague. (Astronauts returning from space have been "quarantined" for varying shorter periods of intensive medical examination, but the term used was "isolated.")]

quark   *Physics.* One of three hypothetical subatomic particles having electric charges either one-third or two-thirds those of an electron, and believed to be the basic building blocks of matter—at least until the next hypothesis. [A tribute to the literacy and whimsy of our physicists: faced with three mysterious unknowns, some physicist bethought himself of James Joyce's mysterious and untranslatable phrase from *Finnegans Wake* "three quarks for Mr. Marks."]

quarrel[1]   An angry dispute or cause for dispute. *I have no quarrel with him.* And verb forms *to quarrel, quarreling, quarreled, —* adj. *quarrelsome* Given to dispute. [Root sense: "with labored breath." IE *kwes-*, to breathe hard, to gasp → L. *queri*, to complain. OF & ME *querele*, a dispute, a complaining.] **querulous** Peevish. Given to complaining. [The form *quarrel* occurs by XVI, but *querele* remained in alternate use into XVII.]

quarrel² The short, more or less square-headed arrow of a crossbow. *buzzing flights of quarrels*. [XIII. < It. *quadrello*, little square (thing) < L. *quadrus*, square. (Also, since XV, as a term in architectue, a small square or, more commonly, diamond-shaped pane of glass in a latticework window.)]

quarry¹ A place from which building stones are obtained. [XIV *quarrer* < OF *carrière*, stonecutter < L. *quadrus*, square, *quadratarius*, worker who squares off marble.]

quarry² The object of a hunt. *Huntsman, what quarry?* [ME *quarre*, *quirre* < OF *curée*, *cuirée*, the part of the kill (the plucked guts) given to the hunters' hounds; but with the root sense: "Skinful," Fr. *cuir* being "leather." See also Eng. *cuirass*, leathern armor. Perhaps it was once huntsmen's custom to flay a slain deer on the spot, and in gutting it, to pile the entrails on the hide for the dogs to eat. One would think the hounds would eat the fresh hide along with the entrails, but Shakespeare certainly used *quarry* for "heap of guts" in *Coriolanus*, I, i:

> Would the nobility lay aside their ruth
> And let me use my sword, I'd make a quarry
> With thousands of these quartered slaves, as high
> As I could prick my lance.]

quarter *v.* To lodge. To provide with lodgings. To assign to **quarters** Lodgings. (As on a military post, or in billeting soldiers in a town.) [< L. *quadrus*, square. With special sense: "four-walled place," i.e., a room.] **give quarter** To spare the lives of captured enemies, soldiers or civilians. **no quarter** Short form of **give no quarter** To kill all who are captured. [I have seen references to an agreement (never specified) between European armies to permit the ransom of P.O.W.'s for one quarter of their annual pay. I am, however, wary of this explanation, the more so in that I cannot find any evidence to support it. I suspect, moreover, that there is an internal absurdity. Soldiers' pay was mostly loot and prize money. The whole annual pay of a common soldier or of junior officers (almost invariably the landless younger sons of the gentry) would not cover the cost of black bread and water during the arrangement of the ransom payment. Noble and wealthy captives, on the other hand, were held for ruinous ransoms. *To give quarter* is, at root, to lodge, i.e., to permit to live, if only in a jail or pen.]

HISTORIC. A black flag flown by an attacking force was the traditional "no quarter" signal. (See also *roger: Jolly Roger.*) At the Alamo (1836), the Mexican commander, Gen. Antonio Lopez de Santa Anna, signaled no quarter by having relays of musicians play a traditional "death air" over and over throughout the twelve-day siege. Jim Bowie probably died humming it.

quasi An adverbial hyphenated prefix signifying "as if but not genuine." *the quasi-literate chitchat of the media.* [< L. *quam*, as; *si*, if.]

NOTE. The German doublet *als ob*, as if, expresses not fake authenticity, but more nearly "the willing suspension of disbelief," the *as-if reality* of the esthetic experience by which we come to know Anna Karenina as if she were a historic personality, an actual unit of the population, just as she becomes a part of our emotional census.

quay (Pronounced as if *key*.) A solid embankment used as a landing and mooring place for vessels (as distinct from a wharf or pier, a structure built over and extending into the water). [Of obscure Gmnc. origin, perh. < *kag-*, fence, mound, embankment. ME *keye*, key. Akin to *key*, small island (KEY WEST). Also, but rarely, *cay* (influ. by Sp. *cayo*, key.]

queen 1. The feminine counterpart of a king. 2. In various games, a powerful but never all-powerful card or playing piece. 3. A preeminent woman, usually of less than wholly admirable achievement. *Jean Harlow was once a Hollywood sex queen. I guess Jackie O. has become queen of the jet set.* 4. *Entomology.* The high ovulator of hive or hill. 5. A homosexual, usu. the transvestite passive or feminine sex partner, but see *The Queen's Vernacular: A Gay Lexicon,* by Bruce Rodgers, in which *queen* refers to any gay person. [An up-and-down word. Ult. < IE *gwen-*, woman; which remains a neutral designation in Gk. *gynē*, woman (GYNECOLOGY). But via Gmnc. → OE *cwene*, still "woman," or "wife," but with the additional designation (from a male-dominant society) "slut, slattern." Sc. *quean, queen* has the primary sense "young woman" but also "slattern, slut." And so the survival of the pejorative senses 3 and 5, though sense 1, and its extension in 2, reach for the top of the social scale.]

queer [First attested early XVI. Prob. < Gmnc. *quer,* oblique ("not straight, not normal"). Perh. ult. < IE *ter(kw)-,* awry, twisted; whence L. *torquere,* to turn, (TORQUE, TORTURE, NASTURTIUM).] *adj.* Unusual ("twisted from the norm"). —*n.* 1. *Slang.* A homosexual. [Most recently replaced by *gay,* but speaking for the Society of Overaged Heterosexuals Who Would Yet Enjoy Gaiety, and with no particular malice toward homosexuals, I insist on resenting this usurpation of a word to which I once had full and fair right.] 2. *Crim. slang.* Counterfeit money. **shove the queer** To pass counterfeit money. —*v. Slang.* To spoil, to mar, to upset a plan. *Keep this up and you'll queer the deal.* **be queer for** *Slang.* To be abnormally attracted to. *Helen Cafferty is queer for rationality.*

quibble 1. To equivocate. 2. To obscure the issue by belaboring petty details. (See *anise and cumin.*) [Root sense: "to talk like a lawyer"— if, as is likely, derived from L. *quibis,* nominative plu. of *qui,* who, both being common terms in legal documents with the sense now expressed "party of the first part" and "party of the second (etc.) part." Hence by association with the obfuscations of legal language. Obs. Eng. *quib,* pun, was prob. based on **squib,* a brief literary lampoon.]

quick 1. Alive. *the quick and the dead.* Hence, 2. (In various exts. of the sense "not inert":) Animated, responsive, rapid. *quick-witted, quick-tempered, quicksilver, quick-step, quick-freeze.* [< IE *gwei-,* alive, to live, has produced disguised cognates, all with the same sense, in three distinct evolutions. 1. With g/k and suffixed *-k-* in Gmnc. → OE *cwic,* alive. 2. With g/b and suffixed *-yo-* → prob. intermediate form *bwei-yo-* → Gk. *bios,* life. 3. Variant *(g)wei-* suffixed *-wo-* → intermediate stem *wei-wo-,* with w/v → L. *vivere,* to live, *vita,* life.]

   to the quick In the fixed form *cut (one) to the quick* To offend (wound one's emotions) to the very core of feeling. Hamlet: "I'll observe his looks. I'll tent him to the quick." [In the root sense: "to the very core of being."]

   quicksand [Root sense: "responsive, not inert."] A pocket of sand that tends to swallow anything that falls into it. (The age-old mystery of quicksand was only recently explained and the phenomenon reproduced in the laboratory, the gist of it being that water must be rising through the sand, as from a buried spring, the upward flow tending to keep the particles spread so that they yield readily to heavy objects.]

quidnunc   A prying busybody. [L. *quidnunc*, what now?]

quilt   A bed cover made of stitched-through padding. [L. *culcita*, feather bed. OF *cuilt*, ME *quilte*. The sense shift from bed to bed cover is not securely dated but prob. occurred in OF, prob. influ. by the German style of bed-making in which the principal cover is a small sack partly filled with feathers.] **to quilt** 1. To make a quilt. 2. To pad as in quilt-making. **quilted** Padded and stitched through the padding, as in ski jackets and Chinese army cold-weather uniforms.

quinsy   A severe inflammation of the tonsils, sometimes leading to throat abscesses. The term, now rare, was in common use through Am. XIX as a general term for any sore throat. [Root sense: "what strangled the dog." < Gk. *kuon*, dog; *ankhein*, to strangle → Gk. *kunanchē*, Late L. *quinancia*, OF *quinencie*, ME *quinesye*.]

quisling   A traitor who turns against his own people to serve an occupying enemy. [After Maj. Vidkun Quisling (1887–1945), a Norwegian Nazi who served the occupying German forces as a puppet governor.]

qui vive   Alert. Especially in *on the qui vive* Watchful. On the alert. (The form "on the alert" contains a root redundancy. See *alert*.) [Fr. *qui vive*, "live who?" had the effective sense "which side are you on?" and was once the standard form of the French sentry's challenge.]
    HISTORIC. The standard acclamations of another day were *vive le roi:* (long) live the king; *vive le duc:* (long) live the duke. Assume that the king and the duke were at war, one side shouting for one, the other for the other. *Qui vive* would then have the sense: "for whom do you say *vive?*" i.e., which side do you support?

quiz   *n. School system.* A short, usu. impromptu written examination. —*v.* To interrogate. *The police quizzed the slain mobster's chauffeur.* (But the act of so interrogating is never called a "quiz.") [First attested by OED in 1782 with the sense "eccentric person." The term spread rapidly with such sense extensions as: "a hoax, a practical joke, a mockery, an oddity, to heckle." The sense "to interrogate" is Am. and not attested before 1886.
    An anecdote published in 1791 relates how a Dublin theater manager named Daly bet that he could create a new word and have it accepted. He is supposed to have won his bet by papering

Dublin overnight with posters bearing the single word QUIZ? Neat—as is most folk etymology—but the word was already in existence in 1791, and for good measure, the same story was later told of P. T. Barnum. *Quizzical,* as attested by the dating, is not the source of *quiz,* but a development from it. Some refer *quiz* to L. *quis,* who, what; but elementary Latin had been available in England since the Middle Ages, and how is one to explain *quis* → *quiz* at so late a date? As guessing games go, and the original sense of the term considered, I favor the derivation < Fr. *exquise,* an exquisite (fantastic) person; but attestation is lacking and one must conclude "origin unknown."]

quiz show A TV (or radio) show in which panelists answer questions competitively for prizes. *quiz kid* A child with a high I.Q. and a tendency to be aggressive about it. [After an early (1950's) TV quiz show with children as the panelists, and with a permanent core of bright adolescents who mugged for the camera. Dr. Joyce Brothers, who still—as of 1979—appears on TV talk shows, is a survivor of this adolescent zoo.]

quorum In committees and other bodies authorized by legal fiat or by by-laws, the minimum number that must be present (usu. a majority) in order to transact business. [L. *quorum,* of whom (genitive plu. of *qui,* whom. The effective sense is "of which number of persons." The legal form in appointing English justices of the peace, c. 1400, read: *quorum vos . . . unum esse volumus,* of which (number) we wish you to be one. Each man so appointed was then called a *quorum* ("one of whom the body was constituted"). The shift to the present sense ("minimum number of whom is required") occurred c. 1600.]

quotidian 1. The literary (fancy) word for "daily." (And as such, without pejorative connotation. But:) 2. Humdrum. Commonplace. [And sense 2 is locked in the roots. < L. *quot,* how many; *diēs,* days → *quotidiē,* every (blessed, endless, humdrum) day; *quotidiānus,* daily.]

q.v. Which see. [L. *quod vide. The indictment,* q.v., *does not refer to Nixon by name.* (q.v., normally italicized, is here in Roman type because it occurs in an already italicized passage.)]

rack and ruin 1. Total destruction. 2. *Ext.* Bankruptcy. [The earlier form, here corrupted, was *wrack and ruin,* which must dispose of the sometimes suggested *rack,* instrument of torture. *Wrack* < *wreck* with particular ref. to ship's wreckage washed ashore. < OE *wraec,* retribution, vengeance, punishment. Ult. < IE *wreg-,* to hunt down and punish. With g/k in Gmnc → the OE form (WREAK).]

radio In today's primary sense, an apparatus for receiving through the atmosphere electrically induced rays and for converting them to sound. [Earlier, as Marconi's invention (patented March 1897), *wireless telegraph.* And *wireless* is still current in Brit. for what Am. calls *radio.*

The 1925 edition of Webster's *New International Dictionary* does not list *radio* as a noun, but only as a prefix denoting "of or in connection with a radius, ray, or radiation" (as in anatomy, *radiocarpal;* in physics, *radioactive;* in technology, *radiotelegram*).]

HISTORIC. I am told that the election returns of the 1923 presidential campaign, won by Warren Gamaliel Harding, were the first to be partially broadcast. In 1927, the Hoover-Smith voting results were fully covered, but as one indication of the then scarcity of radio sets, I can attest that I was one of a crowd of about 200 who stood in the snow of election night in front of a cigar store and newsstand in Medford Square, Medford, Massachusetts, to hear the returns transmitted from the transom above the store's front door.

rag [Ult. < ON **rogg,* a tuft. So Sc. *to rag,* to winnow ("to work the tufts").] *n.* A scrap of cloth. ["Torn and ragged" (as a tuft).] *the rag content of paper.* 2. Contemptuous term for a newspaper. ["Worthless scrap."] —*v.* 1. To tease. 2. To scold. [If akin to the Sc. sense, above, the kinship is unattested. More likely from the sense "to pick at, to tear" as in reducing cloth to rags.]

ragpicker 1. A scavenger who seeks out rags to sell. 2. *Ext.* One who seeks out trash of any sort. *Hedda Hopper is Hollywood's busiest ragpicker.*

the rag game Am. c. 1900. The garment industry.

ragtag and bobble tail The rabble. Any shabby and worthless person or group. [Redupl. based on *rag* (with *tag* end) and exuberant addition.]

ragtime A heavily syncopated form of jazz. [< *ragged time.* See also *tiger: Tiger Rag.*]

have the rag on 1. To be menstruating. Hence, 2. To be in a bad humor. *The boss has the rag on this morning.*

take the rag off the bush To behave outrageously. Almost invariably in the exclam. *well, if that don't take the rag off the bush* [Sthrn. regionalism. Sometimes said to refer to spreading laundry on bushes to dry: only the meanest and lowest of thieves would steal it. But I suspect a ref. to skinny-dipping, leaving one's clothes on a bush. The one meaner and lower act of thievery would be to steal those clothes, leaving one naked and a long way from home.]

rags to riches A formula of the mid XIX Am. success story of the poor but piously avaricious young man who struggles free of economic oppression to become an economic oppressor. [Associated with Horatio Alger (1834–1899). Alger, the half-demented product of a repressive father who was a Unitarian minister and an inflexible puritan, wrote some 130 juvenile potboilers beginning in 1867, to become the most widely read author in human history. The first of them was *Ragged Dick,* on which *rags to riches* is based. All Alger's books run to the basic formula (rarely with any variation): poor boy scorned by rich boy → poor boy works and saves → rich boy plays and squanders → poor boy grows rich and happy → rich boy grows poor and miserable. I have several times seen it reported that Alger died penniless. The fact is he died affluent but psychotic and miserable, his father's inflexible discipline having forever warped his psyche.]

raining cats and dogs Raining violently. [A free-for-all idiom; where nothing is known, anything may be guessed, and everything has been. My guess, no better than another, is a reference to the cat scratch of rain on a roof or on forest vegetation and the dog roar of wind and thunder. When lightning runs more or less horizontally, as I have seen it do in Kansas, it does literally hiss. The expression has precedent in various Nordic forms.]

ramify   To make more complex. [Root sense: "to grow more branches, to branch out." < L. *ramus,* branch. Ult. < IE *(we)rad-,* which combines the senses "root" and "branch." Thus L. *radix,* root. The stem suffixed *-m-* in Italic → *rad-m-,* and with *d* suppressed by *m* → L. *ramus.*]

NOTE. Richard Wilbur, in a small nature poem dedicated to Robert Frost, "Seed Leaves," describes a plant shoot so new as to lack definition. A stem and two leaf buds, it could yet become anything from an herb to a tree. The poem concludes:

> Then reaches for the sky
> And starts to ramify.

The sweet counterpoint of the root sense "branched" and the evolved sense "complexity" is a striking instance of language used at something like its whole depth. Few readers are prepared to respond to language so precisely used, largely because language study has all but disappeared from the schools. Almost any college graduate of c. 1900 would have recognized *ramus* at the root of "ramify." Very few of today's graduates will recognize it. One purpose of this browser's dictionary is to reawaken this too long lost sense of the roots of language. (See also the note following *influence.*)

rampage   (Accent on first syllable.) A fit of destructive anger. *go on a rampage* To fly into a frenzy of destruction. [< Sc. *ramp,* to rear up, originally with ref. to a terrified horse. *Rampage* can imply bloodshed but is more specific to destruction (as a horse kicking at its stall or carriage may kill but its primary concern is to batter its way out of confinement). It is akin to *run amuck* and *go berserk,* but these latter two idioms primarily imply carnage rather than destruction of property.]

ranahan/rannie   A ranch hand, a cowboy. [Though a common term, it has been curiously omitted from most dictionaries. I have, in fact, found it listed only in Berry and Van Den Bark's *An American Thesaurus of Slang.* Origin unattested, but the variant form there listed, *ranchan,* suggests that the term is a corruption of *rancher's hand,* ranch hand.]

ranch   Once implied an acreage on the scale of open range, and specific to the grazing of cattle. Has now become a western synonym for farm or orchard, as *chicken ranch, walnut ranch.* [< Sp. *rancho,* a large southwestern landholding for cattle grazing. But with the root sense: "a row (of outbuildings)."] *dude ranch* A horse ranch converted into a vacation activity for paying guests. [*Dude* for "dressed up," i.e., nonworking, person.]

NOTE. The root *ranch* branches in surprising ways. Sp. *rancho*, Am. *ranch*, as above, "a row, a rank (of outbuildings)." Or alternatively, "an ar(range)ment." The variant stems *ranch-, rank-, rang-* imply "in straight rows," but are akin to OHG **hring*, ring, tier, a circular arrangement. The French, being generally unable to pronounce Gmnc. *hr*, alter it to *har-*, whence *harangue*, a long, loud, characteristically repetitive speech. Which in turn is cognate with It. **aringo*, a ring in which show horses perform or are exercised (going round and round, as does a harangue).

rap 1. In early XVIII Ireland a counterfeit half farthing or halfpenny. [Jonathan Swift noted in 1727 that raps were becoming more and more common, but that small coins were so scarce that even these counterfeits were accepted. (They were finally proscribed by a proclamation read and posted May 5, 1737.)] 2. *Ext.* Any worthless thing. *not worth a rap* Worthless. *not care a rap* Not care at all. [In later XVIII *rap* had some adjectival currency with the sense "counterfeit"; so a *rap halfpenny*, a counterfeit halfpenny. (And certainly a counterfeit halfpenny or half farthing is about as close to zero as money can come without going out of existence.)]

NOTE. In India, the cash columns of ledgers were headed *r., a., p.* for *rupees, annas, paise,* by analogy to British ledgers headed £., *s., p.* for pounds, shillings, pence. Folk etymologies have seized upon this *r.a.p.* as the explanation of *rap*, explaining that Indian money was scorned as nearly worthless. There is, however, no trace of such a usage in British India. And there is the fact that many a British *nabob* made a huge fortune by converting these allegedly worthless r.a.p.'s into pounds, shillings, and pence.

rascal A scamp. (Certainly something less than a villain. No one, for example, has ever thought to call Hitler a rascal. And in fact the term is often used affectionately for one who has misbehaved in an endearing way.) [But at root: "one of the cruddy rabble," and specifically "one with a filthy skin disease" (a crud-scratcher), possibly with ref. to the lesions of advanced syphilis, assumed by aristocrats to be the price the rabble paid for its depraved lifestyle (but ask Henry VIII, who died of the royal form of the same crud). Ult. < IE *red-, rad-*, to scrape, scratch, gnaw → L. *radere*, with same senses; p.p. *rassus* → Provençal *rasca*, rash, crud → ME *rascaille*, the cruddy rabble.]

razor   An instrument for shaving. [Root sense: "scraper." Ult. < IE *rad-*, to scratch, to gnaw. L. *radere*, to scrape. OF *rasor*, ME *raso(u)r*, razor.]

Occam's razor In logic, the process of cutting away all terms not essential to the argument. [Named for William of Occam, or Ockham (d. 1349), Franciscan philosopher and *Doctoris Singularis et Invincibilis* among the doctors of the Roman Catholic Church, so called in deference to his mastery of logic. Occam did not invent this principle of logical argument, but applied it with a subtlety and precision previously unknown. The principle, formally stated, is *Entia non sunt multiplicanda praeter necessitatem.* Terms (entities) should not be multiplied except from necessity. Or in short form: The least proof suffices.]

razor clam Up to c. 1935 a common (but now rare) species of clam with a straight shell about five inches long and a bit over one-half inch wide at maturity. [Because the shell resembles a pocket case for an old straight razor, or the razor itself when folded into its handle.]

red tape   The finicky and often exasperating procedures of bureaucrats in handling papers. [Because in British government offices before the development of modern filing systems and computers (and in some countries, still), presumably related documents were gathered into bundles and tied together before being placed in cubbyholes or on shelves. The British bureaucrats used red ribbon, called tape, for binding documents; hence, *red tape* as a name for the whole fussy procedure of filing, misfiling, and searching out.]

reduplication   The tendency in many languages to alter or intensify the sense of a word by repeating it with a slight alteration. So It. *così-cosà*, like this–like that, with functioning sense: "so-so." L. *nolens-volens*, willing or not. Black Am. *zoot suit.* In Yiddish, contemptuous dismissal is often expressed by reduplicating with *schm-* replacing the first consonant; and so in Am. Yiddish patois, *fancy-schmancy.* And in a wide range of Eng. forms: e.g., *double trouble, fiddle-faddle, hip-hop, hodgepodge, humdrum, roister-doister, shilly-shally, willy-nilly.*

reg-   A pervasive IE root with the senses: "straight, to move straight ahead, to lead straight" and hence, "to take the lead, to command, to rule." Whence:

1. Stem unchanged → L. *regere*, with all root senses → REGAL,

REGENCY, REGIME, REGIMEN, REGION ("area ruled"), REIGN, DIRI-
GIBLE, INCORRIGIBLE, and less obviously, SURGE (< *sub-*, under;
regere, to go forth; hence, "to come up from below").

From the p.p. *rectus* with the sense "straight" → RECTITUDE,
RECTOR, RECTUM ("where the intestines become straight"),
RECTIFY ("to set straight"), CORRECT, DIRECT, ERECT (and see
alert).

And the agential *rex,* king ("one who leads, rules") → common
male given name REX.

2. From stem *reg-,* L. *rex* → OF *roi(x),* king → ROYAL, VICEROY,
ADROIT ("according to right"), ADDRESS ("to set straight, to set
right, to direct the aim"), DRESS ("to prepare oneself in proper
order": cf. military command *right/left dress*), CORDUROY.

3. From the stem suffixed *-l-* → L. *regula,* rule ("straight piece
of wood used as a measure") → REGULAR, REGULATION, RULE (prob.
via intermediate **re(g)ule* → OF *reule,* ME *riule,* rule).

4. Stem *reg-* with g/k in Gmnc. → OE *rīce* (the *c* being a kappa),
realm → BISHOPRIC, Ger. REICH, ELDRITCH ("elf-ruled"). And with
g/h in Gmnc. and suffixed *-t-* → OE *riht,* right (RIGHT, RIGHTEOUS).

From variant IE stem *rak-* via Gmnc. → OE *racu,* rake ("thing
with straight teeth, thing that makes straight rows") (RAKE). From
the same stem nasalized in Gmnc **ranc-* → RANK ("row, tier, placement in a hierarchy"). And from the variant stem *rek-* via Gmnc.
→ OE *gerecenian* (*ge-* as collective prefix), to set things straight
(RECKON).

5. By various windings from Sanskrit variant *raj-* and into Eng.
as a gift of the British Empire: RAJAH, RANI, RYE (Romany chief,
gentleman; given some Eng. currency by the title of George Bar-
row's novel *Romany Rye*).

religion   Belief in the existence of God. (A once simple definition
now troubled by the theological announcement that God is dead.)
religious adj. Pertaining to religion. —*n. Now rare.* A person of
the cloth. *a religious (person). religiously* 1. *At root:* According
to the prescribed rules of religion. 2. *But more commonly in the
extended sense.* By undeviating habit. *He is at his desk religiously
by 7:00* A.M. [< L. *re-,* intensive and frequentive prefix; with *ligare,*
to bind. Hence, to bind oneself to a rule. And exactly so used by
Brown in the title of his *Religio Medici,* the rule that binds physi-
cians, the doctor's rules of conduct. And the earliest sense was
not "religious faith" but "the act and condition of binding oneself
to the rule of a given church order"; *a religious,* in this sense,
being a member of a church order. Archbishop Trench fixed the

original sense precisely, in 1888, in quoting a passage from a decree of the Fourth Lateran Council, 1215 (italics mine):

> . . . ne quis de cetero *novam religionem* inveniat, sed quicunque voluerit *ad religionem converti,* unam de approbatis assumat.

> . . nor, henceforth, let any *new religion* be introduced, but let whosoever wishes *to convert to a (new) religion* join one of those (already) approved.

The decree was specifically aimed at stopping the proliferation of monastic orders *(religionem),* not against "religion" as we now use the term.]

rhinoceros　Any of the several species of large, grazing pachyderms marked by one or two horns on the snout. [Root sense: "horn (on the) nose." < Gk. **rhis-,* nose (combining form *rhinos*); *keros,* horn. Gk. *rhinokerōs.*]

righteous　*Negro and (adopted) mod slang.* Powerful. Impressive. Important. Dangerous. "He has also busted some righteous criminals." —From the script of *Chips,* a TV cops-on-wheels series. ("Righteous criminals" = dangerous felons.) [Prob. originally in the religio-moral admonition to strive for the good, as in "Joshua done his righteous best." I take the sense shift from "moral power" to "power admired as an end in itself, though evil," to be characteristic of Negro militant anger. And cf. *outrageous, mother.*]

rigmarole　Long-winded gobbledygook. [XVIII Brit. A modified form of earlier *Ragman rolls,* legal documents (and their obscurantist language) on scrolls of parchment < yet earlier *Ragmane rolle,* a legal adaptation of the Flemish-French name **Ragemon le bon,* a medieval party game played with parchment scrolls containing descriptive verses, riddles, and other clues, from which the players were probably to guess identities, or relationships, or situations. the game seems to have been popular in northern France. I have been able to locate no detailed account of it, nor is one critical to the etymology, and there is the fact that descriptions of games are usually more detailed than useful, but I will yet offer to take over two days of Purgatory from the scot of any reader who can supply me with a reasonably lucid decription, or the reference to one.]

ring　Conspiratorial association. [Secret inner circle.] *ringleader* Chief conspirator. [Attested 1550.] *ringer Chiefly in horse racing.*

A look-alike superior horse entered in place of and under the name of an inferior performer, the obejct being to ride the tipped odds. [Origin in doubt. If *ring* is associated with conspiracy, as in the first two instances cited, a reasonable speculation would follow. *To ring in,* to inject an element surreptitiously, has a long slang history. The 1811 *Dictionary of the Vulgar Tongue* defines *ring the changes* as "When a person receives silver in change to shift some good shillings and put bad ones in their place. the person who gave the change is then requested to give good shillings for these bad ones." *Ring the changes* is prob. a whimsical play on bell ringing and on the ring of good silver coins when thrown on the counter, but it is also an instance of *ring* with the sense "to substitute one thing for another."] **dead ringer (for)** One who exactly resembles another. [Almost certainly from *ringer,* but in the forms *dead ringer, dead ringer for,* implies resemblance only, with no suggestion of switch-and-swindle.]

rip   1. To tear, as a piece of cloth. 2. To act speedily. [→ IE *reup-,* to snatch. With p/f in Gmnc. → OE *rēafian,* to snatch away from, as in taking loot. To tear, to snatch, to wrest away from, are all actions connoting speedy action. So *to rip along,* to speed.] **rip off** *Mod slang.* To steal.

   rip- Intensive prefix implying powerful as well as speedy action. So **rip-roaring, rip-snorter.**

ritzy   [< The Ritz, the name of a chain of luxury hotels, the first of which was established in London by César Ritz (1850–1918) of Switzerland.] Swanky. Posh. Elegant. The ultimate in chic and high living. (But so used only by those who cannot afford the Ritz and who think of it, therefore, as an upper-crust ultimate. Those who feel at home at the Ritz would think of *ritzy* as a lower-class word with connotation of "putting on the dog." **acting ritzy** Putting on elegant airs. **don't get ritzy with me** Don't affect false airs with me. **this ain't the Ritz** Said in scorn to one who objects to plain-folks accommodations.

rival   A competitor. [< L. *rivalus,* one who lives on the banks of the same river. < *rivus,* river. A word that offers a tantalizing glimpse into prehistory. Was the dispute over water rights from the very beginning? Did the *rivalus* and his ancestors live on the same side or across the river from? If across, old winding rivers regularly shift banks, altering natural boundary lines, and so one more cause of dispute.]

river: sell one (be sold) down the river   1. To put (be put) in a hopeless situation. 2. *Ext.* To betray. [XIX Am. with ref. to the practice of selling unruly (or otherwise undesirable) slaves at a reduced rate to traders who took them down the Mississippi to sell as field hands on Delta plantations, the work there being hard, the living conditions unhealthy, and the hope of escape or betterment reduced to near zero.]

Robin Hood's barn   Sherwood Forest. [XII. Folk whimsy. Because it was there he "stabled" his horses and kept his "cattle" (i.e., the deer he poached).] *go (be led) all around Robin Hood's barn* 1. To go (to be led) a fool's chase all around a thing but never to it. [For to be led *around* the forest when Robin was *in* it was to be kept away from Robin.] But now more commonly, 2. To take the long way round. *We had to go all around Robin Hood's barn to get here.* [Sense 1 is clearly the original; sense 2, an ext. by association.]

robot   1. In the theoretical science-fiction future, an electromechanical humanoid. (Simple robots are already programmed for certain mechanical tasks. Science-fiction theories foresee self-repairing robots with electronic brains capable of original thinking.) 2. A drudgingly mechanical person lacking in human nuance. *robotic* Operating within narrowly fixed mechanical limits. [< Czech *robota,* a serf, a drudge. Into English (and most major world languages) < Karel Čapek's enormously popular science-fantasy play *R.U.R.* (for "(R)ossum's (U)niversal (R)obots"), 1923, in which robots developed by a decaying human society to do its work for it destroy their creators and take over as the successor species.]

roger   1. *Roger.* A man's name 2. *Rogers.* A surname. ("Of Roger, son of Roger.") [< OHG *Hrodgar,* famous spearsman < *hrod,* renown; *gar* < *gairu,* spear.] 3. *Air Force voice code.* The letter *R,* which in Morse code signifies "received." So, in short form, a pilot replying "Roger" by voice code is saying "Your message (command) has been received." (In more recent voice code, "Affirmative.") In WWII, also: *Roger Willco* Received (your command). Will comply. 4. *Ext.* In general usage, expresses agreement, approval, affirmation. —*v. Slang, now rare.* To fuck; esp. to bugger. [I have never found this verb listed in any dictionary. It was a standard part of my adolescent back-of-the-barn New England vocabulary. I have asked numerous men of about my age if they knew "the slang verb 'to roger,' " and about one out of every four or five responded in the sense here given. My own recollection and something like a 20 percent agreement is not exactly a firm and final attestation. As some slight confirmation, Partridge, *Slang,* lists the noun form as meaning "penis" from c. 1650. As conjecture only, I ask if this sense is a survival of the root sense: "great spearsman" (sexually eager male), as expressed in today's slang by great *cocksman.*]

NOTE. While this book was in proofs I finally found an attestation in William Byrd's *Secret Diary:* "I rogered my wife."

Jolly Roger   The traditional pirate flag of the XVI–XVII Spanish Main, a black field (signifies "no quarter"), usu. with a white skull and crossbones superimposed (also meaning "no quarter"). [All dicts. gloss as origin unknown, and perhaps that must be the final gloss. If, however, slang *to roger,* to bugger, can be tolerated; *jolly* is an established Brit. intensive, and the whole idiom may jolly well mean *jolly well up yours,* a firmly piratical sentiment in both intention and tone.]

ROK   Rarely *R.O.K. In Korean War.* A South Korean soldier. [An acronym of *(R)epublic (o)f (K)orea.* Replaced the ealier, invidious *gook. Arvin* (< *(A)rmy of the (R)epublic of (V)iet (N)am)* similarly labeled the armed forces of South Viet Nam during the years of that other disaster.]

ropes: to know the ropes   To be knowledgeable and adept in any given situation. [Commonly said to be of maritime origin, with the sense: "to understand the rigging of a sailing vessel (as only a seasoned seaman could)." And this explanation seems to speak clearly for itself. But the use of *ropes* for *lines* is, to the best of my knowledge, unprecedented. Have I missed some earlier maritime form, *to know the lines?* Or is the origin lubberly and only attributed to maritime Eng.?]

rosemary   An aromatic evergreen shrub indigenous to Mediterranean Europe; used as an herb in cooking, and also as an aromatic. In the language of flowers it stands for remembrance (because evergreen and long-lasting when dried). *Rosemary* A common given name for a girl. [Based on L. *ros marinus,* dew of (from) the sea. With typical Brit. slovening of foreign words, *ros* → rose, *marinus* → Mary; whence the new sense "Mary's flower" (*rose* being earlier generic for "flower"; see *primrose*). And though the folk imagination is capable of a natural poetry, this transformation of "sea dew" into "Mary flower" or "Mary rose" is hardly an example of that imagination at the top of its bent, as in, for example, "day's eye" for *daisy*.]

roster   A list of names. *duty roster Army*. The list of officers and men available for duty, together with the duties assigned to each. [Root sense: "a gridiron," because it, like the paper on which names were listed, consisted of a series of parallel lines. Into Eng. in XVIII < Du. *roosten,* to roast; *rooster,* grill, grating, gridiron used in broiling over an open fire. (*Gridiron* for *football field is an Am. ext. The metaphoric ext.* < *grill* → lined *paper* had occurred in Du. before the word passed to Eng.)]

Rotten Row   A bridle path in London's Hyde Park. [Relevant to Am. only as an especially notable example of what happened to foreign words in Brit. before the language came to us. A corruption of Fr. *route du roi,* for the various English kings who used to ride there.]

roué   Variously, 1. A profligate scamp. 2. An unprincipled lecher who will stop at nothing. (Sense 1 is now primary in Am.) [Ult. from L. *rotare,* to turn a wheel → Fr. *rouer,* to turn a wheel, but also, to turn on the wheel, with ref. to execution by being broken on the wheel, which in XVIII France was the punishment reserved for the most heinous of criminals, these being called *roués,* those executed in this way for their crimes.]
    HISTORIC. Louis XV of France was five years old when he inherited the throne upon the death of his grandfather Louis XIV in 1715. The Duc d'Orléans (d. 1723) was appointed regent and surrounded himself with a palace guard of congenial (to him) rogues he called his *roués,* explaining that every one of them properly deserved to be broken on the wheel. The *roués* accepted the name but insisted that it described their loyalty to their great patron, every man of them being prepared to endure anything— including the wheel, if need be—in the service of the Duc.
    For a similar self-seeking redefinition on another social level, see *beat generation* and Kerouac's insistence that *beat* derived from *beatitude*. (Blessed are the phrase-makers, for they shall be called the children of Madison Avenue.)

round robin   1. *Primary sense in Am*. A tournament in which every player plays every other. 2. *Loose ext*. A letter circulated in turn throughout a group, e.g., a committee, each member passing it on, often after adding comments. 3. *Root sense, and as far as I know, now obs.* A petition signed in circular order so that no signer can be said to head the list. [*Robin* altered from earlier *riban, ribon,* ribbon; *round* refers to the circular arrangement of signatures. An idiomatic evolution by association. Ribbons and signatures are both, though in different senses, affixed to documents, and here the name of one attachment serves for the other. In mid XVI *round robin* was a derisive name, its origin unknown, but its nature evident in this OED citation from 1555: "railing . . . against the sacrament, terming it Jack of ye boxe, the sacrament of the halter, round Robin, with lyke unseemly terms." But in this sense *round robin* has dropped out of the language, and our term is from XVII nautical usage.]

HISTORIC. First organized by Henry VIII, the British Navy was a far-reaching sea power in XVII and its captains were figures of life-and-death authority. Sailors moved to present a petition of grievances did so only under unbearable conditions and in fear and trembling, arranging their signatures in circular order so that no man could be signaled out as the first to sign. The resort to such an expedient would seem to point to a practice among earlier captains of calling out the first man to sign, or the first two or three, declaring the complaint to be mutinous, and resolving it by hanging the leaders of the mutiny. Even a British captain might hesitate to hang his whole crew.

rucksack   A canvas backpack. [A direct borrowing from Ger. *Rucksack,* backpack, based on *zu(ruck),* back.]

ruction   A riot. A to-do. [Early XIX, following the Irish Insurrection of 1798; altered rendering of *insur(ruction).* Some seek to derive the form from L. *rectus,* belch (ERUCTATION), but the sense and the dating clearly favor the derivation from *insurrection.*]

rum go   (Primarily Brit. but understood in Am.) An odd event. A wry or outlandish twist to things. [*Go,* event, happening ("something going on"); *rum* altered from Romany (language of the Gypsies) *rom,* man. At root: "a Gypsy thing"; hence, "a queer thing."]

HISTORIC. The Gypsies (at first thought to be "E(gypsie)ns") seem to have appeared in England c. mid XV, and their presence is well attested by early XVI. The poverty of feudal England spawned many tramps who camped and poached along country roads, begging, swindling, and robbing, as they could; and every sort of city cutthroat and flimflam man. There soon developed a wary but active tradesmen's alliance between the Gypsies and these British rogues, and many Romany terms passed into thieves' cant, some only briefly. *Rum go,* an impure term, is one that endured. Two direct borrowings that have endured (see both) are *shiv* and *posh.*

S

sa- IE *sa-*, repletion, satiety, is the base of several clusters of English words and idioms.

One simple evolution has been from *sa-* suffixed *-d-* or *-dt-* in Gmnc. → OE *saed*, tired, weary → modern Eng. *sad*, sorrowful. In all these terms, the sense "heavy," though never primary, is always implicit. Thus IE *sa-*, replete, is "heavy with food"; OE *saed*, weary, is "heavy with fatigue"; and Eng. *sad*, sorrowful, is "heavy of heart." It was primarily in folk usage and dialect that this sense of *sad* as *heavy* was made explicit.

It is this second, folk evolution that explains the following idioms. ***fate struck him a sad blow*** Fate struck him a heavy blow. ***this bread has sad streaks in it*** This bread (because the dough was not sufficiently kneaded) has some heavy (unrisen) streaks in it. [I first heard this idiom in sthwstrn. Virginia in an area that had been heavily settled by Germans. Whatever the sequence of survival, it is clearly related to earlier British:] ***sad bread*** Unleavened bread (heavy because not lightened by rising). ***sad cake*** A cake, usu. a fruit cake, that has had rum or brandy poured over it (making it heavy). And there are two other survivals of this sense that require more detailed attention:

sad iron (Commonly in the plu. because these irons are used in pairs.) [*Sad*, heavy. Because these irons were heavier than the flat irons they replaced. Flat irons had firmly affixed handles and were square in the stern. Sad irons, aside from being heavier, had off-on handles, and tapered fore and aft like whale boats. One handle did for two sad irons. While iron A, the handle attached to it, was being used for ironing, usu. through a damp cloth, iron B, without the handle, was left on the cast-iron stove to heat. When A no longer gave a light sizzle in passing over the damp cloth, it was put back on the stove, the handle snapped off and attached to B; the ironing going forward by alternating irons in this way. Sad irons are common items at showings and sales of Am. antiques.

Sad Sack WW II. The antihero of the popular cartoon *The Sad Sack*. He was the gentle, worthless, dreamy, stupid, likable, lost G.I. soul of the yardbird forever confused by the army, who always ended up with the dirtiest jobs; Uncle Sam's pathetic born loser. [This capitalized form < earlier *sack of guts, sad (sorry) sack of guts,* a worthless, loutish, lumpish person.]

In a third evolution, IE *sa-*, suffixed *-t-* in Italic → L. *satur*, replete, whence SATE, SATIETY, SATISFACTION, SATIRE, and commonly confused with this group, though not of it, SATYR. The last two need detailed treatment.

satire Now labels any derisive writing, dramatic enactment, or oratorical lampooning, but earlier with specific connotations that can only be accounted for historically (see note). [< L. *satura* (femine plu. adjectival form), replete, heaped high; *lanx* (nominative plu.) platters. The *satura lanx* were the heaped platters of mixed fruits set forth in the early Roman Fescennine Festival.]

HISTORIC. The Fescennine Festival, a sort of bacchanalia that lasted several days, was imported from northern Italy, where it seems to have combined harvest and fertility rituals of immemorial tribal origin. The festival was marked by feasting, dancing, and above all by the fact that slaves and servants were licensed to mock their masters, who were under a taboo that prevented later retaliation.

From these taunts, jingles, and goat-footed capers developed the tradition of Roman poetic satire, a tradition of rough ridicule. Early satires were in mixed meters and these were somehow associated in the minds of the poets with the mixed fruits of the *satura lanx*. Though *satyr* (see below) is not a related word, it was taken to be, and the goatiness of the satyrs was also associated with the crudeness of early poetic satire.

In time, poetic satire became a sophisticated tradition. The taunting and reviling of the Fescennine Festival, however, passed from mockery to vilification to blasphemy (even the gods were impugned) to black-magic maledictions and the casting of spells and hexes. These offensive practices were, in time, even forbidden by law. It was probably the general distaste that led to this legislation which finally brought about the abandonment of the rite.

satyr A mythological creature of gross appetites, half man, half goat. [As noted, the word influ. early satire, but by accident, Gk.

satyros, satyr, being so much like L. *satur,* replete, as to suggest a connection. Gk. *satyros,* however, is < Illyrian *heteris or **hetis,* satyr. The similarity to L. *satur* came about because Illyrian words with initial *h* underwent a regular shift to initial *s* in passing into Gk.]

sack: give the sack   To fire, to discharge from employment. ***get the sack/be sacked*** To be fired. [In late XVIII England, esp. in textile mills, mechanics provided their own tools. Hence, to be given a sack, or to be told to get a sack, meant "gather up your tools and go."]

sacrament   A solemn church rite. [But L. *sacramentum* had a long pre-Christian history, as set forth (here, in shortest form) by Trench in a series of lectures published in 1882. 1. *In Roman law.* Money or property pledged by both parties to certain litigations, the loser of the suit forfeiting his pledge to the use of a temple (to this remote extent, the religious connotation was in the term from the start). 2. The solemn oath taken by a Roman on entering military service. (And still required by all armies.) 3. *Ext.* Any solemn oath. 4. Borrowed into the Christian vocabulary; at first specific to baptism (enrollment in the church militant), then extended to all solemn church rites.]

sacred cow   1. *Hindu religion.* The cow as a taboo animal. Its flesh may not be eaten by Hindus (see *bullet: bite the bullet* and historic note on the Sepoy Rebellion); nor may devout Hindus interfere with or confine a cow. Even when it wanders into a street market and eats the produce off the counters or out of the street peddler's basket, it must be permitted. The practice is probably a survival of some immemorial tribal totemism crossed with the belief in the reincarnation of a great soul of early times that returned as a cow. 2. *Metaphoric ext.* Any person too sacrosanct to be criticized or opposed. *Eva Perón was once Argentina's sacred cow.* (When a thing becomes so sacrosanct, it is usu. referred to as a *white elephant:* see *white.*) [India, Hinduism, and sacred cows may seem remote from western tradition. Yet through the Middle Ages the pig was held to be sacred to St. Anthony, and in Florence well into XIV, the pigs of St. Anthony (from his monastery) roamed freely, cleaning out gardens and the booths of street markets, the faithful being forbidden to interfere with them. The pig is still the standard symbol of St. Anthony, as the wheel is of Catherine (see Catherine wheel).]

St. Nicholas   See *Christmas*, historic note.

salt   [IE *sal-*, salt, unchanged → L. *sal*, salt, the L. form surviving in many Eng. words, as *salad, salami, salary*. The IE base, suffixed *-t-* in Gmnc. → OE *sealt*, ME *salt*.]

salt of the earth The best people. Specifically, the Lord's chosen; they who give God His most relish in creation. [Christ so called his disciples, Matthew 5:13.]

salt a mine To place ore in the facings of a played-out mine in order to trick a buyer into thinking the mine is rich. [In Am. c. 1880 in Colorado, the commonest method of salting was to load a muzzle-loading shotgun with gold dust and bits of nuggets, and shoot that charge into the rock faces. The form is whimsical: salting the mine makes it "tastier."]

salt away 1. *Literal.* To preserve meat by salting it. 2. *Metaphoric.* To put by (usu. money) for future use.

a salt/an old salt A sailor, an old sailor. [As if salted and preserved by the sea.]

Attic salt Classical wit. [L. *sal*, primary sense "salt," also meant "wit." *Scipio omnes sale superabit:* Scipio surpassed all others in wit.]

a covenant of salt An unbreakable and everlasting agreement. [Salt as a symbol of incorruptibility. Numbers 18:19. 2 Chronicles 13:5.]

eat a man's salt To break bread with another as his guest. [In the ethics of many societies, the act bound guest and host to eternal friendship. And see preceding entry.]

borrow salt Sthrn. (Akin to preceding.) To be offered bed and board for the traditional three days of hospitality. To expect to be offered such hospitality simply by turning up at someone's door. [Prof. Miller Williams of the Univ. of Arkansas reports his father, an Arkansas Methodist minister, as saying that he could "borrow salt" in any town in the county.]

not worth one's salt Not worth much. [At root: "not worth one's *salarium* (salt allowance)"; see *salary*, below.]

with a grain of salt In full form: *take (a thing said) with a grain of salt.* To react skeptically. To accept a statement with reservations. [Whimsical. As if, by adding a grain of salt to a statement that, like suspect meat, stinks a little high, one might just manage to swallow it. But not, as often stated, < *cum grano salis.* The Latin, rather, is an effort to appear learned by translating the Eng. phrase.]

salary A fixed stipend for work performed. (In general, white-collar workers receive an annual *salary;* laborers, a weekly wage; and professionals, a fee for specific services.) [In early Rome, soldiers and civil servants received a regular salt ration. (Salt is still a state monopoly in some European countries, as, for example, Italy.) Later an annual *salarium* (salt allowance) was paid in cash.]

   salt cellar A dish, sometimes quite an elaborate affair, placed on a table to hold salt. In addition to its utility, it was often an intricate centerpiece. (Not to be confused with the now common but much later salt shaker.) [The term, an etymological redundancy, has the sense: "a salt dish for salt." Eng. *salt;* with *cellar,* Anglicized form of Fr. *salière,* salt dish.]

   below the salt In an inferior social position. [In ancient custom, the usu. elaborate salt cellar served as the centerpiece of a lord's table, the lord sitting at its head. (I don't know this to be so, but assume that there must have been small salt dishes, prob. filled from the "cellar," else how would the lord, at some distance from the centerpiece, get his salt?) The most honored guests sat nearest the lord, "above the salt," i.e., between him and the salt. Persons of inferior position were placed on the other side of the centerpiece, and were said to be "below the salt." "Above the salt," however, never came into general usage to designate a person of high social standing.

   salad A dish of seasoned and dressed vegetables. (Later also *fruit salad,* and with various meat, fish, and seafood (and other) additions. But at root a vegetable dish. [And etymologically, based on L. *sal,* salted dish (of greens). And so:] *salad days* The days of one's crisp, green flowering. [Coined by Shakespeare, *Antony and Cleopatra,* I. v: "My salad days/ When I was green in judgment."]

Salt River   A tributary of the Ohio, rising in Kentucky. *up Salt River* Gone forever. [Am. early XIX, when river piracy was a cottage industry of the poor but provident river-rat native. The especially winding course of the Salt River made it difficult to navigate and its forested banks made it easy for pirates to ambush any pursuer. The Salt became a natural base for these river pirates, for once the rich booty of the Ohio had disappeared up Salt River, it was beyond pursuit, gone forever off the face of the earth.

   Following the Civil War, the idiom acquired a political application to candidates who had been defeated and who then disappeared from public view. This shift was perh. influ. by *up the creek,* but *up Salt River* is a separate idiom.]

Sam Hill In some such formula as *what in (the) Sam Hill are you doing?* or *do you think you're doing?* [A common XIX minced oath: *Sam Hill* for *damned hell.*]

Santa Claus See *Christmas,* historic note.

sarcasm A cutting remark. [Perh. better rendered "a fangy remark." The word has more or less gentled since its origin in Gk. *sarkazein,* to rip flesh with one's teeth, to gnaw, to bite one's own lip. *Sark-* is the Gk. stem meaning "flesh" (SARCOMA, SARCOPHAGUS).]

sarcophagus A stone coffin. [The term is rare in Am. because such coffins are now rare. It yet remains an exact label. At root: "body eater," because, as evidenced when old sarcophagi were opened, only bones were left, the flesh having been eaten away. < Gk. *sarx,* flesh; *phagein,* to eat.]

sardonic Derisive. Sarcastic. Leeringly cynical. *sardonic smile* A cynical leer. [But at root: "an anguished grimace." Gk. *Sardonios,* the island of Sardinia. On it grew a plant called by the Romans *herba Sardonia,* Sardinian herb/grass. If eaten, this plant caused muscular constrictions, including a distorted grinlike grimace of pain. In current usage the connotation of pain has disappeared along with the capital *S* of Sardinia.]

Saturday night special A cheap handgun. [So called because Saturday night in Metropolis is rush hour in the emergency wards for the victims of both street crimes and crimes of passion. (But see also *Mother: Mother's Day* for another crime-spree occasion.)]
    HISTORIC. Despite existing laws that control the importation of handguns, a quirk in the federal law permits the unlimited importation of gun parts. Anyone is free, therefore, to import all the parts for a cheap pistol, and to assemble them into whole guns, crudely made but effective enough to kill at close range, as in an argument or a stickup. Thus, within the wisdom of the law, one has a legal right to assemble any number of illegal guns that one has no legal right either to own or to sell, except in the spirit of underground, inner-city free enterprise.

sawbuck A ten-dollar bill. *double sawbuck* A twenty. [Because the X of Latin 10 looks like a sawbuck or sawhorse.]

scab 1. The crust over a healing wound. 2. A nonunion worker, esp. one who crosses picket lines to report for work. [Sense 2, though a late evolution of emergent militant labor unionism (c. 1900), is a survival of the XIII sense "skin disease," prob. by association with smallpox, eruptions caused by plague, and syphilitic skin lesions; whence, XVI, one of the rabble, loathsome person (see *rascal*). Ult. < IE *skep-, sker-*, to scratch, to cut. Via Gmnc. → OE *sceabb*, scab; and as the *c*-kappa altered toward ME → SHABBY. (Cf. MD *schabbe*, slut.)]

scaff　*n.* Food. —*v.* To eat. [< Erse & Sc. **scaff*, food.]
　　NOTE. I first heard this word in the 1930's when my brother-in-law, the late Thomas William Fennessey, a first-generation Irish-American brought up in South Boston, while strolling with me past a cafeteria, said, "Let's scaff." I assumed it to be a South Boston Irish idiom. I did not hear the term again until some twenty years later, when my NYC cabdriver, presumed to be Jewish on the basis of the name on his hack license, said, "I scaff raisins by the handful all day long." I concluded he had borrowed the form from an Irish friend. So the melting pot.

schmaltz　Sentimental trash. *adj.* **schmaltzy** Stickily sentimental. [Root sense: "rendered animal fat." < MHG *smaltz*, rendered fat (MELTS); Yiddish *schmaltz*, chicken fat (as the commonest article of the Jewish kitchen and Mama's chicken soup); the final reference being to the stereotyped Jewish Mama, and to her sentiments, views, and tastes.]

schneider/schneid　1. Primarily in gin rummy, which is usually played as a set called a *Hollywood*, consisting of three *streets* (games) of, usually, 200 points each. To schneider is to complete one or more 200-point streets before the opponent has scored a point on that street, the loser then paying double the stake. 2. Any lopsided victory in which the loser does not score. (In baseball, for instance, 1–10 is not a schneider, but 10–0 will certainly do for one—and 10–1 will not. [Ger. *Schneider*, tailor < *schneiden*, to cut. Into Am. via Yiddish. In the garment industry (the rag game), a *schneider* is the man who cuts many layers of fabric at once to size and pattern, the pieces to be sewn together for ready-to-wear clothing. Since a mistake can be costly, a *schneider* must be an expert craftsman. The sense "expert cutter" certainly functions in sense 1. In gin rummy a player may *knock the hand* under certain circumstances; i.e., lay it down and declare himself low man. If his opponent, after playing off cards on the knocker's exposed melds, then has an equal or lower count, the knocker is *cut* or *undercut* and loses the difference in count, plus 25 points, plus a box worth 25 points in the final tally, though it does not count toward the game score of 200.]

scholar   One who studies. [Nor would a modern reader sense any contradiction in "hard-working scholar"; yet the root sense is "leisure." < Gk. *skholē:* 1. leisure; 2. a work of leisure; 3. a gathering place (an informal school) where men of leisure met for discussion. So the phrase:] ***a gentleman and a scholar*** A man of leisure and of learning. [The phrase being a pure survival of the root sense.]

HISTORIC. The root sense offers a fair glimpse into one aspect of Greek society, in which the labor of slaves permitted the cultivation of philosophy and the arts by men of leisure.

scotch a rumor   To suppress a rumor; lit., to cut it off. [Not etymologically related to Scotland. < OF *escocher,* to cut, to scratch. See *hopscotch.*]

scot-free   Without payment or penalty of any sort. Usu. in the form ***get off scot-free*** [ME *scot,* tax, fine, penalty; < ON and Frankish *scot,* tax; and akin to OE *scot, sceot,* an arrow shot (SHOT). The prob. connecting sense is "thing (in OE *sceot,* an arrow; in *scot,* money) sent away from oneself." Cf. similar idiomatic force in Am. *shoot the works,* to bet the whole amount.]

Scott: great Scott!   Exclam. of surprise, astonishment. [< Ger. *grüss Gott,* praise God (a form of pious greeting: cf. Eng. *goodbye* < God be wi' ye). < Ger. *grüssen,* to greet; and in this context, to praise (to address God being to praise him). The form does not occur in Brit. It must, therefore, be assumed to be an Am. (XIX) rendering of the greetings exchanged by German immigrants, the sense being associated with the loud heartiness of the call, rather than with the sense of the original Ger. (And note the survival of the double *t* as in Ger. *Gott,* God, rather than the single *t* of Eng. Scot.)]

screw¹   *n.* 1. A conical metal fastener with a continous spiral cutting edge and a variously slotted head to accommodate a screwdriver. 2. *Nautical.* A propeller. 3. *Crim. slang.* A prison guard, jailer, turnkey. [Because it was jailers who once turned the thumbscrews in extorting confessions.] 4. A miser. *He's an old screw.* [And cf. obs. *to screw down,* to drive a mean, hard bargain; to squeeze for the last farthing.] 5. *Now rare.* A twist of tobacco, or a small quantity of loose goods contained in a twist of paper. [Based on IE *sker-, skr-*, to cut (SCAR, SCRAPE), but not with any sense of "spiral cutting edge," for the concept of the screw was unknown to ancient Aryans. Metal screws, as we know them, are a product of mid XIX technology. Even nails, it is well to remember, were rare in early America, as witness the pegged joints of colonial carpentry, and the fact that Jefferson, in building Monticello in late XVIII, had to establish his own forge-and-factory for making nails by hand.

Intermediate between the IE root and the metal fastener we call a screw is L. *scrofa,* sow ("animal that cuts—i.e., scrapes—the ground in rooting"). Whence OF *escroue;* earlier Eng. *screw,* sow. The connective to the modern metal fastener is by association with the screw tail of the sow.

Nor is the "screw of Archimedes" relevant. His device was a water pump consisting of a spiral tube wound about a crank shaft: when the crank was turned in the right direction, water rose inside the tube. Archimedes called his device *peri helion,* near helix, approximate helix. It was not called *screw of Archimedes* until XVII Brit., by which time *screw,* spiral-turned thing, had evolved from *screw,* sow.

The OED's first citation of the word is from a 1404 inventory listing: "Item 1 rabitstoke cum 2 scrwes." (For *rabitstoke* read *rabbeted stock: stock* in carpentry and mechanics, the material from which a worked piece is cut; *rabbet,* a groove.) The inventory describes a large, probably hardwood nut with two bolts. Such hardwood devices, sometimes reinforced with iron straps, were used in medieval siege machinery, and may have been known to the Romans.]

to screw To turn tight. To set firmly in place. [So Lady Macbeth: "But screw your courage to the sticking place/ And we'll not fail." Prob. a ref. to thumbscrews.]

have one's head screwed on To be sensible. [Not inclined to lose one's head, as might happen if one were:] *to have a screw loose* To be mentally unconnected. [Poor mental function follows, as in a machine that is not properly assembled.]

to screw up/to screw a thing up To make a mess of things; to get it all twisted. [And influ., of course, by *screw²*, to fuck it up.]

screwball 1. *Am. Late XIX. Baseball.* A twisting, erratic pitch, effective in deceiving batters, but hard to control. 2. *Ext.* An erratic person. A zany.

screwy Mentally twisted. [Dating uncertain, but almost certainly predates *screwball.* In common sign language, *screwy* is signaled by rotating one finger along the side of the temple.

thumbscrew An instrument of torture consisting of a box that fits over a thumb or finger, a threaded hole, and a wing bolt for turning down on the finger, the pressure gradually increased to force the victim to confess. [The first OED citation is dated 1715 and clearly specifies a metal device, establishing the fact that craftsmen were by then capable of threading relatively small nuts and bolts.]

twin screw Said of a vessel that has two propellers (and hence two drive shafts and sets of boilers). **Twin Screw U.** The United States Naval Academy at Annapolis. [Midshipmen's joke. The USNA is basically a school of naval engineering for the study of twin screws under a thumbscrew discipline by which midshipmen get double-screwed in the sense of screw². (The United States Military Academy at West Point is stodgily nicknamed The Trade School. But the Air Force Academy at Colorado Springs is more jauntily known as Sky Blue U. or Aluminum U.)]

screw² Synonymous in all contexts with *fuck,* which see. [Reticent lexicography has left this usage untreated. First listed by Capt. Francis Grose, *A Classical Dictionary of the Vulgar Tongue,* 1785, who offers for it: "to copulate," and by association with obsolete *screw,* sow, "a common prostitute." (Prob. an ancient coupling, for it is widespread in the Romance languages, as in Italian *scrova,* sow, prostitute.)

In this sexual sense, the word is traceable to L. *scrofa,* sow; the sense being reinforced by the similarity to L. *scrobis,* vulva, ditch; and again by the sow's screw tail, twisting pertly above the animal's cleft. (Cf. Yeats: "Love has pitched his mansions/ In the place of excrement.") This triple interplay underlies the English term. *Screw* is, perhaps, a slightly minced form of *fuck,* as in *If your girl asks why your fucking is all screwed up, tell her it happened in a Roman pig's ass.* (But note that the sense is identical if *fuck* and *screw* are reversed.)]

scrimmage [Earlier interchangeable with (military) skirmish, which was originally It. *scaramuccia.* Later, in Italian farce, *Scaramuccio* was a stooge who tangled with *Arlequino* (Harlequin), the straight man, and always lost to him. The Fr. form is *Scaramouche.* In Am. usage today, *scrimmage* is a word in transition.] 1. Originally (after the root sense) the head-on contact and tussle of a football play. And this sense survives in **line of scrimmage** The yard line on which opposing teams line up, from which the ball is put into play, and from which gains and losses are measured. But increasingly, 2. Specific to a football practice session in which the squad divides into two teams as if in an actual game; this sort of practice session as distinct from one in which the players simply run through the signals.

scut book   *In hospital shop talk.* The daybook in which senior doctors list "dirty work" for interns, as urinalysis, stool tests, and other disagreeable tasks that do not really advance an interne's medical education. [At root: "shit book." Prob. most immediately < Sc. *scuttal,* a pool of filthy water (urine-related at base); and *to scutter,* to make a mess of, to botch, to smear (feces-related at base). So to Eng. *scut,* the stubby erect tail of a rabbit or deer (anus-related). The *scut* root, along with *skate* in *cheapskate* and *skite* in *blatherskite,* all derive < OE *scittan,* to shit; the *c*-kappa passing intact into dialect and Sc., the *sc* altering to *sh* in ME.]

Scylla and Charybdis   (The *c* of Scylla is silent; the *ch* of Charybdis is a kappa.) In the Strait of Messina, which divides Sicily from the toe of the Italian boot, Scylla is a dangerous rock on the Italian side; Charybdis, a whirlpool on the Sicilian side. The rapid current through this strait has made the passage legendary as a peril to shipping. Hence, **between Scylla and Charybdis** Caught between two mortal perils. Between a rock and a hard place. (Many ships in seeking to avoid one peril of this passage have been lost to the other. In Greek myth both perils were personified as monsters that fed on men.)

sea cook: son of a sea cook   (Like *son of a gun* can imply either affection or rejection.) 1. A guy. In rough, male, affectionate greeting, esp. with "old," a good guy. But, 2. A mean, nasty stinker. [And *stinker* is, in the root sense: *"son of a skunk."* < Algonquinian *shekakua,* skunk. (Lit. "little mammal that pisses" < *shek-,* to piss; *akua,* small mammal.) The etymology is unattested, but the following note is as sound a conjecture as can be accommodated to the known facts.]
　　HISTORIC. Early settlers of the Atlantic coast, having regular dealings with Indians, had to develop some form of pidgin for dealing and trading, and naturally acquired a stock of Indian words, or—to be more exact—of words mangled from the Indian originals. The Indians around the Massachusetts Bay Colony used for *skunk* something approximating *s'qunk,* and this form was rendered ap-

proximately *see-konk* by the earliest settlers. Hence, *son of a see-konk,* (stinking) son of a skunk.

In time, as the Indians were pushed westward by the armed kindnesses of the white man, the younger generations lost contact with them and with their languages. My conjecture is that they heard the grandfathers say something like "son of a see-konk," and that lacking any association with "see-konk," gestalt-modified the term (see *gestalt*) to a near-familiar pattern. *Sea cock* was a standard pattern of maritime Eng., but *cock,* penis, is old slang, and this modification was prob. inhibited by Puritanism, whence the alternate modification to *sea cook,* a term that can readily imply a disreputable and cantankerous person, and yet one who does set out the food; whence the ambiguity of the evolved sense as opposed to the wholly pejorative original sense.

second [IE *sekw-*, to follow (which if pronounced phonetically is evidently the root of SEQUEL, SEQUENCE, and less evidently of SUIT, PERSECUTE, ENSUE). → L. *sequi,* to follow; *secundus,* the one after (following) the first. *Secundus* was the title of the general second in command to Scipio Africanus; and that name, surviving in It. *Secondari,* may well be the oldest traceable family name in European history, though the late John Secondari, author of *Three Coins in the Fountain,* who put by his title to become a U.S. citizen, and who was once a prominent TV newscaster, may have been the last of the line.] *adj.* Immediately after the first. —*v.* To support a motion once it has been made. —*n.* An assistant, earlier in a duel; now most commonly in prize fighting, one who aids the fighter between rounds.

section eight/Section Eight/section 8/Section 8 1. The section of U.S. Army regulations dealing with fitness for military service and with discharge for mental incompetence (if that is still possible, given the example of Army brass) and for neurotic or psychotic unfitness. 2. A discharge under the provisions of this section. 3. An erratic or crazy person. *Stay away from him—he's a section eight.*

senate An elected legislative body. In U.S.A. the final expression of the boondocks imbalance designed to destroy the theory of representative government. [Root sense: "legislative assembly of the senile." < L. *senatus,* senate < *senex,* old.]

sez A phonetic spelling of *says.* [A curious form that originated in Boston c. 1825, when the local wits made a waggish fad of "murdering" Inklish. (See note to *O.K.*) The form was carried on by writers in dialect. It appears frequently in George Ade's *Fables in Slang*. It survives mainly in the lettering of comic-strip dialogue, its function being to show that the speaker is illiterate. And to be sure, one who writes *sez* for *says* qualifies as a doubtful speller. But how, in rendering dialogue, does a phonetic spelling of a properly pronounced word indicate illiteracy? Sez who?]

shambles [Through many windings, the best root sense is: "stout-legged table on which a butcher used to display cuts of meat," or alternatively: "butcher's block." Ult. < IE *skabh-*, underpinnings, to prop, to bear the weight of; with nasalized infix *-n'* → L. *scamnum*, bench, *scamellum*, little bench (stout construction implied) → OE *scamel, scaemel*, same sense; but in ME *shamel*, a butcher's block; in XV, in plu. form ("an assemblage of butcher's blocks"), a butchershop. In XVI *shambles*, a slaughterhouse.] Always with *a*, *a shambles* (plu. form, sing. article). 1. A scene of bloody disorder. 2. *Loose ext.* Any disorder. [Strictly speaking, gore is implicit, but Am. usage systematically ignores that implication; and so *the field of Gettysburg was a shambles*, was a scene of bloody disorder, now takes rank with *Junior, your room is a shambles*, it is untidy.]

   shamble/to shamble along/shambly Forms expressing awkward, ponderous, shuffling motion. [< earlier *shamble legs*, thick legs, a ref. to the heavy underpinnings of a butcher's block.]

shank's mare   One's own legs. *go by shank's mare* To walk. [Sometimes *Shank's mare*, as if "the mare belonging to a person named Shank." The idiom is folk whimsical. The same whimsicality is at work in *Adam's ale*, for water.]

shanty   A shack, a hovel. (A *shanty* if for human habitation; a *shed*, for animals or for storage.) [Irish *sean tig (se* pronounced as *sh)*, old house (implies general disrepair); *tig* < IE *(s)teig-, (s)tig-*, sharp, pointed; with derivative senses: "stake, paling," hence, "inclosure, marked-off place" (and note that terminal *-ig* tends to evolve to *-y*, as in OE *lustig* → Eng. *lusty*). *shanty Irish Am. XIX*. Derogatory term for Irish immigrants driven by poverty to accept the most menial labor and to live in shacks. [Later, as distinct from *lace-curtain Irish* to label those who had prospered enough not only to have a house but to hang lace curtains in the windows as a mark of gentility.] ***shanty town*** A rural slum, or a huddle of improvised shacks at the edge of a city. The term is sometimes, but improperly, applied to the company-owned housing of mining towns and the like, most of which did at least have a water connection and, later, electrical connections, features not properly parts of a shanty. (See *Hooverville.*)

shavetail   *U.S. Army.* A second lieutenant. With original reference to one just out of West Point and on first duty assignment with the cavalry. [From U.S. cavalry custom of shaving the tails of untrained mules and horses as a warning to handlers that these animals were not broken to army ways and were unpredictable and potentially dangerous.]

Sheeney   A bigot's offensive term for a Jew. [The form is unattested but I will dare assert without qualification that it derives from Ger. *schön,* beautiful, which in Yiddish is rendered *shane;* with ref. to a Jewish peddler holding up some object from his pack and inviting admiration by saying, "Shane, eh?" Hence, the often used phrase adapted as a label for the user.]
    HISTORIC. To label "strange" people by a characteristic phrase is a standard language device. The French once called the English *les goddons* because British soldiers in France said *Goddamn* so often. In WWI, Fr. *les sombiches* had some currency for American soldiers who kept saying *son of a bitch.* And in Rumania up to WW II, when every traveling salesman was likely to be a German, a traveling salesman was a *wiegehts* < the repeated Ger. *wie geht's?* how goes it, their standard form of greeting. So, of a Jewish peddler, "Here comes another shane-eh," modified to *Sheeney.* Also *Sheeny.*

sheets to the wind   Now usu. ***three sheets to the wind*** Lurchingly drunk. But earlier ***two sheets*** and ***one sheet*** were in use to indicate degrees of drunkenness. And even ***four sheets*** has been attested, but *three* and *four* are lubberly extensions by those who have not sensed the seagoing precision of the idiom (see below). [In maritime Eng. *sheet,* a line from either of the two lower corners of a square sail to the spar. (The upper lashings of such a sail are not properly sheets.) When a sheet came loose, it and the sail were said to be *to the wind* (i.e., flapping, not secured). When one sheet is to the wind, one corner of the sail flaps loose, and the ship, responding badly to the helm, lurches. When the sail is two sheets to the wind, it has torn loose from the lower spar, and the lurch is increased. Since, technically, there are only two sheets, three sheets to the wind is a hyperbole, and four sheets to the wind redoubles it; which may be said to lack logic but to be, by that much, better suited to label drunkenness.]

sherry   A fortified tawny wine ranging from very dry to cream-sweet, usu. about 20 percent alcohol by volume, or 40 proof (which is about the alcoholic content of a whiskey highball). [Because the production of this originally Spanish wine centered on Jerez, Spain, earlier Xeres, called Sheres by the Moors, and *sherris* was the XV Eng. form.]

shibboleth   Now, any partisan catch phrase used for identification or in denouncing the opposition. So *to hurl one's shibboleths upon.* But originally, as used by Jephthah's men, a test word used to identify the fleeing Ephraimites. [Hebrew *shibboleth,* stream, ear of corn.]

HISTORIC. Judges 12:5–6 recounts how the Gileadites applied the test:

> And the Gileadites took the passages of Jordan before the Ephraimites; and it was so, that when those Ephraimites which were escaped said, Let me go over; that the men of Gilead said unto him, Art thou an Ephraimite? If he said, Nay;
>
> Then said they unto him, Say now Shibboleth: and he said Sibboleth: for he could not frame to pronounce it right. Then they took him, and slew him at the passages of Jordan: and there fell at that time of the Ephraimites forty and two thousand.

In just this way, during the *Sicilian Vespers* (which see) of 1282, the French were identified and put to death, the shibboleth being It. dial. *cecceri,* chick peas.

shifferrobe   I must take this word backward from Flannery O'Connor's short story "The Train": "His ma . . . had her walnut shifferrobe in there." I took it to be a regional corruption-engulfment of *chiffonier* and *wardrobe,* and had my guess confirmed by Peter Taylor, who recognized the term immediately as sthrn. regional, though I cannot find it listed in standard dictionaries. The piece is a free-standing two-door wardrobe with drawers behind one door *(chiffonier)* and a space for hanging clothes behind the other *(wardrobe).* That Flannery O'Connor's was a fairly imposing piece of furniture is attested by the fact that "his ma" paid $30 for it in days when that was a substantial sum.

shindig   Earlier, still surviving. *shindy.* A boisterous social gathering. A hoedown. (Implies drinking, shouting, and violent dancing.) [Into mid XIX Am. from Irish immigrants. Perh. based on Irish *shinty,* a violent form of field hockey. Onions, *Oxford Dict. Eng. Etymol.,* says that a common cry in the game was "Shin ye!" or "Shin t'ye!" but does not explain its meaning. A friend who "has the Gaelic" tells me they prob. mean "stay on your own side of/behind the puck (or you'll be penalized for being off side)." He himself, however, is not certain and the point remains to be clarified. Whether or not intermediately based on *shinty,* prob. ult. < Gaelic *sinteag* (in which *si* is sounded *shi*), to leap around, skip, gambol.]

Shinola   Registered trade name of a brand of shoe polish once commonly sold in cans about the size and shape of a hockey puck, but some smaller in all dimensions. *not know shit from Shinola* Be totally stupid. [c. 1900. Vulgar exuberant. If a can labeled Shinola were to be packed with shit, the contents would look like brown shoe polish, but it would take a man of less than average sensibility to shine his shoes with the stuff and not notice certain differences that would make him a standout when he showed up for the dance.]

shinplaster   Worthless paper money; originally Confederate money. [1863. With ref. to Confederate money: ". . . bills of smaller denomination being known as 'shinplasters' because a soldier once used a fistful to cover a tibia wound."—Shelby Foote, *The Civil War,* vol. II.]

shipwreck   1. The destruction of a ship. 2. A wrecked ship. [Root sense: "ship breakage." It is possible to distinguish between shipwreck (the breaking up of a ship) and foundering more or less intact as by swamping or capsizing, though once the ship is lost, one is left a distinction without a difference. Yet "breakage" is the gist of it. So OE *scipbryce,* shipbreak. So the intermediate XV form *shipbreche* (with *brech-* pronounced as in *breakfast*); labial *b* swallowed by labial *p*; then *w* inserted under influ. of *wreck,* wrack.]

shiv   Dagger. Knife. [Romany *shiv, chiv,* the form and sense unchanged. Established in thieves' cant by XVIII in Brit.]
   HISTORIC. The first Gypsies reached Britain by c. 1500. By late XVI they had formed a wary tradesmen's alliance with British rogues, a number of Romany words passing into Brit. thieves' cant, and some later into standard usage. See *rum go, posh.*

shiver   *Maritime*. To bring a vessel into the wind until the sails flap and quiver. [ME *chevelen, shiveren*, to quiver, to have one's teeth quiver as from cold. < OE *ceafl*, jaw.] **shiver my timbers!** *Exclam.* May my ship's beams and masts quiver (and break) in the howling of the storm. [Pseudo-nautical invention of Frederick Marryat in *Jacob Faithful*, 1834. Later adopted as cricket jargon: *to shiver one's wicket*, to knock over one's own wicket.]

Shock Language (A Note)   Every language sets aside certain words and expressions as taboo, not to exclude them, but the better to reserve them for situations of stress. When the hammer hits the thumb, "Tut!" is generally inadequate, but the taboo words are ready for use.

Each language ethos sets its own taboo restrictions, often in ways that may seem arbitrary. In the Catholic countries of Europe the taboo has been on blasphemy, which is simply the act of associating a sacred name or object with something low. In Italian, for example, *porca madonna*, lit. "pig of the madonna" (and with low side associations), is still a shocking blasphemy to many people. It is in this way that a Spanish mule skinner can curse for twenty minutes without repeating himself: he need only free-associate vulgarities, from the Triune top to the habits of local nuns.

The shock language of Roman Catholic England followed this tradition. Chaucer inveighed against blasphemy and profanation. Of the rioters he wrote, "Christes holie bodie they to-rente," which is to say they tore apart Christ's holy body with such (to us mild and quaint) oaths as *Zblood! Znails! Zwounds!* (His blood! His nails! His wounds!) Men should not so abandon themselves, Chaucer declares. Yet he is easy enough in his use of the basic Old English words of bodily function, now snickered at by schoolboys.

After the break with Rome, English gradually shifted from the rich resources of blasphemy and profanity, and based its taboos on references to bodily function expressed by the Old English rather than the French-Latin word. So *rectum* is acceptable in discussing medical symptoms, but *asshole* is shocking.

Aside from this difference of connotation between Norman French and Old English, however, there are only a limited number of body functions and the resources of the genitourinary and digestive systems are soon exhausted. It is for this reason that the shock language of English is so colorless by comparison to the resources of, say, Spanish, which leaves an angry man all Heaven to assault.

shoddy   *adj.* Trashy. Worthless. [But originally a noun. In early XIX
Yorkshire dial. the noun (of unknown origin) had two senses, of
which the first was prob. the earlier: 1. Inferior quarry stone. 2.
Coal with poor burning qualities. Then, during the Am. Civil War,
the term, still a noun, was applied to label the inferior clothing
supplied to Union soldiers by profiteering suppliers. And so to
the current adjectival sense.]

   HISTORIC. From *The Civil War,* vol. II, by Shelby Foote:

> *Shoddy* was . . . used to designate an inferior woolen yarn made from
> fibers taken from worn-out fabrics and reprocessed, then later as the
> name of the resultant cloth. "Poor, sleazy stuff," one of Horace Gree-
> ley's *Tribune* reporters called it, "woven open enough for sieves, and
> then filled with shearsmen's dust"; while *Harper's Weekly* referred
> to it as "a villainous compound, the refuse and sweepings of the shop,
> pounded, rolled, glued, and smoothed to the external form and gloss
> of cloth, but no more like the genuine article than the shadow is to
> the substance. . . . soldiers on the first day's march or in the earliest
> storm, found their clothes, overcoats, and blankets scattering to the
> wind in rags, or dissolving . . . under the pelting rain."

shrewd   Calculating. Cunning. Ingenious. Astute. Equipped to survive in this world. [But these senses are from XVI only. Earlier
the root sense clustered about "wicked-mean-harsh." Origin ambiguous. Perh. < *shrew,* ounce for ounce the meanest mammal
in existence, whence *shrew,* vile-tempered person (later specific
to a woman). Perh. from *beshrew thee,* damn thee. In either case,
the sense evolution from *wicked-mean-harsh* to *able to survive
in this wicked world* is from the purest folk sensibility. See *ninny.*]

shrift   Absolution granted after hearing a confession, subject usually
to penance and communion. [As verb, *shrive, shrove, shriven.* <
L. *scribere,* to write. Root sense: "to write in the book of the Lord
(or of the Recording Angel) that one's sins have been removed."]

   give one short shrift *Now.* To snub. To get rid of with the
least possible ceremony. But earlier. To perform the ritual of confession in a curtailed way.

   HISTORIC. Curtailed rites may be justified under various conditions, as for a criminal found guilty of so odious a crime that he
is held to be unworthy of full rites at his execution. Or the hearing
of the confession might be curtailed if the priest feels that a man
about to be executed is simply playing for time. Or, less directly,
a parish priest might simply cut off a loquacious penitent who is
more gabby than sinful.

But there were many other precedents for withholding full rites, as in the burial service of a person suspected of being a suicide. In *Hamlet,* Ophelia is buried with "maimèd rites" as a possible (though not absolutely proven) suicide. Persons adjudged to be contumacious (but not excommunicated) were also buried with clipped ceremony, *a lumi spenti,* with unlit tapers—i.e., in the dark of God.

shuck [Am. dialect. Prob. altered from *chuck* with sense: "thing to be chucked out."] *n.* An outer covering, as a corn husk. And as fixed idiom: ***shuck oysters*** To open oysters. [Force open (so to speak, "remove") the shells.] —*v.* To remove the outer covering or husk. ***shuck down*** *Usu. intrans.* To strip (oneself) naked. As a command: ***shuck it (off)*** Strip yourself naked.

not worth shucks Worthless. [Not worth the part to be thrown away.] ***shucks!*** Exclam. of mild vexation. [Equivalent to "rot."]

sic 'im/sic 'em Verb forms are *sic, sicced, siccing* and also *sick, sicked, sicking.* Command used in setting a dog or dogs on a person, persons, or an animal. [Now means "attack," but in the earlier form *seek him, seek them,* the command to a dog to trail a scent. Cf. *harass.*]

Sicilian Vespers A bloody uprising of the Sicilians against their French rulers on Easter Monday 1282. [So called because the prearranged signal for the slaughter was the vesper bell.]

HISTORIC. In the dynasty of the Capetian kings of France (987–1328) it became traditional to name the first son either Philippe or Louis, and to designate the next son Charles d'Anjou. A traditional prerogative of these second sons was the Kingdom of Sicily or the Kingdom of the Two Sicilies (Sicily and Naples, or in effect, everything in Italy south of the Papal States). These kingdoms were given to them less to rule than to plunder as part of their royal allowance.

The Sicilians rose against this oppression determined to kill every French man, woman, and child on Sicilian soil, the test word being It. *cecceri,* chick peas. *Di cecceri,* the Sicilians commanded all strangers—"Say 'chick peas.' " And if the pronunciation sounded foreign to the Sicilian ear, the stranger died on the spot.

See *shibboleth,* used in exactly this way by Jephthah's men when they slew the Ephraimites.

sierra   A sawtooth range of geologically new mountains. [Sp. *sierra* < L. *serra*, saw.] There are no Sierra Catskills, those mountains being old and worn down to rounded contours. The essence is expressed in Roy Campbell's "The Albatross," in which the bird, flying down a coastal range, is made to think: "The ranges moved like long two-handed saws/ Notching the scarlet west with jagged lines."

signature   One's name as subscribed to a document in one's characteristic handwriting. *legal signature* Such a subscription in the legally registered form of one's name. (Nicknames, stage names, etc., may be made legal, but the legal name usually derives from one's registered birth and marriage records. The form *T.(I.O) J.(I.O) Jones*, with *I.O.* for "Initial Only," is a legal name. The "S." of Harry S. Truman is an I.O.) [Though *signature* now denotes something like "John Hancock," the root sense, still visible in *to sign*, is: "the act of affixing one's sign." (When the signature is written apart from a document it is called an *autograph*.]
   HISTORIC. Through the Middle Ages, literacy was the almost exclusive possession of the clergy and documents were formalized by making one's sign in the presence of witnesses, usually in the form of an *X*. (See *kike*.) *X*, moreover, was a fixed symbol of Christ and of the cross. (See *Christmas*.) The act of attaching this sign, therefore, was one of solemn avowal in Christ's name. Alternatively or additionally, illiterates of high social rank solemnized documents by pressing their signet into wax dripped on the paper. This attestation by sign and seal was also used by literate officials to solemnize documents, and the practice persists in important legal documents.

signify   To indicate. *significant* Of some importance. Worth indicating. [The evolved sense is: "to indicate orally or in writing." The root sense, however, refers to signs, primarily to signs one makes oneself, as in sign language, but also referring to omens and portents. < L. *signum*, sign; *facere*, to make; whence *significare*, to make a written mark in evidence of, to attest. (And so *signature*, which see.)]

silly   *adj.* Lacking good sense. Inane. Foolish. [IE *sel-*, happy, favored by fortune. Via Gmnc. and with collective prefix *ge-→* OE *gesaelig*, happy, i.e., at root: "all happy, happy in every way" (akin to Ger. dial. *saelige*, luck. In evolving to ME *seely*, acquired the sense "blessed, elect of god, saved soul, saintly," and became common as an epithet for a saint, whence, through the intermediate sense "not really of this world," to the folk-rueful sense "too foolish for this world." And see *ninny.*] —*n.* A person who lacks good sense. *Don't be such a silly.*

    knock one silly To beat out of one's senses. *Silly Putty* Registered trade name for a silicone compound that looks like putty but acts in unpredictable ways. [As if "foolish putty."] *silly sauce/silly syrup* Any intoxicant. [Because it makes the drinker silly. *Syrup* a variation of *sauce. Sauce* for alliteration and cf. *to lap up the sauce,* to drink greedily.]

sin   A religious transgression. (In earlier societies sin and crime were the same, but by the time Jesus said "Render unto Caesar, etc." *God's law* and *man's law,* though akin, were distinct at many points.) [IE *es-,* to be. L. *esse,* to be (ESSENCE). Via Gmnc. the same root yields Eng. *yes,* with the root senses: "so, it is so, it exists." In a variant of the Gmnc. root suffixed -*n-* → *es-n-* (prob.) *(e)s'n-* → OE *synn,* sin ("thing asserted or confessed to be so").]

    HISTORIC. How ancient is the religious doctrine of inherent sinfulness, or *original sin?* The derivation of *to be* and *to sin* is certainly a clue to the workings of earliest man's mind, an etymological glimpse beyond history. Certainly, wherever there have been tribal mores (later to develop into elaborate religious systems and earlier at least partly traceable to the pack behavior of primates) there have been individuals to violate them. Rules and the concomitant breaking of rules are from the first of man's being.

sincere   Honest. Without subterfuge. [One of the most persistent of folk etymologies derives this word from L. *sine cera,* without wax; explaining that Roman stoneworkers, lacking power tools (they had in fact plenty of water-mill power, slaves, and animals), had trouble polishing marble to a mirror finish. Devious dealers, therefore, rough-polished their stones, then waxed them to make them smooth and shiny; whereas those honest merchants who had truly polished announced their product to be *sine cera.* The account is neat, and even ingenious, as with most folk etymology, but Roman builders were not fools, and any man who tried to make a living by selling them waxed marble was studying to starve.

    To return to etymology, the stem is IE *ker-,* to grow. So *Keres, Ceres,* the earth goddess, goddess of crops ("she who makes things grow"). In the zero-grade form *kr-* → L. *crescere,* to grow (CRESCENT, EXCRESCENCE); the same stem visible in Eng. *increase. Sin-* < *syn-,* the syncopated combining form of Gk. *sym,* with. Hence, "to grow together (as one thing; without adulterants)."]

sirloin   A choice cut of beef or venison from above the loin and between the rump and the porterhouse. [OF *sur*, above; *loigne*, loin. In XVI the forms were *surloyne, surloyn.*]

NOTE. As commonly claimed by folk etymologists, some drunken prince may have been so pleased by his roast that he tapped it with his sword and dubbed it Sir Loin; but if so, only after the name had evolved in OF and passed into ME. The more interesting question (to which I can find no answer) is: why did *sir name* (second name of a knight) change to *surname* (which see), while XVI *surloyn* was changing to *sirloin?* Wurds can go absird ways.

six   [< Gmnc. **seks;* OE *siex, sex, six.*] Arabic 6; Roman VI.

six of one, half a dozen of the other Said of any two things taken to be the same, or of a distinction without a difference.

at sixes and sevens Usu. defined as: In disorder. [Not arranged in neat numerical sequence but with the 6's and 7's jumbled together.] *Yet the one sense always known to me has been:* In dispute. At 'tis-'taint with one another. [As in heated argument, with one person shouting *six* and the other *seven;* or with one shouting *even* and the other *odd.*]

sixty   Six times ten. [The suffix *-ty* was *-tig* in OE and indicated "times ten," akin to Ger. *-zig;* as *dreizig*, thirty ("three times ten").]

go like sixty 1. Drive at great speed. 2. Do anything at great speed. *As usual, she was talking like sixty.* 3. To go great guns, to zip through a task with ease. [Based on 60 mph, a possibility introduced to man first by the railroads, and then by the automobile. In this jet-and-rocket age, 60 mph may seem slow enough, but in XIX the near-mystical equation of a mile and a minute seemed the formula of a miraculous new possibility.]

sixty-four-dollar question The big question. [From the title of a 1950's TV giveaway show in which contestants were started with $2, which they could parlay to $4, $8, $16, $32, by answering questions, and then to the big $64 final prize by answering correctly the BIG question. (As a measure of TV BIG, the scale soon went to $64,000. Today, if my inattention serves me, one such show offers a top prize of $100,000—or a free sex-transformation operation; whichever comes first.)]

sixty-nine n. and corresponding *v.* Simultaneous oral sex between two people. [< Fr. *soixante-neuf,* the sex partners conceived as a prone six lying on a supine nine.]

skedaddle 1. To light out in a hurry. 2. To break and run from battle. [A Civil War coinage, and one that seems to have been in about equal use by both sides. There are many dialect precedents, as Brit. *sket,* rapidly (akin to *scat*), *daddle,* to walk unsteadily. Also *scatter, rattled.* One is free to speculate, but the exact origin remains unknown.]

skiddoo *A command.* Get out of here—fast. [Prob. based on *skedaddle.* Either coined or popularized by comic strip cartoonist A. Dorgan, c. 1890].

  23 skiddoo From c. 1900 into the 1920's, an obsessive catch phrase often with no specific meaning except to show that one was "slick" enough to know the catch phrase and to say it knowledgeably, as when a pretty girl walked by. Otherwise the basic senses were: 1. Scat. Get out of here. 2. Well, let's go, boys! [In the earliest form, *1-2-3 skiddoo,* as if a variant of *1-2-3 go* in starting a race. The "in" thing of the catch phrase was that the race-starting cadence was altered. Instead of 1-2-3, evenly spaced, the count ran *one,* then pause, then *tu-three* (very rapidly), and *skiddoo.* Later, the *tu-three* rendered as *23.* It wasn't really much of a joke, but the idiots who make much of such catch phrases aren't much to begin with.]

Skid Row Earlier, and still used in Oregon and Washington: *Skid Road.* 1. The area of a large city inhabited by alcoholic derelicts. [They are on the skids and headed down.] 2. The flophouse center of a large city where itinerant workers line up at the numerous employment agencies looking for work. (The areas of senses 1 and 2 are much the same.) *on Skid Row* The condition of being an alcoholic derelict. Down and out and busy trying to drink oneself to death. [These senses, however, are a late evolution. In the earliest form, c. 1890, in northwestern lumbering, a corduroy road with partially embedded logs laid transversely about five to ten feet apart, and sometimes greased, to aid in hauling logs to water. The first sense shift, to "shabby street or section of a city," seems to have occurred (?) in the 1920's, prob. in Seattle, when an abandoned lumbermen's skid road became a street lined with cheap bars. As late as 1944 the form remained *skid road* and meant "run-down strip of a town with flophouses, cheap bars, and employment agencies for unskilled labor." The alteration to *Skid Row* and the specific association with winos is post-WW II.]

slantandicular [Whimsical Am. variant of *perpendicular.*] 1. Not vertical. 2. Askew; all messed up. *You've got it all slantandicular.*

[Of a class with such exuberant whimsies as *absotively, posilutely, absogoddamntively, posihootintootinlutely.*]

slave A person who is the property of another. [Based on *Slav,* because the eastern slavs were early enslaved by military conquest. It was so that Russia became a land of native serfs owned by ruling families of foreign origin. So L. *sclavus,* Slav, slave. It. *schiavo,* Fr. *esclavo,* and Ger. *Sklave,* slave; but this last is a borrowing. The Gmnc. stem for *slave* is the mysterious **calc-* (see *marshal*) and the native Gmnc. word for the western Slavs is *Wend.*]

    slave bracelet A small ornamental chain of precious metal, sometimes set with stones, worn about the ankle by a woman as a love token from the man who "owns" her. (Clark Gable gave one to Carol Lombard with the inscription "Heaven's above!") [*Bracelet* is, of course, based on L. *bracchium,* arm, but "armlet for the ankle" is as literate as a jeweler needs to be. The symbolic language is clearly enough "fettered by love."]

    slave (away) To work hard.

    Britons never, never will be slaves So the proud assertion of "Hail, Britannia." But the early English *esne* was, in fact, a chattel property. And there are numerous references to black slaves being bought and sold in XVIII England. A newspaper of Nov. 30, 1771, reports the sale of a "negro boy" in Richmond for 32 pounds. It may have been the last of such commerce, for in 1772 the Court of King's Bench outlawed slavery in England; and on Aug. 28, 1783, Parliament abolished slavery in the British West Indies (after appropriating a huge sum to reimburse slave owners, who took the money and worked their ex-slaves in economic peonage).

    white slavery Coercive prostitution on the scale of organized crime. [Am. Late XIX. The Mann Act of 1910 (after Congressman James R. Mann, 1856–1922), prohibiting the transportation of women across state lines for "immoral purposes," was specifically aimed at syndicates of "white slavers." Well-intentioned but semantically distraught, the act was chiefly used for blackmailing men of N.J. and Conn. who took consenting girls to NYC for an overnight or weekend tryst. The act was repealed shortly before WW II.]

sly-boots A cunning person. [One who sneaks up on you noiselessly (cunningly). In XVI *smooth boots. Sly-boots* and *sly-cap,* which are synonymous, are attested in XVIII.]

smart aleck/smart alec/smart Alec   A wise guy. A practical joker. (And often with the sense:) A wise guy who outsmarts himself. [Am. first attested 1865. *Alec, Alex < Alexander* might suggest "the would-be great," but this is conjecture, and a common man's name as a generic term for "guy" has ample precedent in Jack, a good Joe, a weary Willie, and Tom, Dick, and Harry, among many more.] *smartalecky adj.* Inanely sassy.

sn-   Snakes and snobs sneak through the snow, perhaps to prove that not all English words beginning with *sn-* refer to the nose or snout, but many do, the *sn-* root occurring in many IE compounds referring to the snout, and so to the teeth, a snout being, in one sense, a nose with teeth in it. With this IE root in mind, the following words fall more or less easily into etymological place:
   snack n. 1. Food eaten between meals. 2. A hasty light meal. —*v.* 1. To eat between meals. 2. To eat lightly and hastily. [< MD *snac, snack*, to eat hastily and furtively. Root sense: "to snatch with the teeth."]
   snap v. To bite. To seize with the teeth as a dog. *Hence, many extended senses:* 1. To break off sharply. 2. The sound made in breaking a thing off, or in biting down on one's own teeth. 3. An easy thing. [Easily broken off.] 4. A sudden motion. [As in biting sharply.] And so: *snap out of it, snap shot, snap to* (come to attention sharply), *snap decision, to snap up, cold snap, ginger snap.* [MD *snappen*, to seize with the teeth.]
   snarl v. To growl. (*Ext.* To speak angrily.) —*n.* A growl. [Obs. Eng. *snar < MHG snarren*, to growl.]
   snatch To seize. [As with the teeth. Akin to *snack*.] *Slang.* To kidnap. —*n. Slang.* The vagina. [Conceived in vulgar euphoria as an organ forever eager to seize and swallow a penis.]
   sniff   *n.* A short, sharp inhalation through the nose. *Hence.* An expression of contempt. —*v.* To smell. To make an effort to smell. *sniff out a crime* To detect evidence of wrongdoing. [ME *sniffen*, same senses, is ult. echoic of a short, sharp inhalation through the nose.]
   sniffle v. To inhale repeatedly through the nose, especially through a clogged nose. [Frequentive of *sniff*.] *the sniffles* 1. A head cold. 2. A fit of sobbing. [Both involve repeated sniffing.]
   snip [Du. *snippen*, to bite off, to cut off, to tear off.] To cut off. *tin snips* Shears for cutting sheet metal. *snippet* 1. A small (bitten off) piece. 2. A child. ["Small piece" of a person.]
   snivel Variant of *sniffle*, but implies tearful whining. [ME *snyflung*, nasal mucus.]

snoop [Du. *snoepan* (pronounced as if Eng. *snoopan*), to root around like a pig. Hence, with the double sense: 1. To eat furtively (root for food). 2. To poke one's nose into. It is sense 2 that functions in Eng.] *v.* To pry into (stick one's nose into) other people's business. —*n.* 1. A prying person. 2. A detective.

snoot Slang. Nose. [Variant of *snout*. ME *snute*.] *snooty* Haughty. ["With nose in air."] *have a snootful* To be drunk. [Image of an animal with its snout in water and lapping it up so eagerly it fills its nose.]

snooze *v.* To sleep. —*n.* A nap. [Origin uncertain. Root sense prob.: "To breathe through the nose."]

snore To breathe loudly in one's sleep. [ME *snoren*, to snort.]

snorkel [< Ger. dial. *Schnorchel*, a snout.] A tube for breathing under water. Originally an air pump developed for submarines, permitting them to take in fresh air without surfacing.

snort [See *snore*, above.] 1. A strong exhalation or inhalation through the nose. Hence, 2. An expression of contempt. 3. Loud laughter. *have a snort* To have a drink. Especially to drink whiskey neat, "knocking it back over one's teeth." [As if not drinking, but inhaling sharply. See *schnapps*, below.]

snot 1. Nasal mucus. 2. A worthless person. [Earlier forms unattested.]

snout 1. The nose and mouth of an animal. 2. The human nose. [See *snoot*, above.]

snub [Root sense: "To cut off, to cut short (as if bitten off)." ME *snubben*, to rebuke, to chastise.] *v.* 1. To ignore or to deal with curtly. [To cut courtesy short.] 2. To check sharply. To bring up short. *to snub a rope.* —*n.* A social slight. *snub nose* A short ["bitten off"] upturned nose.

snuff [Variant of *sniff*, but with the primary sense "to cut off."] *v.* 1. To cut short. *snuff a candle* To extinguish by cutting off the charred wick. 2. *Slang.* To kill. ["To cut short a life"] *snuff porno* A pornographic movie in which sexual perversion culminates in the murdering and dismembering of the sexual victim; sadomasochism stuff. —*n.* Finely powdered tobacco to be sniffed up into the nose or placed against the gums for absorption through the mucous membranes. [< Du. *snuftabak*, sniffing tobacco.] *up to snuff* Fit and able. ["Well enough to take snuff." Cf. the New England regional answer to "How are you?" which runs, "Able to sit up and take nourishment": Healthy enough to function.]

snuffle Heavy breathing, as through a partially blocked nose.

In Ger. and Yid. the *sn-* root is commonly rendered *schn-*, whence the following:

schnapps Hard liquor. [A direct borrowing from Ger. In German custom, liquor is drunk neat and tossed off in a gulp. (See any Erich von Stroheim movie.) Hence, the root sense: "to bite, to snap." Cf. *snort,* above.]

schnauzer A snarly breed of German terrier, bred in toy and regular sizes. ["Snout hound." So Ger. *Schnauze,* snout.]

schnorrer A beggar. A whining nuisance. [Yiddish. Akin, in form, to snore, but < MHG *snurren,* to hum, to whine. Because professional Jewish beggars used to whine through the nose while strumming a small lute.]

schnozzle Also *schnozola/schnoz Slang.* The nose. [Implies "large nose," the sense prob. influ. by comedian Jimmy Durante, he of the enormous nose, who billed himself as "The Schnozz" and "The Great Schnozzola"; but first into Eng. < Yid. *schnoitzl,* little nose < Ger. *Schnauze,* nose; with *l* dim. ending.]

(And see *sneeze,* which resembles this *sn-* group, but is from other sources.)

snake　　1. The legless reptile. 2. A low, treacherous, sneaky person. *snake hips* A lithe dancer. [IE *sneg-,* to creep. With g/k in Gmnc. → OE *snaca,* snake.]

snake in the grass 1. A concealed enemy. (But has gradually acquired the sense:) 2. A friend who betrays. [This sense shift may be from the idea of encountering danger in one's own fields, i.e., where least expected. The image is very old. Some take it to be a ref. to the snake that tempted Eve while pretending friendship. But non-Christian Virgil uses the same image in the *Third Eclogue: "Lauret anguis in herbis":* "a snake lurks in the grass." Dante, who knew every line of Virgil, says of Fortune (*Inferno,* VII, 84): *"é occulta come in erba l'angue":* "she (her workings) are hidden like a snake in the grass." The image is prob. from a source that much predates both pagan and Judeo-Christian, both traditions drawing from it. Note that Dante intends no least flicker of humor, but that Eng. "snake in the grass," in a highly formal context, injects an incongruity that touches risibility.]

sneeze　　(*n. & v.*) A violent involuntary expulsion of breath caused by irritation of the mucous membranes. To expel breath in this way. [Would appear to be an *sn-* word (see *sn-*), but is so only by clerical error. Ult. < IE *pneu-,* to blow (PNEUMATIC, PNEUMONIA). With p/f in Gmnc. → OE *fnēosan,* to sneeze ("to blow"). But the long *f* of early script, identical with the long *s,* caused a clerical error in transcription whereby *fnēosan* became late OE *snēosan* → ME *snesen,* to sneeze.]

it's nothing to sneeze at It is of some consequence; even of very great consequence. *I know you have a good job, but a free extra billion is nothing to sneeze at.* [I don't know why *to sneeze* = a negligible response, but as in the instance given, the offer might merit something more than a sneeze by way of acknowledgment.]

snide Nastily sarcastic. Given to cutting remarks. [First noted c. 1850, occurring in both Brit. and Am. with the sense: "counterfeit, sham," possibly with an earlier ref. to clipped coinage. Early developed the sense: "pertaining to sharp practice." [Universally glossed as of unknown origin. But why have all lexicographers failed to consider as the source Ger. *Schneider,* tailor ("one who cuts"), the transmission to Brit. and Am. being via Yiddish. Ger. *schneiden,* to cut. In gin rummy *to schneider, to schneid* is to complete a game before an opponent has scored a point (which is the unkindest cut of all).]

snob One who looks down on others he takes to be his inferiors in caste, refinement, wealth, or accomplishments. [Root sense, XVI (of unknown origin): "an apprentice boy, esp. a shoemaker's apprentice." The sense evolution is prob. accounted for by the fact that the shoemaker's *snob,* in serving gentlemen, developed an affected imitation of their manners, and learned to look down on other apprentices, who lacked his "refinement."]

snollygoster 1. A shyster. 2. Any devious and disreputable person. [Am. dial. Obsolete until Harry S. Truman (president 1945–1953) used the word in a remark to the press, sending the fourth estate running to dialect dictionaries. As I recall the follow-up stories, a few reporters traced it to XIX dialect "shyster," but no one tracked it all the way home to Ger. *schneller Geist,* fast-moving spook; by way of Penna. Dutch variant *schnelle geiste, snelle gaster,* boogieman ("spook that darts about seizing bad children"—and going bump in the night).]

sod buster A farmer of the western plains. [Post–Civil War Am. With ref. to those who staked out land claims for farming west of the Mississippi under the 140-acre allowance of the Homestead Act authorized Jan. 1, 1863 (same day as Lincoln's Emancipation Proclamation), the act looking ahead to the postwar settlement of the West. Because before farming it was necessary to plow (bust) the sods of virgin buffalo grass that once covered the plains. And prob. partly influ. by the fact that the first houses built by settlers in this almost treeless land were made of mud-daubed sods, somewhat in the manner of adobe houses.]

solecism   An impropriety, esp. in the forms of speech. *Billy Carter is a social solecism.* [Based on a touch of Athenian snobbery. (See *barbarian.*) Athenians went forth to colonize Soloi in Cilicia, Asia Minor. In time the Greek there spoken began to vary from Athenian Greek, the stay-at-home Athenians, scorning every such variation, labeling it *soloi kismos,* "in the manner of Soloi." British blimps who visited the U.S. in XIX, first encountering American English, generally had the same stupidly snobbish reaction to all Am.-evolved words, idioms, and variants.]

somatic   Of the body as distinctive from the nerves and brain as the responsive and cognitive systems. [Gk. *sōma,* body; and related *sōmata,* slaves ("mere ignorant bodies").]

somersault   [< L. *supra,* above; *saltus,* a leap. OF *sobresault, sombersau(l)t.* In XVI Eng. both *sobersault* and *somersault* are attested.] *n.* 1. An acrobatic leap and turn, head over heels, to land on one's feet. 2. *Ext.* Any complete reversal. *Once he had the job, Sandy's attitude did a somersault.* —*v.* To fall or roll end over end. *The car went off the road and somersaulted down the slope.*

sorry   [OE *sārig,* sad, painful; with regular shift of OE terminal *g* to *y* in Eng. Ult. < IE *sai-,* painful.] *adj.* 1. Feeling sympathy for the distress of another. 2. Rueful. Apologetic. Abashed. 3. Inferior. *a sorry excuse for a human being.* (And cf. *a poor excuse for a man.* Both based on the idea of inferiority as that for which one must apologize and vice versa.) 4. Causing pain, sadness. *the sorry news of the* Titanic. And note, 5. *A recent conversational evolution.* What's that? What did you say? (As if "Sorry, I wasn't listening: please repeat.")

S.O.S.   The international Morse code distress signal. [C. 1900. Often, but wrongly, explained as an acronym of *Save Our Ship, Save Our Souls, Sure Of Sinking,* etc. The signal . . . . - - - . . . was chosen as the distress call because it is distinctive, and easy to transmit even by a wounded radioman or by an amateur with only the slightest knowledge of Morse code.]

soup and fish   White-tie dinner clothes. [XIX Am. < *soup and fish,*
an elaborate dinner; prob. a variant of *from soup to nuts,* a formal
dinner with many courses.]

southpaw   A lefty. Originally a left-handed pitcher. By extension,
any left-handed person and especially an athlete. [From the self-
elaborating impulse of sportswriting that calls a baseball a *spheroid*
and the home team *the local aggregate.* This one coined in 1880's
by Finley Peter Dunne, who was then a young sportswriter for
the *Chicago News.* This whimsy is based on the fact that the Chicago ball park was then laid out with home plate to the west.
Hence, a left-handed pitcher would be hurling the spheroid with
the "paw" on his south side. But despite the self-conscious artful-
ness of this sort of thing, *northpaw* has never come into use.]

speakeasy   *Prohibition era.* An illegal saloon. [A metaphoric flight
based on the idea that one must speak softly to avoid attracting
the attention of the police. The fact is that no such place could
function except with the knowledge of corrupt cops, who stopped
by regularly for a drink and to collect their bribes.] Also ***blind
pig*** and common c. 1900 but obs. during Prohibition era: ***blind
tiger.***

specter of the Brocken   A phenomenon of light refraction and diffrac-
tion, now commonly seen in flight when the shadow of an airplane
cast on a cloud appears magnified and circled by a rainbow aura.
Before aviation the phenomenon was so rare as to be thought
magical. In Europe the specter was long associated with der Brock-
enberg, the highest peak in the misty Harz Mountains of Germany.
There, when the sun was low, observers often marveled at their
shadows so cast on cloud faces. The ancients took the mountain
to be a magic place because of this phenomenon, and Walpurgis-
nacht and the annual May 1 witches' sabbath ceremonies were
performed there (as they are still imitated as a tourist attraction).
Goethe set one of the scenes of *Faust* on the Brocken.

Spic   Derogatory name for a Spanish-speaking person. [Prob. based
on mockery of the mispronounced *no spic (speak) the Eenglish.*
The bigotry that derides the way foreigners speak and then distorts
that way of speaking into a name for them is an ancient word
process. See *barbarian, gringo.*] ***Spic and Spanish*** A Puerto Rican
dude. (See *spic-and-span.*)

spic-and-span   (Properly *spick-and-span,* but the influ. of *Spic and Span,* well-established trade name for a detergent, has all but fixed the first spelling as standard Am.) In immaculate order. Spotlessly, spanking, brand-new clean. [< Earlier *spick and spannew,* said originally of a new ship (new in every spike and piece of wood). *Spick,* nail, spike. XIII *span-new, spannew* < ON *spannyr,* new (clean, fresh) as a freshly shaved wood chip. But though the elements of the term are traceable to earliest English, the compound dates from XVII, prob. based on XVI Du. *spiksplinternieuw,* new in every nail and splinter. Akin to Ger. *nagelneu,* nail-new.]

spiel   1. A glib sales pitch or come-on, as by a side-show barker. 2. Any drawn-out, self-seeking account. (And all corresponding verb forms.) [Ger. *spielen,* to play; *Spiel,* a game. In Am. with the sense: "at play," i.e., not serious, i.e., false.]

spitting image An exact likeness. *He is the spitting image of his father.* [A corruption of *spit and image, spit 'n' image,* which were formulas of the most ancient practices of black magic and the casting of spells by hex dolls, in which any harm done to the doll is transferred to the hexed person. The two basic principles of such hexing were: 1. Anything that was once part of a person, or that was intimately associated with him, retains a power over him. 2. Anything that resembles a person has a power over him. Hex dolls, therefore, were made as symbolic resemblances (power 2), and bits of his or her hair, spit, feces, nail parings, clothing, etc., were incorporated into the material of which the doll was made (power 1). *Spit,* therefore, on the first principle; *image,* on the second. See Rossetti's "Sister Helen" for a late hex poem: Sister Helen, in melting the wax doll she made on these principles, causes her victim to waste away.]

spoof   A mild hoax or good-natured satire. [< *Spoof,* name of a half-nonsensical, bluffing card game invented and popularized by English comedian Arthur Roberts (1852–1933), the name being his coinage. Give Roberts credit for an excellent ear: his coinage somehow manages to sound like what it means, and in being so accepted, it has survived to become a standard word in Brit. and Am.]

spoonerism   An involuntary transposition of sounds when speaking, esp. of the initial sounds of words. *Hesitant Proover* for *President Hoover.* [After William A. Spooner (1844–1930), English university don and cleric, who was notably given to such tang tungling.]

stake   [IE *steig-*, sharp, pointed. With g/k → hypothetical Gmnc. stem *st'k-* → OE *staca*. In Gmnc. the root idea "pointed" became associated with "pointed length of wood." (In a similar sense shift IE *bherdh-*, to cut, became Gmnc. *b'rd-*, cut piece of wood. Both shifts are probably related to the fact that the early Teutons were tree worshippers. See *board*.)] 1. A pointed stick or log driven into the ground, most commonly to mark a boundary point, but also as a support or for attaching a tether; and in early usage, the post to which wretches were lashed for whipping or for burning. 2. *Exts*. [From the idea "marked-off property" to "valuable thing."] *a*. A share in a financial venture. *to have a stake in*. *b*. *Often in plu*. An amount wagered. *They play for high stakes*. *c*. A prize in a competition. *the Belmont Stakes*. (And corresponding verb forms.)

at stake At hazard. *to stake* 1. To support with stakes, as a plant. 2. To mark off property lines. (Usu. *to stake out*.) 3. To advance working capital in a venture. *stake-out Police*. A watch (also the scene and the duration of such a watch) set in anticipation of a crime or of arresting a wanted person.

grubstake XIX Am. prospecting. (n. & v.) A supply of food and equipment advanced to a prospector in return for a stated share of any ore he may strike. To supply in this way.

pull up stakes 1. To abandon an enterprise and move on. 2. *Ext*. To leave. 3. *Lit*. To pull up the boundary stakes and walk off one's land. [Stakes as boundary markers were in use in Eng. in IX: *mid stacum gemearcod*, lit. "with stake ge-markèd." Later, English boundaries were commonly marked with stones. (See *butt-: butts and bounds*.) But stakes are mentioned as boundary markers in various XVII and XVIII Am. documents. *To stake a claim* was common in XIX Am. prospecting and land settlement. (The area claimed literally marked with stakes—or stones—and registered accordingly in the land records.) *To drive stakes* was to post one's boundaries. Bret Harte, 1862, has the related *to move stakes*, in mining, to pull up stakes of an unrewarding claim, to drive them again in another place. *To pull up stakes* is simply an idiomatic reversal of *to drive stakes*, but let it be noted as an "as-if" idiom; for it is unlikely that a man abandoning a piece of land in disgust, or at least in anticipation of claiming much better land to the west, would go to the trouble to seek out and pull up his boundary markers.]

HISTORIC. Free land was available in the U.S. through all of the XIX, and settlers could claim homestead sites into the early XX. A man, having failed in the East, might abandon his land there to claim a new farm in Ohio, later abandoning that to try again in Missouri, later possibly to try again farther west. *To pull up stakes* became idiom as a description of this migrant pattern.

stalk [Prob. based on IE *ster-*, to creep up on. Via obscure Gmnc. evolution to OE *stealcian*, to steal up on. ME *stalken*. In XVI with the senses: 1. To pursue relentlessly. 2. To advance with deliberate, measured strides. All these senses function in current usage.]

    stalking horse Politics. 1. A candidate put forward to hide the candidacy of another, in whose favor he will withdraw. 2. *In various loose extensions.* A candidate put forward to test the political climate. A candidate put forward to divide the opposition. Any device used to conceal one's true political intentions. [But originally a horse trained to walk toward deer while concealing a hunter who walked behind it or at its off shoulder; because deer will not take alarm at a riderless horse. Later a movable screen or blind used in lieu of such a horse. Both devices, of unknown antiquity, were meant to get an archer or a javelin thrower close enough to the game for an effective shot. In XVIII, with the development of an accurate long rifle, close stalking was no longer necessary, and stalking horses fell out of use.]

stalwart *adj.* Strong. Staunch. Worthy. —*n.* 1. Powerful and resolute person. 2. Active and unswayable supporter of a cause. [Root sense: "worthy of a place (esp. in a company of soldiers, workers, supporters of a cause)." < OE *stael*, place (STALL); *wierthe*, worth, worthy.] And so the radical pun: *The winner of the Derby is a stalwart horse.*

stamping ground 1. A place where horses and other ungulates, both domestic and wild, tend to congregate. [So called because ungulates commonly paw the ground when they are standing in groups and not feeding.] 2. *Ext.* A familiar place. A haunt. *one's old stamping ground* A once frequented place.

starboard/larboard See *board.*

Star Chamber [In Norman Fr., *chambre d'estoilles;* ME *sterred chambre*, starred chamber.] 1. A large room in Westminster Palace, the ceiling of which must once have been decorated with stars, though all trace of them is now lost. 2. Beginning c. 1400, a court of royal officers that sat there with special powers, and under rules that gave it wide latitude in extorting confessions. 3. As the Court of Star Chamber, from c. 1500 until its abolition in 1641 by the Roundhead Long Parliament, an inquisitorial court, usu. but not always sitting in Westminster Palace. 4. Any arbitrary court.

HISTORIC. The arbitrary use of the Court of Star Chamber by Charles I (crowned 1625, beheaded by order of Cromwell 1649) was one among many other reasons for the English Civil War.

Star Chamber proceedings Any court, board, or investigating body convened to "railroad" those who are called before it.

stash   Anything stored away in a safe and secret place. *to stash (away)* [Early XIX Am. Prob. formed by combining *store* and *cache*.]

steward   One who manages the affairs of others or of another, as *estate steward, ship's steward, shop steward.* [Like *marshal, butler, chamberlain, constable,* a word that has changed social connotation dramatically. OE *stīgweard,* keeper of the hall (a court officer). But also and as attested by the surviving ME form *styward,* a swineherd ("warder of the sty"). *Stig* and *sty* both connoted "inclosed space." Prob. ult. < IE *steig-,* a boundary marker (STAKE). It was by threading this ambivalence from keeper of the sty to keeper of the great hall that the swineherd founded a dynasty as a *stigweard, styward, Stuart* king.]

stiff   [IE *steibh-, steip-,* compacted, hard, stiff. With p/f in Gmnc. → OE *stif,* stiff.] *adj.* Inflexible. Rigid. —*v. Slang.* 1. To knock cold. [As if to knock to rigor mortis.] *I'll stiff you.* 2. To cheat. To con. *He stiffed me out of a week's pay.* [To do one out of, by analogy to doing one in.] —*n. Slang.* 1. A corpse. [Body in the state of rigor mortis.] 2. A guy. [Conceived simply as a present body.]

working stiff A common laborer. [Conceived simply as a body that does work. Cf. *able-bodied seaman.*] *little stiff* A guy of no real consequence. (And so the hoary old vaudeville turn: *B Banana:* I'm a little stiff from bowling. *A Banana:* I don't care where you're from, you little stiff.)

stiff necked Obdurate. Unyielding. [In Exodus 32-34, "a stiff-necked people" appears four times; twice again in Deuteronomy 9, and finally in the NT, Acts 7:51, it is thundered as: "Ye stiffnecked and uncircumcised in heart and ears." At all points it labels those who refuse to yield to God's law.]

stirrup   A loop, usu. metal, for the foot. It is attached to the end of a strap attached to the saddle, and is used for mounting a horse, and for control when riding. [In nautical English, a loop of rope suspended from a yard to provide sailors with a foothold when working a sail. In this nautical sense some such form, though unattested, may be of considerable antiquity, but the first paradigm is OHG *stegareif*, step-rope ("rope to step into or to stand on").] **stirrup cup** 1. A hunt cup served to the riders after they have mounted. 2. *Ext.* One for the road.

HISTORIC. There are no forms of the word before XII *because the stirrup was not invented until prob. late XI.* The invention was a major technical breakthrough and radically altered the use of cavalry, thereby altering the basic forms of warfare. In allowing cavalrymen to stand while riding, and to lean far to either side, the stirrup more than doubled the range at which they could wield a saber. All illustrations of early cavalry, back to the Greek and Middle Eastern, show riders with their legs simply adangle, requiring them to sit the horse more or less squarely. The wonder is that so simple a device took so long to hit upon.

stool pigeon   1. *Police and crim.* An informer, either an underworld spy paid in money for favors, or an implicated criminal who informs on his accomplices in return for a release or for reduced charges. 2. *Loose ext.* A tattletale. [*Stool,* here, altered from obs. *stale,* a decoy. (Akin to *stall,* an assigned place. And see *stalwart.*) Hence, in earlier usage, a live or imitation bird fixed in place to decoy (and associated sense "to betray"). In XVI a *stale* was a prostitute who served as a thief's decoy. So Shakespeare, *Much Ado About Nothing,* "a contaminated stale." The sometimes offered explanation that decoy birds were commonly tied to stools is self-evident nonsense.]

straight jacket   A corrupted form of *strait jacket.* A canvas jacket with long arms that can be tied together in back to restrain the arm movements of demented or violent people. *in straits* In confining or limiting circumstances. Commonly said of one's finances, but originally, of course, *straits* signified a narrow sea passage, as in *Straits of Magellan.* [Ult. < L. *stringere,* to squeeze, to draw tight. In It. *stringere la mano* (lit. "to squeeze the hand") is to shake hands. The Eng. form is from the L. p.p. *strictus* by way of It. *stretto,* confined, squeezed; and when used as an adjective, narrow.]

stump   [ME *stumpe* < MLG *stump.* Ult. < IE *stebh-,* tree trunk, post.] 1. The part of a tree trunk still rising from the ground after the tree has been felled. 2. *Ext.* The remainder of a limb after an amputation. 3. *Related.* An artificial limb, esp. a wooden leg. —*v.* To walk heavily, as if on a wooden leg.

HISTORIC. The foregoing are all the senses common to both Brit. and Am. In Am., however, there is a whole range of "stump" idioms traceable to the long process of clearing forest land for farming. The land was once covered with the stumps of newly felled trees. In the XIX Midwest one might easily spend a lifetime without ever being far from a stump. Gone now, those stumps have left their presence in idiom.

stump juice Moonshine whiskey. [Whimsical. As if the stuff were brewed in the rotted hollow of a stump (a conception perhaps reinforced by its taste). But association with the woods clearing in which whiskey was brewed, in the beginning to be close to a fuel supply for the distillation, later to avoid detection by revenue agents.]

stump jumper A yokel. [Whimsical. As if he made his way cross country by jumping from stump to stump. The idiom is identical in pattern to *clodhopper* and *ridge runner.*]

take to the stump To campaign politically. [Lit. "to make a speech." Because a man who wanted to make a speech needed only to mount one of the stumps that were forever near at hand. So, also:] *to stump* To campaign by making speeches in many different places. *to stump the boondocks* To campaign for the back-country vote.

to stump/to be stumped To baffle, to be baffled by. *it has me stumped* It has me baffled, blocked, defeated. [In this sense, from the back-breaking labor of pulling stumps out of the land after the trees have been felled; mainly with ref. to a stump that won't be budged, partly with ref. to a plow hung up on a partly cleared stump or underground root.]

to be up a stump To be treed. [By bastard association with "up a tree." An animal might force a man to climb a tree and then force him to remain there in an uncomfortable and sometimes precarious situation, but obviously a stump would not be far enough out of reach for safety.]

stumpy adj. Short and squat. —*n.* A short and squat person. 2. A person with an artifical leg (on which he stumps around).

sub rosa 1. In secret. 2. *Common ext. from the idea of secrecy to the idea of covert ill doing.* In evil conspiracy. [L. *sub rosa,* under the rose. The sense derives from the Greek myth of Harpocrates, god of silence, to whom Cupid gave a rose, pledging him to guard all the secrets of Aphrodite, i.e., of lovers. In the Middle Ages and into the Renaissance, a rose hung over a meeting or a dinner table signified that nothing said there was to be repeated. It has also long been common to carve a rose above a confessional booth to symbolize the secrecy of the sacrament.]

subtle   Of fine texture, nuance, discrimination. [Prob. originally a weaver's term with ref. to passing the shuttle under *(sub)* the material *(tela)*. So L. *subtilis*, which has the same sense as the Eng. word. The ME forms were *sutil, satil*, the *b* reemerging from the Latin form (which would have been known to anyone able to write) c. 1400.]

su-ee   The basic form of the hog call, not only in Am. but in various European countries. [< IE *su-*, pig. Early suffixed *-i-*, whence It. *suine*, Ger. *Schwein*, Eng. *swine*. A pure root survival, but explainable in part as a modification of *sow-ee*, the *-ee* functioning as a naturally protracted syllable when shouting, as in *John-ee, Bill-ee.*]

Sunday   The Christian day of rest. [The "seventh day" (Genesis) on which the Lord rested from the labor of the Creation.] In the English calendar the day corresponding to It. *domenica*, Fr. *dimanche*, in which the root sense is "the Lord's day." [But the Eng. root sense is: "day of the sun," rendered in OE as *sunnandaeg*. The English week is adapted from the Scandinavian, which at first consisted of five days (Tuesday through Saturday) but which added a "sun day" and a "moon day" under influ. of the Roman calendar.]

   Sunday   best/Sunday-go-to-meeting   clothes   One's best clothing. [In earlier America, where farmers lived in rough work clothes, the expression implied a single suit or dress, usu. the clothes in which one had been married, and which were carefully set aside for churchgoing, ritual occasions, and to be buried in.] ***Sunday punch Boxing.*** A fighter's most powerful punch. [By analogy to *Sunday best clothes*, his carefully hoarded best. And also, whimsically, the punch with which he puts his opponent to "rest with the Lord, his labors done."]

   sundae A dish of ice cream with various more or less elaborate toppings. [H. L. Mencken, *The American Language*, traces the term at some length, and persuasively, to Two Rivers, Wisconsin, 1890, and to an ice cream parlor run by E. C. Berners. It was he, according to Mencken, urged by a customer named Hallauer, who first put chocolate syrup over a dish of ice cream. On this specific point, Mencken may have been indulging in a bit of folk etymology, for to put some sort of topping on ice cream is at least as natural as to pour cream on sliced peaches, a practice that certainly cannot be traced to a single origin. Mencken is correct, however, in tracing *sundae* to George Giffy, who operated an ice cream parlor in nearby Manitowoc. Mencken explains that a dish of plain ice cream was the standard treat, but that a festively topped dish was the "Sunday best" reserved for the once common ritual of stopping for ice cream after church. The variant *sundae* is an advertiser's standard well known to operators of nite clubs and to the manufacturers of Kashew Ka-runchies.]

superette   A small supermarket. [Am. c. 1950. An etymological absurdity meaning "a little big," yet almost inevitable within that self-sequential illogic we call idiom. Early grocery stores tended to be small and to center on a counter. The customer, standing in front of the counter, told the clerk what he wanted, and the clerk located it and set it on the counter. The first supermarkets were, by comparison, enormous stores, whence their name; but their most distinct feature was the checkout counter, to which self-service customers wheeled the items they had selected. Supermarkets, moreover, were usually chain stores. Independent grocers, in an effort to compete, imitated their checkout system; but unable to achieve the size of the chain stores, they called themselves "super" to signify the checkout method, with the dim. suffix *-ette* to indicate that they were small.]

supercilious   Haughty. Disdainful. Contemptuous. [Root sense: "above the eyebrows." Effective sense: "with raised eyebrows." < L. *cilium*, eyelid; with *super→ supercilium*, eyebrow ("thing above the eyelid").] *As Truman Capote grows balder, his superciliousness begins to rise past the top of his head and to reach for the nape.*

surname   Family name or patronymic. In now common practice, the inherited portion of one's name. (See also *cognomen, given name, nickname.*) [Originally *sir-name*, because—and beginning only c. XII in England, and only slowly—such names, usually an estate designation, were used by knights and nobles.]

HISTORIC. As a point of historical reference, King Arthur's knights were known by just their first names, as Sir Bors, Sir Mordred, Sir Launcelot. Only after the Norman Conquest did it become customary to add a "twa-name" (a second name), usually

formed on the name of the knight's landholding, the common
formula being "Sir X of Place-name," though such warrior names
as Fortinbras ("Armstrong") developed soon.

swa(r)n/I swa(r)n   1. An intensive. *I swa(r)n I had it just a minute
ago.* 2. Exclam. *Well, I swa(r)n! well, I'll (I) be swa(r)n* [Early
upper New England regionalism with ambiguous Brit. dialect
roots. Perh. < *I'se warn ye,* but the form "I'se," though common
in sthrn. U.S., is without precedent in New England. Prob. < *I'll
be sworn (to the truth of what I'm saying).* In New England *swarn*
usu. emerges as *swan,* the omission of the *r* being paht of a regulah
patte'n theah, if you get the idear.]

sweetheart contract/sweetheart arrangement   1. Favoritism by public
officials in granting contracts, esp. the awarding of such contracts
without open bidding. 2. *Labor unionism.* The equivalent in making settlements with favored employers. [Dating uncertain. Prob.
in use at least by 1900. The "sweetheart" contractor endears himself variously by kickbacks, by return of favors, by exerting favorable political influence, and by assisting in the machine's election
campaigns.]

swindle   *v.* To defraud. —*n.* A scheme for defrauding. *Agential form:
swindler.* [But the sense "to cheat" is a late evolution. Ger.
Schwindler, the paradigm, was originally "a giddy person" < OHG
suintilōn, to have fits of dizziness, to be subject to fainting spells.
First applied with this root sense to a merchant who took dizzy
risks, it implied not dishonesty but brashness. (His money management was enough to make one's head swim.) But since those who
bought shares in the speculations of such a man regularly lost
their money, a *Schwindler* became "one who made money disappear," whence, when the money was one's own, "a cheat."]

sycophant   A toady. One who will stop at nothing to win the favor
of a rich or powerful person. [< Gk. *sukon,* fig; *phantes,* one who
shows (agential form of *phanein,* to show) (PHANTASY). But what
is the fig, and how shown? On this question gentility has led lexicographers to obscurantism.

At one point in ancient Greek history, the exportation of figs
was heavily taxed; and though it seems an unlucrative enterprise,
informants (we are told) took to exposing fig smugglers. There is
also the fact that among the Greeks the "sign of the fig" was
the standard gesture in accusing a person before a magistrate.

Most authorities have argued, therefore, that the fig shower made this gesture in exposing fig smugglers in order to ingratiate himself with a magistrate.

Perhaps, but the sign of the fig is an immemorial obscenity, and still used in Mediterranean Europe. It is made by clenching the fist with the thumb (penis) pushed out between the first and second fingers (labia). In effect, it means "Fuck you—rudely." Dante so uses it in *Inferno,* XXV, 1–3:

> When he had finished, the thief—to his disgrace—raised his arms with both fists making figs, and cried, "Here, God. I throw them in your face!"

Fig, moreover, signifies "vagina" in several Mediterranean languages, and one need only split a hairy purple fig to see why. (And so: *not worth a fig, not care a fig.*) Genteel evasion aside, the *fig,* here, is the *fig shower's* own anus, which he *shows* by bending over bare-ass to offer his all to his master.]

sympathy   1. A sharing of like feelings. [Gr. *sym,* with; *pathos,* feeling. Hence, fellow feeling.] 2. *But often in Am.* Feeling sorry for. So: **sympathy card** A greeting card of condolence sent when there is a death in the family.

NOTE. It. *simpatico,* sharing in one's feelings. (As a substantive, *un simpatico,* a congenial fellow.) So Fr. *sympathie.* Neither has the sense, now common in Am., "to feel sorry for." In 1942 André Maurois, French novelist and biographical critic, autographed a book for a midwestern five-by-five spinster: "With the understanding (I think he meant Fr. *connaissance,* personal acknowledgment) and sympathy (Fr. *sympathie*) of the author." In Am., however, the sense emerges as something like "Understanding your problem, I feel sorry for you." The title of the book was *Women Without Love.*

(*Empathy,* a related form with Gk. *en-,* in, into, which here takes the syncopated form *em-* in front of *p,* is a rarer word and largely restricted to psychology and literary criticism—the condition of reading oneself into the situation of another, but with this difference: a biographer can bring himself to empathize with Caligula, but never to sympathize with him.)

tadpole   A polliwog. [*tad,* toad; *pole,* head (as in *poll tax*). Hence, "toad head."]

tail   [IE *dek-* refers to tresses and to the bushy caudal appendages of many mammals. With d/t and k/g in Gmnc. → OE *taegl, taegel,* and with common g/y from OE to Eng. → ME *tayle,* tail.] 1. The caudal appendage of many animals, including birds, lizards, fish. 2. *Ext.* Thing attached to. *tail of a kite.* 3. *Ext.* Thing that comes last. *tail end, tail of a plane.* 4. Thing left behind by a process, as smelting. *tailings of a smelter, a mine.* 5. *Special sexual ext.* Thing that takes place in the end. So **piece of tail** A sex act. A woman conceived as a vaginal sheath. [Akin to slang, *to get it in the end.* Because the sex organs occur more or less where an animal's tail is attached. "Love has pitched his mansions in the place of excrement." —W. B. Yeats.]

    tail along To follow as a tag-along rather than as a participant. ***tailspin*** *Aviation.* The fall of an airplane in which the tail rotates more or less eccentrically; or the same maneuver under aerobatic control. 2. *Ext.* A loss of emotional control. [Because in early light aircraft, before modern trim devices, a tailspin often resulted in a fatal crash, the plane spinning out of control.] ***tail wind*** *Aviation.* A following wind.

    with tail tucked between one's legs Cowardly; retreating abjectly. [As if a frightened dog. And see *coward,* which is at root: "tail-tucked person."]

    heads or tails Refers to coinage, one side of which has been traditionally stamped with a portrait or with a symbolic creature. [*Heads* for portrait, side on which the head appears; and so *tails* as the side opposite the head.]

    HISTORIC. In most coinage, and traditionally in U.S. coins, the date is shown *heads* and the value and national identification is shown *tails.*

As a minor etymological exercise, the idiom *at face value* must refer to paper money and must, therefore, be relatively recent, prob. dating from latter half of XIX in U.S. Paper money was in use in China by XIII as recorded by John de Plano Carpini, who traveled in Mongolia 1245–1247 and who was prob. the first European to see this form of money. The Continental Congress issued paper money during the American Revolution and then defaulted on it, bringing it into disrepute in U.S. And though in early XIX there were issued government bearer notes and bank notes backed by the reputation of the issuer, the first greenback dollar bills (payable to the bearer in silver on demand) were not issued until 1863 and were only slowly accepted in general use.

Tammany/Tammany Hall   [Named after Tamanend ("the friendly") XVII Delaware Indian chief who was especially well disposed toward white men. (Even the noblest of savages can be wrong.)] The model of Am. big-city political machines.

HISTORIC. Founded in 1789 as a fraternal organization, Tammany gradually took to politics, and Tammany Hall became a popular place for political meetings. William Marcy ("Boss") Tweed (1823–1878) took over the organization in 1859 and developed it into the ruthless Democratic machine of New York City, himself emerging as the symbol of corrupt boss politics. The last power of Tammany, already diminished, may be said to have ended in the 1960's with the arrest of Carmine de Sapio, the last Tammany-connected NYC politician of any consequence.

tandem   One behind the other. End to end. Lengthwise. (For whatever reason one can imagine, there once were tandem carriages drawn by two horses hitched up fore and aft.) [< L. *tam*, so, so much; *-dem* (demonstrative suffix), that → *tandem,* so much. When used in ref. to time, the sense was "exactly then, at just that point in time." But in an XVIII Brit. university joke, rendered "at last, at length" (as one slow minute following upon another; whence "one behind the other." Brit. univ. jokes, one gathers, were not required to be funny but only Brit.]

Tap City   Gambler's argot. The gambler's ghost town. Where he is when he has lost the last of his money. [*Tap* < *tapped out*, originally said of a keg from which the last drink has been tapped. *City,* where one lives; hence, in slang, "where one is at; the condition in which one lives." (Mod slang, c. 1970, made obsessive use of "ville" in this sense, as in *Squaresville, Dullsville, Nowheresville* to describe the mental frame within which one lived.)]

NOTE. In most regular back-room games, a player who has lost all his money can say "I'm Tap City," and thereupon be allowed to draw a small amount from the pot or the house for carfare and for snacking money. He may then raise new funds and return to the game, but only after he has paid back the tap.

Nevada casinos have a similar arrangement for gamblers who have gone broke. The casinos are closely aware of winners and losers. I have it from Harold Smith of Harold's Club in Reno that a gambler who has gone Tap City in his club is not given cash (with which he might too likely go next door and start gambling again), but a chit to be presented at the Greyhound bus depot, where it will be honored for a bus ticket. (The usual destination from Reno is San Francisco.) By arrangement with Greyhound, the bus driver will also give him a few dollars for food when the bus has reached the first rest stop in California; and, at destination, streetcar or local bus fare home from the Greyhound terminal.

task force 1. *Naval.* An irregular force assembled from various regular units for a specific strike or task. 2. *Ext. Police work.* A special unit so assembled for a specific purpose, upon completion of which all police officers are returned to their regular duties. 3. Related extensions of the term in governmental investigative work, emergency action, etc.

tattoo 1. *Armed services.* A sustained even drumbeat once used as a military signal for lights out (and fires); and in some ceremonial formations, esp. at executions. 2. Any similar drumming with one's fingers, a pencil, or other small object. [A gift to the military from Dutch pubs, in which closing time was signaled by a sustained knocking on the bar called the *tap-toe* or *taptoe.* < *tap,* spigot; *toe,* to < *doe toe,* lit. "do to," effective sense "to shut." (Note that Du. *oe* is pronounced as if *oo* in *poop.*) Hence *tap-toe* = *shut-tap time.* And cf. Penna. Dutch *make the door to,* shut the door. (Not to be confused with *tattoo,* indelible design pricked in the skin; which is from Polynesian *tautau, tautu, tatu,* ritual scarification.)]

tawdry *adj.* Flashily worthless. Cheap and tasteless. (In Brit. only, as a noun: flashy, cheap stuff.) [< *Sain(t Audry)* via Brit.-slurred *Sin Taudry* → *tawdry.* Because on her feast day (June 23) a fair was traditionally held at which the most characteristic articles offered for sale were flashily colored and decorated neck scarves of the cheapest material ("tawdry stuff").]

HISTORIC. In her time (d. 679) she was known as Etheldreda. A princess of the East Angles, she became a nun in 672, founded a monastery-nunnery on the Isle of Ely, and served as its abbess. Pious legend has it that she died of a disease of the throat (cancer?), which she interpreted as a fitting retribution for her youthful sinfulness in wearing bright worldly ornaments about her neck; hence, the flashy-cheap neck scarf as her symbol.

tea: dish of tea   Also *saucer of tea* A cup of tea. [In Am. thought to be an importation of Irish immigrants, and perhaps there have been Irishmen who drank tea out of the saucer, though I have never seen it done. But from XVII to XIX in general Brit. usage, *dish* also signified a small bowl without handles modeled on the vessel from which the Chinese drink tea, and *dish*, here, is a survival of that sense.] *not my dish (saucer/cup) of tea* In any context, not to my liking, not to my taste.

teddy bear/Teddy bear   A plush-covered stuffed toy bear. [After President Theodore ("Teddy") Roosevelt. A once well known cartoon showed big-game hunter Teddy sparing the life of a bear cub. The cartoon seems to have inspired a toy-maker, who managed to come up with a bear-cub doll with Teddy's glass-eyed blank expression; so much so that T.R. had small teddy bears made up and attached by a ribbon to some of his large 1904 campaign buttons. The Roosevelts may be the only U.S. family to have given two eponymous words to the language, *alice blue* (which see) having been named after daughter Alice Roosevelt.]

tedium   Boredom. Ennui. [< L. *taedium* < *taedēre*, to make weary, to bore; of unknown (perh. ? Etruscan) origin. But not, as commonly asserted, < *Te Deum laudamus*, Thee, God, we praise, fifth-century Latin hymn incorporated into R.C. mass; this folk etymology asserting the *Te Deum* to represent the boredom induced by all liturgy.]

Tenderloin/the Tenderloin   In post–Civil War NYC, the police precinct west of Broadway between 23rd and 42nd streets, a then heavily Irish vice district. [Whimsically so called because police assigned to the district found such lavish opportunities for graft from gramblers, shady saloon keepers, vice hustlers, and organized criminal gangs that they could forget stew and live on tenderloin. Cf. *to live high on the hog*.]

tenderfoot *Wstrn. Post–Civil War.* 1. A new and uninured arrival on the frontier. A greenhorn. 2. *Ext.* A greenhorn in any context. 3. *Boy Scouting.* The beginning grade of Scouting. [The frontier was not measured by walking distances and it was not a greenhorn's feet that were likely to get tender, but his butt, which was in line for saddle sores. The peculiar stress on footsoreness is a transfer from the first application of the term to cattle that had been driven from Texas to stock ranges in Montana, Wyoming, etc., and that arrived trail weary and foot sore. (Also called *pilgrims* because they had walked so far, and that term was transferred to greenhorns.) These terms were first attested by L. Swinburne, *Scribner's Magazine,* May 1887: " 'Pilgrim' and 'tenderfoot' were formerly applied almost exclusively to newly imported cattle." (In which "almost" is an inaccuracy.)]

tennis   The game, which in all its variants is played with a racket on a standardized court divided in the middle by a net. [Because in the custom of c. 1200 France, the server, on striking the ball, called in OF *tenetz!* and later in modern Fr., *tenez!* lit. *hold!* but in effect, *take it! here it comes!* For *tenez-tennis,* compare *oyez-oyes* (see *oyez*).

termagant   A loud, nagging, shrewish woman. [Bearing in mind that men, being almost exclusively the writers of England, had virtual control of the language, they managed to attach a whole vocabulary of odious terms to women. This one is from *Tervagant, Trivigent, Tervagaunt* < OF *Tervagaun, Tervagaunt;* It. *Trivigante,* a loud, menacing (male) figure of medieval morality plays. This pious invention was said to be a Moslem subdeity-demon, his function being to threaten the pious and to be defeated by them through the power of faith. As a gift of male supremacy, the term had become specific to women by XVI.]

testify   to bear witness. [Based on L. *testiculus,* 1. testicle; 2. little witness < *testis,* witness; because the testicles were (in the end) the little witnesses to one's virility. To swear by one's testicles was an ancient form of oath and survived at least into the works of Villon. It is this oath the King James version of the Bible minces in several references to oaths taken with a hand on one's thigh. Exodus 30:6; Numbers 1:50; 9:15; 17:4. This form, of course, left women nothing to swear by or on, but no one then, including women, much cared.

And so *detest,* at root, "to bear witness against," hence "to curse," and implicitly, "to hate to the bottom of one's balls."]

thug   A violent criminal. Hoodlum. Mugger. Strong-arm killer-robber. [< Hindi, *thag*, a member of the *thugees* < Hindi *thagi*, robbery. Into Brit. c. 1830, a gift of the British Empire.]

HISTORIC. The thugees were not a criminal gang that one might join, but an ancient roving religious clan, or confederation of clans, into which one was born, inheriting religious rites, a specific ethos, and a distinct spoken and sign language. In some ways they resembled the Gypsies, with the difference that they did not cheat and swindle but murdered and buried their victims for gain, the murder, burial, and preparation for attack being religious rituals. There were about 5,000 to 6,000 of them in India in early XIX. Beginning in 1828, British forces moved to eliminate them, killing in police raids, executing after trial, and deporting. By 1852 about 300 remained in controlled centers under police registry, and the thugees had ceased to function as a band of religious murderers.

thunder   1. The growl or clap of air rapidly expanding along the path of lightning. 2. Any loud sound. (For whatever the observation may be worth, in Kansas I have heard this expansion give off not a growl or a bang but a loud, running hiss.) [IE *stene-*, thunder evolved into Gk. *stenein*, to groan aloud, to make a loud sound (STENTORIAN). In the Gmnc. evolution the *s* of the root was dropped and the *t* thickened, prob. to the stem *thun-* → OE *thunar;* ME *thonre, thundre.*]

steal one's thunder   At root, to plagiarize. But the evolved Am. sense is to steal another's bright ideas before he can use them. A comedian who delivers another man's punch line before he can use it himself steals his thunder. [Though accounts vary, all refer the idiom to John Dennis, who in 1709 presented a florid tragedy titled *Appius and Virginia,* for which he developed a sound-effects contrivance that gave forth the sound of thunder with unprecedented success. The theater closed out his play as a failure but kept the thunder machine for the next play to be produced; and when Dennis returned to see the play that had succeeded his, and heard his thunder machine resound, he is reported to have complained that he had been doubly badly used, for the theater had not only closed down his play but had stolen his thunder. The story, though it sounds like folk etymology, is attested.]

tiddlywinks   1. A game played by snapping counters into a cup, pressing them on one edge with another counter or with a coin. Once popular in British pubs. 2. Pointlessly frivolous behavior. *Don't* *try to play tiddlywinks with me* = Don't offer me any foolish answers. [The origin has been obscured by many extensions in XIX Brit. slang, but *wink* is an obvious metaphor for the flash of the counter when it pops from the table. *Tiddly* is ult. from *tittle*, a tiny amount, as in obs. *not a jot or tittle*. In Brit. slang c. 1850, *tiddlywink*, a brothel, an unlicensed grog shop. And later *tiddlywinker*, a petty cheat. In late XIX *tiddlywink* became standard rhyming slang for "drink." The dating of the game is uncertain (prob. early XIX) but it is its name that underlies all other senses.]

tiger The wild cat *Panthera tigris*. [< IE *steig-*, sharp. With common suppression of *s* before *t* → *teig-* → L. *tigris*. In Persian the form is akin to the word for "arrow." Whence the two probable root senses: "the sharp cat" and "the cat that strikes like an arrow."]

Most Am. idioms based on *tiger* are from *faro* (which see), the tiger being a distinctive marking of faro cards, and traditionally, too, on the shoe (also called the tiger) from which the dealer takes the cards. In faro, the most popular XIX Am. casino game, the players bet against the dealer, or tiger. Hence:

buck the tiger To bet against the dealer. To gamble. To take a chance. To take on in any competition. **hold that tiger** Draw successfully against the dealer. Face down the competition. (But see below, *have a tiger by the tail*.) Also a regular refrain in the standard jazz piece **Tiger Rag** Gambler's song in syncopated rhythm. [I.e., in ragged time, ragtime.] **Lucky Tiger** Common XIX Am. name for a gambling casino. [A curious choice in that the *tiger*, the dealer, represents the house. The name would seem therefore to advertise that the house is the lucky one, a poor pitch in attracting suckers. The name, however, early became generalized as a "sporting" man's catch phrase; and it was in this sense that it became the brand name of a line of hair tonics and men's toilet waters.] **blind tiger** Originally an illegal (back room of the saloon) gambling hall. Then c. 1890, a place where liquor was sold illegally. Then also called *blind pig*. During Prohibition *blind pig* was a standard synonym for *speakeasy*, but blind tiger had fallen out of use.

Idioms not based on faro:

three cheers and a tiger Three cheers followed by a shrill yell. [Reputedly the scream of a tiger. This was the common XIX form of huzzah, especially in political rallies.]

tiger 1. A powerful and potentially dangerous person. 2. A physically powerful lover of either sex, conceived as a feral pouncer.

have a tiger by the tail To have one's hands full, and to be in danger of having them bitten off if one lets go. [Perh. from a folk tale on the order of the racist *Little Black Sambo*. Perh. a natural metaphor for a dire predicament, with a force akin to *take the bull by the horns*. But the sources of the idiom may run yet deeper, for wild cats can sometimes be captured by running them to exhaustion and pulling on their tails. Natives of Africa's Serengeti Plain capture cheetahs alive in this way for sale to zoos. The method may not work for all wild cats, but it works for enough to provide a possibly ancient base for the idiom.]

tinker   *n.* One who mends pots. [And so c. 1100. But British tinkers were itinerants and regular flimflam rogues, whence by XV the second sense: rogue, undesirable person, petty thief, Gypsy. Perh. OE *tinn, tin,* tin. But this derivation is uncertain and contradicted by XII variant *tinkler;* and the form may very reasonably be echoic of *tink-tink-tink,* the sound of tools scraping on a tin pot.] —*v.* To fuss about at a mechanism as if to see what makes it work. Implies a mechanical aptitude but no previous knowledge of the particular mechanism. *Let me tinker with it,* let me poke about and see if I can't figure out how to get it running. (And note the Am. double agential form, *tinkerer.*)

    not worth a tinker's dam Worthless. [In preparing to flow solder onto a hole in a pot, tinkers made a dam (a restraining mold) of mud, clay, chewed bread, around and on one side of the hole. This dam held the solder in place until it had set. The dam was then brushed away, as a thing of no further use.]

Tin Pan Alley   The popular-music industry in U.S. as originally based in NYC. [There is no such street name (city planners, please note that there should be), but the industry was concentrated around Times Square, and all music publishers had a tinny piano available for auditions, whence the whimsical notion of an actual alley lined with tinny pianos. I can find no evidence of an earlier *Tin Piano Alley* and am simply guessing that *pan* derives from *(p)i(an)o.* Alternatively *Tin Pan* may be a more or less accurate assessment of the music played in this "alley"—as if by clanking tin pans. The sometimes suggested derivation from *timpani* cannot be flatly refuted but seems to be seriously out of tone.]

tip   1. Advice, especially from an insider. *a tip on the fifth race and straight from the horse's mouth.* 2. Any advice. *let me give you a tip, son.* (This time from, usu., the other end of the horse, the source of most unsolicited advice.) 3. A gratuity for personal services. [The first sense is from XVIII. Origin uncertain, but perh. altered from *tap*, as in tapping someone on the shoulder to attract attention before speaking in confidence, as in offering advice, a hint. The third sense may be an unexplained ext. of the late XVIII.]

NOTE. A common folk etymology explains sense 3 as an acronym for *(t)o (i)nsure (p)romptness,* and explains it as a sign over what we today would call a *kitty*. Nothing supports this assertion. There is no record of any such kitty in British inns and pubs. The derivation was probably suggested by the folk etymology that seeks to derive *cop* from *(c)onstable (o)n (p)atrol* (see *cop*). And there is the simple fact that one does not tip before being served, but only after.

tire   In Brit. *tyre.* [Root sense: "wheel dressing." By aphesis < *attire,* dress; obs. *to tire,* to dress (oneself, one's hair). The essential noun sense until the beginning of the automobile age was "metal rim around a wheel" (i.e., its last accouterment.] A rubber cushion around a wheel that is especially flanged to receive it.

HISTORIC. The earliest automobile tires were of solid rubber, sometimes with transverse holes. Later tires were inflated by inner tubes that kept the air from escaping. Today, unless a variation is specified, the word signifies a tubeless tire. As an example of language concept and variation, the Italian for tubeless tire is *gomma senza camera,* rubber (tire) without (inner) chamber.

spare tire 1. A replacement tire, esp. the one mounted on a fifth wheel and carried in the trunk of a car. (Changing tires was once a motorist's chief occupation, the road kit including rubber patches to be glued over the hole in the inner tube and an often used hand pump for reinflation. I note that I have put in at least twenty years of driving since my last flat tire, and guess that spare tires may soon become a thing of the past. For the time being, however, they are standard equipment.) 2. *Ext.* The roll of fat around the waist of my ugly neighbor, as distinct from the vigorous rondure surrounding mine.

tit for tat   An exchange of equivalents. Originally blow for blow, unpleasantness for unpleasantness, push for shove; and these remain the primary senses, but also, as in banter, mot for mot. (So the much attributed old joke. *Hostess:* Mr. Clemens, I am told you are a great wit, but tonight I shall give you tit for tat. *Mark Twain:* Tat, madam.) [Modified from earlier *tip for tap,* you push (tip) me and I'll strike (tap) you.]

toady One who will do anything to ingratiate himself. A sycophant. [Earlier *toadeater,* a sort of geek used by the medieval medicine man.]

HISTORIC. As part of the medicine-man-quacksalver-mountebank-charlatan's presentation of his cure-all nostrum, the toadeater ate, or pretended to eat, a live toad. Toads were believed to be virulently poisonous, and the toadeater began his act by going into what seemed to be his death throes. The medicine man then gave him a dose of the miracle cure-all, and the toadeater promptly recovered and performed feats of agility to prove the wonders of medicine, and also that there is a sucker born every minute.

toast *v.* 1. (Since XIV.) To brown and crisp a slice of bread by exposure, in one way or another, to heat. (Cf. *biscuit, zwieback.*) 2. *Ext.* To warm before the fire. *toast one's feet.* 3. *Ext.* To pledge, as in drinking. [< IE *ters-,* to dry, to parch. → L. *torrere,* same senses; p.p. *tostus,* dried, parched. Sense 3 is a XVII evolution. See note, below.] —*n.* 1. An acclaimed person. 2. A compliment or acclamation pledged with a drink.

toastmaster At a banquet, the master of ceremonies. He introduces guests and speakers, proposes toasts, and is commonly expected to be a stand-up comedian. The late Harry Hershfield, an unquenchable joke-spout much sought after for this work, used to bill himself as Toastmaster General of the United States. *toast of the town* A much acclaimed person, usu. an actress or a lady of fashion. [Implies that her name is on everyone's lips and that she is pledged in every drink that goes down the hatch.]

HISTORIC. Sense 3 and the forms that have developed from it began with the British custom of putting a piece of highly spiced toast in a glass of liquor, and especially of sherry. The exact dating of this custom is in doubt, but Shakespeare presents pot-valiant Falstaff as one who was fond of his dry sack with a toast in it. Circa 1600 this toast (touch of extra flavor at the bottom of the drink) came to mean a health (a particular good wish and compliment pledged with the drink).

But there are more specific antecedents of *toast, toast of the town.* No. 24 of *The Tatler* offers an account of a revel at Bath in the reign of Charles I (crowned 1625, beheaded 1649):

> It happened that on a public day a celebrated beauty . . . was in the Cross Bath, and one of the crowd of her admirers took a glass of water in which the fair one stood and drank her health to the company. There was in the place a gay fellow, half fuddled, who offered to jump in, and swore, though he liked not the liquor, he would have

the toast. He was opposed in his resolution; yet his whim gave foundation to the present honour which is done to the lady we mention in our liquor, who has ever since been called a *toast*.

This account is supported by the dating and by the fact that in mid XVII a toast was specifically a lady, the extended sense, "any person so pledged," evolving only in XVIII.

Tom and Jerry/hot Tom and Jerry   A hot grog of whiskey, sugared water or milk, and beaten eggs, the whole seasoned with nutmeg. [And this is the only Am. sense, necessarily restricted to people with perverted drinking habits, but the name has a Brit. history beginning with Pierce Egan's *Life in London*, 1821, being the adventures of two young Regency rakes named Tom and Jerry, whence, c. 1825, *Tom-and-Jerry Days* became a label for the Regency (1811–1820). Then, c. 1830: *to Tom and Jerry* To go on a riotous pub crawl. And c. 1875: *Tom-and-Jerry Shop* Also *jerry shop* A disreputable pub. A low London dive.

topaz   A gemstone, a crystal of aluminum silicate, especially prized in its brown-and-pink form. [Gk. *topazos*, topaz < *topazein*, to conjecture.]
    HISTORIC. The topaz came to the ancient Greeks as a trade item of unknown origin. They invested it with mysterious properties and called it "conjecture," because it was said to be found solely on a cloud-concealed island whose location mortal man could only conjecture.
    To extend this submyth a step further would be to say that only the gods could be in the business of mining topaz. But the Greek gods meddled in everything else, and a minor commercial venture in gemstones would not be wildly out of character.

touch and go   1. *Maritime.* Said of a ship that touched a reef or other obstruction while under way but was able to sail on, having suffered no serious damage; hence with ref. to a near wreck. 2. *Metaphoric ext.* Labels any narrow escape from disaster or downfall.

tragedy   Originally, a Greek drama that ended in the death or downfall of the hero; by analogy, any similar outcome in literature or in life. [Root sense: "goat song." < Gk. *tragos*, goat; *ōidē*, song; but the sense in which these roots were understood is not certain. *Satyrs* (mocking choruses of fate) were early associated with tragedy, and later tragedians traditionally wore goatskins. The meter of certain choruses was said to caper goatily. It was once custom to award the prize of a goat to the best reciter (singer). All or any of these goat references may explain the word formation, but none can be asserted before another.]

traipse   To wander about aimlessly (implies slaunchy slovenliness). [Brit. dialect *trapes*. Possibly (but ?) < MD *trappen*, to tramp about. But among the forms listed in Wright's *The English Dialect Dictionary* are *traapes, traapse, trapass*, and *traipass*, at least the last two of which may be akin to trespass, with a possible root sense, then: "to slouch about paying no attention to limits." (But still ?, and in fact ??)

transpire   [Root sense: "to breathe out/across/to." < L. *trans-*, out, across, *spirare*, to breathe.] 1. To take place. To occur. [This is certainly the most common usage in Am., but is held to be questionable by many who seek to use the language precisely.] 2. To come to light. *It transpired that he had been peculating.* [This more acceptable usage is an extension of the root sense in biology and botany:] 3. To emit vaporous waste products through the pores. (In a curious usage by a sports announcer: "Irvin returned to the game in the second half and transpired a new vigor into his teammates." The announcer's intent is usu. expressed by "inspire," and yet the surface error turned out to be etymologically exact, Irvin breathing a new spirit *out* of himself and *across* to his teammates.)

treacle   1. Molasses. (Primarily Brit., but I have in the pantry a can, bought in a U.S. grocery, labeled *treacle*.) 2. A medicinal syrup. (Originally specific to poisonous bites. In this sense Chaucer calls Christ "the treacle for every harm.") [Based on Gk. *therion*, wild beast, venomous beast. Later labeled the remedy for snake bite. ME *triacle*. Whence, the medicine being a sticky syrup, the shift in XVII to label the then newly discovered extract Am. calls *molasses*.]

triage   At field hospitals for battle casualties and disaster victims, the establishment of priorities for treatment by doctors, who set aside those who seem sure to die even if treated at once, and those who seem likely to recover even if treatment is delayed, selecting for earliest treatment those for whom it might make a life or death difference. [A name for the bitterest form of mercy. < Fr.

triage, which is *tri(er)*, to cull, to winnow; *-age*, act of. Akin to TRYWORKS, on American whalers, the area in which oil is tried (rendered) from blubber. Fr. *triage* became specific to the process of separating chaff and broken coffee beans from whole ones, and also as a label for the refuse left by such culling. Then borrowed as a Fr. medical term. Then into English in WWI.]

tribulation   Commonly in the phrase ***trials and tribulations*** which is redundant in that tribulation is a test (trial) of one's character and convictions by hardship. [Ult. < IE *ter-*, to rub. Associated early with the various changing processes of separating grain from chaff. The zero-grade form *tr-* → L. as stem of *tribulum*, a frame in which grain was placed to be flailed. The act of so winnowing was *tribulatio*, which implied no second meaning until it was adopted by pious Christian writers as a metaphor of the suffering gladly endured by the faithful for the good of their souls. Tribulation is not to be confused with punishment, which is retribution for evil. The difference can be illustrated in the sentence: "The faithful gladly bear the tribulations of this world in the hope of escaping the eternal punishment of the wicked."]

triskaidekaphobia   Fear of the number 13, or of any thirteenth thing. *All U.S. hotels are triskaidekaphobic* (they number floors from 12 to 14, omitting 13). Sometimes said to mean "fear of Friday the thirteenth," But Friday is not specified in this donnish coinage. [A whimsical Brit. university invention. Dating uncertain. Based on Gk. *triskaideka*, thirteen; < *tris*, three; *kai*, and; *deca*, ten; and suffixed *phobia*, fear of.]

trivia   Stuff of no consequence, now usu. said of small talk and smaller ideas. [< L. *trivialis*, lit. "of the place where three streets meet"; < *tri-*, three; *via*, a street. Triple intersections of Roman streets formed what Italians now call *un largo*, a wide place, a natural spot for a street market. The sense "of no consequence" came about not so much by association with the produce sold at such markets, as with the chatter of neighborhood gossips and other idlers who met there.]

trophy   A memorial of victory. The earliest sense was "battle plunder," i.e., thing of value, but modern usage implies not the intrinsic but the token value of the prize. [< Gk. *tropē*, I turn (TROPE, HELIOTROPE, TROPIC), with the implied sense "turning point," because after a victory Greek soldiers collected swords, shields, and other gear and plunder and erected a pile on the exact spot at which the enemy first turned and ran.

  trophy hunter 1. A hunter who kills not for food but for prize specimens to be preserved and mounted as ego proofs. 2. *Ext.* In the war between the sexes, a woman who collects men (and their expensive gifts) as a trophy hunter collects specimens, only incidentally, if at all, for the meat.

tsimmes/tzimmes [Yiddish. A meatless stew.] 1. A stew of fruits or vegetables cooked a long time (and much fussed at) over low heat. 2. Any overbusy fussiness about nothing much. *Her son graduates from kindergarten and such a tsimmes she makes of it you would think already he was a doctor.*

Tuesday The day after Monday. [In the Latin calendar it is *dies Martis,* day of Mars; and so It. *martedì,* Fr. *mardi.* And Tiu was the Teutonic god of war, another correspondence. Yet the name *Tiu* is < IE *deiw-, deiu-,* one sense of which is "god" (DEITY), which suggests that Tiu was once the supreme god of the Teutons but was replaced by Woden (WEDNESDAY). Or as Owen Barfield asks in his brilliant *History in English Words,* was Tiu demoted or was he promoted as god of war, patron of the central activity of Teutonic life?]

  HISTORIC. The undisputed derivation of the name *Tiu* from the root that means "god/deity" indicates that Tiu was, at one time, the supreme deity of the Teutons, a position later occupied by *Oden/Woden/Wodin.* In primitive languages tribes call themselves "the people" or "the people of." The root sense of *Teuton* is, not conclusively but probably, "the people who worship Tiu" or "the people of Tiu."

  If, moreover, the *T* of *Tiu* undergoes a standard phonetic shift to *Tz,* it corresponds to Gk. *Zeus pater,* God the father; Sanskrit *Dyaus pitar;* Illyrian *Deipaturos;* and via an intermediate early form *Diespiter* → L. *Juppiter, Jupiter.* Once again, the etymological evidence points not to Mars but to God the father.

  As a further evidence of possible etymological clues to our prehistory, *Woden* corresponds to Mercury, and both *mercuric* and obs. Eng. *wood* (rhymes with *owed*) connote "erratic change of mental attitude, flashing irrationality, madness."

  The etymological evidence leaves no doubt: there was a pre-myth—perhaps back to the very cave mouths of the Stone Age—and the Teutonic and Graeco-Roman mythoreligions are equally descendants.

turkey   1. The bird *Meleagris gallopavo,* indigenous to North America. 2. A sure loser (as turkeys get to be come November). [Yet though the turkey stands next to the eagle as the U.S. national bird, and though it moves into first place come Thanksgiving, both its common and its scientific names derive from foreign sources, the common name deriving from the country of Turkey. The curious misnomer arises from the fact that the Pilgrim fathers took the bird to be a species of guinea fowl, which it does somewhat resemble in its bald wattled head, its grating cry, and its stiff strut. Guinea fowl are native to the Guinea coast of Africa, but had been introduced into England by Turkish traders and were accordingly called *turkey fowls, turkey hens,* and *turkey cocks.* (See *Venetian blind* for a like language process.)

So it is that we celebrate the first of our national holidays under a Turkish brand name. Nor do we come much closer if we use the scientific name, which means *Meleager's guinea cock* or *Meleager's peacock.* Meleager was one of the heroes who sailed with Jason on the *Argo.* Caught up in the jealousies of the gods, he died in the fullness of his powers, leaving his sisters to wail so discordantly that the goddess Artemis changed them into guinea fowl. Happy Turksgiving.]

turtle   The reptile in a box, of the order Chelonia. [Med. L. **tortuca.* It. *tartaruga* is prob. influ. by XVII Fr. *tortue,* tortoise (specifically the large, then newly discovered tortoise of the Caribbean and the Pacific. ODEE cites, from the same time, the variant form *turckle* and guesses it may derive from a Carib word native to the Bahamas; but the Bahamian ref. is uncertain, and I suggest that a more native influ. is from the evolution of *turtledove* (which see).]

   mock turtle A soup usu. based on boiling a calf's head and flavoring to taste, supposedly like green turtle soup. [But the idea "imitation turtle" is whimsical. To the best of my knowledge, there are no turtle-imitating spices.]

   turn turtle Maritime. To capsize. [Because most turtles, and practically all large ones, are helpless when turned on their backs.]

turtledove   1. *In Am.* The mourning dove. 2. *Strictly speaking.* The European dove of the genus Turtur. ". . . The voice of the turtle is heard in our land."—Song of Solomon 2:12. [Of echoic origin. Root sense: "the dove whose cry is tur-tur." So L. *turtur.* And though language groups vary widely in their rendering of echoic sounds (as the sound of the bee is rendered in English *hum* or *buzz*, and in Italian as *ronzolare*), the cry of this dove has achieved something like onomatopoetic unanimity: Hebrew, not an Indo-European language, has *tur;* and Sumerian adds a "hoo" to reproduce the whole three-note cry: *turturhu.* It was in the Gmnc. that some form of *dove* was added to the *tur-tur.* So Swedish *turturdufva,* Du. *tortelduyf,* Ger. *Turteltaube.*] **turtledovery** And rarely **turtledovism** The billing and cooing of doting lovers.

tuxedo   Also *black tie.* Men's tailless formal dinner wear, once worn with a black tie, now gone to the rainbow. [Introduced c. 1890 at Tuxedo Park, a community of the rich on the west bank of the Hudson about forty miles above NYC. It rapidly became a common substitute for the more traditional tails and white tie, which continues as the rather more formal dress for high occasions, though today it is best known as the working clothes of classical musicians. (I sense that *tuxedo* is a fading term, and that *black tie* is no longer apt to the new riot of color. I would guess that *dinner jacket* is the term of the future. Tuxedo Park, it must be noted, is named after an Algonquinian root meaning "wolf." Is a tuxedo sheep's clothing for social values?]

tweed   A woolen fabric. [Root sense: "double thread." By a long and convolute evolution < L. *bilix* < *bi-,* double; *licium,* thread. In OE *bi-* was altered to *twi-* (TWICE) and *lix* to *li, ly* (the vowel in all cases being pronounced as if *ee.* So *twily* → Sc. as *twill* (pronounced *tweel*). In Sc. the thread of *twill/tweel* became snarled on the banks of the river Tweed, the form becoming *cloth of the Tweed,* later *Scotch tweed,* whence *tweed.*]

    tweedy *In Brit.* Country squireish. [Tweed being the usual out-of-doors clothing of the country gentleman.] *In Am.* 1. *Earlier, by association with British gentry.* Anglophiliac. 2. *Later* (and before everything, including sex, fell into blue jeans). Informal and outdoorsy. *the summer-in-Vermont tweedy set.*

tycoon   Great (powerful) person. [In Am. now specific to a financial giant, as John D. Rockefeller was a tycoon and Abraham Lincoln was not, but the root sense was "great prince, great ruler." < Chinese *ta,* great; *kiun,* prince, ruler. Borrowed into XIX Japanese as a title for the *shogun.* The shogunate ended in 1868. Under it, a dynasty of war leaders, purportedly serving the (powerless) emperor, ruled Japan with absolute power.]

Typhoid Mary   1. A person of either sex who spreads a disease he or she is immune to. 2. A jinx. [After the nickname given to Mary Mallon, a XIX Irish immigrant who worked in NYC as a cook.]

HISTORIC. The existence of immune carriers of typhoid infection had earlier been documented in Europe, when in 1888 an outbreak of typhoid fever sent U.S. public health authorities in search of such a carrier. The poor wretch turned out to be Mary, an immigrant girl with no way of making a living except as a cook and domestic. Since there seemed to be no charges on which Mary Mallon could be held, she was released but forbidden to work as a cook, food handler, or domestic. Mary, however, had to eat; and after another outbreak of typhoid fever in N.Y. in 1906, she was once more tracked down and found to be working as a cook under an assumed name. Since there was no known way to change her physical nature as a carrier, U.S. health authorities classified her as a menace to public health and kept her confined and isolated until she died in 1938, probably with some choice but unrecorded reflections on the gifts of the gods.

U

ugly　[ME *ugli, uglic* < ON *uggligr,* ugly. Prob. into English during the Danish occupation.] 1. Displeasing to the eye. 2. Morally repugnant. *Sex rears its ugly head.* 3. Temperamentally disagreeable. *in an ugly mood.* 4. Socially offensive. *ugly behavior.* 5. Threatening. *Those are ugly clouds in the west.*

　　have the uglies To be in a bad mood. **the morning uglies** A hangover.

　　ugly duckling The least attractive child of the family. [In the folk tale as retold in "The Ugly Duckling" by Hans Christian Andersen, a duck hatches a swan's egg along with her own. The changeling cygnet grows up to constant mockery for being ugly, large, and ungainly, as compared to the smaller, fluffier, and more agile ducklings. In time, however, it turns into a beautiful swan. To the insecurity of all childhood the story is a loving reassurance that all will be well in time, but in idiomatic usage, this final triumph is not implied when an ill-favored child is called an ugly duckling. There are limits of credulity. Who, after all, could really believe that Ronald Reagan could grow up to be President?]

umbrage　(Rare except in high literary diction.) Shade. Shadow. [< L. *umbra,* shade, shadow.] **umbrageous** (Even rarer and more formal.) Shady. Shadowy. *One must think twice about people who call a shady slope "an umbrageous declivity."* But survives in the more or less formal idiom **take umbrage** To take offense. To resent. [Root sense: "to be darkened by," i.e., "not to shine upon with favor."]

uncle　[IE *awo-, avo-,* any adult male relative other than one's father. L. *avus,* It. *avo,* grandfather (AVAL). L. & It. *ava,* grandmother, is prob. the first ext. of the root sense to include a female relative, and that only by association with *avus, avo.* L. *avunculus,* maternal uncle. Late L. *aunculus.* OF *oncle,* ME *uncle.*

From XVI to XVIII, frequently *nuncle* by transfer of the *n* from *an uncle* to *a nuncle*. This alteration, common in many English words (see *noncing*), was largely restricted to dial. and to lower-class speech. Yet the tendency seems to be inherent in English, as witness the fact that young Am. babblers still tend to say "some nother time." Hamlet's "married to mine uncle!" preserved the educated form "uncle," yet is all but identical to *married to my nuncle!*] 1. The brother of a parent or the husband of an aunt, the latter being, strictly speaking, an *uncle-in-law* but more commonly an *uncle by marriage*. 2. A common generalized term of respect for an older person, esp. as used by children with ref. to an adult friend of their parents (see *kissing cousin*). Also: 3. *In southern slaveholder's tradition, and still surviving.* The form for referring to or addressing an aged male Negro. 4. A pawnbroker. [Fanciful. As if he were a kindly old relative one turns to when in need.]

Uncle Sam One rendering of the initials U.S. (And note also *Uncle Sugar* as a satirical ref. to U.S. give-away diplomacy.) The familiar cartoon personification of the United States as a lanky, goateed old country squire in a red-white-and-blue high hat and a swallowtail coat. [A complicated evolution, some of which remains in doubt. Though disputed, the original verbal reference may have been to Samuel Wilson, commonly known as Uncle Sam. As an army inspector during the War of 1812, he inspected and forwarded, among other things, the meat packed by one Elbert Anderson, who branded his pork barrels "E.A.—U.S." So the army joke that the pork was sent by Uncle Sam. Whether or not this account is reliable, the name *Uncle Sam* dates from the War of 1812. As a cartoonist's figure, Uncle Sam first appeared in 1830 as a sort of Yankee hayseed, the now traditional form and accouterments having begun to appear only in 1868 in the cartoons of Thomas Nast (1840–1902). The original hayseed figure was based on *Brother Jonathan* (which see), the earlier personification.]

Uncle Tom *In modern Negro usage.* A black who kowtows to whites. Especially one who not only knuckles under, but actually believes in white superiority. [After Uncle Tom, the pietistic and self-abasing old Negro in Harriet Beecher Stowe's abolitionist-tract novel, *Uncle Tom's Cabin.*]

Dutch uncle See *Dutch.*

monkey's uncle In the common exclaim. *well, I'll be a monkey's uncle!* Expresses surprise or mild vexation. [*Monkey* with the generalized sense "foolishness" is attested in Am. by 1792 and was prob. in use much earlier. An intermediate form of this idiom was *well, I'll be monkeyed!* (made of fool of). To be a monkey's uncle is, of course, to be oneself a monkey and (as southern and midwestern idiom has it) "to claim kin."]

my/a rich uncle Common formula for explaining any windfall the source of which one does not care to disclose. So a girl who has got a mink—in exactly the same way minks get them—will say, "I got it from a rich uncle."

say/cry Uncle! In pre-switchblade boys' games, a formula by which a tormentor will release his victim in return for being called "Uncle," i.e., in return for being granted a title of respect, thus establishing the pecking order. [A specimen case of the survival with modification of an ancient formula. Latin distinguished between maternal uncle, *avunculus,* and paternal uncle, *patrue* (lit. "of the father"), the *patrue* having senior status in the Roman patrolineal clan. As far back as the Republic, Roman boys used the formula *patrue, mi patruissimo,* uncle, my best of uncles. Century by century, as the language changed, boys retained the basic formula, adapting it to successive shifts, thus making it as native to Hannibal, Missouri, as it once was to Ostia Antica, and probably to every playground back to the cave mouths of the troglodytes.]

union suit One-piece underwear with a rear drop panel or slit. *Union* signifies *one-piece* as distinct from the earlier common underwear consisting of separate undershirts and drawers. Now usu. associated with heavy underwear, but turn-of-the-century Sears Roebuck catalogues show many variants in weight and length, especially in models for ladies. One 1890's catalogue (not Sears) even offered a union suit with attachable cuffs and dickey, thus doing away with the need for a shirt. [*Union* has prompted many folk etymolo gists to refer the term to the underwear of the Union Army. Army issue, however, was two-piece. The Union Army reference is almost certainly from a once popular story to the effect that Lee showed up at Appomattox in full dress, and that Grant showed up in his Union suit. But this dull enough joke dates to the late 1890's, at which time *union suit,* unknown during the Civil war, had become a common new term. I am indebted to Mrs. Elizabeth Huston of Paris, Ill., for pointing out an advertisement in *Harper's New Monthly Magazine,* Nov. 1897. The sponsor was the Oneita Knitting Mills, Office No. 1, Greene St., NYC, and in it the term "Union Suit" is followed by "(Patented April 25, 1893)."]

untrammeled Free. [As a small language exercise, I once asked fifty English faculty members, in the random order of finding them alone, to give the root sense of the word. Thirty-six related the word to *trampled, untrampled,* six had no opinion, and eight identified it correctly as being from the root sense: "not caught in the net (mesh)." The element *mel-*, mesh, implies woven (as in suit of *mail*), the element *tra-* < L. *tri-*, three; and so L. *trimacula*, triple mesh; It. *tramaglio*, triple-layer fishing net. Via OF *tramail*, ME *tramele* → XVI *trammel net* A fishing net consisting of a fine mesh between two layers of coarse. In Brit. a *trammel* is a restrictive shackle for teaching a horse to amble; and plu. *trammels* labels various restrictive technological devices. (I once had a student, courtesy of the first thirty-six of my faculty members, who wrote of "untrammeled snow.")]

upper crust The elite. [It was etiquette, into XVI, to slice off the upper crust of a loaf of bread brought to table, and to present that slice to the king, or to the ranking person at the table. Hence, the root sense: "one of those entitled to the upper crust."]

HISTORIC. I cannot entirely explain the source or the significance of this ritual, but it is well attested. Wynken de Worde, late XV–early XVI English publisher, specified in his *Boke of Keruinge* (Book of Carving): "Then take a lofe in your lufte hande and pare ye lofe rounde aboute; then cut the over cruste to youre soverayne, and cut the nether cruste, and voyde (dispose of) the parynge, and touch the lofe no more after it is so served."

The passage will do as a specimen of precisely detailed nonexplanation. I have seen, but doubt, the assertion that the crust so cut was used as a trencher: certainly carved wooden trenchers would have been common; and if the "soverayne" got the one trencher, what did the rest use? Yet a XVI rhyme repeats the gist of it: "Furst pare the quarters of the lofe round alle about,/ Than kutt the upper cruste to your soverayne and to him alowt" (*alowt*, allow, allow it).

Whatever the exact function of the upper crust, the custom in XVI England, as in most of Europe even today, was to eat bread by tearing chunks from the loaf (though note that in this ritual Wynken de Worde has set the loaf aside to be touched no more).

urchin A mischievous child. A brat. [In archaic Eng. a hedgehog. < L. *ērĭcius;* OF *herichon;* ME *urchon*, hedgehog. Ult. < IE *gers-*, spiny, to prickle, to bristle. With g/h → L. *(h)ērĭcius*. Because hedgehogs are forever poking about, and do minor damage with their gnawing. So, by metaphoric ext. → brat (minor pest of a child). Cf. *kid*, child, as a similar metaphor. But:] *sea urchin* A bristly echinoderm. [Because its bristles resemble those of a hedgehog.]

valentine   1. A sweetheart. 2. A greeting card sent on St. Valentine's Day, Feb. 14. (Such cards once commonly included comic lampoons, but of late all seems to be sweetness and light in a lace border.) 3. Any Valentine's Day gift.

St. Valentine's Day Feb. 14. A much altered survival of an ancient mid-February fertility ritual, a late form of which was observed in Rome at the Lupercalia. At the climax of this Roman ritual, priests cut bloody strips from the skins of sacrificial animals (goats and dogs) and dividing into two bands (prob. representing the sexes), ran through the Palatine lashing the people, who offered themselves to it because a lash with these whips was believed to be a cure for sterility. [There were two saints named Valentine, both martyred in Rome at different times in the third century, but their connection with the modern observance has nothing to do with what little—which is very little—is known of their lives. The connection seems, rather, to be by a common sort of name association, the name *Valatin* being cognate with OF *galatin*, a gallant, a lover. The idea that saints have been assigned particular functions by chance association with their names seems strange to many, and strikes some of the pious as irreligious. Yet note that Santa Lucia (It. *luce*, light) is the patroness of eyesight in Italy; that function being assigned to Ste. Claire in France (Fr. *claire*, light); and to *der liebe Augenstein* in Germany (Ger. *Augen*, eyes).]

vamoose   *Western, now generally diffused.* To leave on the run. To skedaddle. *As a command.* Get out of here! Beat it! Skat! [Sp. *vamos*, we go, let us go. And see *mosey* from the same source.]

NOTE. *Vamoose* implies rapid motion away from; *mosey*, slow, ambling motion either toward or away from. One is adapted from the whole of Sp. *vamos;* the other, from the last syllable. I can find no historic explanation for this difference and must assign it to the sound values of the two Am. words, *vamoose* being a short-voweled spondee; *mosey,* a dactyl with an opening long vowel and a feminine ending.

varmint   1. A pestiferous creature, as a body parasite or a predatory animal. 2. A despicable person. [Corruption of *vermin,* which see. Though it has to it the ring of Am. colloq., the form is of Brit. dial. origin.]

vast   1. Far-reaching. Labels largeness on a geographic or cosmic scale. And so in extension: 2. Great. *a man of vast experience.* 3. Much. *vast wealth.* [But, as visible in **devastate** (< L. *devastare,* to lay waste), the root sense was, with ref. to wasteland, "empty." Ult. < IE *w'*-, void, lacking. Suffixed -*n*- in Gmnc. → OE *wanian,* to lessen (WANE). With same nasal suffix in Italic → L. *vanus,* void, useless (VAIN). And so the related form *vastus,* empty, arid, desert-like. *The vast Sahara,* or the archaic *vasty deep,* permits the root sense of the word; *the vast reaches of Kansas* does not, Kansas being fertile.]

vaudeville   Theatrical variety performances. (Vaudeville is supposed to have died in the Great Depression of the thirties, but it has in fact only moved to TV, though there one misses the acrobats and the animal acts. [Fr. *chansons du Vau de Vire,* songs of the Valley of the Vire, after the many ditties written in XV by Olivier Basselin and named by him after his birthplace in the Vire Valley. Immensely popular as theatrical music, the songs gave their name to the variety entertainments performed to their strains.]

Venetian blind   A form of slatted window shade. [So called because introduced into most of Europe by Venetian traders; but in Italy Venetian blinds are *persiani* because the Venetians brought them from Persia. And see *peach,* originally "Persian apple" or "Persian fruit."]

verdict   1. The decision guilty or innocent arrived at by a jury at the end of a trial. 2. *Ext.* Any definitive opinion. [Root sense: "a true saying." < L. *vēr(um),* true; *dict(um),* a saying. → OF *veirdire.* ME *verdict.*]

vermicelli   The thinnest form of Italian pasta. It has a diameter about half that of spaghetti. [< L. *vermis,* worm, maggot. It. *vermicelli,* little worms (VERMIN). Hardly the most appetizing of names, but

common usage changes many questionable terms into simple labels. One could hardly sell "boiled little strings" as a menu offering,
yet *spaghetti* is from It. *spago*, with dim. plu. ending; hence, "little
strings." (The *h* is inserted in Italian to keep the *g* hard before
the soft vowels *e* and *i*.)]

vermilion A bright red. [< L. *vermis*, worm, maggot, crawling insect.
Via OF altered form *vermeil* (VERMEIL). Because vermilion dye,
now made of mercuric sulfide, was once made of the bright red
body fluid of the cochineal insect. (VERMIN, VERMICULAR, VERMI
CELLI.)]

vermin 1. Any pestiferous creature, as a body parasite, predator,
or rodent. 2. The whole class of such creatures. 3. A despicable
person, or the entire class of such creatures. [< L. *vermis*, worm,
maggot, crawling insect. Whereby it is clear that the root sense
is "body parasite" and that predatory, gnawing, and otherwise
destructive larger animals were so labeled later, by association
with these more intimate pests. And see *vermilion*.]

very *adj.* 1. Extreme, absolute. *to the very end.* 2. Identical, exact.
his very words, at that very instant. 3. Mere. *The very thought
of it scares me.* And corresponding adverbial senses. (But it is very
true that in the very practice of rhetoric, "very" does not add
very much to very many constructions. —As in the preceding
sentence, each use of "very" can be deleted without changing
the sense.) [Me *verray* < OF *ver(r)ai* (Fr. *vrai*) < L. *vērus*, true.
And note that, with the possible exception of the sense "mere,"
"true" may generally be substituted for "very"—which in a very
true sense is seldom very truly necessary.]

vigorish 1. In loan sharking, the usurious margin of profit consisting
usu. of interest at 20 percent a week, penalties for late payment,
and additional fees enforced by strong-arm tactics. 2. In bookmaking, the percentage set by the bookmaker in his own favor. [Am.
prob. early XX. One of our few terms of Russian origin. With
alteration in Yiddish transmission < Russ. *vyigrish*, gambling gains,
profit. But influ. in Am. by similarity to *vigor*, yielding the associated sense "stronglike," which will do as a fair equivalence of
20 percent interest compounded weekly.]

villain 1. An evildoer, esp. one who takes pleasure in doing harm.
2. *In drama and fiction.* The character who seeks to undo the

protagonist. *the villain of the piece* The one blamed for evil endured or accused of intended evil. [Root sense: "of the villa." The ref. is to a country estate (not of the city), hence, rustic rather than urbane and cultured; and specifically to a serf on a country estate ("one who is the property of the villa"). So Medieval L. *villanus,* serf. By patrician assumption, therefore, a person of low (vile) birth; hence, one lacking in all the virtues the aristocracy claims for itself. The senses "base-born slave" and "base/vile" coexisted till c. 1700, after which the sense "serf/peasant" receded from the word, leaving only "evildoer" and evil-intender."]

virtue 1. Moral purity, especially chastity. *Despite my best efforts, Rusty Sonnek has kept her virtue intact.* 2. Enabling power. *the Christian virtues. by virtue of the authority invested in me.* 3. A specific power or essence. *the healing virtues of the various herbs. His methods have the virtue of simplicity.* [Another male chauvinist word. < IE *wiro-,* man. → L. *vir,* man → *virtus,* manliness. Because in the male-dominant society in which the term developed, the enabling power was manliness, woman being dismissed as *the weaker vessel.* (Note to Rusty: Can't you see that even your virtue is bound to my manliness?)]

make a virtue of necessity To accept imposed conditions as if they were an enabling power.

virtual/virtually 1. In essence if not in fact. [As if sufficient to grant enabling power.] *They are virtually married; they have been squabbling for years.* 2. Almost. *Don't stop now; we're virtually there.*

virtuoso Primarily but not exclusively in music, an artist or performer of great fluency and technical brilliance. (The term is often used to imply a lack of "deeper feeling," but this is a slob's self-defense in the face of brilliance; as if one could achieve virtuosity without feeling deeply enough to endure years of self-demanding discipline.)

vittles Food for human consumption. (Most dicts. enter the sing. form *vittle,* but I have never encountered that sing. except in such arch constructions as "stay and nibble a vittle," which is a deliberate play on the fact that the term is in fact a plural.) [Commonly glossed as a corrupted form of *victuals* < L. *victualis,* of food, genitive of *victus,* food, which is p.p. of *vivere,* to live; hence, with root sense: "what one lives on/by." The form, however, is less a corruption than a simple phonetic rendering.] *victualer Brit.* One who supplies food. (Though within the recognition vocabulary of literate Americans, the term is about as functional as ME *maun-cipal,* which had some of the same sense, or as *sutler,* which was common in the Civil War and after, but which has all but disappeared from use.)

viz.   Namely. (And usually sounded as "namely" when reading aloud.) [Not so much a word as a traditional bit of scholarly jargon. The standardized abbrev. of L. *videlicet,* it is possible to see; i.e., "it follows." < L. *videre,* to see; *licet,* it is permitted (LICIT, ILLICIT). Now rare.]

vogue   1. Fashion. 2. Thing in fashion. *The Cro-Magnon look is all the vogue with college students this year: they are imitating the faculty.* [Into XVI Eng. < It. *vogare,* to row; but with extended senses: "to be going well, to be moving ahead nicely."]

volcano   A laval vent of the earth's magmatic mass, usu. in the form of a cone-shaped mountain formed by the cinders and cooled lava that flow from the opening in its peak. [After *Vulcan,* associated in Greek mythology with the earth-born Titans (see *Pandora's box*). The mechanic of the gods, he had his smithy in the core of the mountain. The smoke and fire of active volcanoes was said to be from his forge.]

𝒲

waddy/waddie *Wstrn.* A cowhand. [MMM cites an 1897 ref. that says rustlers were once so named, but the general sense before and since has been simply "cowboy." Origin uncertain, but the earlier forms *cow waddy,* cowboy, and *top waddy,* ranch foreman, suggest that the term is a corruption of *warden,* guardian.]

waffle A crisp batter cake baked in a more or less honeycomb pattern between two patterned waffle irons. [IE *web-,* to go back and forth, to weave. MLG *wāfel,* Du. *wafel,* honeycomb (WAFER). OE *wafian,* to wave. Sense shift from "back-and-forth motion" to "up-and-down motion (of the hand)." ***to waffle*** *Federalese, since c. 1965.* To evade an issue by double-talk. [On the assumption that federalese responds to human criteria, the form must be based on an extension of *back-and-forth vacillation.*] ***wafflebutt*** *U.S. Army. WWII.* A contemptuous term for the chairborne cavalry from headquarters. [One of the true poems of G.I. slang: the HQ worker conceived as having taken a permanent fundamental impress from the cane seats of army-issue office chairs.]

wagon wheel A silver dollar. [Early XIX. Whimsical hyperbole, silver dollars being round and conceived to be as big as wagon wheels—which they almost were once in purchasing power.]

walk-on (part) *Theater.* An incidental role, as of a messenger, delivery boy, hotel maid. Implies a single brief appearance with few speaking lines, or none. In contrast, see *cameo.* [< Walk on, walk off.]

wall: be driven to the wall To go bankrupt. Especially to be driven out of the securities market. [The root image is of being jostled to one side of a narrow city lane (hence, against the wall) by a carriage or by a group of powerful men who take up the center of the passageway. So *thrust aside* → *no longer in the busy mainstream* → the financial sense, *no longer able to trade in the crowded center of the stock exchange* → (because) *bankrupt.*]

wallop   *n. & v.* A powerful blow. To strike a powerful blow. [Akin to *gallop,* which yields the intermediate sense: "to strike with the force of galloping hoofs," but ult. < Gmnc. roots *wal'-,* well; *hl'p-,* leap (LOPE), and so the root sense: "to leap (run) well."] *pack a wallop* 1. To be capable of a powerful punch. [*To pack,* as if that power were carried about like a piece of luggage.] 2. *Generalized ext.* To be powerful. *Fred Shrallow's cocktails pack a mean wallop.*

wandering Jew   A European folk tale theme blown up by superstition. There are various apocryphal references to Jews who offended Christ at the time of the crucifixion and who were doomed to wander the world as outcasts, forever in sorrow. But what is that theme if not a twice-told condemnation of the Jews as Christ-killers doomed to perpetual exile and rejection for their sin?

European Jews were commonly forbidden to own land. Many, therefore, had to earn their living as back-pack peddlers. Dressed in their Orthodox garments and wearing long beards, all of them must have seemed much alike to the Christians. Inevitably a peddler would show up who seemed to match exactly the description in a story told by great-great-grandfather. Was that not evidence that this very man had been wandering for at least a century, still unchanged? But why for just one century? For two. Forever. An outcast on earth to the end of time. The folk imagination once set off is unstoppable.

(For obvious reasons, various plants used as ground cover are called *wandering Jew.*)

war   *n. & v.* Armed hostilities between social groups or by parties within a social group. To engage in such hostilities. [Ult. based on IE *uer-, wer-,* to speak; the eventual sense evolution to *war,* via Gmnc., prob. being "to utter forcefully, to demand, to enforce a demand." But Italian *guerra,* war, though also based on Gmnc. *wer-, wers-,* has been influ. by L. *gerere,* to carry, to bear, in the L. fixed form *bellum gerere,* to wage (carry on) war, and this bastardized *gw-* has been transmitted, sometimes with initial *g,* sometimes with initial *w,* to a family of Eng. words with widely varied meanings, as below.]

*war/ward/warden/wardrobe/warrant/warrantee/guarantee/
guard/guardian/guerrilla* All these words with their variously
derived senses are akin to It. *guerra,* war; *guardia,* guard, in both
of which It. gu- is pronounced *gw-.* **war** As above, is based on
Gmnc. *wer-.* **ward** Person under custodial care of a guardian; and
warden Person of custodial authority, are both based on It.
guardiano with the g sound suppressed. **wardrobe** A clothes cupboard, and by ext. one's total supply of clothing, < It. *guardaroba,*
originally closet for storing stuff, then clothes cupboard, has similarly suppressed the It. g. **warrant** (in OF *garant*) is a mixed case
deriving < Gmnc. via the Frankish. **warrantee** and **guarantee**
Obvious siblings, one suppressing the g, the other the w. **guard**
and **guardian** came into Eng. from Fr., in which the suppression
of the w is standard. **guerrilla** (which see) is < Sp., in which *gw*
is retained, though the w is suppressed in Eng.

The foregoing is only a partial explanation of this distributed
gw- sound. The interrelation of Eng. *warrant,* OF *garant,* and
the Gmnc. stem *wer-* is evidence of some further shifting affinity
in this family, to which I can find no further clue.

war department   *Out-with-the-boys bravado.* One's wife. [Because
she is in charge of hostilities. Dating ?? Prob. late XIX.]

ward heeler   Derogatory name for a minor local politician or political
errand boy, his duty being to keep in touch with people and matters within a ward and to report to his political boss. [Based on
heel as command to a dog to follow close behind.]

Waterloo   1. A village a few miles south of Brussels. There Bonaparte
suffered his final defeat. Hence, 2. Generic for a total and final
downfall. *meet one's Waterloo* To be totally defeated.

NOTE. As a specimen of sense extension, an odd quirk. Napoleon's disaster was Wellington's ascendancy, Waterloo being the field
of England's long sought great triumph. Why has English chosen
the idiom as if from Napoleon's view? Had it chosen the Wellingto-
nian view, the idiom might as readily have meant "to triumph
gloriously," or "to repulse evil." The question is not to answer
but to ask, perhaps toward the realization that language does what
it does because it does it.

weed   *Obs.* A garment. [Root sense: "thing woven < IE *wedh-,* to
weave; via Gmnc. → OE *wāed(e),* cloth, garment.] Survives only

in *widow's weeds* (Always in plu.) A widow's black mourning clothes. [The black armband worn by men in mourning is also, at root, a weed, but *widow's weeds* has usurped the term, and such black strips are simply called armbands or mourning bands.]

week　1. The calendar period of seven days from Sunday through Saturday, or from Monday through Sunday. 2. Any seven successive days. *a week of anxiety.* 3. Seven days after a designated time. *a week from Tuesday.* (In Brit. this thought is expressed *Tuesday week.*) 4. A calendar period of seven days designated for some special event or observance. *inauguration-week activities, fund-raising week.* (In 1975, Governor Byrne of New Jersey proclaimed a John Ciardi week in early March, followed by a Battleship New Jersey Week. I have never understood the connection, especially since both weeks were part of Rutgers Basketball Month.) [IE *weig-, weik-,* to turn, to bend. Prob. with ref. to the phases of the moon, but see historical note. Via Gmnc. *w'k-* → OE *wicu, wice,* ME *wike, weke, week.*]

　　work week The now (commonly) five working days of the standard *forty-hour week.* (But *four-day week* and even *three-day week* are commonly heard in labor discussions, usu. not with the intent of working only three or four days each week, but to start overtime pay after the third or fourth day.)

　　Historic. The Babylonians worked out a seven-day week roughly corresponding to the phases of the moon. In other cultures, however, *week* has been a variable concept. In some cultures *week* has been related to *market days* (a notion roughly corresponding to *work week*). The *Encyclopaedia Britannica,* without specifying further, notes that in some African languages the same word is used for *week* and for *market.* The early Scandinavian week consisted of Tiu's day, Woden's day, Thor's day, Frieda's day, and Saturn's day, a Sun's day and Moon's day being added under Roman influ. and not until c. VIII or IX.

wench　1. XIII. A girl or young woman. 2. XIV. A servant, menial, and by ext., a wanton. Whence *go wenching* To go whoring. [Rare in Am. In all senses implies a menial or low person. OE *wenscel,* child (of either sex); ult. < IE *weng-,* to curve, bow, twist; with the sense: "person who has not yet firmed and grown straight." (Cf. the root senses of *pusillanimous.*) The ext. from "unformed person" → "changeable (inconstant) person" → "wanton" seems natural enough. Between OE and ME the word became specific to a female, but the sense "not worth much" is from the root.]

werewolf   Count Dracula's dog. In spook legend, a man who changes at night into a ravenous wolf that eats men, usu. under compulsion of the full moon, resuming human form by day. Prob. a semi-mythological figure personifying rabies. [OE *werewolf, werwolf* is a bastard form, the first element based on L. *vir,* man; the second on Gmnc. *wulf,* wolf. The Gmnc. is an adaptation of the L. *lycanthropus,* wolf-man < Gk. *lukos,* wolf; *anthropos,* man (LYCAN-THROPE, LYCANTHROPY).]

west   Where the sun sets. [< IE *wespero-,* night, nightfall (VESPERS). It. *levante,* east ("place where the sun rises") (ELEVATE), and *ponente,* west ("place where the sun goes down") (DEPONE), are based on the same sort of reference.] *Mae West Since WWII.* An inflatable rubber life vest slipped over the head at the top, and secured by straps at the bottom. When fitted with a collar, this flotation device is designed to keep a person's head above water during sleep or unconsciousness. Usu. inflated by a CO_2 cartridge of the sort used in seltzer bottles, but can also be inflated by one's breath. [After Mae West, erratic theatrical genius of the prewar era and once sex goddess of the pneumomammaliaphiliacs, because these vests, when inflated, kept the wearer's chest buoyantly buxom.] *gone west* Dead. *he has gone west* He died. [Early XIX Am. Based on the Indian belief that the Happy Hunting Ground (the Indian Heaven) lay to the west, beyond the setting sun. (And cf. Wordsworth, "Tintern Abbey," ll. 93–97,

> And I have felt
> A presence that disturbs me with the joy
> Of elevated thoughts; a sense sublime
> Of something far more deeply interfused,
> Whose dwelling is the light of setting suns.)]

wetback   A Mexican who has entered the U.S. illegally (usually assisted by or contracted for by unscrupulous vegetable growers who pay subminimum wages for the stoop labor of these pickers, and who abuse them in other ways, threatening to turn them over to the immigration authorities if they protest). [Because the common means of entry is by wading the Rio Grande, in which they are assumed to have wet their backs, though in many places the river is so shallow that *wetcrotch* or even *wetshoe* might be as accurate.]

whatchamacallits   Am. is rich in words for "no-name somethings" and for words that will not come to mind, a class of words largely ignored by our dictionaries. One sequence of the more obvious such words is: *whatchamacallit* What(ever) you may call it. *whatsis* A what-is-it (whatever it is). *whosis* Whoever it is, whatever his name is. The self-evident *whatsisname.* And the more or less archly elaborate variants: *whatsisface, whosispuss,* and *whatchamaface.*

Some words of this class can be traced at least speculatively. *dingus* [Certainly based on Ger. *Ding,* thing. Into Eng. from Afrikaans during the Boer War.] *dingbat* [Lit. "thing bat." In Brit., a throwing thing, throwing stick. (Cf. *brickbat.*)] *gadget* [Perh. < Fr. *gâchette,* the catch of a lock.]

And of uncertain origin. *doodad, doohickey, gismo, gizmo, thingumajig, thingumbob, thingumdoodle, flapdoodle.* See also *framis.*

whipping boy   One who gets the blame and the punishment for whatever happens, guilty or not. Implies that this honoree is innocent

HISTORIC. Boys of noble birth were commonly turned over to tutors, who supervised their education, training, and moral and religious character. All boys will misbehave, and princelets, as specially privileged persons, even more so. Misbehavior had to be punished, but the person of the young prince was sacred. Commonly, therefore, the royal sprig was brought up with a gentleman companion of his own age who was required, among other things, to take upon himself the whipping for the young prince's misbehavior, the prince being required to watch the punishment. The theory seems to have been that the two boys would become such loving companions that the princelet could not bear to see his friend being punished in his royal stead. In practice, watching someone else suffer for a royal mistake was probably a gratifying training in the nature of royal prerogative—and let the bounder be grateful for the privilege of taking such distinguished licks.

whiskey   (So in Am. and Irish usage; but Sc. and Canadian *whisky.*) 1. A hard liquor distilled from grain with an alcoholic content of at least 40 percent (80 proof), which is approx. twice the alcoholic content of sherry. 2. A drink of this liquor. *Bartender, give me a whiskey.* [Root sense: "water of life." Distillation was simultaneously developed by the Irish and the Arabs in IX (see *alcohol*). The Irish named the distilled product in Gaelic *uisga beathe,* water of life → Sc. *usque baugh,* dial. *whiskybae,* and by contraction *whisky, whiskey.* A like root sense works in Scandinavian *akvavit* < L. *aqua vitae,* water of life; and in Russ. *vodka,* dim. form of *voda,* water, hence, at root: "the little water (so dear to us)." In Amerind pidgin *firewater* expressed somewhat the same sense with a different metaphoric base.] **whiskey-head** *Primarily XIX Black English.* (Also *juice-head.*) An alcoholic. [*Whiskey* combined with *head,* addict.]

whistle   (*n.* with corresponding verb forms.) 1. The act of expelling the breath shrilly and with more or less modulation. 2. A mechanical device for producing a sound of this sort. 3. An early tubular musical instrument. (*Tin-whistle bands* are still popular among the tin-eared Erse.) [OE *hwistle.* < a generalized Scandinavian echoic root with various senses having to do with the shrill expulsion of breath, as Old Norse *hvisla,* whisper; Swedish *vissla,* whistle; Danish *vissla,* hiss.]

   whistle bait The sort of girl girl-watchers watch first and longest. [She attracts (baits) whistles of admiration, invitation, and generalized acknowledgment of the mystery of proportion.]

   whistle stop 1. *Am. railroading.* A station (town) at which trains stop only when signaled. [Because the train acknowledges receipt of the signal by blowing its whistle.] 2. *Ext.* Small town on the railroad. (See *jerkwater.*) 3. *Ext. Politics.* (Late XIX and up to c. 1950, when TV became the effective campaigning medium.) In campaigning by train, a stop made in a small town to permit the candidate to orate from the rear platform of the train. It was common to pretend that such stops were unscheduled (the candidate having been suddenly filled with a desire to see dear old Jerkwater again), but they were often set up by advance agents or by telegraphing from the train well in advance, for what is a candidate without a crowd on hand, and, if possible, a brass band? Also *to whistle stop* To campaign in this way.

   whistle for it/let him (go) whistle for it/go whistle Formulas of rejection. Imply that anyone may whistle but few are answered. [Some ascribe the idiom to nautical usage, asserting that becalmed sailors used to whistle for a wind. Such a custom is likely, and would be a survival of primitive magic in which like attracts like, the hissing of breath causing the air to move. But the custom is only ambiguously attested. A more persuasive source is in the now lost reference to *whistle tankards,* originally large earthenware tankards holding up to six pints, the handles of which had a built-in whistle for summoning a refill (if the barmaid ever got around to it). Such tankards were once common in Dorsetshire pubs and were perhaps the work of a local potter, but if so, their use spread, an ornate silver whistle tankard dating from c. 1650 having been recently catalogued among Yorkshire antiques.]

wet one's whistle To have a drink. [Though the idiom may be sufficiently explained by the fact that it is hard to whistle when one's mouth is parched, it has specific and less visible antecedents going back to at least XVI. *Whittle,* scythe, has long been generalized Brit. dialect. *To whet the whittle* was to pause to hone the scythe. Mowers took a jug of beer or of cider to the fields with them, and the pause to whet the whittle was an occasion for having a pull on the jug.]

white The chromatic opposite of black. The color of innocence and goodness as opposed to the black of sin and evil. (See *black and white.*) [IE *kweid-,* brightness, whiteness. With k/h and d/t in Gmnc. → OE *hwit,* white. (And note the side evolution to OE *hwaete,* wheat, "the source of white flour.") ME *white* reverses the OE *hw* but preserves its pronunciation.]

white elephant 1. *Lit.* In India, where elephants shared some of the status of sacred cows, a rare grayish-white specimen believed to have special religio-totemistic powers. 2. *Ext.* A burdensome possession, esp. a gift one cannot dispose of for fear of offending the donor. [After rajahs' practice of presenting their nobles with sacred white elephants as a mark of esteem (and perhaps to get rid of them). The recipient was left with the honor of the gift, and with the burden of maintaining an elephant too sacred to be put to work or even to keep confined, and whose damage to property one was forbidden to prevent; and with the further burden of keeping the thing in perfect condition lest the rajah come to visit and find that his gift of honor has been badly treated. (Anyone want three rare kids? I promise to make no tours of inspection.)]

white feather Cock fighting. The least trace of white plumage was and is said to be the mark of a badly bred cock with no fight in it. Handlers who found a trace of white on a cock would, of course, trim it away or dye it for concealment, but breeding would tell and a cock that turned and ran betrayed its poor strain. Whence *show the white feather* To betray cowardice. To run from the fight.

white lie [White for innocence.] A lie told without malice, usually with intent to spare someone's feelings.

white man's burden [After Rudyard Kipling's poem "The White Man's Burden," 1899.] British Empire. The conquering Briton's obligation to sweat in tropical exile in order to supervise the orderly plundering of his conquests, with a few missionaries thrown in to sanctify the process.

whited sepulcher A hypocrite. [At root, a whitewashed tomb.]

HISTORIC. The Jews held that a tomb was desecrated if a stranger, and particularly an infidel, came near it. Most Semites avoided the places of the dead superstitiously (and perhaps because old burial practices made them places of infection). It was custom among the Jews, therefore, to whitewash tombs at intervals to make them a more visible warning for strangers to stay away. Matthew 23:27 converted the custom to metaphor with the sense it now has: "Woe unto you, scribes and Pharisees, hypocrites! for ye are like unto whited sepulchres, which indeed appear beautiful outward, but are within full of dead men's bones, and of all uncleanness."

white tie Full fork-tail evening formal wear for men. [Earlier *evening dress*. *White tie* is early XX, evolving to distinguish this once standard dinner wear from *black tie* for the new tailless *tuxedo* (which see).]

whitewash *n*. 1. A temporary coating of lime dissolved in water with a whitening agent added, once commonly used on fences, outbuildings, stucco, stones, etc. Glue and sizing added to the mixture make for a more durable coating, but even then the coating weathers rapidly. 2. The act of protecting a person's reputation by coating his defaults with an aura of purity. —*v*. To gloss over a person's defaults, giving them an aura of purity.

too poor to paint and too proud to whitewash Self-relishing sthrn. rhetoric describing an impoverished but intransigent southern gentlemen with aristocratic antecedents or pretensions.

whoopee Riotous festivity, as in painting the town red. [*Hoop, whoop*, a loud cry (echoic); with *yip-yip-yip-ee*, Indian war cry. Both connoting energetic enthusiasm.] **out to whoop it up** In a mood for a wild revel. Out on the social equivalent of an Indian war raid. **Whoopee!** A humor and cheesecake magazine popular in the 1930's. **making whoopee** 1. Engaged in a wild revel. [Whooping it up.] 2. Having a torrid love affair. [Walter Winchell, once popular Broadway gossip columnist, conceded that he may not have coined *whoopee*, but claimed *making whoopee* as his coinage. He was wrong on both counts: he had no slightest claim to having originated *whoopee*, nor to sense 1 of *making whoopee*.

He did assert and popularize sense 2. But let the glory be fractionally his, and may he rest in perpetual rumor.]

whore [Let wives make what they will of the root sense: "desired woman" < IE *ka-*, desire, to desire. With k/h and suffixed *-r-* in Gmnc. → OE *hōre*, whore. And by a similar process → L. *carus*, *cara*, dear, dear one; and likely influ. by *caro*, flesh.] *n.* Hired sexual meat. —*v.* To make use of such meat.

   whoredom The generalized meat market. *whorehouse* A bordello. (A specific meat market.) *whoremaster* 1. One given to such meat. 2. A pimp. *whorish* Blatantly for sale.

widdershins/withershins *In loose usage.* Counterclockwise. *But specific to the casting of spells in Teutonic witchcraft.* A circular motion against the course of the sun. (Reversal is an element in all demonism: cf. the black mass, a devil-worshipping ritual in which the mass is performed backward.) [The first element, *widder*, via Sc., is < Gmnc. *wid-*, *wider* (Ger. *wieder*, back, reverse, again), contrary to, against, in reverse; second element, *sin*, voyage, journey, course taken. MHG *widdersinnes*, contrary to the course of (with ref. to the sun).]

widow A woman whose husband has died. See also *grass widow*. [Root sense "(woman) divided from (her husband)." < IE *weidh-*, to divide, to put a distance between (WIDEN, WIDE). Suffixed *ewo-*, *evo-* in Gmnc. → OE *widuwe*, widow. (In the Latin evolution, IE variant stem *widh-*, with negative prefix *dis-*: *dis-widh-* → L. *dividere*, to divide.)] *widower* 1. As an associated form, a man whose wife has died. 2. As agential, a killer ("man slayer who causes women to become widows"). *the widow-maker* A common epithet for the sea as the swallower of men.

   In typesetting *a widow* is a length of set type that will not fit into the space available. ["Thing left over."]

widow's peak A down-pointed triangle of hair in the middle of the forehead. [Sometimes associated with XVI and earlier caps, resembling the headdress of some nuns, and having such a projection in front; these once worn by widows in mourning. But such a headdress was itself prob. suggested by the ancient superstition that women with such a hairline were marked for early widowhood (and were therefore not to be sought as wives).]

widow's walk A commonly railed-in platform on the roof of more or less imposing American colonial houses. They were built either around or next to chimneys, with access through a dormer or a trap door in the roof. [So called because the wives of ships' captains were said to walk there when a ship was due, in the hope of catching first sight of their husbands' returning sail. A pretty legend, and these walks were in fact so used along the coast, but they may also be found on imposing houses far inland. Wherever they occurred they were stocked with barrels of water and buckets for putting out grease fires in the flues, such fires being a common danger in chimneys that drew off the fumes from cooking fires. To whatever extent these walks were used as coastal lookout points, they were built with chimney fires in mind.]

wig: big wig   An important person. [See *high horse.*]
   HISTORIC. The custom of wearing ornate men's wigs began c. 1690 with the aging Louis XIV of France (1638–1715). Noted in his youth for his luxuriant hair, he took to elaborate wigs in sparse old age (and after all, a crown must feel uncomfortable on a bald head).
   Louis's courtiers naturally aped his custom, but just as junior executives today do not drive cars bigger than the boss's, they chose their hairpieces according to their rank in the pecking order: the bigger the wig, the more important the man.
   The custom of wearing wigs as a mark of gentility persisted, in more modest form, into the early XIX in U.S. George Washington (died 1799) wore a wig. As part of the intricate tradition of British law, judges wore simple white wigs long before the time of Louis XIV.

willies   Always with *the* An eerie uneasiness. The creeps. [Am. XIX but now also Brit. Origin uncertain. Perh. < *willy-nilly* via "it gives me the willy-nillies," but no such form is attested.]

wiseacre   A smart aleck. [At root: "a soothsayer." < IE *weid-*, to see, to know → modified Gmnc. stem *wis-* (Gm. *weissen*, to know); *sago* (SAGE), one who speaks → *wis-sago*, one who sees and speaks, i.e., a seer, a soothsayer. The connective sense between this and modern sense is "know-it-all."]

wisecracker   A flippant, sassy, know-it-all person. [Late XIX Am. variant of *wiseacre* (see above). Into common Brit. usage c. WWII.]
crack wise 1. To make wise cracks. 2. To be impudent. [In this form remains purely Am.]

wont   Used to, inured, accustomed. Usu., if not invariably, with an infinitive. *It was his wont to stop by the churchyard* = it was his custom. (And so in Brit. novels into XIX, but in Am. most commonly met in the New England regional form:) **wonted to** used to, accustomed to. *The work is hard but I'm wonted to it.* [< ME *wonen,* to dwell, to abide ("to continue in one place"), and so: to accustom, to become accustomed ("to continue in one way"). *Wont* and *wonted* are p.p. forms of *wonen.*]

wool: all wool and a yard wide   1. *Of cloth.* Unadulterated by lesser fibers and of full measure. 2. *Ext. Of a person.* Genuine and reliable.

wool: dyed-in-the-wool   Steadfast. *Jimmy Carter is a dyed-in-the-wool washout.* [A more accurate phrasing would be *dyed in the yarn,* but idiom follows its own sequential illogic. As now phrased, suggests dyeing the fabric before the suit is cut. But the real intent is that the yarn be dyed before the cloth is spun because the texture of the woven cloth might interfere with the deep absorption of the dye.]

wool: pull the wool over one's eyes   To hoodwink. [The modern phrasing of this idiom suggests a visored cap, which was unlikely in early England. The earlier phrasing *to pull the wool over one's ears* more accurately suggests a woolen stocking cap, and is more nearly akin to the synonymous *hoodwink* (which see). *Over the ears* certainly implied pulling the cap down over one's whole head, leaving one blinded, hence, easily duped.]

woolgathering   Erratically shifting reverie.
    HISTORIC. In the grinding poverty of feudal England, peasants of an estate were permitted to gather from bushes and hedges the tufts of wool snagged from passing sheep. (See *boot; hook or crook.*) For many of the rural poor these tufts were the only source of homespun clothing. Hardly a high-yield occupation, woolgathering was left to children, who naturally made a game of it, leaping about with no fixed direction, but from tuft to tuft as they caught sight of it. Playfully erratic and producing very little, woolgathering provided an apt metaphor for the daydreamer's state of mind.]

Wop   Pejorative name for an Italian. Also as an adjective. *wop food.* [< It. south-of-Rome dial. *guappo,* dude. Into Am. c. 1900. Mencken cited *guappo* as a common form of greeting among It.

immigrants. It was never that, but rather a jovial exclamation when a man showed up in his flashiest Sunday best: *che guappo!* what a dude! Mencken may have confused it with the southern dial. *(g)uaglio,* boy, which was a common intimate greeting form. (The commonly offered derivation < *W(ith) O(ut) P(apers),* with ref. to immigrants at Ellis Island, is nonsense.)]

HISTORIC. Every tribe has had its term of contempt for the tribe across the river. Gk. *barbaros,* stranger, enemy, means at root: "those who say bar-bar-bar when they talk." Sp. *gringo* (from *griego,* Greek) has the same root sense of contempt for the way others talk. (See *gringo.*) Among the most common ethnic pejoratives in Am. are: *Bohunk,* Bohemian-Hungarian; *Canuck,* Canadian; *Chink,* Chinese; *Frog,* Frenchman; *Gook, Slope, Slant,* Pacific Islander or Oriental; *Greaser,* Spaniard, Mexican; *Guinea,* Italian; *Honky, Honkie,* white person; *Hunky,* Hungarian; *Jap,* Japanese; *Kraut, Squarehead, Fritz, Jerry,* German (and extended to the Dutch and Scandinavians); *Nigger,* Negro; *Russki,* Russian; *Spic,* Spaniard; *Yid, Hebe, Kike,* Jew—and so to the vision of brotherly love through a gun sight.

wrangler   A cowboy. [Into SW Am. c. 1870 < Sp. *caballerango,* horse groom, horse handler. Reinforced by *to wrangle,* to bicker—a reasonable metaphor for the work one does with (and against) a stubborn and half-broken horse.]

wrong side   Etymologically, the left. [By ancient association with the right as the side of honor. So *dexterous,* deft (at root: "right-handed"); *sinister,* devious, threatening (at root: "left-handed").] ***get out of bed on the wrong side*** Said of one who appears to be in a bad humor, [A good example of an idiom that holds to an earlier specific meaning after the form has been so altered that it no longer expresses the still more or less understood original meaning. A superstition traceable at least to Roman times held that bad luck would follow if, on getting out of bed, one first touched the floor with the left foot. The idea "bad humor" follows naturally from the idea "jinxed." But only by association with this fixed sense of *wrong side* has the superstition anything to do with one side or another of the bed. In a private informal survey over the years, I have asked hundreds of people to interpret this idiom. None could, and very few thought it had anything to do with right and left. Most guessed it to mean "arose with the worse side of one's character dominant."]

wrote the book on   Knows everything there is to know about the thing referred to. [Am. Dating? But *book* here is specifically "technical manual" of the sort that accompanies a new machine or technical system, and since elaborate systems are comparatively recent, I guess the idiom to be no earlier than WWI, and perhaps later.]

X

X/x 1. The 24th letter of our alphabet, corresponds to Gk. chi. 2. Roman numeral 10. 3. *Math.* Unknown quantity. [First so used by René Descartes, *Géométrie*, 1637 (along with *y* and *z*). But there was precedent in the work of Arabian mathematicians, who so use Arab *shei*, a thing, something, in Sp. written *xei* (and note that the earliest form of *X* was the Phoenician symbol *sāmekh*, which stood for *s*. Sp. *xei* was translated into It. as *cosa*, thing, unknown thing, the abbreviation *co.* being read aloud as an *X*. (Cf. *viz.*, commonly read aloud in English as "namely.")] 4. *In correcting school papers and in proofreading.* A symbol of error. 5. A symbol for "delete." So *X, X's, X'ing, X'd, X-out.* 6. *When witnessed or in extremis.* A legal signature. [Originally because a sign easily drawn by an illiterate, but also as a form of oath, *X* symbolizing the cross and signifying "testified by the cross of Jesus."] 7. As above, a symbol of Christ and of the cross. 8. *In love letters.* Stands for a kiss. 9. *On road signs.* Takes the place of "cross." So *X-ing, Deer X-ing, Children X-ing, X-Walk*, and the common:

X

Children

Walk

To which Ogden Nash added the line, "Happy children ride." 10. *In the dialogue balloons of comic strips, often mixed with stars, planets, and exclamation points.* Signifies "unprintable" language.

XX/XXX In cartoon and comic strip convention, a bottle so marked is a bottle of hard liquor.

[I have not been able to trace the first use of this convention in Am. cartooning. It was almost certainly sometime in XIX, and based on the practice of British breweries in marking their products *X, XX, XXX*, and even, though rarely, *XXXX*, each added *X* indicating a higher alcoholic content. The practice prob. corresponds to the use of stars in indicating the strength and quality of brandy.]

xantho-   Also *zantho- Prefix.* Yellow. *xanthin* A yellow vegetable pigment. [Gk. *xanthos,* yellow.]

xeno-/zeno-   *Prefix.* Foreign, foreigner. *xenophobia* The irrational distrust of foreigners; hence, rabid nationalism. [Gk. *xenos,* stranger, foreigner. But also: guest ("stranger in the house"). *As an adj.* Odd. Strange.

xero-   (Also *zero- Prefix.* Dry. *Xerox* Trade name of a dry-copier machine. *xerophagy* The eating of dry food only (dry Lenten fare) as a form of fast. [Gk. *xeros,* dry.]

Xmas   Christmas. [Though commonly frowned upon by grammarians as slovenly and by the pious as profane, *X* has ancient antecedents as a symbol of Christ and the cross, so much so that illiterate Jews at Ellis Island refused to sign with an *X,* insisting instead on making an *O,* called in Yiddish *kikl,* little circle.]

X-ray   A relatively high-energy stream of photons. [X here for "unknown." Hence "unknown ray." Translation of Ger. *X-Strahlen.* So called because when W. C. Roentgen (or Röntgen) discovered the phenomenon in 1895, its effects could be noted but its nature was unknown.] *X-ray/X-ray photo* A photo taken on a plate sensitized to X-rays, which have varying penetrative powers, passing easily through most tissue but substantially blocked by bone, and somewhat less so by the density of organs. Hence, *to X-ray* To take such a photo. *X-ray eyes* A metaphoric application to what was earlier called "a penetrating gaze." Also applied to people who "mentally undress" members of the opposite sex.

xylo- Also *zylo- Prefix.* Wood. [Gk. *xulon,* wood.] *xylophage* A wood eater, as the beaver and various insects. *xylophone* A percussion instrument of chromatically arranged wooden bars played by striking with mallets.

XYZ Affair From 1798 to 1800, a time of tension and of maritime brushes between U.S. and France. In 1797 President John Adams sent three delegates to France to work out an agreement on contested maritime rights. The delegates reported to Washington that they had been approached upon their arrival by three French agents, who demanded a large bribe and a loan from the U.S. before negotiation could begin. The delegates sent home their correspondence with these agents, who were designated X, Y, and Z when the file was published. The French government denied the authenticity of the correspondence, took offense at its publication, and got its hair up, though only briefly. It is bad manners to publish the truth, but in diplomatic circles nothing goes out of date faster.

𝒴

yabyum   The Beat Generation's form of the orgy, in which more
or less all the girls present at a "rap-cum-pot-cum-pills-cum-medi-
tation" session were available for witnessed copulation. [In the
intricate ritual of Zen, the yabyum was an annual fertility ritual
involving copulation witnessed by priests. The Beats, in the name
of Zen spirituality, made a party game of it.]

yacht   An indeterminate label for a sleek-lined, fast vessel, with sails,
and/or power, usu. privately owned, and primarily for pleasure
cruising and for racing. [< Du. *jaghte* < *jaghtschip*, hunting ship,
sea raider. Akin to Ger. *Jaeger,* hunter. The ancestor of the yacht
was the fast, light pirate ship developed for raiding coastal shipping; a vessel based on the traditional Viking ship but with modifications for greater speed and for boarding overtaken victims. Eve-
lyn's *Diary* entry for Oct. 1, 1661, mentions the first yacht in
England, a gift of the Dutch to Charles II (who, a few years earlier,
had been a penniless outcast in exile in the low countries):

> I sailed this morning with his Majesty in one of his yachts (or pleasure
> boats), vessels not known among us till the Dutch East India Company
> presented this curious piece to the king.]

yahoo   (Pronounced *yā'-hoō* in common Am., and less often with
an *a* as in *harbor.*) A crude, mannerless, and brutal person. [In
Swift's *Gulliver's Travels,* 1726, one of a degraded humanoid race
representing humanity and contrasted to the ruling Houyhnhnms
(pronounced, as if by a whinnying horse, *hwin' -ms*), a race of
highly cultured horses dedicated to philosophy and to ideal justice.
Though kept alive by lexicographers, *Houyhnhnm* remains a mar-
ginal term in English because it is all but impossible to spell without
looking into the dictionary. *Yahoo,* on the other hand, despite
its literary origin, is firmly fixed not only in Brit. but in Am. colloq.

Note as evidence of its naturalization in Am. that it need not be capitalized. (Webster's is not wrong in citing it with an upper-case *Y* but is certainly retrograde in not permitting the lower-case form.) *Houyhnhnm,* on the other hand, is always capitalized, an evidence that it is not an accepted loan word. (See note on loan words under *loan/lend.*)]

Yankee 1. *Original sense, c. 1650.* An Englishman in North America. Hence, 2. A New Englander. 3. A citizen of the United States. 4. *In sthrn. usage since the Civil War.* A Northerner. 5. *In early XVIII but soon passing out of use.* A fine thing. *a Yankee cider, a real Yankee cider.* 6. An American abroad. *The Yanks are coming.*

Though the most common of Am. formations, *Yankee* has never been satisfactorily etymologized, and nothing less than a condensed essay will address its origins.

To begin with, it is probably a converging evolution, one simplest derivation being from Du. *Janke,* Johnny. So *Connecticut Yankee,* Connecticut Johnny, one of those Johnnies from Connecticut. And Janke, Yanke, Yankee is amply attested in colonial Du. both as a surname and as the name of a ship. Also Du. *Jan Kase,* John Chease, a belittling epithet.

There is, however, another evolution, from Indian sources, and James Fenimore Cooper was certain of it in a footnote to his *Deerslayer,* 1841:

> It is singular that there should be any question concerning the origin of the well-known sobriquet of "Yankee." Nearly all the old writers who speak of the Indians first known to the Colonists make them pronounce "English" as "Yengeese." Even at this day it is a provincialism of New England to say "*E*nglish," instead of "*I*nglish" [???], and there is a close conformity of sound between "English" and "Yengeese," more especially if the latter word, as was probably the case, be pronounced short. The transition from "Yengeese" thus pronounced, to "Yankees," is quite easy. If the former is pronounced "Yangis," it is almost identical to "Yankees," and Indian words have seldom been spelled as they are pronounced. . . . The liquids of the Indians would easily convert *en* into *yen.*

Others have applied Cooper's essential argument in explaining the derivation of *Yankee* from Fr. *Anglais,* English. Various scholars of Indian languages, however, have argued more learnedly than I can follow that the phonetics of Indian speech would not permit such a development from either *English* or *Anglais.* And Cooper, for all his absolute assurance, failed to note that an earlier form, mentioned by Washington Irving in 1830, was *Yanokie.*

Prof. Edward Taube of Racine, Wisc., has long studied Algonquinian place names and the Algonquinian languages, and I am indebted to him for the first useful clues I have been able to find on the Indian origin of the word. I digest the following explanation from Prof. Taube's unpublished [!!] paper, *Yankee, "This Stranger,"* and from two long letters I have received from him. The material is unfamiliar and the explanations complicated, but I believe Prof. Taube has solved the problem that has vexed etymologists for over 300 years.

1. Roger Williams, *A Key into the Language of America,* London, 1643, cites Algonquinian *Awaunaguss* (lit. "this stranger") as meaning "Englishman." The plural form is *awaunagussuck,* the elements being *awau,* these; *nagussuck,* they are strangers.

2. When Capt. John Mason, at dawn on May 26, 1637, staged a retaliatory raid that wiped out a Pequot village, the startled warning cry of the first Indians to see his party was, as he reported, *Owanux! Owanux!* (also spelled *Wanux*), Englishmen! Englishmen!

3. Primitive languages, those of the Indian among them, make common use of extreme contraction. Fanny Hardy Eckstrom, *Indian Place Names of the Marine Coast,* notes of Indian words: "they are subject to such condensation that from a root of a half dozen letters the root may be pared down to one or two."

4. Prof. Taube read *ng* and variant *nk* as such an extreme contraction of Awaunaguss, based on the central *nag, n'g.* He sees *nag* as itself a slightly less contracted form. Prof. Taube writes:

> Awaunagus, awenoch, wanux, wenoch, Yanokie, Yankee, etc. are all distinct and independent descendants of the same Algonquinian ancestor, each one mutilated a little but differently during its individual transfer from the Algonquinian spoken word to the English written record.

There yet remains a puzzle. The first edition of Brewer's *Phrase and Fable* notes that Cromwell was lampooned as *Nankee Doodle* and that his March on Oxford (1642) was satirized in the ballad: "Nankee Doodle came to town upon his little pony,/ Stuck a feather in his hat and called it macaroni." [So for our first "national air," which has been variously identified as an old Central European, Polish, and Spanish folk air.]

No other source I know mentions Nankee Doodle. Was Brewer having one of his rare lapses? His later editors may think so, for Nankee Doodle does not appear in later editions.

The account of Capt. Mason's 1637 raid suggests that *Yankee* had not yet emerged. It also suggests that in the thirteen years since the first Dutch trading post on the site of what is now Albany (1824), Du. *Janke, Yanke* had not come into use. The dating suggests either that some previously unnoted *Nankee* lurks in the wings, or that Brewer was in error in this case. The dating also casts some doubt on the common derivation from the Dutch. It is the derivation from Algonquinian "this stranger" that remains persuasive.

yegg   A safecracker. [All sources join in deriving this term from John Yegg, usu. described as "a famous safecracker." Perhaps a better crime buff than I can run him down, for despite his alleged fame, he does not appear on any of the noted criminal lists I have been able to search.]

yo   In armed services, one of the standard responses to a roll call. [Curiously overlooked by lexicographers, though a common form. Cf. *yo-ho-ho,* the old chanty refrain. Answers to a roll call are varied in rapid succession, as *"here! ho! yea! yo!,"* almost any sound being answer enough. Perh. a combination of *yea* and *ho.*]

you-know-who   *Colloq.* Ref. to a person known to both the speaker and the person addressed, the function of the idiom being to assert intimacy. So on postcard, *Having a wonderful time in Niagara Falls with you-know-who.*

Yule/Yuletide   See historic note to *Christmas.*

Z

zany *adj.* Farcical. Clownish. Bizarre. —*n.* A clown, a fool. [The fond diminutive of the common Italian name *Giovanni* is *Gianni,* rendered in dialect *Zanni,* and in the tradition of Italian farce, the name in this form became standard for a clown-stooge; whence It. *zanni, zani,* buffoon.]

Zen/Zen Buddhism A Chinese and Japanese form of buddhism that asserts "the All" to be uncontainable in scripture but attainable by revelation after long and rigorous discipline and meditation. (Cf. Protestant conscience versus R.C. pronouncement.) [Japanese *zen,* meditation.]

HISTORIC. "Zen" came into common Am. mention in the 1960's when the Beat Generation, an antiestablishment subrevolution of manners, proclaimed its revelation to be based on Zen. There is small evidence, however, that the young rebels had any substantial grasp of Zen concepts or any taste for its lifetime of demanding discipline. The Beats, rather, raided Zen writings for bits and pieces of ritual and teaching that would justify what they wanted to do to begin with. See *yabyum* and the conversion of a Zen fertility ritual into a party game. In quoting Zen, moreover, the Beats could cite both abstrusely and on authority a system of beliefs their parents knew nothing of and were therefore unable to rebut. Whatever the counterassertions of Beat spokesmen, Zen was, for them, less a religion than a way of shutting out mother and dad as poor square slobs.

zilch Nothing. *The score stands at twelve–zilch. I went to the track and got zilched. All you'll get from Betty Jo Potter is zilch; unless, that is, you ask her.* [From *Ballyhoo,* popular Am. humor and cheesecake magazine of the 1930's. It featured a series of cartoons in which more or less undressed girls in compromising positions exclaimed, always wide-eyed, "Oh, Mr. Zilch!" Mr. Zilch, however, was never shown, except as a pants leg protruding from behind a sofa, or as a heap of clothing on the floor. He became the ubiquitous little man who wasn't there. Hence, the nothing man. Hence, nothing. (Cf. *framis.*)]

zip [Echoic.] 1. A short hissing hum as of an arrow, crossbow bolt, bullet. 2. Quickness. Vigor. [By association.] *zippy* Fast. Intensely lively. Snappy. Tangy. *Bill Sloane used to mix a zippy martini.* *zip along/by/away* To move rapidly.

Zip Code A five-number designation for each of approximately 100,000 postal delivery areas in the U.S. It was intended to reduce errors in mail sorting and to permit automated sorting, but the U.S. Post Office is like marriage: the more one pays for the service, the less service one gets. [Asserted to be an acronym for *Z(one) I(mprovement) P(rogram)*, but obviously *zip,* implying speed, came first, the awkward long form being then concocted to fit the purported acronym.]

zipper 1. One who zips. Also a more or less common nickname for an especially speedy athlete. *Zipper White.* 2. A slide fastener that meshes or unmeshes a series of interlocking plastic or metal teeth.

HISTORIC. This now pervasive fastener first came into widespread use in the late 1930's, but was first developed for use on shoes by the American gadgeteer Whitcomb L. Judson in 1893. Developed and refined for more general uses c. 1913 by Gideon Sunback, it was first bought in large quantities by the War Department in WWI. It was given its now established name c. 1920 by an executive of B. F. Goodrich, who, according to Wallechinsky and Wallace, *The People's Almanac,* praised the device as quite a "zipper."

zip your lip WWII posters. Fasten your mouth shut. *zip up/ unzip* To close/open a zipper. *zip me up* Fasten my zipper for me. (Said usu. by women whose dresses have a zipper in the back and hard to reach.)

In slang, additionally, *zip* is "nothing." *Minnesota won 23– zip* = The score was 23–0. In golf, an expert player asked his handicap may answer "zip," meaning he gets no handicap strokes. [Perhaps because to zip up is to shut out. But perhaps influ. by *zilch* (which see), which may be substituted in either usage given.]

zoot suit An extravagantly sharp man's suit, the coat of which hangs almost to the knees from a tightly tailored waist, broad lapels, and heavily padded shoulders. It is worn over full-cut trousers that taper to the ankles. A wide-brimmed hat, and a watch chain hanging to the knee and even below it, are essential accessories. [C. 1939. Louis Lettes, a white tailor of Memphis, Tennessee, designed and made the first of these suits for students of Booker T. Washington High School; and they, in characteristic Negro rhyming slang, dubbed them *zoot suits*. Within a year they had become a national fad among members of the jitterbug set, but were succeeded, all too soon, by the Government Issue of World War II.] *zooty adj.* Sharp. Snappy. Snazzy.

zwieback   A form of German sweet bread first baked as a loaf, then sliced and toasted; most commonly available in U.S. in packages of the toasted slices. [Root sense: "twice baked." < Gmnc. *zwi-*, two; Ger. *backen*, to bake.]